THE ARTIST'S GARDEN

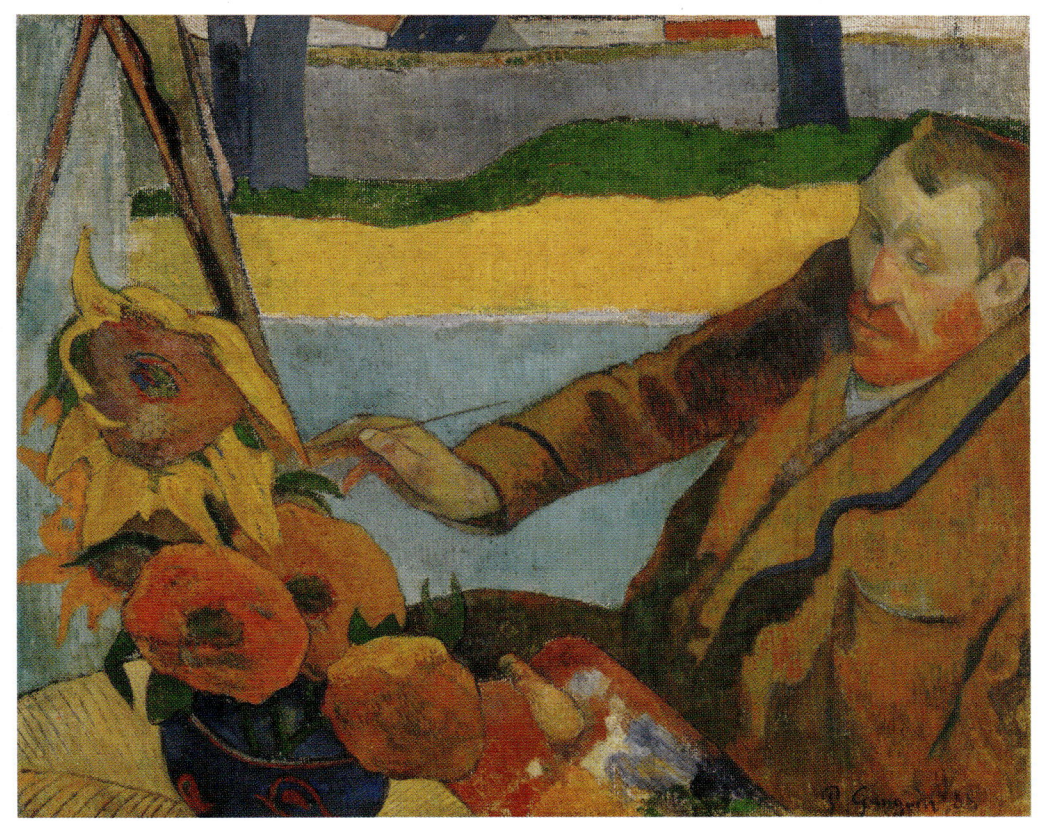

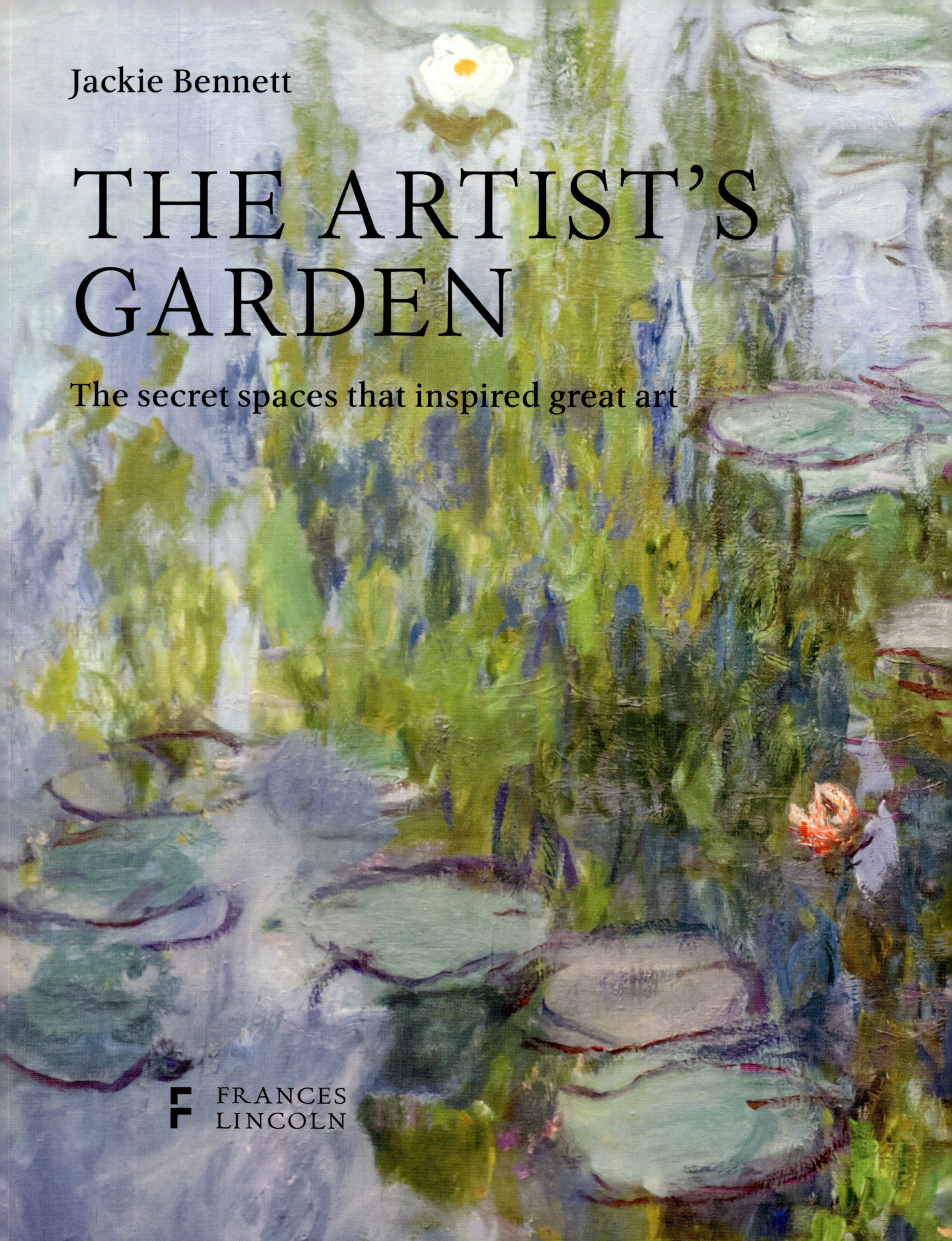

Jackie Bennett

THE ARTIST'S GARDEN

The secret spaces that inspired great art

FRANCES LINCOLN

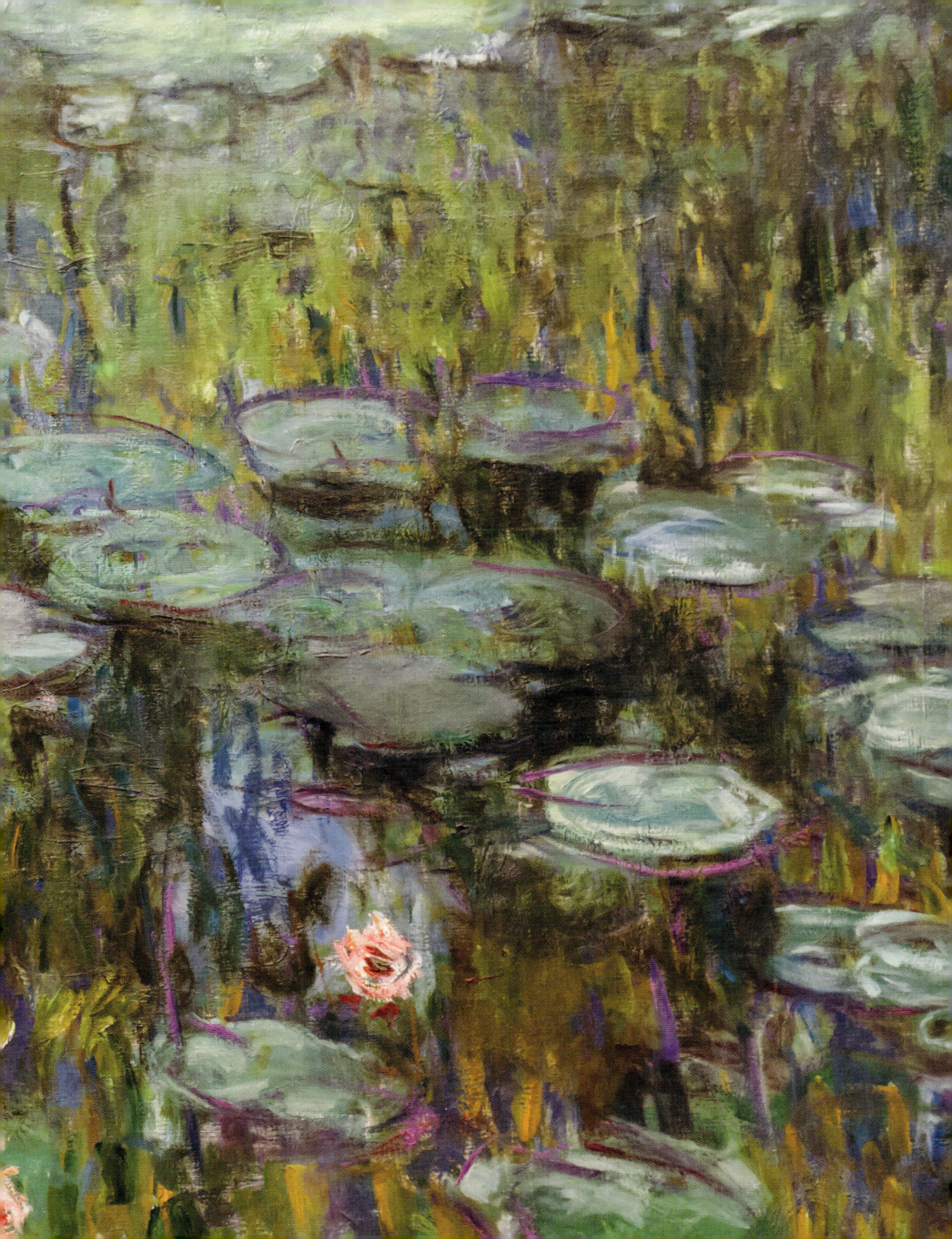

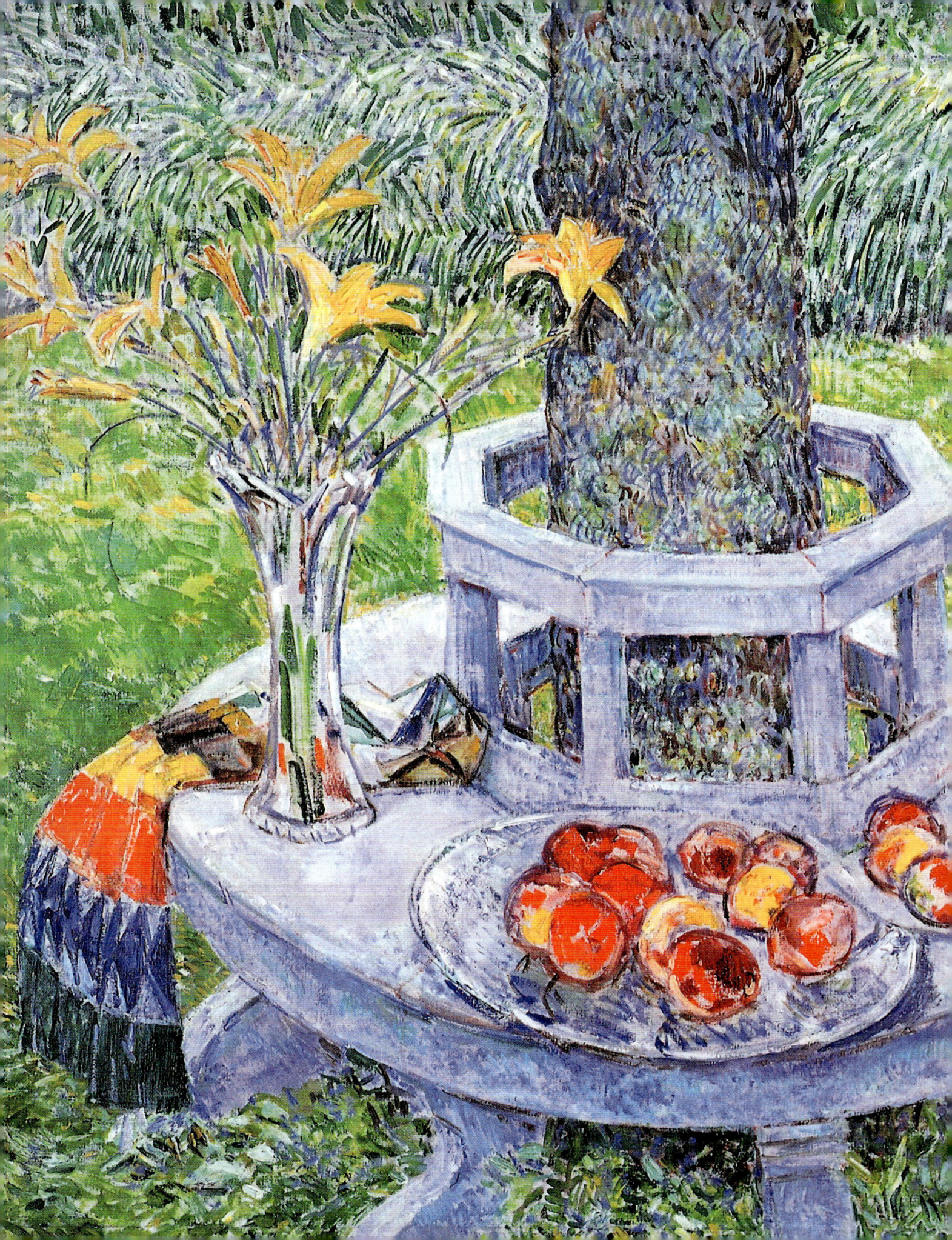

Contents

HALF-TITLE *Van Gogh Painting Sunflowers* (1888) by Paul Gauguin.
TITLE PAGE *Water Lilies* by Claude Monet (1915).
LEFT *Mrs Hassam's Garden at East Hampton* by Frederick Childe Hassam (1934).

Introduction

THE MOST ALLURING IMAGE of an artist at work is surely one where he or she has come out of their studio, set up their easel on the garden path, pulled on a hat to shade their eyes from the sun and taken their brush and palette in hand. What could be more inspirational for a painter – amateur or professional – than to work surrounded by the sights and sounds of a garden, capturing its beauty and form?

Spending time in a garden can be a transformative experience, but what exactly is an artist looking for when they set up their easel outside? One may paint the garden figuratively, while another will use it as a trigger for emotions that are expressed in an abstract way. Clearly, one of the great advantages of a garden – as opposed to a still life, for example – is that it is constantly changing, offering different colours, shapes and views throughout the seasons. A garden also changes from year to year, providing endless possibilities for new features or angles to paint; Claude Monet's garden at Giverny is the prime example of how one garden can be the catalyst for hundreds of great paintings. A garden can also allow an artist to learn, mature, and perfect a technique, returning to the same *motifs* year after year – Monet painted little other than his water garden in the last decades of his life.

Having a garden, and being able to grow the plants that interest you close at hand, is something many artists aim for. And it is these real gardens, created by some of the world's finest artists, from Renoir and Cézanne to Salvador Dalí and Frida Kahlo, that form the subject of this book. Through their flower gardens, olive groves, vineyards, and vegetable plots we can discover so much more about the artist than we might see at first glance in their paintings.

The relationship between artist and garden is often a complex one. The French Impressionists Pierre Bonnard, Gustave Caillebotte, and Claude Monet, who all lived and worked in the Seine valley in the late nineteenth century, were knowledgeable gardeners, as much in love with their plants as their art. Paris-based artists, including Pissarro, Manet, Renoir, Gauguin and Monet, were highly competitive and vied to paint each other's gardens. Other painters would 'borrow' gardens for their own purposes, such as the renowned American Impressionist Frederick Childe Hassam, who spent idyllic summers in

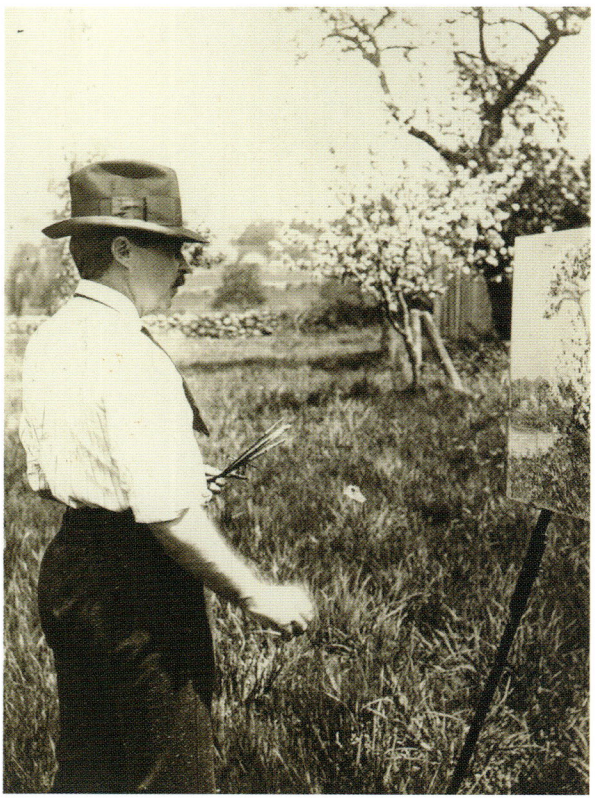

the artists' colonies of Old Lyme in Connecticut and at Celia Thaxter's garden on the Isles of Shoals in Maine.

A number of artists approached garden-making with a carefully considered design philosophy; for example, Rubens made a Baroque garden and house in Antwerp, and the German Impressionist Max Liebermann built a new house and garden on Lake Wannsee near Berlin. For others, it was a case of embracing an existing place, as Renoir did when he saved an ancient olive grove in the South of France from developers. The garden could also be a training ground, somewhere to improve their craft, with a ready supply of flowers and *motifs* to hand. A young Paul Cézanne, for example, honed his skills painting his father's garden in Aix-en-Provence in the south of France.

ABOVE American Impressionist Frederick Childe Hassam painting apple trees in the garden at Old Lyme in Connecticut.
RIGHT One of the first artists to work only outdoors, Claude Monet captured his wife Camille and son Jean in *Woman with a Parasol* (1875).

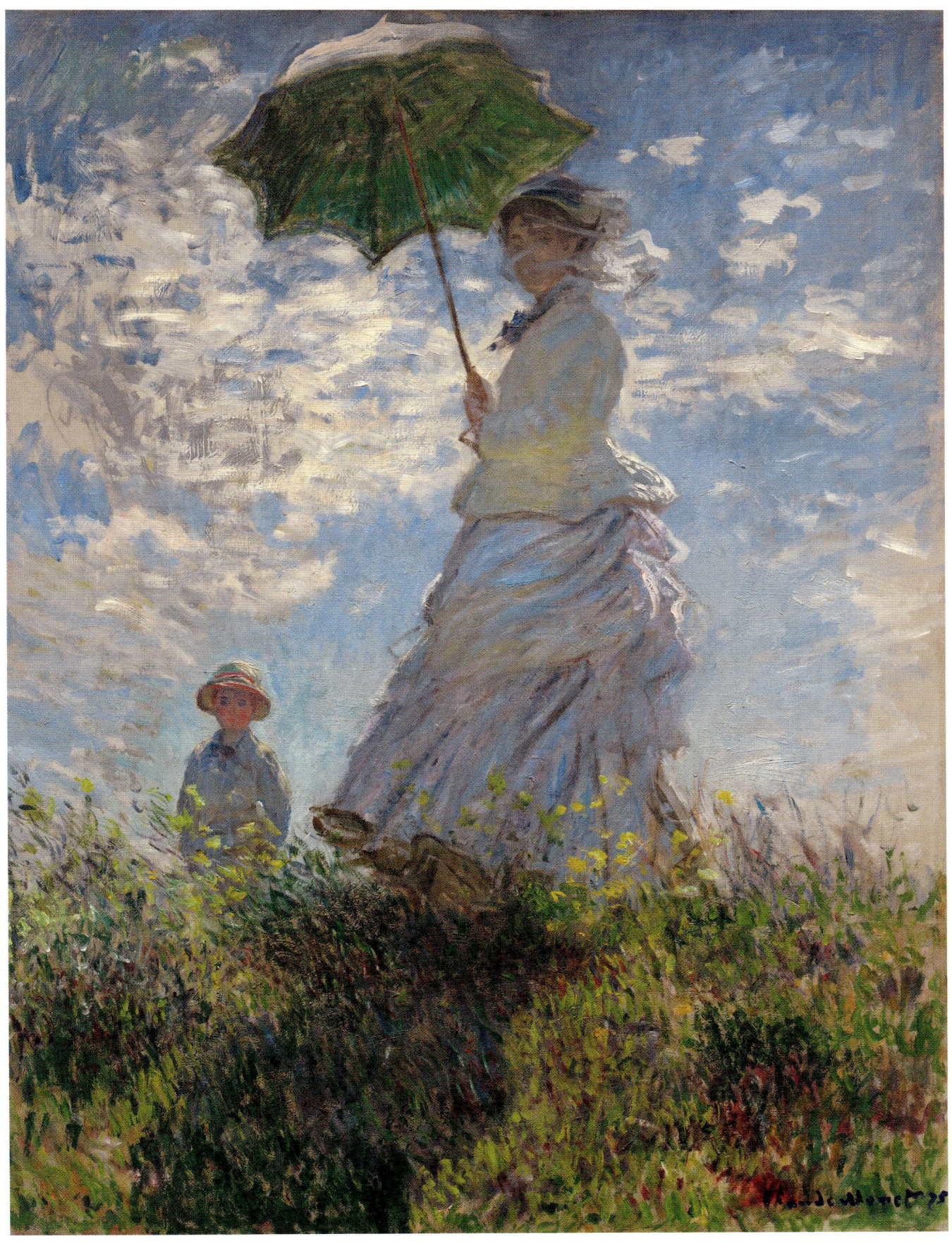

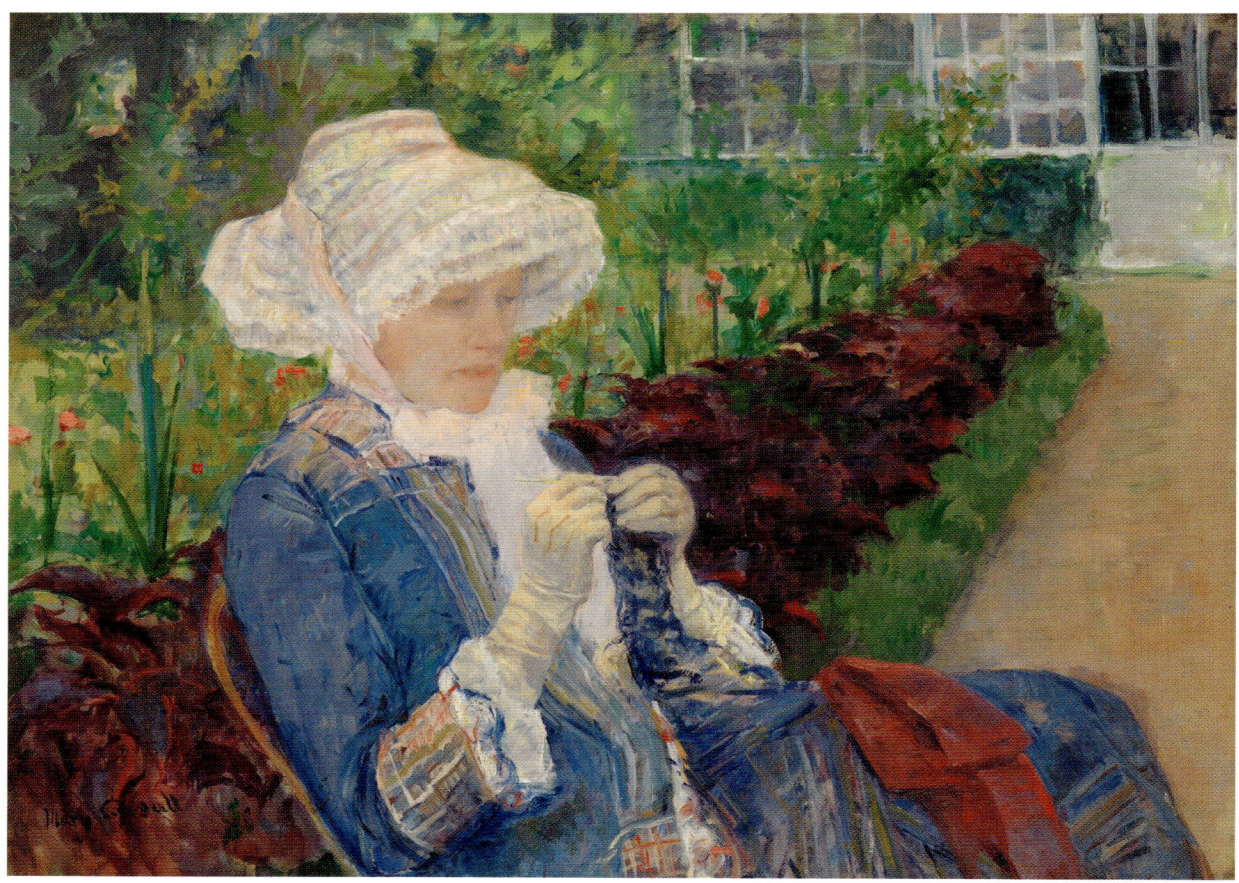

WORKING *EN PLEIN AIR*

Painting outdoors is a relatively recent phenomenon and only became possible as paint technology improved. For the 'Old Masters' of Europe, flower blooms had to be cut and brought indoors to be painted, where they were arranged in vases or placed in the hands of their sitters, always looking rather awkward and presumably very difficult to keep looking fresh.

In Renaissance Italy, artists ran communal workshops, known as *bottega*, where apprentices and pupils prepared canvases, mixed colours and learned from the great masters. Leonardo da Vinci spent his early career in a *bottega* in Florence, while Rubens became a great master himself, teaching Van Dyck and others, and running a thriving workshop from his house and garden in Antwerp. Sketching was possible outdoors, but putting paint on to canvas or wood was always carried out in the workshop. Mixing colours was a messy and dangerous business, as

mineral pigments had to be ground by hand and combined with oils to make the paint. Filled with varnishes, solvents, paints, and additional ingredients that included ground glass and beeswax, a pre-nineteenth-century workshop would have looked rather like a chemist's laboratory.

Watercolours were the first artists' materials to become genuinely portable when, in 1781, William Reeves invented his patent 'cakes' – hard blocks of paint that could be carried around and reconstituted *in situ*. Ready-mixed oil paints were becoming more widely available too, but they were still not really portable. Landscape painter J.M.W. Turner spent many days near his country

ABOVE *Lydia Crocheting in the Garden at Marly* (1880) by American-born artist, Mary Cassatt, depicts her sister at Marly-le-Roi, just outside Paris. Cassatt was influential in bringing Impressionism to America.
OPPOSITE Édouard Manet's *Claude Monet in Argenteuil* (1874) shows the artist painting on his small boat on the River Seine.

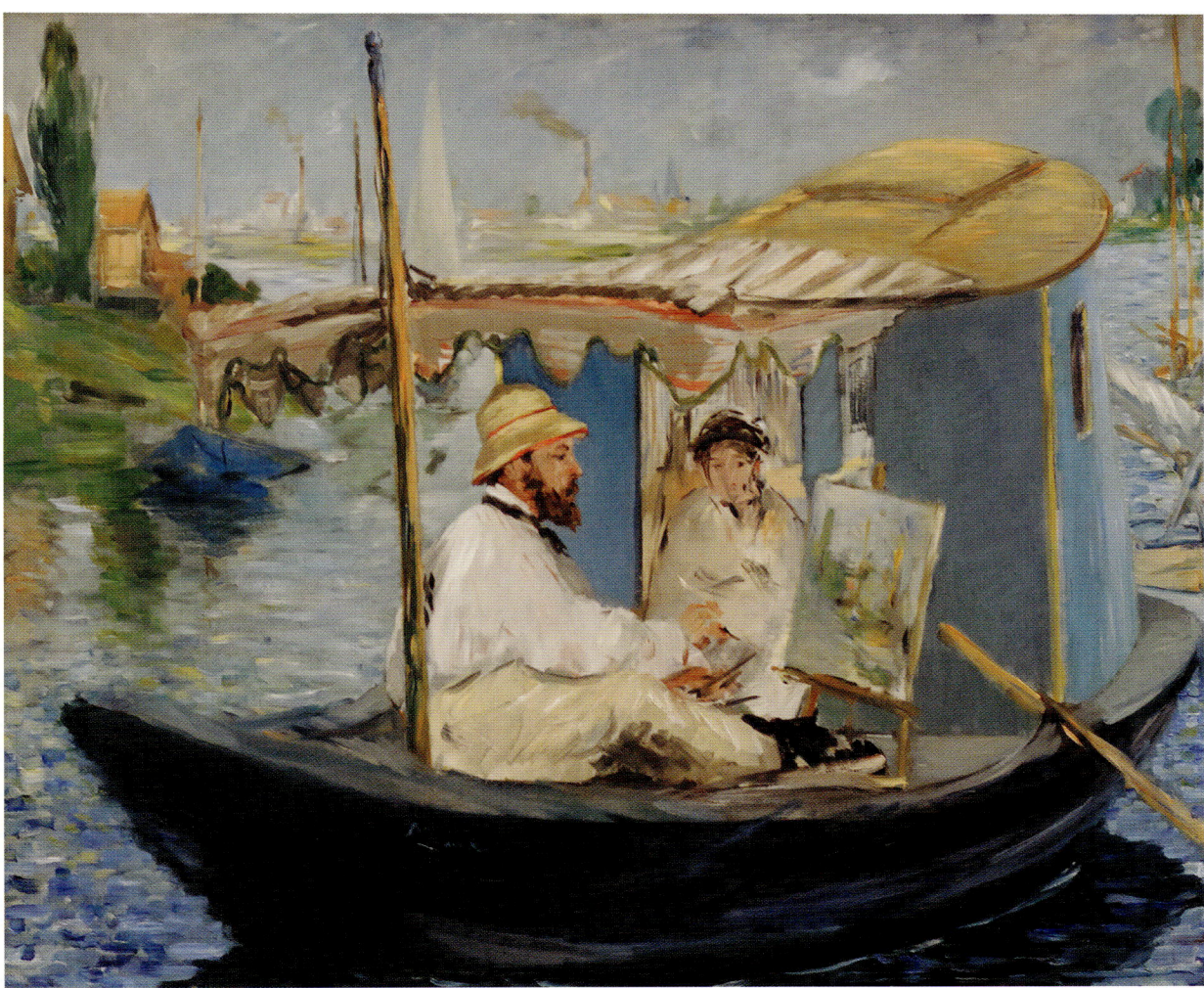

house in Twickenham with his friend, William Havell, experimenting and trying to prove that oil paints could be used successfully outdoors.

The invention by American portrait painter John Goffe Rand of a metal tube that could hold oil paints provided a real leap forward, but that would not come until 1851, the year Turner died. These flexible containers finally allowed painters to work freely outdoors – *en plein air* – a term that became synonymous with the Impressionist movement. From this point on, everything changed and painters of gardens and landscapes could experiment with the freer application of paint outside.

The Impressionists were foremost among an elite group of artist-gardeners, combining the two great art forms. Impressionism as a term was initially one of derision – it came about when Monet's painting, *Impression, Sunrise*, a hazy depiction of his home town of Le Havre, was shown in an alternative Paris exhibition in 1874. A critic writing

about the paintings, which also included work by Berthe Morisot, Cézanne and Degas, sarcastically referred to them as 'impressionist'. The term was embraced by the artists and the press and became one of the most influential art movements of the nineteenth and early twentieth centuries – filtering into Germany and Spain and across the Atlantic to America. What all these artists shared was a love of outdoor painting and a new way of looking at their subject matter.

GARDEN INSPIRATIONS

It may seem obvious, but to have a garden, you also need a relatively settled lifestyle – not something artists are particularly known for. Henri Le Sidaner, who created a wonderful rose garden in Picardie in northern France, P.S. Krøyer, known for his garden paintings in the seaside town of Skagen in northern Denmark, and Joaquín Sorolla, whose courtyards in Spain's capital city Madrid were his

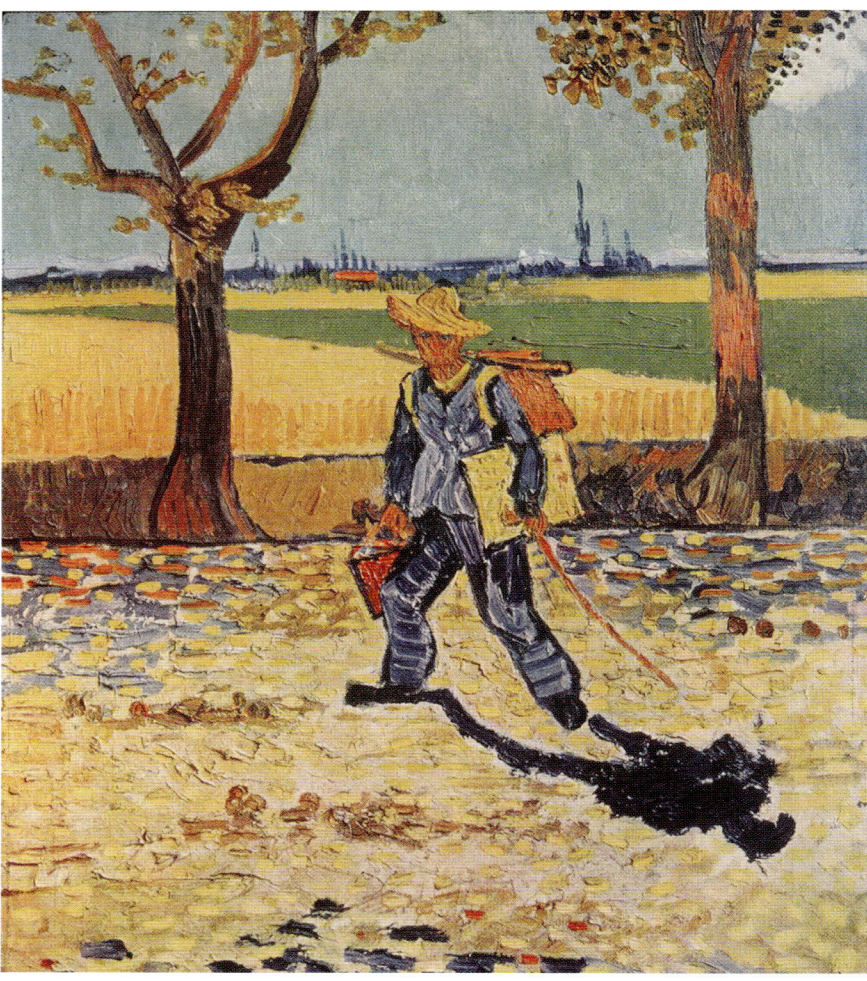

passion, were all secure in their professions as painters and could afford to establish homes and gardens. These artists, and many others, benefitted from the technical innovations of the previous centuries and were able to create – and paint – their own gardens and those of their friends in a relatively leisurely way.

Other painters never had that luxury. The creator of arguably the greatest images of sunflowers, poppies and irises, Vincent van Gogh, never had a garden of his own. However, after leaving the Yellow House in Arles where, following an argument with the painter Gauguin, he had mutilated his own ear, Vincent entered the Saint-Paul de Mausole asylum in Provence. The garden there covered about two acres, with a circular fountain and geometric paths giving way to wilder, more wooded areas. From his first day of admission in May 1889, Vincent set to work painting the purple irises and spring-flowering shrubs. Although his periods of calm were fleeting, he painted continuously, completing more than 150 works in the year

he stayed there. Among them are some of the most dazzling paintings the art world has ever seen: star-studded skies and richly coloured images of flowers. When Van Gogh returned to Auvers-sur-Oise near Paris, he created three great paintings of the garden of another artist, the late Charles-Françoise Daubigny, which Vincent himself believed were among his most carefully considered works.

Even artists not known for their flower paintings or depictions of gardens admit to their influence on their work. The abstract art of Henri Matisse, for example, was informed by the garden he was making at Issy-les-Moulineaux, a suburb of Paris. It was the flowers, he said, that branded the chromatic shapes on to his mind's eye. He had a studio built in the garden to ensure he was always in close contact with the brightly coloured blooms. Matisse claimed that when he held his paintings next to the flower beds, the colours of the latter would always make the paintings look dull. Other painters were similarly dazzled by the colours of a garden. Modernist artists, like Raoul Dufy

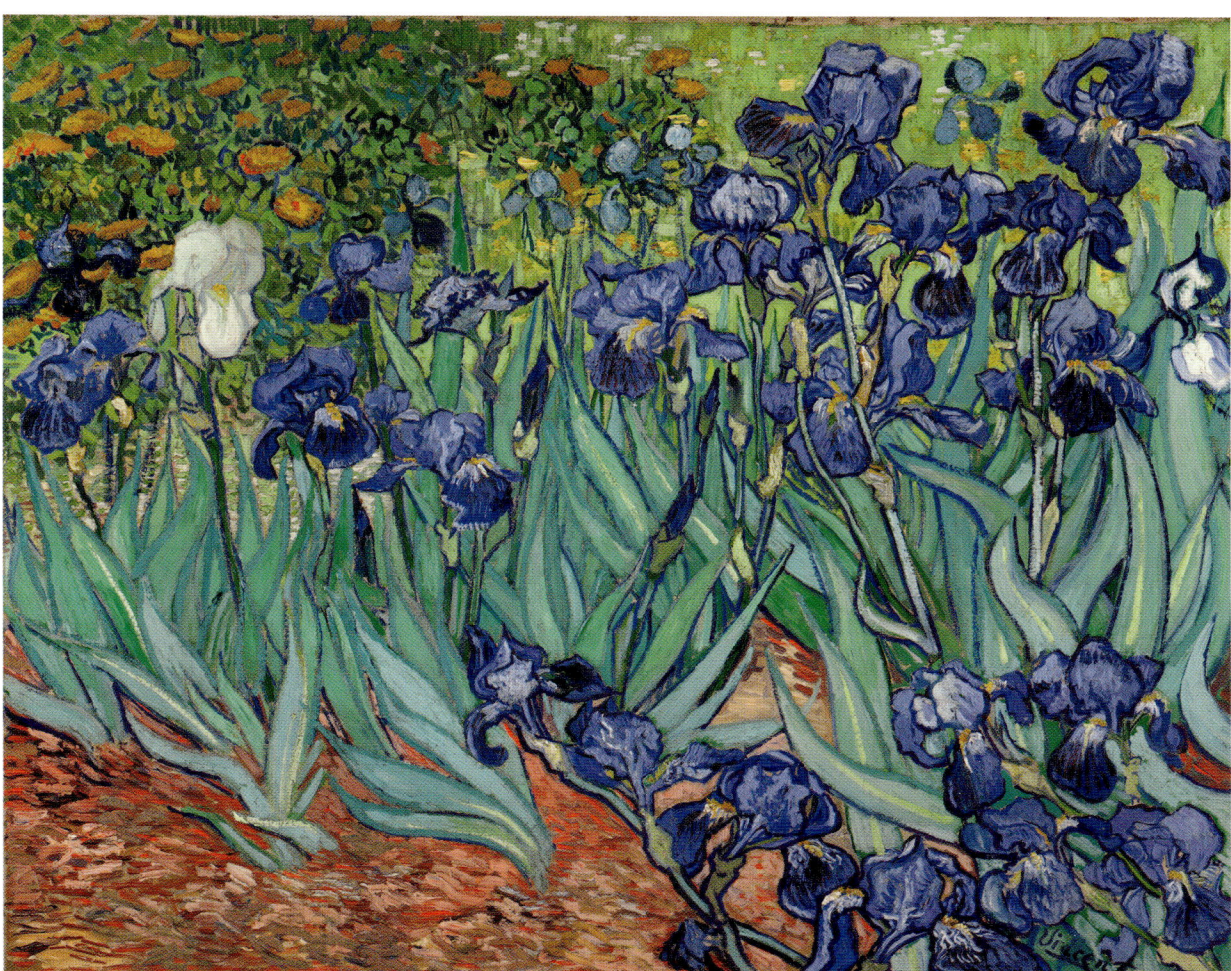

and Paul Gauguin, were inspired by their travels abroad to exotic gardens, particularly those in North Africa and the South Sea islands. Their work sought to find the universal, metaphysical aspects of nature within a garden, rather than to depict a particular place.

GARDENER-ARTISTS

Two of the masters of abstract art, Paul Klee and Wassily Kandinsky, were also avid gardeners. Klee gardened in Switzerland, while Russian-born Kandinsky threw himself into making a garden in Bavaria with his partner, Gabriele Münter, prior to the First World War. All these artists recognized and absorbed the creative energy that came from tending and making a garden – Klee would go further to say that he actually felt like a plant himself, believing that creativity flows through a human as sap flows through a tree, from the ground up.

By the mid-twentieth century, to be an artist-gardener was a recognized lifestyle. One British artist who lived the dream was Cedric Morris, a great plantsman, iris breeder and painter of gardens. His life in East Anglia captured the imagination of a new generation of art- and garden-lovers and his images of irises are perhaps the closest a British painter has come to rivalling Van Gogh or Monet. In the 1940s, Morris and his partner, Arthur Lett-Haines, ran an art school from their home at Benton End, which became known as 'The Artists' House'. The garden not only attracted artists, but also the great gardeners of the twentieth century, including Vita Sackville-West and Beth Chatto. Morris's obsession with plant breeding manifests itself in his paintings, many of which depict the bearded irises he bred, including those with 'Benton' in the name, such as 'Benton Cordelia', 'Benton Lorna' and 'Benton Farewell'. While Morris's irises are long gone from Benton End, many have been saved and are available once again.

Morris was typical of many artists in wanting to attract like-minded people around him. From the late nineteenth and throughout the twentieth century, artists' colonies

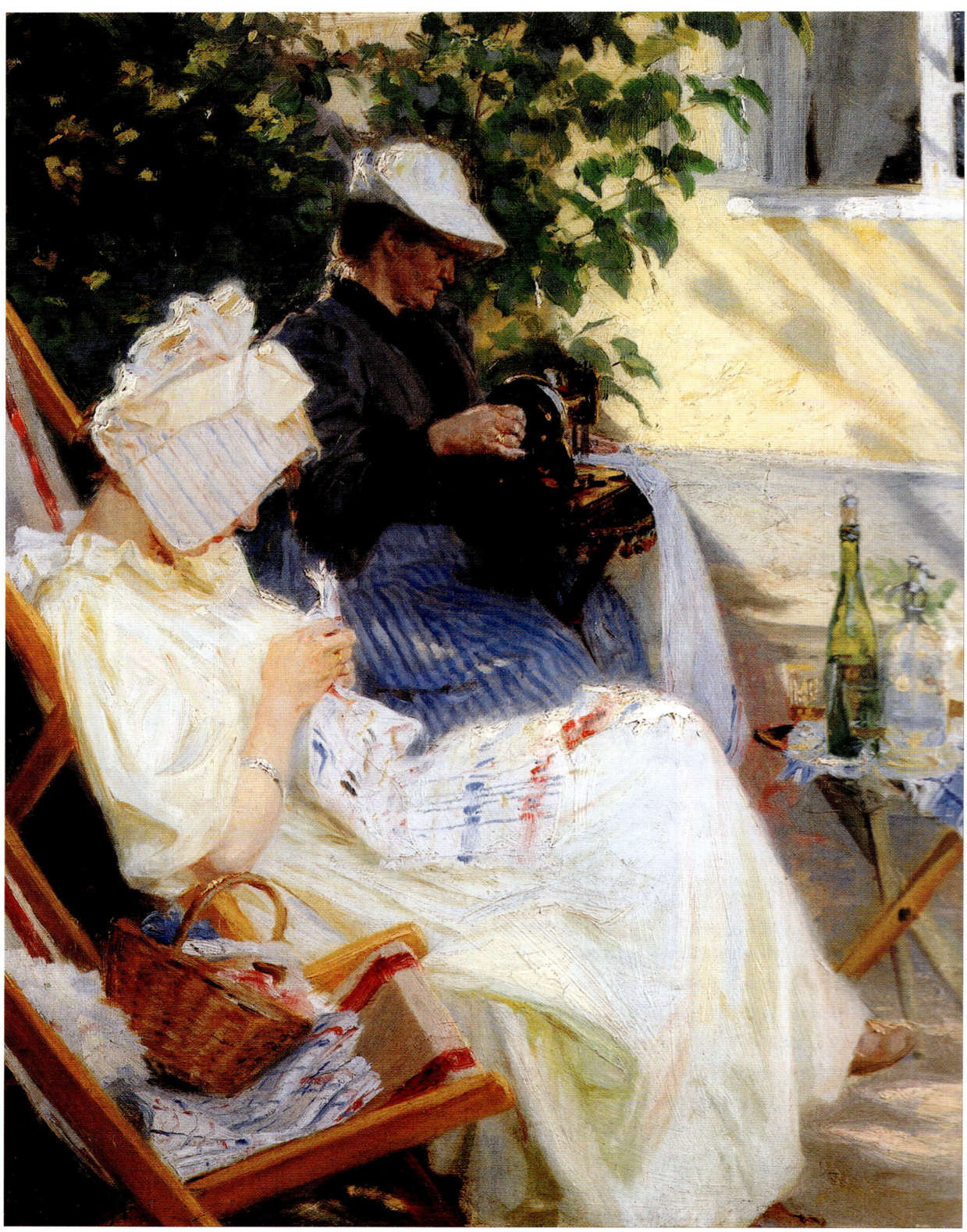

The Artist's Garden

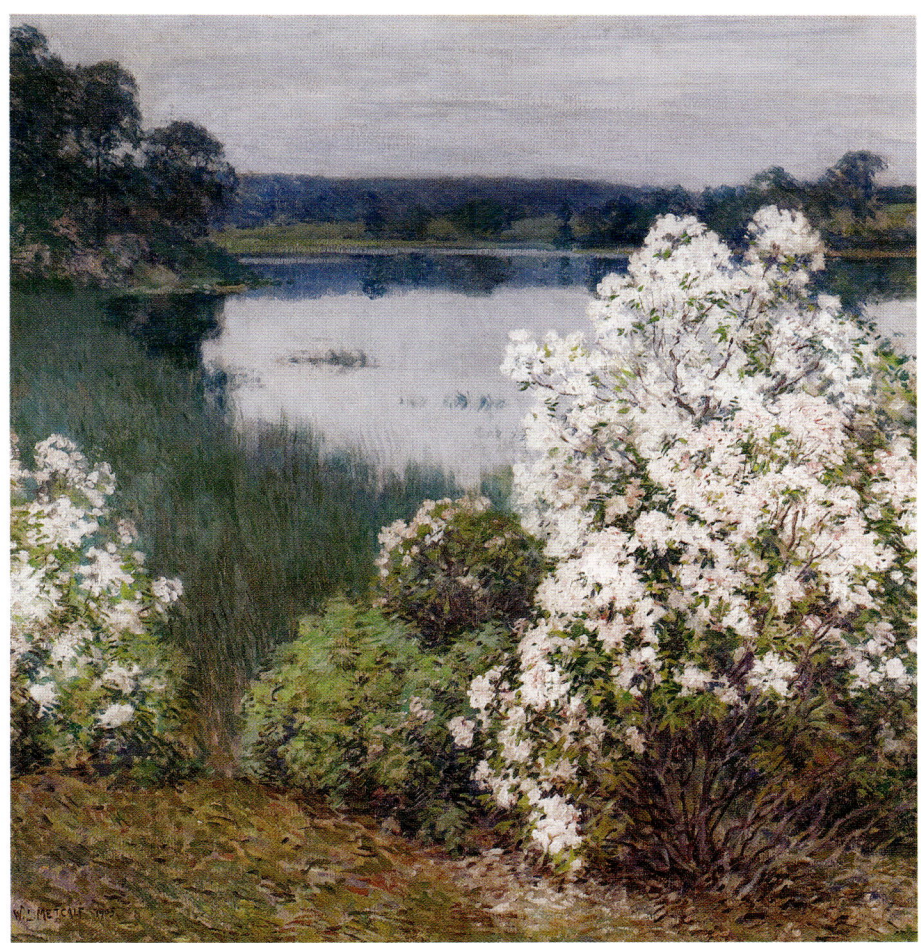

OPPOSITE *Two Women in the Garden* (1891) by P.S. Krøyer. At Skagen, in the north of Denmark, artists gathered each summer to paint, often featuring their own gardens or those of their friends.
LEFT *Kalmia* (1905) by Willard Metcalf shows *Kalmia latifolia* in flower in the grounds of Florence Griswold's boarding house in Connecticut, where he spent the summer months working with fellow artists.

sprung up throughout Europe and in America. In England, the Arts & Crafts designer William Morris retreated with his family and friends to Kelmscott Manor in Oxfordshire; in Scotland, the Glasgow Boys (and Girls) gathered at the home of E.A. Hornel in Kirkcudbright; and in the eastern USA, Impressionist artists met in summer houses, where the gardens were not just decorative, but essential to their art and wellbeing.

NATURAL SANCTUARIES

Painters are no more immune to world events than anyone else, but where they often turn in a crisis – political or personal – is to a place of their own making, somewhere enclosed that provides them with an escape, nourishment and a source of inspiration: a garden. This was particularly true of Frida Kahlo, living in Mexico City in the late 1930s. Her garden at The Blue House, which was so integral to her unconventional life and work, also provided a sanctuary for the exiled revolutionary Leon Trotsky. Likewise, Emil Nolde retreated to a small village on the Danish/German border, where he created a vibrant flower garden during the turmoil of the Nazi period. Even in a tranquil corner of England, the garden at Charleston in Sussex provided the Bloomsbury artists with the chance to make an alternative life and avoid conscription during the First World War.

This book is a journey to find the gardens, studios and houses lived in, and created by, great artists – places that still exist today, and that are open to visitors. The first part concentrates on the painters who chose to live alone or with their immediate families, while the second part is devoted to those living close to one another in artists' communities. All these painters – singly and collectively – were inspired by the basic act of growing fruit, flowers and vegetables. They managed to combine garden-making with their art; as gardens fed into their work, their art flowed into their gardens. Walking the paths that they walked and spending time in these gardens helps us to understand the day-to-day life of the artists and, more importantly, their paintings, which ultimately transform and transcend reality.

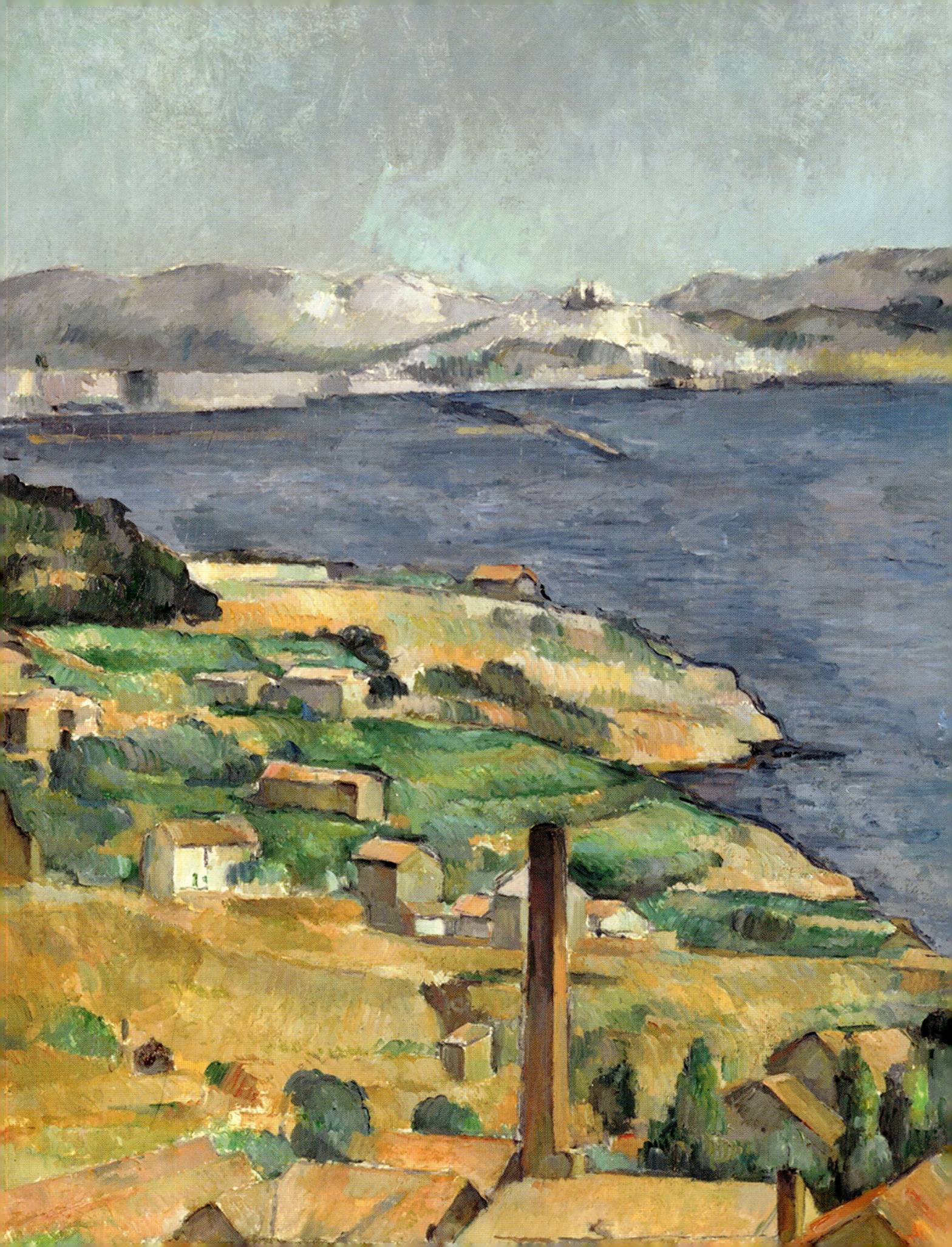

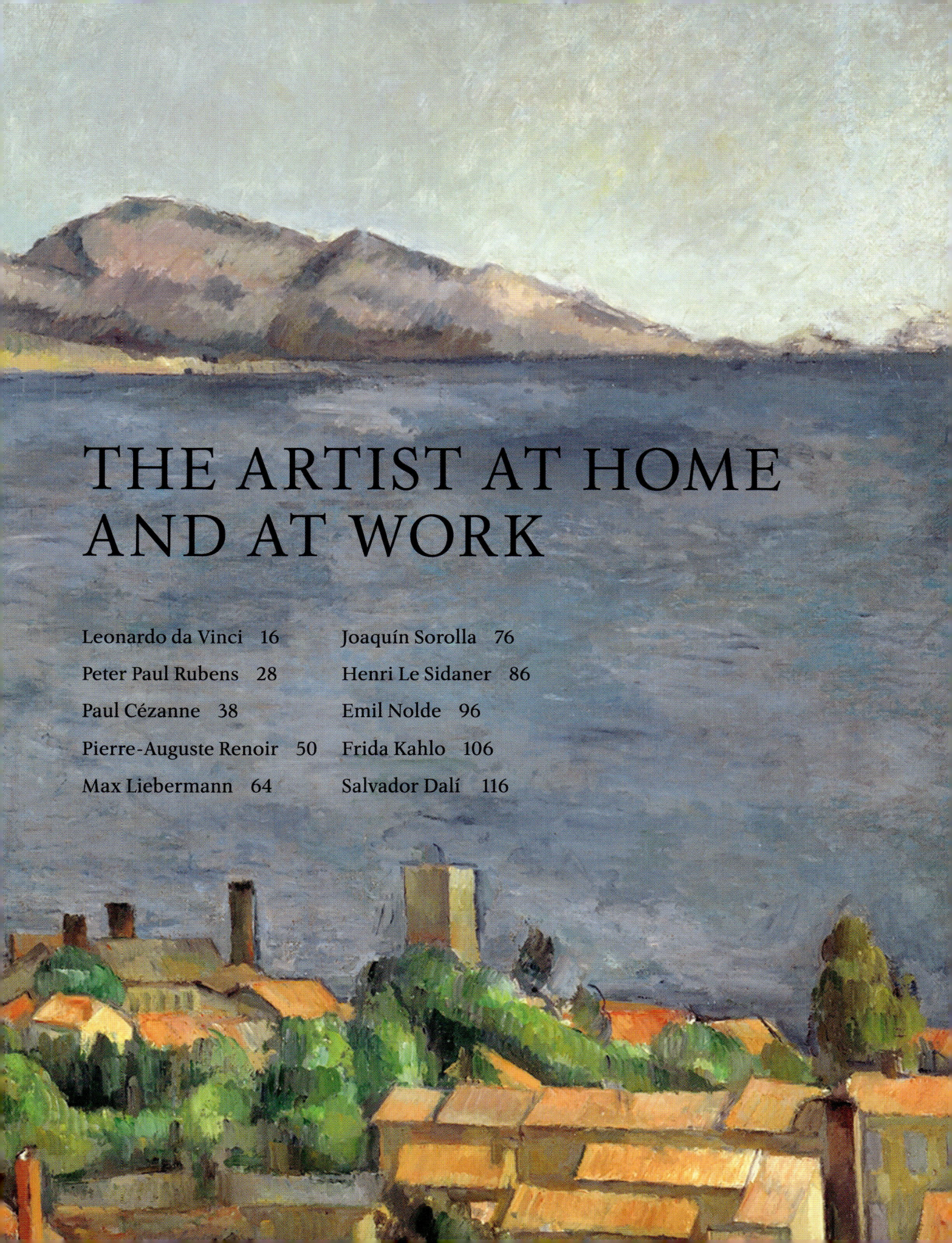

THE ARTIST AT HOME AND AT WORK

Leonardo
da Vinci

Amboise, France

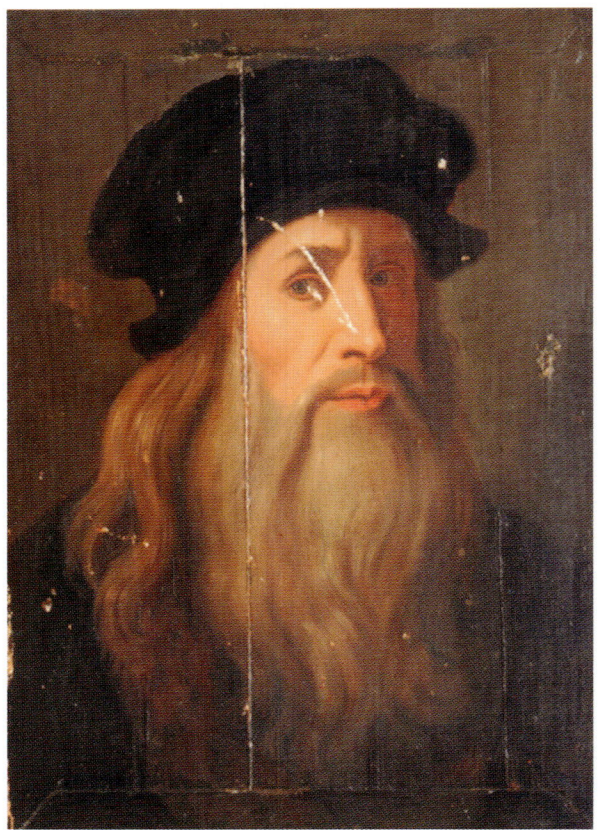

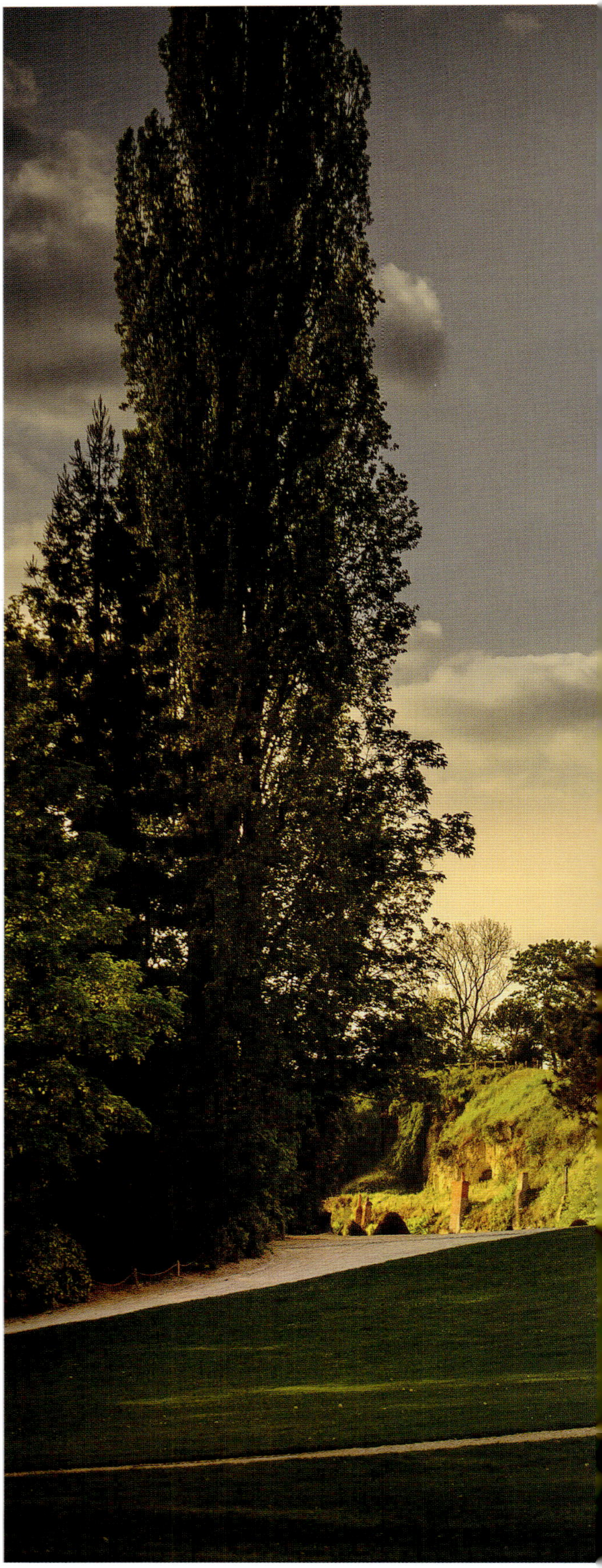

THE MAN WE KNOW simply as 'Leonardo' will be remembered not only as an artist, but also as an inventor, military architect, botanist, engineer, cartographer, sculptor and philosopher. Although he was brilliantly talented, Leonardo was not a prolific painter and few of his artworks survive today – his writings and polymathic mind will perhaps prove to be more enduring

ABOVE This early sixteenth-century self-portrait is thought to have been painted when Leonardo da Vinci was in his early fifties.
RIGHT The Italian artist spent the last years of his life at the Château du Clos Lucé in the Loire valley at the invitation of King François I.

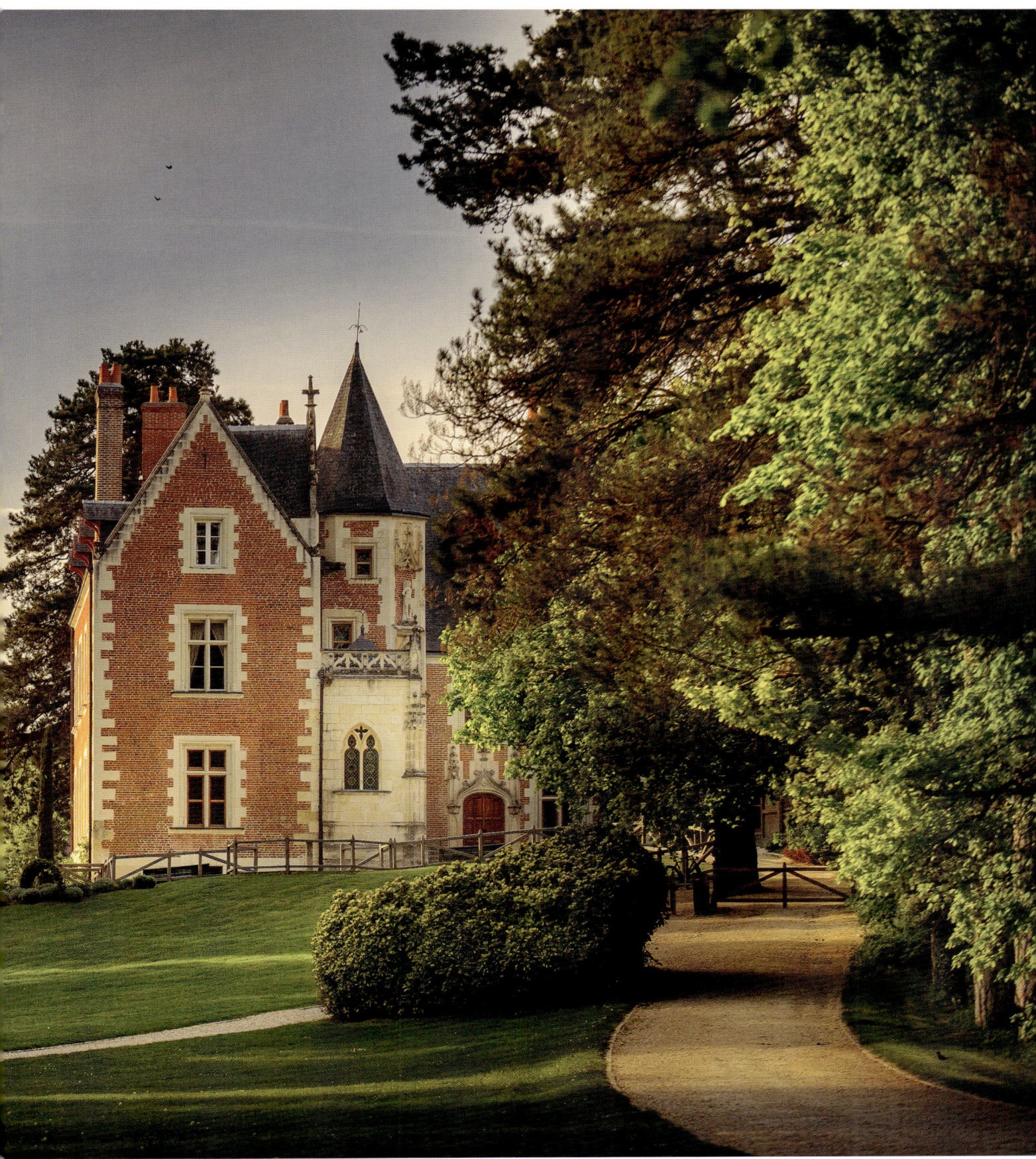

than his painting of *The Last Supper* on the walls of the Santa Maria delle Grazie convent in Milan. Yet there is one work that has captured the public's imagination like no other. The *Mona Lisa* is not only Leonardo's most famous painting, it also holds clues to the theories he held about the intimate connection between nature and the human body. A keen botanist, moving to Le Clos Lucé in France confirmed Leonardo's passion for the natural world and particularly for plants, which he studied closely at his home by the Loire, where he spent his final years.

EARLY PATRONS

Leonardo da Vinci took his name from the commune of Vinci, where he was born in the village of Anchiano, not far from Florence. The son of Piero da Vinci, a successful notary, Leonardo was born illegitimately to Caterina, a servant in his father's house. When Leonardo was five years old, his mother was no longer able to support him and placed him permanently with the da Vinci family. He was raised by his paternal grandparents and an uncle, who took the boy horse riding around the Tuscan countryside. It was there, among the Montalbano hills, that Leonardo discovered the natural world and grew to believe that every part of man corresponded with every part of nature.

Taught to paint in Florence by Verrocchio, Leonardo's career never followed a straight path. At the age of twenty-four he, along with several other members of Verrocchio's household, was prosecuted for homosexuality, although the charges were later dropped. By the time he was thirty, he was receiving commissions for large religious works and, in 1482, he won the patronage of Ludovico Sforza, the Duke of Milan. In a famous letter to the Duke, Leonardo claimed that he could '*construct bridges which are light and can be easily transported … drain water from moats … contrive catapults and weapons for firing arrows … and carry out sculpture in marble, bronze and clay.*' This confidence was not arrogance; he was a skilled practical engineer with a fantastically inventive mind.

Leaving Milan when the French invaded in 1499, he went on to sell his services to Cesare Borgia – the

infamous politician and commander of the Papal armies. In 1503, Leonardo was commissioned by the Florentine minister of justice Piero Soderina to paint one of two wall paintings for the Palazzo Vecchio, the city hall in Florence – the other was by Michelangelo. The paintings celebrated famous Florentine victories; Leonardo's was the Battle of Anghiari, fought in 1440, and on the opposite wall Michelangelo worked on the Battle of Cascina.

Michelangelo was the younger and, by all accounts, the more efficient artist and there were rumours of rivalry and jealousy. In the end, neither artist finished their commissions: Michelangelo was called away to paint the Sistine Chapel in Rome, while Leonardo's painting failed when he experimented with a paint and plaster mix, which melted when he tried to dry it out more quickly using braziers. Nevertheless, the years between 1500 and 1505 were Leonardo's most productive for painting, and it was

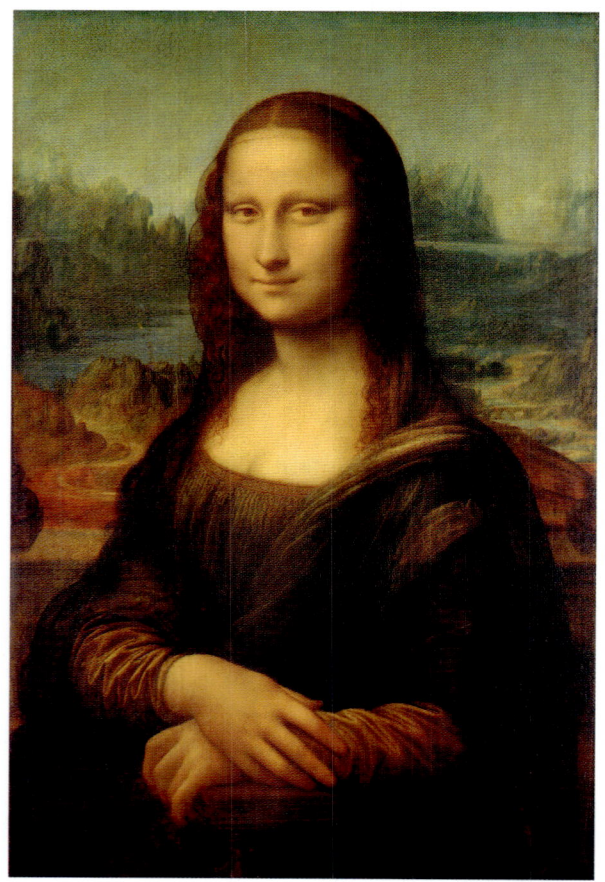

RIGHT The *Mona Lisa* or *La Gioconda* (1503–05) is Leonardo's painting of Lisa Gherardini, the wife of a Florentine official.

Restoring Leonardo's Vineyard

In 1498, Leonardo's patron, the Duke of Milan, gave the artist a small vineyard, close to where he was working on his troublesome masterpiece, *The Last Supper*, in the convent of Santa Maria delle Grazie. Every morning and evening, while walking across the vineyard to and from his work, Leonardo would check on his sixteen rows of vines. A year later, when his patron was captured by the French, Leonardo managed to reclaim the lease and subsequently kept the vineyard for the rest of his life.

The rectangular vineyard, measuring 60 by 175 metres/197 by 574 feet, miraculously survived 500 years of development and has been restored and replanted with the original vine stock. The aim is to preserve the historic grape varieties, especially the *Malvasia aromatica* grape which, following DNA testing, proved to be the one grown here in the late fifteenth century. The vineyard, gardens of the neighbouring house and orchard opened to the public in 2015, and wine is once again produced in the traditional way using grapes from *La Vigna di Leonardo*.

On his deathbed, Leonardo would not forget his own small patch of Italian soil, dividing it between two servants, one of them his long-time pupil, Salaì (Gian Giacomo Caprotti da Oreno), who had lived with Leonardo for twenty-five years in Milan and Rome, before the artist's departure for the Loire valley in France.

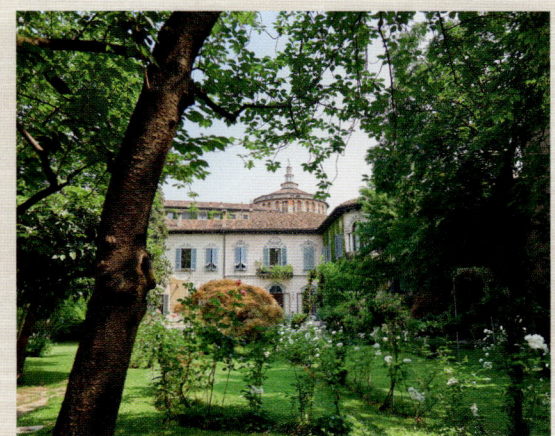

La Vigna di Leonardo in Milan

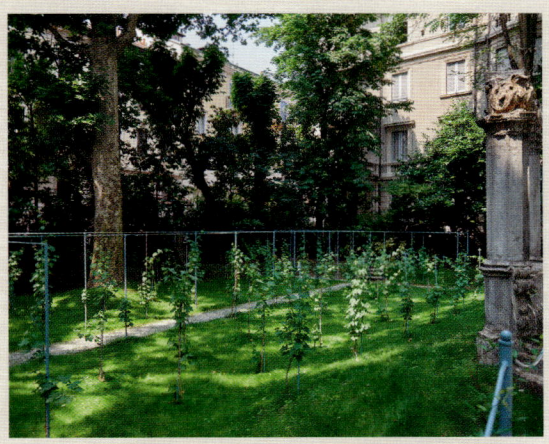

Malvasia aromatica vines

during this time that he painted a portrait of a Florentine official's wife, known as *La Gioconda* or *Mona Lisa*. He never sold the painting and kept it for the rest of his life.

BY ROYAL INVITATION

A decade later, Leonardo's star was falling in his home country. While he was no longer able to do the physical work of a military engineer, his paintings were being surpassed by those of Raphael and Michelangelo. He was attracting less patronage and few commissions. In contrast, the French were just discovering Renaissance artists and they were highly sought-after, particularly by the nobility and royal family. Leonardo probably met the young King François I of France in 1515, and the following year, the King invited him to live in France, appointing him *peintre et ingénieur,* with a pension of 1,000 golden *écus* per year – a fortune, which Leonardo was not in a position to refuse.

In August 1516, aged sixty-four, Leonardo set off across the Alps to France, travelling by mule with his companions, Batista Vilanus, his cook, and Francesco Melzi, his long-

Leonardo da Vinci
(1452–1519)

The Chateau du Clos Lucé in the town of Amboise was Leonardo da Vinci's final home and the last place he worked. Aged sixty-four and almost forgotten in his home country of Italy, he was invited to live in the chateau by King François I. He brought with him three of his most important paintings and worked on his botanic drawings with the intention of creating a herbal, as well as running a workshop for other artists. When he died, Leonardo probably left the enigmatic *Mona Lisa* to one of his assistants, who possibly sold it to the King, which is why to this day the *Mona Lisa* remains at the Louvre in Paris.

Five hundred years after his death, his genius and legacy to art, architecture, anatomy, science and engineering, is immeasurable. More and more of his ideas, drawings, sketches and his leaps of imagination are proving to be workable in the twenty-first century.

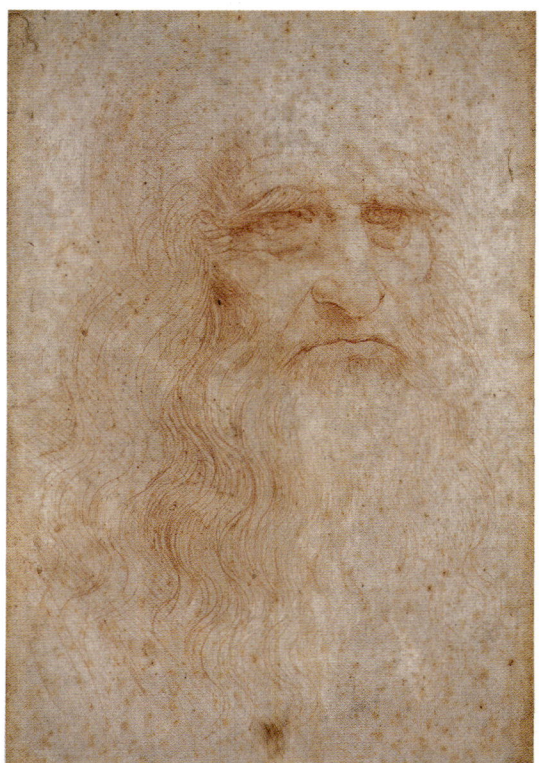

Portrait of a Man in Red Chalk (circa 1510) in the Royal Library, Turin, is thought to be a self-portrait of Leonardo da Vinci, aged about sixty.

time pupil, who also received a pension from the King of 300 *écus*. With them went Leonardo's most treasured possessions: his notebooks, drawings and three paintings – *The Virgin and Child with Saint Anne*, the unfinished *Saint John the Baptist*, considered to be his last masterpiece, and *Mona Lisa*, the one painting he never let out of his sight.

The King accommodated Leonardo within view of his castle at Amboise on the River Loire, in a handsome brick and stone fifteenth-century chateau owned by his mother. By placing Leonardo in his mother's home, François, who had only recently taken the throne, was clearly looking to the older and wiser man for guidance and paternal advice. Aged just twenty-two and with no father of his own – Charles Count of Angoulême had died when François was just two years old – he wanted Leonardo close at hand.

Leonardo and his companions set up home at the chateau, renaming it Le Clos Lucé (enclosure of light) and one of his first works after arriving there in October 1516 was a drawing of the view across the river to the King's spectacular castle. Leonardo continued the same workshop or *bottega* system that he had used in Italy, setting up studios in the downstairs rooms for assistants and pupils and encouraging a multi-disciplinary approach. It was essentially a workshop of apprentices, each learning different trades, including painting, sculpture, theatre design, and iron-, silver- and goldsmithing. The pupils had access to painting and drawing materials, and were able to draw directly from nature in the gardens.

The type of garden at the chateau at that time is not known, but it would probably have included kitchen and formal gardens, pastureland, vineyards (Leonardo had left behind his own vineyard in Milan), fishponds, pigeon lofts and beehives. The *pigeonnier*, which still exists, has one thousand roosts, suggesting that Le Clos Lucé was a large estate, as each pigeon needed a hectare/2.5 acres of land for gleaning (feeding). Pigeons were valued not only as meat, but also for their eggs, feathers and manure.

LEONARDO'S GARDEN LEGACY

The Château du Clos Lucé came into the ownership of the Saint Bris family in 1855, who enhanced the parkland with plantings of plane, oak and ash trees, sequoias, and conifers. The chateau and grounds were opened to the

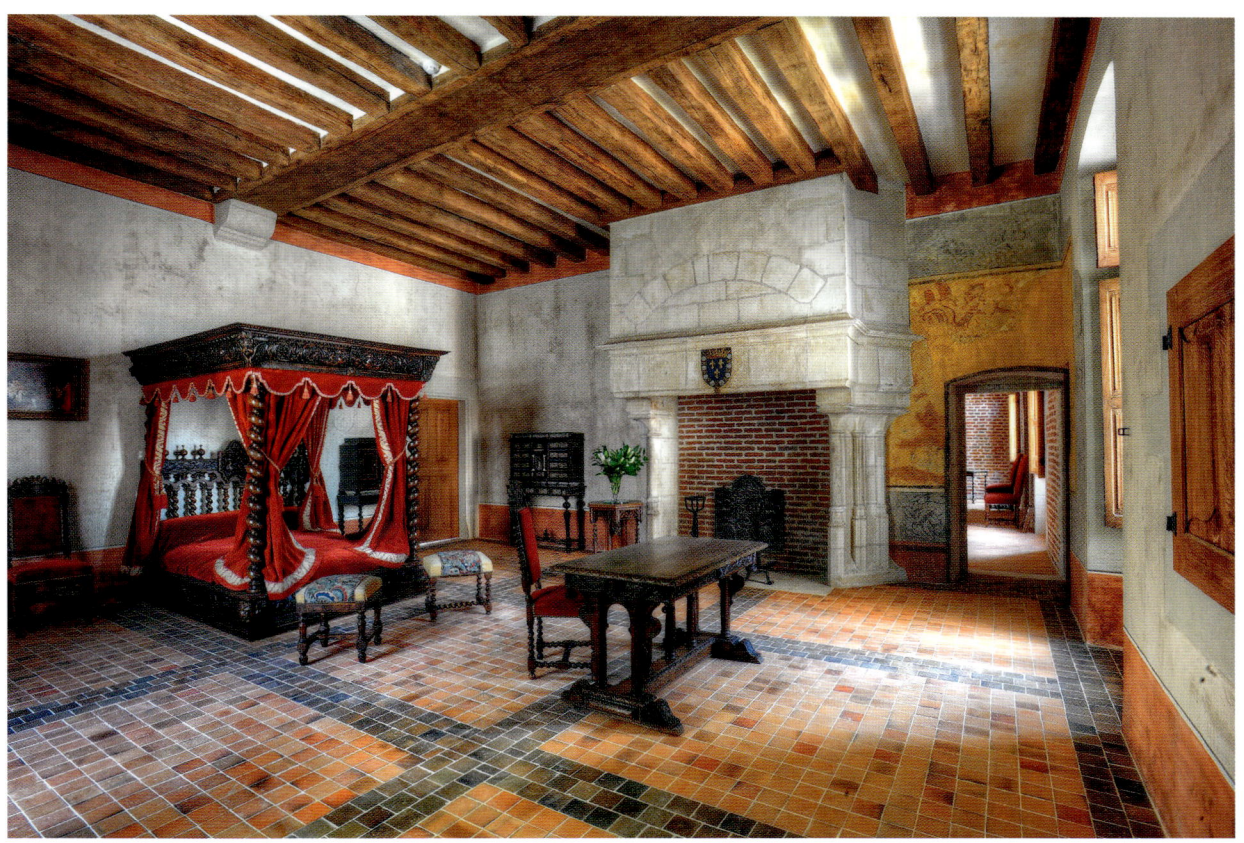

ABOVE Leonardo's spacious bedroom at Le Clos Lucé was on the first floor.
RIGHT The artist operated a studio system at the chateau, with his assistants and pupils sharing the downstairs rooms.

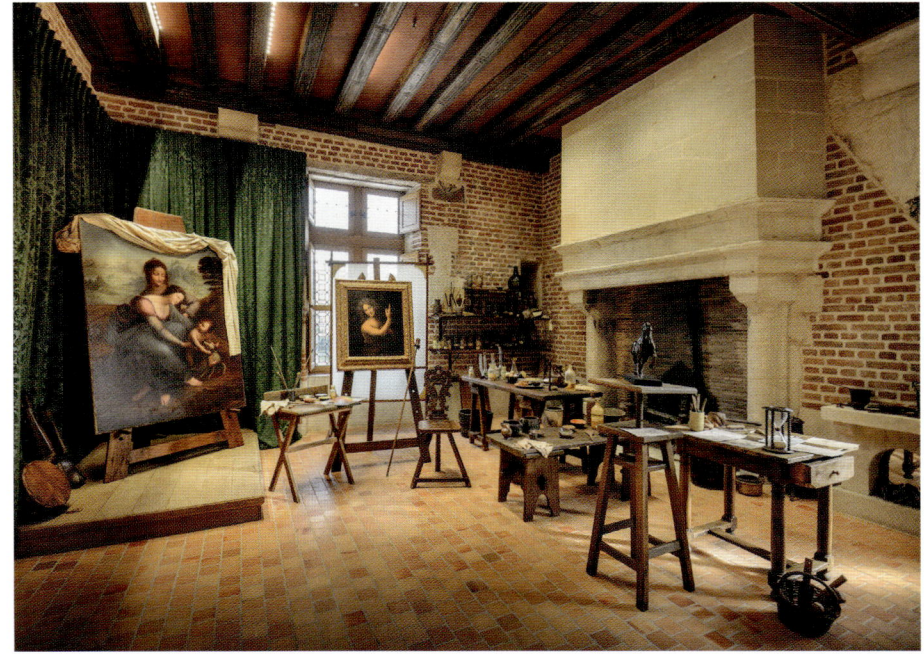

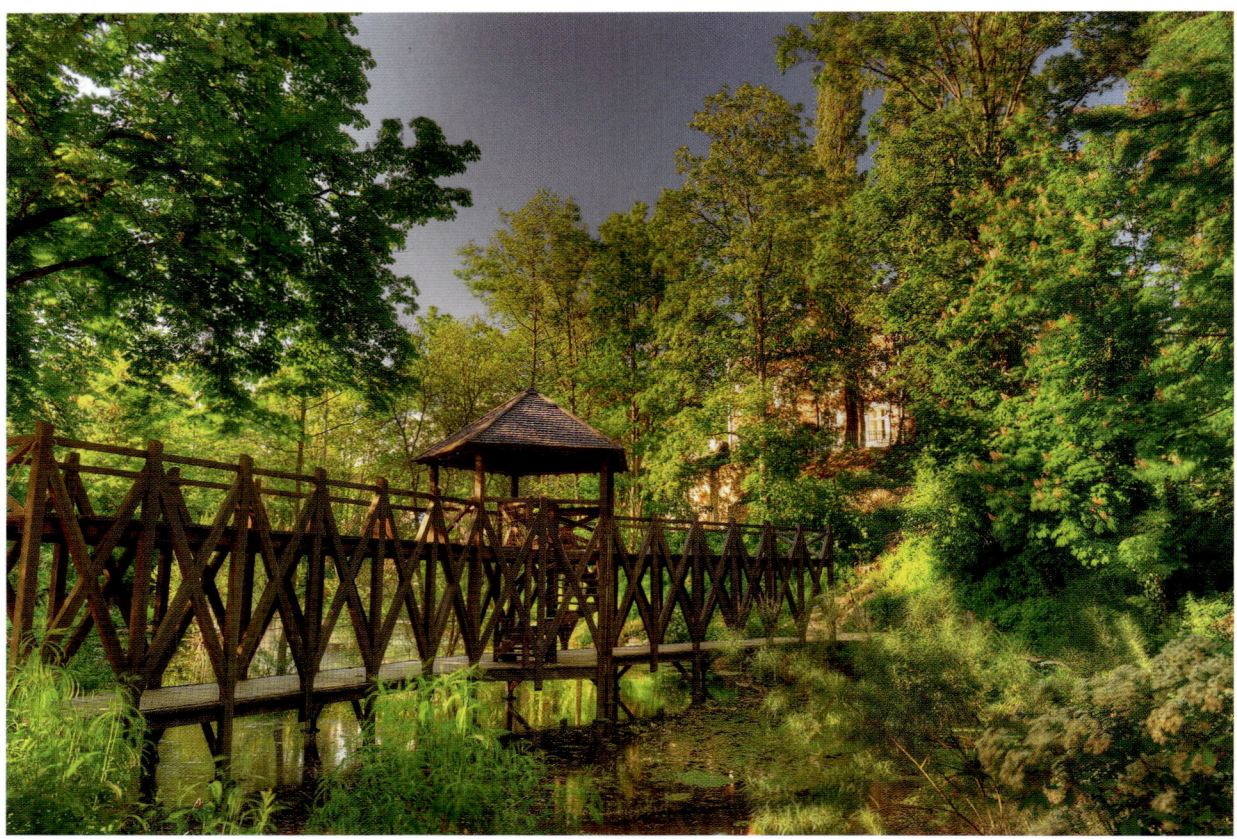

*"The air moves like a river
and carries the clouds with it."*
LEONARDO DA VINCI (1482–1519)

ABOVE The water garden at Le Clos Lucé,
designed in 2008, includes a two-level
bridge built to an original Leonardo design.
RIGHT (CLOCKWISE FROM TOP LEFT)
The replica of Leonardo's Golden Horn
Bridge; *Ligularia przewalskii* growing in
the water garden; *Rosa* Mona Lisa; the lower
water gardens; the Renaissance-style
parterre; the *pigeonnier*, containing
a thousand pigeon roosts; the ancient
mill in the grounds of the chateau.

public one hundred years later, in 1954. In the late twentieth and early twenty-first century, the current co-owner, François Saint Bris, with his brother and sisters, have overseen a regeneration of the gardens that aims to capture Leonardo's spirit and energy. This includes a terrace, potager and water garden, as well as the ongoing conservation of the nineteenth-century park.

On the terrace, a Renaissance-style parterre has been executed by Bernard Vitry, an architect of historical monuments and landscaper, with a water feature made up of geometrical shapes. Box- and yew-edged compartments are filled with the red *Rosa* Mona Lisa, which was developed in 2000 by rose breeders Meilland and trialled at Château du Clos Lucé before being released worldwide. The rose is disease resistant and repeat flowers from late spring until autumn.

The water garden is a fresh interpretation of Leonardo's place in history. Designed in 2008 by landscape architect, Olivier van der Vynckt, it was inspired by some of the 120 architectural and engineering plans that Leonardo drew – most of which were never realized. One was for a two-level bridge, a design developed in response to the plague that ravaged Europe in the late fifteenth and early sixteenth centuries. Leonardo saw the filth and squalor in the cities and thought that people's health would be improved if they walked on the upper

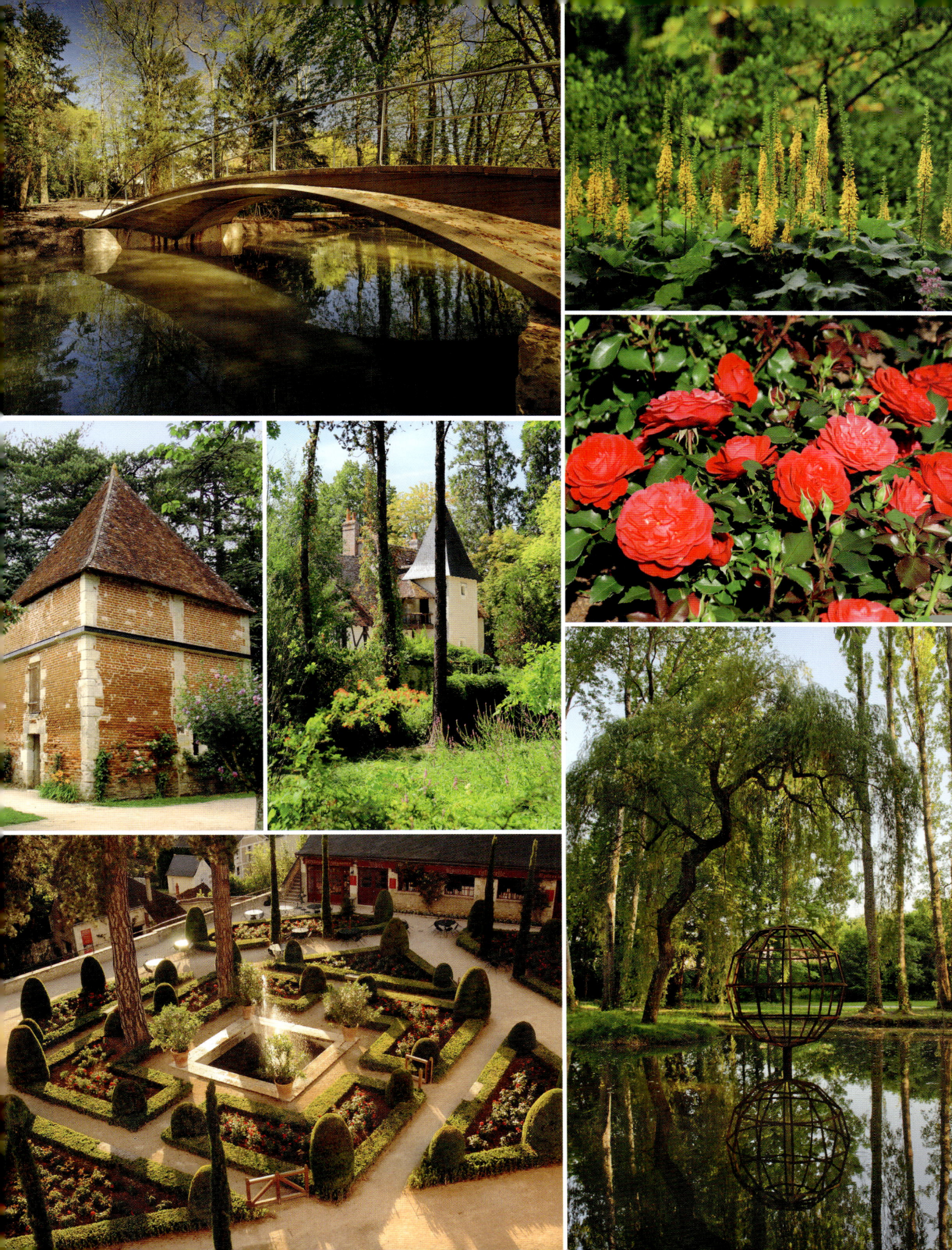

bridge, well away from the animals and carts, which would use the lower bridge, with the sewers running below that. The wooden construction at Le Clos Lucé is the first time Leonardo's bridge idea has been put into practice and it serves as a good lookout point over the water, with its whirlpools, or *tourbillons*.

The philosophy of Le Clos Lucé is evolutionary and organic – no chemicals are used anywhere – but it is also about adapting what nature provides rather than imposing a gardener's will on the land. This was also a key tenet of Leonardo's thinking: the idea that nature must be studied for what it can teach us rather than trying to 'domesticate' it.

The Clos Lucé park is, in part, laid out on clay marshland and it is still prone to flooding from the Amasse – a tributary of the Loire. A bridge has been built at the lowest point, following the design of Leonardo's Golden Horn Bridge of 1502. One of his many ingenious designs, it was drawn for the Sultan of Istanbul and intended to span the Bosporus river, which runs through the Turkish capital. The bridge was brilliant in architectural terms, using two parabolic arches

to combat the problem of crosswinds, and tall enough to allow a ship in full sail to pass beneath it. Sadly, like many of Leonardo's visionary ideas, it was never built. However, in 2016, Clos Lucé, with Norwegian artist Vebjørn Sand and a team of thirty carpenters and craftspeople, constructed the bridge in wood for the first time at one-tenth of its planned original size (Leonardo intended it to measure 10 metres wide by approximately 360 metres long/33 by 1,180 feet), proving that the design was workable and perfectly in scale.

THE SELF-TAUGHT BOTANIST

Leonardo had an extensive knowledge of botany, as shown in the sketchbooks he brought with him from Italy, which were filled with detailed botanical drawings. While at Clos Lucé, he hoped to produce a herbal, and the forty existing drawings of wild plants that would presumably have been in the book show that it was another of his great schemes that never quite made it to completion. Had it done so, the herbal would have ranked among the first in western Europe. Among his sketches

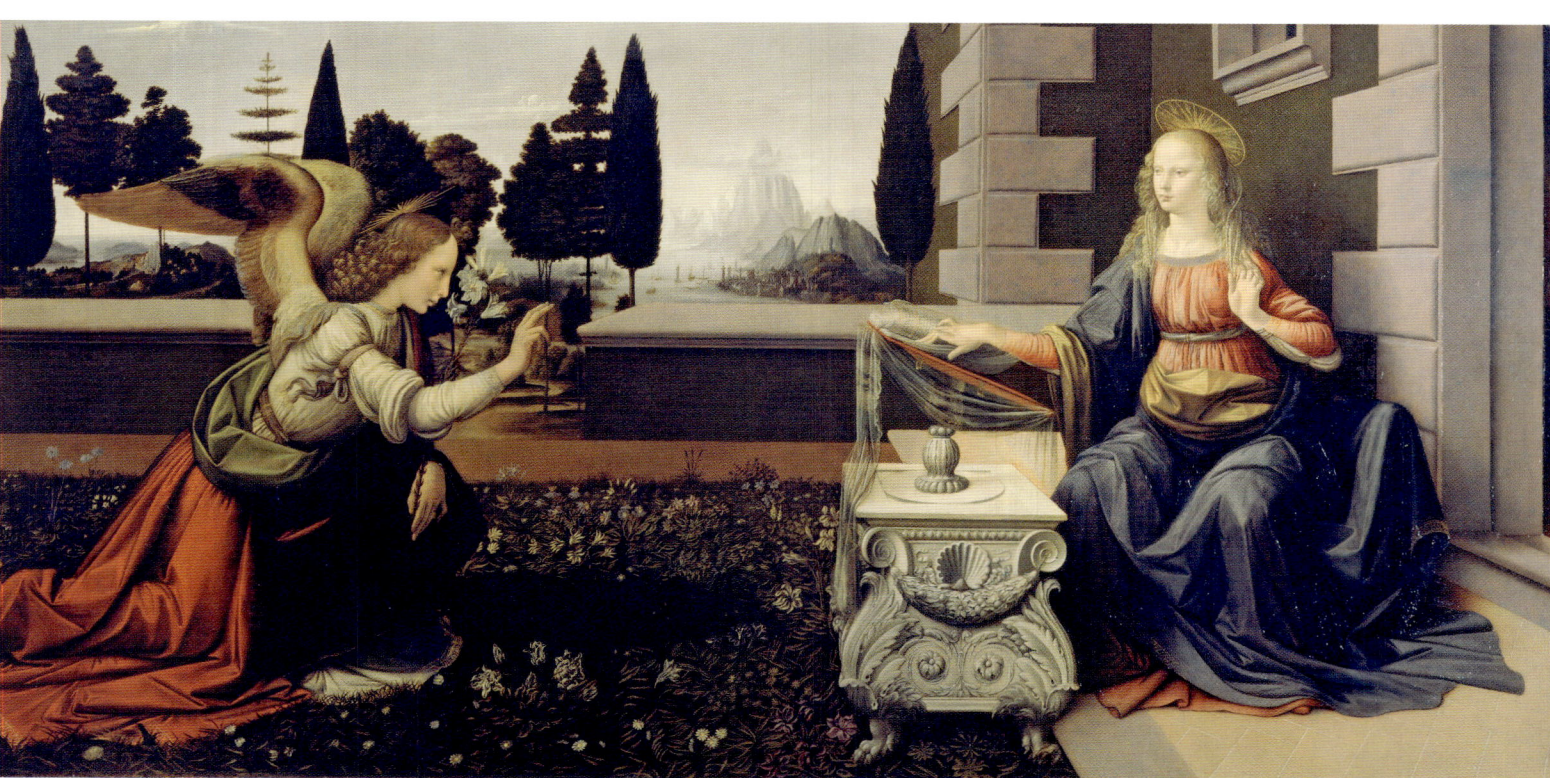

are many of the trees and shrubs he would have found on the marshy ground in the chateau's park, such as alders (*Alnus glutinosa*), guelder roses (*Viburnum opulus*), arum lilies (*Zantedeschia*), yellow flag irises (*Iris pseudacorus*), ferns and violets, as well as *Cyclamen repandum* and the Madonna lily, *Lilium candidum*.

The Madonna lily appears in his painting, *Annunciation* (circa 1472) that hangs in the Uffizi gallery in Florence. The first version of *The Virgin of the Rocks,* painted around 1480, also features several clearly visible plants, including the tufted pansy (*Viola cornata*) where the child's hand lies, aquilegias and yellow flag irises (*Iris pseudacorus*). These are all botanically accurate and would have been copied from the preparatory drawings of the plants made in his sketchbooks.

THE *MONA LISA* STORY

According to Don Antonio de Beatis, Secretary to the Cardinal of Aragon, who visited Leonardo at Clos Lucé, the artist had three paintings in his possession, and one of these was *Mona Lisa*. Research in 2016 showed that Leonardo made sketches for one of the other paintings he brought with him – *The Virgin and Child with Saint Anne* – and altered it while at the chateau, so it seems that the artist never wanted to finish his paintings and perhaps also contemplated changes to *Mona Lisa* in his final years.

The identity of the woman in Leonardo's famous painting is not really a mystery – she was Lisa Gherardini, the wife of a wealthy Florentine official, Francesco del Giocondo – but who or what the painting represented to Leonardo is something we will probably never know. The outer dress the woman is wearing has been identified as a *guarnello* – sometimes worn in pregnancy – and, as Leonardo was separated from his own mother at the age of five, this adds another layer of poignancy to the portrait.

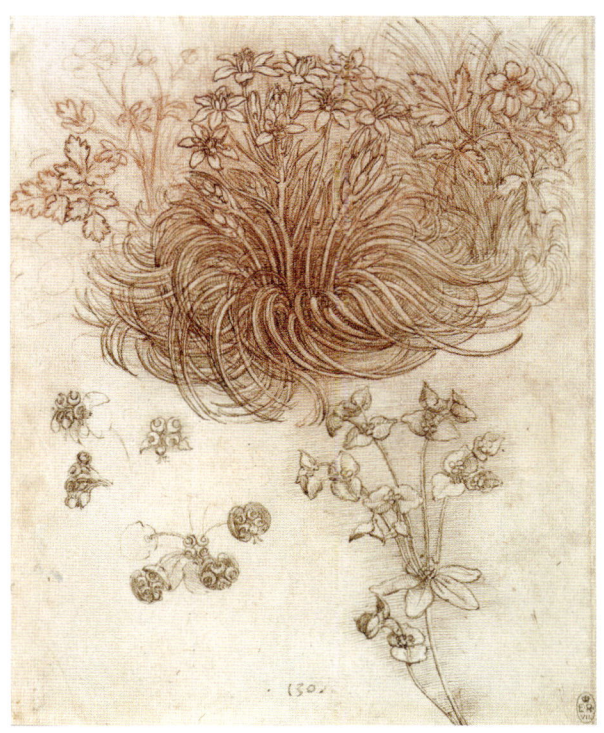

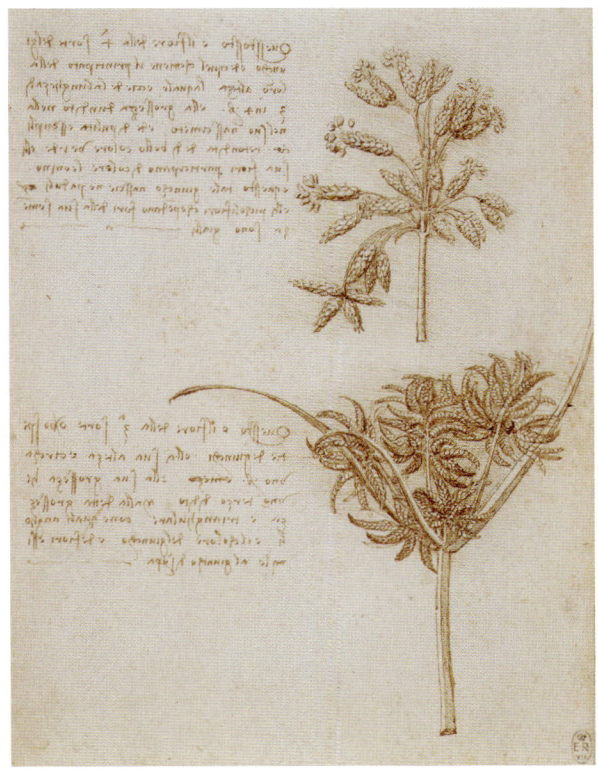

LEFT In the *Annunciation* (circa 1472–75) Leonardo, working with Verrocchio, shows his botanical knowledge in the bed of flowers and Madonna lily (*Lilium candidum*) held by the angel.
RIGHT, ABOVE Star-of-Bethlehem (*Ornithogalum umbellatum*), and wood anemone were among the drawings Leonardo intended to compile into a herbal while he was living at Clos Lucé.
RIGHT, BELOW Leonardo does not name the two types of rush or sedge drawn here, but he depicts them in fine botanical detail.

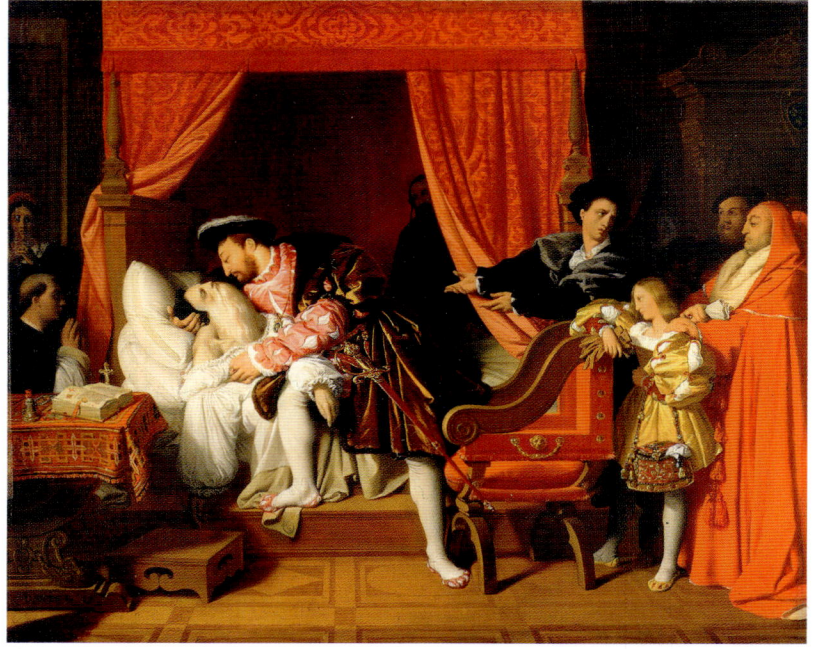

LEFT The story of Leonardo's close bond with the French king is encapsulated in a much later painting, *Francis I Receives the Last Breath of Leonardo da Vinci* (1818) by Jean-Auguste-Dominique Ingres – a copy of which hangs in the bedroom of the chateau.

RIGHT This screen print of the *Mona Lisa* hangs in the gardens at Le Clos Lucé; Leonardo never parted with his most famous painting.

REFERENCES TO NATURE

In his painting of *Mona Lisa*, Leonardo embedded symbols representing all his theories on how nature reflects the way the human body works. These include the tree in the Tuscan landscape, which celebrates his belief in the way sap rises through a plant or a tree, just as blood flows through the veins of a human body; the rocky, eroded landscape suggesting physical decay; and the flowing water evoking the passage of time.

Ten days before his death at the chateau, it is thought that Leonardo bequeathed *Mona Lisa* to his assistant, Francesco Melzi, indicating the closeness of their bond. Subsequently, King François I bought it from Melzi and the painting has remained in France for 500 years. In 1911, it was stolen from the Louvre in Paris and offered to an antique dealer in Florence, who alerted the authorities. *Mona Lisa* has since been returned to her former home in Paris, where millions of people go to see her every year.

Back at Le Clos Lucé, in the bedroom of the chateau, hangs a later painting, depicting a distraught François I at the bedside of the dying Leonardo da Vinci. The sentiment was accurate, if not the image, as François was not in Amboise when the artist passed away on 2 May 1519. Leonardo was buried in the Royal Chapel of Amboise across the river, close to the gardens that had, in a small way, inspired his last works.

LEONARDO'S TIMELINE

1452	1482–99	1499	1502	1503	1516	1519
Leonardo born, the illegitimate son of Piero da Vinci, near Florence	Works in Milan for Duke Ludovici 'Il Moro'; in 1494 starts work on *The Last Supper*	Flees Milan with his assistant Gian Giacomo Caprotti (Salaì); works as a military architect and engineer	Employed by Cesare Borgia as his military architect; travels throughout Italy	Begins the *Mona Lisa* in Florence and works on one of a pair of wall paintings at the Palazzo Vecchio	Accepts invitation of King François I of France to take up residence at Château du Clos Lucé at Amboise	Dies on 2 May at Château du Clos Lucé

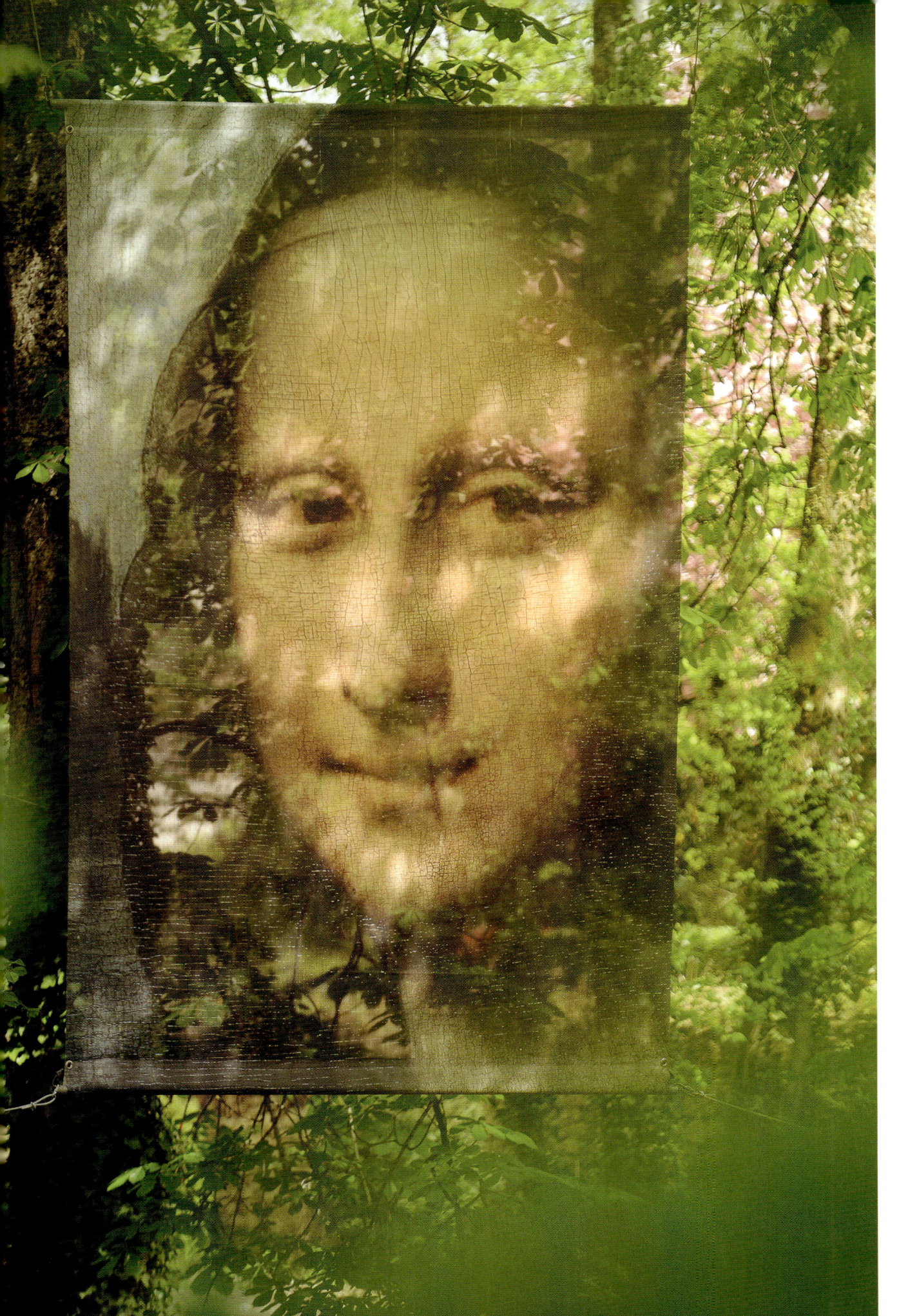

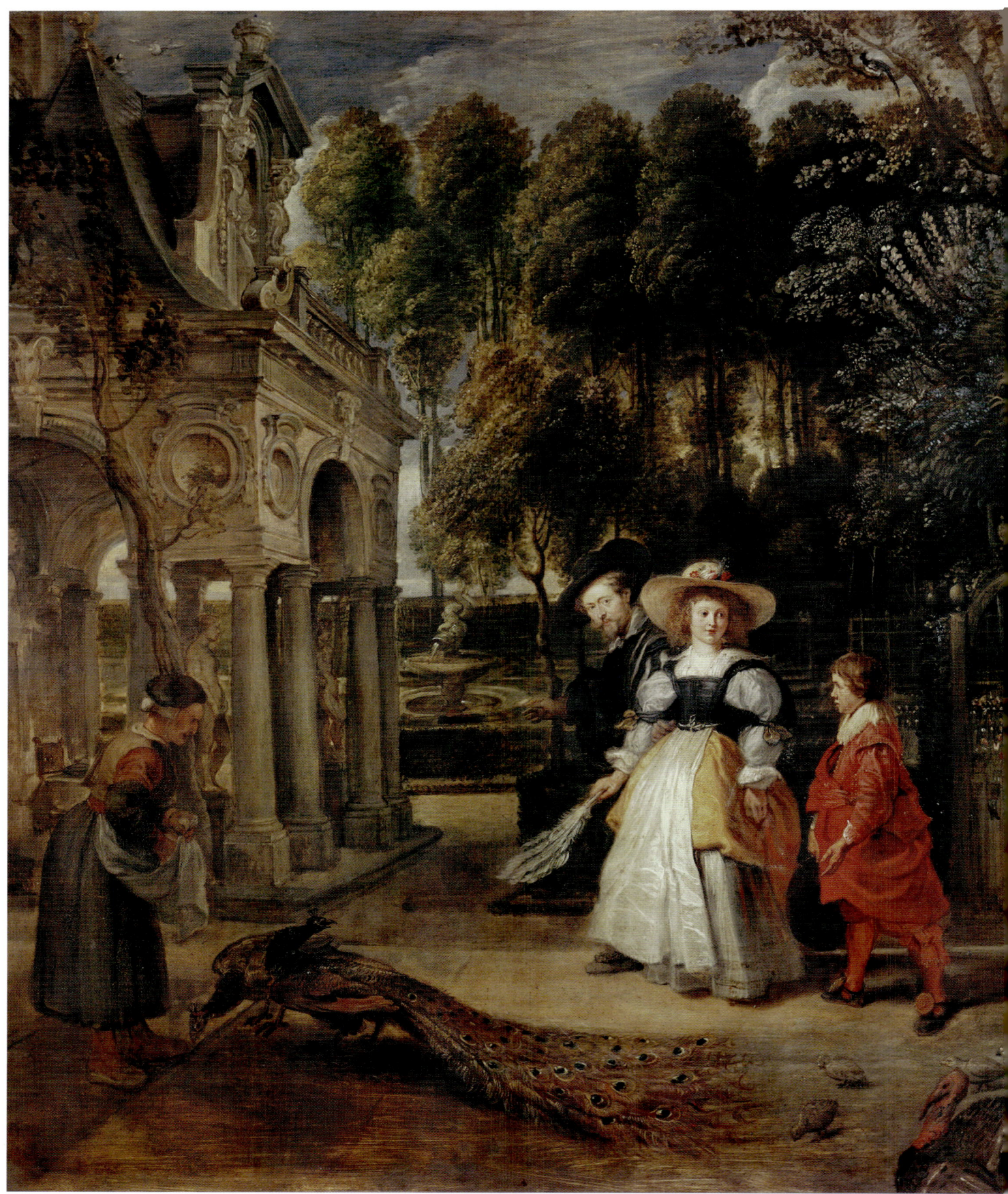

Peter Paul Rubens

Antwerp, Belgium

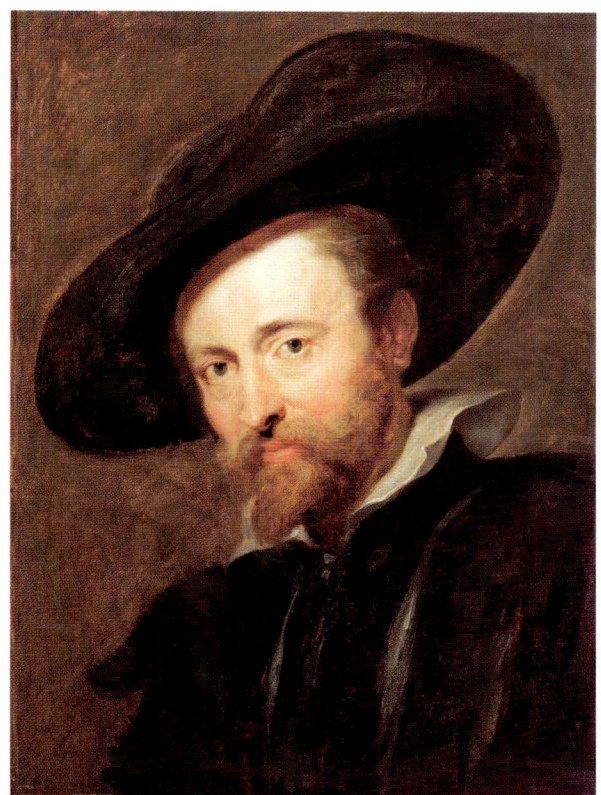

PETER PAUL RUBENS was the undisputed master artist of his age. He spoke six languages and, as a religious and court painter, moved in diplomatic circles, while turning his hand to everything from architecture and garden design to printing. At the age of twenty-three, having been admitted to the prestigious Antwerp Guild of Saint Luke for artists, he left the city for Italy, spending eight years in Mantua, Genoa and Rome.

LEFT *The Walk in the Garden* (circa 1630) shows Rubens with his second wife Helena and his son Nicolaas. Painted shortly after his marriage, it represents a garden of love, but also mirrors his own garden in Antwerp.

ABOVE Rubens' *Self Portrait* (circa 1628–30).

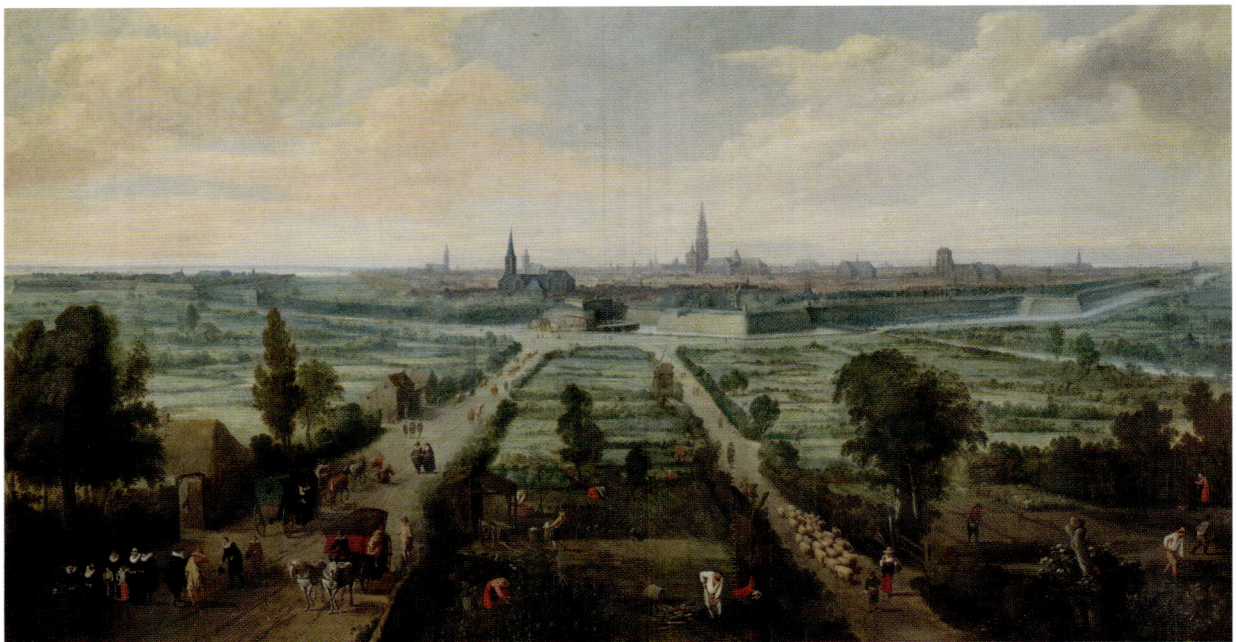

It was this fusion of Flemish and Italian influences that shaped Rubens' work and, through him, made Antwerp the centre of Baroque art in the Low Countries. Rubens was also a garden maker and, although plants and flowers do not feature in many of his paintings, he was a keen amateur botanist, building up a collection of reference works to expand his knowledge.

EARLY LIFE

Rubens' father was a Protestant lawyer and former magistrate who had been forced to flee Antwerp due to religious persecution. He was also alleged to have had an affair with the wife of William of Orange and was banished to Siegen in Germany, where Peter Paul Rubens was born in 1577. After the death of his father, the young Rubens, aged ten, returned to Antwerp with his mother and siblings and attended the Latin school, where he was taught humanism and languages. Given his background, his choice of occupation was surprising, but he showed artistic promise and at fourteen went to study under the landscape painter Tobias Verhaecht and later under Otto van Veen, who introduced him to Antwerp society and probably suggested he make a study tour to Italy.

In 1609, a year after returning from his travels, Rubens was appointed court painter to the Spanish royal house of Albert and Isabella, then ruling the southern Netherlands from Brussels. Unlike other court painters, he retained his independent status and worked from his home town of Antwerp, rather than Brussels. In the early seventeenth century, Antwerp comprised a jumble of closely packed low houses to the east of the River Scheldt, dominated by the towering gothic cathedral. When, in 1610, Rubens decided to build his own house, he chose a site with large grounds on the edge of the crowded city, looking away from the river and out over the fields. The house was to become one of the most substantial properties in Antwerp, outshone only by the Elzenveld monastery with its medicinal garden, and the cathedral itself.

THE ARCHITECT AND DESIGNER

Rubens and his wife, Isabella Brant, whom he had married in 1609, bought the land on the Wapper for the fairly modest sum of 8,960 guilders, plus 'one painting by his hand' – an indication that Rubens' work had considerable value. There was an old Flemish house on the plot, which Rubens intended to expand, but to design and build his own house, he needed to study architecture, and so he set about teaching himself. In time, he became a great authority on the subject (publishing a work in 1622 on the Palazzi di Genova), although the Rubenshuis in Antwerp would be his only complete building project.

During the next seven years, he expanded the original house, adding a grand portico, a semi-circular gallery for his collection of sculptures, a large painting studio, and a library, where he built up a huge collection of books on every subject from botany to philosophy. Rubens' style

*"I have not yet made
up my mind whether
to remain in my own
country Flanders or to
return forever to Rome."*

PETER PAUL RUBENS (1609)

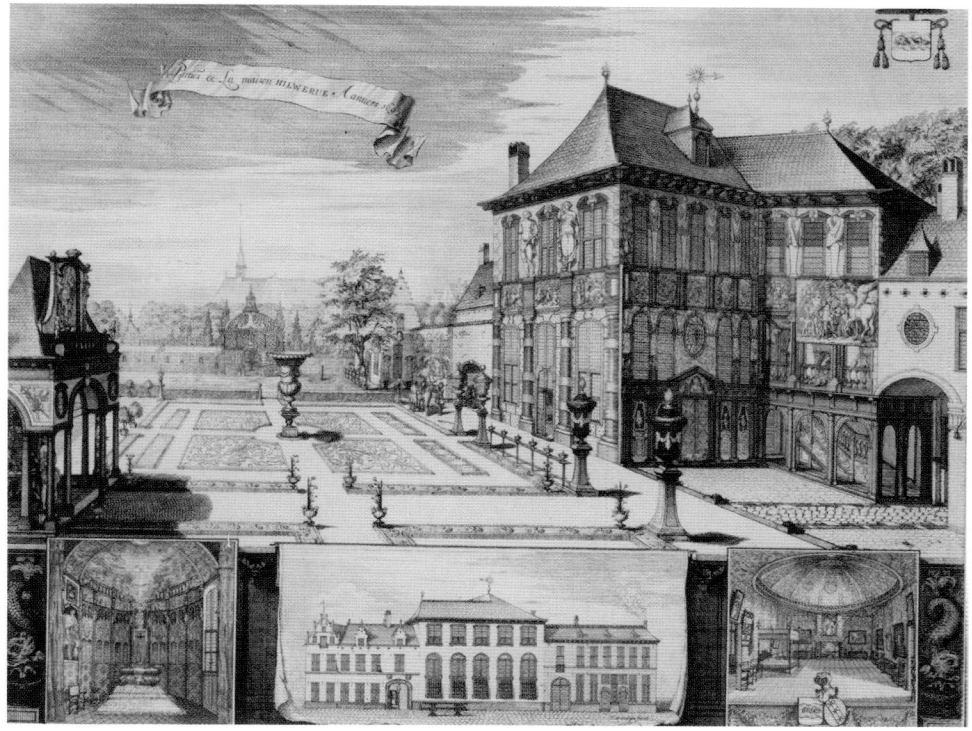

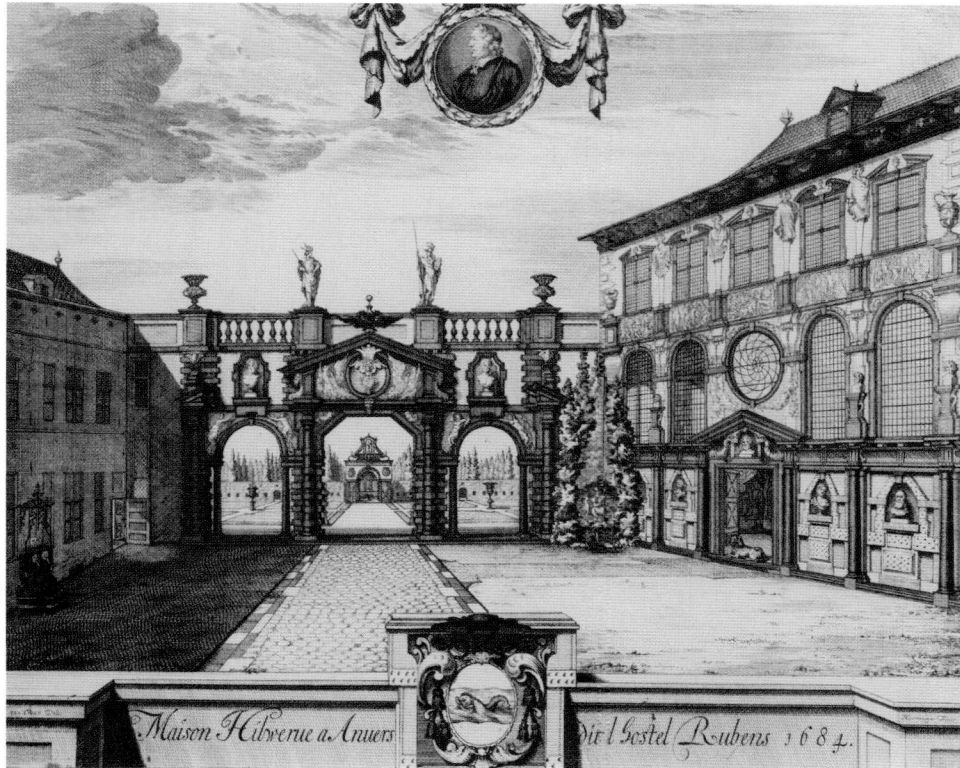

OPPOSITE *View of Antwerp* (1656)
by Jan Wildens portrays the city
built around the River Scheldt.
RIGHT, ABOVE The 1692 engraving,
The Rubenshuis in Antwerp,
by Jacobus Harrewijn, shows
the pavilion and a later (post-
Rubens) garden.
RIGHT, BELOW The earliest
depiction of Rubenshuis is the 1684
engraving by Harrewijn showing the
grand portico and garden beyond.

Peter Paul Rubens
(1577–1640)

Born in Germany, Peter Paul Rubens moved to Antwerp at the age of ten with his mother and five siblings after his father's death. In 1609, he married Isabella Brant and bought the house later known as Rubenshuis in 1610, which he redeveloped and extended.

In his studio at the house, Rubens ran a system very similar to those of his Italian predecessors, Raphael and Michelangelo, employing assistants (including the young Anthony van Dyck) to meet his growing number of commissions. He would execute preparatory oil sketches, which the assistants then worked up on a large scale, with the master retouching the final painting. Rubens employed painters, but also encouraged sculptors, engravers and printers to assist him, collaborating on joint works and learning new techniques from them.

The house in Antwerp was also home for Rubens' collections of art and curiosities, while the garden was an important public area, enjoyed by his many visitors.

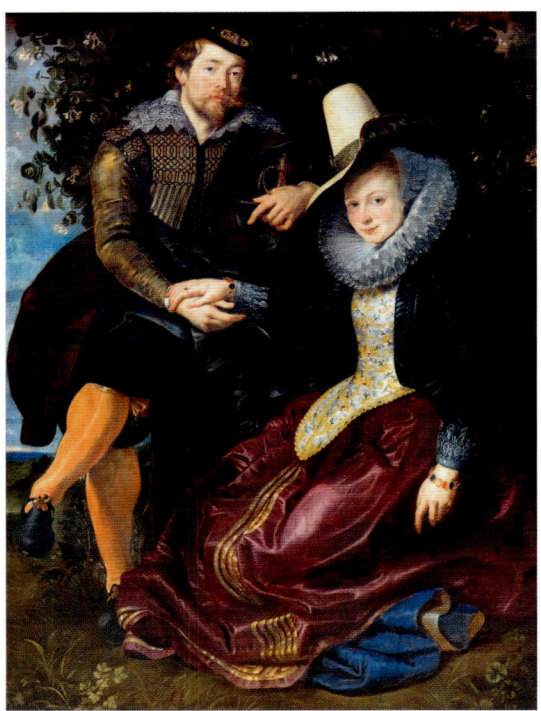

The Honeysuckle Bower, self-portrait with Isabella Brant (circa 1609).

of architecture had not been seen in the Low Countries before: he was creating a *palazzetto* – like those he had seen in northern Italy, as depicted by the great Renaissance painter Raphael – with Roman architectural influences, particularly in the exterior elements. Rubens designed his house to be a meeting place for the *cognoscenti*, patrons and art collectors of the city and beyond, as well as a home for Isabella and their children.

Some images from the seventeenth century have helped to recreate the house and garden that Rubens built. Two engravings made by Jacobus Harrewijn in 1684 and 1692, after Rubens' death, show the old Flemish house in shadow to the left, with the focus on the parts that Rubens built, including the studio extension, gallery, and grand portico. This was the time of illusion and at Rubenshuis the influence of the Renaissance painter Paolo Veronese, who played with architectural elements for artistic effect, is evident, and it is likely that the windows and pillars would have been painted on the façade as *trompe l'oeil*.

IN SEARCH OF RUBENS' GARDEN

Baroque garden style, with its focus on decoration, was just coming into vogue when Rubens built his house, and paintings of these gardens had become a genre in their own right by the mid- to late seventeenth century. In Harrewijn's engravings the viewing axis runs from the entrance gate, through an inner courtyard, via the portico, and down to the pavilion, so the eye is deliberately drawn towards the garden. A later seventeenth-century painting recently came to light and adds a little more detail and colour; in it, the landscape looks as if it goes on and on, reflecting the view from Rubens' garden over open fields.

Today, the only remaining original parts of Rubens' grounds are the portico and garden pavilion. The portico connected the old Flemish house to the new studio wing and was modelled on the triumphal arches and entrance gates to the parks of Rome. The central passage is a direct copy of the *Porta Pia* – the city gate in Rome designed by Michelangelo, with its unusual 'broken' arch. Above the arch, Rubens placed two Roman deities: Mercury, the god of entrepreneurs, and Minerva, the goddess of art and wisdom. The portico – which features in a 1621 painting of Isabella by Anthony van Dyck, one of Rubens'

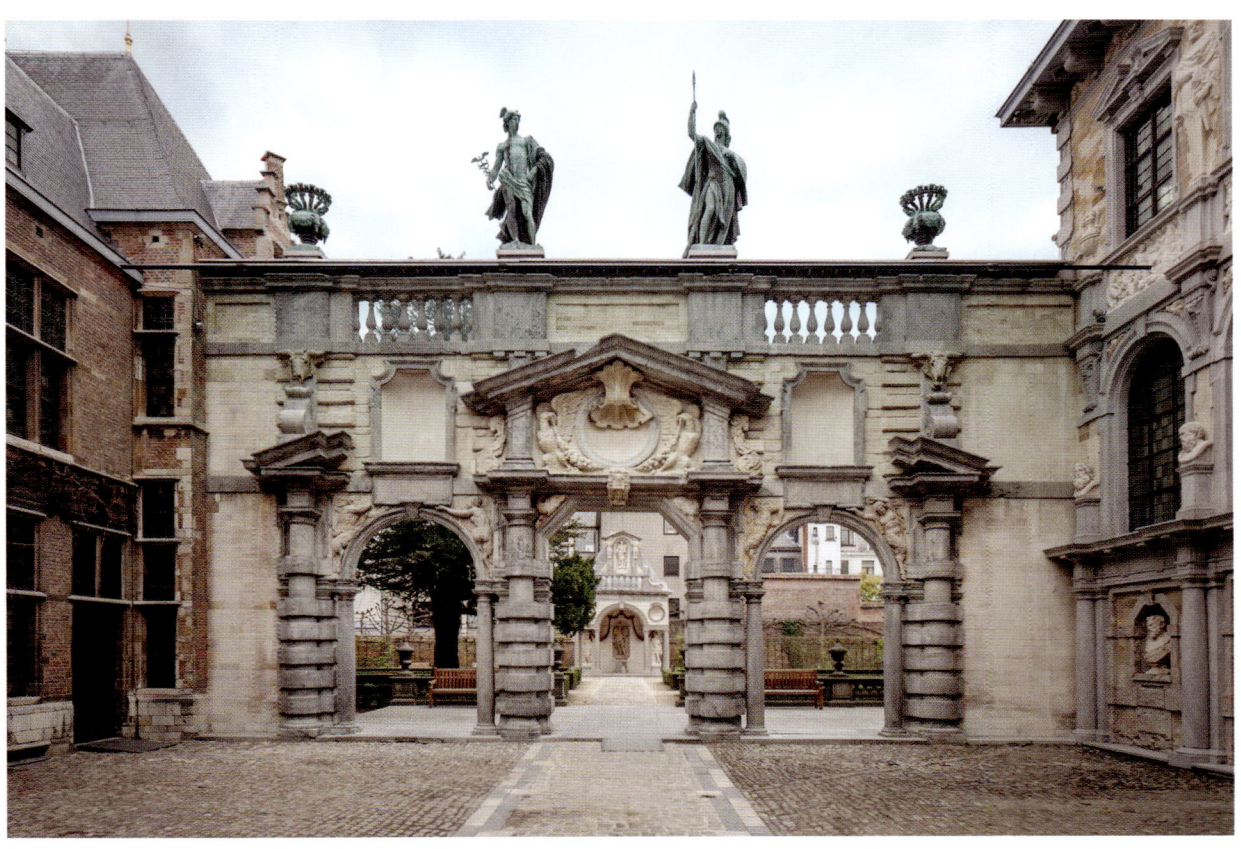

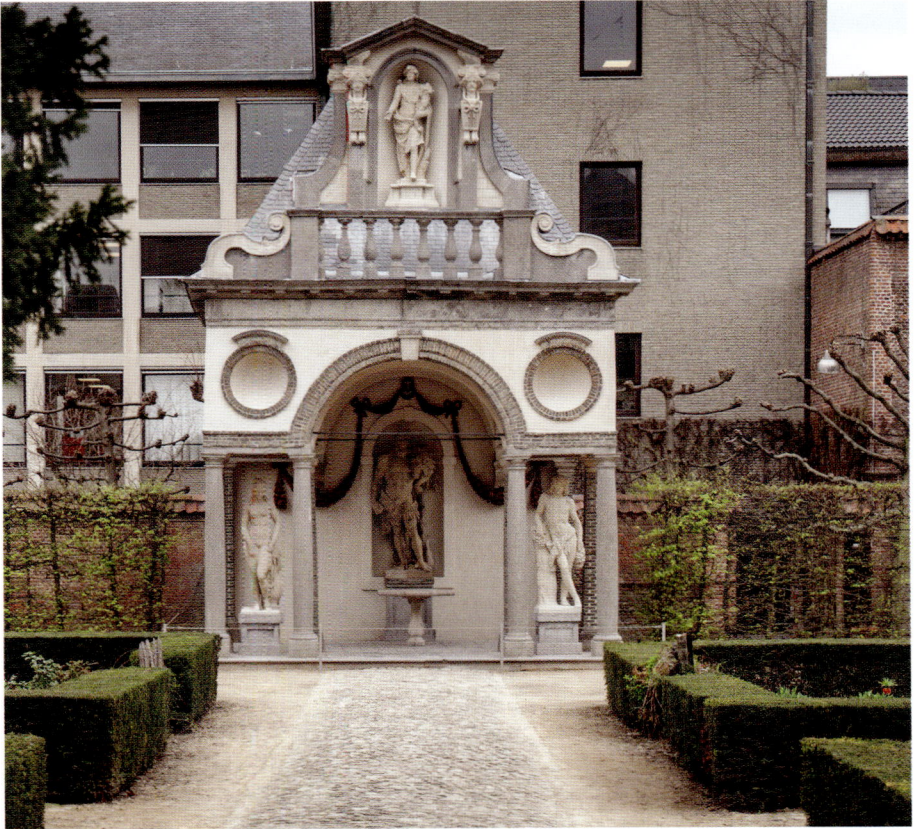

ABOVE The portico at Rubenshuis is based on the triumphal arches of Rome, which Rubens had visited as a young man.

LEFT A statue of Hercules takes central place in the garden pavilion, where Rubens entertained the *cognoscenti* of Antwerp.

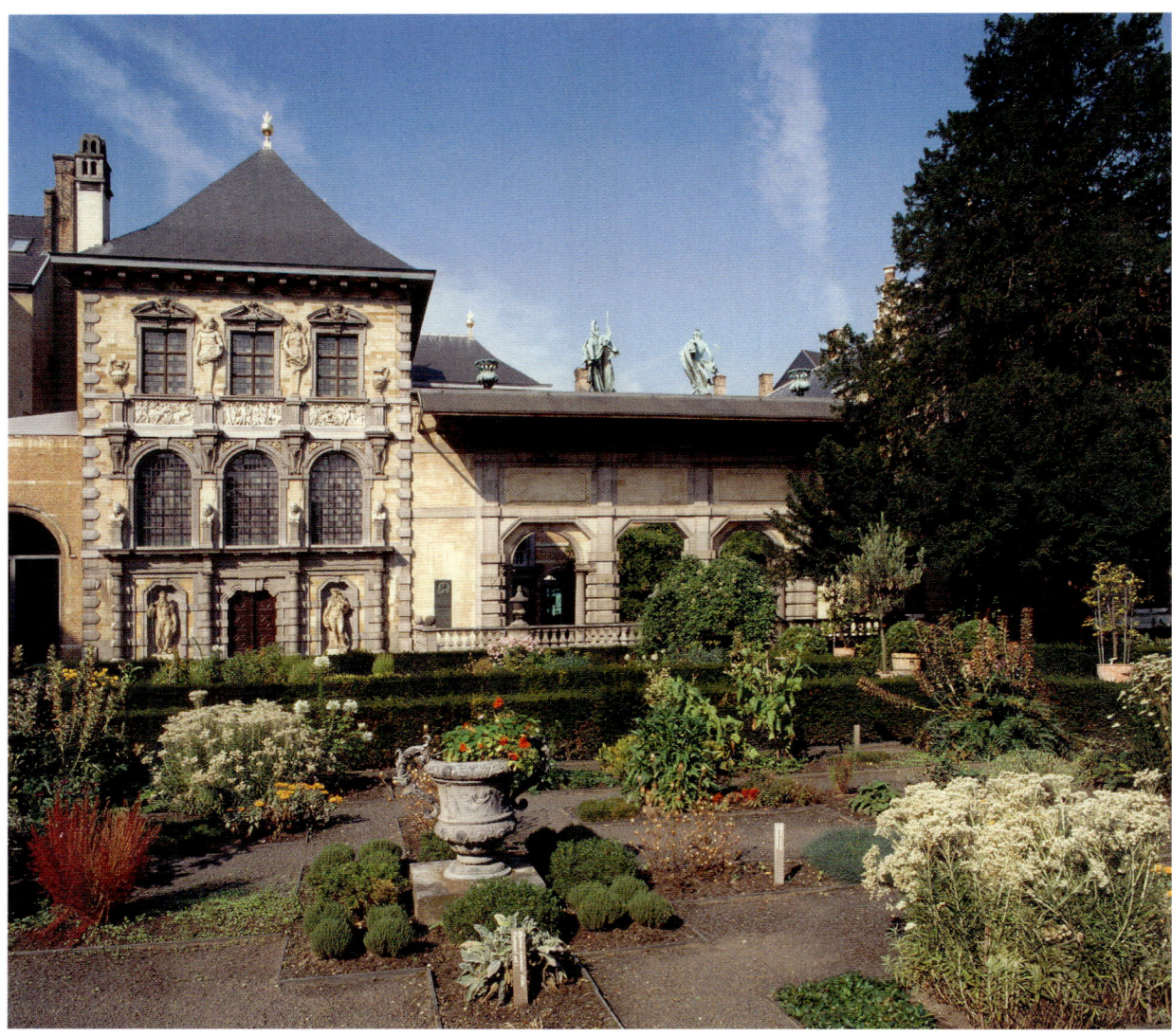

most successful pupils – announces that Art and Wisdom will give way to Nature (the garden) and Virtue, in the figure of Hercules, who stands inside the garden pavilion. The arches separate culture from Nature – an important tenet of humanist thinking, the tradition Rubens had been taught as a boy and which he followed throughout his life. Skilled at this type of elaborate design, in 1635 he was commissioned to design a 'theatrical set' to herald the entrance of the new regent Ferdinand into Antwerp, with arches, facades and painted panels lining the streets.

Harrewijn's engravings are somewhat misleading when it comes to the garden. The subsequent owner, Canon Hendrik Hillewerve, probably commissioned the fashionable French-style garden shown in the engravings, rather than keeping the one Rubens designed. The artist would have included Roman and Baroque elements, with clear vistas and statuary, *trompe l'oeil* and Classical references, and research also shows that there was a fountain with dolphins in the western corner and a grotto. The existence of the grotto is known because in the 1684 engraving it has been placed inappropriately in a corner of the courtyard, next to the studio extension – artistic licence by Harrewijn on behalf of Canon Hillewerve, who was keen to make sure all the Rubenesque elements of his house and grounds were included in the picture.

Rubens employed several gardeners, including one called Willem. After the death of Isabella from the plague and his remarriage to the young Helena Fourment, he bought a castle known as Het Steen as a country residence and began spending more time there. Het Steen featured all the landscape elements that were not feasible in the town garden, including a large pond, terraces and extensive orchards and plantations of trees. However, not everything grew well in the country, and while at Het Steen, Rubens wrote asking that Willem send figs and oranges from the garden in Antwerp, where these more tender trees would have benefitted from the protection of its walls.

Like Elizabethan and early Jacobean gardens in England, the one at Rubenshuis would have been for show – with low hedges of myrtle (*Myrtus*), southernwood (*Artemesia*) or box (*Buxus*), wooden pergolas and painted screens, together with geometric beds where special and expensive plants, such as tulips, peonies and roses, could be displayed. Exactly what form the beds took is open to interpretation. Rubens was a contemporary of the architect and painter Hans Vredeman de Vries who worked in Antwerp and executed many garden plans, so it is possible the artist drew ideas from de Vries' *The Book of Perspective,* published in 1604–05.

Rubens instructed himself in whatever task he was undertaking and would have also owned herbals and other volumes on plant science to help him make informed choices about the garden. Rubens' love of plants was also evident in his art collection, which included flower paintings by his friends Jan Brueghel the Elder and Daniel Seghers. Flowers, and particularly bulbs, such as tulips, scillas and irises, were valuable commodities, and by including neat beds where they could be displayed, Rubens was following a trend among the wealthy citizens of Northern Europe.

THE RENAISSANCE MAN

In his self-portraits, Rubens was always careful to depict himself as a gentleman, never as a working painter. He cultivated this self-image partly to reflect his new passion for collecting, owning and displaying art and artefacts, as

LEFT The area behind the house is the subject of ongoing research to discover what style of garden Rubens may have created.
BELOW One of a series of allegorical paintings depicting the senses, *Smell* (1617–18) was a collaboration with Jan Brueghel the Elder, who provided the flowery backdrop to Rubens' figures.

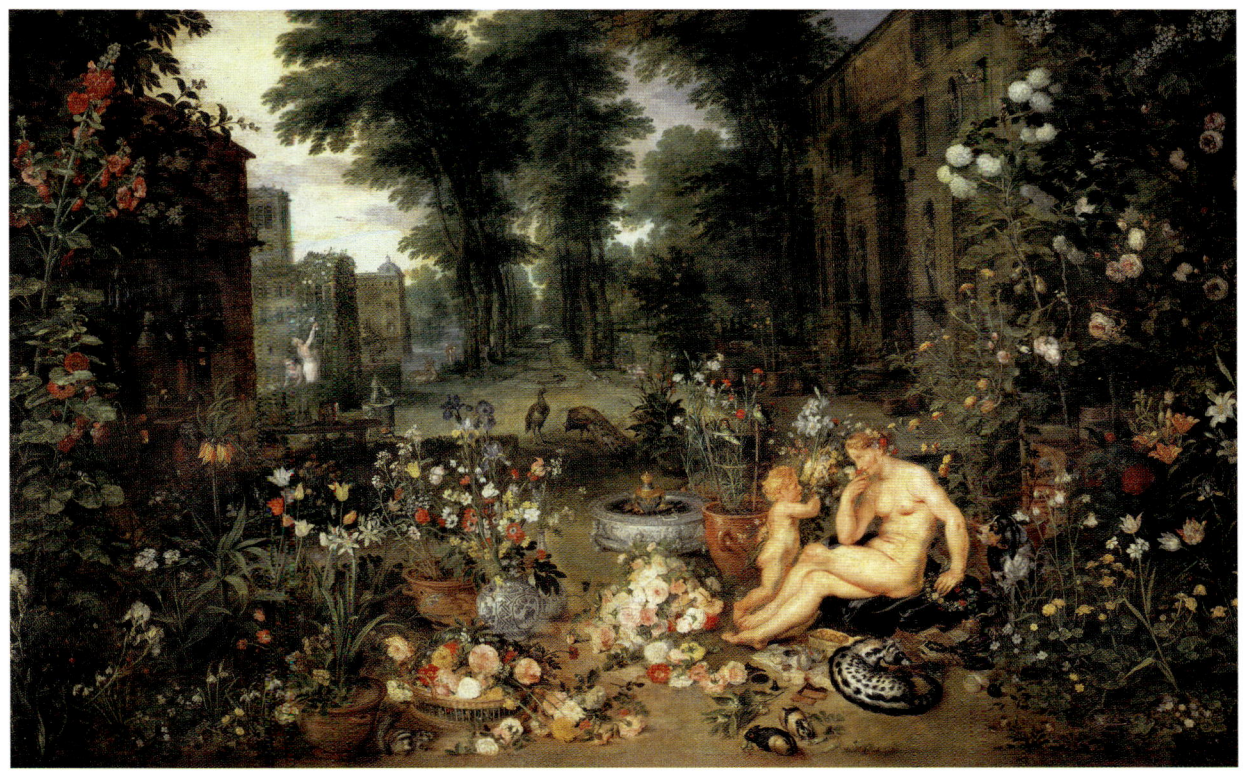

were the other burghers of the city. But Rubens surpassed them all by acquiring paintings by Titian, Raphael, and Frans Snyders, and sculptures by Petel and Duquesnoy, as well as sundials and pieces of antiquity. His centrepiece was an antique marble bust of the Roman philosopher Seneca – the father of Stoicism who advocated restraint and composure as the answer to life's ups and downs. Rubens bought the bust back with him from Italy in 1608 and it featured in several of his paintings. He died believing he had the real thing, but when an original bust of Seneca was discovered in 1813, experts had to agree that Rubens, like many other collectors, had bought what is known as a pseudo-Seneca – a good likeness of an old philosopher, but not the first-century Roman statesman.

Rubenshuis was a meeting place for painters, printers, draughtsmen and sculptors, as well as writers, and Rubens drew inspiration from them all, often collaborating on projects. He was a close friend of Balthasar Moretus of the Plantin-Moretus family, who ran the largest printing firm in Antwerp and also had a substantial home and garden, and of Nicolaas II Rockox, Antwerp's polymath mayor. It was a house of lively debate, where art, science and philosophy were the topics discussed. The important areas were the shared spaces: Rubens' studio, the gallery, the portico and, vitally, the garden, where visitors could stroll, visit the grotto and the fountain, or sit in the pavilion and look back to the house. Here, the separation between man and nature were clearly visible. These were the spaces Rubens wanted people to see and, as a true believer in the Renaissance, he put man at the centre of his world.

BELOW The art cabinet (or gallery) and semi-circular sculpture gallery beyond display some of the works Rubens amassed during his lifetime.
RIGHT The *Gallery of Cornelis van der Geest* (1628) by Willem van Haecht depicts the art collection of one of Rubens' friends and patrons.

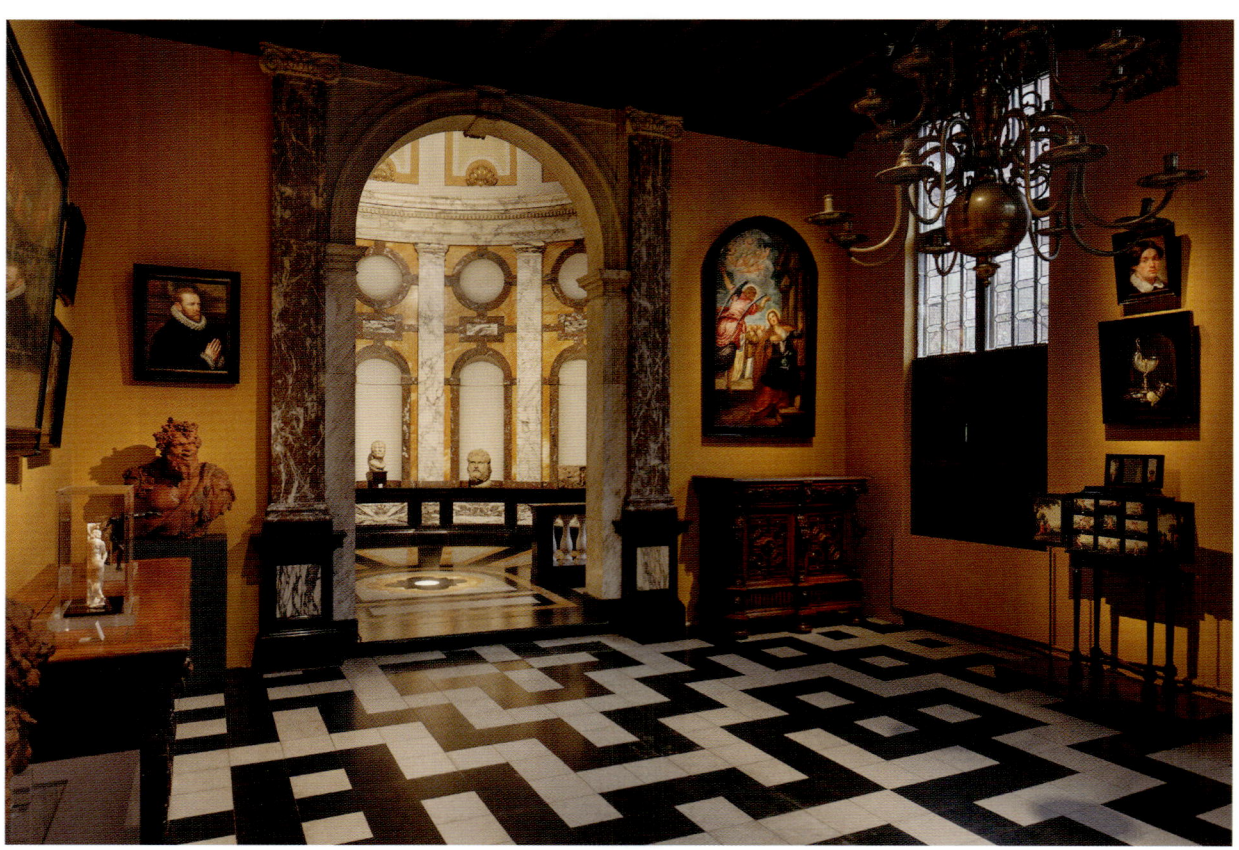

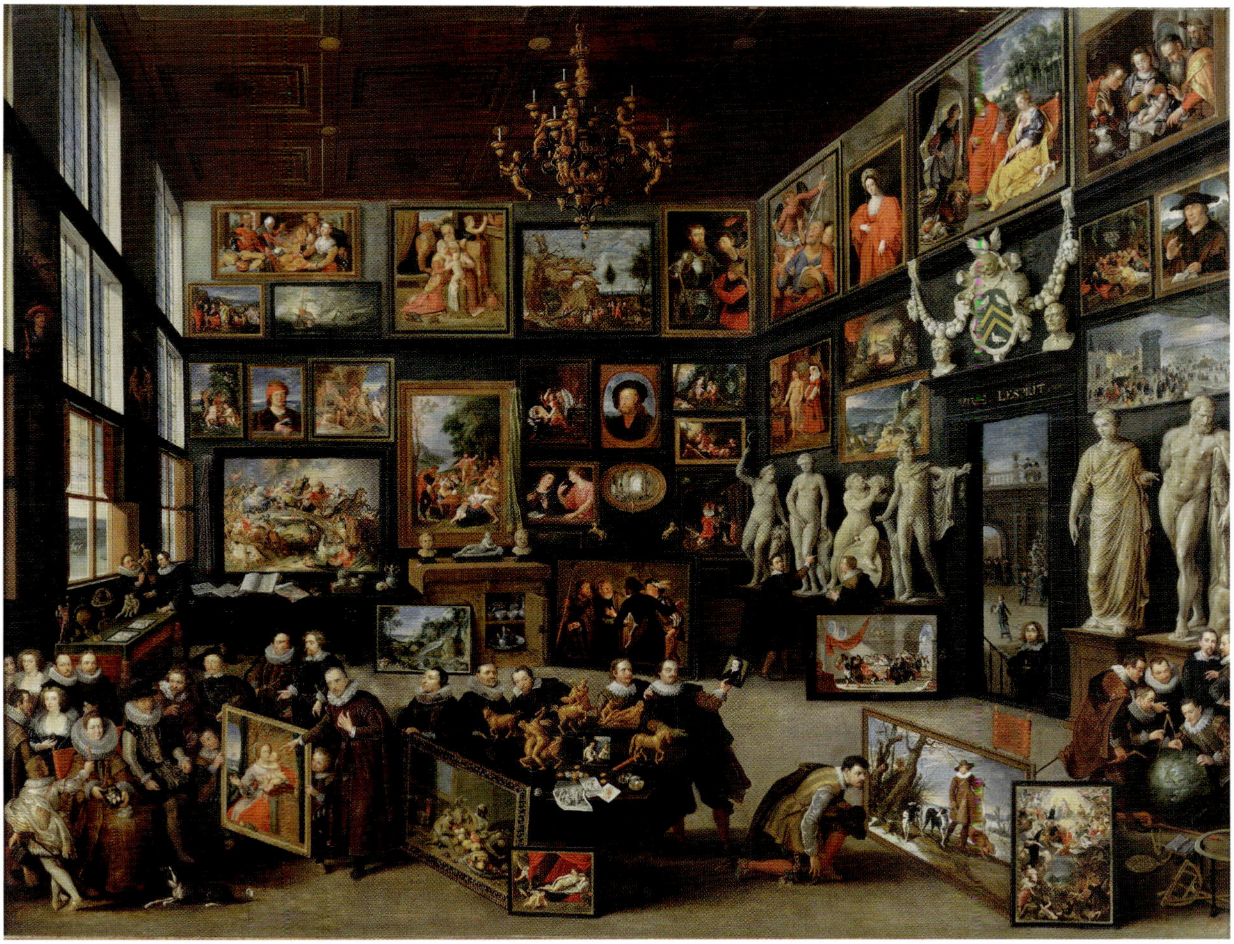

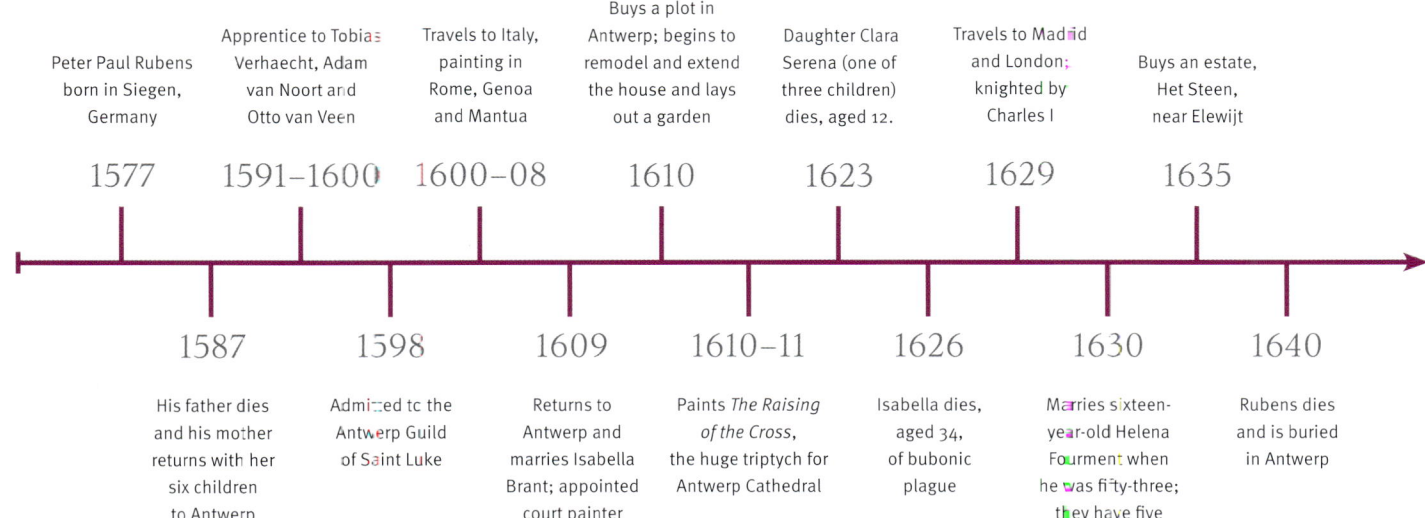

RUBENS' TIMELINE

Peter Paul Rubens born in Siegen, Germany

1577

His father dies and his mother returns with her six children to Antwerp

1587

Apprentice to Tobias Verhaecht, Adam van Noort and Otto van Veen

1591–1600

Admitted to the Antwerp Guild of Saint Luke

1598

Travels to Italy, painting in Rome, Genoa and Mantua

1600–08

Returns to Antwerp and marries Isabella Brant; appointed court painter

1609

Buys a plot in Antwerp; begins to remodel and extend the house and lays out a garden

1610

Paints *The Raising of the Cross*, the huge triptych for Antwerp Cathedral

1610–11

Daughter Clara Serena (one of three children) dies, aged 12.

1623

Isabella dies, aged 34, of bubonic plague

1626

Travels to Madrid and London; knighted by Charles I

1629

Marries sixteen-year-old Helena Fourment when he was fifty-three; they have five children

1630

Buys an estate, Het Steen, near Elewijt

1635

Rubens dies and is buried in Antwerp

1640

Paul Cézanne

Aix-en-Provence, France

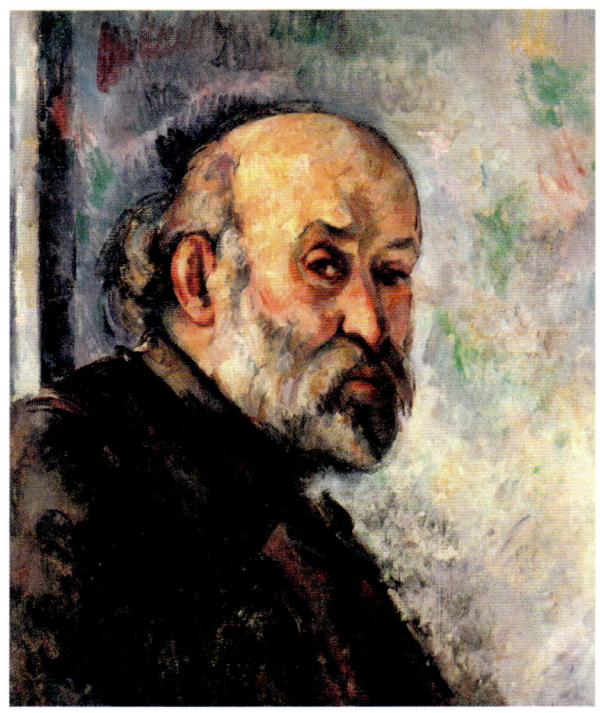

APPLAUDED BY HIS CONTEMPORARIES for his unconventional style and artistic skill, Cézanne is renowned for his mesmerizing landscapes, inspired by his parents' garden and the countryside around his home town of Aix-en-Provence in southern France.

Cézanne was an innovator, crossing artistic boundaries and shining out from the many other talented French painters of the time. He never followed any specific movement or genre, always taking his own direction, whether in his native Provence or while working in Paris. The great Impressionist painter Claude Monet owned more paintings by Cézanne than by any other artist, while Camille Pissarro was his close friend and painting

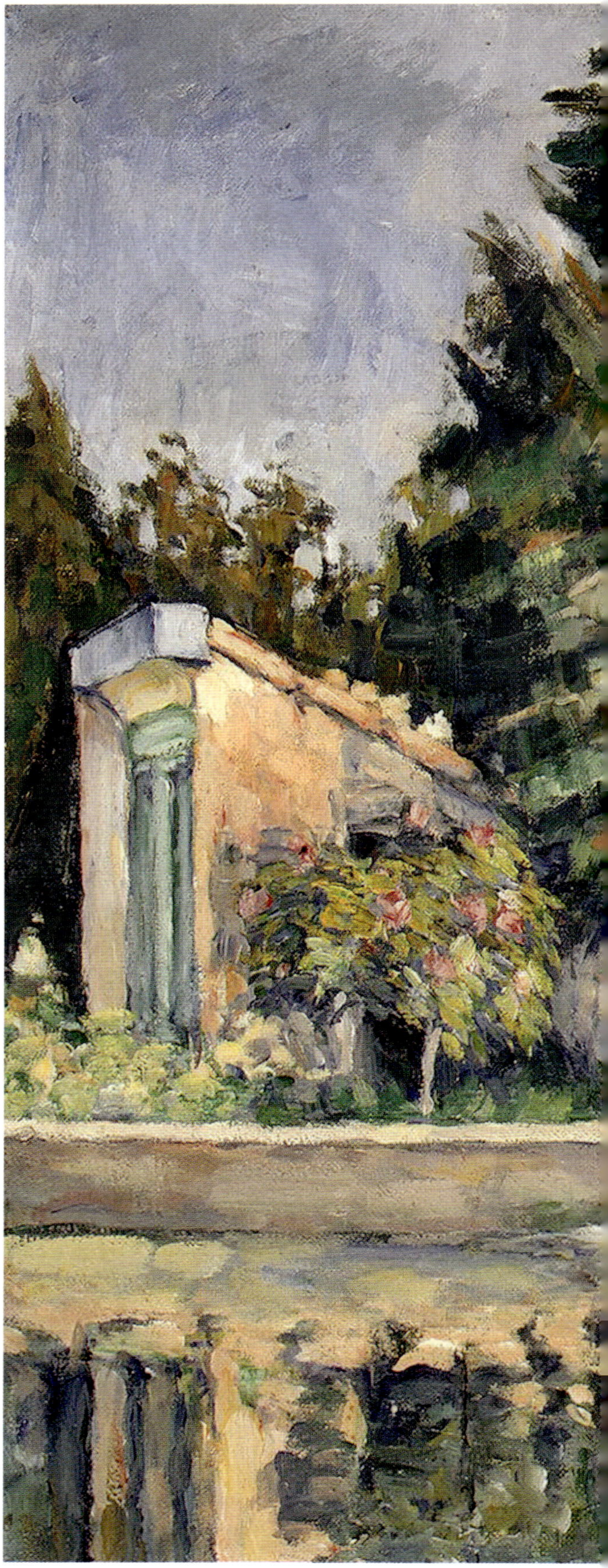

ABOVE This *Self-Portrait* (1895) of Cézanne aged fifty-six is one of many the artist painted during the course of his lifetime.
RIGHT *The Pool at Jas de Bouffan* (1876) depicts the gardens of the house owned by Cézanne's father, who later had a studio built here for his son.

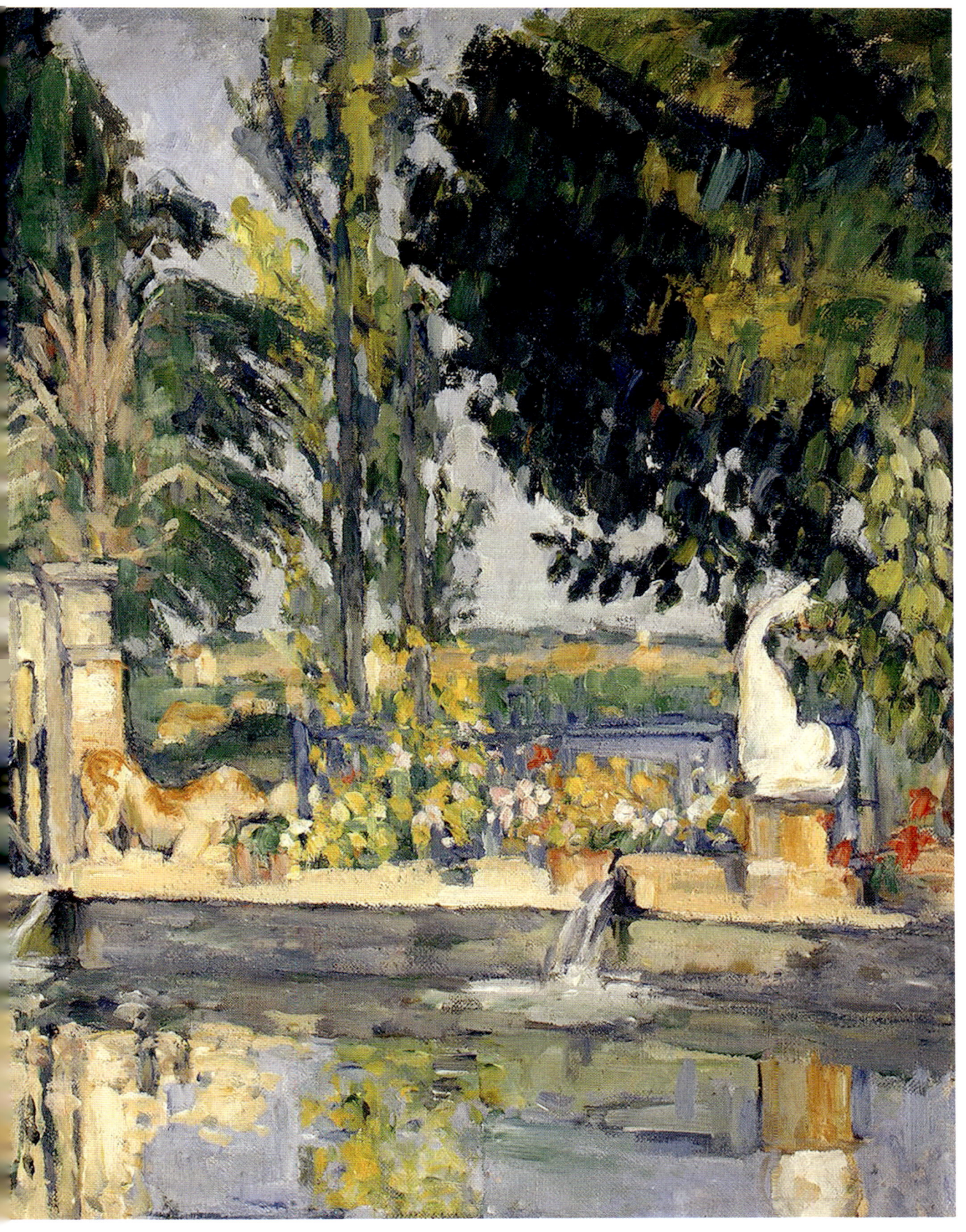

Paul Cézanne
(1839–1906)

One of the most sought-after artists in the world, Paul Cézanne is often described as a Post-Impressionist but, in fact, he bridged a period between the Impressionists – including Monet, Renoir and Pissarro, whom he knew well – and the Modernist artists, such as Matisse, Georges Braque and Picasso. He spent his youth in Aix-en-Provence, travelling to live and work in Paris in his twenties and returning there periodically throughout his life. Cézanne's latter years were spent in Provence, where his studio became a place of pilgrimage for other painters. Yet despite his skill, Cézanne didn't have his first one-man show until he was fifty-six. His work was often underestimated by critics, but he never doubted his own talent and, although his father described him as 'profession-less', he was greatly admired by his peers, who vied to paint with and learn from him. His subject matter was regional – the people and the landscapes of Provence – but his influence was to become international, extending far beyond the land of his birth.

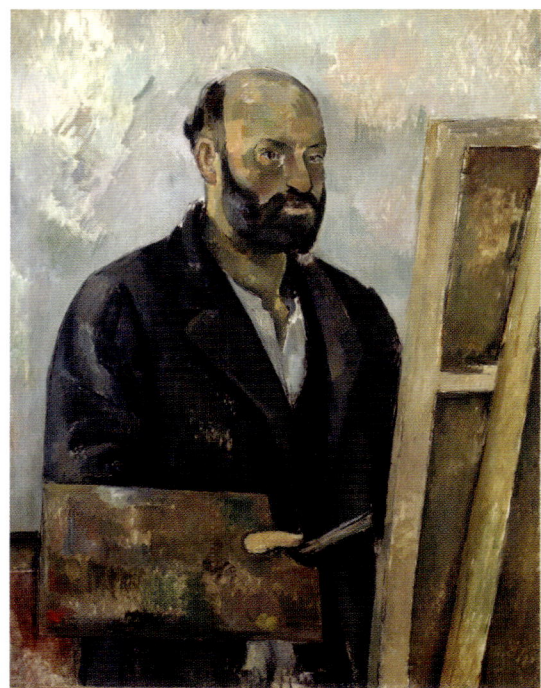

Self-Portrait with Palette (circa 1890).

companion, and Pierre-Auguste Renoir became a lifelong colleague and correspondent. Paul Cézanne was, quite simply, the artists' artist.

EARLY YEARS
Born in Aix-en-Provence, the son of a hat-seller turned banker, Paul Cézanne grew up among the pine trees and rocky hillsides of south-western France, with the writer Émile Zola as his playmate. The natural landscapes of Provence, and particularly its olive groves, pines, and pistachio and fruit trees, played a special role in his life, and they would continue to provide inspiration for his paintings throughout his career.

In 1859, when Cézanne was twenty, his father, Louis-Auguste Cézanne, bought a large villa, Jas de Bouffan, on the outskirts of the town. He initially sent his son to law school, but Paul had other ideas. He dropped out after a couple of years, and moved to Paris, where he began mixing with many of the leading painters of the day.

Despite Cézanne senior's disappointment with his son's choice of career, he gave Paul permission to paint full time and provided him with an allowance to do so. Now financially secure, Cézanne travelled back and forth between Aix and Paris, where each season his work would be consistently turned down by the jury of the Paris 'Salon' – the influential exhibition held at the *Académie des Beaux-Arts* in the capital.

WORKING AT HIS FATHER'S HOUSE
Back home in Aix, Cézanne's father was playing the country gentleman, having acquired fifteen hectares/37 acres of land around his villa for 85,000 francs. The eighteenth century house now had its own meadows, cultivated land and a separate farmhouse where the labourers lived.

Cézanne's surviving paintings of Jas de Bouffan give us a good idea of the gardens his father had taken on. Originally laid out in the seventeenth century by the Maréchal de Villars, they were embellished by the Gaspard de Truphème family in the mid-eighteenth century, who made the pool and added an orangery overlooking the water. An avenue of chestnut trees led up to the house where the family lived. Cézanne senior employed labourers and gardeners to maintain the gardens and farm

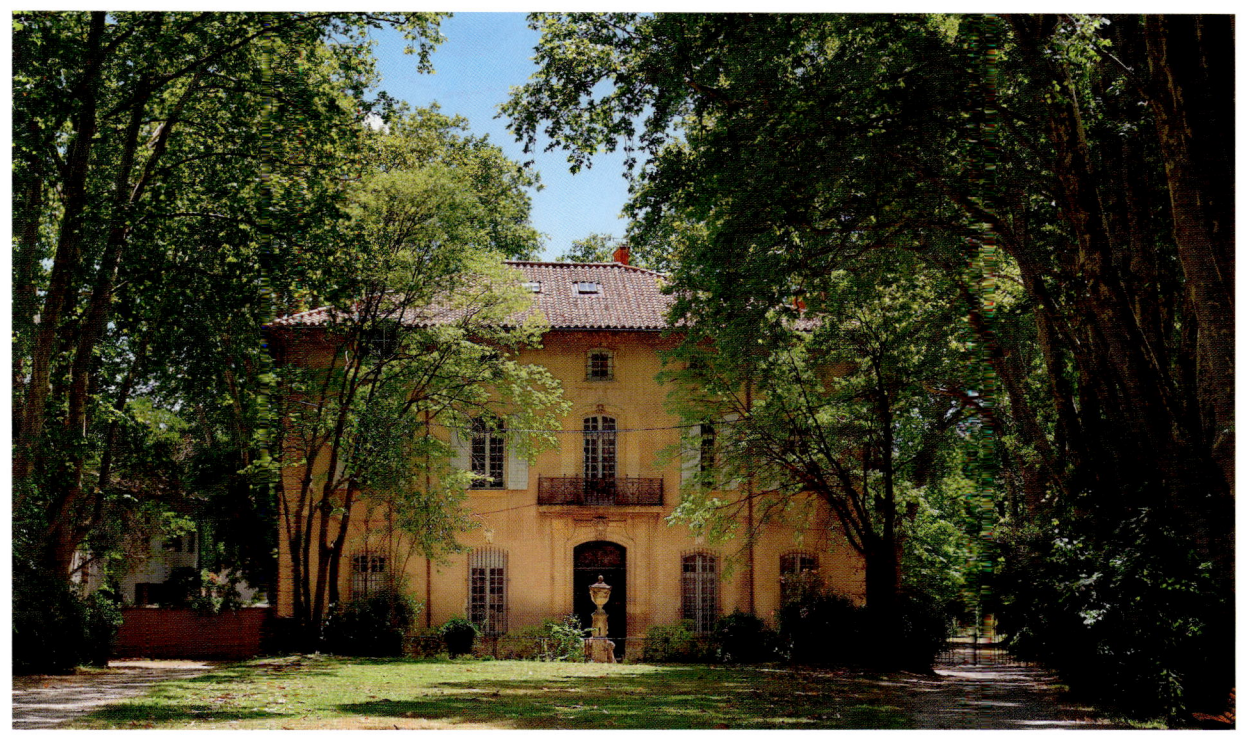

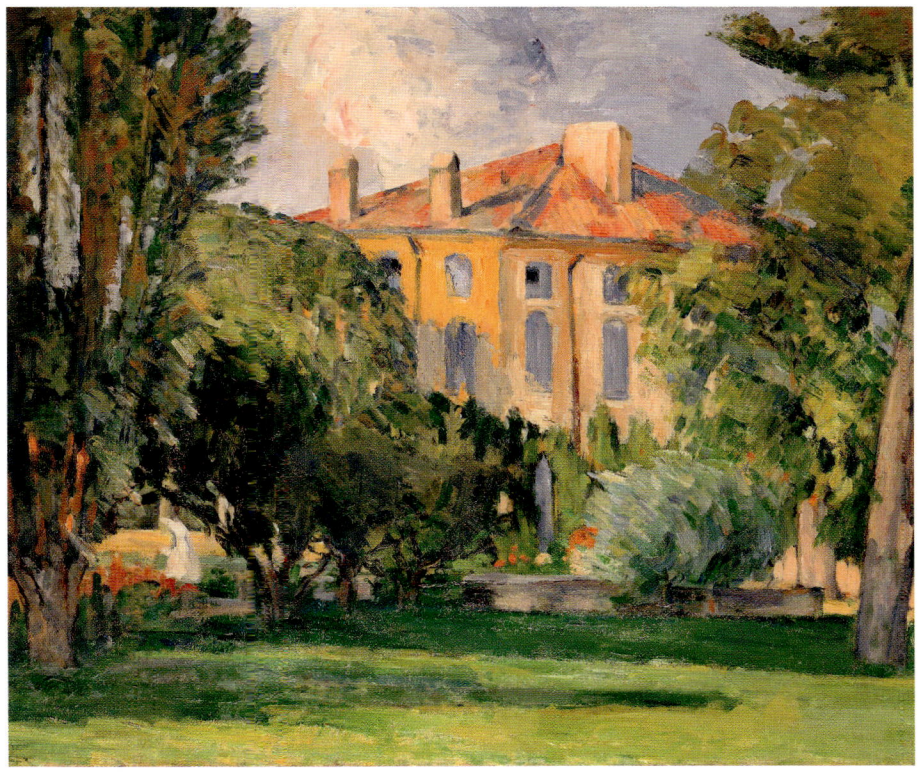

ABOVE Bought by his father in 1859, the elegant building and extensive grounds at Jas de Bouffan reflected Cézanne senior's rising fortunes.

LEFT *The House at Jas de Bouffan* (1876–78). The painting shows the house surrounded by the tranquil gardens that became the artist's sanctuary.

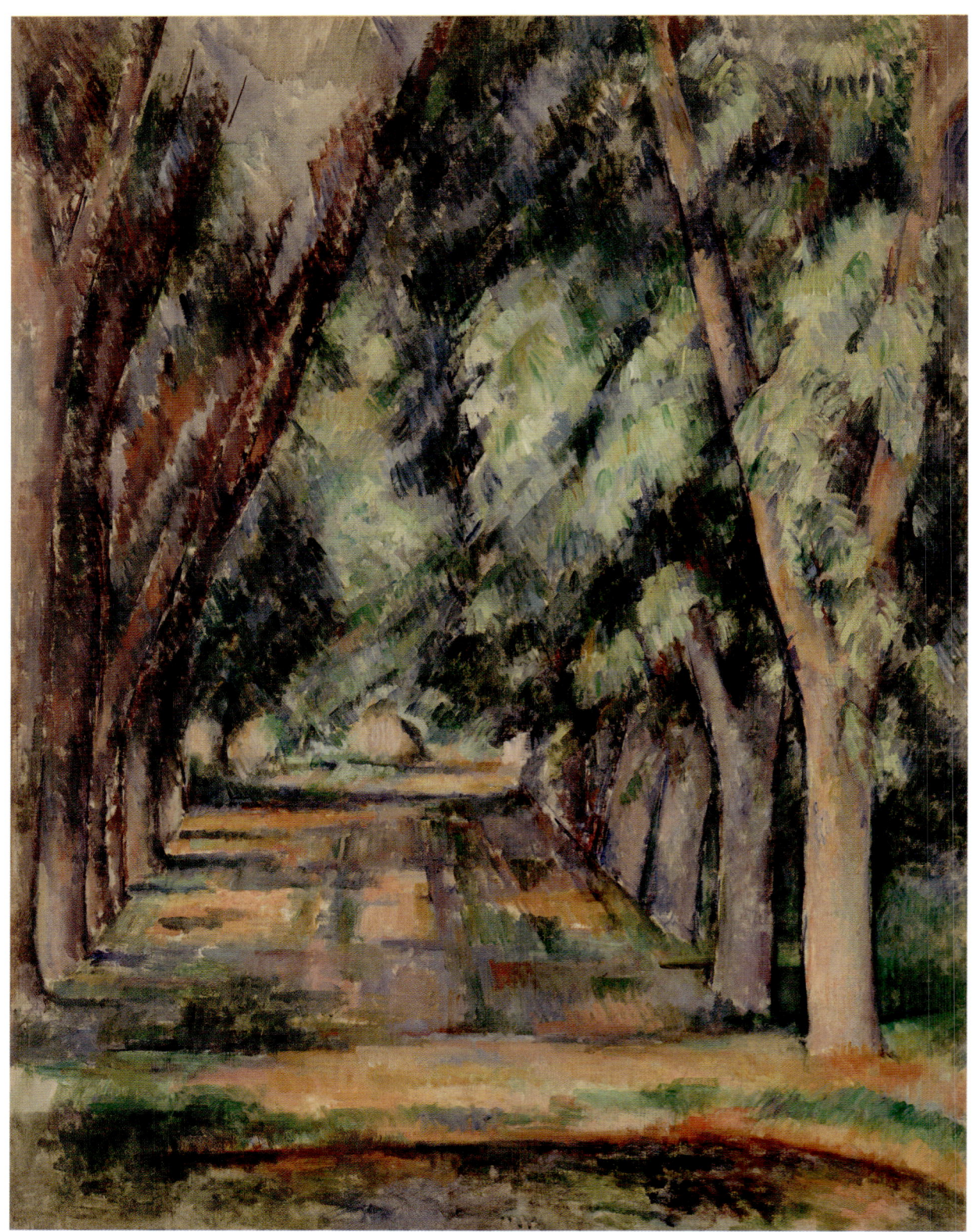

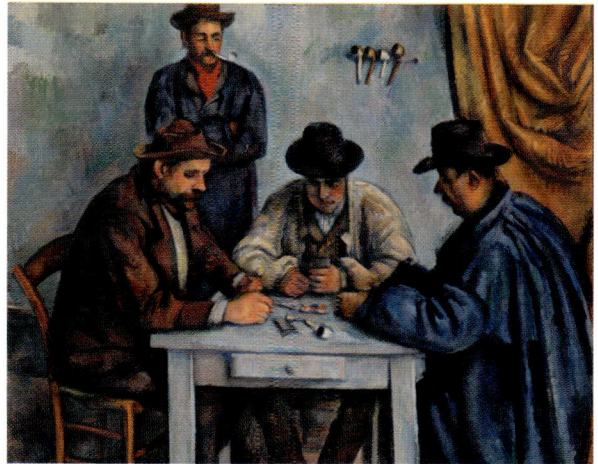

buildings at Jas de Bouffan, although there is evidence that the house itself was fairly run-down.

For son Paul, the family home at Jas de Bouffan was a sanctuary, a place where he could escape from the intensity of Paris. His work shows his close attachment to both the landscape and the people there – as well as painting the gardens, the farm labourers would later become the models for one of his most famous series of paintings, *The Card Players* (1890–95).

To prove his talent to his father – and his commitment to his craft – Cézanne painted straight on to the walls in the grand drawing room of the house, a project he worked on for a decade or more. The most impressive was a series of five panels on the curved alcove apse, depicting the four seasons, with a portrait of his father in the centre. In response, his father had a studio constructed for him on the upper floor of the house, with an enlarged north-facing window breaking the line of the eaves.

Over the next thirty years, Cézanne would paint some thirty-six oils and seventeen watercolours of his father's

LEFT *The Allée of Chestnut Trees at Jas de Bouffan* (circa 1888). ABOVE Cézanne used labourers on his father's estate as models for *The Card Players* (1890–92) – one of a series of similar studies. RIGHT *Madame Cézanne in the Conservatory* (1891) shows the artist's wife, Hortense Fiquet, at Jas de Bouffan after the death of Cézanne's father, who disapproved of the marriage.

house, its gardens, pool and statues, and the lines of chestnut trees. However, the full extent of his work at Jas de Bouffan will never be known. When the house was sold in 1899, Cézanne was devastated and built a bonfire in the garden, burning all the canvases that were stored there – mostly early work that perhaps he did not want to come on to the art market.

FAMILY AFFAIRS

Back in Paris, Cézanne had met and fallen in love with Marie-Hortense Fiquet, an artists' model and seamstress. Unbeknown to his father, the couple lived together in Paris and in 1872 she bore him a son, also called Paul. His mother knew of the affair, but kept it a secret so that Cézanne senior would continue to bankroll the artist.

Cézanne began to paint alongside his friend Camille Pissarro at Pontoise, a community just outside Paris, and nearby at Auvers-sur-Oise, where Cézanne, Hortense and little Paul lived for a while. His *en plein air* paintings, which he completed while there, were exhibited with works by

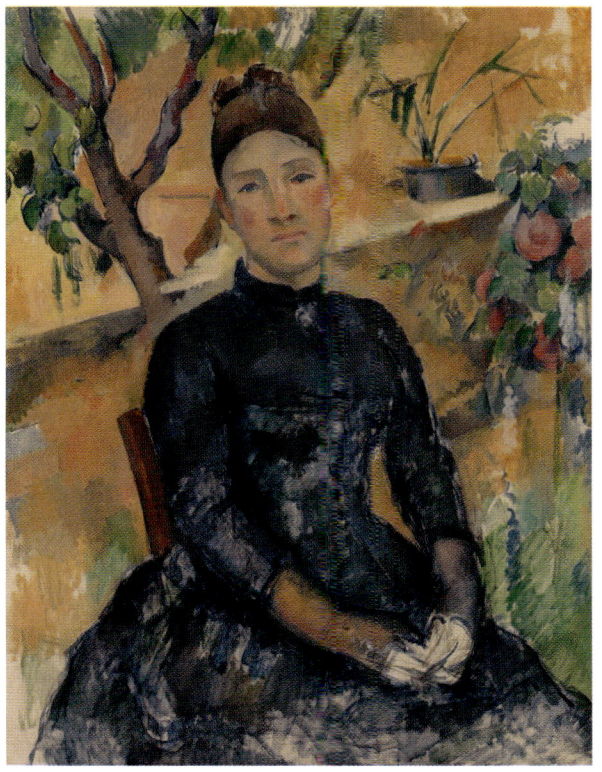

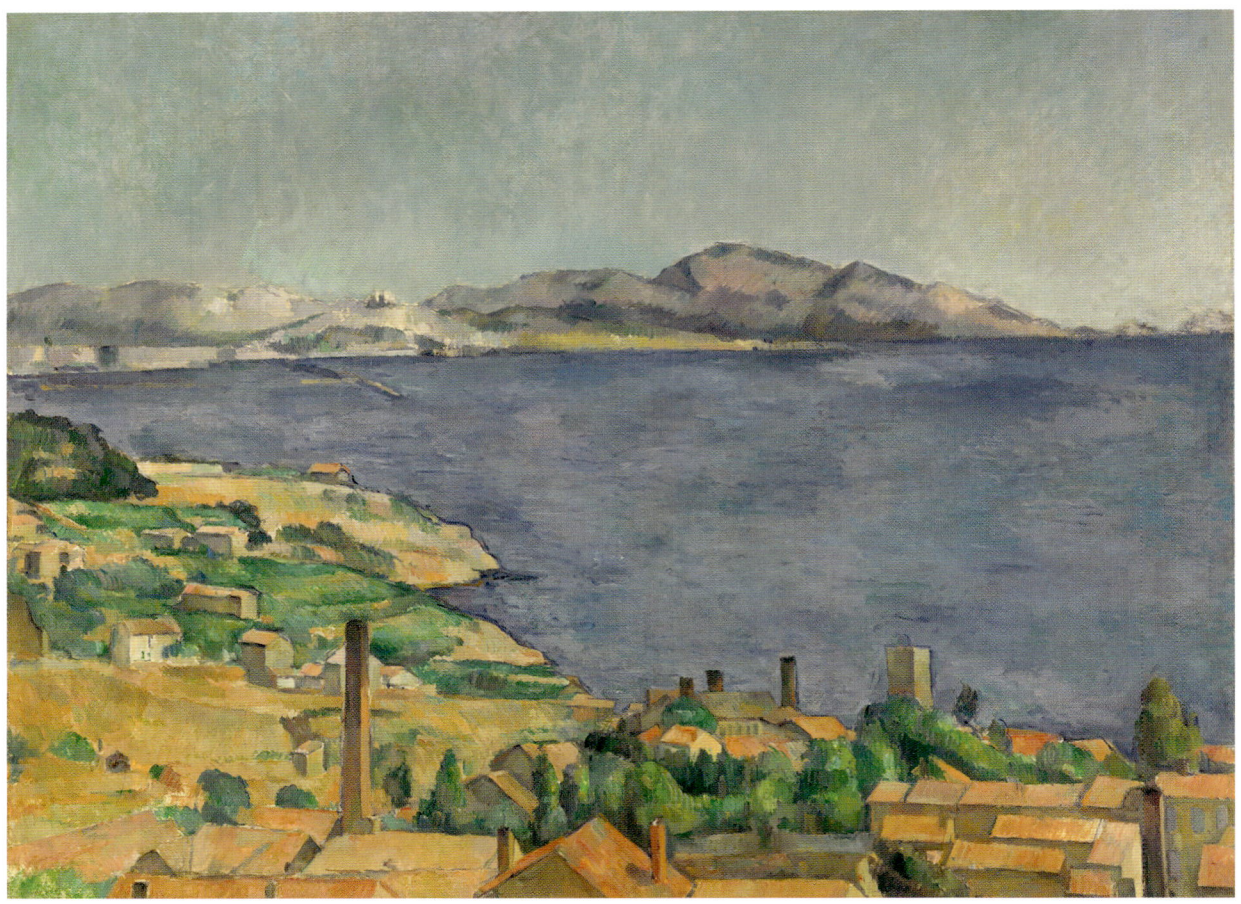

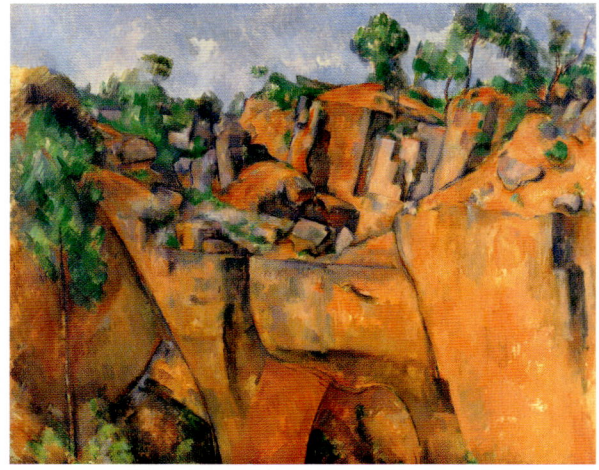

TOP *The Gulf of Marseilles Seen from L'Estaque* (circa 1885);
Cézanne loved this little fishing village, where his mother owned
a house, enthusing over its red rooftops and the blue sea.
ABOVE *The Quarry at Bibémus* (1895), where Cézanne rented
a stone *bastidon* (cabin) from which he painted the red rocks
and vegetation.
RIGHT Les Lauves, photographed in 1935.

Monet and others in the first and the third 'Impressionist'
exhibitions of 1874 and 1877, although Cézanne never
really fitted in with this breakaway group of artists and
continued to develop his own unique painting style.

INSPIRING LANDSCAPES

It was around this time that Cézanne also became
interested in painting views of the Mont Sainte-Victoire, a
mountain ridge in Provence, which can be seen from many
of the villages around Aix. He painted the motif repeatedly
for many years, working his way around the Provençal
landscape, always trying to find the perfect angle.

In 1882, Renoir joined Cézanne at his mother's summer
house in L'Estaque, a seaside village near Marseille, and the
following summer both Renoir and Monet accompanied
him on a tour of Provence, where his capacity for walking
miles, carrying easel and paints, had become legendary.
He also had many temporary cabins and stopovers
throughout the region, where he would store canvases
and items he may need for a day's painting. Cézanne was
known by his contemporaries for his measured approach

to his paintings, often pausing – interminably it seemed to other artists who worked alongside him – between each brushstroke to achieve the desired effect.

As well as painting the rocky, pine-covered landscapes of Provence and the mystical mountain of Sainte-Victoire, Cézanne found a new motif: the Bibémus Quarries. A romantic hillside setting on the outskirts of Aix, Bibémus was formed when two tectonic plates collided during the Jurassic period. The area was mined from Roman times until the early nineteenth century for sandstone and clay, which were used to build the town of Aix. As a child, Cézanne knew about the famous working quarries at Bibémus, but, when he started to paint there, they were practically abandoned and already yielding to nature, the rocks scattered with self-seeded pines and broom.

From the *bastidon* (stone cabin) that he rented at Bibémus, Cézanne produced eleven oils and sixteen watercolours of the quarries over a period of around five years. It is widely believed that this work, which includes *The Quarry at Bibémus* (1895), as well as the paintings he produced at L'Estaque, inspired the start of the Cubist movement and future artists, such as Georges Braque.

LATER LIFE AT LES LAUVES

After a turbulent love affair with another woman, Cézanne finally came back to Hortense and married her in 1886, the same year his father died. His mother lived on at Jas de Bouffan, where the couple were now welcome, but Cézanne's relationship with Hortense deteriorated during the last few years of the nineteenth century and she eventually went to live separately with their son Paul.

During this period, Cézanne was living an itinerant life, dividing his time between Jas de Bouffan and his other lodgings and cabins. One of his favourite sites was the Château Noir, just outside Aix, where he rented a room. This neo-Gothic castle, which was built in the nineteenth century but designed to look like a Gothic ruin, intrigued Cézanne, and he made several paintings of its grounds, including *The Pistachio Tree in the Courtyard of the Château Noir* (1900).

After the death of his mother in 1897, the family home at Jas de Bouffan had to be sold (for a little less than his father had paid for it) and the proceeds were divided between the artist and his two sisters. On 16 November 1901, Cézanne took possession of a 7,000-square-metre/75,348-square-foot plot of land along the Le Chemin des Lauves, an isolated road above the town of Aix. At the age of sixty-two, he was going to live alone and embarked on a project to build his own studio in the landscape that he loved.

The south-facing, sloping plot at Les Lauves was planted with olive, fruit and fig trees and backed on to the Verdon Canal. Cézanne was attracted to the place because of its uninterrupted view to the south-west of Mont Sainte-Victoire and he commissioned a simple dwelling to be built there. His architects initially misunderstood the artist's intentions and built a decorative villa – horrified, he had the balcony and ornamentation removed to leave a plain, farm-style building that suited his needs and aesthetic vision. Although the land cost just 2,000 francs, the construction work took ten months and cost the artist a further 30,000 francs. The new building had two rooms downstairs – a kitchen and small office – while the upstairs was devoted to the studio, illuminated by both south- and north-facing windows.

Cézanne moved into his studio at Les Lauves in 1902 and told everyone how much better he was working there than in the town. He would leave his flat on the Rue

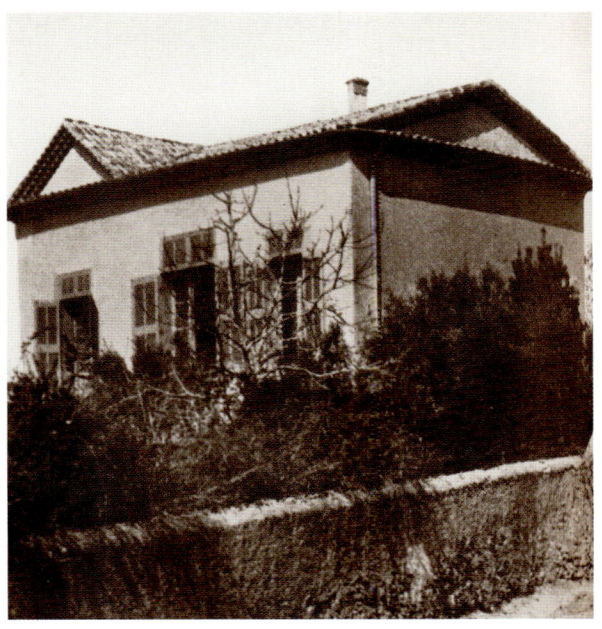

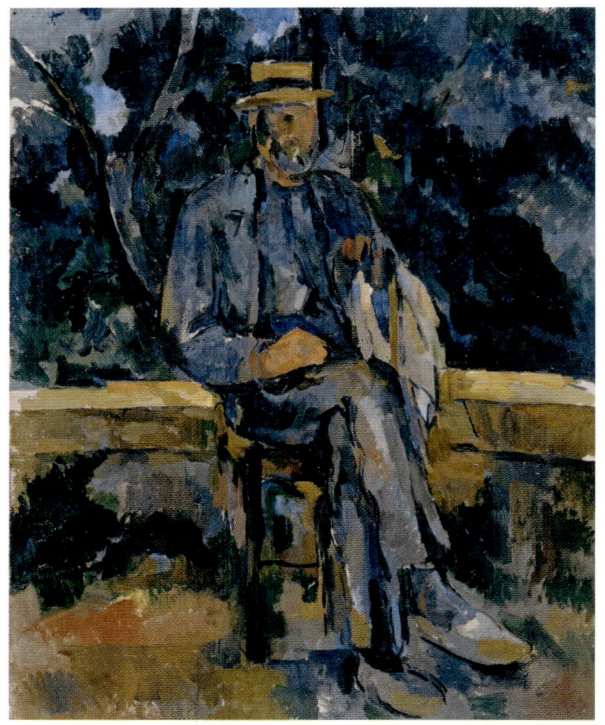

Boulegon in Aix every morning at 6.30 a.m. to walk up to Les Lauves, only returning to the town to eat and sleep. Within the fruit garden there was one tree that Cézanne singled out: an ancient olive in the courtyard, around which he had erected a low wall to protect it during the building work. He imbued this tree with spiritual properties, touching it, speaking to it, and even kissing it when he left his studio in the evening. He felt it was an old friend and wanted to be buried at its feet.

Cézanne was very contented at Les Lauves and produced much of his finest work there, including *Les Grandes Baigneuses*, his last still lifes, several paintings of Mont Sainte-Victoire as seen from the bottom of his property, and a handful of watercolours of the garden and its terrace.

Although Cézanne was not strong enough to work in the garden, he enjoyed its surroundings and the privacy it gave him to paint. He employed a gardener, Vallier, to tend the olives and figs and Vallier also became the subject of one of Cézanne's greatest portraits. In his last letters, the artist expressed how sad he was about the length of time

"Nature is very beautiful. They can't take that away from me."
PAUL CÉZANNE (1905)

ABOVE The model for *Seated Man* (1905–06) was Vallier, the gardener at Les Lauves who looked after Cézanne in his latter years.
RIGHT *The Terrace of the Garden at Les Lauves* (1902–06). Cézanne often made preparatory watercolours before working in oils.
OPPOSITE Cézanne's studio at Les Lauves, with the notebooks, artifacts and furniture that still remain in the house today.

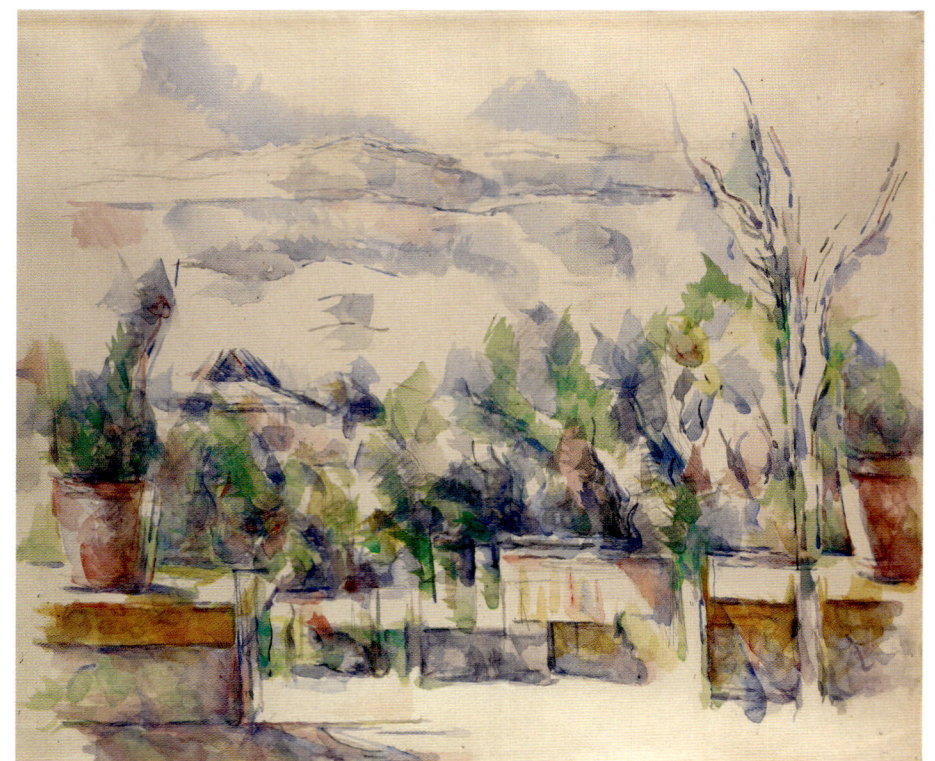

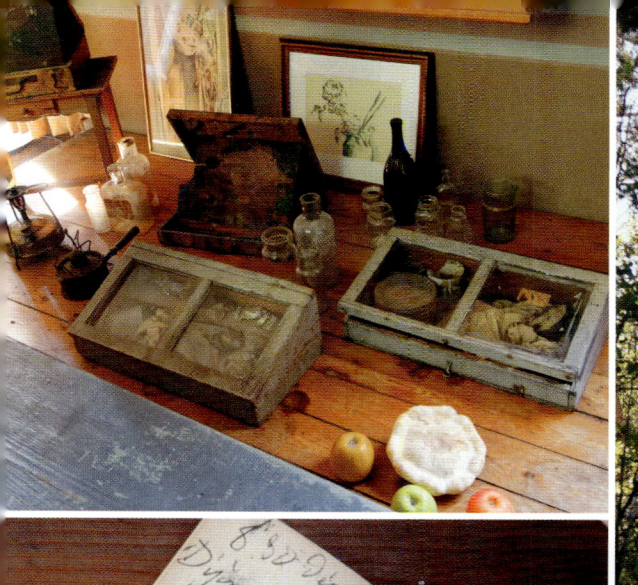

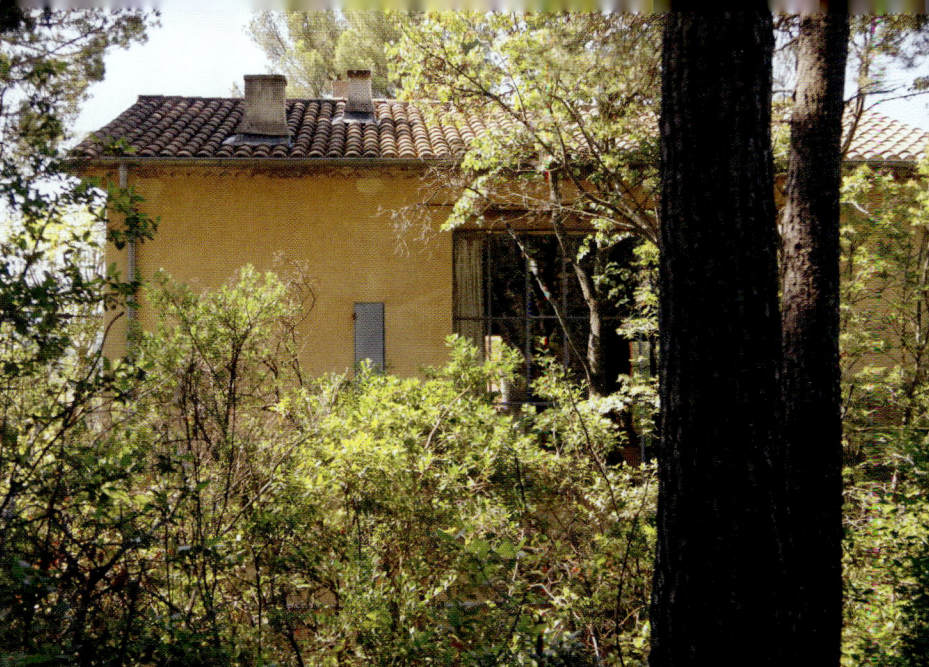

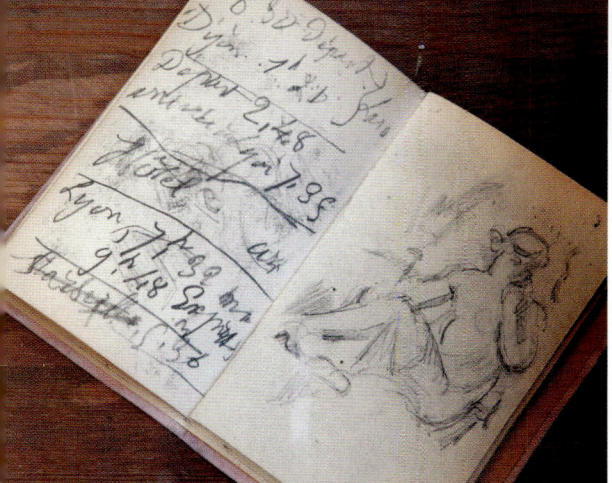

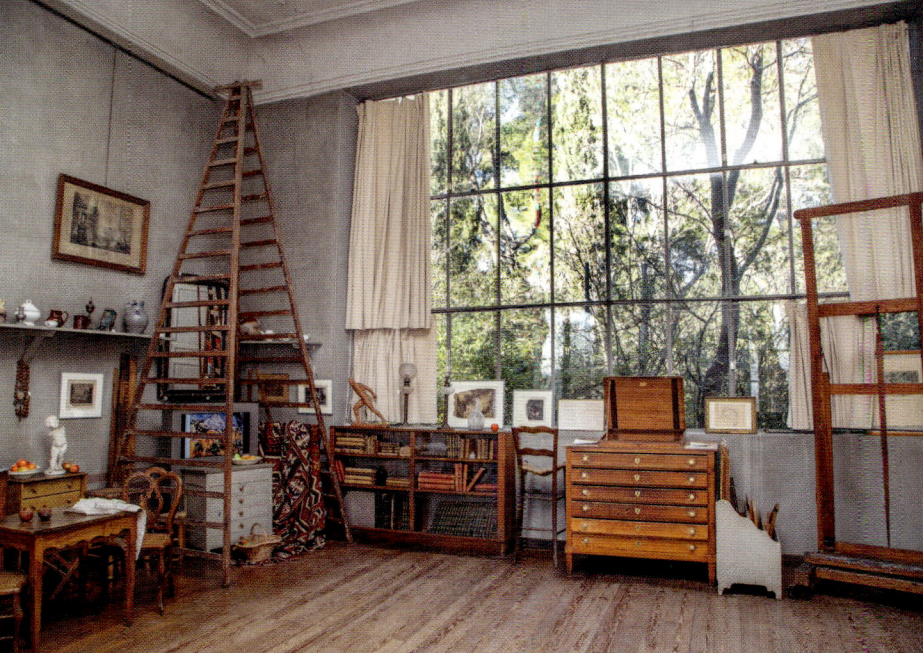

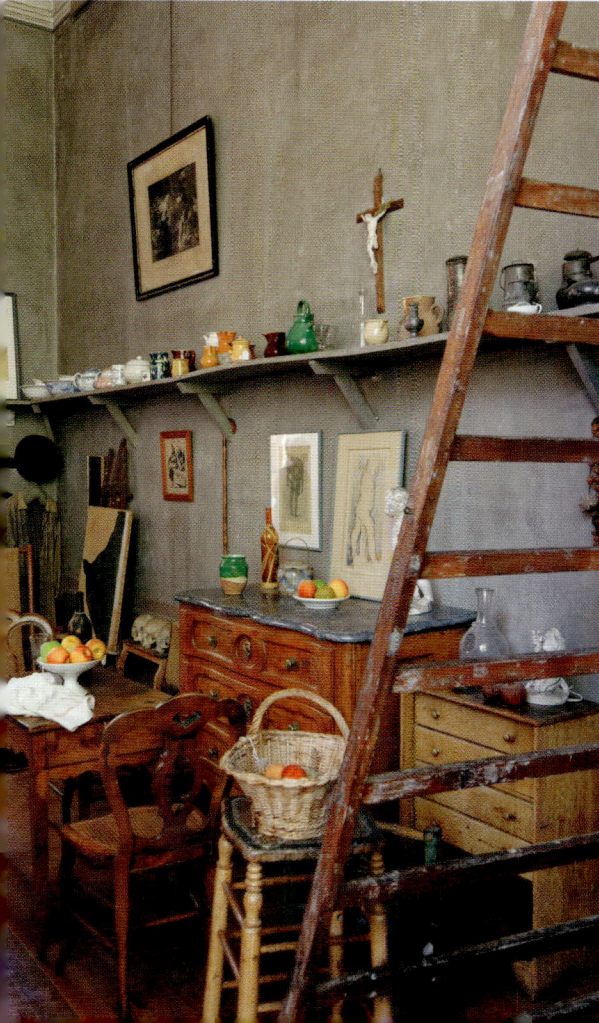

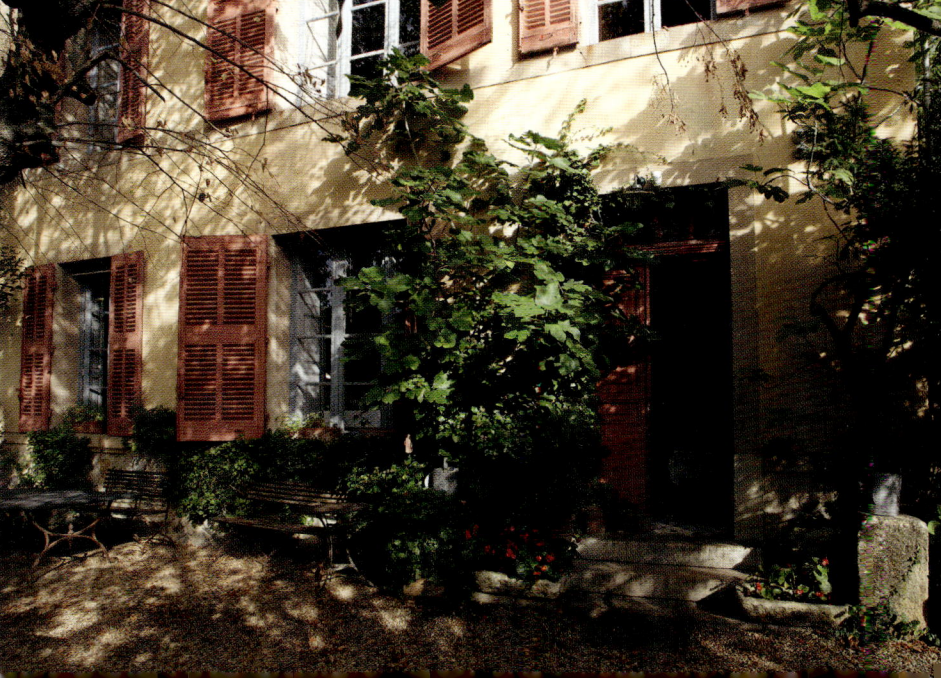

the portrait of Vallier was taking him. The gardener, in turn, complained that his sittings for this painting, and for several other portraits, were so long that he didn't have enough time for his own work.

Cézanne's last painting trip was just a few hundred metres from his garden, where he went to work on *Jourdan's Cabin* (1906). Later that year, in October 1906, he was caught in a storm and was carried back, unconscious, to Aix by cart. The next morning, still unwell, he walked back up to the studio, sat under a lime tree and worked on his portrait of Vallier. He died a few days later of pleurisy.

AFTER CÉZANNE

In September 1907, just one year after his death, Cézanne's paintings were exhibited in a retrospective in Paris at the Salon d'Automne. Cézanne fever – which would make him one of the most sought-after artists for the next hundred years and more – had begun.

In 1921, Les Lauves was bought and lived in by a famous Provençal character known as Marcel 'Provence', who wrote about Cézanne and kept his studio exactly as it

was, until his own death in 1951. The building was saved from developers by a group of American art lovers who fund-raised and opened it to the public, welcoming poets, artists, historians and fans from around the world, including, in 1955, Marilyn Monroe.

Unlike his studio, Cézanne's gardens suffered greatly after his death. The olive trees at Les Lauves were removed after they were damaged by storms in 1956, while the house and gardens at Jas de Bouffan fell into disrepair until 2018, when a major restoration programme of Cézanne's properties began. This work is ensuring that the places the artist knew are finally receiving the attention they deserve.

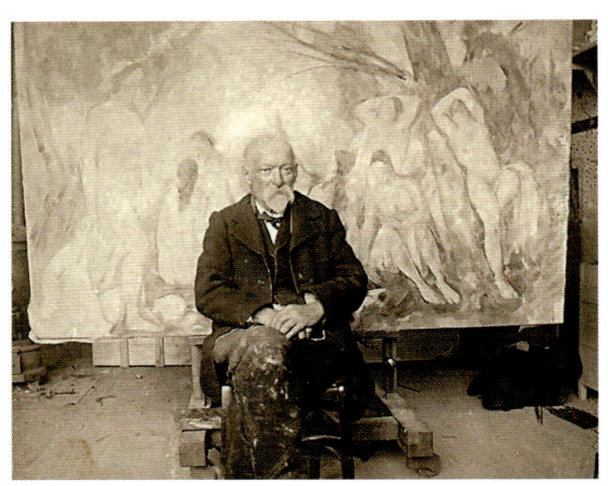

RIGHT Paul Cézanne photographed in his studio at Les Lauves two years before his death.
OPPOSITE *Mont Saint-Victoire* (1904); Cézanne returned again and again to paint this mountain ridge close to his home.

CÉZANNE'S TIMELINE

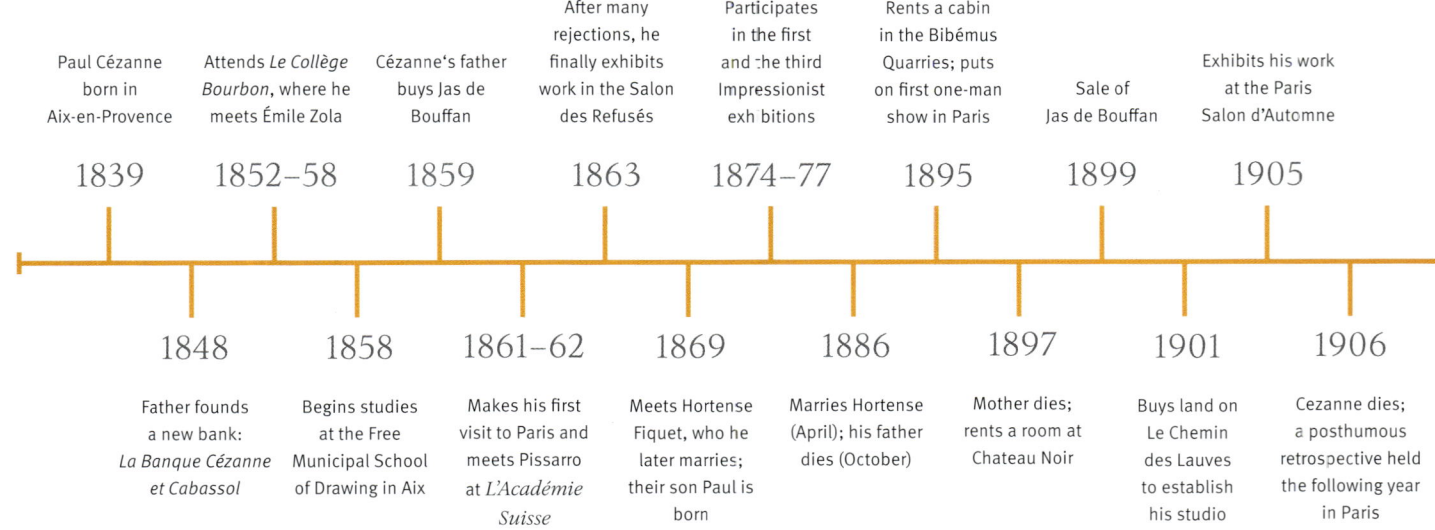

1839	1852–58	1859	1863	1874–77	1895	1899	1905
Paul Cézanne born in Aix-en-Provence	Attends *Le Collège Bourbon*, where he meets Émile Zola	Cézanne's father buys Jas de Bouffan	After many rejections, he finally exhibits work in the Salon des Refusés	Participates in the first and the third Impressionist exhibitions	Rents a cabin in the Bibémus Quarries; puts on first one-man show in Paris	Sale of Jas de Bouffan	Exhibits his work at the Paris Salon d'Automne

1848	1858	1861–62	1869	1886	1897	1901	1906
Father founds a new bank: *La Banque Cézanne et Cabassol*	Begins studies at the Free Municipal School of Drawing in Aix	Makes his first visit to Paris and meets Pissarro at *L'Académie Suisse*	Meets Hortense Fiquet, who he later marries; their son Paul is born in 1872	Marries Hortense (April); his father dies (October)	Mother dies; rents a room at Chateau Noir	Buys land on Le Chemin des Lauves to establish his studio	Cezanne dies; a posthumous retrospective held the following year in Paris

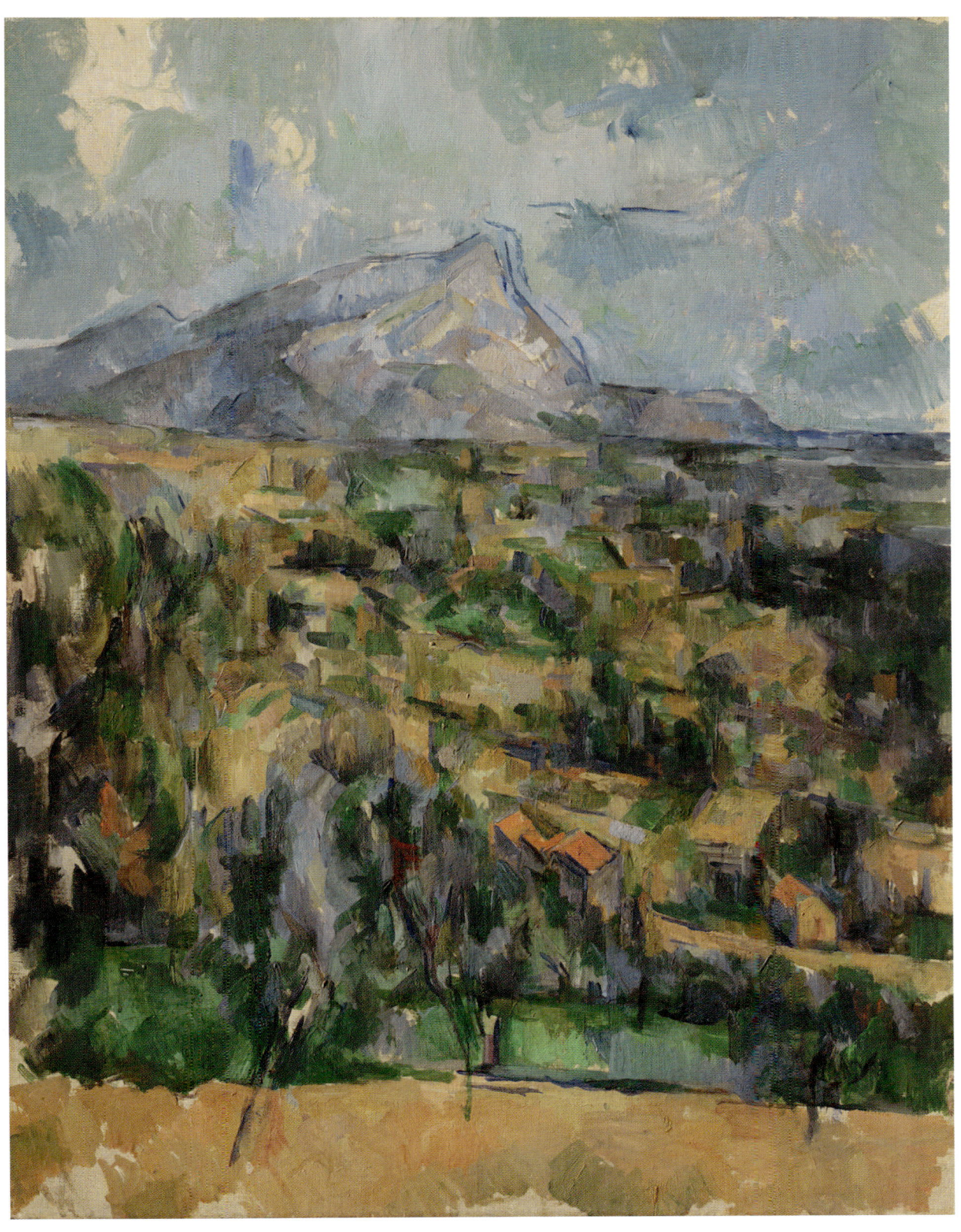

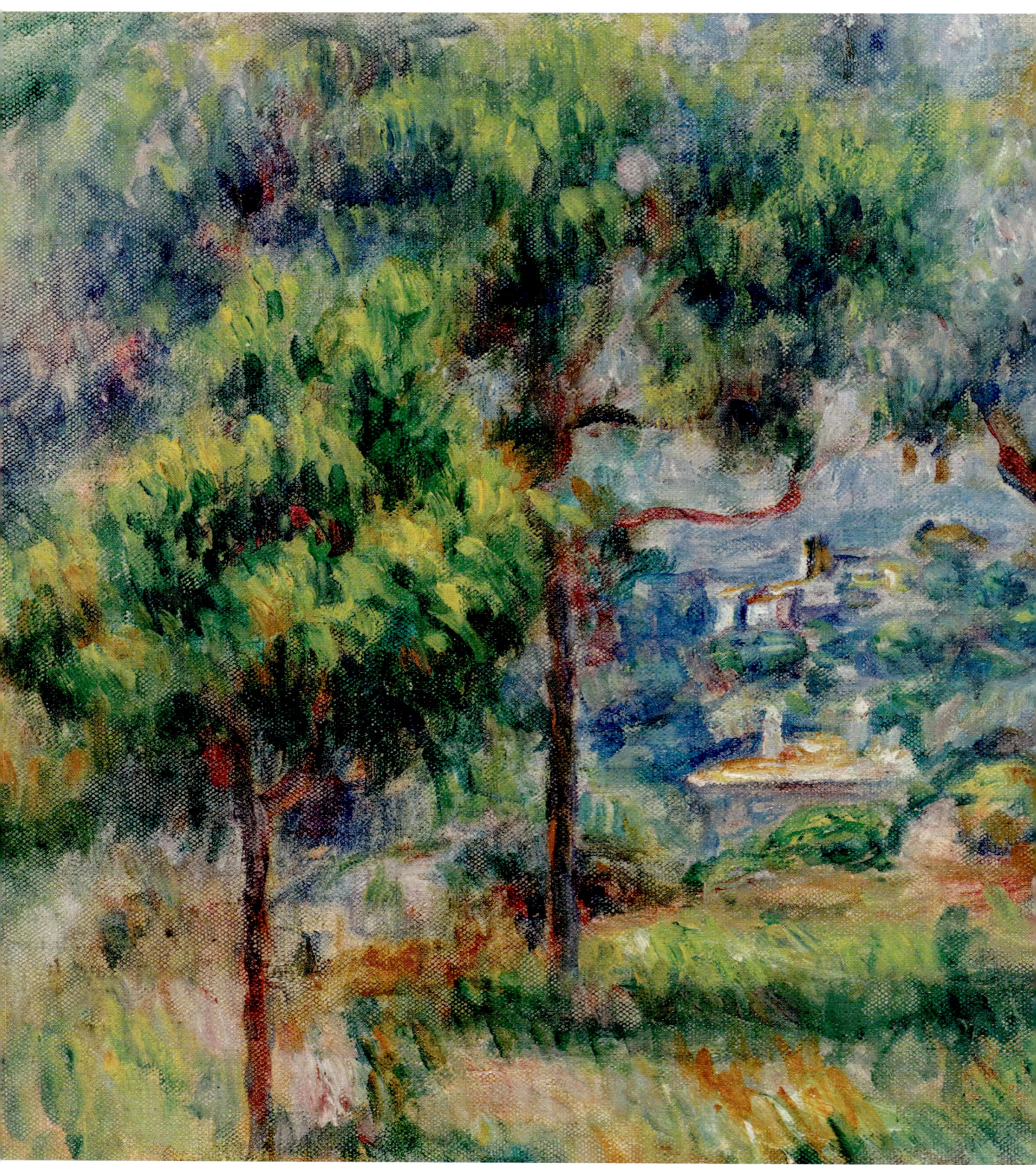

The Artist's Garden

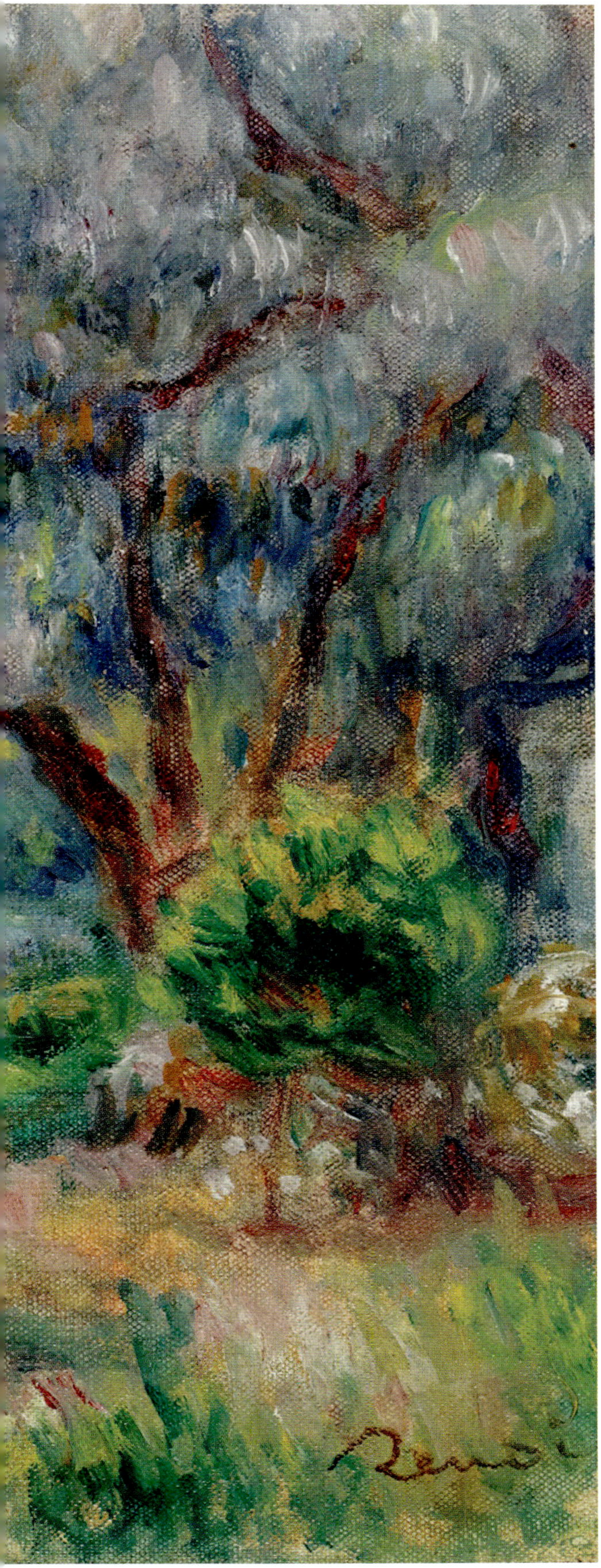

Pierre-Auguste Renoir

Champagne and La Côte d'Azur, France

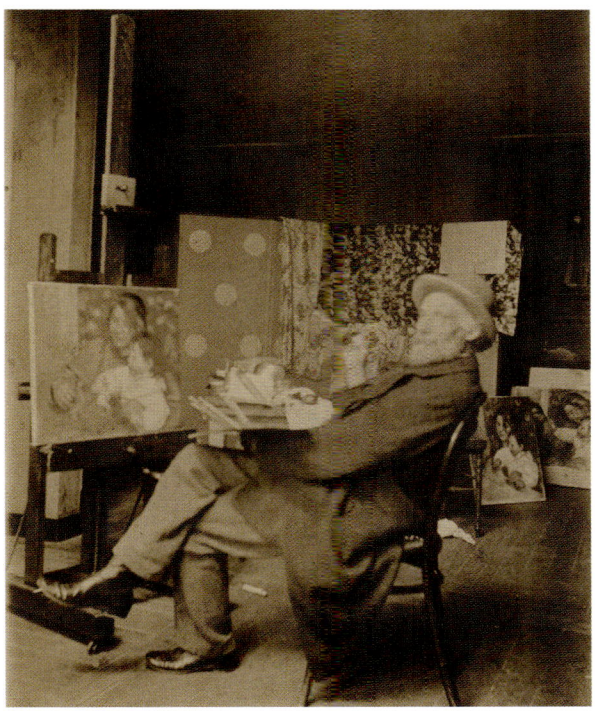

ORN THE SON of a tailor in Limoges, a town famous in the nineteenth century for its ceramic industry, Pierre-Auguste Renoir was not destined to become an artist. His first job was painting flowers on china in a porcelain factory where the owner recognized his talent and encouraged him to take drawing lessons. Renoir then prepared for entry to the École des Beaux-Arts and by the age of twenty one, he was living in Paris and

ABOVE This photograph of Renoir, taken around 1895, shows the artist working in the living room of his summer house in Essoyes, Champagne, where he painted until he built a studio in the garden. LEFT Renoir's *Paysages des Collettes* (circa 1907) was painted from his terrace at Les Collettes on the Côte d'Azur.

studying in the studio of the Swiss artist Charles Gleyre, where he befriended three other young painters: Frédéric Bazille, Alfred Sisley and Claude Monet. With no financial support, Renoir struggled to buy materials, but along with Monet, several of his paintings were selected by the Parisian art dealer Paul Durand-Ruel for inclusion in the first 'Impressionist' exhibition of 1874. He also began painting people and portraits during this time, which he knew would attract commissions and bring him income.

In 1880, in the heat of Paris' *Belle Époque*, Renoir and his friends would gather in a little restaurant on the river, to the west of the city. On Sundays, La Maison Fournaise also offered an escape for girls working in the city, including waitresses, shop assistants and seamstresses from Paris' fashion industry. One of these dressmakers was a girl from the Champagne region, Aline Charigot, who would not only feature in much of Renoir's work, but whom he would also later marry. It was said that Renoir was painting the face of Aline before he had even set eyes on her.

At the restaurant, Alphonse Fournaise, the son of the owner, organized boating trips for the customers, which Renoir captured in some of his greatest paintings, including *Le Déjeuner des Canotiers* (*Luncheon of the Boating Party*; 1881) where, in the foreground, Aline is seen clutching a little dog and wearing flowers in her hat. Two years later, she is clearly the dishevelled, carefree countrywoman in the *Danse à la Campagne* (*Country Dance*; 1883).

NATURE'S INSPIRATION

Although best remembered for his paintings of people, and particularly women, Renoir also developed an early interest in gardens – he painted Monet in his garden at Argenteuil in 1873 (see page 134), and completed several paintings of the naturalistic gardens behind his studio in Montmartre, including *Woman with a Parasol in a Garden* (1875) and *The Garden in the Rue Cortot* (1876). His 1876–7 painting, *Chemin Montant dans les Hautes Herbes*, with its landscape dotted with poppies, is probably Renoir at his most 'impressionistic', while his still lifes, *Bouquet* (1879), *Bouquet of Chrysanthemums* (1884) and *Pommes et Fleurs* (1895), also demonstrate his mastery of botanical detail.

Aline encouraged his love of nature and gardens. She came from Essoyes, a village in the Champagne region,

and the Renoirs spent every summer there, eventually buying a property where Renoir designed his first garden. Later in life, they moved to an olive farm at Cagnes-sur-Mer in the south of France – the garden there provided a relaxing space for the family and also became an important source of inspiration for the artist, offering him a way of expressing his affinity with the natural world.

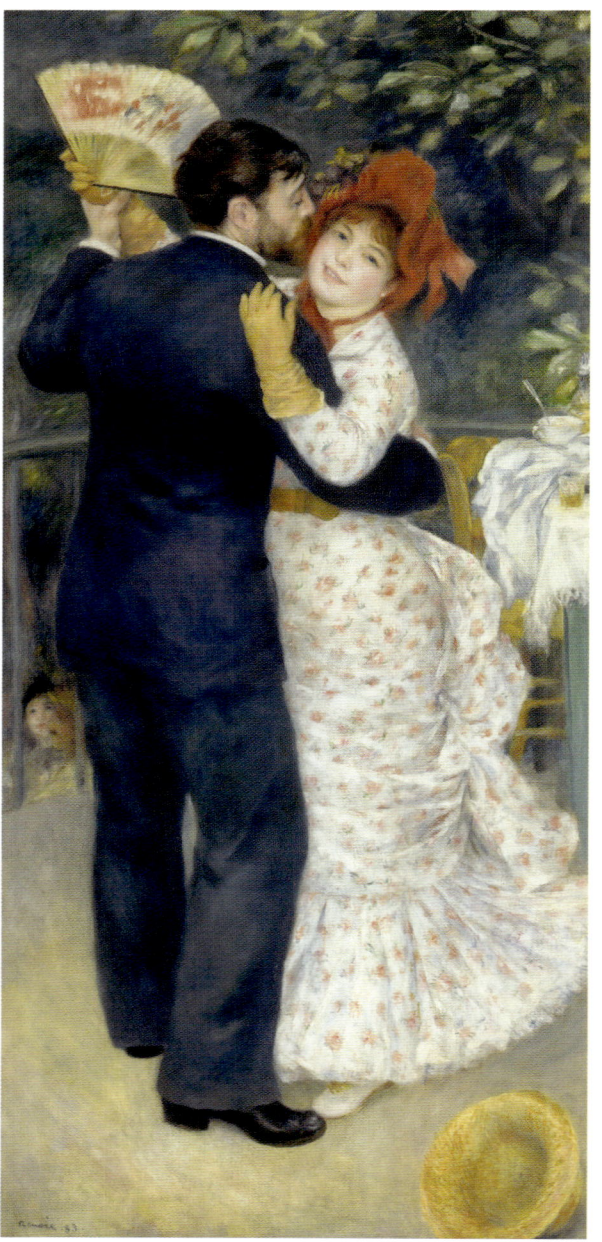

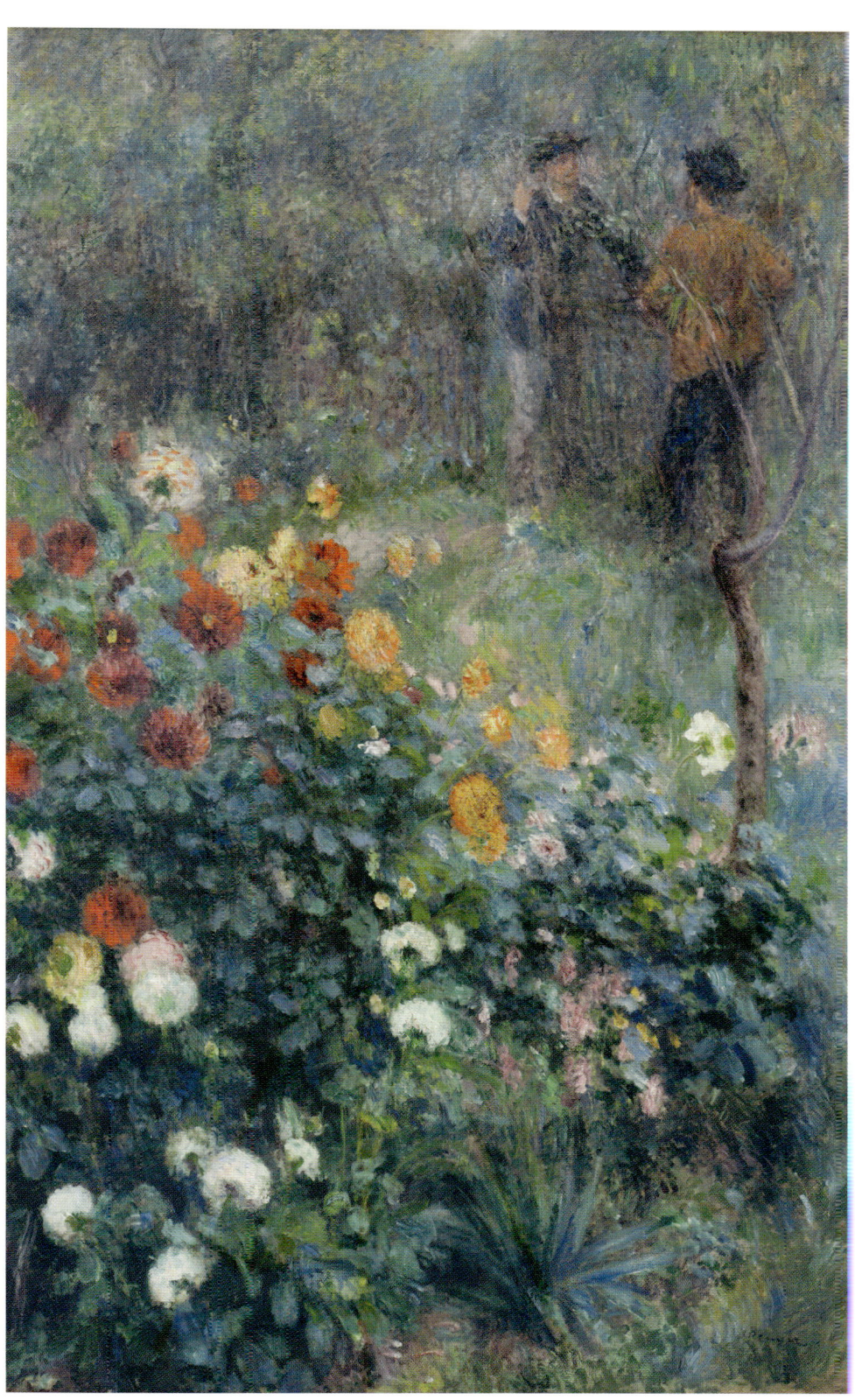

OPPOSITE Aline Charigot, whom Renoir would later marry, was the model for *Country Dance* (1883).
LEFT *The Garden in the Rue Cortot* (1876) is one of several paintings of the gardens close to Renoir's studio in Montmartre, which he completed while living in Paris.

Pierre-Auguste Renoir
(1841–1919)

Renoir was born in Limoges in 1841 and, as a young man, he travelled to Paris and mixed with a set of forward-thinking artists, including Claude Monet and Frédéric Bazille, who soon marked him out as something special. After living in Paris in a series of apartments in the artists' district of Montmartre, Pierre-Auguste and his wife Aline bought a house at Essoyes in the Champagne region in north-east France, making it into a summer home for their growing family. Here, the simple life, good food, and country traditions became as important to Renoir as the light and paints he used to create his artworks. This search for simplicity was later compounded by the move in 1908 to the south of France, where the olive grove and gardens of their home, Les Collettes, offered the couple warmth during the winter months. Both houses stayed in the Renoir family for many years – their youngest son, Claude, lived on at Les Collettes until the 1960s and Sophie Renoir (the artist's great-granddaughter) lived in the Essoyes house until 2011.

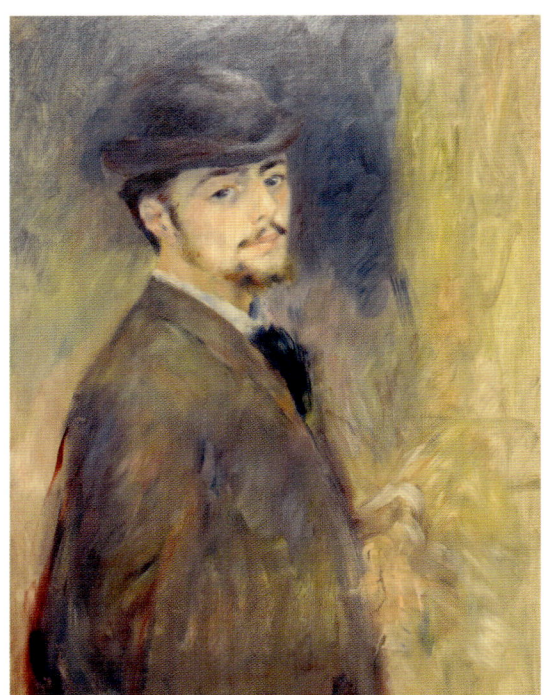

Self Portrait (1876) of Renoir as a young man.

DISCOVERING CHAMPAGNE

Renoir made his first visit to Essoyes a few years after the couple's first son, Pierre, was born in 1885. Since becoming a mother, Aline had been eager to return to her home and she finally persuaded Renoir to accompany her. He was enchanted with this village by the Ource, a tributary of the Seine, and during that first summer he painted one of his most famous works, *Les Laveuses* (*Washerwomen*; 1888), inspired by women he saw rinsing their clothes in the river.

For Aline, settling in Essoyes was a lifelong dream. Her father had left the family for America when she was small, and her mother was forced to find work in Paris as a seamstress, leaving Aline behind in the care of an aunt and uncle. As soon as she was old enough to work, Aline followed her mother to Montmartre, but to return as the wife (the Renoirs married in 1890) of a successful painter was a coup. In 1896, they found a property to buy – the house of a *vigneron* (winemaker) with an attached barn that they could renovate and make into a substantial family home. When their second son, Jean, was born, Aline's sixteen-year-old cousin, Gabrielle Renard, joined the family as the baby's nanny, and went on to became Renoir's most celebrated female nude model for the next two decades.

Renoir loved the house and garden in Essoyes, with its orchard and vegetable patch, and found everything he needed in the village. He liked the fact that it was not easy to travel to (taking a full day from Paris) and he was also inspired by the range of subjects he had available to paint. He was particularly drawn to the river, which he described as 'molten silver', but mostly he loved the people, with whom he felt at home. Renoir was happy leading a 'simple life' in Essoyes, and the family would spend the summers at the house there up until a few months before his death.

A COUNTRY GARDEN

Renoir painted his country home, *La Maison d'Essoyes*, in 1906, which gives us some clues about the garden he made there. The artist had a dislike of anything formal and hated neat English lawns, which he found too clinical. His own garden was a model of simplicity – a productive space, with fruit trees, vines, vegetables, salads and some cottage flowers. At that time, it extended only as far as the outdoor studio – about 0.15 hectares/16,145 square feet. Initially,

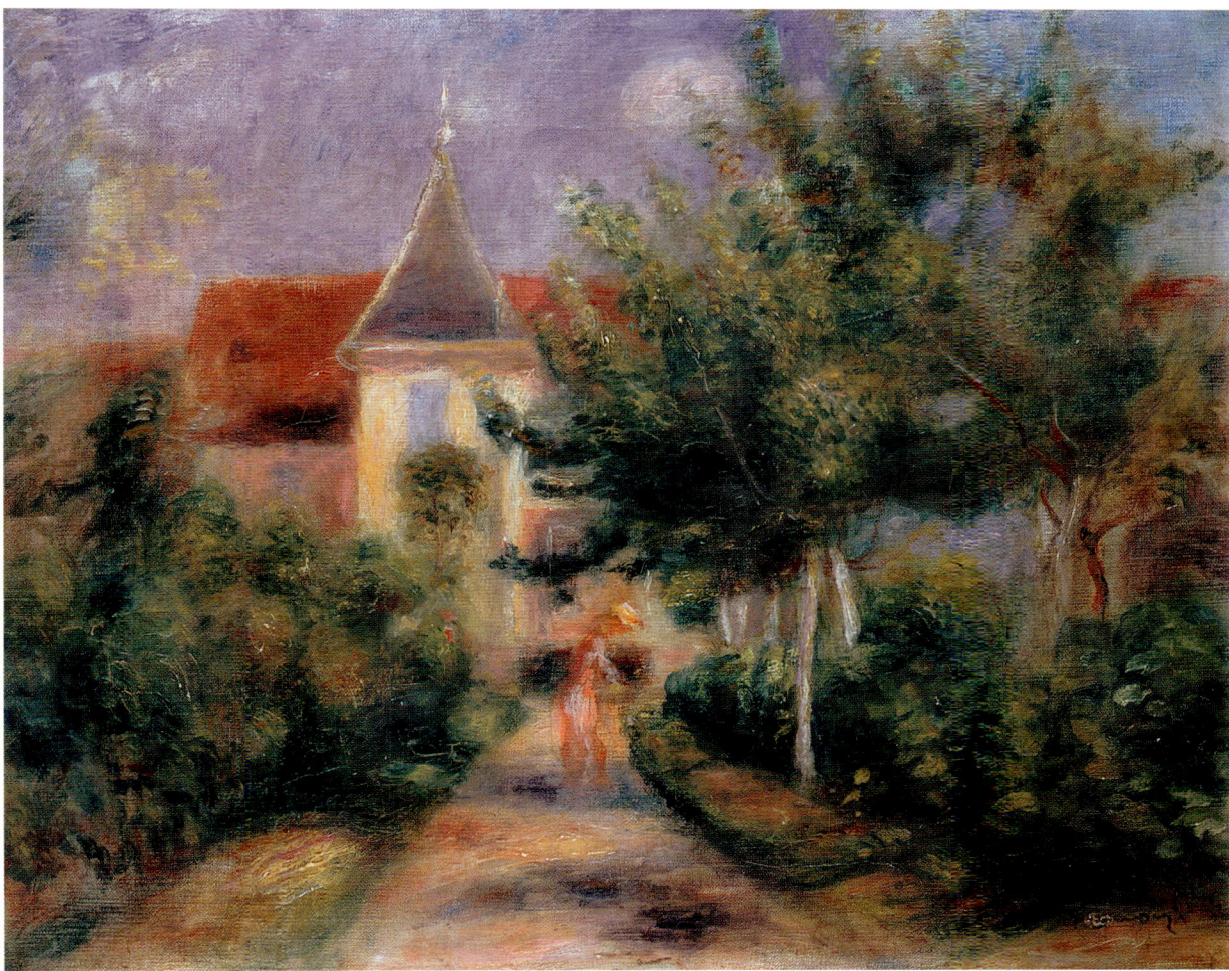

Renoir painted in the main living room but when their third son, Claude, was born in 1901, he built an outdoor studio at the end of the garden, with an external staircase to the first floor. Jean Renoir, who went on to become a celebrated filmmaker, recalls that his father was never too busy for the children. They were always encouraged to play outside and make a noise, even when he was working, as if the sounds of their laughter helped rather than hindered him.

While Renoir painted, Aline, enjoying her new status in the village and with plenty of money to spend, began a major renovation of the house, adding a grand staircase encased in a tower to connect the two floors. Letters written by her show that she was in charge of the build and kept on top of it, even when they were back in Paris.

While Aline oversaw the house improvements and created memorable meals from the garden, Renoir concentrated on his love of light and the play of the foliage, whether it was the silver willows (*Salix alba* var. *sericea*) near the river, or the horse chestnut tree in the courtyard behind the house – now long gone, but replaced by a sweet gum (*Liquidambar styraciflua*).

Renoir was, by this time, in his sixties and although Aline was twenty years his junior they were both suffering physically – she with diabetes (which she refused to help through diet) and he with rheumatoid arthritis. They decided to spend the winters in the south, settling in Cagnes-sur-Mer. His painting of the Essoyes house and garden in 1906 could well have been a reaction to their imminent departure, knowing that his health would probably not allow many more visits to the village, where the summers may be benign, but where winter temperatures frequently drop well below freezing.

After Renoir and Aline left their house at Essoyes, it stayed in the family when they passed it on to their eldest son, Pierre. The last member of the Renoir family to live in

ABOVE *La Maison d'Essoyes* (1906), Renoir's painting of the house and garden he and Aline created in Essoyes.

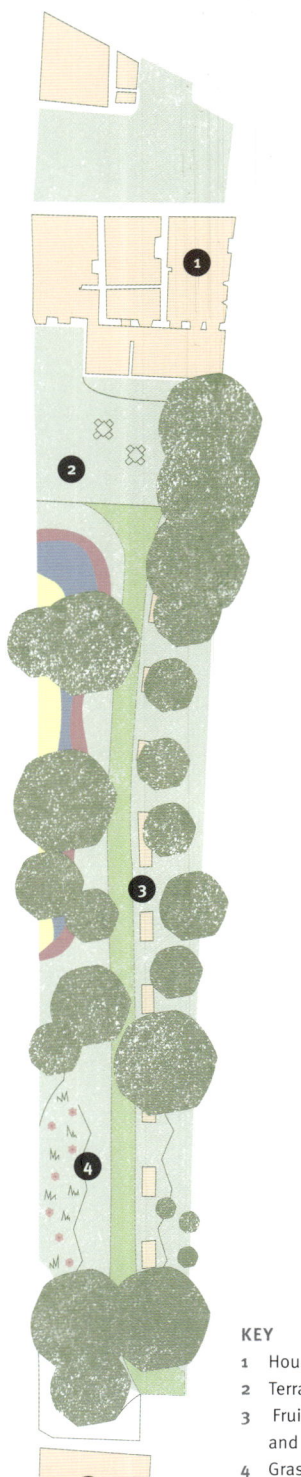

the house was Pierre Renoir's great-granddaughter, Sophie, who sold it to the *Commune d'Essoyes* in 2012, along with much of its contents, including Aline's kitchen table, Renoir's bed, and most of the original furniture. After five years of detailed research, the house was renovated and opened to the public in 2017.

RESTORING THE GARDEN

When the commune acquired the property, the garden was overgrown and dominated by hydrangeas. Another piece of land had been added in 2010 to accommodate a visitor centre and this was planted up by Paris landscaper, Alice Tricon. However, in what had been Renoir's original garden, a lawn covered most of the plot, boundaries had collapsed, the fruit trees needed attention and there was little left of the potager. The town, along with the visitor organization, *Du Côté des Renoir*, decided to create a new garden that would be easier to maintain and more accessible. The job fell to landscape designer Nicolas George who, tasked with creating the new space, still wanted to retain the Renoirs' presence, while making a garden that would function well for visitors.

George reinstated the path along traces of the original route leading from Renoir's studio back to the house. Flanking the path, the artist's 1906 painting of the garden shows a narrow band of turf, edged on one side by low shrubs and roses, and on the other by fruit trees and a potager. George has replicated the potager with a new planting of vines and currant bushes and reintroduced the grass border.

While the plants have changed, the designer has been careful to retain the lightness of the planting, and its balance of masses and voids. For lightness, there are *Gaura lindheimeri*, achilleas, astrantias, scabious and geums, as well as grasses, including *Stipa tenuissima, Panicum virgatum* and *Pennisetum villosum*. For solidity, George has planted hydrangeas, roses, peonies, alliums and dahlias. In terms of colours, Renoir reputedly used no more than seven or eight colours on his palette at any one time, which included yellow ochre, rose madder and viridian, believing that to extend beyond this was to over-complicate things. The planting reflects Renoir's methods by also using a restricted palette, picking up on colours that feature in his paintings.

THE LURE OF THE SUN

In 1959, the filmmaker Jean Renoir returned to his father's home in Cagnes-sur-Mer to make *Le Déjeuner sur l'herbe* (*Picnic on the Grass*). A documentary made at the time shows him talking to camera in front of the old farm and he would later write a memoir (*Pierre-Auguste Renoir, Mon Pere*) about his time at Les Collettes with his brothers, Pierre and Claude, and his parents, Pierre-Auguste

RIGHT (CLOCKWISE FROM TOP LEFT) Renoir's second-storey studio at the end of the garden in Essoyes; the living room where the artist initially painted; Aline's household bills and letters; Renoir's studio interior; the new garden designed by Nicolas George; the family kitchen.

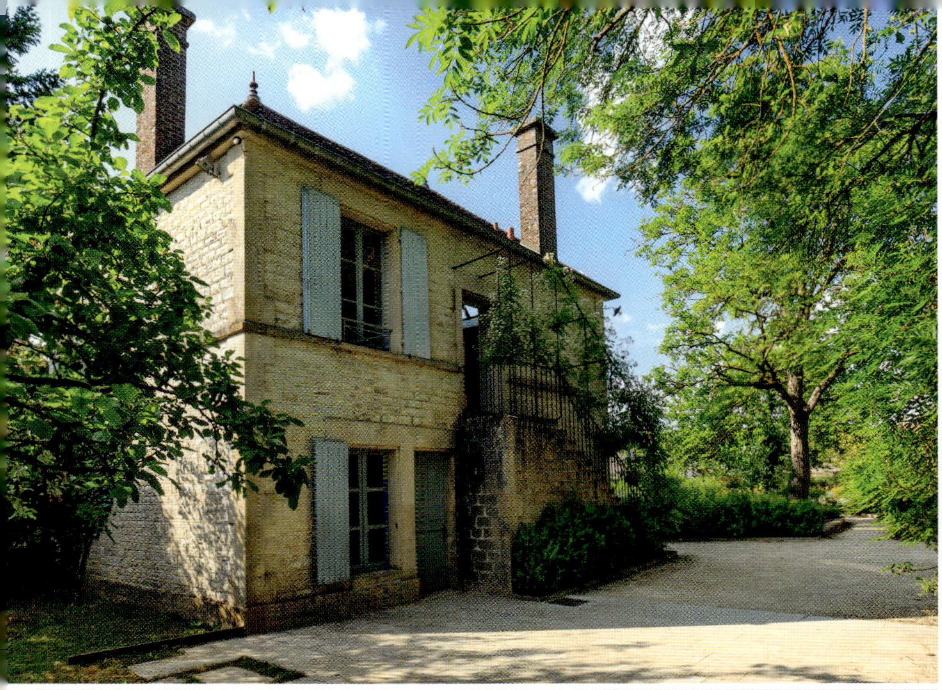

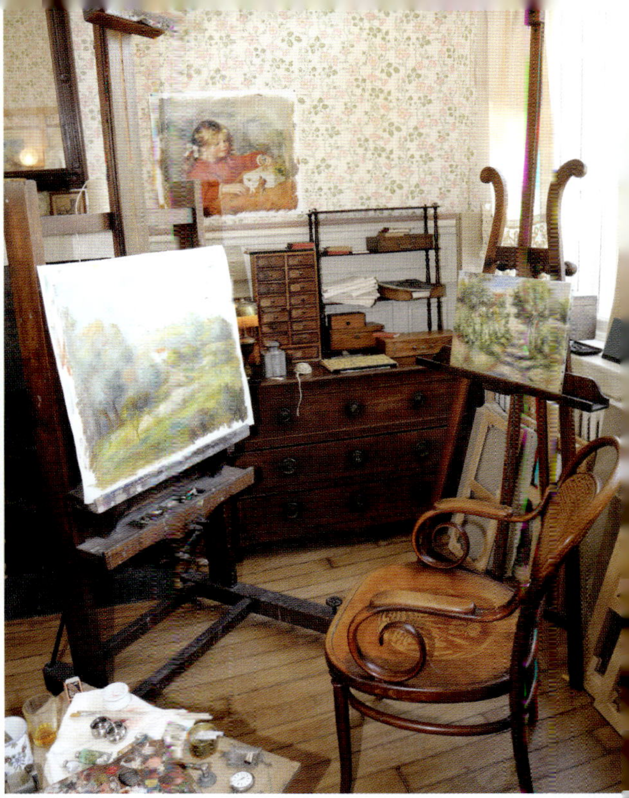

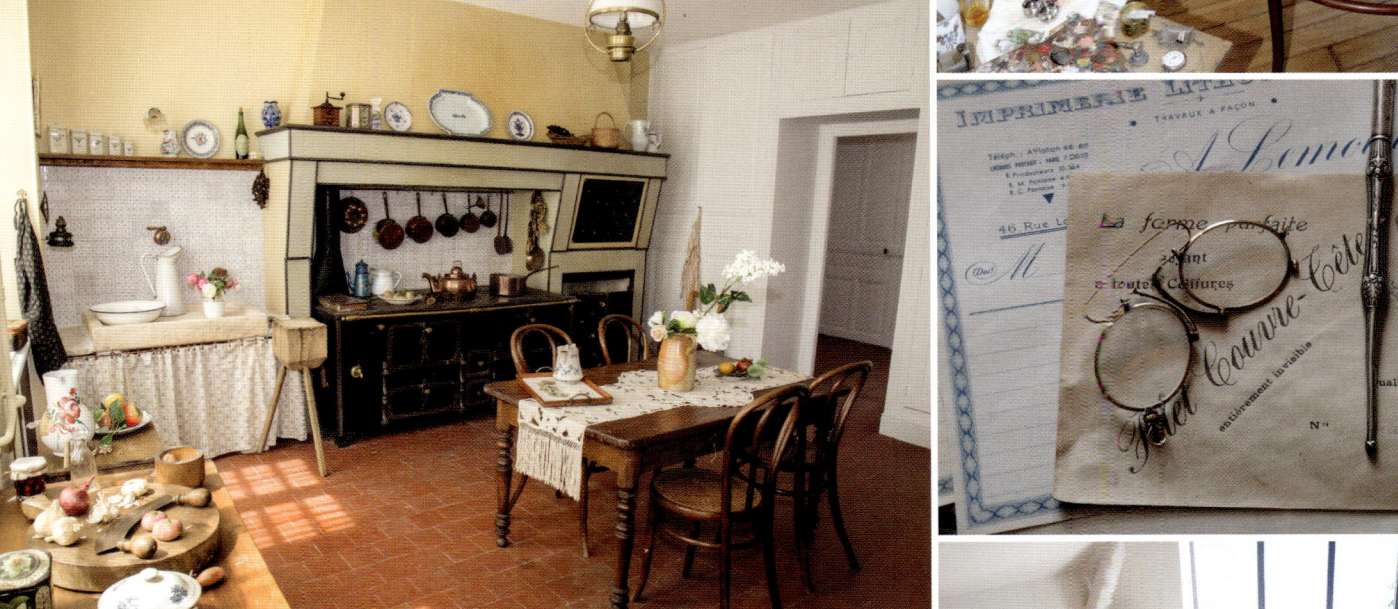
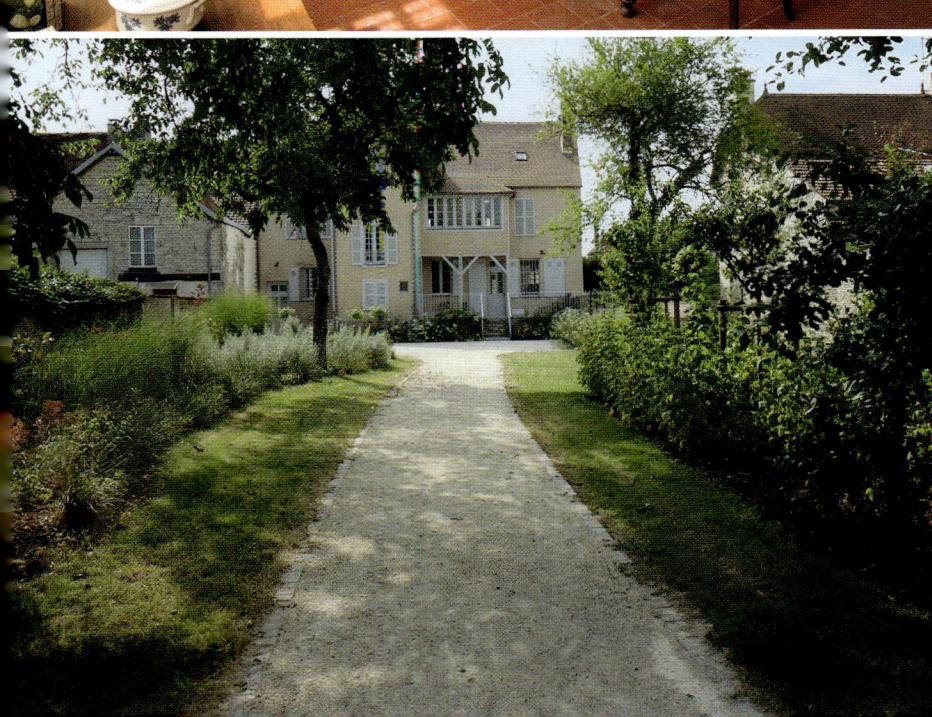
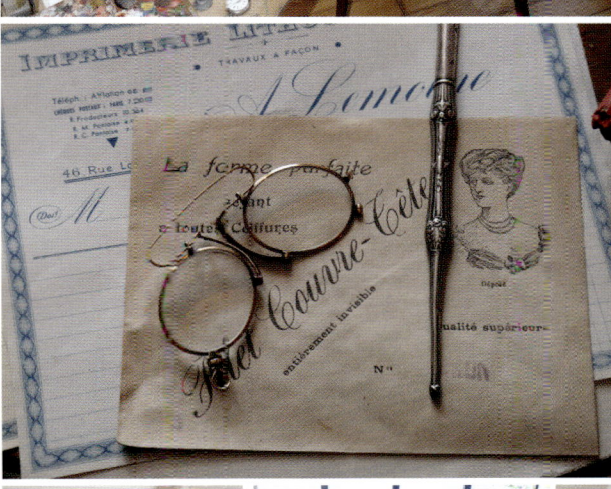
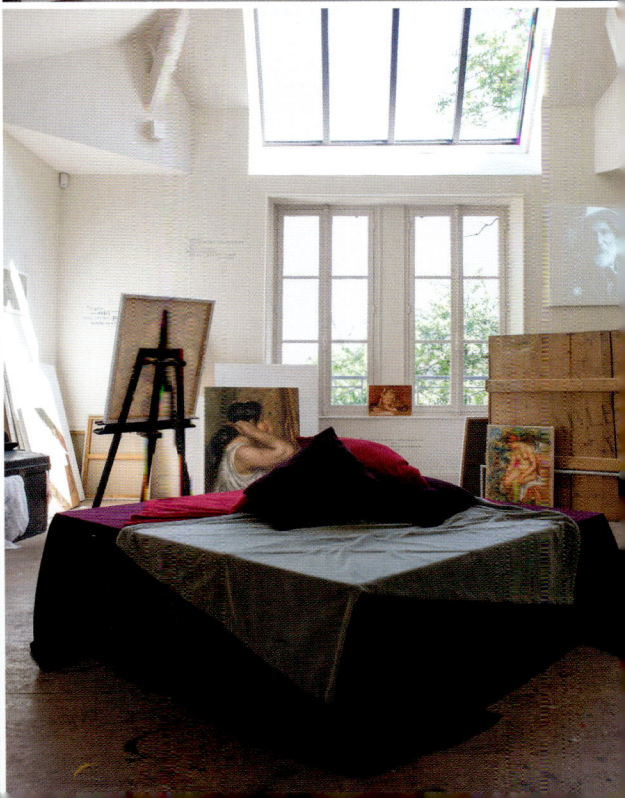

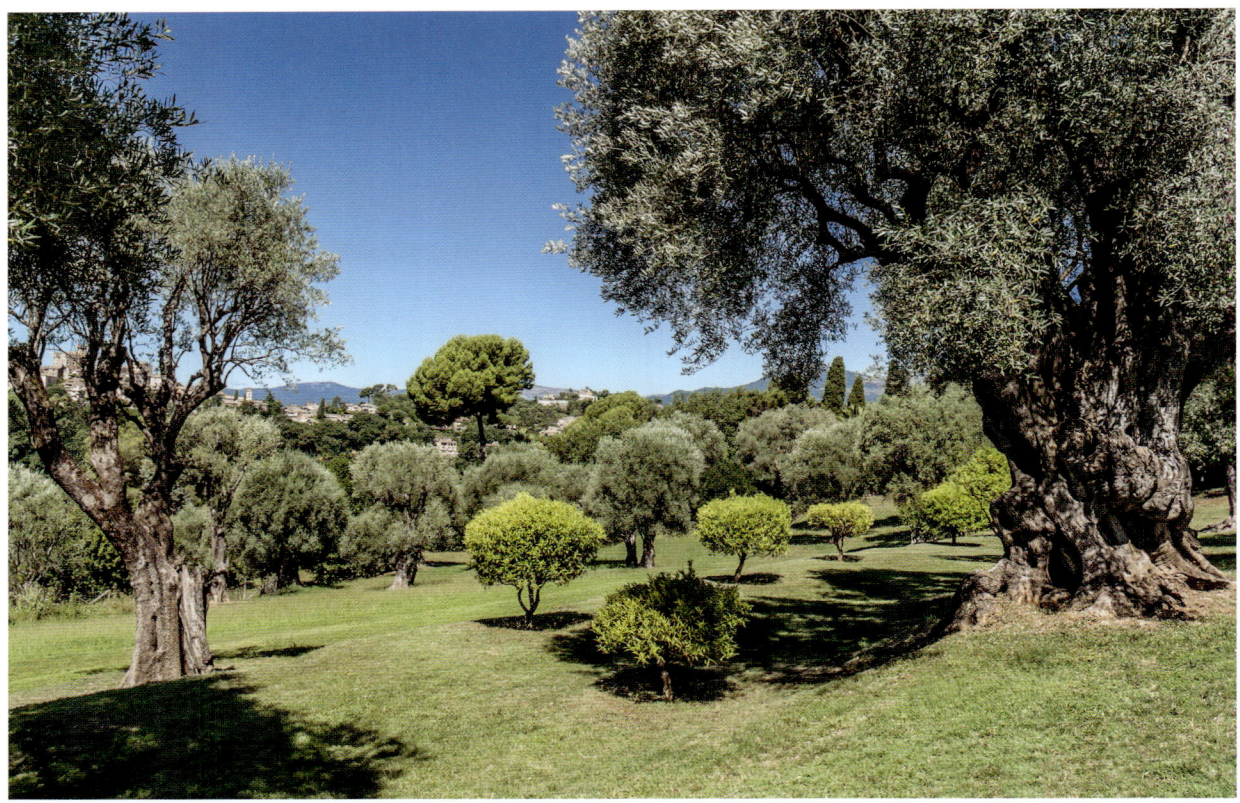

ABOVE Renoir painted from this spot in his old olive grove at *Les Collettes*, looking towards the nearby medieval village of Haut-de-Cagnes on the Côte d'Azur.
OPPOSITE The windows from the upper floors of Renoir's house looked over the terrace of orange trees towards the Mediterranean.

and Aline. According to Jean, finding Les Collettes coincided with his mother's wish for a permanent home, and his father's need to rest in a warm climate to relieve his advanced rheumatoid arthritis, which had already deformed his hands and made walking difficult. When the couple heard that a hillside of old olive trees near Cagnes-sur-Mer was about to be bought by a property developer (who intended to fell the trees to make napkin rings), Renoir senior put in a bid.

The Renoirs bought the farm in June 1907 for 35,000 francs, with long-term tenants living in the small farmhouse on the property. Over the next ten years, they bought up further parcels of land, until they had around eight hectares/ twenty acres. At sixty-six years of age, Renoir had no thought of roughing it and in November 1907 he commissioned a spacious 600-square-metre/6,460-square-feet, modern family house on three levels. He wasn't looking for ostentation, but he was looking for functionality – its windows and terraces needed to make the best of the views down to the Mediterranean sea in one direction and up to the medieval village of Haut-de-Cagnes in the other and, most importantly, the full-length windows should open directly on to the garden.

As the house was being built, garden terraces were also created. An upper terrace, level with the house, was laid with gravel and planted with shrubs, while a lower terrace featured orange trees surrounded by rose bushes and

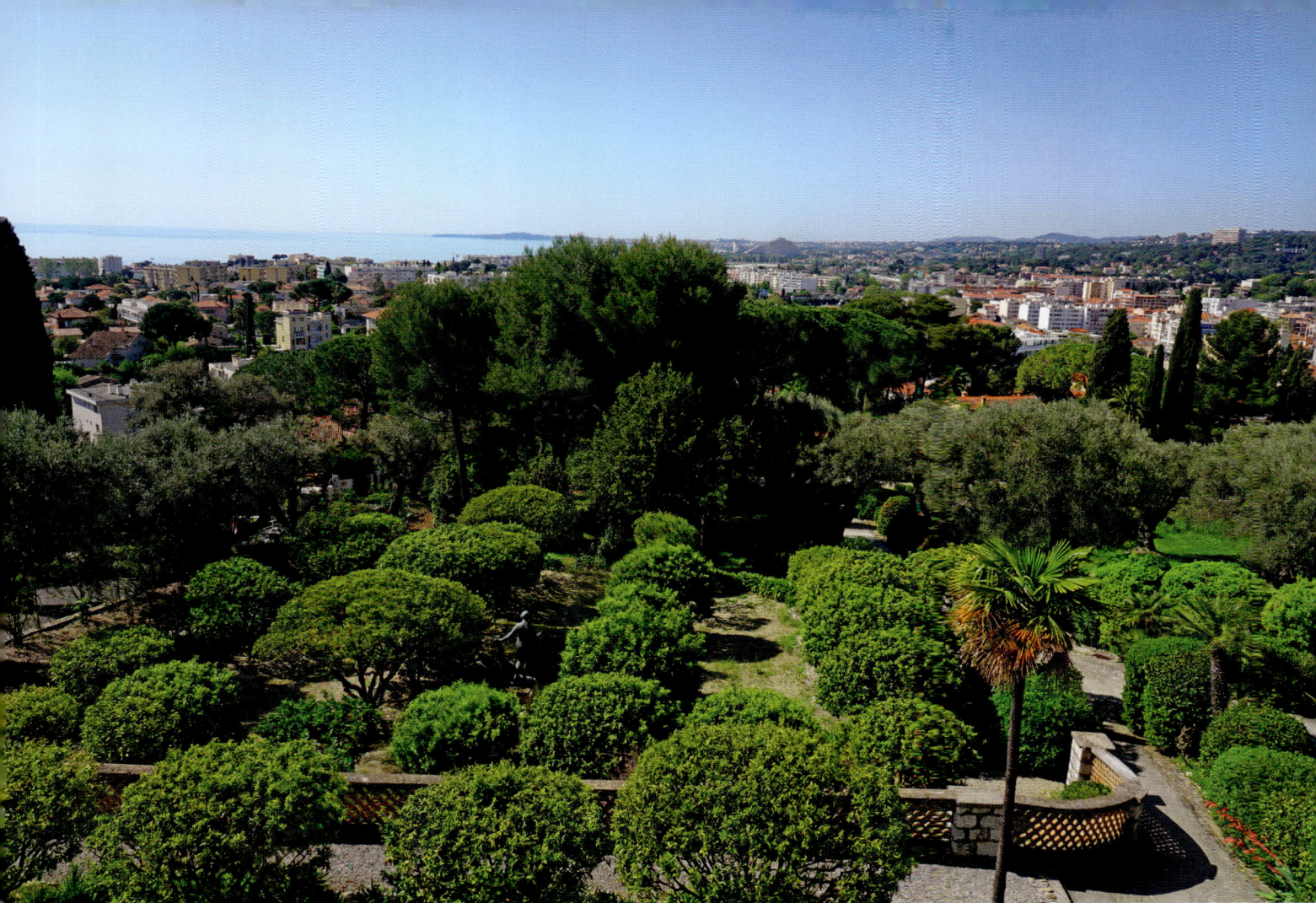

a bougainvillea, together with a plumbago trained against the walls. Aline also planted an orchard, and receipts kept by the family detail her gardener buying seeds for carrots, peas, spinach and celery for the potager, as well as artichokes and tomatoes. She planted a small vineyard for winemaking, and reared fowl and rabbits for the table. Other produce included figs, a carob tree (very important during the war years as a coffee substitute), lime blossom from *le tilleul* (lime trees/*Tilia cordata*) and *la bourrache* (borage/*Borago officinalis*) for making *les tisanes* (herbal teas). What was – and still is – extra special about Les Collettes is its olives. The trees were said to have been planted by soldiers of Francis I (circa 1530) but local tradition pushes the date back a further 300 years – and there may well have been an olive grove on the site in the 1200s. Many of the 150 trees growing there today are of a venerable age.

The tenant farmers on the farm were an Italian family who introduced the Renoirs to a simple life that revolved around the gathering of orange blossom from March to May (a lucrative crop for the perfume makers at Grasse), followed by the olive harvest in November, and a winter crop of bitter and sweet oranges. Renoir strongly believed in traditional values and, wary of scientific progress, he loved these seasonal harvests and the idea of being self-sufficient and living in tune with nature – for him, there were no *mauvais herbes*, or weeds, only wild

"We are in the process of planting like La Fontaine's old man . . . the green peas are doing well, and so are the potatoes. So for the moment it's perfect bliss."
PIERRE-AUGUSTE RENOIR (1908)

and beautiful grasses and meadows. His son Jean's film picks up on this theme, which pokes fun at the modern obsession with science as the answer to everything.

A PLACE TO PAINT

Renoir came to Les Collettes to paint every year in winter from 1907 until the end of his life. While he continued to paint figures, he began to work on more landscapes, using his trademark swift brush strokes. His largest studio was purpose-built on the top floor of the house with a full-length, north-facing window. Here, there was room for his wheelchair and a stage for his models.

Renoir also had a second studio on the top floor, a smaller room with east-, west- and north-facing windows, to bring him closer to the natural outdoor light. According to Jean Renoir, his father liked having a space for painting where the light wouldn't fluctuate as it did outdoors, but where he would be as close to nature and the garden as possible. In 1916, Renoir had an outdoor studio built in the garden to the north of the house – a simple wooden structure on a stone base. When he died, there were more than 700 paintings, drawings, watercolours, engravings

and sculptures in his three studios, giving some idea of his prolific output, even as he aged.

Despite his increasing disability, Renoir continue to develop his artistic techniques and wanted to turn his two-dimensional drawings and paintings into three-dimensional forms. For the first time in his life, he could afford to work in bronze and other materials, but physically it was impossible since, by then, his hands were so badly distorted that he had to wear bandages to stop his fingernails digging into his palms. To fulfil his ambition, he began a collaboration with Richard Guino, a young sculptor from Catalonia who worked on some thirty-seven sculptures at Les Collettes, including the *Venus Victrix*, which stands on the lower terrace.

Renoir's sons were encouraged to take up arts and a kiln and pottery were built for them on the edge of the land. On returning to Les Collettes after the First World War, Pierre (who became a successful actor) and Jean (the filmmaker), used ceramic art as a release from their traumatic experiences, although it was the youngest son, Claude, or 'Coco', who took to it most successfully and made his living as a ceramicist, working from the property. Claude married Paulette Dupré, the daughter of the French family who succeeded the Italians on the farm and one of Renoir's models. The couple lived on at Les Collettes until 1960, when it was offered to La Ville de Cagnes-sur-Mer.

LIFE AT LES COLLETTES

Jean Renoir's description of life at Les Collettes bathes it in a golden light and, indeed, as the painter aged, it became a destination for every artist and celebrity of the time, including the art dealer Paul Durand-Ruel, the painter Modigliani and the sculptor Auguste Rodin (who arrived in March 1914, accompanied by Lady Victoria Sackville-West – the mother of gardener Vita). Rodin owned several of Renoir's paintings and believed his

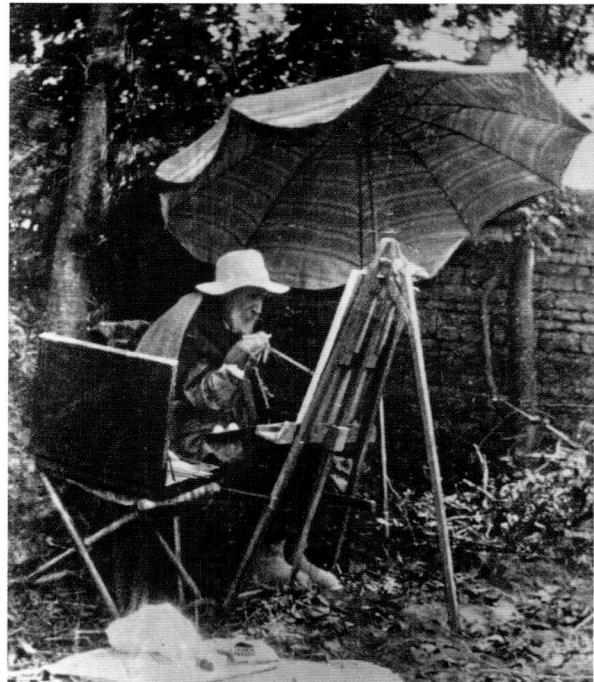

LEFT Renoir sometimes ventured outdoors to paint, but mainly favoured the steady light of an indoor studio.
RIGHT (CLOCKWISE FROM TOP LEFT) Renoir's house at Les Collettes was the family home from 1908 until the 1960s; the olive groves that inspired the painter; the original farmhouse at Les Collettes; the garden in early summer; the view from the garden towards Haut-de-Cagnes.

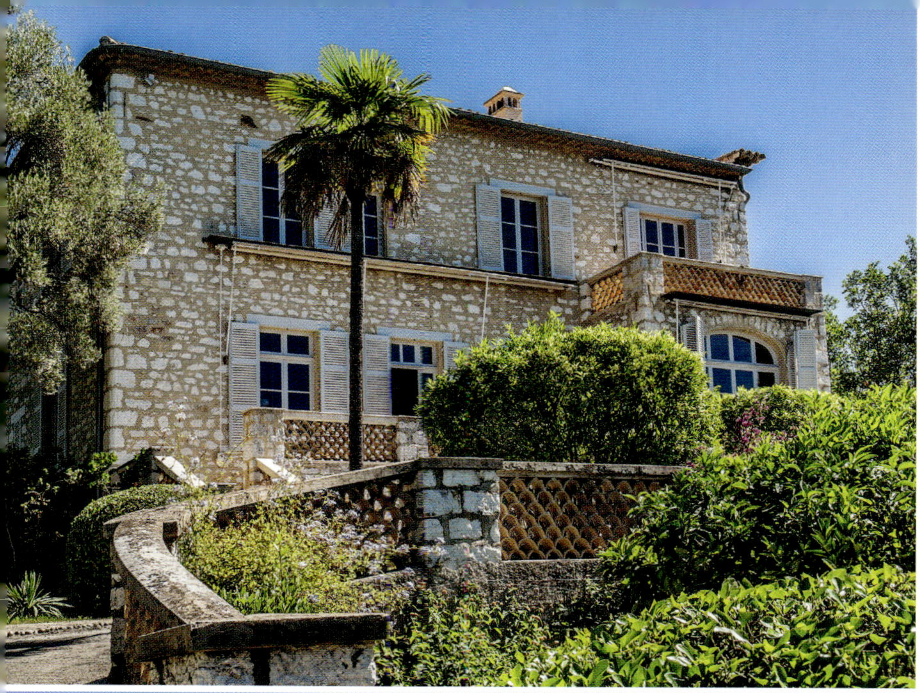

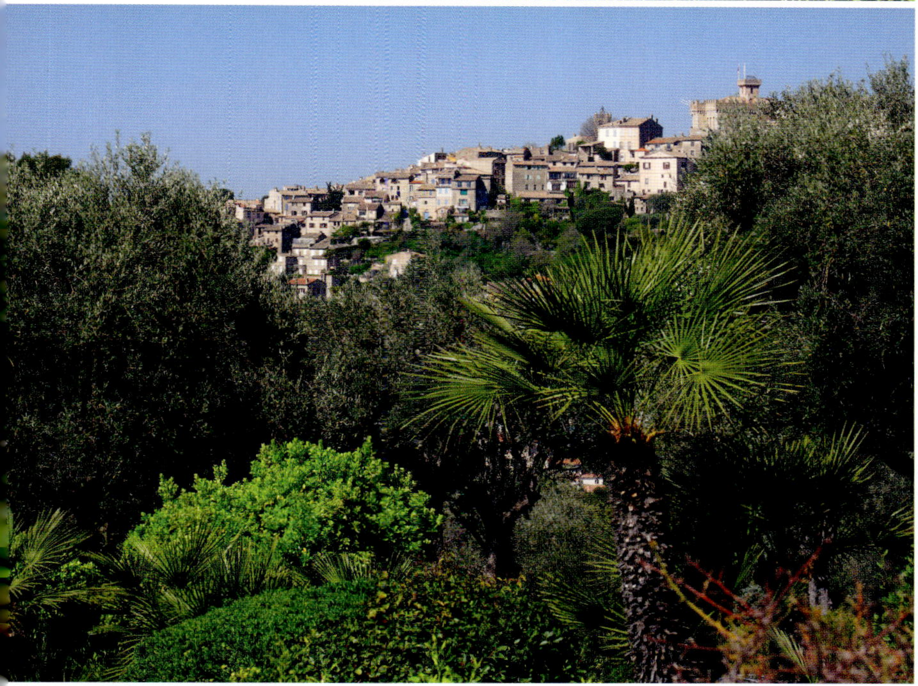

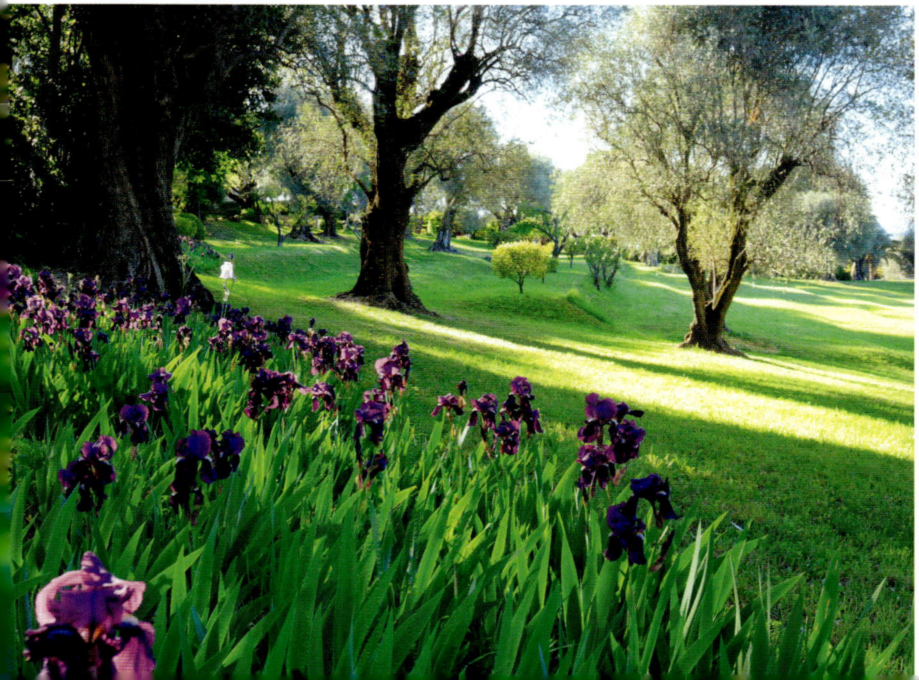

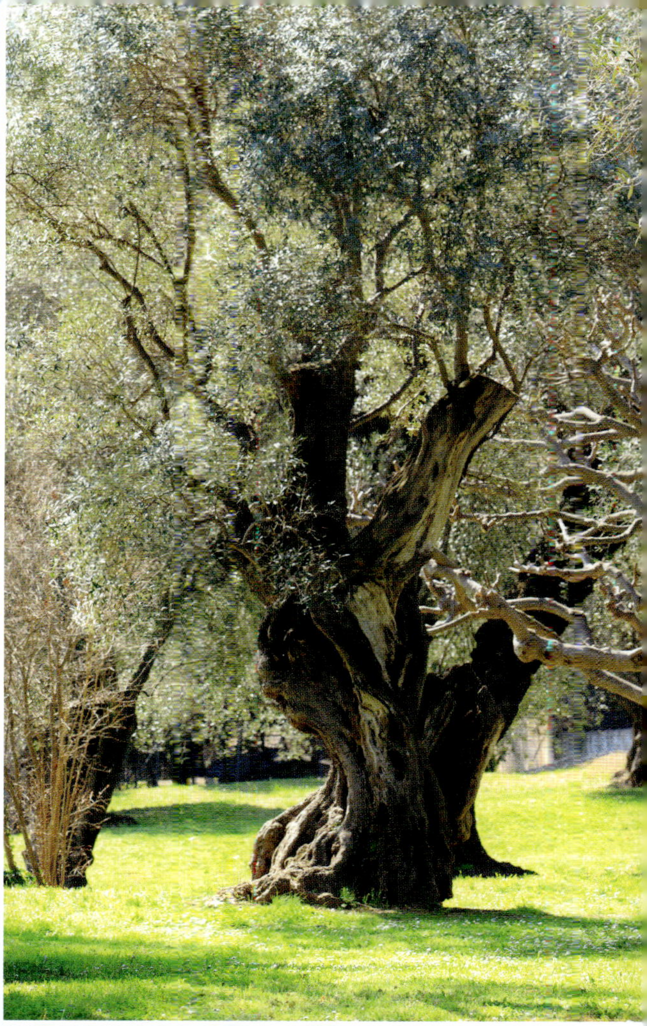

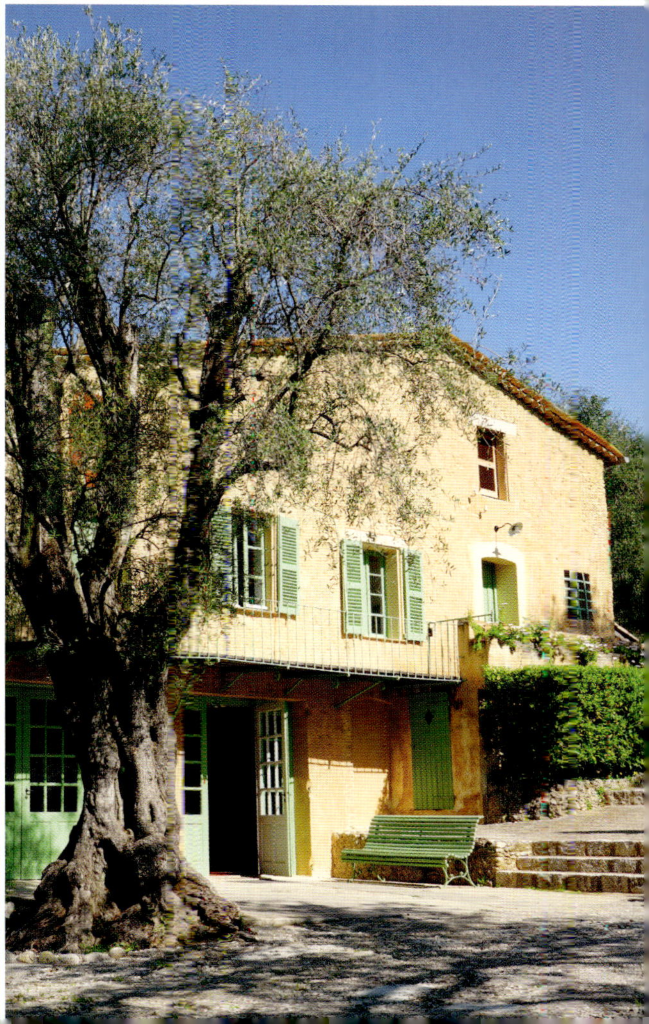

friend was one of two great painters – the other being Van Gogh. The cosmopolitan visitors had to mix with family and locals, such as Madeleine Bruno, the vegetable seller from Cagnes-sur-Mer, who became Renoir's model.

We owe a particular debt to the painter, Albert André, an old friend of Renoir's, for leaving us with a record of the gardens at Les Collettes. His *Le Jardin de Renoir* and other scenes provide a unique record of the property, including *Les Oliviers aux Collettes* (1910), which shows an olive workers' shed, no longer there. As Renoir aged, André painted his friend repeatedly, showing how the artist worked, bent over the canvases from his wheelchair or sedan chair, which was often carried out into the garden.

During Renoir's latter years, lack of mobility limited his ability to get out and about. However, he left two memorable paintings of his home in the south: *Paysages des Collettes*, painted in 1914, showing the old town in the distance framed by two ancient olive trees – a view you can still take in today – and *La Ferme des Collettes*, painted in the same year. These mark a return to impressionism in his work – by the time of *La Vue des Toits du Vieux Nice* (*The Rooftops of Nice*), painted in the winter of 1917, he is displaying a more architectural style.

The Musée Renoir and La Ville de Cagnes-sur-Mer continue to rediscover and buy Renoir's paintings from this period of his life to hang once more in Les Collettes. Renoir's views may have been swallowed up by the sprawl of the Côte d'Azur, but enough remains of this olive-clad hillside to show the colours and clear light that drew him, and many other artists before and after him.

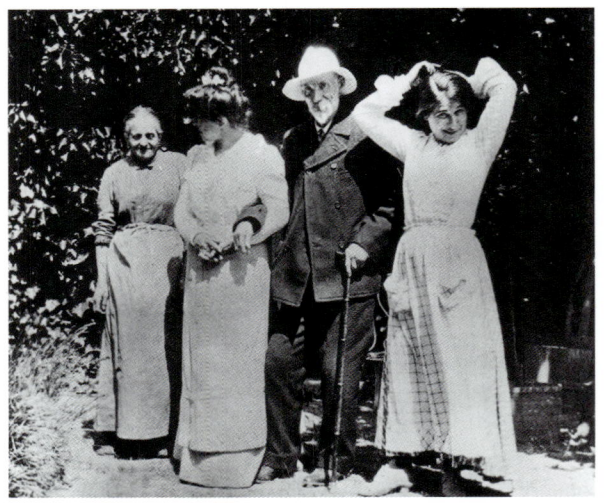

LEFT Renoir had a close circle of friends and family, including his model Gabrielle Renard, pictured far right.
OPPOSITE Renoir's painting of the farm, *La Ferme des Collettes* (1914), marked a return to his earlier impressionistic style.

RENOIR'S TIMELINE

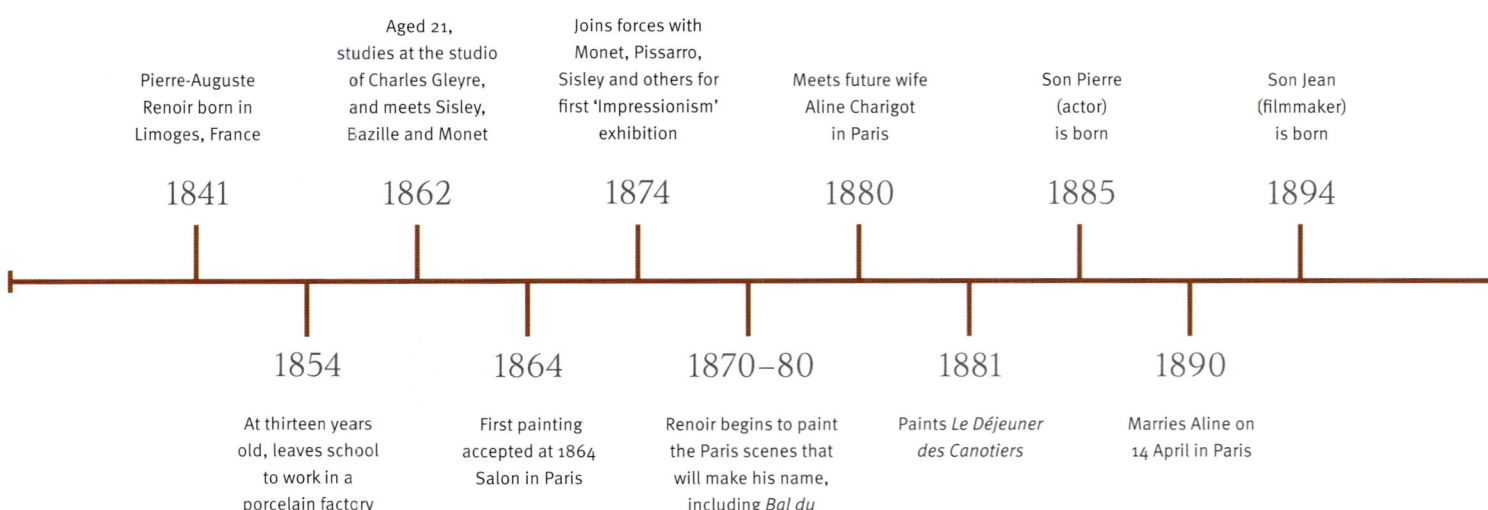

1841	1862	1874	1880	1885	1894
Pierre-Auguste Renoir born in Limoges, France	Aged 21, studies at the studio of Charles Gleyre, and meets Sisley, Bazille and Monet	Joins forces with Monet, Pissarro, Sisley and others for first 'Impressionism' exhibition	Meets future wife Aline Charigot in Paris	Son Pierre (actor) is born	Son Jean (filmmaker) is born

1854	1864	1870–80	1881	1890
At thirteen years old, leaves school to work in a porcelain factory	First painting accepted at 1864 Salon in Paris	Renoir begins to paint the Paris scenes that will make his name, including *Bal du Moulin de la Galette*	Paints *Le Déjeuner des Canotiers*	Marries Aline on 14 April in Paris

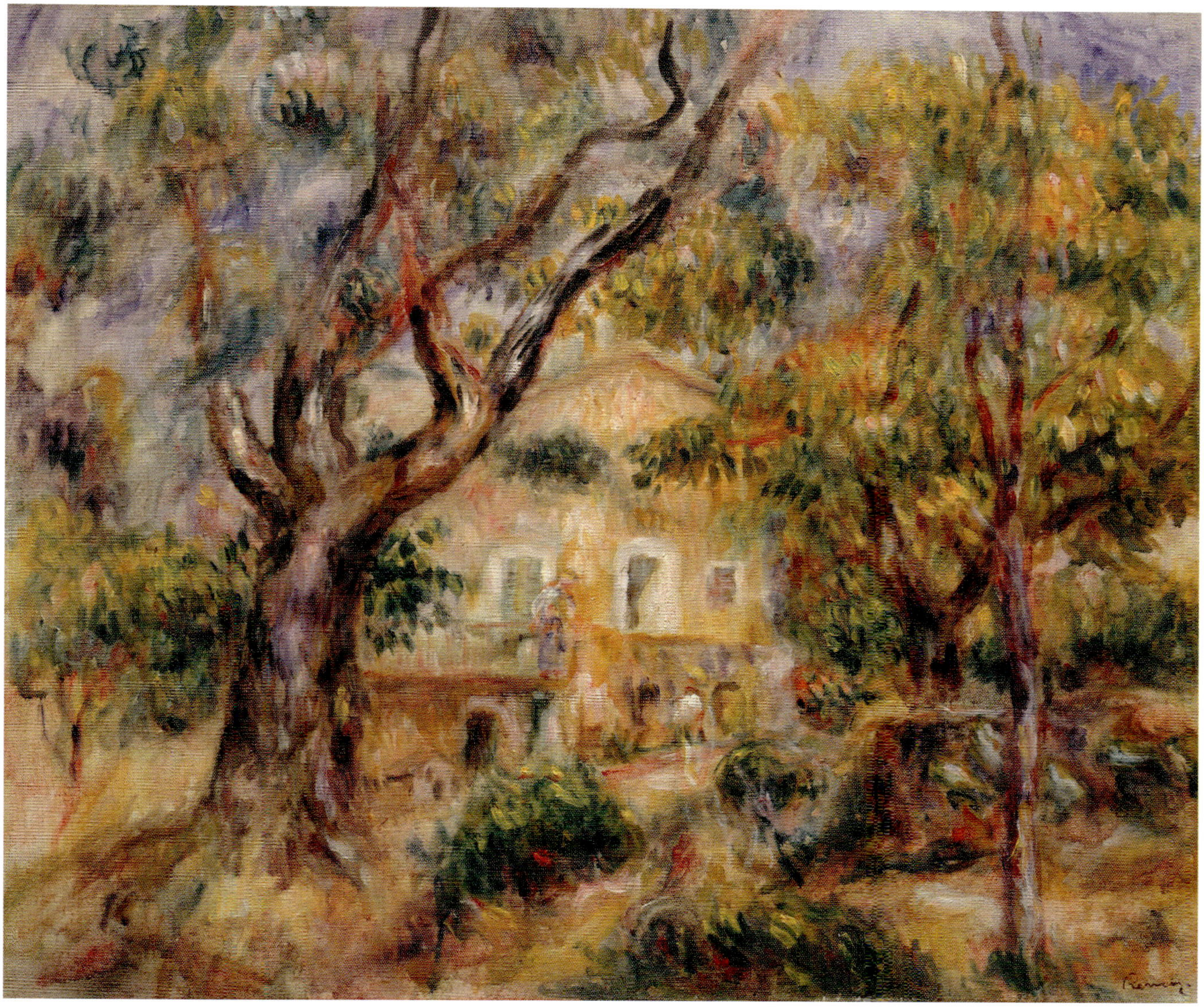

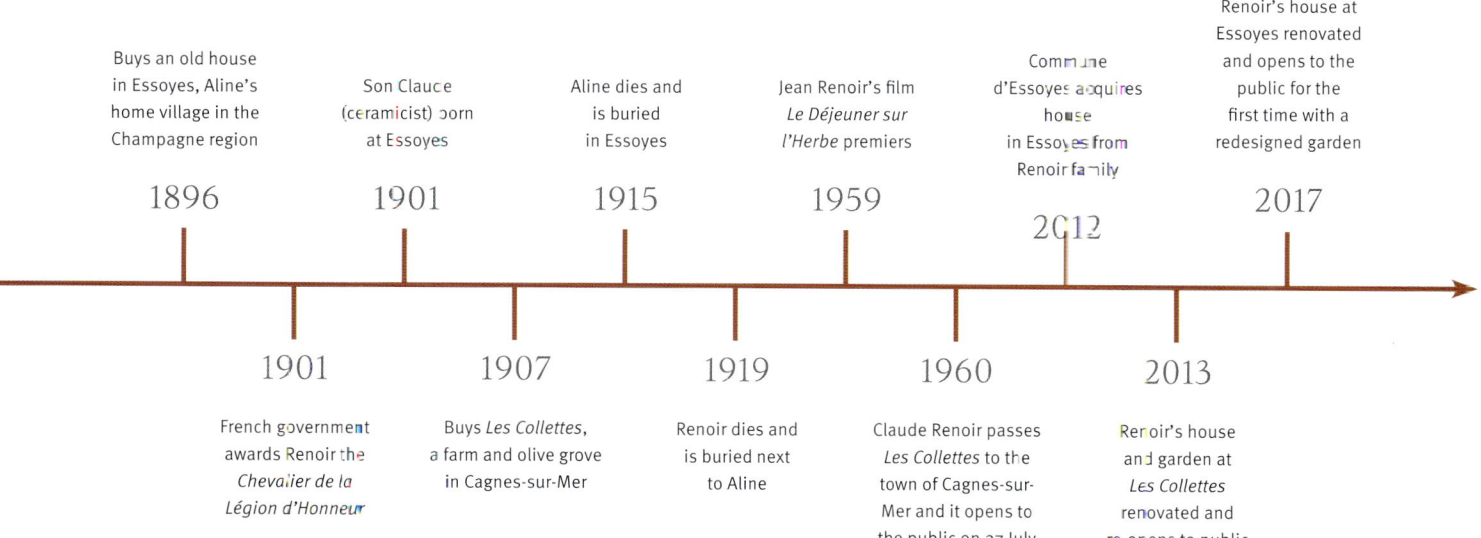

1896
Buys an old house in Essoyes, Aline's home village in the Champagne region

1901
Son Claude (ceramicist) born at Essoyes

1915
Aline dies and is buried in Essoyes

1959
Jean Renoir's film *Le Déjeuner sur l'Herbe* premiers

2012
Commune d'Essoyes acquires house in Essoyes from Renoir family

2017
Renoir's house at Essoyes renovated and opens to the public for the first time with a redesigned garden

1901
French government awards Renoir the *Chevalier de la Légion d'Honneur*

1907
Buys *Les Collettes*, a farm and olive grove in Cagnes-sur-Mer

1919
Renoir dies and is buried next to Aline

1960
Claude Renoir passes *Les Collettes* to the town of Cagnes-sur-Mer and it opens to the public on 27 July

2013
Renoir's house and garden at *Les Collettes* renovated and re-opens to public

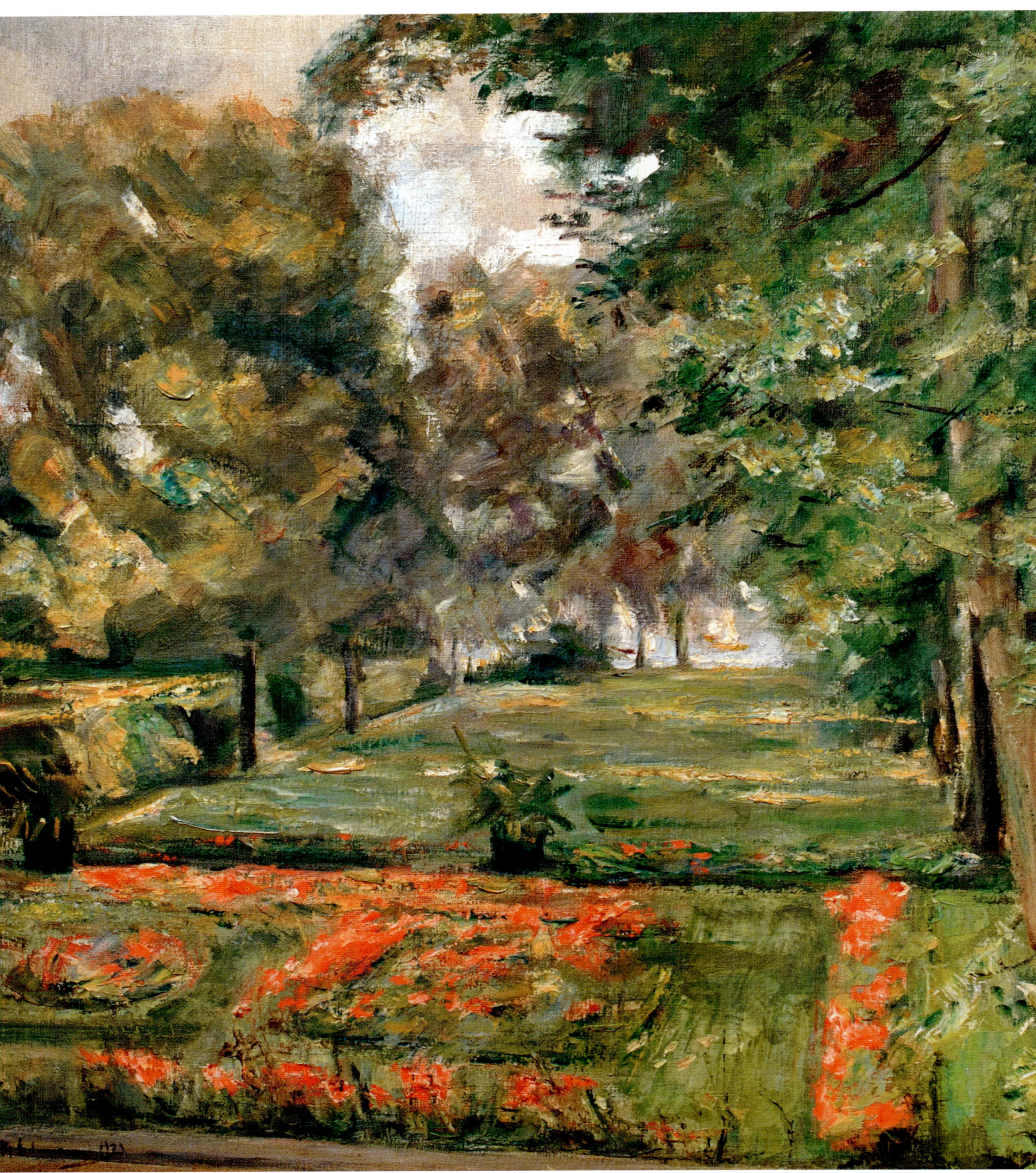

The Artist's Garden

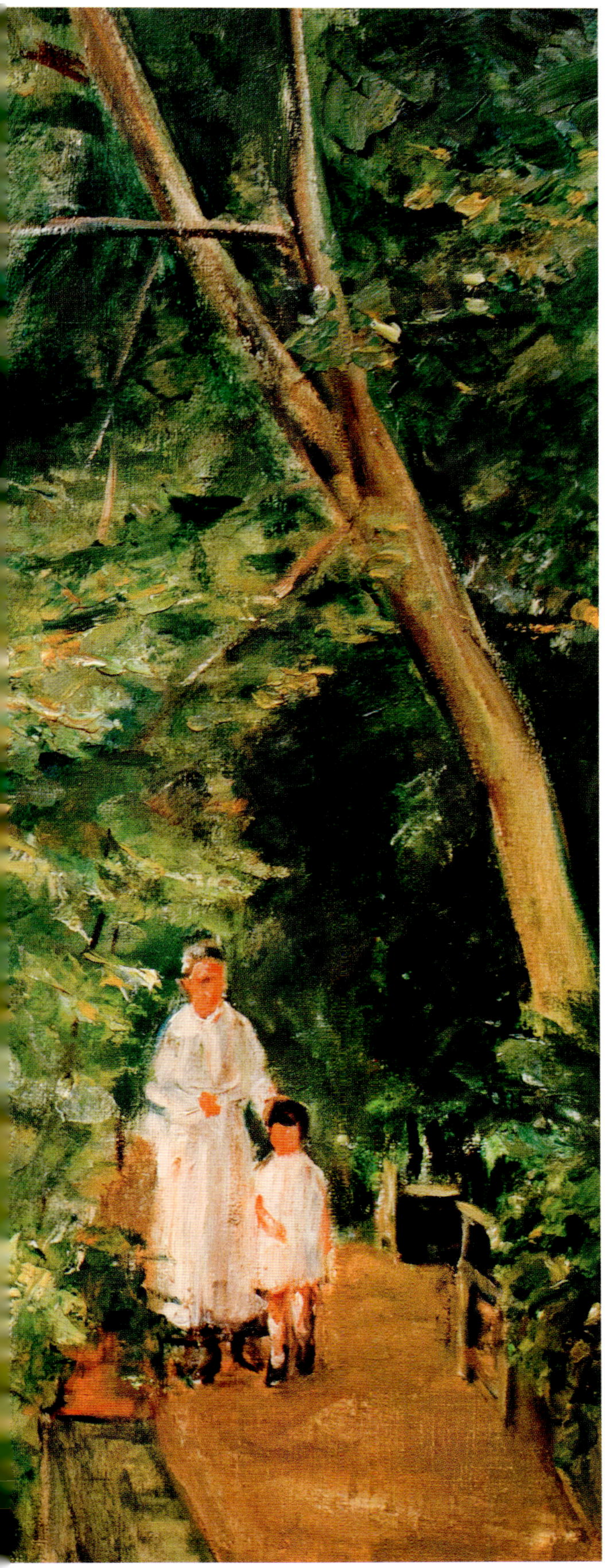

Max Liebermann

Lake Wannsee, Germany

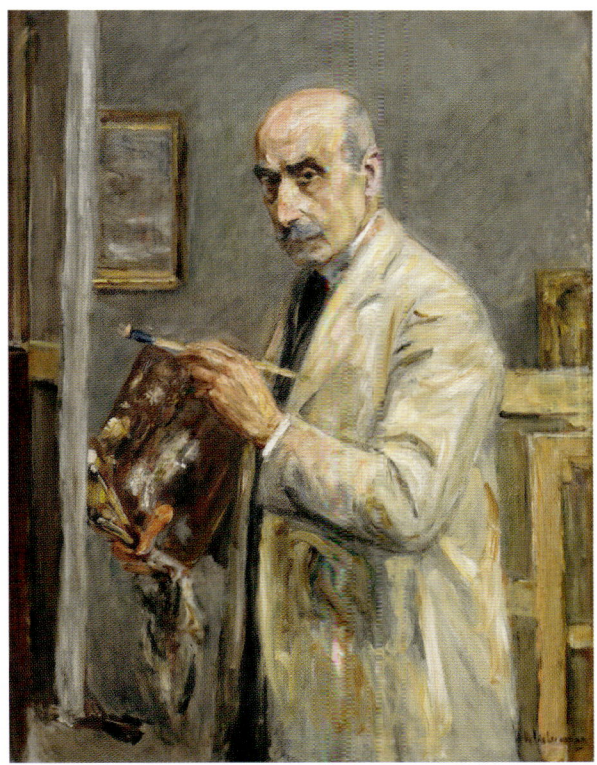

A LEADING LIGHT of German Impressionism, the Jewish artist Max Liebermann was a founding member of the Berlin Secession, a breakaway group of artists who produced some of the most progressive exhibitions the conservative art world of late nineteenth and early twentieth century Europe had ever seen. Yet he lived through a period of great change in his homeland – change that ultimately would have a devastating effect on his home, work and family.

LEFT *The Artist's Granddaughter with her Governess in the Wannsee Garden* (1923) depicts Liebermann's garden on the lakeside near Berlin.

ABOVE *Self-Portrait in Painter's Overall* (1922). Portraits of himself and the garden he made were among Liebermann's favourite subjects.

"Come and visit my little 'castle by the lake'. It is not looking pretentious, but I think it looks like me."

MAX LIEBERMANN (1922)

LAKESIDE DREAMS

Liebermann began his career by painting realistic scenes of simple peasant life in Holland, but soon became inspired by the work of Manet in France, and began to paint in a brighter, lighter style – one that was perfectly suited to his favourite subject matter: parks and gardens. In particular, the landscapes and gardens at his home at Lake Wannsee were to provide the main subjects and inspiration for his later work.

Born in Berlin in 1847, Liebermann was the son of a textile manufacturer. He followed his dream of becoming an artist by attending the influential Grand-Ducal Saxon Art School, Weimar, in Germany and then travelled to Paris and Munich. On his return to Berlin, he took his place among the established art circle, becoming a professor at the Prussian Academy of Arts and a founding member of German Impressionism.

In 1894, he inherited his father's house in central Berlin, along with a sizeable fortune. Financially secure, he lived in the house with his wife, Martha Marckwald, and daughter Käthe, but longed for a summer house in the country where he could paint in peace. It was fifteen years before he fulfilled that dream, but in the spring of 1909 he took the first step by purchasing a plot of land overlooking Lake Wannsee.

This area of lakes and wooded islands to the south-west of Berlin had long been an escape for city dwellers and the peninsula of Wannsee was a favourite spot for wealthy Berliners to build their second homes. Liebermann had strong ideas about what his new villa and garden should look like, and it would be in marked contrast to what he thought were the ostentatious displays of power and wealth he saw in the houses going up along the waterfront. He bought a 7,000-square-metre/75,347-square-foot plot facing east across Wannsee, and commissioned architect Paul A.O. Baumgarten from Alfred Messel's practice to help him realize his ideas. Although commissioning the foremost

BELOW, LEFT The west front of the house in 1911, shortly after it was completed.
BELOW, RIGHT The Hedged Garden on the east side, with its armillary sphere.

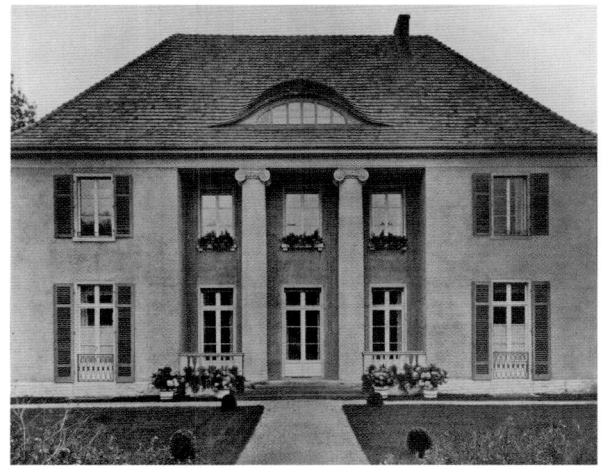

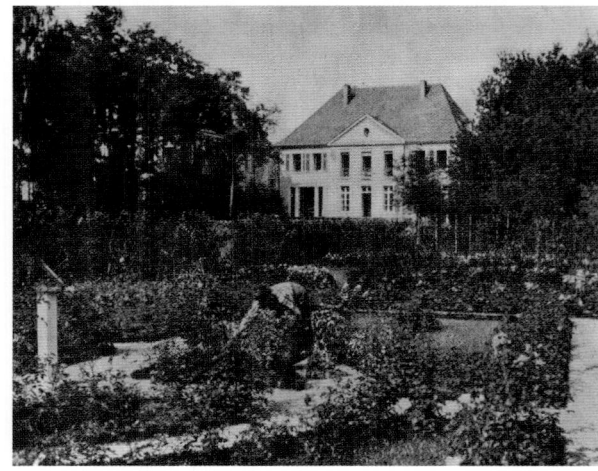

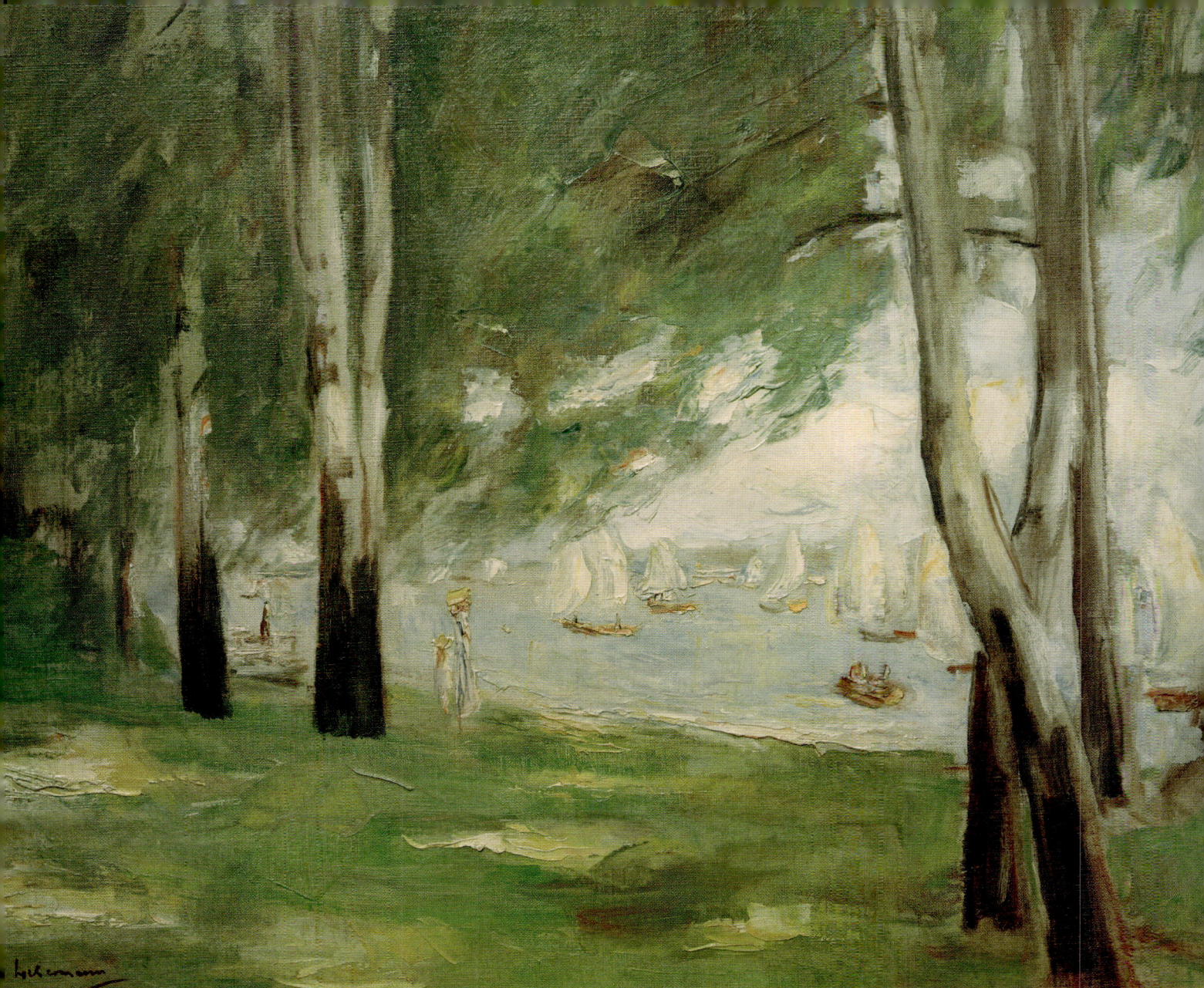

practice in Germany (Baumgarten would go on to design the imposing Villa Marlier– infamous as the venue for the Nazi's Wannsee Conference in 1942 – just a few plots down), Liebermann had no intention of building the kind of neo-Baroque house that was fashionable at the time. He was soon sketching over Baumgarten's drafts, indicating his preference for a classical house that would sit modestly alongside its neighbours.

THE HAMBURG INFLUENCE

While planning the house and garden at Wannsee, Liebermann corresponded regularly with his close friend Alfred Lichtwark, the first director of the Art Museum (Kunsthalle) in Hamburg. Lichtwark had shown Max and Martha around Hamburg during their frequent trips to the city, introducing them to the eighteenth- and nineteenth-century country villas on the outskirts, styles that

ABOVE Liebermann's painting, *Birches on the Wannsee to the East* (1924), with its many sailing boats in the distance, shows how popular this lakeside resort was for Berliners wanting to escape the city. The Liebermann family spent every summer here from 1910 until the artist's death in 1935.

Max Liebermann
(1847–1935)

When Max Liebermann left school, he first studied chemistry but soon abandoned this to pursue his love of painting at the Grand-Ducal Saxon Art School, Weimar. His first works, in the realist style, were of poor and working people in Holland and Paris, but after returning to Berlin, he increasingly depicted the leisure classes and his colours became more luminous. One of the founding members of the German impressionist group known as the Berlin Secession, he would go on to paint 200 oils and similar numbers of pastels and drawings of his garden on Lake Wannsee, where he spent every summer from 1910 until his death in 1935. Always a central figure in German cultural life, he was ostracized by the Nazis, but died before the Holocaust. In 1938, his wife Martha and private collectors from Germany and Switzerland sent eighteen works of art by Liebermann to London for the Twentieth Century German Art exhibition, held in support of Germany's so-called 'degenerate' art.

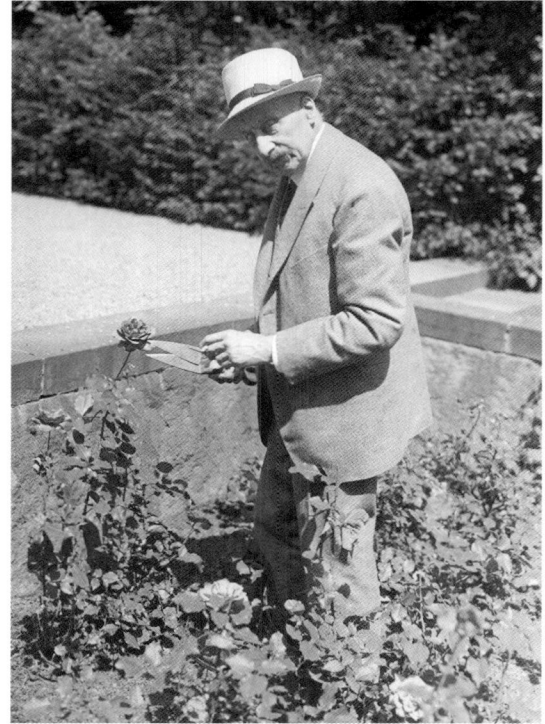

Liebermann gathering roses, 1932.

would be reflected in Liebermann's new home. The artist also admired the house of Goethe in Weimar and sketched an almost exact copy of its pointed roof and roundel window on Baumgarten's drawing of the east façade.

This meshing of styles led to an interesting, if unconventional, house. Set in the centre of the plot, it divided the garden into two almost equal halves. The central axis led through the front garden and the middle of the building, then out into the back garden to the lake. It was a house designed for living, with a dining room that opened on to the terrace, where the family ate outside, and a large, north-facing, barrel-vaulted studio on the second floor for painting. Compared to its neighbours, with their turrets and grand entrances, the Liebermann Villa was unostentatious, symmetrical and compact.

BREAKING WITH TRADITION

In 1909, Liebermann sent Lichtwark the first sketches of his ideas for the garden, about which they would correspond for the next five years. Garden design at the time was stuck in a very predictable rut. The landscape architects knew what their clients wanted: smaller versions of noble or royal gardens which, to Liebermann's mind, were ridiculous. Lichtwark and modern architects, such as Peter Behrens, saw that plots were getting smaller, yet the ambition was still to include waterfalls, grottoes, parks and landforms, in a poor imitation of an eighteenth-century English landscape garden.

By the early twentieth century, Art Nouveau ideas in Germany were emanating from places like Darmstadt and culminated in Applied Art Fairs in Düsseldorf in 1904 and the influential Garden Exhibition of Mannheim in 1907. In 1908, Liebermann was on the jury to choose a design for the Schiller Park in Berlin, which was awarded to a modern architect, Friedrich Bauer. As Liebermann expressed in his letters to Lichtwark and others, these new modes of design fed into his ideas for his own house and garden.

RIGHT A strong axis, flanked by flower beds, runs through the kitchen garden and down the hallway of the house to the lake. Liebermann was influenced by a new design movement that believed gardens should be informed by the geometry of the house.

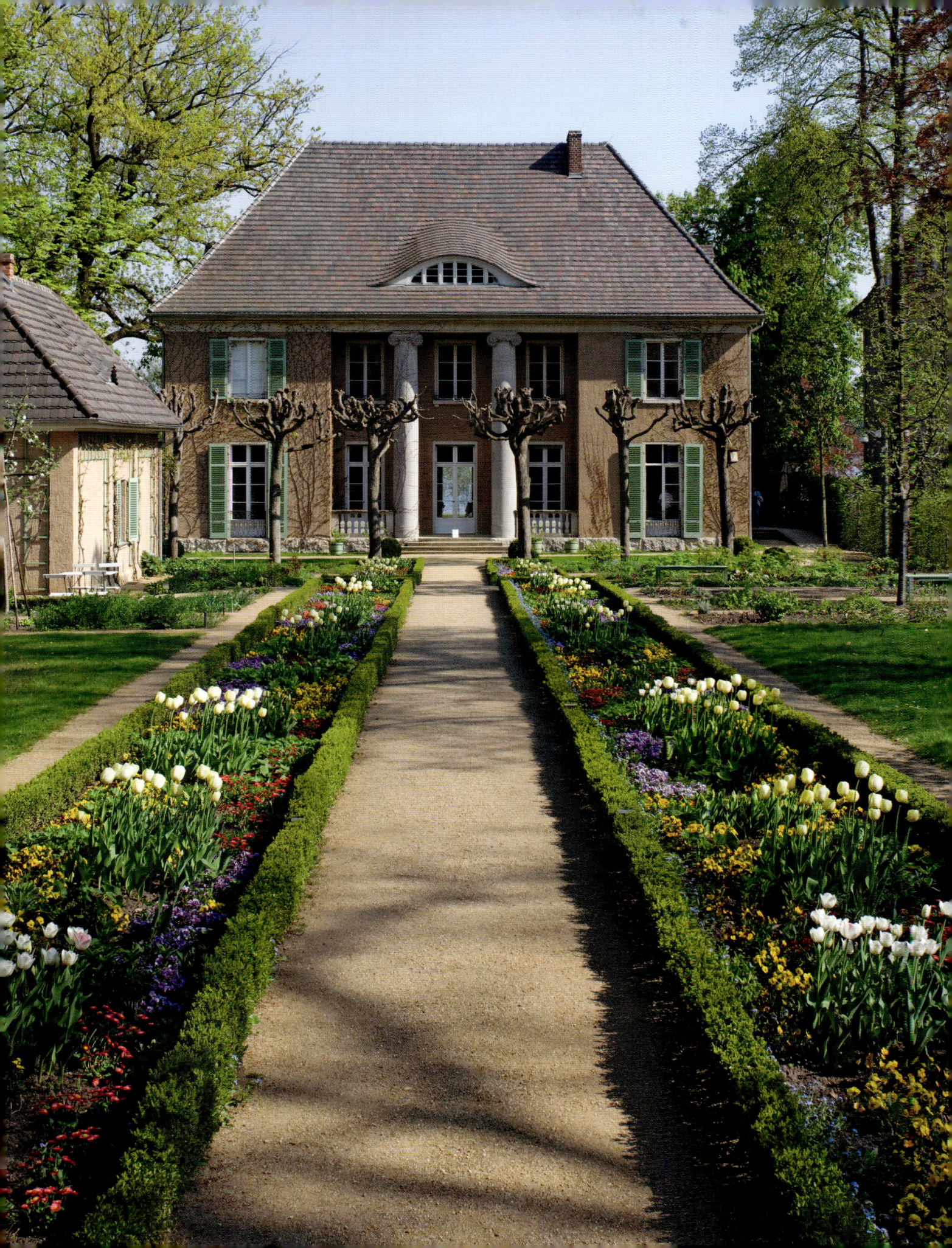

THE GARDEN AT WANNSEE

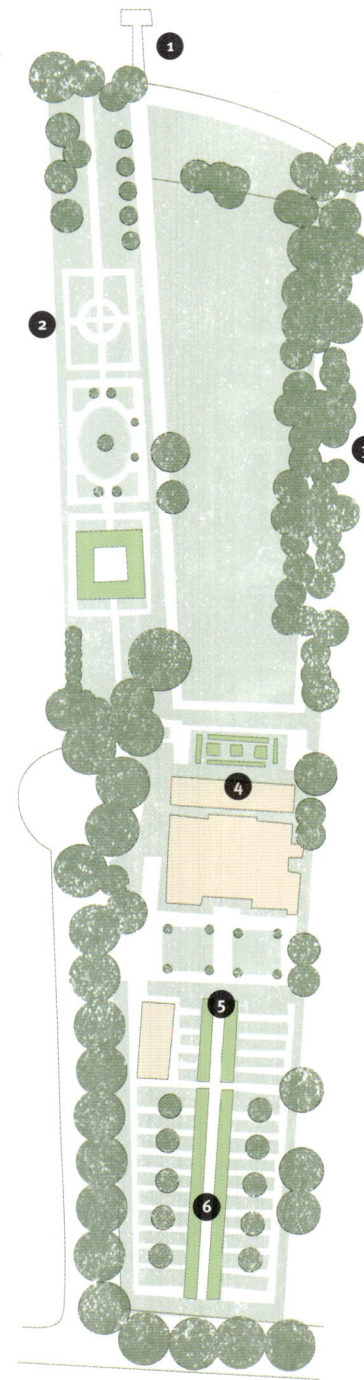

KEY

1 Jetty and Tea Pavilion
2 Hedged garden
3 Birch path
4 Terrace
5 Lime stilt hedge
6 Flower and vegetable garden

AN UNCONVENTIONAL GARDEN

New concepts were beginning to filter in from England, with the writings of William Morris, Gertrude Jekyll and William Robinson breaking with conventional 'grand' ideas for houses and gardens. The influences of these English writers, continental Art Nouveau and Modernist architecture all combined to give a new direction to German garden design. This school of thought saw gardens as formal spaces, informed by the architecture of the house. Geometry was important, with hedges, steps, paths and terraces defining the space – features that almost always appear in Liebermann's paintings of this period.

In Germany, the new movement would be led, not by professional landscapers, but 'amateurs', such as artists, architects, ceramicists, museum directors like Lichtwark, and writers. Lichtwark had introduced Liebermann to the farmers' gardens near the River Elbe in Hamburg and Liebermann was struck by their functionality. People designed their gardens to suit their needs: vegetables for food, herbs for medicines and flowers for pleasure. It was, of course, an idealized view – neither Lichtwark nor Liebermann could imagine living off the land, keeping livestock, or farming for survival. But the Hamburg effect was strong and explains why the artist's garden has two such distinct areas.

In the front garden, facing the street, Liebermann filled the entire space with a vegetable and flower garden. Broad beds on either side of the central path were planted with colourful annuals and biennials, and beyond these were discrete beds for vegetables, salad leaves and perennials. The whole plot was enclosed with lilac and jasmine hedges and, to disguise the gardener's cottage on the boundary, Liebermann planted a line of eight stilt lime trees.

By siting the functional garden, with its rows of potatoes and courgettes, next to the road where it could be clearly seen, Liebermann was making a deliberate statement – this garden was for practical daily use, something that must have shocked the neighbours in this exclusive suburb of lawns and driveways.

At the back of the house, Liebermann ensured nothing would spoil the view of the lake. Here, he designed a generous terrace for entertaining and a lower flower terrace, featuring box-edged compartments filled with yellow and purple pansies in spring, and dark red pelargoniums in summer. Lichtwark advised the Liebermanns to keep the grove of birch trees that ran down one side of the plot to the lakeside and consequently the path leads straight through them to the water's edge.

A circular bench gives a clear view to a sculpture by August Gaul, a friend of the artist and member of the Berlin Secession, while, on the waterfront, Liebermann built a small jetty and tea pavilion. The final flourish, installed when the artist was able to widen the plot slightly with the purchase of additional land, was what he

RIGHT, CLOCKWISE FROM TOP LEFT The parterre beds on the terrace; the armillary sphere in the hedged garden; cottage garden planting in the flower garden; the birch path; the view from the terrace towards Lake Wannsee; the lime stilt hedge.

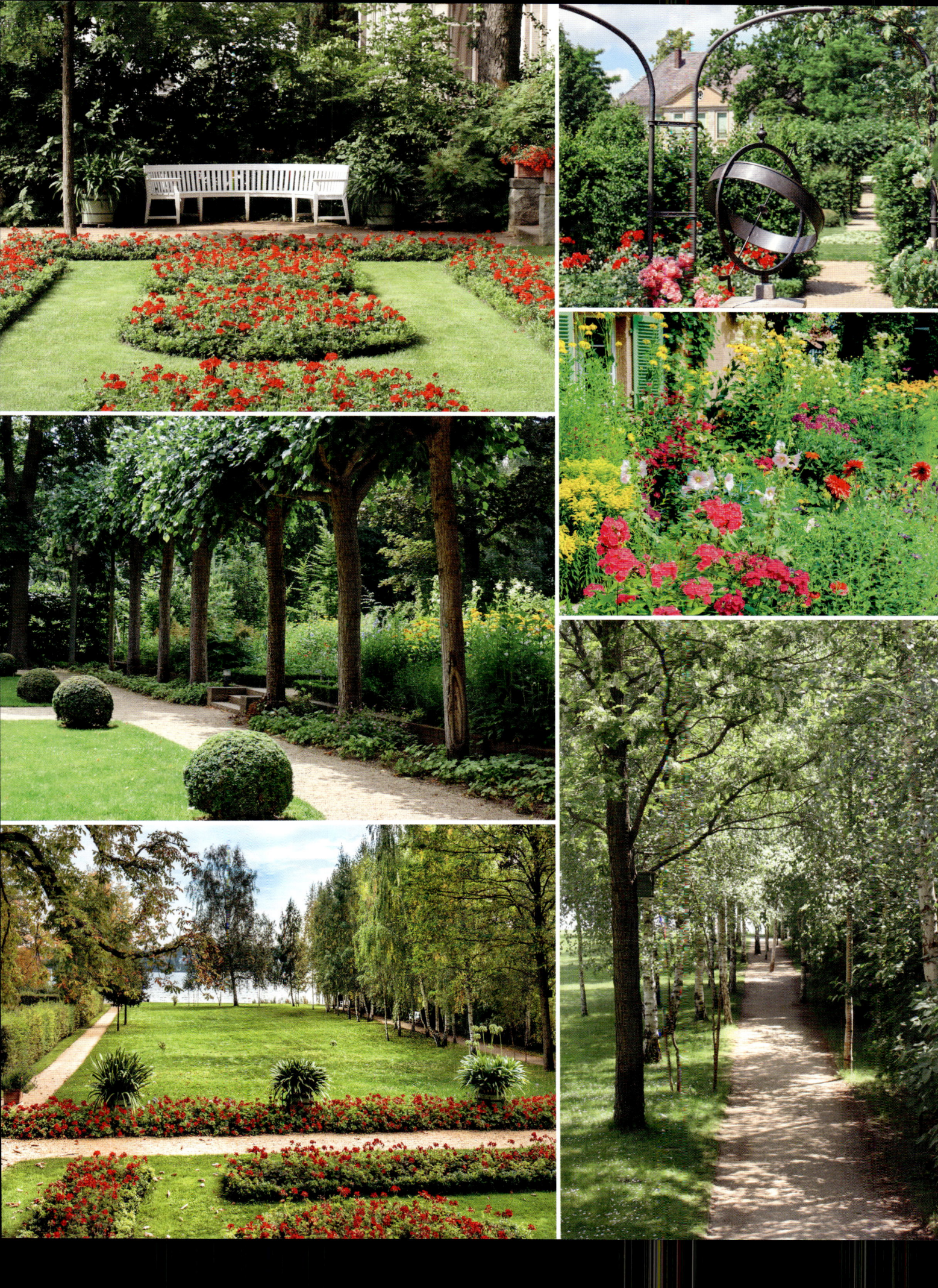

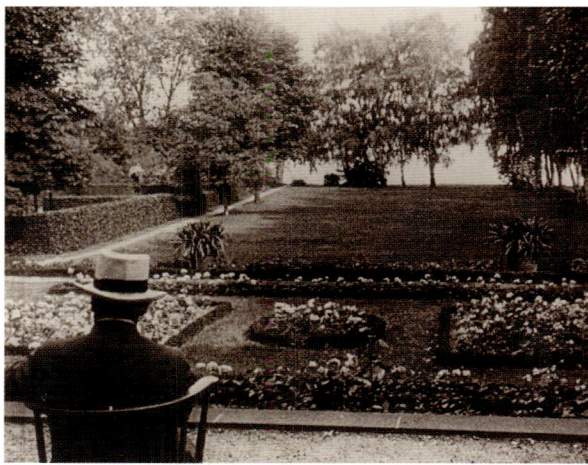

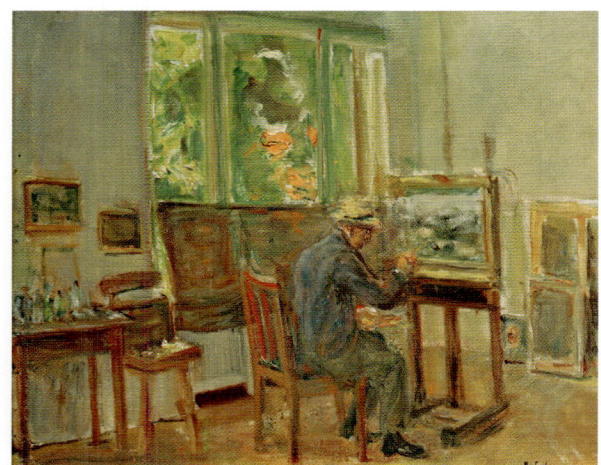

ABOVE, LEFT Max Liebermann in 1924 looking out over the flower terrace towards Lake Wannsee. He wanted to ensure that nothing spoiled the view of the water.

ABOVE RIGHT *Self Portrait in the Studio* (1930) shows the artist's large, light work space at his lakeside home.

called a 'hedged garden of three parts'. Using hornbeam hedging, he created three compartments: one for a *carré* (square) of stilt lime trees, one for roses, and one simply planted with clipped hornbeam for structure. A strong axis was vital and in this space it leads through the three compartments to an armillary sphere.

THE ARTIST'S RETREAT

The Liebermann family moved into the house at Wannsee on 26 July 1910 when Max was sixty-two and they spent every summer there for the next twenty-four years. Liebermann produced at least 200 oil paintings and similar numbers of pastels and watercolours of the garden, never tiring of the same subjects. Aspects of the garden would be painted again and again, just as Monet was doing at Giverny. Unlike Monet, however, Liebermann always included some architectural element and never featured flowers alone, so borders always have a glimpse of a house, building, path, steps or terrace, and occasionally the figure of a gardener. Nevertheless, his brushstrokes are loose and colour is allowed free rein as he, like his fellow artists in the Berlin Secession, Lovis Corinth and Max Slevogt, moved towards Impressionism. Whenever possible, they all worked outside, and with the garden as the *motif*, this was very easy for Liebermann to do, although he would generally finish his paintings inside in the studio.

DARK CLOUDS LOOMING

By the early 1930s, the idyllic summers spent on Lake Wannsee were numbered. After thirteen years as President of the Prussian Fine Arts Society and a pillar of Berlin cultural society, Liebermann resigned his post in 1933 as a protest against the practice to exclude Jewish artists. He died two years later, having become increasingly ostracized by the very people and institution who, on his eightieth birthday, had named him an honorary citizen of Berlin. By 1940 his widow Martha was forced by the National Socialists to sell the villa, which

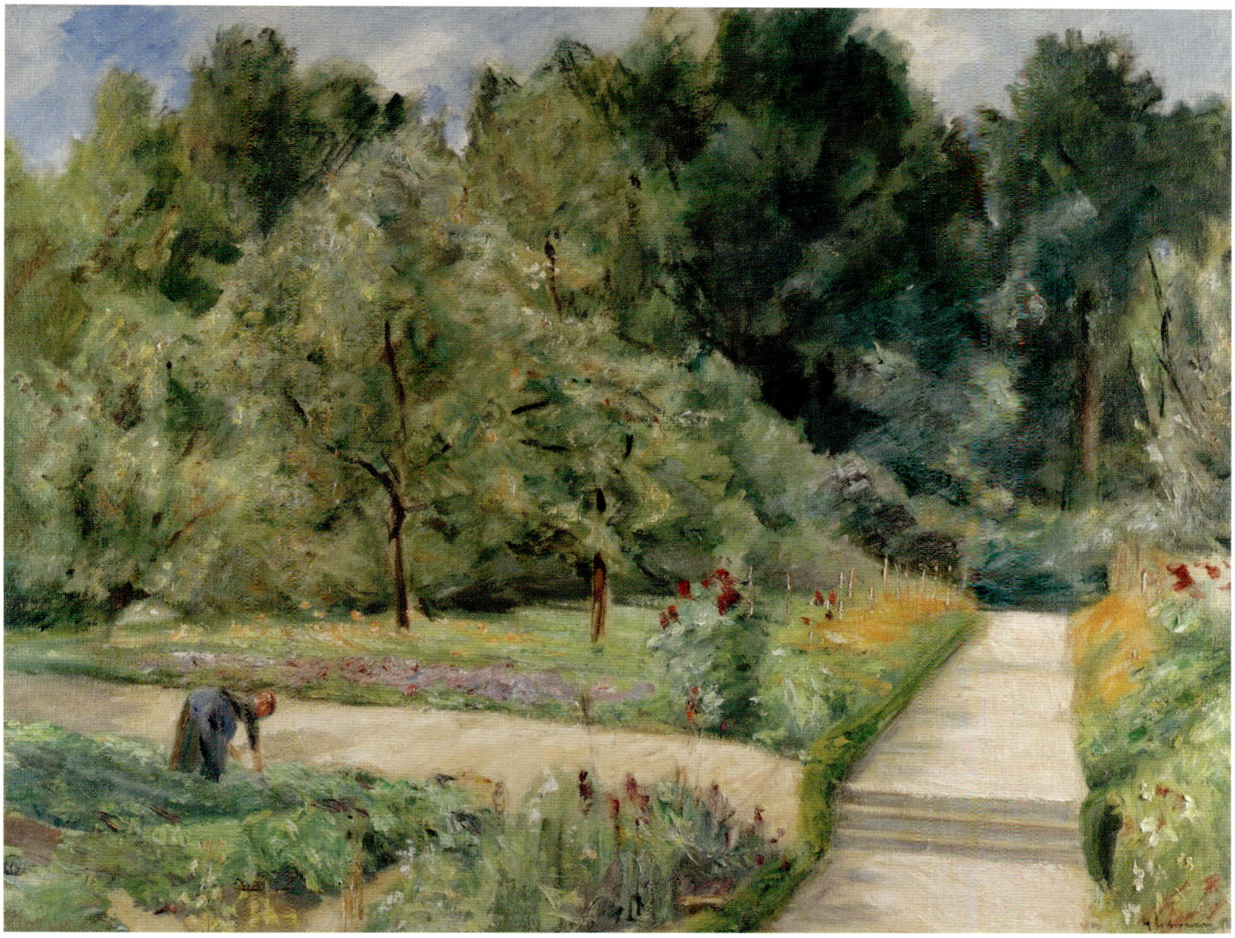

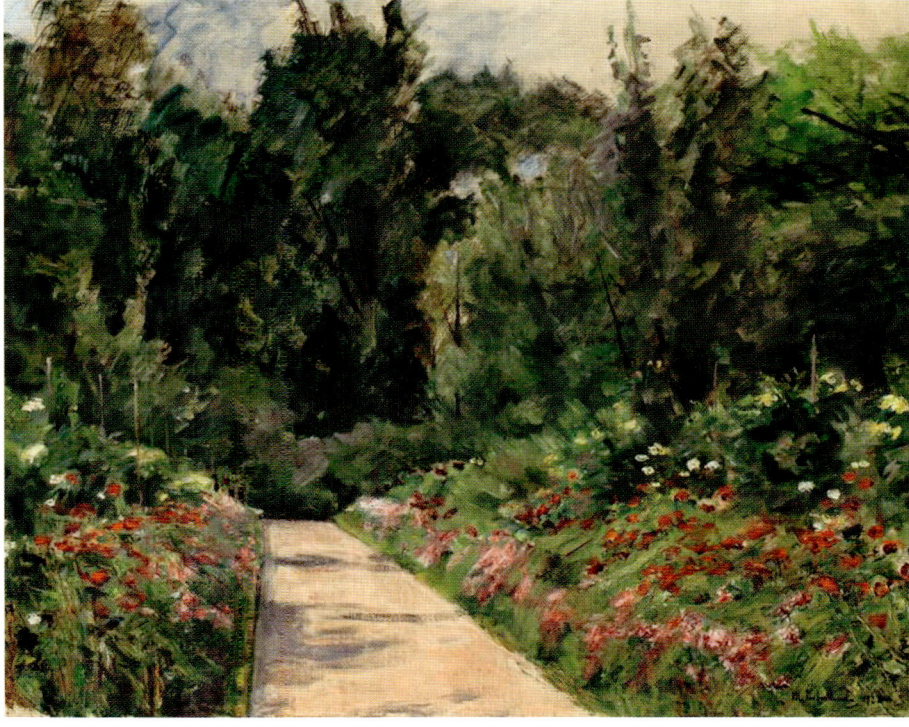

ABOVE AND LEFT Two versions of *The Useful Garden in Wannsee to the West*, the first painted in 1921 (above) and the second in 1922 (left). Liebermann painted the same garden *motifs* repeatedly, capturing them in different seasons and light.

was requisitioned by the Postal Service as a training ground for female followers. Although her daughter and granddaughter had fled to America, Martha moved back to their Berlin house and on 5 March 1943 she received an order of deportation. On the same evening, after writing letters to friends, she took her own life, aged eighty-six.

A PHOENIX RISING

After the Second World War the villa and its garden were used as a hospital. Parking lots were built at the front and in the 1970s a scuba diving school occupied the house, installing jetties and other structures on the lakeside. When, in 2002, the Max Liebermann Society finally took charge of the villa, there was little remaining of the garden, other than the tall lime hedge and a chestnut tree. The home of one of Germany's foremost artists had been forgotten, but there was just enough remaining, including the retaining walls, terrace steps and remnants of the hornbeam compartments, to make a restoration viable.

Liebermann's paintings of the garden from almost every angle were vital to the reconstruction process, while photographs, taken in 1927 when Liebermann celebrated his eightieth birthday on the terrace, also helped. From 2002 to 2006, the Society fundraised and invited volunteers to help recreate a garden that the Liebermann family would probably still recognize, with its new birch trees, restored thatched tea pavilion and vibrant kitchen garden. The restoration of Liebermann's Villa has not only created the focus for a celebration of his life, but it has also placed his garden at the heart of all that he believed in.

RIGHT The flower and vegetable garden has been restored to Liebermann's design – with strong geometry but relaxed planting of dahlias, annuals, and herbs flanking the path.

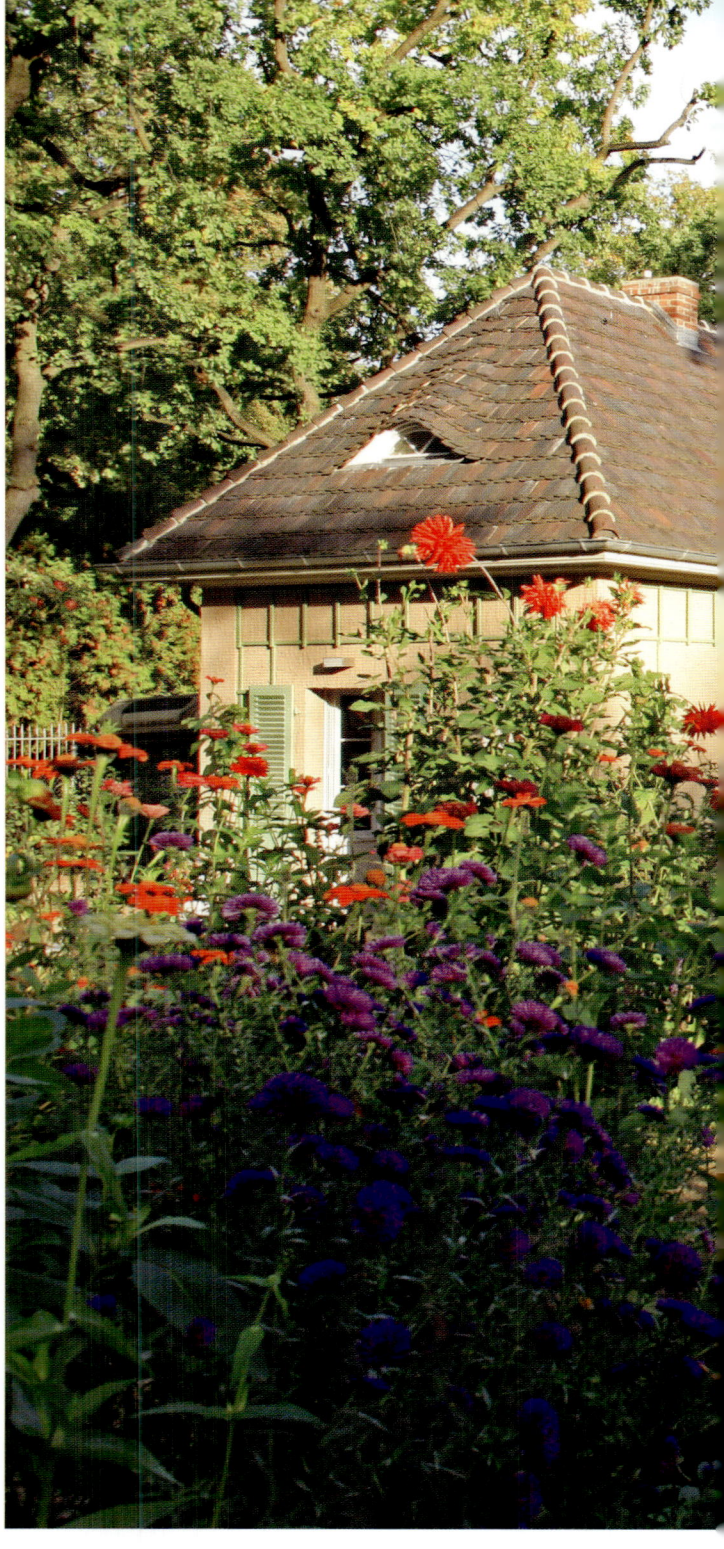

LIEBERMANN'S TIMELINE

1847	1869	1884	1894	1897	1898	1909–10
Max Liebermann was born the son of a wealthy Jewish textile manufacturer in Berlin	Studies at the Grand-Ducal Saxon Art School, Weimar; travelled to Paris and Munich	Returns to Berlin; marries Martha Marckwald; daughter Käthe born in 1885	Death of his father; Inherits house on Pariser Platz, Berlin, where he has lived since 1892	Appointed Professor at the Royal Academy of Arts, Berlin	Made President of newly founded Berlin Secession	Liebermann villa built; every summer spent here from now on

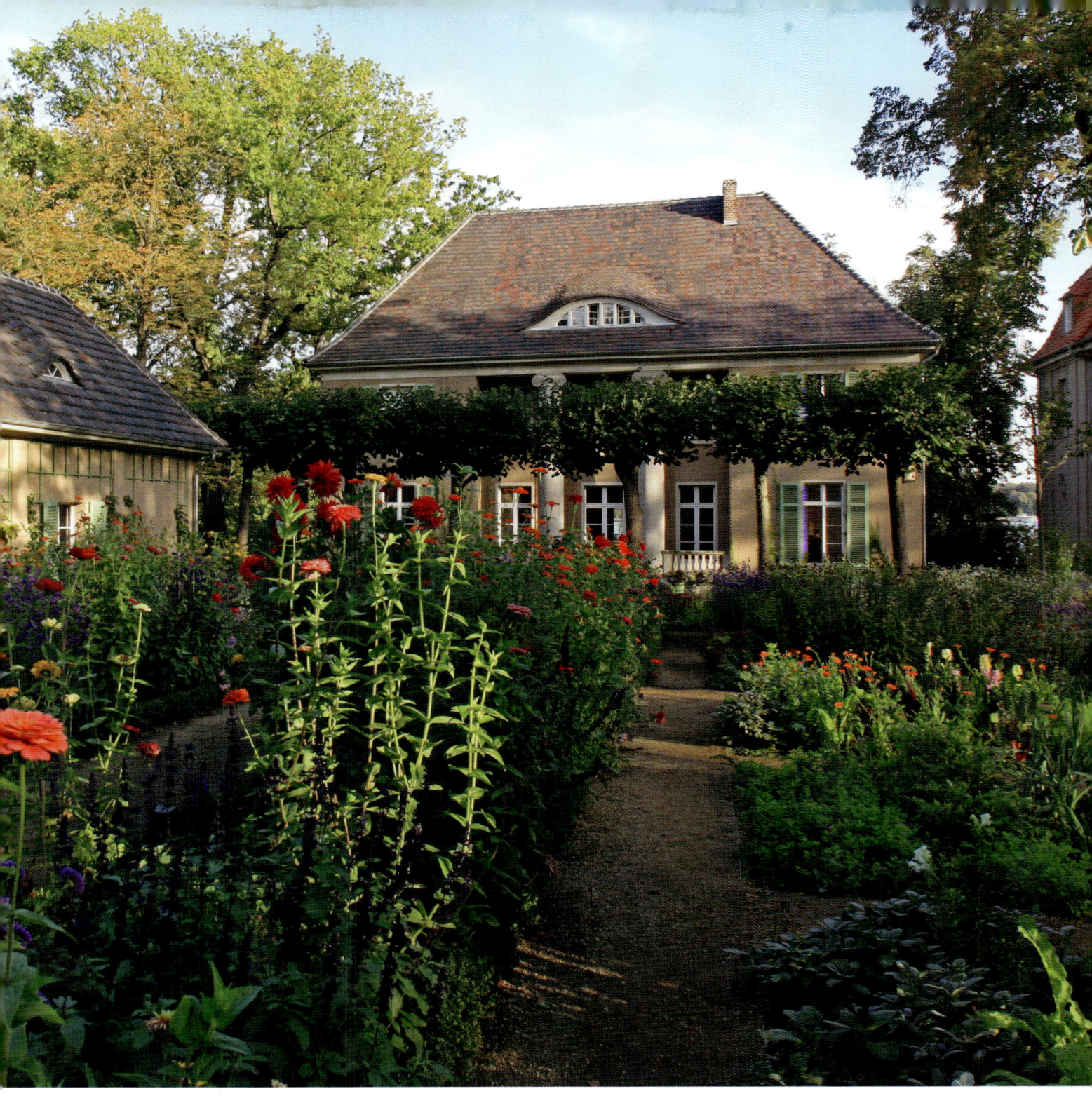

Made President
of the Prussian
Academy of Arts,
Berlin; resigns
in 1933

Named an honorary
citizen of Berlin

Died in house on
Pariser Platz, Berlin

Liebermann Villa
requisitioned by
National Socialists

In March, his wife
Martha takes her
own life

Max Liebermann
Society founded; work
begins on restoring
Liebermann's Villa
in 2002

The Villa
opens to the public
and receives
European Heritage
Award

1920   1927   1935   1940   1943   1995   2006

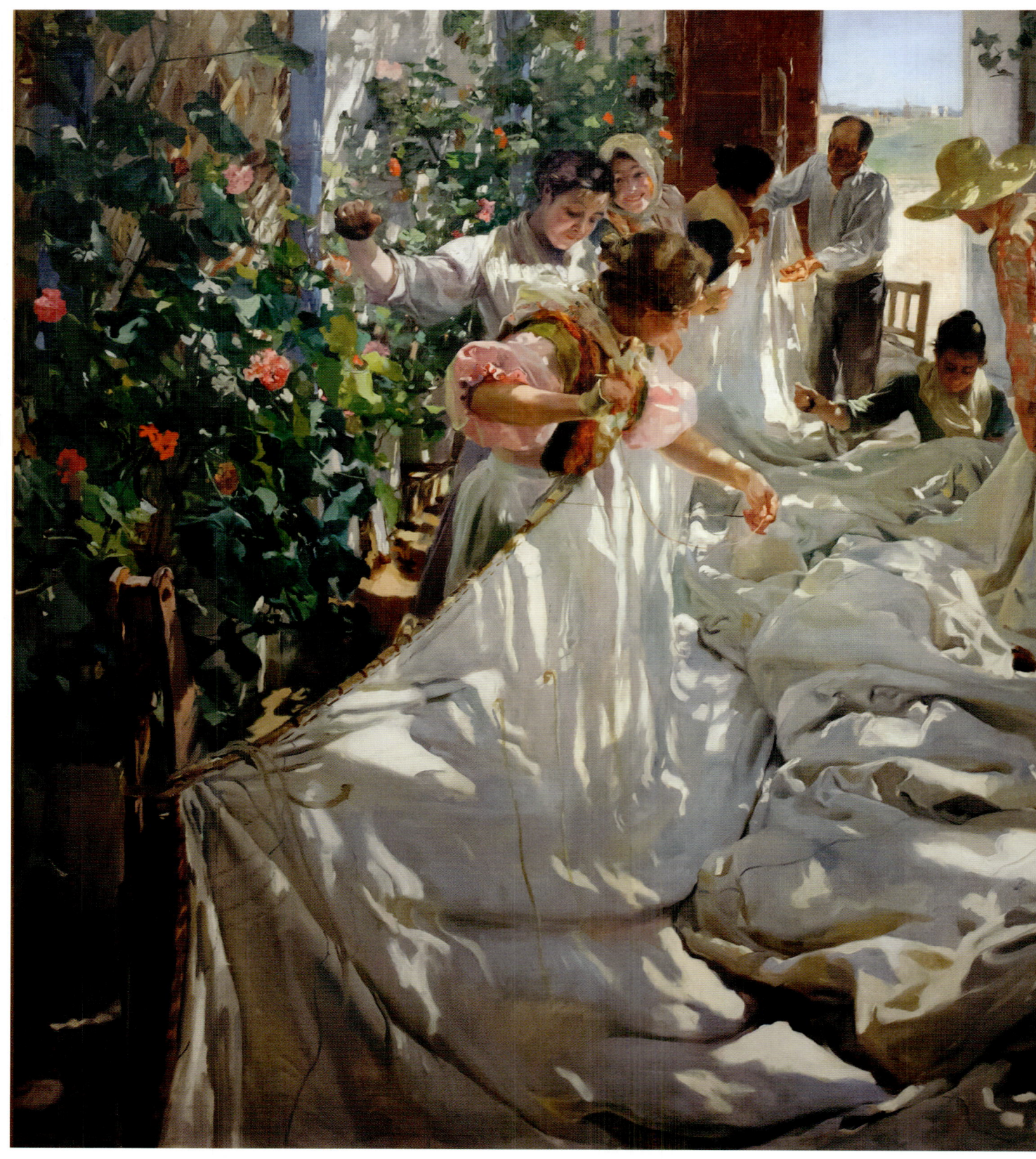

ABOVE One of Sorolla's most celebrated paintings, *Sewing the Sail* (1896) cemented the artist's reputation as the Spanish 'master of light'.

RIGHT *Self-Portrait* (1909) was painted at the height of Sorolla's success, in the same year he had his first exhibition in America.

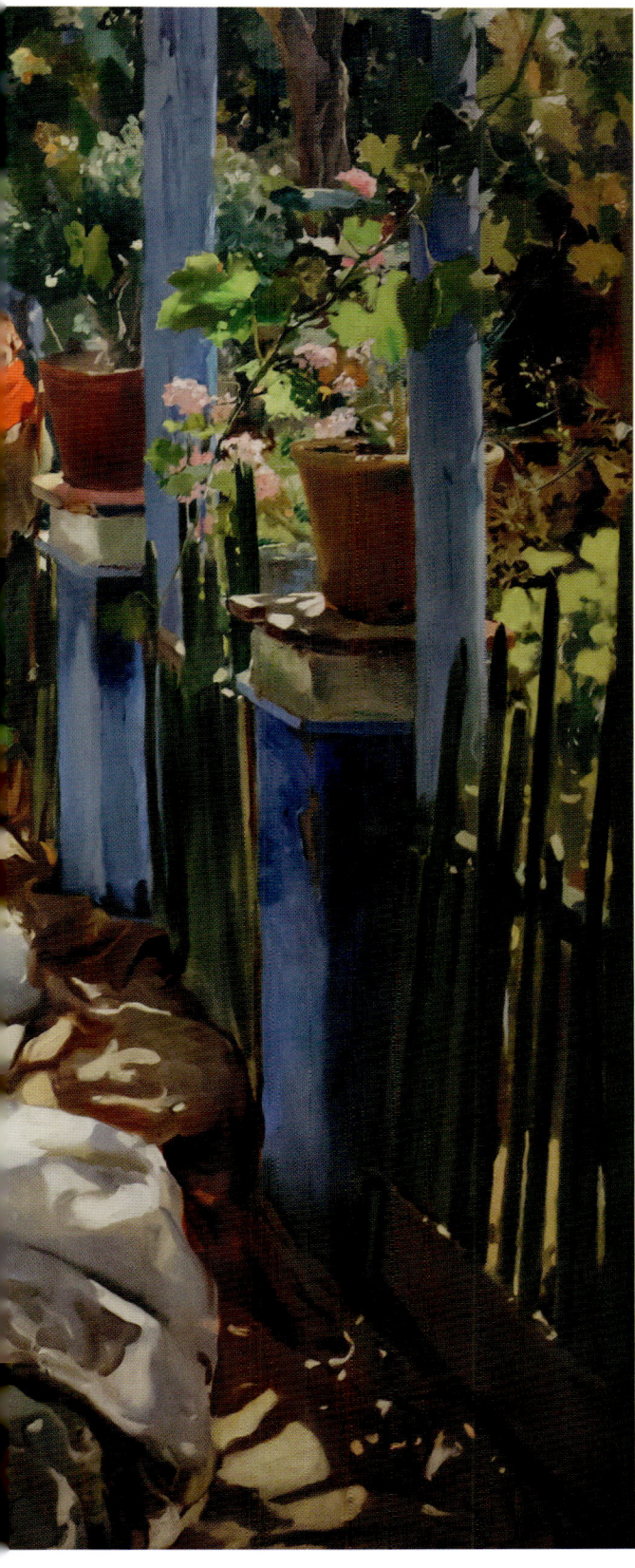

Joaquín Sorolla

Madrid, Spain

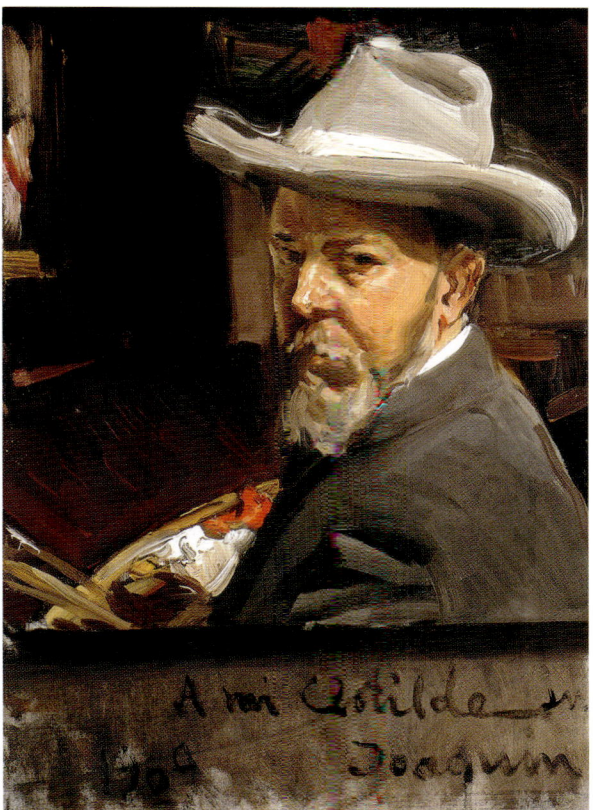

THERE ARE MANY great Spanish artists, but only one who merits the title 'master of light'. Working at a time when photography was in its infancy and just beginning to fire European imaginations, Joaquín Sorolla became obsessed with the nature of light and made it his mission to produce paintings that were as impactful as the new photographic images.

Sorolla was celebrated for his paintings of children, animals and working people on the beaches of his home town of Valencia, but his work also included portraits, landscapes and, increasingly, garden scenes. He had a love of nature and the outdoors, and the great gardens of Granada and Seville became his subjects. As a mature man, he also designed and planted his own garden in Madrid, which inspired many later paintings.

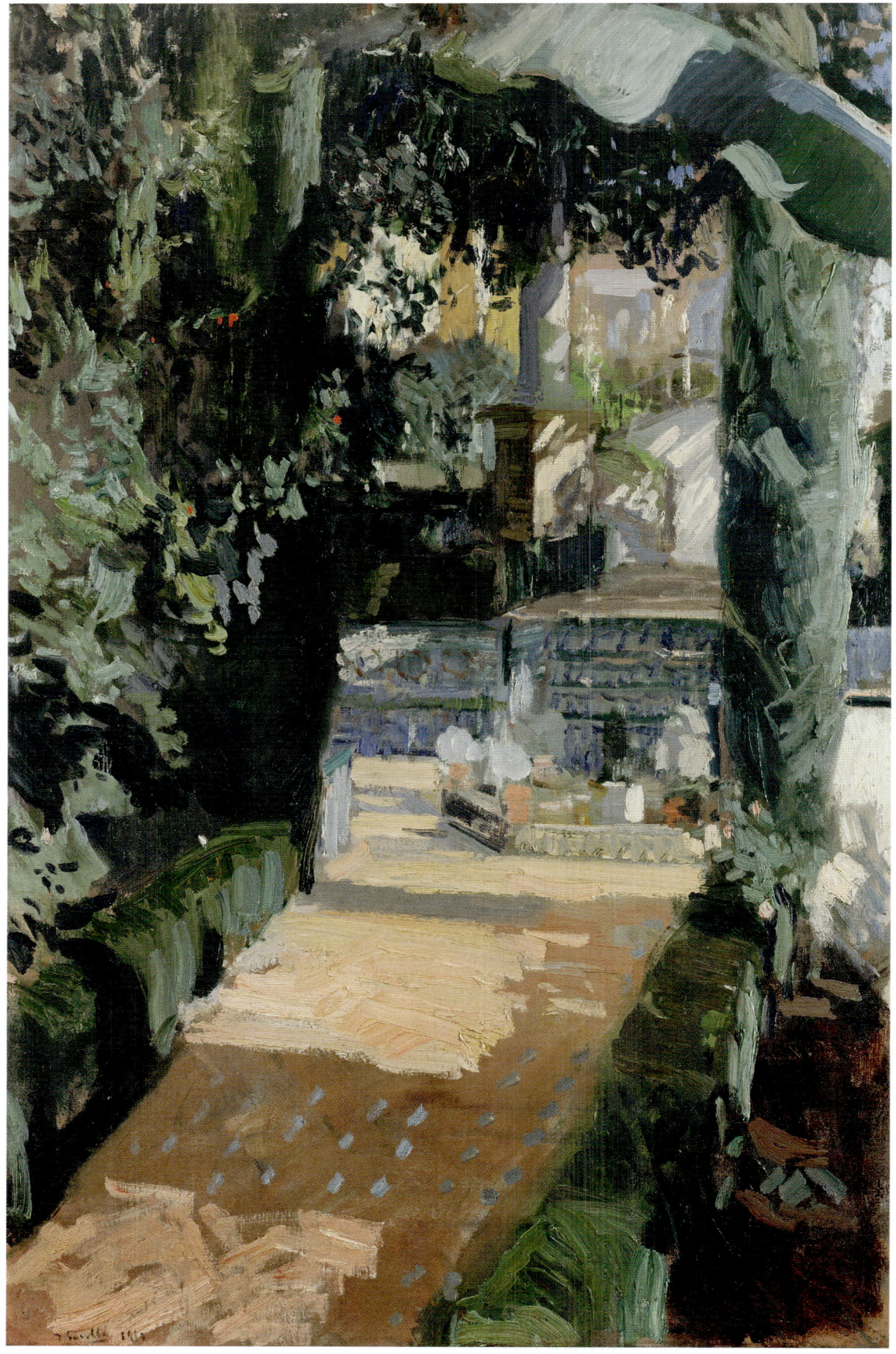

CAPTURING THE LIGHT

Joaquín Sorolla y Bastida was born in 1863 in Valencia to parents who died in an outbreak of cholera when the boy was just two years old. Brought up by an aunt and uncle, he was apprenticed to his uncle, who was a locksmith. At that time, thirty-five per cent of the population of Valencia were illiterate and had little education, but Sorolla was lucky and he attended school and also drawing classes, where his artistic talent emerged.

By the age of fifteen, he had secured a place at the *Real Academia de Bellas Artes de San Carlos* in Valencia and was also working and given an allowance by the leading photographer, Antonio García. As well as providing financial and moral support, this connection with photography would prove to be seminal for Sorolla, who was both enamoured by and frustrated with his patron's art – during his lifetime, he amassed a large collection of photographs of all kinds. It was inevitable, perhaps, that the twenty-year-old Sorolla should fall for García's daughter, Clotilde, but it proved to be a great and enduring love match and in 1889 the couple moved to Madrid.

Sorolla had always found joy in painting outdoors. While in Valencia, he captured people working on the beaches – a life that was fast disappearing from the town, where oxen and horses had been used to haul in the boats for hundreds of years. Although Sorolla disliked painting in the studio, when he moved to Madrid, it was sometimes necessary during the hard winters, but whenever possible, he would go outside, often using his children – Maria, Joaquín and Elena – as models. In 1906, when his eldest daughter Maria contracted tuberculosis, a friend lent him an estate in the Pardo mountains, where she could benefit from the pure air. His painting of her there, *Maria Painting in El Pardo* (1907), touchingly captures her working at an easel with a box of colours on her knee. By the summer of 1907, Maria had recovered and featured in his painting *Maria en los Jardines de la Granja* (1907).

The artist also spent time in the south of Spain (as did his contemporary, John Singer Sargent, with whom he

LEFT *Court of the Dances, Alcázar, Sevilla* (1910). Courtyards intrigued Sorolla, and he drew inspiration from the designs of those he saw in southern Spain for his own garden in Madrid.

Joaquín Sorolla (1863–1923)

Brought up in Valencia by his aunt and uncle after the death of his parents, Joaquín Sorolla moved to Madrid as a young man with his wife Clotilde, shortly after their marriage in 1888. His portraits, scenes of people working along the Spanish coastline, and his larger commissioned works in America, made Sorolla one of the most successful painters of his day. His work straddled figurative, Impressionist and Luminist styles, but he was mainly interested in capturing the light and mirroring the realistic effects produced by the new art of photography. As Sorolla's fame grew, he and Clotilde were able to build their own house and garden in Chamberi, a suburb of Madrid, where they moved with their children in 1911. Although Sorolla travelled extensively for his work, he always returned to Madrid and increasingly used his own garden as a source of inspiration.

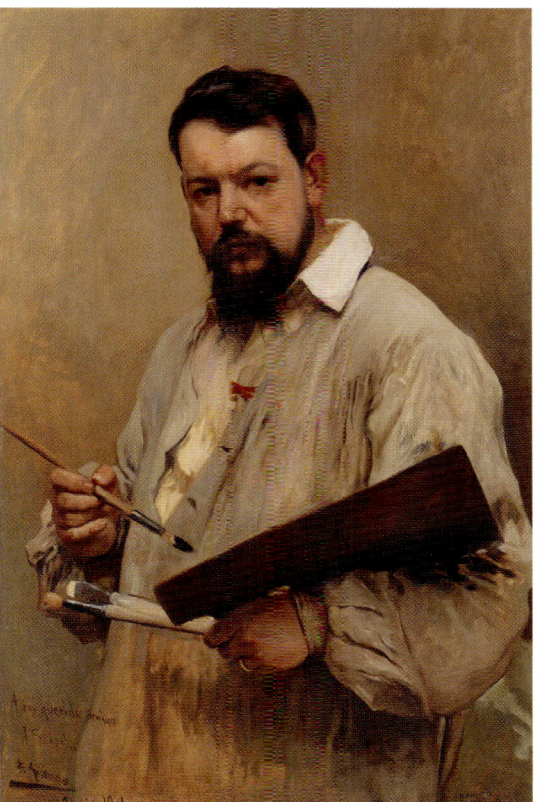

Joaquín Sorolla (1901) by José Jimenez Aranda.

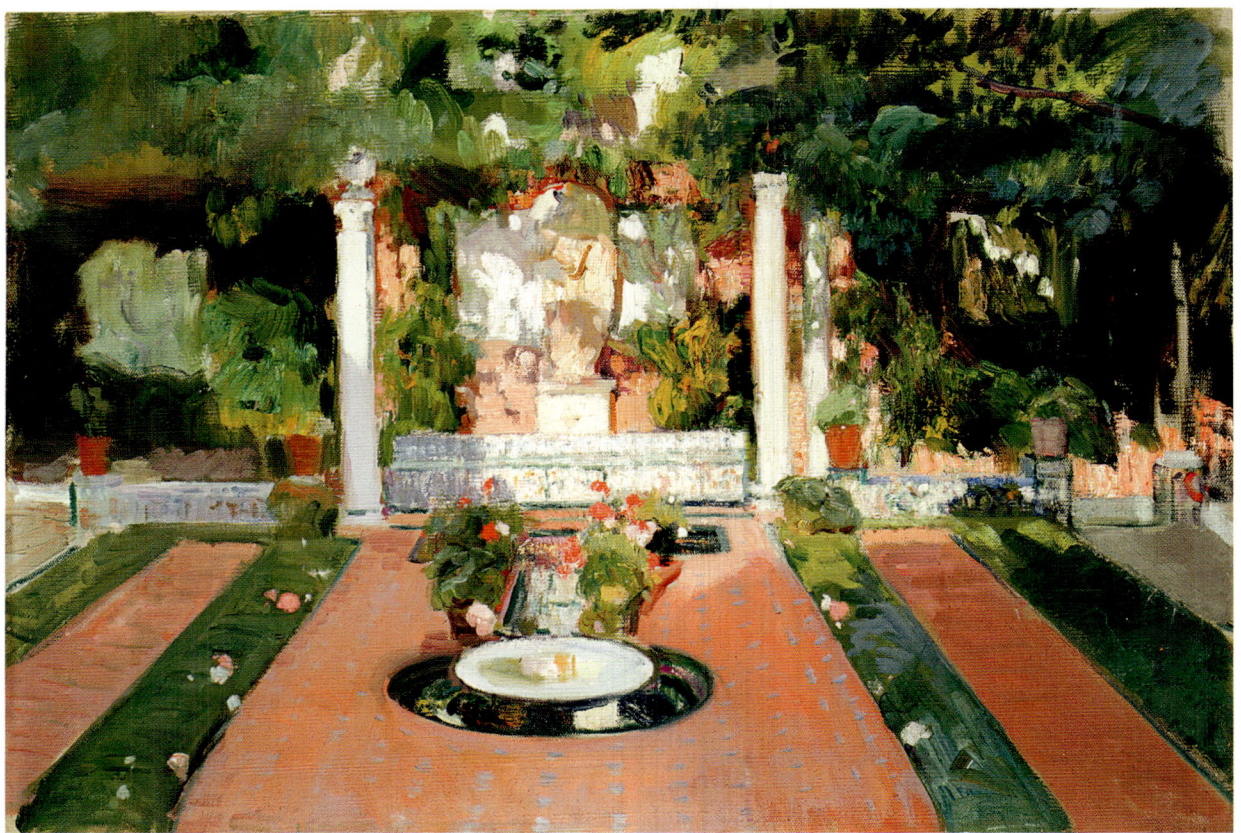

ABOVE *Garden of the Sorolla House* (1918), shows the pool and rill in the Second Garden, influenced by the artist's visits to Granada.

is often compared) and painted several scenes of the Alhambra in Granada in 1909 and Alcázar in Seville a year later, reinforcing his interest in gardens as a *motif*, which would remain with him for the rest of his life.

MAKING A HOME IN CHAMBERÍ

By 1911, the Sorollas were in a financial position to build their own house at No. 37 Paseo del General Martinez Campos in Chamberí, a leafy suburb of Madrid. Feeling the need for a more comfortable and workable home, Sorolla designed and oversaw the construction of the house, studio and a new garden, which would prove to be not only a sanctuary for the family, but also a source of new inspiration for his painting.

The house reflects Sorolla's connection to southern Spain, with its internal Andalusian-style courtyard, planted with cypresses and oleanders, featuring a fountain in the centre. Sorolla also celebrated traditional crafts, using blue and white tiles from the Triana factory of Seville in the courtyard, and panels of green and yellow tiles along the inner passageway. The panels were from the Talavera de la Reina factory, owned by his friend, the ceramicist Ruiz de Luna, who was reviving traditional tile-making. Sorolla's workspace, accessed from external steps, included a room for preparing and storing canvases and a studio with a high ceiling that looked down on the inner courtyard. Not just a space for working, the studio was also for entertaining and showing clients his paintings.

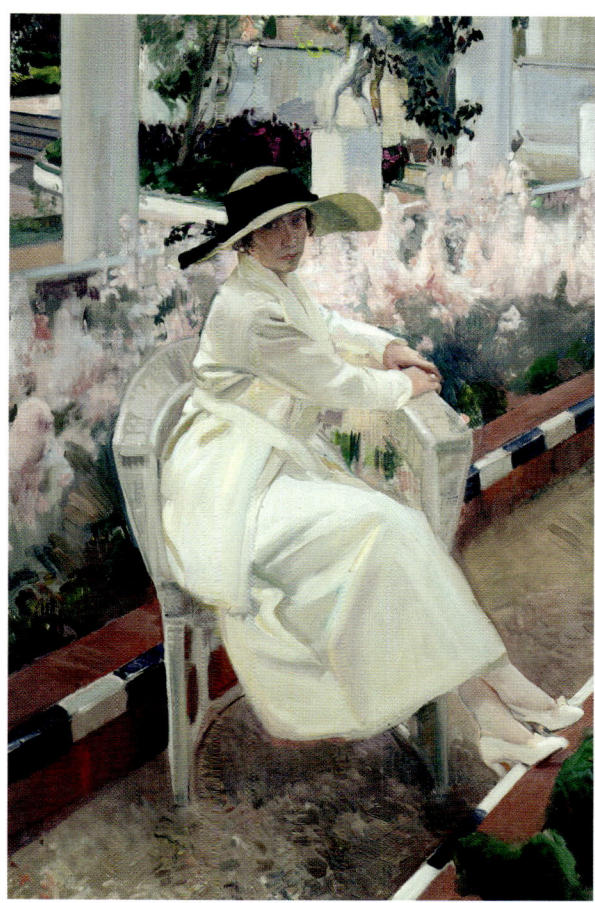
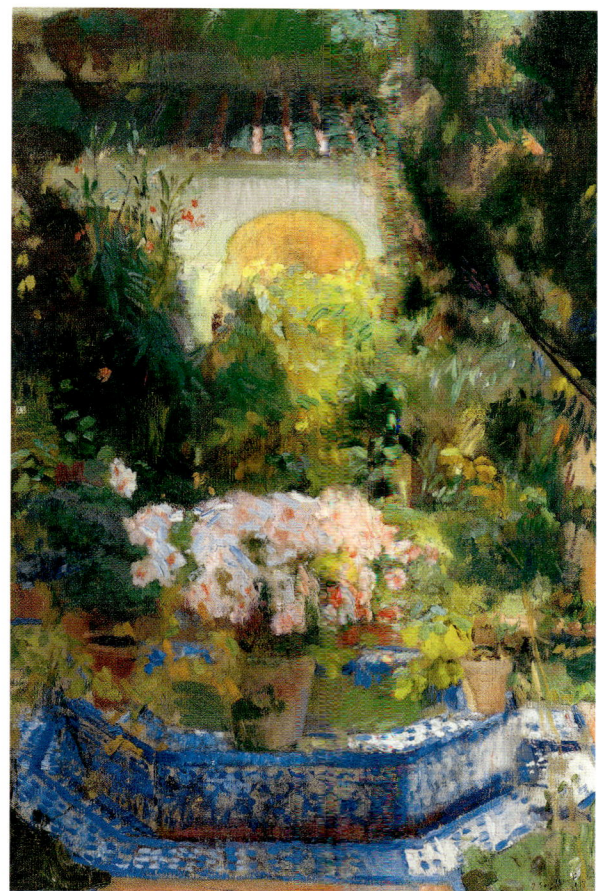

CREATING A GARDEN TO PAINT

When planning his own garden, Sorolla was inspired by the Islamic gardens he had seen and painted in Seville and Granada. The presence of water, strong architecture and intimate spaces are the hallmarks of the external courtyards, which he designed generally for outdoor living, but, more specifically, as spaces where he could paint.

The 'First Garden' at the front of the house was, perhaps, most influenced by the Alcázar of Seville, with steps leading up to the main entrance, now flanked by an orange tree and a palm (*Trachycarpus fortunei*), which were planted later. On the north wall, overlooking a small rectangular pool, Sorolla installed a large masonry seat decorated with new tiles he had ordered from the Mensaque factory in Seville. In each corner of the garden, low formal hedges of box and myrtle enclosed beds of scented, standard roses, while the paths were tiled with terracotta squares, inset in the neo-Spanish style with smaller, decorated pieces.

While working on the entrance, Sorolla also laid out the garden closest to the working areas of the house – now known as the 'Third Garden'. The main feature he included here was a large lily pond, now presided over by a bronze sculptural group, *Fuente de las Confidencias,* by Francisco Marco Díaz-Pintado, installed in 1975. There is also a substantial pergola, where Sorolla liked to set up his painting equipment, and plantings of shrubs, including rhododendrons, hydrangeas and azaleas, edged with low box hedges. In several of his paintings, the distinctive blue

ABOVE, LEFT Blue and white tiled edging is visible in *Clotilde in the Garden* (1919–20), which depicts Sorolla's wife, the daughter of photographer Antonio García. ABOVE, RIGHT Sorolla was passionate about using traditional ceramic tiles, which feature in *The Courtyard of the Sorolla House* (1917).

THE GARDEN AT CHAMBERÍ

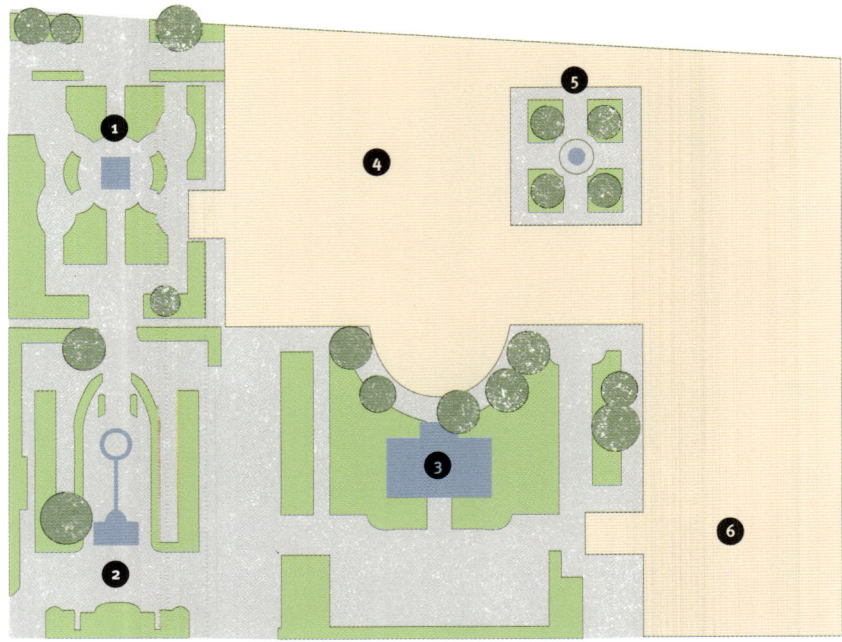

KEY

1 The First Garden
2 The Second Garden
3 The Third Garden
4 Sorolla's house
5 Andalucian-style inner courtyard
6 Artist's studio

RIGHT, CLOCKWISE FROM TOP LEFT The First Garden; the Andalucian-style inner courtyard; the tiled staircase leading to Sorolla's studio; the pool and bronze sculpture in the Third Garden; a tiled stone bench; The Second Garden; stone fountain and trough on the house wall; a copy of an original bust of the artist by Mariano Benlliure now stands under the pergola.

and white tiled edging used in this garden is clearly visible – particularly in his 1919 painting of Clotilde, which shows his wife sitting in front of a long border of pink wallflowers.

On his last trip to Granada in the winter of 1917, Sorolla began researching ideas for a new garden he was making at his home in Madrid (the Second Garden). This garden leads on from the First and links it to the Third Garden, and its design worried Sorolla the most – he made repeated drawings of it showing different ideas.

The Second Garden includes the clearest references to the Alhambra, but with some suggestions of Roman culture in its white pillars topped with sculptures. It is defined by the channel running north–south, featuring small fountains that cool the courtyard and set off the white planting of jasmine, pelargoniums, hydrangeas in pots, standard roses and, a more recent addition, Mexican orange blossom (*Choisya ternata*). The Roman statue at the end of the vista was a gift Sorolla received in 1916.

Although planned separately, the three spaces are linked by the features and materials Sorolla used – the steps, tiled paving, stone columns and benches, terracotta pots and sculptures, and the use of water in each of the gardens.

PLANTS WITH MEANING

Like many garden-makers, Sorolla sought out plants from places that meant a lot to him. From Granada, he ordered myrtle cuttings (*Myrtus communis*) for the hedges. He also included trees and plants that held special significance. One example is a *Cercis siliquastrum*, noted for its prolific display of pink blossom in spring. Known as the tree of love, Sorolla planted one at the front of the house in Chamberí when he and his family moved there in 1911. His earlier painting *El árbol del amor* (1902–04) also features a *Cercis siliquastrum*.

The garden became a focus for relaxation for Sorolla and his family, but it was also a source of more intimate settings for his paintings. This was a recognized trend among Spanish painters of the time and, by choosing to work outdoors, Sorolla was following in the footsteps of Mariano Fortuny (1838–74), who also spent time at the Alhambra in Granada in order to paint plants more accurately. Altogether, Sorolla produced around 140 paintings of gardens, including his own, which became an increasingly important and immediate source of ideas and creativity as he grew older.

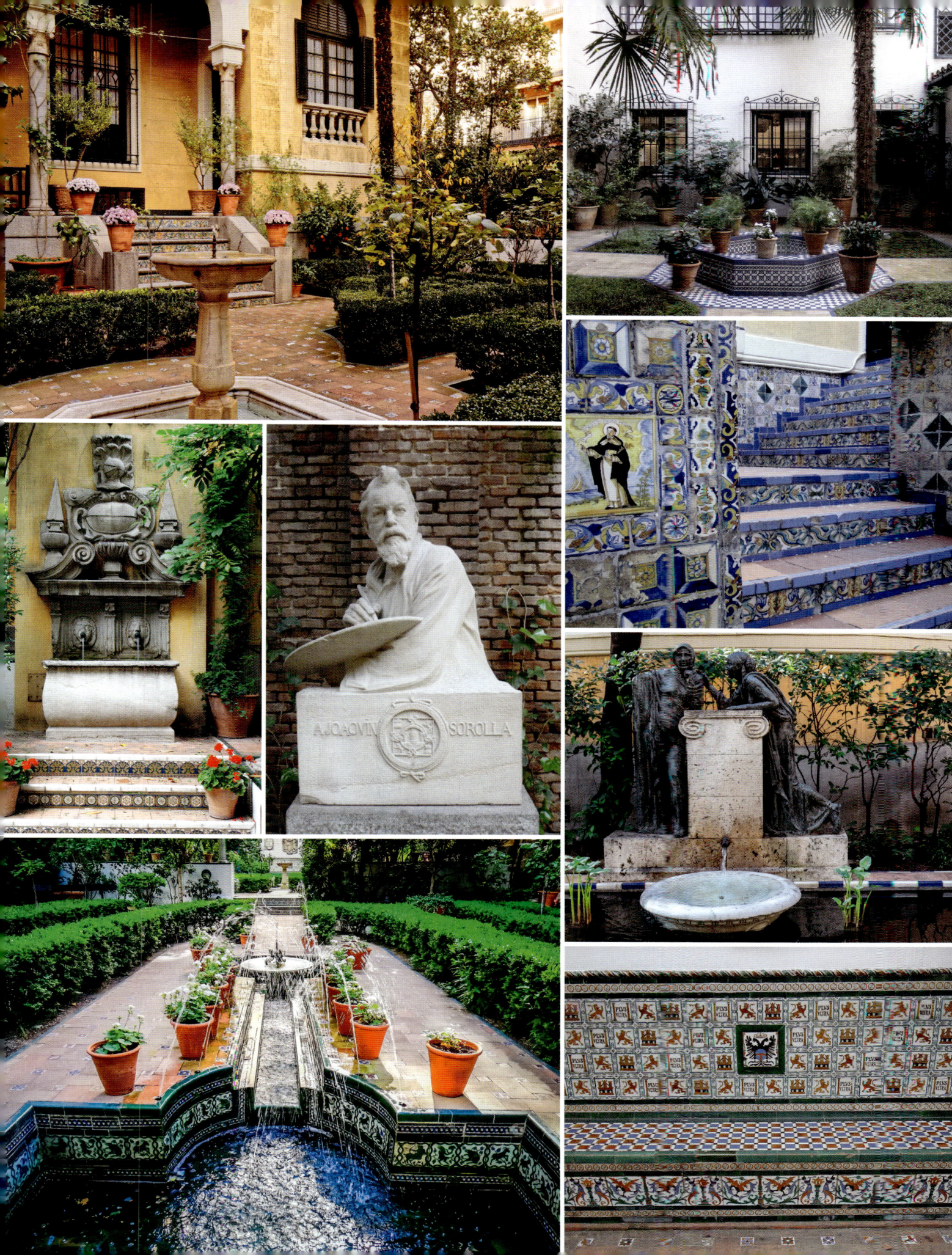

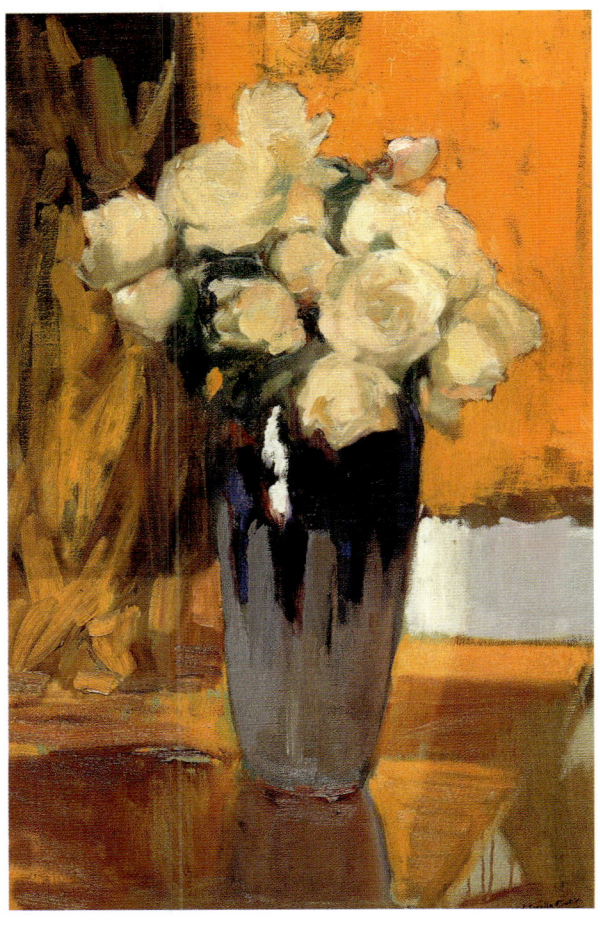

VISION OF SPAIN

The work that absorbed much of Sorolla's later life would be an epic in more ways than one. Through the connections of his wealthy patron, Archer Milton Huntington, he was commissioned by the Hispanic Society of America to complete a series of paintings, known as *Vision of Spain,* to decorate the Society's library in New York. Interest in Sorolla's work in America had been sparked by two travelling exhibitions of paintings: one in 1909, which attracted crowds of over 150,000, and another in 1911. His new brief was to capture the atmosphere of Spain's regions, from the Basque Country to Andalusia. He began work in 1912 on the fourteen four-metre/twelve-foot-tall canvases and the commission would take him seven years.

Travelling to and working in different regions of Spain, as well as going back and forth to America for exhibitions, took its toll. He wrote repeatedly to Clotilde that life on the road and his workload were exhausting him, mentally as well as physically, and that his moments of energy were like 'fleeting sparks'. Sorolla returned from his travels, thin and ill. He suffered a stroke in 1920 while painting under the pergola in the garden, after which he remained paralysed. He would never paint again. A photograph of his daughter Elena's wedding in June 1922 shows the family on the terrace overlooking the garden he had planted – the painter, a depleted but still central figure.

His monumental work, *Vision of Spain,* took until 1926 (after Sorolla's death) to be fully installed in the Hispanic Society of America's Museum and Library in New York and measures a staggering 200 metres/656 feet in length.

Chamberí remains a leafy part of Madrid, although the turn-of-the-century architecture has been replaced by late twentieth-century residential housing. Casa Sorolla is a walled sanctuary, much shadier than the artist would have known it, the trees and buildings serving to block out the sun. Clotilde donated the house and garden, just as they were, to the Spanish government and they opened to visitors in 1932. Today, Sorolla's home is still a sought-out destination on Sundays, when all of Madrid's museums are free to enter. Sorolla's bust stands under the pergola, and the great and the good of Madrid continue to gather in his studio – just as they did in his heyday. The master of light has found his time again.

SOROLLA'S TIMELINE

1863	1878	1888	1890–95	1909–17	1909	1911
Joaquín Sorolla y Bastida born in Valencia, Spain; parents die two years later	Studies at *Real Academia de Bellas Artes*; mentored by photographer Antonia García	Marries García's daughter, Clotilde; they move to Madrid in 1889	Three children born, Maria, Joaquín and Elena	Travels regularly to Alhambra and Seville	First exhibition in the USA	Builds house and designs garden in Madrid; second exhibition in the USA

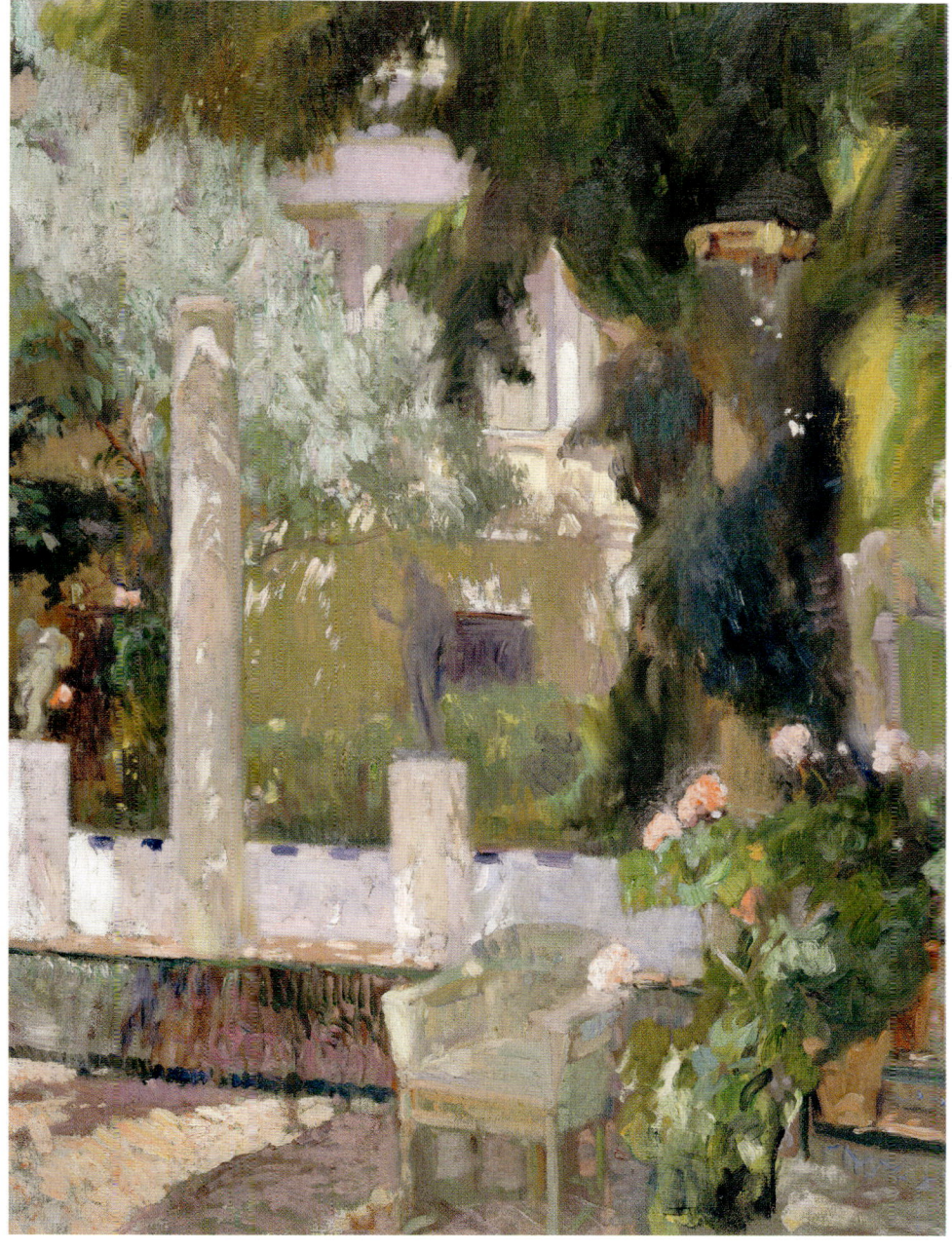

OPPOSITE *White Roses from my Home Garden* was painted in 1920, the year in which Sorolla had to stop working altogether, after he suffered a stroke.

LEFT One of Sorolla's last paintings of the garden was *The Gardens at the Sorolla Family House* (1920).

Begins tour of Spain for a commission for Hispanic Society of America

Visits Alhambra in Granada and plans a new garden for his house in Madrid

Completes the *Vision of Spain*

After suffering a stroke in 1920, Sorolla dies, aged 60

Museo Sorolla opens in Madrid at the artist's former home

First retrospective exhibition in the USA

Fully renovated Vision of Spain Gallery opens at the Hispanic Society, New York

1912 1917 1919 1923 1932 1989–90 2010

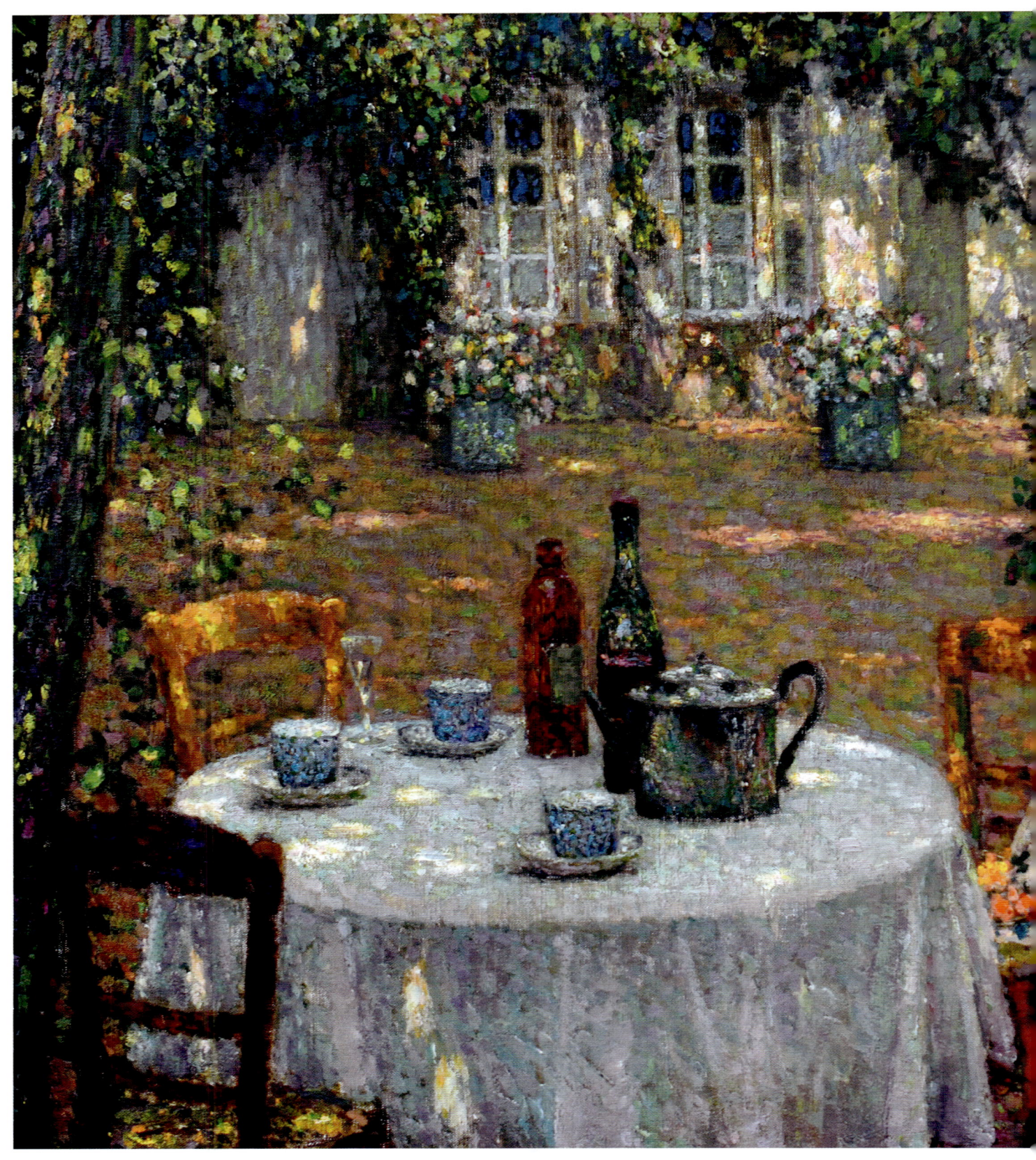

ABOVE *The Table in the Sun* (1911), painted in the courtyard of Le Sidaner's home, *Le Presbytère*, illustrates the intimate subjects that defined his work.

RIGHT Le Sidaner, pictured here, circa 1930, at his house in the village of Gerberoy, where he worked from a studio in a converted barn.

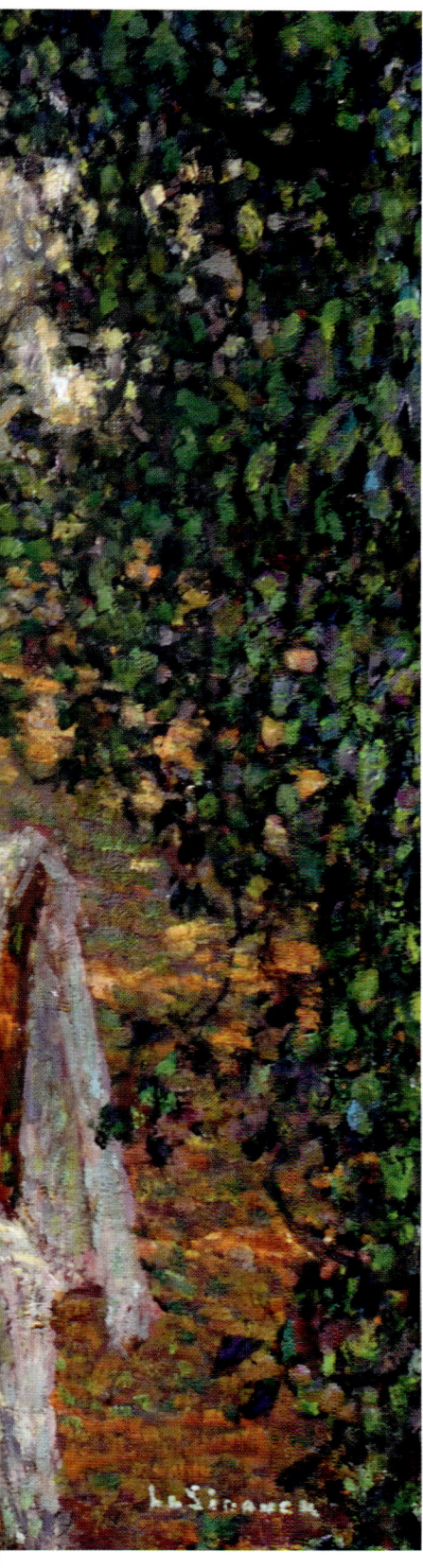

Henri Le Sidaner

Gerberoy, Picardie, France

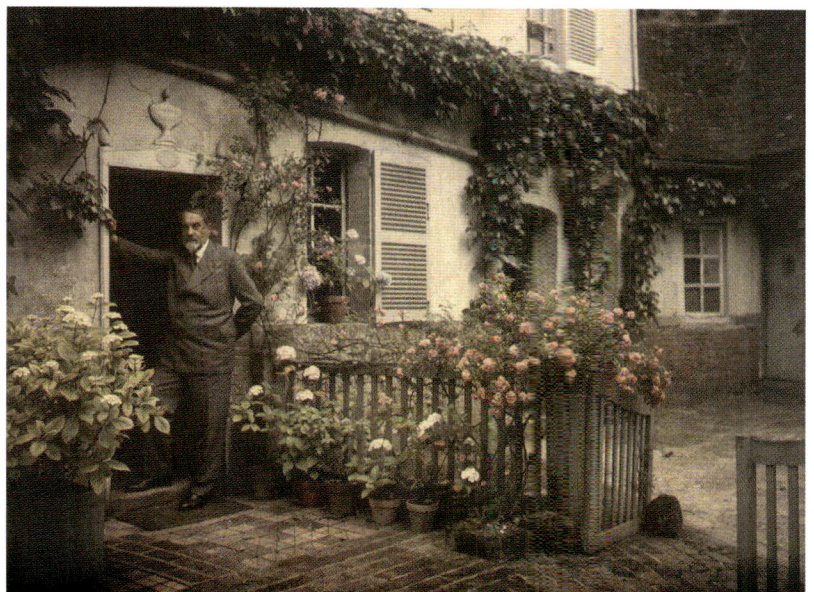

A CONTEMPORARY OF CLAUDE MONET and Édouard Vuillard, Henri Le Sidaner was as successful as these great artists during his lifetime, but his fame diminished after his death and his work is now less well-known. Although not an Impressionist, many of whom were renowned for working *en plein air*, Le Sidaner became a painter of gardens, particularly his own in Picardie, taking his place among an elite group of gardener-artists.

Critics have called his style Post-Impressionist and his technique Pointillist, but, in fact, Le Sidaner did not like to be labelled or wish to belong to any group at all. 'If you want to call me anything,' he once said, 'call me an Intimist.'

BREAKING WITH TRADITION

It seems that Le Sidaner, even during his youth, never followed a conventional path. Born in French Mauritius in 1862, he came back to France with his parents to live in Dunkirk on the Pas de Calais coast. His father was a shipping broker, so an artistic career was probably not encouraged by his parents, but undeterred he took himself off to Paris where, after being turned down several times, he was finally admitted to the prestigious *École des Beaux-Arts*.

In 1885, bored and stifled by the city, he joined an artists' colony at Étaples on the Opal Coast in northern France. There he met Eugène Chigot and Henri Duhem – who would both become lifelong friends – and together they painted the sea, harbour and town, always looking for that elusive quality of light.

Henri Le Sidaner
(1862–1939)

Although Le Sidaner worked in Paris, Brittany and Versailles, as well as in London and Venice, it was his house and garden at Gerberoy in northern France that inspired most of his paintings – at least ninety finished oils and pastels and fifty studies were of his home there. Many featured the White and Rose gardens, and the terraces where the family ate and entertained friends, who included Rodin, Chigot and the Belgian poet Émile Verhaeren. In later life, when his guests had gone home, the elderly Le Sidaner would return to his studio to capture the atmosphere of the garden where his friends had sat long into the evening. His favourite subjects were the intimate spaces around the house, particularly at dusk as the light began to fade. A few of his paintings still exist in French galleries, but most are in private collections and galleries in Rome, Bilbao, Madrid, Cologne, New York, Chicago, Philadelphia and in Britain.

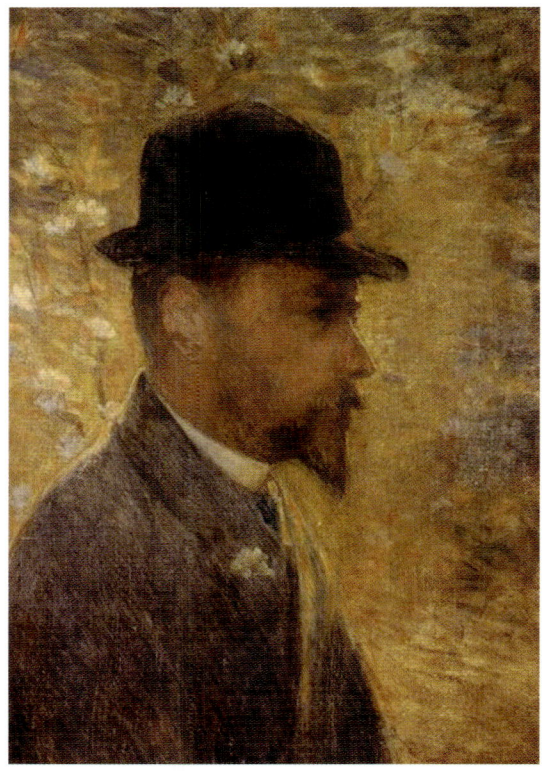

Henri Le Sidaner (1894), a portrait by Marie Duhem.

THE MOVE TO GERBEROY

Le Sidaner soon became restless again and left Étaples, eloping with a young Parisian called Camille Navarre, whom he later married. The couple settled in Versailles to the south-west of Paris and in 1899, with his paintings selling well, Henri signed a contract with the established Georges Petit Gallery in Paris. For the next thirty years, wherever he painted, all of his work would be packed up in wooden crates and delivered to Petit to be sold.

The park of Versailles seem to have ignited an interest in gardens as a subject for Le Sidaner's work. Now a family man with two young boys – Rémy and Louis – he took his children to see the historic gardens created by André Le Nôtre for the Sun King, Louis XIV. Yet the scale of the park, with its vistas and grandeur, did not inspire him. He sought more intimate subjects: a flight of steps, a gatehouse, small pavilions, gates and doorways, courtyards, a jet of water against a backdrop of spring blossom. Even before he came to Versailles, the figures that had led some critics to define him as a member of the Symbolism art movement had all but disappeared from his paintings. His work and his life were about to take a new turn.

Always happier in the country than in the town, Le Sidaner began looking for a property where he could develop his painting in a new direction. The sculptor Auguste Rodin suggested the beautiful cathedral town of Beauvais in northern France, but another friend, the ceramicist Delaherche, directed him to the nearby village of Gerberoy, which Le Sidaner first visited in March 1901.

The artist was completely entranced by this sleepy medieval village, with its old houses and little bridges over the river Oise. He rented, and later bought, a long, two-storey house adjoining the church, which had formerly housed a religious community. His home, Le Presbytère, was built on the ruins of an old medieval castle and for the next three decades, this would be his family's summer home and the source of his new passion, gardening.

CREATING A GARDEN

The move to Gerberoy confirmed him as an 'Intimist', a group of artists who adhered loosely to an Impressionist style, but who chose more homely subjects, such as house interiors, windows and terraces, rather than landscapes.

Making Light Work

Le Sidaner would begin a painting either outdoors or in the *atelier d'été* (summer studio) and finish it in his indoor studio, which he had made by converting one of the old barns. Obsessed with the light at dusk, *le crepuscule*, he became skilled at capturing that particular time of day. He explored the play between the darkening exterior and the light from the windows, which he painted orange, a bold move for the time. One of his earliest works on arriving at Gerberoy was *The Table in the White Garden* and he would go on to paint hundreds of similar settings throughout his life, always trying to convey the perfect light.

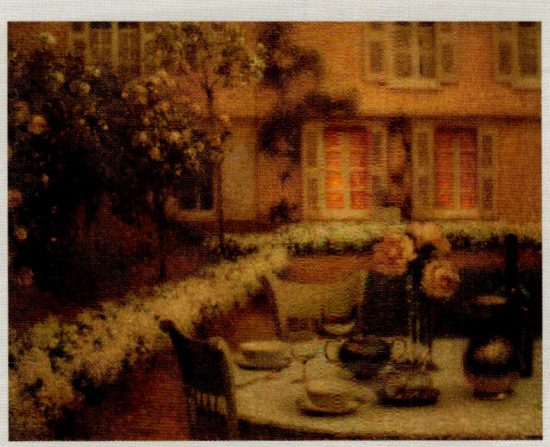

The Table in the White Garden (1906)

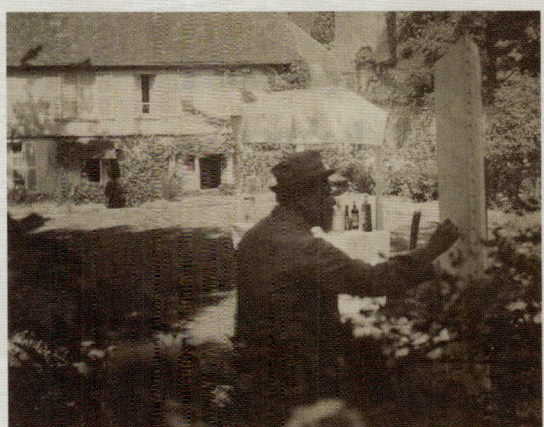

Le Sidaner painting in the garden, 1920

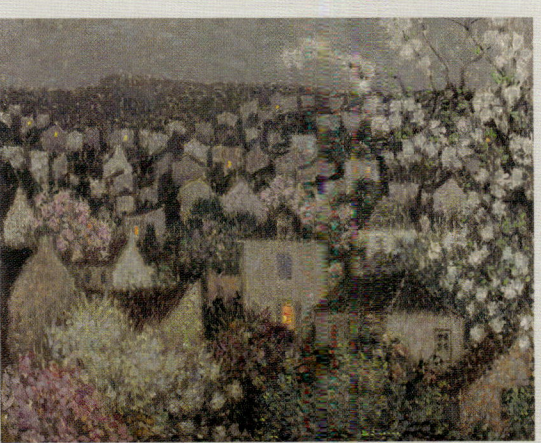

May Evening (1934)

Le Sidaner increasingly wanted to capture the garden at his new home in Gerberoy. Equally important to him was the quality of the light and, after successful attempts to paint twilight, moonlight and sunrise in Paris, these dual obsessions informed Le Sidaner's work until his death.

He set out to make a series of monochromatic areas in the garden. The original plot that came with the house was to the front, where he created a White Garden (thirty years before Vita Sackville-West's famous White Garden at Sissinghurst in Kent). Henri then bought up additional plots, enlarging the garden piece by piece until he had acquired 3,000 square metres '32,292 square feet. Each area was colour themed: above the White Garden, he made a Yellow Garden with golden box and yellow roses, and a Blue Garden, using *Perovskia*, hardy geraniums and the almost blue rose 'Pacific Dream'. He bought perennials from local growers and sourced roses and azaleas from nearby Beauvais.

Much of the garden comprised the ruins of the medieval castle on which it was built, and he re-used the old stones

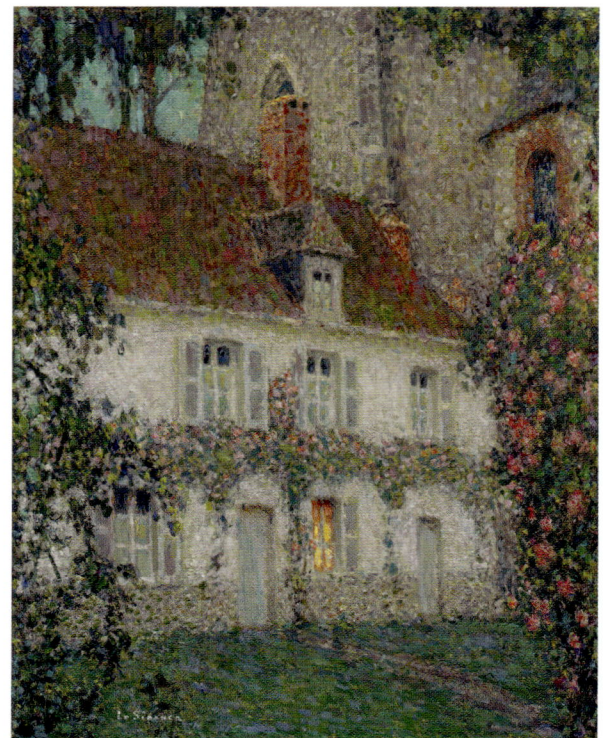

"My love of painting is so great that I love every painter ... provided he is sincere."

HENRI LE SIDANER (1931)

to create terraces, protected by stone balustrades. Just prior to making the gardens at Gerberoy, Le Sidaner had been painting in the Borromean Islands in Italy and there is a clear Italian influence in the terraces he built. Known as 'the garden of falling rocks', he planted them with roses and hydrangeas – he liked the latter for their wide range of flower forms and colours, although it was the white mopheads that he favoured most.

Throughout the garden, he placed old ecclesiastical statuary that he had recovered during the build. Later, he was able to buy areas of the castle's original defensive ditches and, at the edge of the site, he used an old round tower as the base for a pavilion with a domed cupola roof, inspired by the Temple of Love at Versailles. This structure, with its verdigris roof and wooden columns, offered him and his guests far-ranging views across the Picardie countryside.

THE ROSES OF PICARDIE

Le Sidaner made a rose garden on the upper terrace, using the new cultivars of the day, such as the dark pink rambler, *Rosa* 'Excelsa' (1909), and the slightly lighter pink 'Dorothy Perkins' (1902), both floriferous doubles. He commissioned the local blacksmith to make metal arches that he had designed to support the roses. In places these arches were only 1.5 metres/5 feet high, too low for tall visitors to pass under, but much better for viewing the flowers up close. The design of the garden is strong, with clear geometry and vistas leading the eye through the tunnel of roses to a central pedestal and basin, inspired

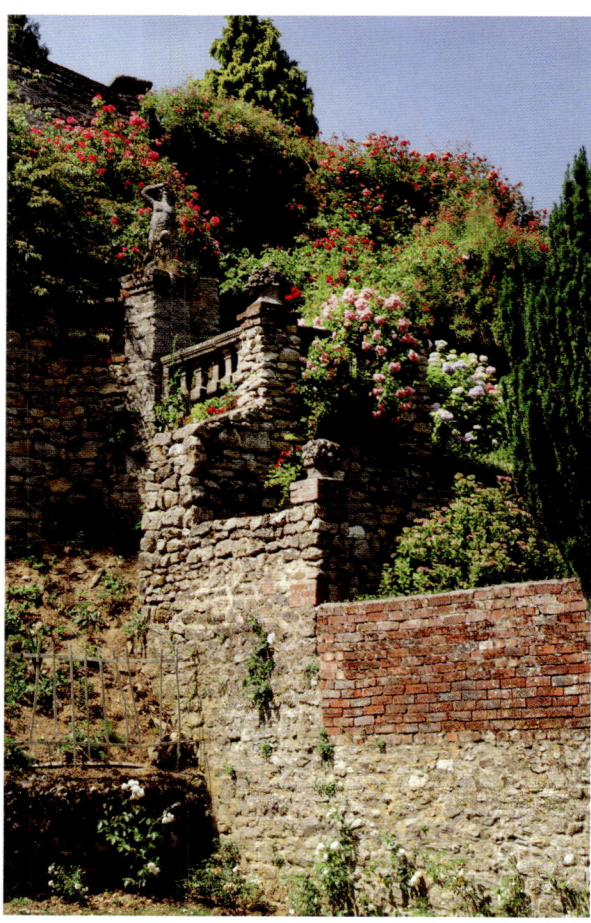

LEFT, ABOVE *The House by the Church, Gerberoy* (1932).
LEFT, BELOW Inspired by Italian designs, Le Sidaner described his rose terraces as 'the garden of falling rocks'.
RIGHT, ABOVE The White Garden was the area Le Sidaner completed first, on the level plot of land in front of the house.
RIGHT, BELOW *The White Garden at Twilight* (1913) shows the lawn edged with Le Sidaner's favourite white hydrangeas.

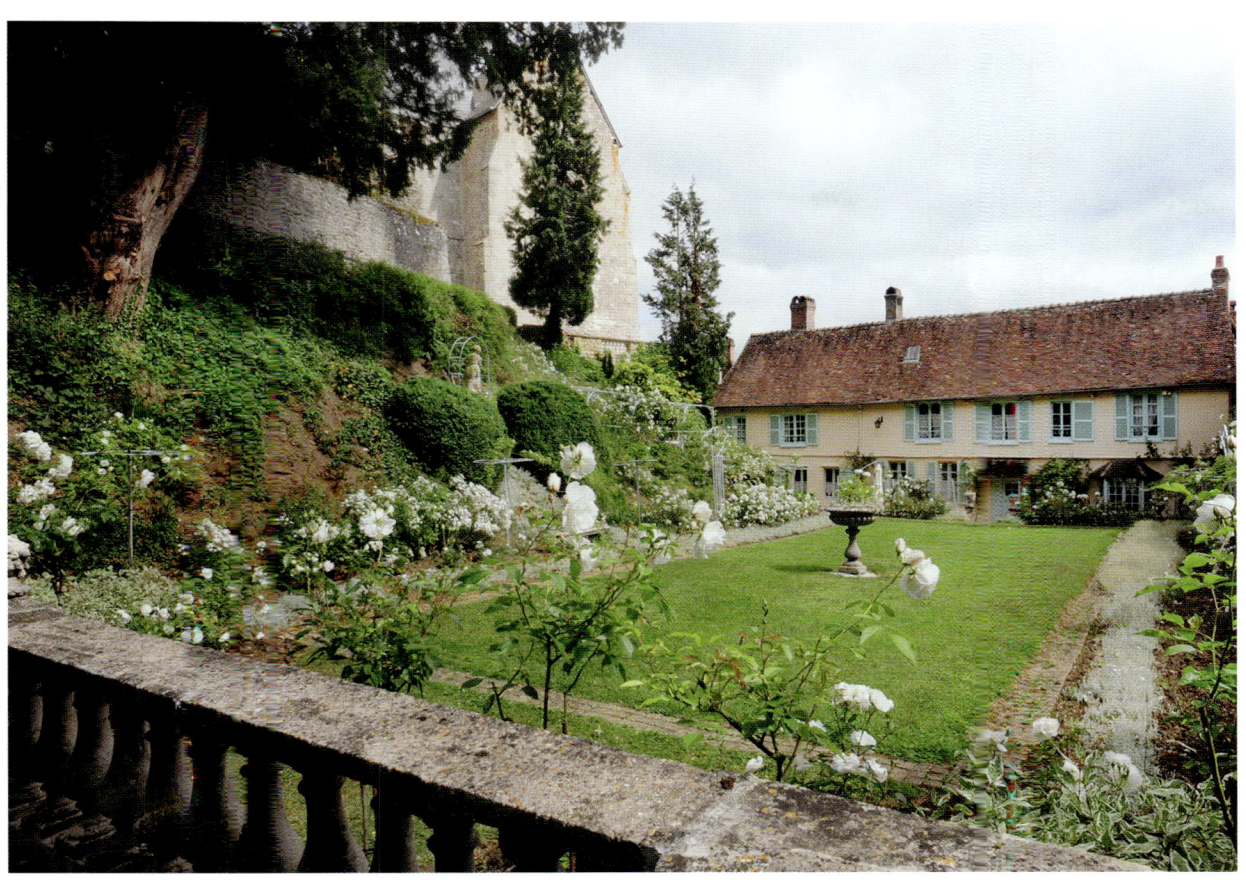

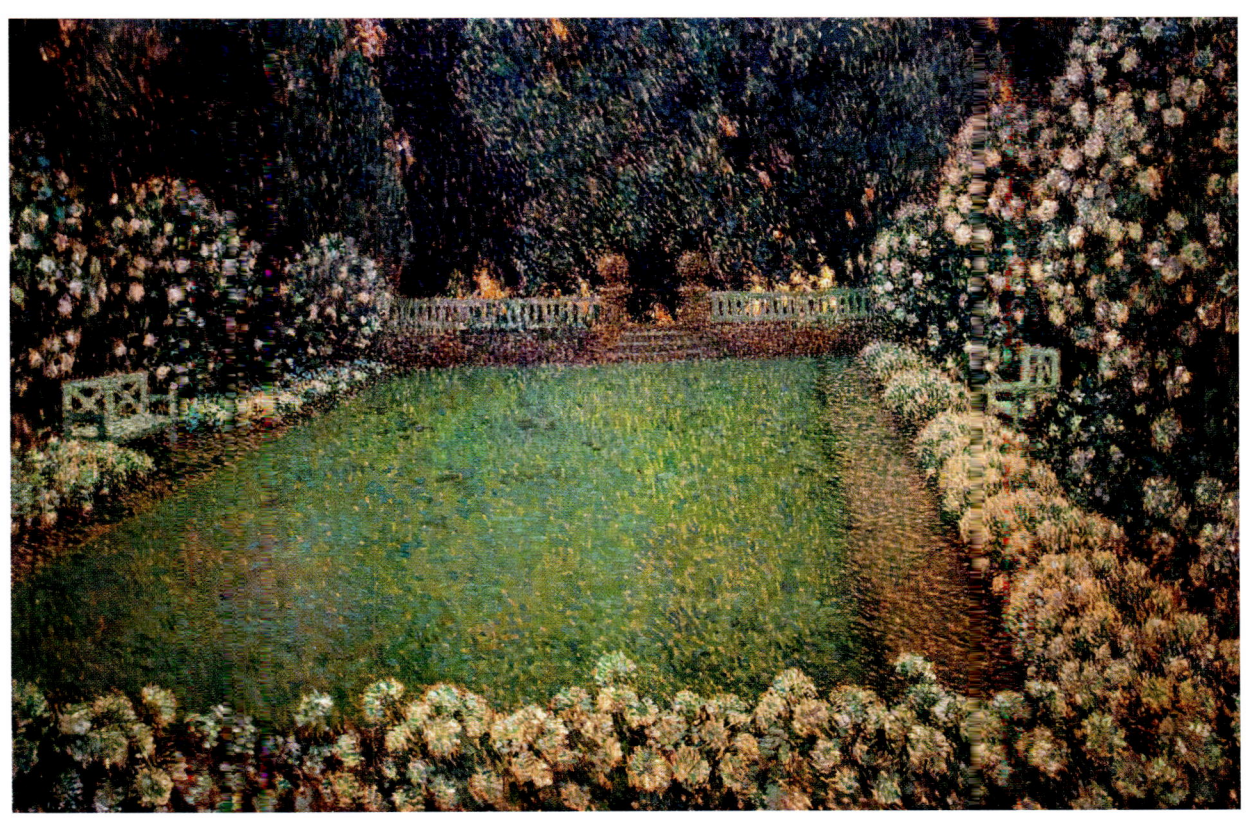

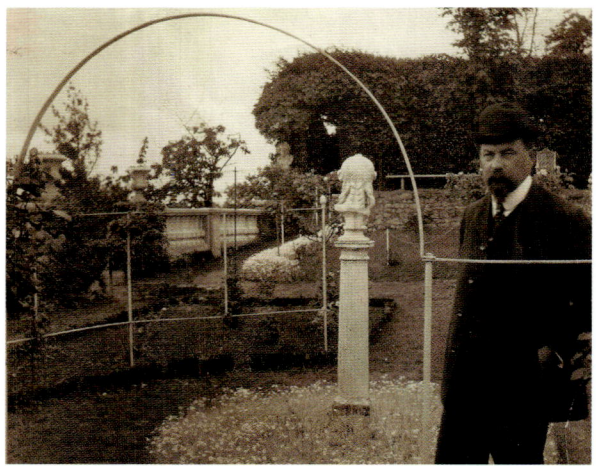

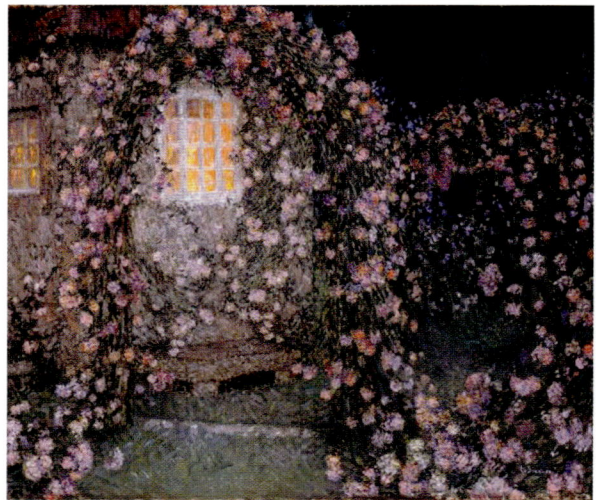

by the formal gardens he had seen in Italy and possibly Hampton Court Palace, which he visited in 1908.

The poignant lyrics of the song, *Roses of Picardy*, penned in 1916 by a British soldier pining for his French sweetheart, have cemented the flower's association with this part of France, but 'rose fever' had begun long before the war and was in no small part due to the influence of Le Sidaner. Shortly after arriving in Gerberoy, the artist persuaded the town dignitaries to plant two rose bushes – one in front of the *Mairie* and another in front of the square. Then, in 1904, he asked the people of Gerberoy to plant two roses each outside their houses, which, in the main, they did. Soon, the already picturesque village was filled with flowers (the colours carefully orchestrated by Le Sidaner so as not to clash) and the artist instigated the first *Fête des Roses* in 1908. The festival is still held in Gerberoy on the third Sunday in June, when the streets are festooned with flowers and floats.

OUT FROM THE SHADOWS

During his lifetime, Le Sidaner exhibited and sold some 4,000 works in France, other European countries and the USA. Yet he was all but forgotten in France for fifty years, after the Georges Petit Gallery that handled his paintings closed down in 1931. Most of his works were sold abroad, particularly to William Henry Singer Junior, an American art collector. The timing of Le Sidaner's death in July 1939 also diminished the artist's legacy in his homeland. His two sons were caught up in the ensuing war and when Rémy, the eldest, returned to Gerberoy to keep his father's memory alive by maintaining the gardens, he found that Le Sidaner's plans, as well as sixty studies painted on wood, had been used to light fires by the occupying troops.

In time, the house and garden at Gerberoy were passed down to Etienne Le Sidaner, the painter's grandson who, with his wife Dominique, have been responsible for bringing the garden back to its former glory. In 2008, seventy years after the artist's death, Dominique began a restoration project, with the aim of opening up the property to the public. Raising funds and using volunteer help, the weeds and overgrowth were cleared away to reveal the garden Le Sidaner had created. All the old roses were still *in situ* and where possible, they were revived –

TOP Henri Le Sidaner designed low metal rose arches to ensure the flowers would be close to the viewer as they passed beneath them.
ABOVE *The Rose Garden at Dusk* (1923) captures the soft light illuminating the flowers as evening falls.
RIGHT (CLOCKWISE FROM TOP LEFT) The inner courtyard of *Le Presbytère*, where Le Sidaner set many of his intimate paintings; the Rose Garden on the upper terrace; *Rosa* 'Pacific Dream'; the steps leading up to the Blue Garden; a bust of Henri Le Sidaner by Félix Alexandre Desruelles; the castle ruins were used to make terraces topped with a viewing pavilion; *Rosa* 'Excelsa'.

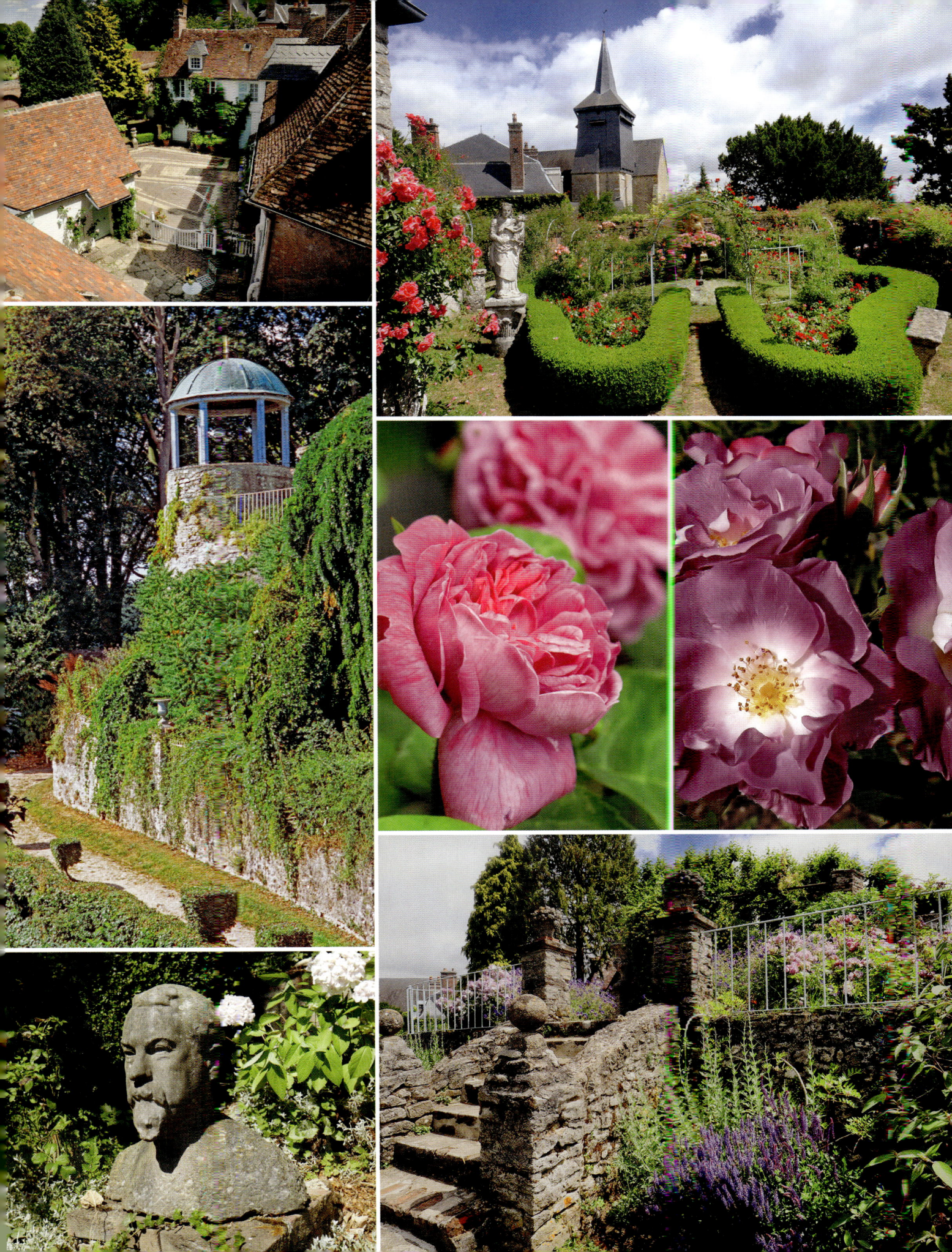

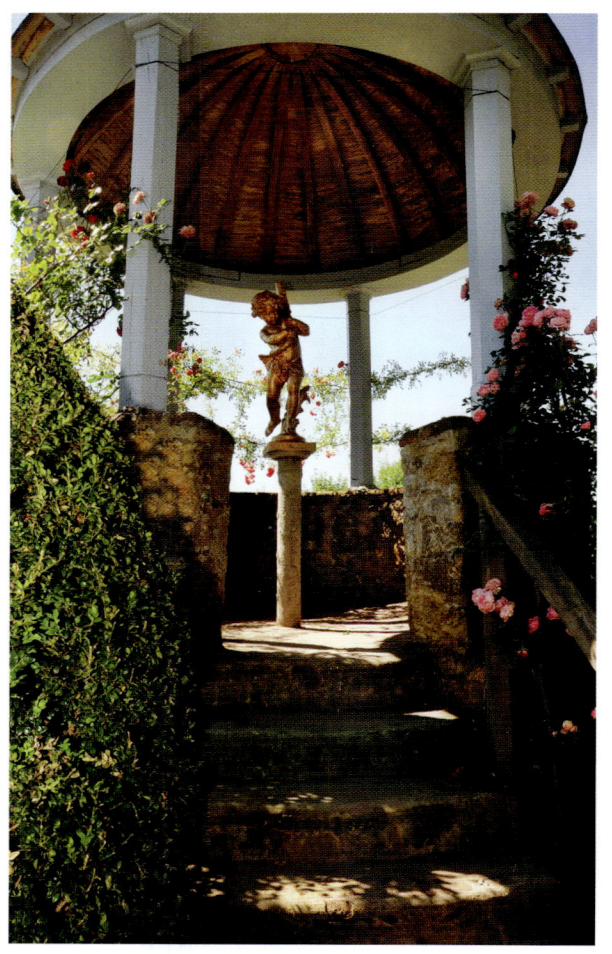

new roses that have been added are of the same period. The walls were also made safe and the Temple of Love restored. The garden opened to visitors a couple of years later and in 2013 it was named a *Jardin Remarquable*. This accolade is given to the best gardens in France and in Gerberoy there are two: Le Sidaner's and the nearby Jardin des Ifs, with its ancient yews.

Gerberoy itself has been awarded the status *of Les Plus Beaux Villages de France* – the only one in Picardie – and is therefore attracting more and more visitors. Happily, the cobbled, uneven paving and narrow streets, mean that it is inaccessible to cars. It was its very fragility and intimacy that attracted Henri Le Sidaner to the village and, for now, those features are protected. He would probably have also been proud that, in the twenty-first century, his paintings have been hung alongside Monet's and other great French artists in galleries around the world. Like the garden, Le Sidaner's work has, at last, emerged from the shadows.

LEFT The Pavilion was built on the ruins of a medieval tower and topped with a domed roof to echo the Temple of Love at Versailles.
RIGHT *The Tower with Lanterns* (1926) brings together Le Sidaner's love of intimate garden spaces and his interest in painting at dusk.

LE SIDANER'S TIMELINE

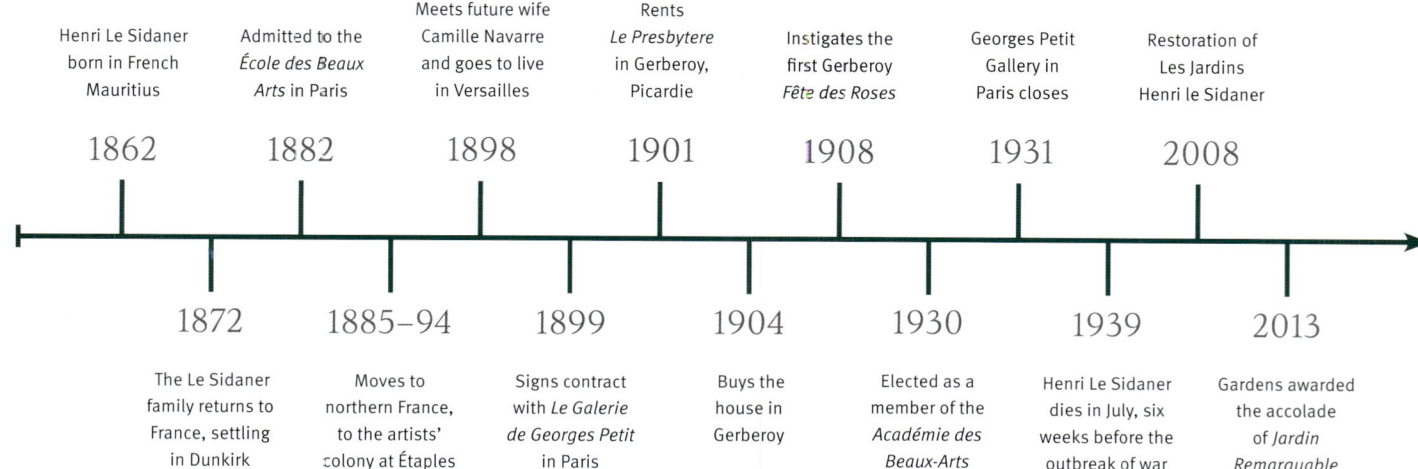

1862	Henri Le Sidaner born in French Mauritius
1872	The Le Sidaner family returns to France, settling in Dunkirk
1882	Admitted to the *École des Beaux Arts* in Paris
1885–94	Moves to northern France, to the artists' colony at Étaples
1898	Meets future wife Camille Navarre and goes to live in Versailles
1899	Signs contract with *Le Galerie de Georges Petit* in Paris
1901	Rents *Le Presbytere* in Gerberoy, Picardie
1904	Buys the house in Gerberoy
1908	Instigates the first Gerberoy *Fête des Roses*
1930	Elected as a member of the *Académie des Beaux-Arts*
1931	Georges Petit Gallery in Paris closes
1939	Henri Le Sidaner dies in July, six weeks before the outbreak of war
2008	Restoration of Les Jardins Henri le Sidaner
2013	Gardens awarded the accolade of *Jardin Remarquable*

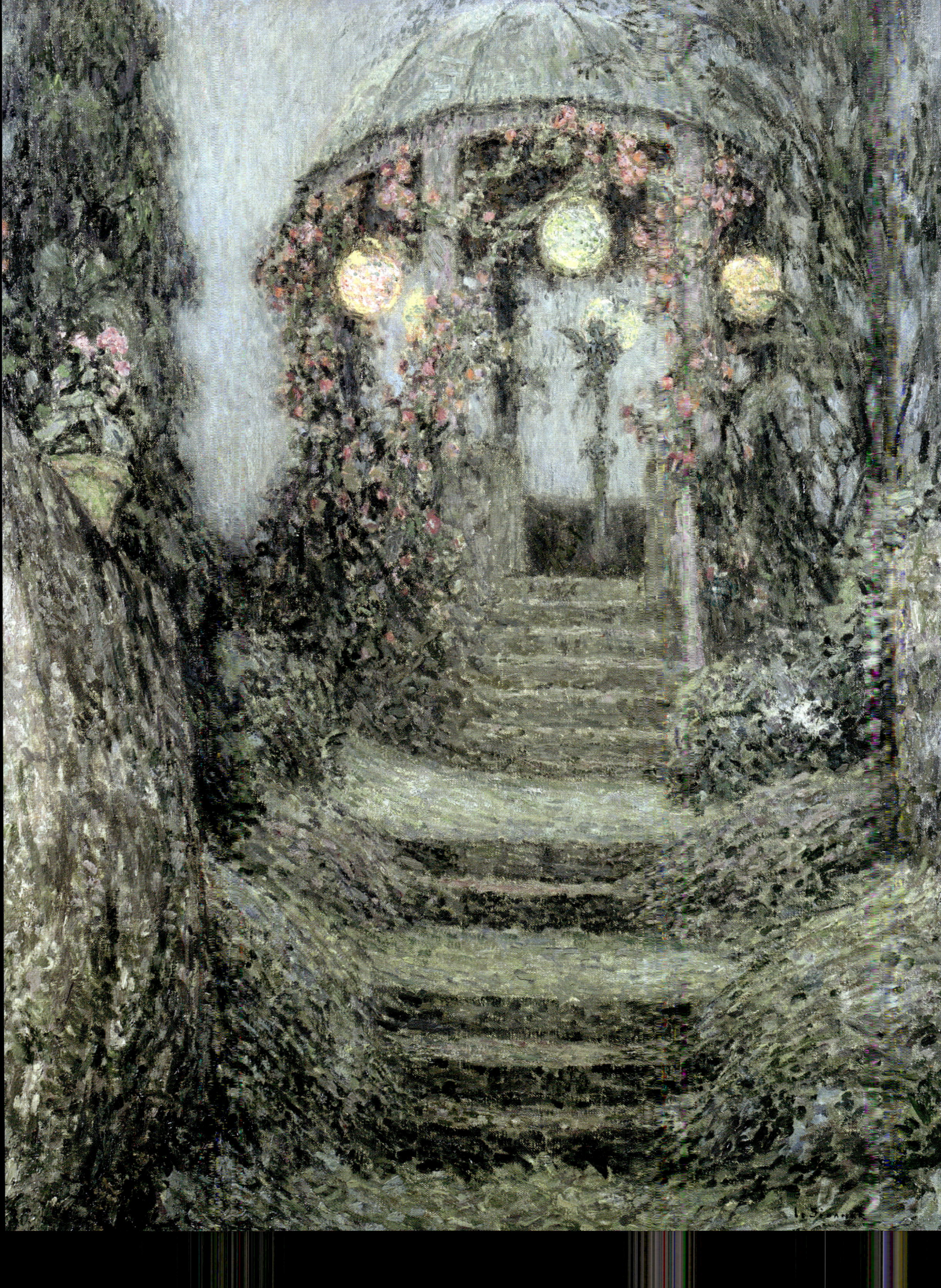

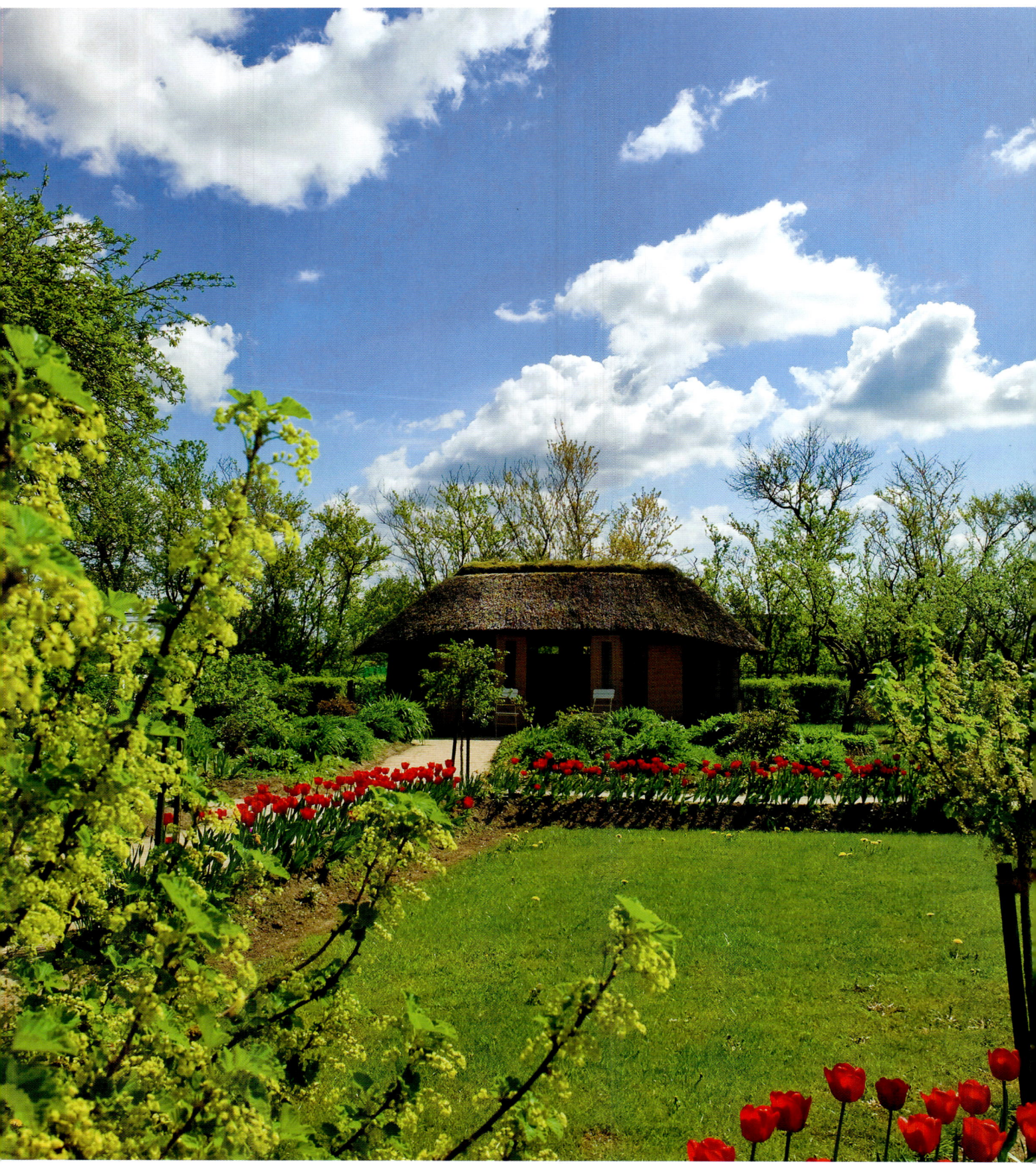

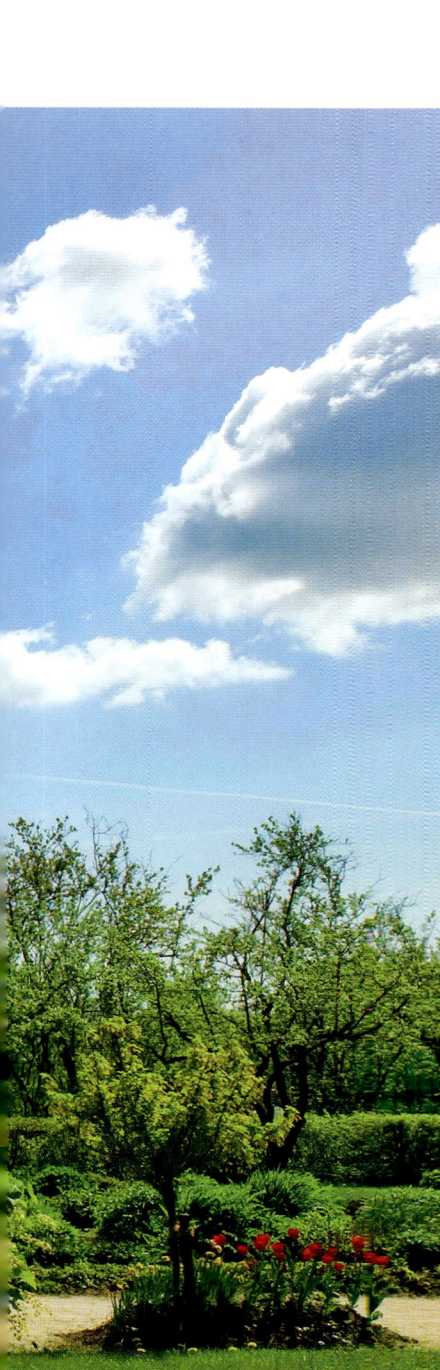

Emil Nolde

Seebüll, Nordfriesland, Germany

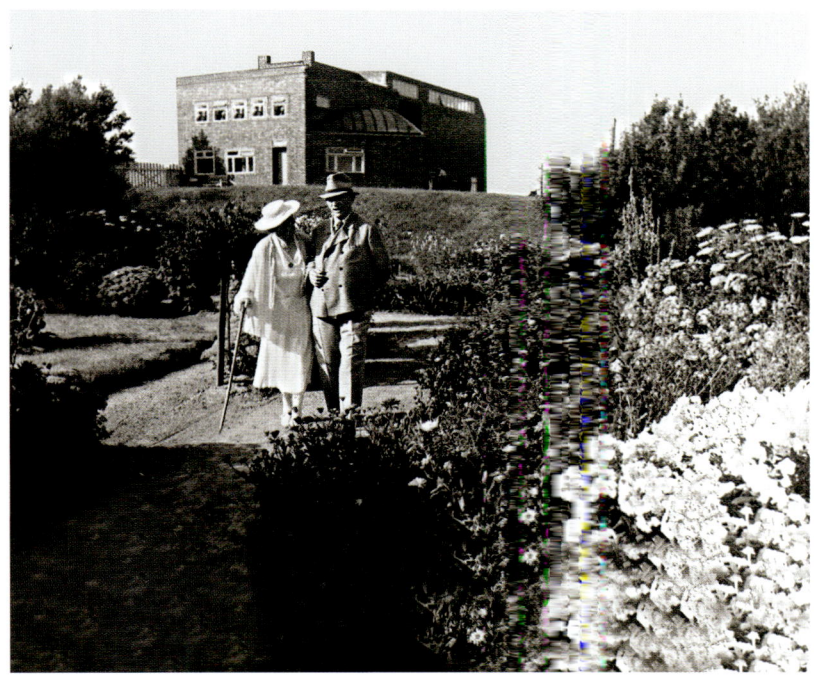

ONE OF THE MOST DARING and dazzling painters of the early twentieth century, Emil Nolde was a leading light in the German Expressionist movement, and experimented with a wide range of different subjects, from controversial Biblical scenes to seascapes, landscapes and vibrant flowers. He lived through the turmoil of the Nazi period and from 1927 made his summer home at Seebüll on the German/Danish border, staying there full-time from 1941. It was his final wish that people would see the house and garden he had created on the marshy land close to the coast, and find the peace and artistic renewal that he had experienced there.

Born Emil Hansen in the village of Nolde in Schleswig-Holstein, the artist's father wanted him to work on the family farm, but young Emil had other ideas and went to train as a woodcarver instead. By 1892 he had taken a job as a technical drawing teacher in Switzerland and published a successful series of postcard cartoons – work that gave him the financial independence to follow his heart and become a painter. In 1901, he spent the summer in the fishing

ABOVE Ada and Emil Nolde in 1941 in the garden they made at Seebüll.
LEFT Emil Nolde designed a garden around his new house, which he built in 1927 on the German/Danish border. It included this thatched garden house, known as 'Little Seebüll'.

Emil Nolde
(1867–1956)

Emile Nolde was the son of a farmer but made his own way in the world of art. Trained as a woodcarver, he went on to become one of the most celebrated Expressionist painters of his day. In the summer of 1926, he and his wife Ada discovered Seebüll, a marshy landscape close to the coast on the Germany/Danish border. The following year, the couple began building a house in a modernist style, designed to make a statement in this northerly landscape of water meadows and uninterrupted skies. The garden they created in front of the house was neat and formal, and filled with a succession of seasonal flowers that provided material for many of Nolde's colourful paintings. During his time at Seebüll, the artist produced thousands of oils and watercolours, including many of the flower garden he had designed.

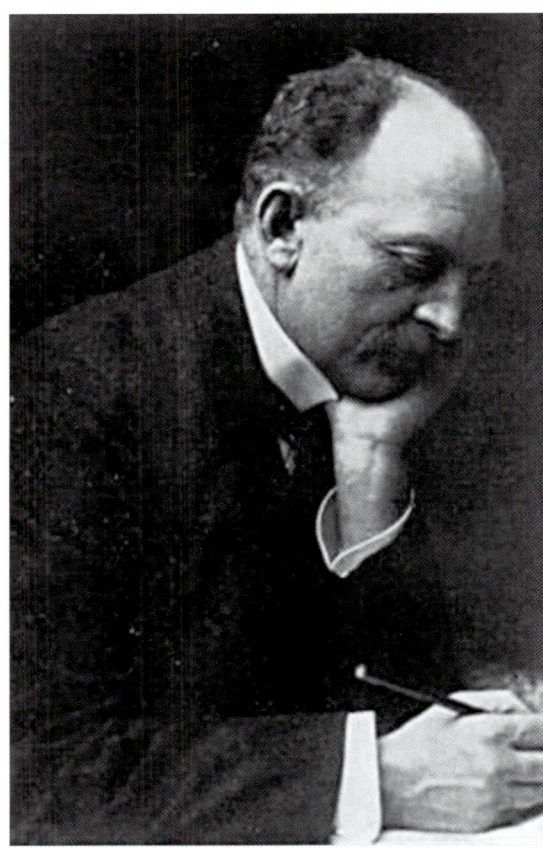

Emil Nolde in 1909.

village of Lild Strand in northern Jutland and there he met the twenty-two-year-old Danish actress, Ada Vilstrup. The couple began courting and were married the following year just outside Copenhagen. Shortly afterwards Emil and Ada Hansen changed their surname to that of Emil's birthplace – Nolde – linking him ever closer to his native landscape.

The Noldes found they could live cheaply on the island of Alsen (now Als) in the Baltic Sea, and in 1903 they rented a thatched fisherman's cottage there, where Emil built a rudimentary studio from wooden planks jutting out into the water. The sea seems to have inspired the way in which Nolde was able to connect with colour. He describes how he 'went back to grey' to discover its nuances in the landscapes and seascapes he was painting during this period, renewing his confidence in his use of colour.

Over the following seven years, Nolde emerged as the leading painter of Expressionist art, his work becoming increasingly colourful and thought-provoking. He was also, briefly, a member of two influential artists' groups of the time: the Dresden-based *Die Brücke* (The Bridge) in 1906, and a less happy period with the Berlin Secession, led by Max Liebermann (see page 64) which turned down one of Nolde's religious paintings, *Pentecost* (1908).

GARDEN OBSESSIONS

Nolde always felt most at home when close to the North Sea and the Baltic coastal landscapes of Jutland. As well as painting seascapes he became obsessed with gardens as a new subject matter for his work, using them to experiment with and discover a range of different styles. In his memoirs, he ascribes the germ of his garden paintings to an exact time and place: the summer of 1906, on the island of Alsen. He talks about how he was magnetically drawn to the bright red of the roses and subsequently painted more and more flowers, always seeking their depth of colour.

He painted his own cottage, which was situated at the edge of a beech wood and had a small flower garden, in *Man under Trees* (1904) and *Roses in Front of the House* (1907). He then went on to paint the gardens of his neighbours, becoming increasingly bolder in his use of

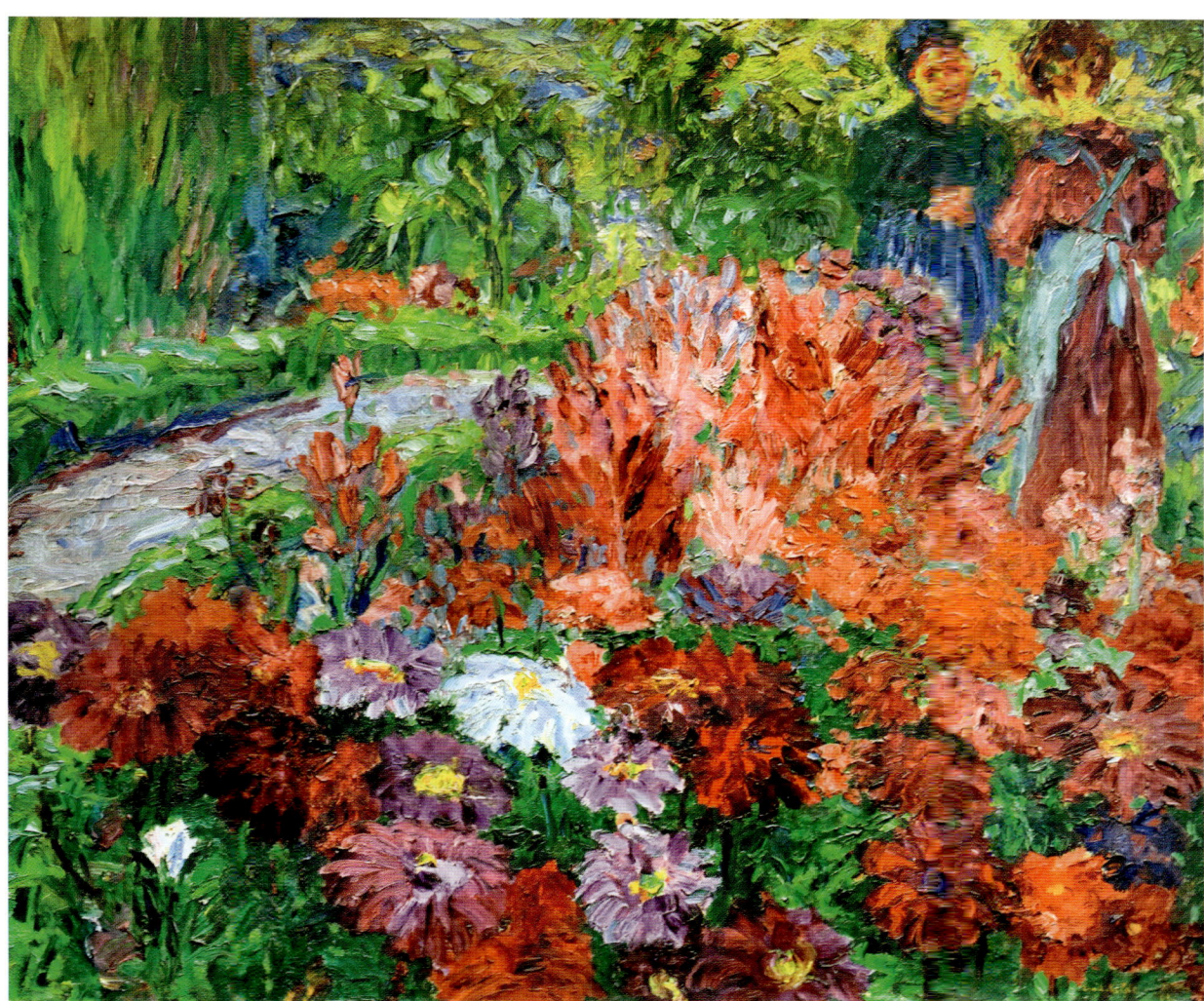

colours and experimental techniques, as seen in *Young Woman* (1907) and *Conversation in the Garden* (1908), in which he depicts his subjects among vibrant flowers.

In 1916, Emil and Ada were able to buy their own home on the western coast at Utenwarf. They bought a farmhouse which came with a mature, south-facing garden, where the couple made a pond and planted flower borders. They filled the garden with many colourful plants, including lilies, peonies, irises and roses. On his return from trips to Berlin or Copenhagen, Nolde describes how the glowing colours of the flowers welcomed him home. During this period he made a whole series of studies in chalk of his poppies, sunflowers, irises, lilies and crown imperials.

THE HOUSE AT SEEBÜLL

In 1920, the northern part of Nolde's homeland of Schleswig-Holstein became part of Denmark, while the south remained in Germany. Utenwarf was on the Danish side of the new border and when landscape drainage schemes threatened their home, Emil and Ada decided to look for a new place to live. In 1926, they discovered a grassy knoll or *terp* in the otherwise uninterrupted landscape of Nordfriesland. *Terps* were ancient, man-

ABOVE *Flower Garden* (1908). From the summer of 1906 onwards, Nolde began to find his inspiration in gardens, sparking a passion for flower colour that would strengthen as the years passed.

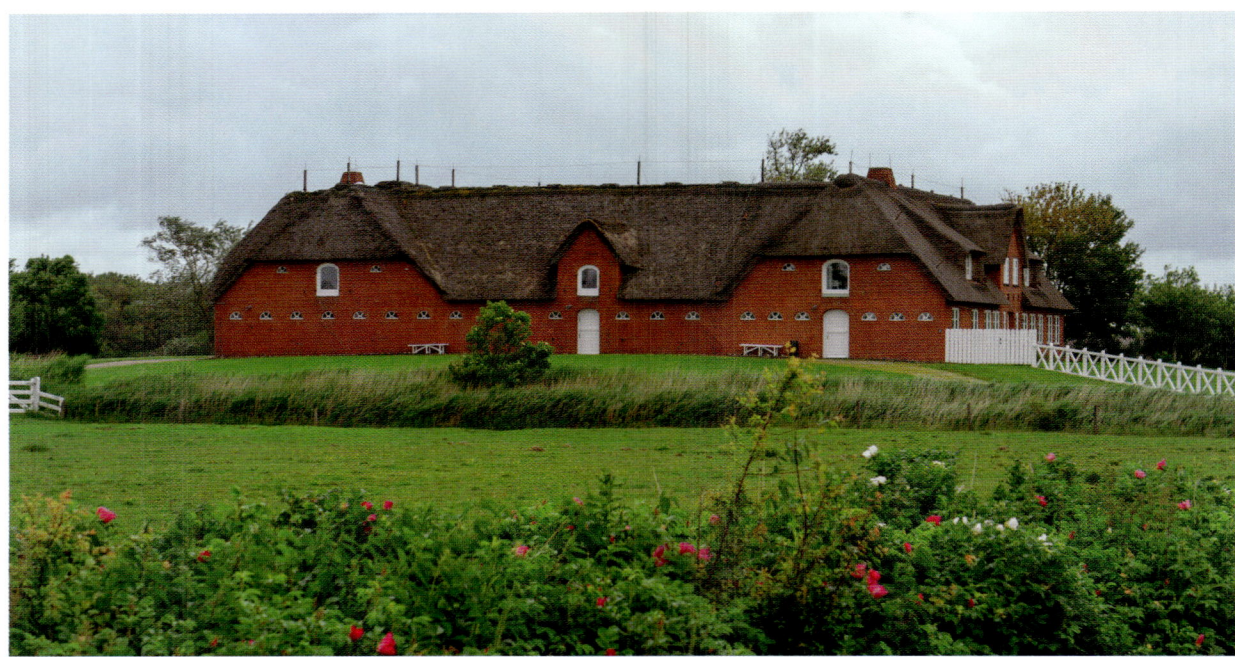

made mounds used as safe dwelling places in Friesland and other parts of northern Europe that were prone to flooding. In his autobiography, Nolde claimed that he and Ada looked at one another in total agreement and said, 'this is our place'.

They chose the site because it gave expansive views over the undrained, marshy landscape, which was still in its natural state. They began building a modern house on top of the knoll, using distinctive red bricks from Bockhorn, and named it 'Seebüll'. The layout followed the path of the sun, with a bedroom in the east for the morning light and the living room in the west catching the evening rays. Although stark from the outside, the house interior was colourful, with painted walls covered in woven textiles made by Ada.

By the time the Noldes settled at Seebüll, they were already experienced garden-makers. On Alsen Island and at Utenwarf Nolde had adapted the gardens with his own planting schemes, but at Seebüll he relished the chance of laying out a brand-new garden exactly to his own design. However, the plot had little to commend it. In essence, it was a badly drained field, with an oval-shaped pond beneath the mound, which had been used for watering

cattle. The wet clay soil had to be made usable by adding tons of sand. At first, Nolde despaired of what he should make of it, but then, while working on his sketchbook, he drew his and Ada's initials, A & E, subtly entwined. Suddenly, he saw the design unfold and planned a curved hawthorn hedge enclosing a secret flower garden, the beds following the outline of the letters A & E – a design that was not obvious on the ground, but something that Ada and Nolde enjoyed keeping as a secret between themselves.

Nolde laid out the paths using stakes and supervised the planting of shrubs and trees, often moving them around himself until he was satisfied with their positions. Reed fences were put up to protect the plot from the wind until the hedges gained height, and the planting was brightly coloured and designed with flowers to paint from summer through until autumn.

Today, the gardens at Seebüll are little changed, having been carefully tended for the past half a century or more as the Noldes would have done. The flower garden, with its small oval pool and simple water jet, is full of rich reds, golds, purples and yellows, while the thatched garden house, known as Little Seebüll, where the couple loved to sit and look at the garden, is painted ochre yellow.

THE GARDEN AT SEEBÜLL

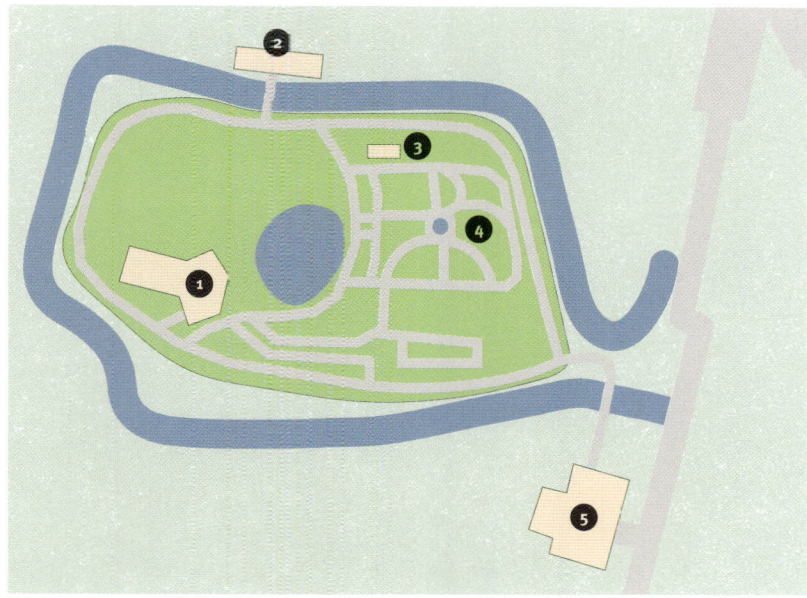

FAR LEFT In 1926, Emil Nolde purchased the thatched farmhouse, Seebüll Hof, and lived there with his wife, Ada, while their new house was being built.

BELOW The Noldes chose Seebüll because of its wild and marshy landscape, building their new house on a mound and laying out the garden below the old cattle pond.

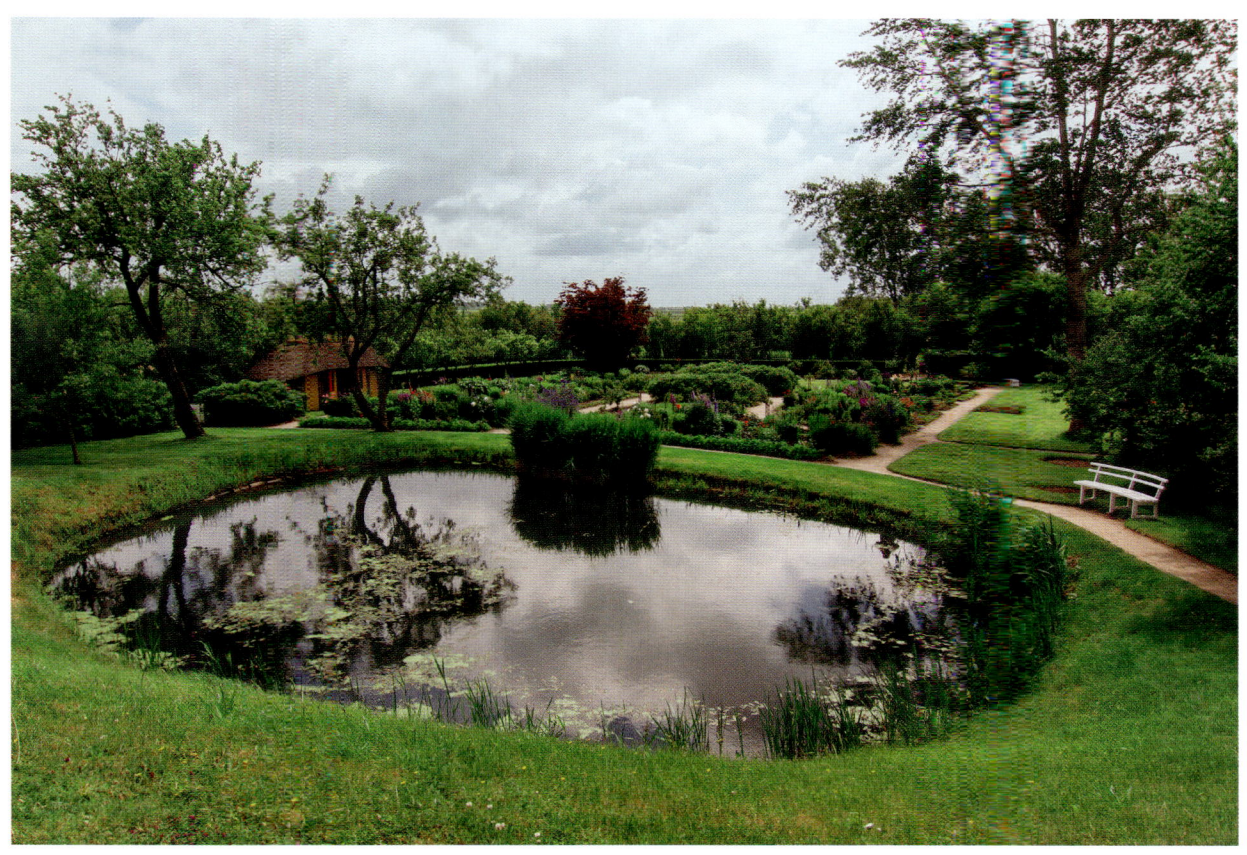

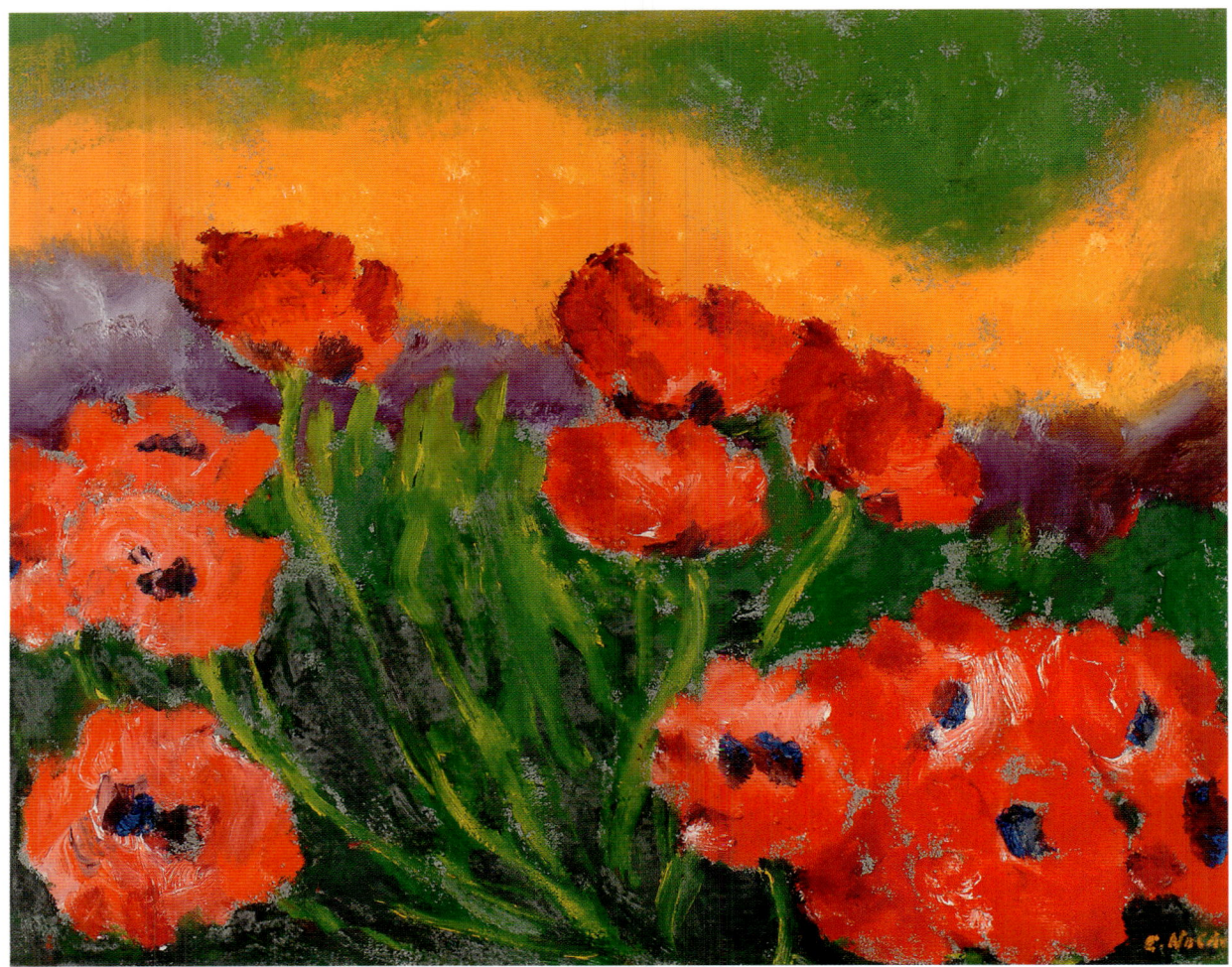

ABOVE *Poppies* (1950) is typical of Nolde's later work, and sets the saturated colour of the flowers against glowing skies.

RIGHT, CLOCKWISE FROM TOP LEFT The flowers in Nolde's garden include bi-coloured lupins; foxgloves, daylilies and achilleas adorn the garden today; Nolde loved to paint bright oriental poppies; red poppies create highlights in front of the thatched garden house; the pompon *Dahlia* 'Moor Place'; *Geranium magnificum;* pot marigold (*Calendula officinalis*).

The hawthorn hedges in the garden have matured, as have the fruit trees that the couple enjoyed. Quinces, wild plums, damsons and Mirabelle plums have now been supplemented with local apples, such as 'Agathe von Klanxbüll' and a rare variety, 'Renette von Seebüll'.

By 1927, when Nolde was sixty, his studio on the first floor of the Seebüll house was finally completed. It was the first indoor, purpose-built studio he had ever owned. He rarely let anyone, even Ada, into this workspace, believing that an artist's studio should be a haven and never allowed to be 'frivolously defiled'.

FAVOURITE FLOWERS

During Nolde's time at Seebüll, three flower groups dominated his artistic life: dahlias, sunflowers and oriental poppies. These bright blooms all spoke to his love of colour. In spring, bulbs, primulas and globeflowers (*Trollius*) began the cycle of life, followed by a large range of oriental poppies (*Papaver orientale*), known in Germany as the Turkish poppy, planted together with *Verbascum olympicum*, hardy geraniums, peonies and argyranthemums. By late summer, the dahlias and sunflowers (*Helianthus annuus*) provided the biggest impact, alongside pot marigolds (*Calendula officinalis*), love-lies-bleeding (*Amaranthus caudatus*), and strong yellow blocks of the coneflower, *Rudbeckia fulgida*.

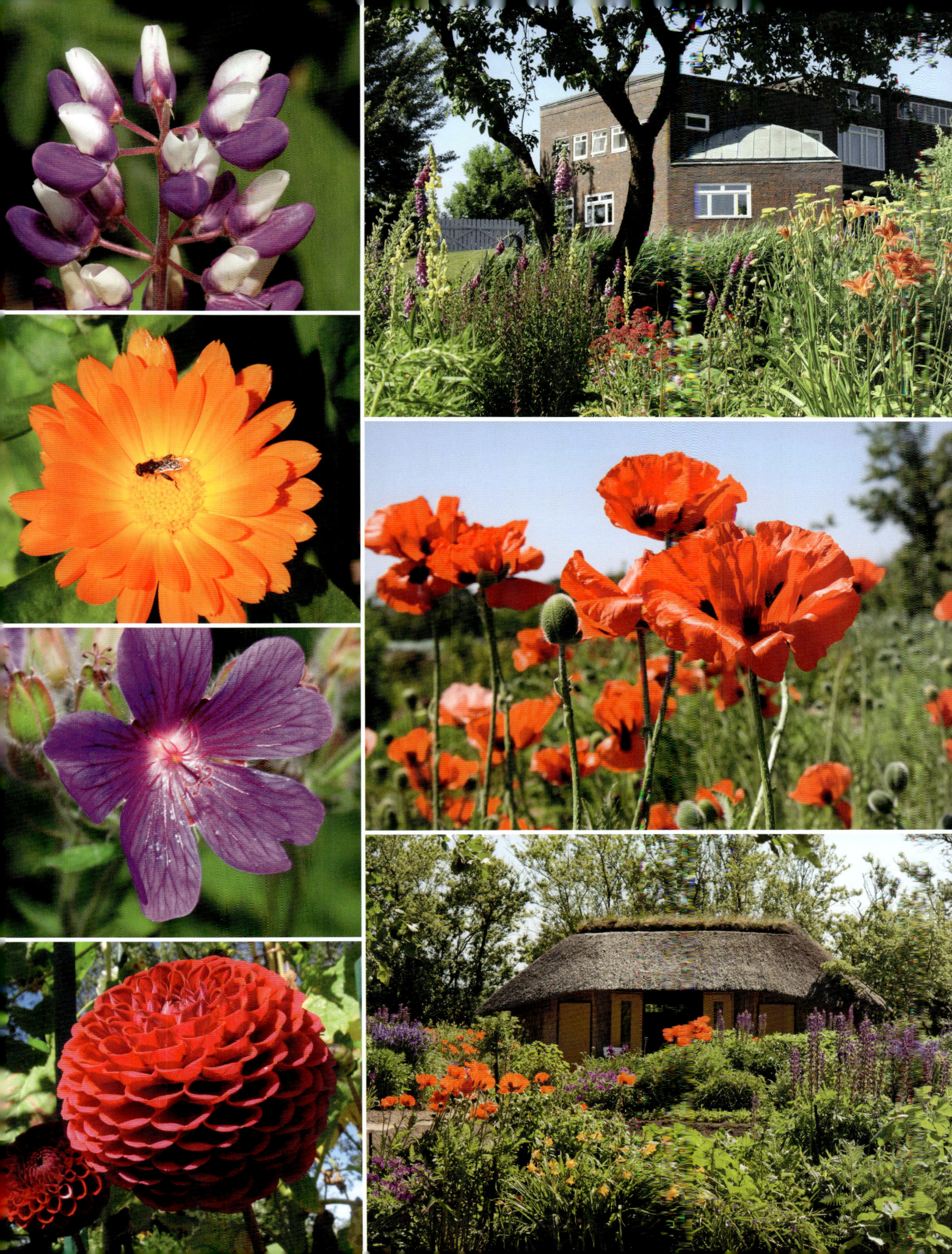

DARK DAYS

Nolde sympathized with Hitler's National Socialists until the end of the Second World War, joining his local branch in 1934 in the belief that his own art could genuinely become an 'art for the people'. In the 1930s, he had been admitted to the Prussian Academy of Arts and in 1932 has taken part in the *Neuere Deutsche Kunst* exhibition in Cologne – the last modern art exhibition to be staged in pre-war Germany. However, in 1937 more than 1,000 of Nolde's works were removed from museums and twenty-nine of his paintings were included in the infamous Degenerate Art exhibition, *Die Ausstellung Entartete Kunst,* in Munich. This was part of a general purge to remove all artworks that the Nazis considered anti-German or 'degenerate'. Hitler's antipathy towards contemporary art forms knew no bounds, and even supporters of the regime were not immune.

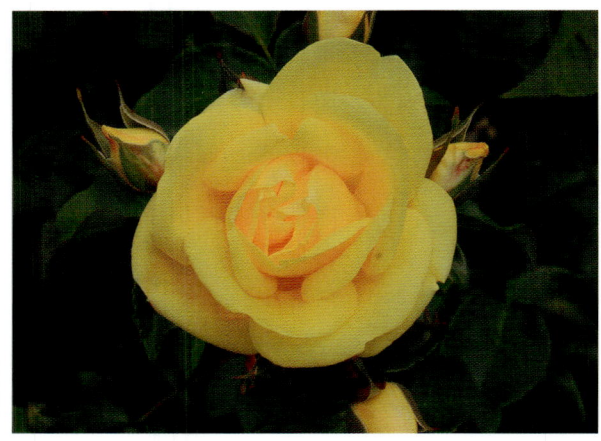

Nevertheless, the Noldes remained in their German home, choosing not to emigrate to either Denmark (they both had Danish citizenship) or Switzerland, and built an air-raid shelter in the garden to protect Nolde's artwork from bombing. He was expelled from the Reich Chamber of Visual Arts in 1941, but continued to paint, producing oils and, as materials became scarce, a large number of small format watercolours.

After the war, Nolde continued to paint in oils until 1951 and worked in watercolours until 1956. After Ada died in 1946, he married twenty-six-year-old Jolanthe Erdmann, with whose help he was able to continue living and working at Seebüll. In his final years, he completed the plans for the *Stiftung Seebüll Ada und Emil Nolde,* which would run the estate after his death and, as they had intended, Ada and then Emil were interred in the garden in the old air-raid shelter among their flowers. Today, the gardens grow the twenty-first-century yellow rose named after the artist, *Rosa* Emil Nolde, surely an accolade this master of colour would have enjoyed.

LEFT *Rosa* Emil Nolde honours the artist's love of flowers and was bred in Germany in the early twenty-first century.
RIGHT The strong colours of red *Lychnis chalcedonica* and yellow verbascums dominate the planting in front of Nolde's modernist house.

NOLDE'S TIMELINE

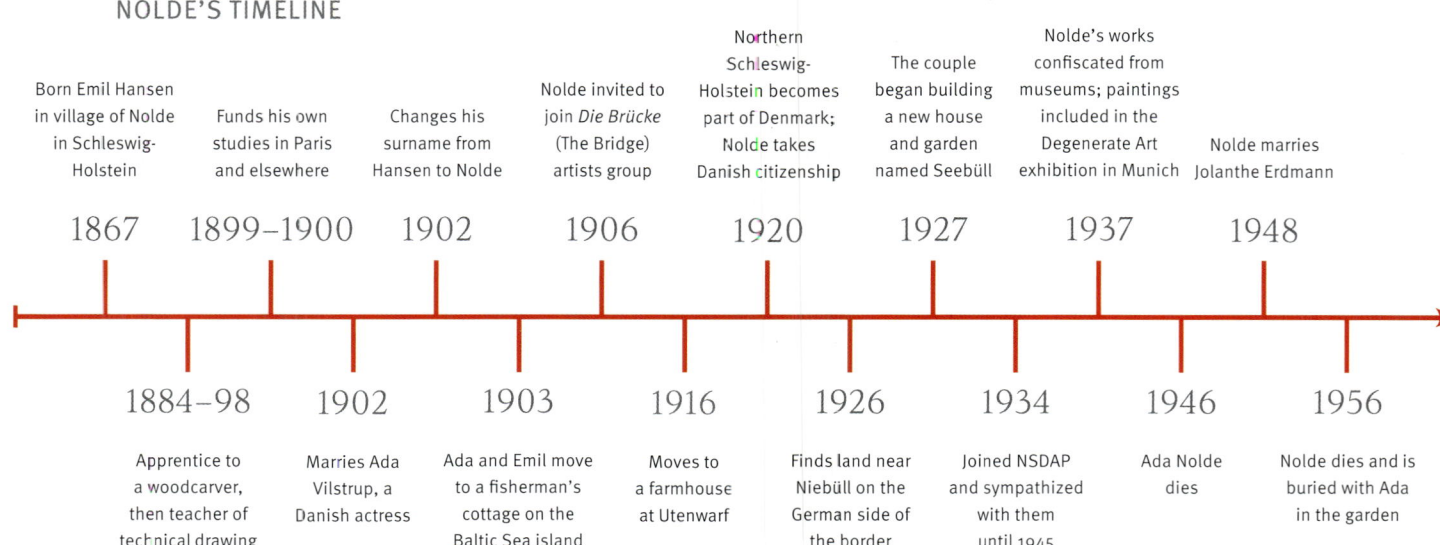

Born Emil Hansen in village of Nolde in Schleswig-Holstein — **1867**

Funds his own studies in Paris and elsewhere — **1899–1900**

Changes his surname from Hansen to Nolde — **1902**

Nolde invited to join *Die Brücke* (The Bridge) artists group — **1906**

Northern Schleswig-Holstein becomes part of Denmark; Nolde takes Danish citizenship — **1920**

The couple began building a new house and garden named Seebüll — **1927**

Nolde's works confiscated from museums; paintings included in the Degenerate Art exhibition in Munich — **1937**

Nolde marries Jolanthe Erdmann — **1948**

1884–98 — Apprentice to a woodcarver, then teacher of technical drawing in Switzerland

1902 — Marries Ada Vilstrup, a Danish actress

1903 — Ada and Emil move to a fisherman's cottage on the Baltic Sea island of Alsen

1916 — Moves to a farmhouse at Utenwarf

1926 — Finds land near Niebüll on the German side of the border

1934 — Joined NSDAP and sympathized with them until 1945

1946 — Ada Nolde dies

1956 — Nolde dies and is buried with Ada in the garden

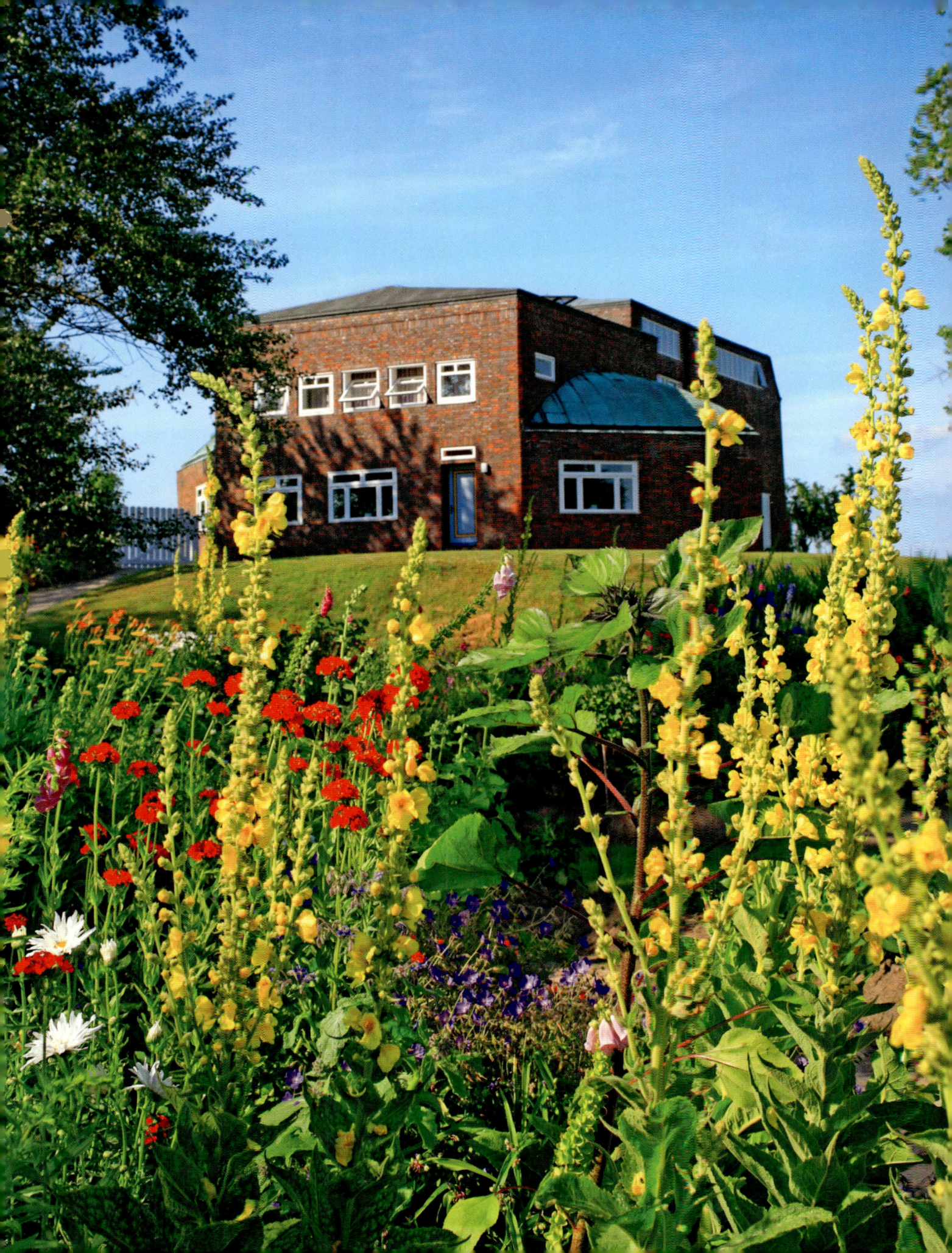

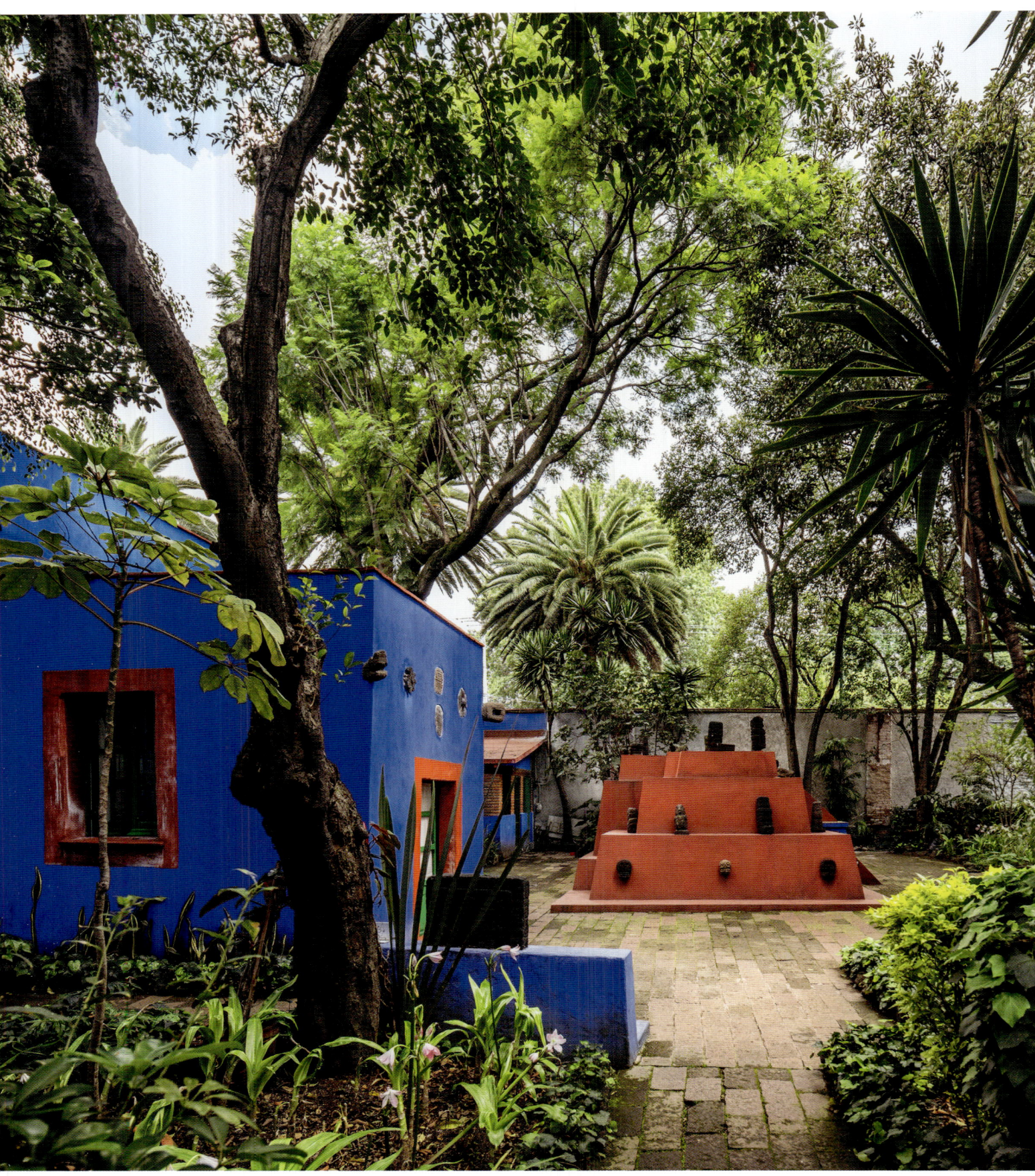

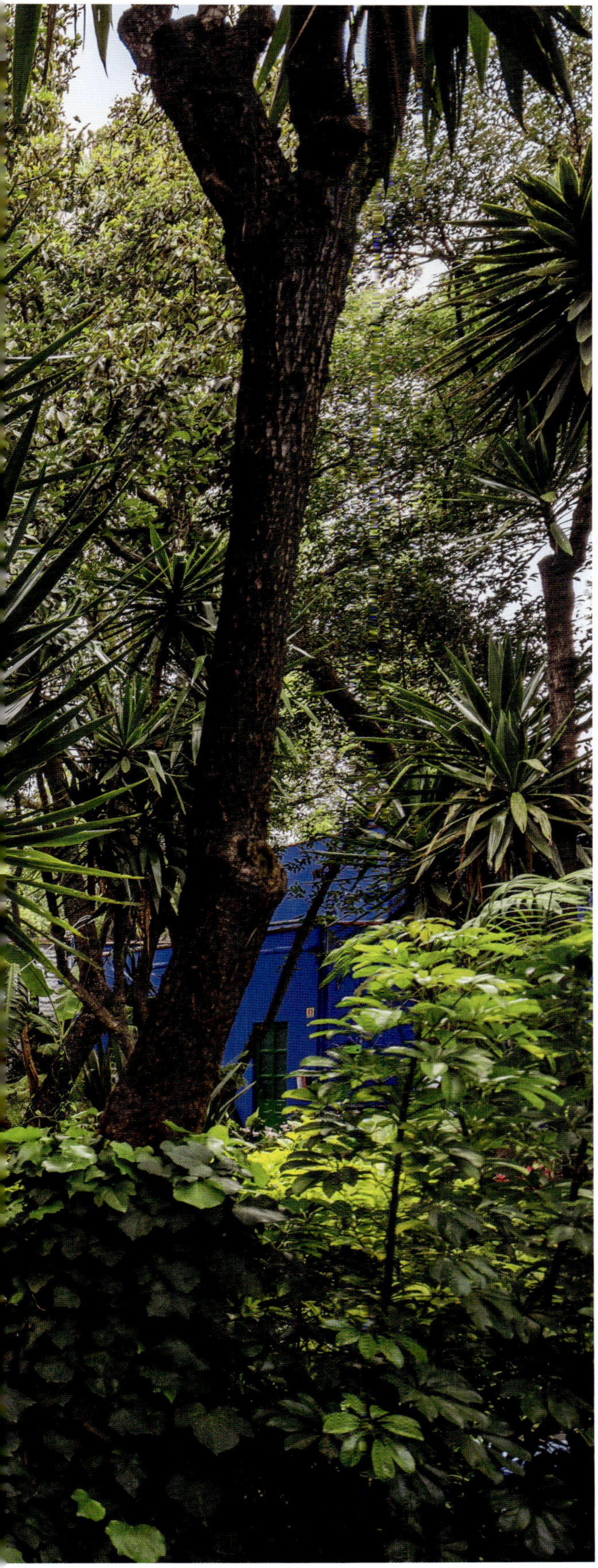

Frida Kahlo

The Blue House, Coyoacán, Mexico

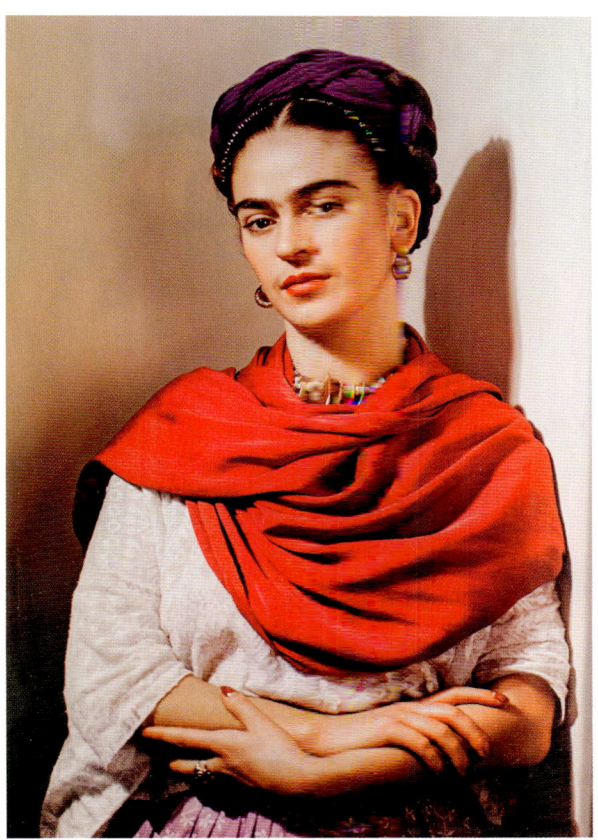

THE WORK OF MEXICAN ARTIST, Frida Kahlo, was overlooked for many years, until the late 1970s when its relevance to feminists and political activists brought it to the attention of a wider international audience. Today, she is celebrated for her autobiographical work, which describes the emotional and physical pain she suffered throughout her adult life. Described as a Surrealist, she made art in her own unique style, using her

ABOVE Frida Kahlo, photographed in 1939 by Hungarian photographer, Nickolas Muray, with whom she had a ten-year relationship.
LEFT The Blue House was not only a sanctuary for Frida Kahlo during her troubled life, but also a refuge for revolutionary Leon Trotsky.

Frida Kahlo
(1907–1954)

The Mexican artist, Frida Kahlo, is renowned for making her life a work of art. Everything she did, particularly after her marriage to Diego Rivera, became noteworthy. Rivera was the more famous artist during their lifetime, but it is Kahlo's work that has received the most attention in the late twentieth and early twenty-first centuries. Her paintings range from conventional watercolours to Surrealist masterpieces and, in life, she was flamboyant, displaying her inner self through her choice of clothing, her house and garden, and her collection of folk art. She embraced Mexican post-revolution values and celebrated her multicultural ancestry. Living through, and being part of, intense political turmoil, Kahlo always put herself in the middle of the action, rather than remaining on the sidelines. During her lifetime she created around 200 works of art.

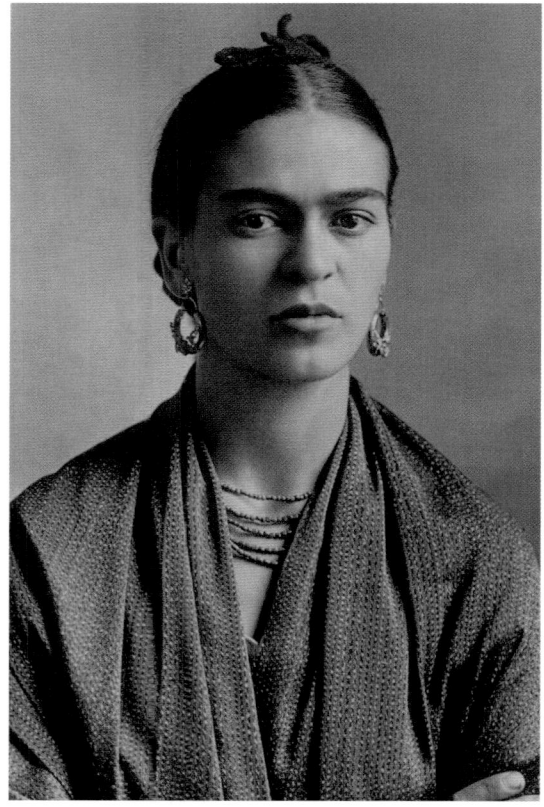

Frida Kahlo, photographed in 1932 by her father, Guillermo Kahlo.

home and garden in Coyoacán, now a suburb of Mexico City, both as three-dimensional artworks and as the subjects for her paintings.

THE BLUE HOUSE

Frida Kahlo's house in Coyoacán, where she was born and where she died, offers a lasting legacy of her life and work. Known as The Blue House, to say it was no ordinary home is certainly an understatement. Kahlo decorated the brightly painted walls with religious and Mexican folk art and, in the garden, spider monkeys, parrots, and a young pet deer vied with dogs and cats for the attention of Kahlo and her husband, the artist Diego Rivera. It was a house that saw physical tragedy, emotional heartbreak and political turmoil, but in later years, it was also filled with the laughter of friends and an abundance of flowers, collected from the garden Kahlo and Rivera made there.

When Frida Kahlo's story began at the beginning of the twentieth century, Coyoacán was a small rural town, named centuries before by the pre-Columbian peoples, the *Colhuas*, as 'the place of the coyotes'. Kahlo's parents bought a plot of land to build a house there in 1904, and were early settlers in what was a new neighbourhood with good links to Mexico City. Her German-born father, Guillermo Kahlo, had arrived in Mexico in 1890 to work in the fashion jewellery business, and later became a noted photographer. Frida was born three years after Guillermo moved to Coyoacán with his second wife, Matilde, and the artist had two older half-sisters born to his first wife, María Cardena, who had died in 1897. The family all lived together in the city at what would later become known as La Casa Azul, The Blue House.

The Kahlos' house was on a 1,200 square-metre/12,917-square-foot plot, close to the town square. It was built to a Mexican design often used for the properties of the middle classes in the pre-revolution period: single-story, laid out in a U-shape around a courtyard, with an orange tree in the middle. Privet trees were planted close to the exterior to shade the long windows and a high wall separated the property from its neighbours. The house had four bedrooms and the all-important *patio*, with a surrounding low wall, which over the years became adorned with traditional terracotta pots and indigenous Mexican plants.

THE BIRTH OF AN ARTIST

Some of Frida Kahlo's earliest memories would have been of the turbulent political events taking place in Mexico, initiated by the uprising against President Diaz that began on 20 November 1910, and politics was to play a significant part in her life. She was also influenced by her father's profession. Kahlo used to accompany him to his studio, where he taught her how to capture images and to develop and re-touch photographs. She watched as he experimented with his photographic self-portraits, sowing the seeds for her own brand of autobiographical art.

At the age of fifteen, while enrolled at the prestigious National Preparatory School in Mexico City, Kahlo was planning to become a doctor – she had already shown an aptitude for biology, especially anatomy and botany. It was at school that she also first saw the charismatic thirty-six-year-old Diego Rivera, who had been commissioned to paint a mural in the school's theatre. Recently returned from Europe and a new member of the Communist Party, he fascinated Kahlo, who watched him as he worked on the mural, *Creation*.

But fate was about to intervene. In September 1925, Kahlo suffered an horrific accident when the bus she was travelling in was crushed by a trolley car. Several people died and Kahlo's injuries were extensive – she was impaled by a metal handrail and spent many months in hospital recovering. When she was well enough, she was moved back to her home where, bored and still in severe pain, her parents encouraged her to start painting – using a mirror, she went on to produce self-portraits from her bed. Kahlo never returned to school after the accident. Her spine and pelvis had been so badly damaged in the crash that she would have to endure many years of painful operations and never fully recovered from her injuries.

Kahlo started to paint watercolours of scenes in her home town and portraits of herself, family and friends. During this time, she also sought out a radical, intellectual group of people and in 1928 she joined the Communist Party. A close friend, the communist Italian photographer Tina Modotti, also reintroduced her to Diego Rivera. Now separated from his wife, Rivera and Kahlo began a relationship. She wanted to become better known as an artist and he encouraged her to keep painting and to find her own direction.

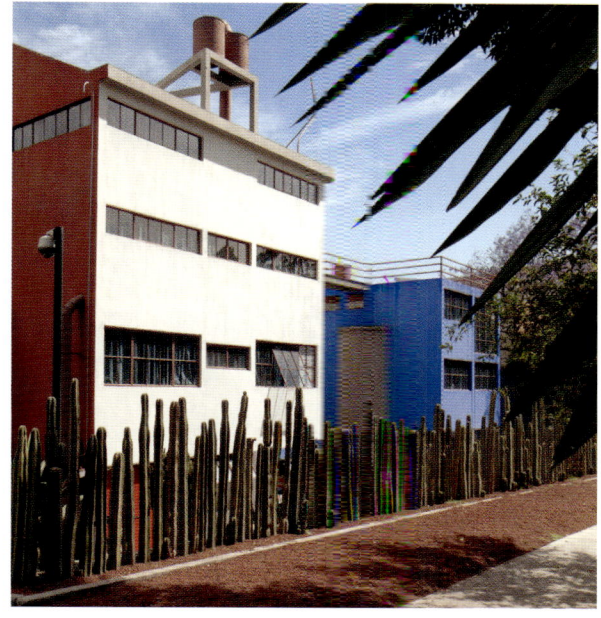

TRAVELS ABROAD

Kahlo and Rivera married in August 1929 in the town hall at Coyoacán close to her home. She wore traditional Mexican costume, a way of dressing that she would embrace for the rest of her life. They set up home in Mexico City and Rivera paid the mortgage on the house in Coyoacán to give her parents financial security – in 1930, the property was transferred to Kahlo's name.

The couple spent a year in the United States, staying in New York, San Francisco and Detroit, while Rivera fulfilled his commissions. Kahlo continued with her work, which included an uncharacteristically realistic watercolour of Central Park in New York. They returned in 1933 to live in San Ángel in two interconnected houses and studios that had been designed for them by Juan O'Gorman.

Now heavily involved in radical politics, in 1937 Kahlo offered her home in Coyoacán as a safe house for the Russian revolutionary Leon Trotsky and his wife Natalia Sedova, who were hiding from the Stalinists. She and Rivera fortified the house for them, blocking up the windows that

ABOVE In 1931, Frida and her husband Diego Rivera had interconnected houses at San Ángel in Mexico City, with studios designed for them by the architect Juan O'Gorman.

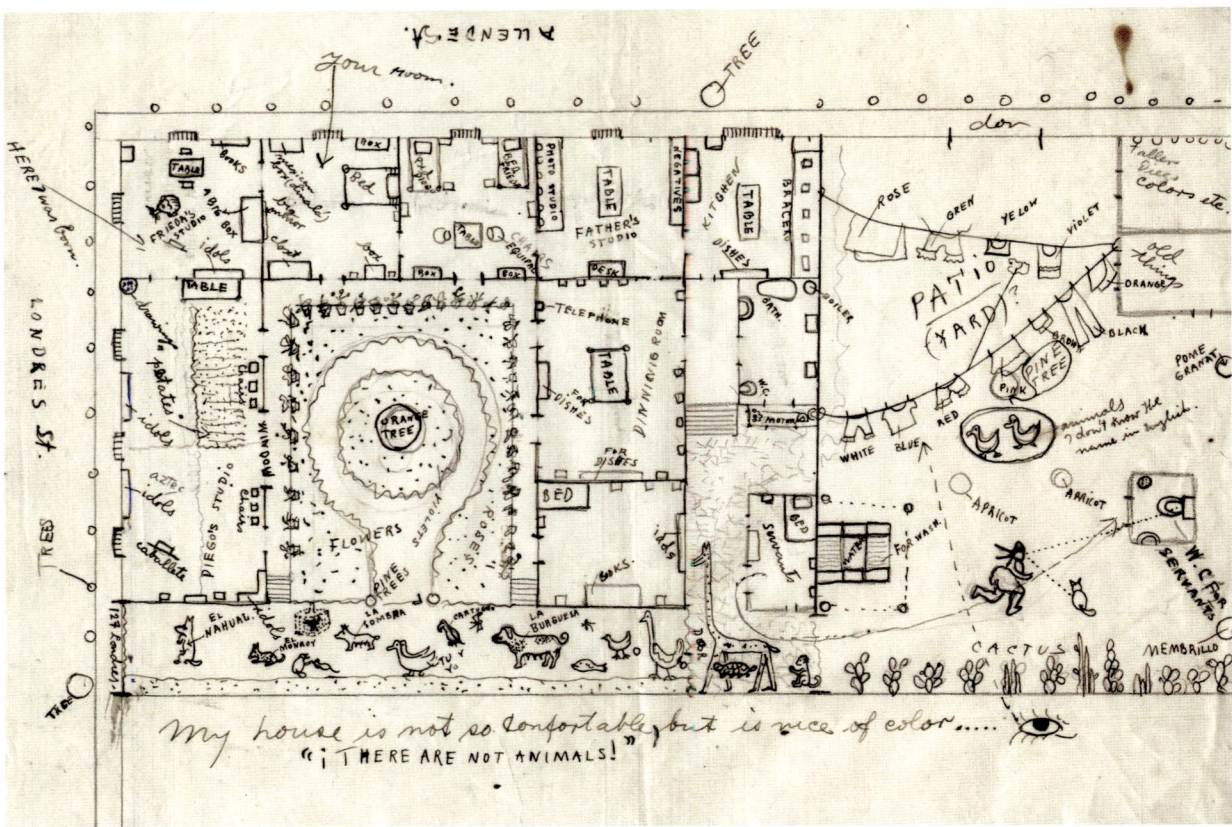

faced the street so that the inner courtyard, with its cacti and succulent plants, became a haven for the beleaguered couple. Rivera bought the plot next door as extra security, so that the garden grew in size from 200 to 1,000 square metres/2,153 to 10,764 square feet. The exterior walls of the new plot were plastered and painted a strong shade of cobalt blue and from then on it was always known as La Casa Azul – The Blue House.

RETURNING HOME

The course of Kahlo and Rivera's marriage never ran smoothly. He had many sexual partners, as did Kahlo, including an affair with Trotsky that lasted six months. The leading proponent of Surrealism, André Breton, admired Kahlo's work and the three couples: the Riveras, the Trotskys and the Bretons, travelled together around Mexico.

In 1938, Kahlo put on a show at the Levy gallery in New York, well known for its Surrealist works. At that time, she was having an affair with the photographer Nickolas Muray, which more or less sealed the fate of her marriage to Rivera and the couple divorced in 1939. She travelled to Paris later that year and the French government bought her painting *The Frame* – the first work by a twentieth-

century Mexican artist in their public art collection. But with war looming, she travelled back to Mexico, where the Trotskys had moved out of The Blue House to another property close by, allowing Kahlo to return to her old home. This period of turmoil in her personal life fired Kahlo's creativity, as she channelled her angst into her art.

Kahlo then went to Los Angeles for a rest cure, and on her return, her doctor encouraged Rivera to take care of her. Subsequently, the couple remarried in December 1940 and agreed it should be a union based on mutual respect for each other as people and as artists.

THE GARDEN REVIVED

Kahlo and Rivera lived at The Blue House, together with Rivera's assistant Emmy Lou Packard, and it was at this time that Kahlo drew a plan of the property to show Emmy Lou where she would be living. The plan was full of details about what the house and garden meant to the artist. Most

ABOVE Frida Kahlo drew this plan of The Blue House and its garden, lovingly detailing all the plants and animals to be found there.
RIGHT Christian symbolism, Mexican folklore, and a love of nature combine in *Self-Portrait with Thorn Necklace and Hummingbird* (1940).

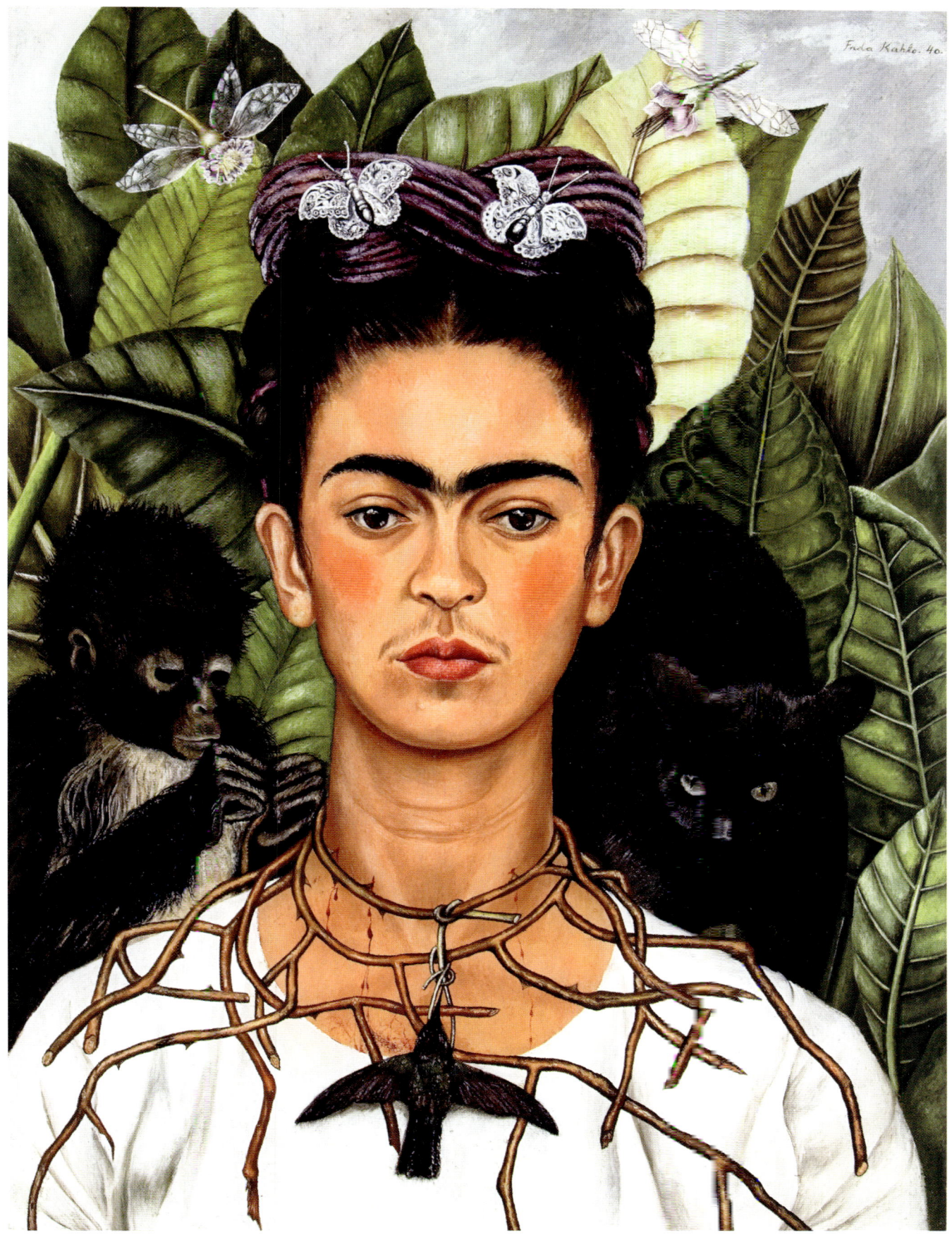

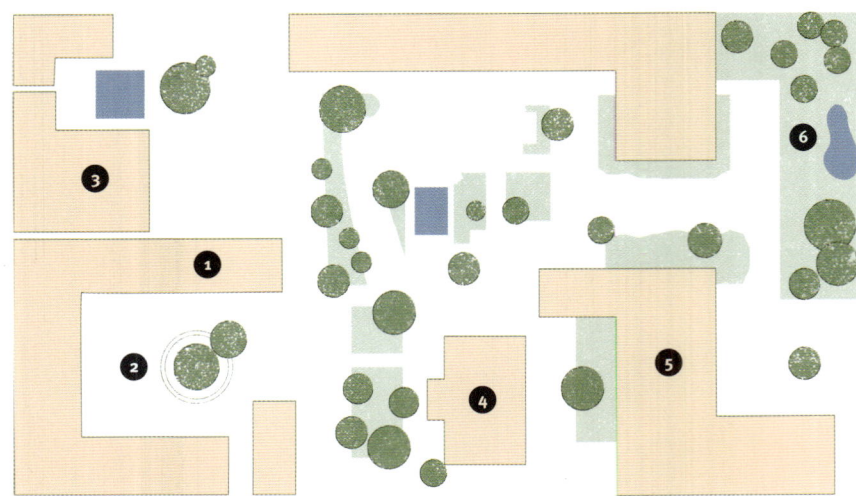

"How we painted the house [at Coyoacán] and the Mexican furniture – all that influenced my painting a lot."
FRIDA KAHLO (1950)

RIGHT, CLOCKWISE FROM TOP LEFT
The Studio extension was designed in 1946 by architect Juan O'Gorman; the strong colours and indigenous plants in the courtyard found their way into many of Kahlo's paintings; the kitchen retains the Mexican utensils used by Kahlo; many of the original trees, including the old pine, marked on Frida's drawing (see page 110) are still alive; the space beneath the studio held more examples of the couple's folk art.

significantly, Kahlo labelled every plant and tree in the courtyard garden, which included roses, violets, a pine, and pomegranate, apricot and quince trees.

The property was all on one level, making it possible for Kahlo to walk around it on crutches and, later, to navigate the garden by wheelchair. She and Rivera spent many hours outside, planning and discussing the placement of their collection of pre-Hispanic art, some of which was displayed on a stepped pyramid. From 1937 onwards, Kahlo used The Blue House garden in many of her paintings: the menagerie of animals, the bougainvillea and passion flowers that clambered up the walls, and the native plants, such as agaves, cacti and yuccas, are all important components of her artworks. Wherever possible, Kahlo also portrayed herself wearing or surrounded by plants and flowers.

In 1946, Rivera bought an additional plot to the east of The Blue House and built what is now known as The Studio, a modern building designed by functionalist architect Juan O'Gorman. This part of the garden was a place for nature, away from the busy courtyard that was always full of people. The plants and artefacts were contained by low walls, made of the local volcanic rock from the lava fields of the Xitle volcano.

THE FARM AT EL PEDREGAL

In 1942, Kahlo decided to buy her own slice of countryside at El Pedregal, south of Coyoacán. Mexico had joined in the Second World War and Rivera and Kahlo thought they could be self-sufficient and become farmers. But Rivera also had other ideas for the cactus-ridden landscape. He bought more land and planned a museum, which he later called Anahuacalli ('House of the valley of Mexico' in Nahuatl language), to display his collection of art. He consulted architect Frank Lloyd Wright and designed the museum together with Juan O'Gorman, planning

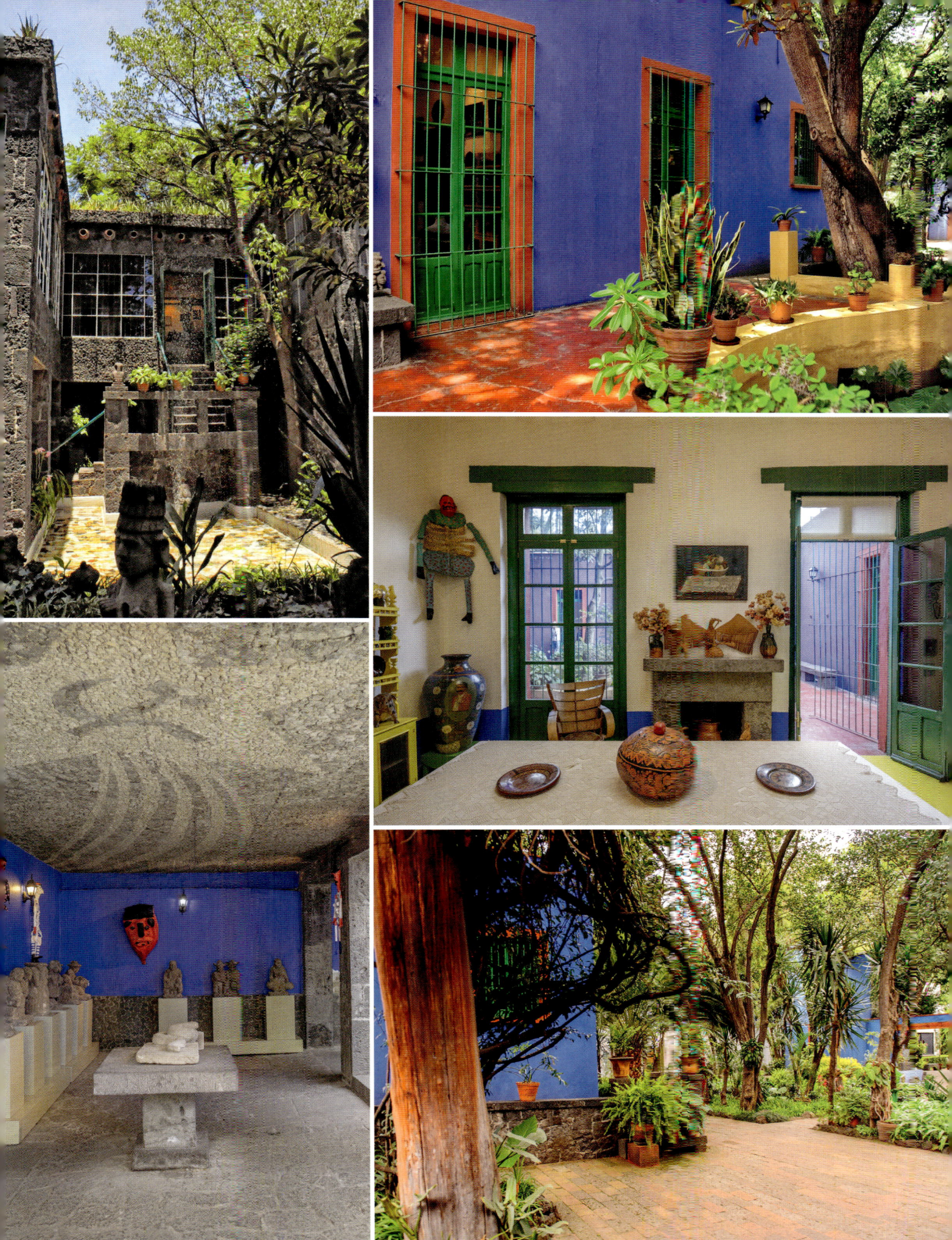

an organic building that would blend with the landscape. The project would absorb him for the next fifteen years and was unfinished at his time of death in 1957.

Kahlo, meanwhile, concentrated on making The Blue House her own creative project, with her trademark use of colour, from the pots of succulents to the orchids hanging from the trees. Her last years were dominated by ill health,

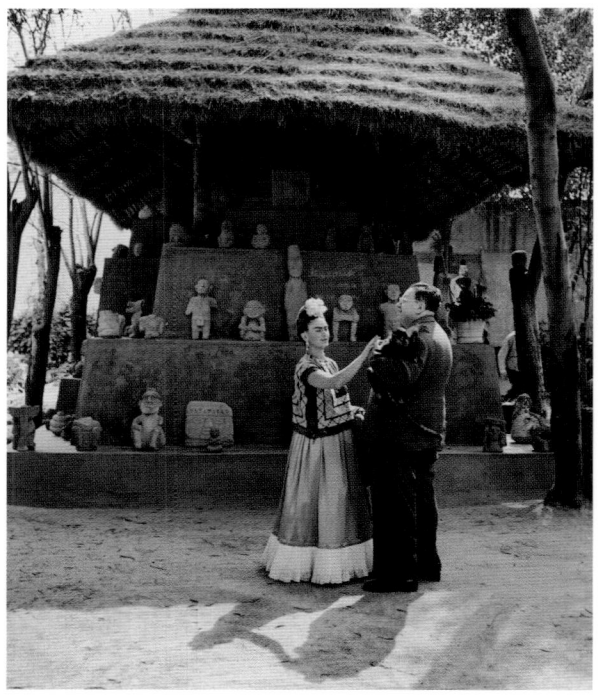

but she continued to receive visitors when well enough. Art students, painters, writers, her sisters, nephew, and niece all came to stay, while the children of the cooks, gardeners, and nurses were encouraged to play in the garden. Despite her pain and her tempestuous relationship with Rivera, it became a happy home and one she wanted to share.

The Blue House garden today is almost as Kahlo and Rivera left it – their artefacts, ornamentation and pre-Hispanic art remain in their original positions. Plants decay and are replaced, of course, but the eclectic nature of the space has been retained; a space dedicated to their shared love of Mexican art, culture and history.

Frida Kahlo's work was not widely appreciated during her lifetime, and her only solo exhibition in Mexico was held in 1953, a year before her death. Since then, her star has risen, and in the twenty-first century she has taken on iconic status in Mexico and around the world. One of Kahlo's still lives held at The Blue House is a colourful depiction of watermelons, which she signed *Viva la vida* (Long live life) shortly before passing away, aged just forty-seven – a demonstration of her insatiable passion for the natural world in the face of almost unbearable agony.

LEFT The artists' sense of theatre extended to the garden, where they displayed Rivera's collection of pre-Hispanic art on a stepped pyramid.
RIGHT The Studio on the upper floor of the extension built by Rivera is filled with Kahlo's artwork and equipment. As her health failed, her work focused on the life-enhancing colours of fruit, flowers and nature.

KAHLO'S TIMELINE

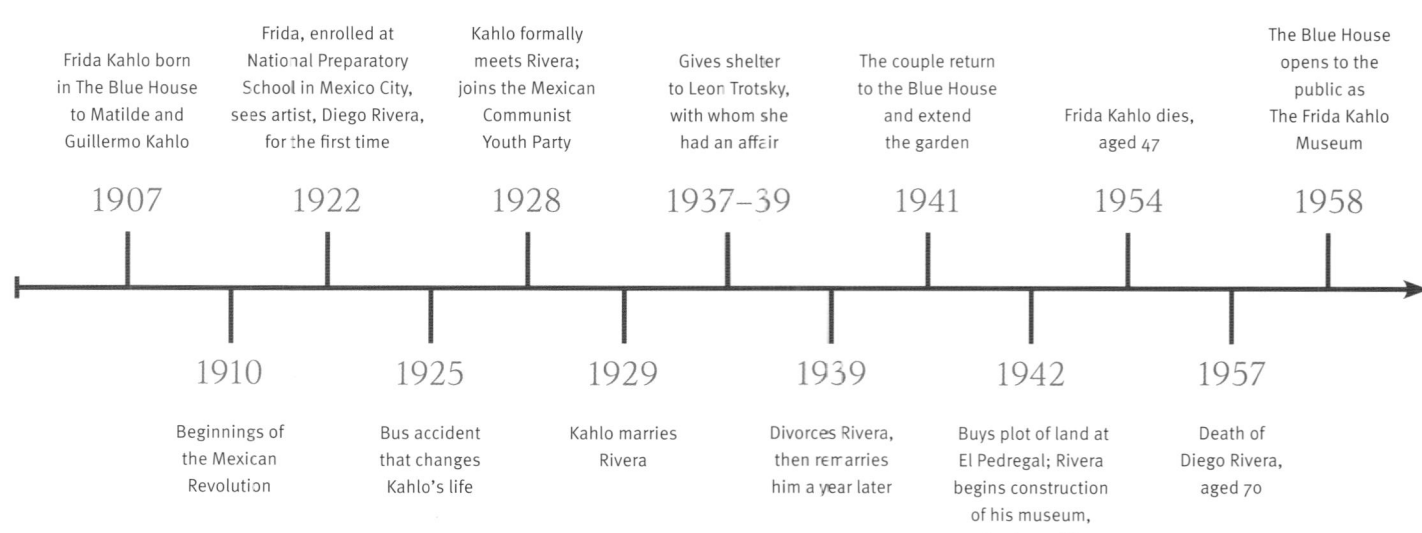

Frida Kahlo born in The Blue House to Matilde and Guillermo Kahlo
1907

Frida, enrolled at National Preparatory School in Mexico City, sees artist, Diego Rivera, for the first time
1922

Kahlo formally meets Rivera; joins the Mexican Communist Youth Party
1928

Gives shelter to Leon Trotsky, with whom she had an affair
1937–39

The couple return to the Blue House and extend the garden
1941

Frida Kahlo dies, aged 47
1954

The Blue House opens to the public as The Frida Kahlo Museum
1958

1910
Beginnings of the Mexican Revolution

1925
Bus accident that changes Kahlo's life

1929
Kahlo marries Rivera

1939
Divorces Rivera, then remarries him a year later

1942
Buys plot of land at El Pedregal; Rivera begins construction of his museum, Anahuacalli

1957
Death of Diego Rivera, aged 70

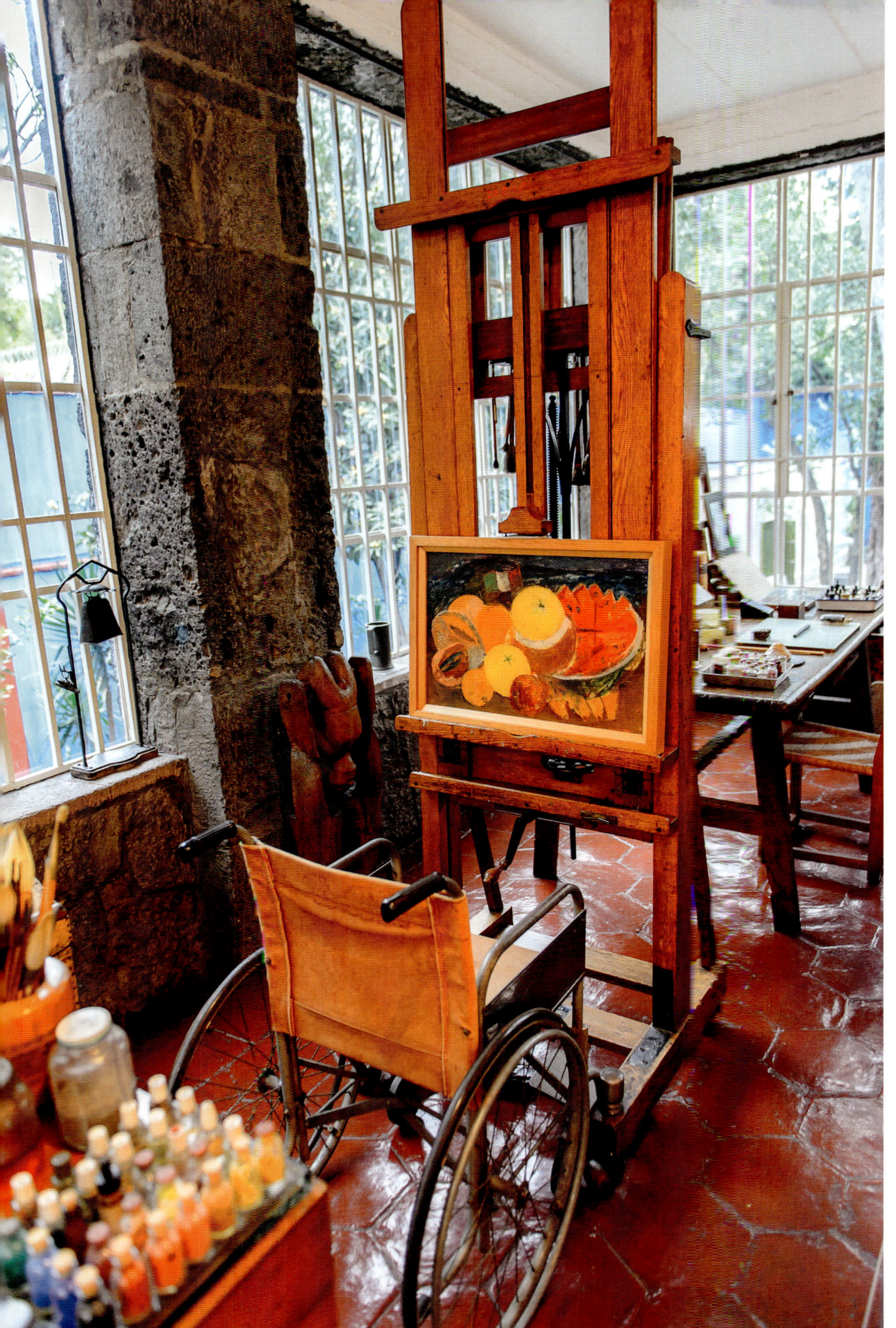

Salvador Dalí

Portlligat and Púbol, Spain

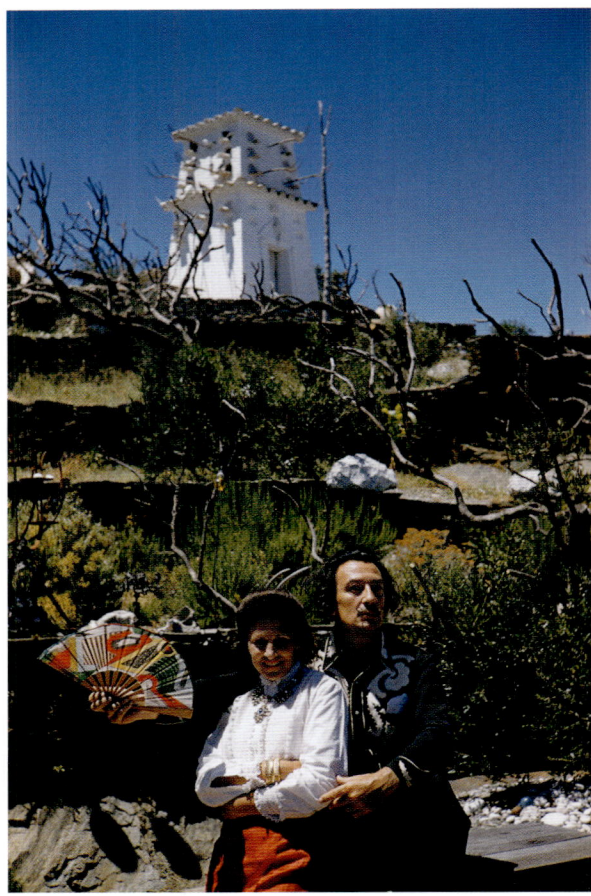

ONE OF THE MOST FAMOUS artistic personalities of all time, Salvador Dalí defies categorization. Sometimes grouped with the Surrealists, a movement he left while in his twenties, he described himself as a 'genius' and there probably is no better epithet for a man whose whole life was an artwork. A sculptor, creator and painter, he shocked, surprised and delighted his audiences in equal measure. In a life

ABOVE Salvador Dalí with his wife Gala below the dovecote and terraces at their home at Portlligat on the north-east coast of Spain. RIGHT Dalí created his house by the sea, little by little, from a collection of traditional fisherman's huts set within an olive grove.

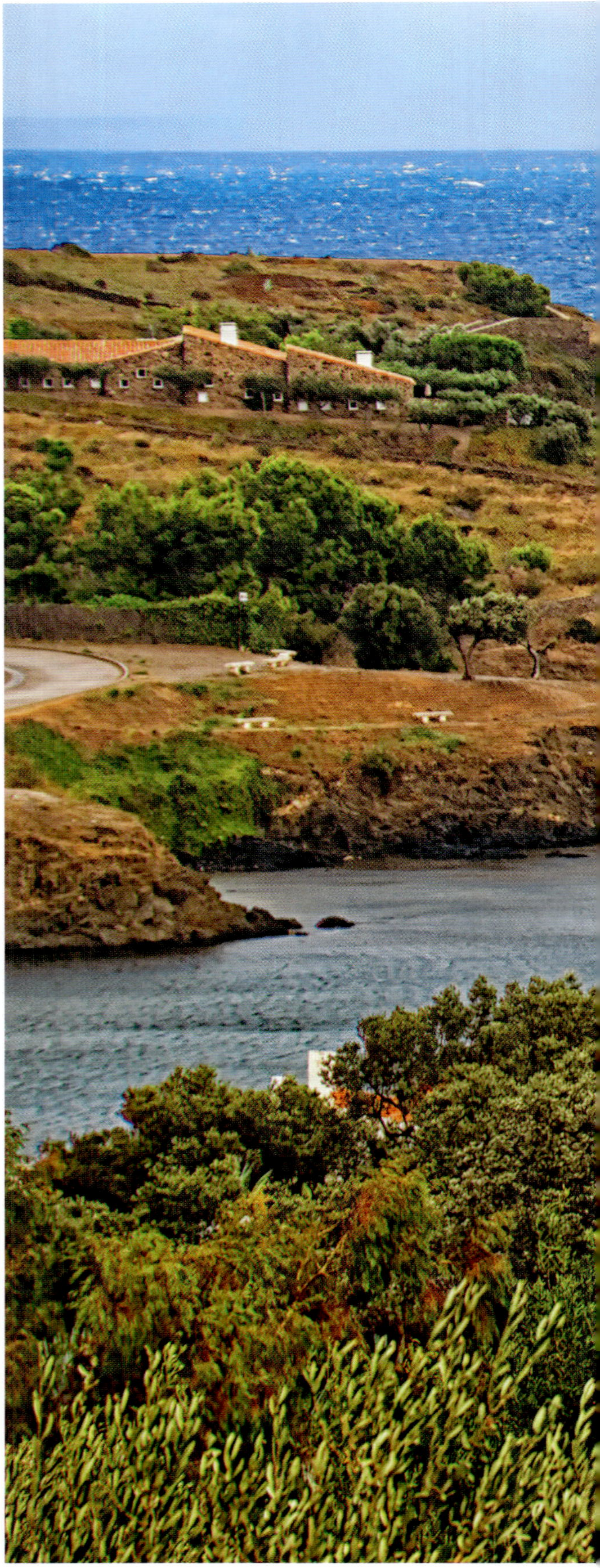

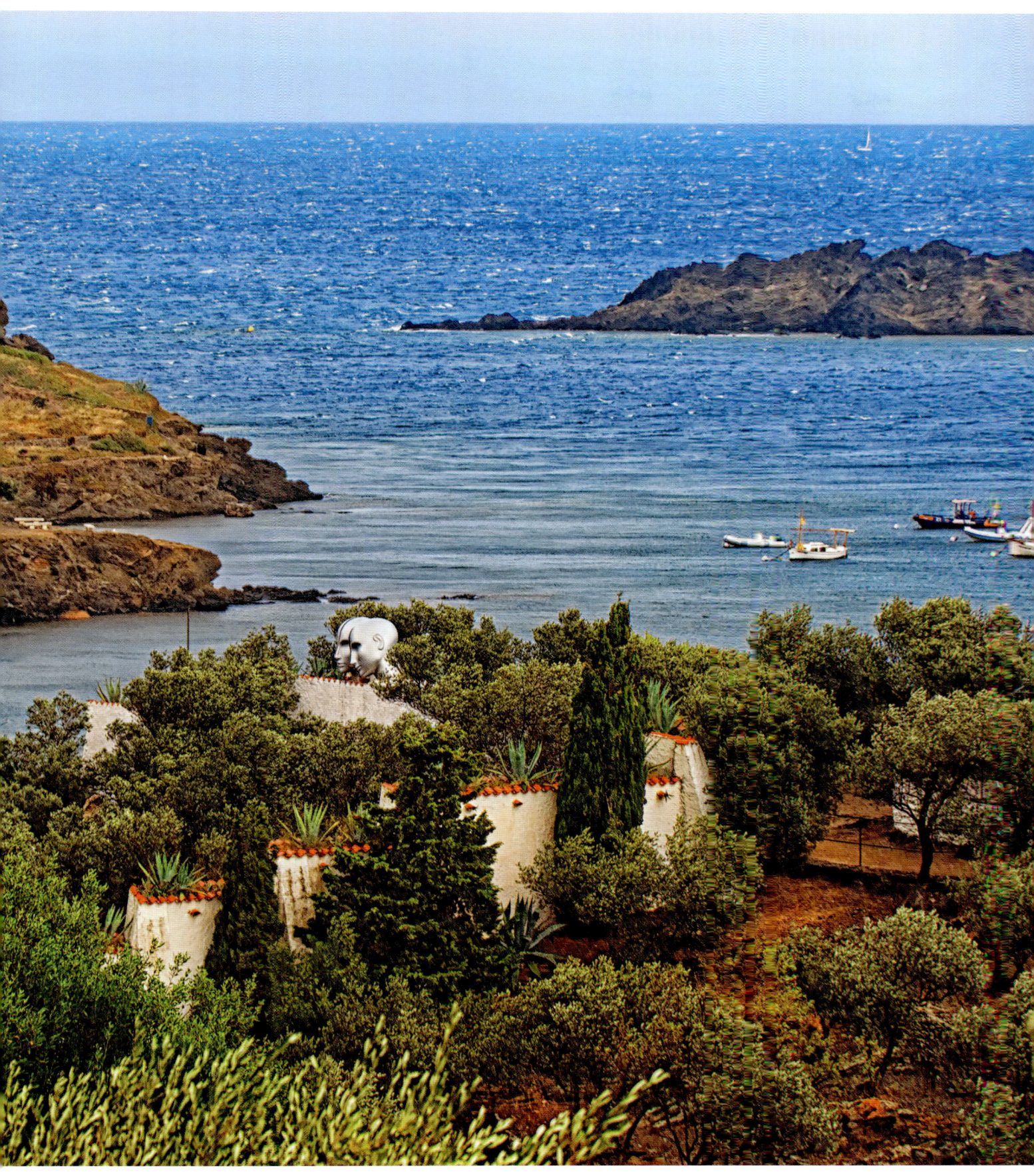

Salvador Dalí
(1904–1989)

Dalí's work spans the Surrealist movement of the 1920s and 1930s to the Pop Art era of the 1960s and 1970s, embracing theatre, film, sculpture and installation art. He studied drawing in Figueres and Madrid and became a painter, but soon his whole life would be a carefully orchestrated artwork. Dalí designed and created his own museum and theatre in his home town of Figueres, which would become his lasting legacy. His home at Portlligat was his private residence for fifty years, while the castle at Púbol, which he renovated for his wife Gala, was a later obsession. He spent his last years at his Theatre and Museum in Figueres, where he was buried in his own mausoleum in 1989 below the stage.

Among the many paintings Dalí produced while living in Catalonia are *The Persistence of Memory* (1931), *Figure and Drapery in a Landscape* (1935), *The Christ* (circa 1951), and *Gala Placidia* (1952).

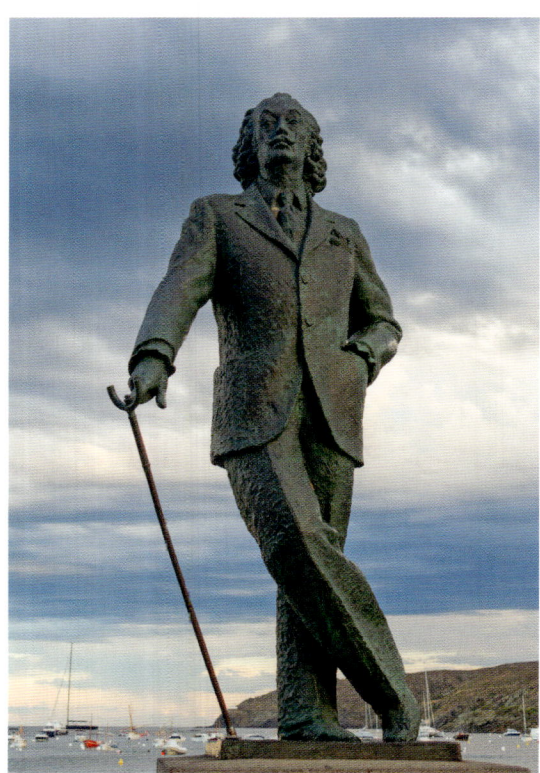

A life-size bronze statue of Dalí in the town of Cadaqués.

spanning most of the twentieth century, Dalí's work was inspired by the areas around his home in the north-east corner of Spain. He defined his own geography, but it roughly equates to the region of L'Empordà in Catalonia and includes Figueres, where he was born and buried; Portlligat, which was, in his own words, the centre of the universe; and Púbol, where his beloved wife had her own retreat at Gala Dalí Castle – albeit one designed and orchestrated by her husband.

FINDING PORTLLIGAT

Dalí always maintained that to understand his paintings, you had to understand Portlligat. This cluster of former fisherman's workshops near Cadaqués, the town where his father was born, took on a special meaning for the artist and, through him, for the rest of the world.

In 1930, Dalí bought a tiny one-room building on the coast at Portlligat; this run-down *barraca* (hut) with a leaking roof had been used previously to store fishing gear. Over the next fifty years he would buy a total of ten of these *barraques,* using six to make his house, which evolved organically, room by room, each one a little higher up the cliffside. Every *barraca* came with a plot of land, where the fishermen would have tended a few vegetables in summer and collected olives in winter, which Dalí turned eventually into a garden.

Dalí's wife Gala was born Elena Ivanovna Diakonova in Kazan in Russia. Ten years older than him, she had previously been married to the poet Paul Éluard, by whom she had a daughter, Cécile, born in 1918. She met Dalí in Cadaqués in 1929, and after they spent their first summer together with mutual friends, including René Magritte and his wife, they were never apart. The couple were married in a civil ceremony in 1934 and again in a Catholic church ceremony in 1958.

As well as being Dalí's muse, Gala also handled the practical arrangements in the house and garden. She adored the yellow everlasting flowers (*Helichrysum stoechas*) that grew wild in the olive groves around their home. The predominant colour throughout the property is yellow and when these plants flowered in May and June, she filled the rooms with bowls full of the sunny blooms. As the flowers dried, they gradually faded to a buff colour,

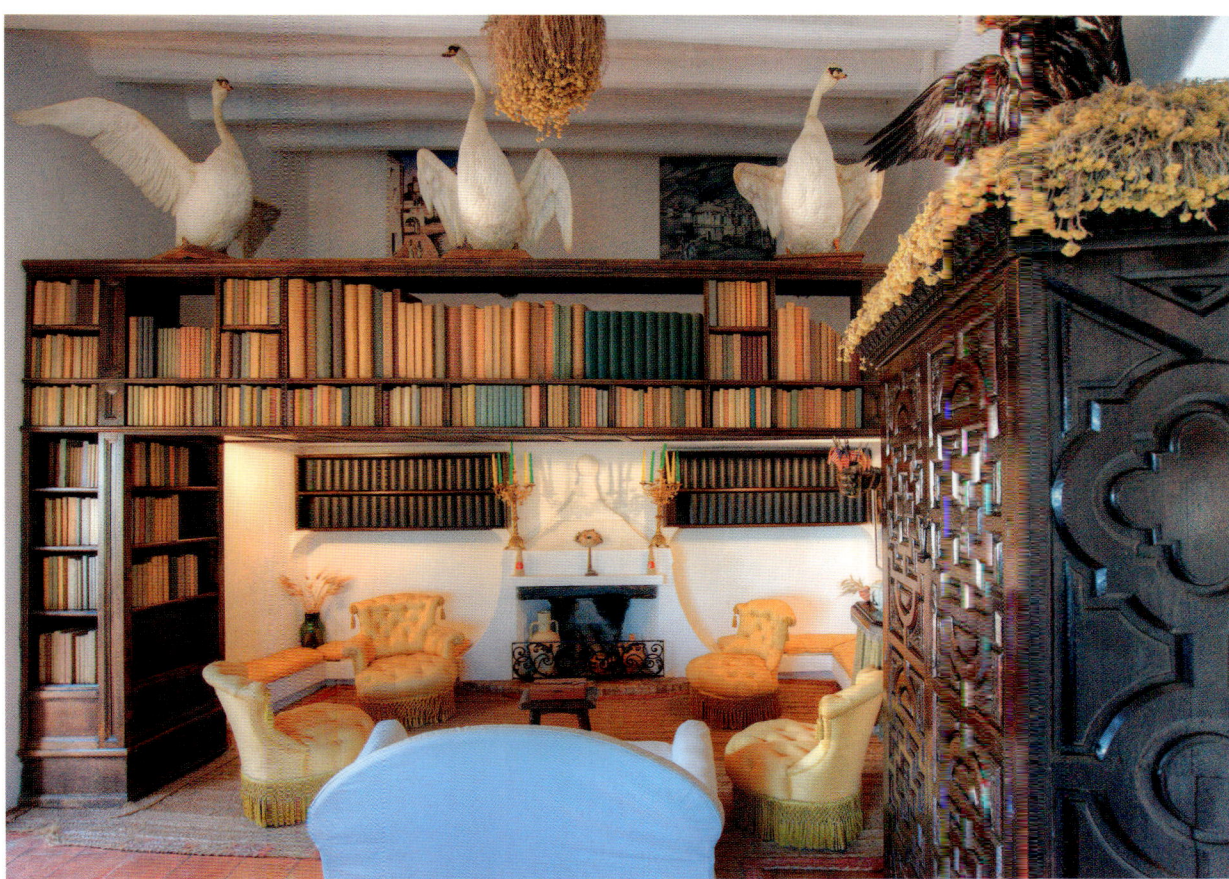

and she would then weave them into garlands and drape them over the curtain pelmets, where their aromatic scent (which also probably kept insects at bay) filled the house.

Dalí wrote many times of the special light at Portlligat and he also believed that when there, he was the first man in Spain to see the sun rise. In the couple's bedroom he angled a mirror so that from his bed, which was on the left, closest to the sea, he could see the sun come up over the horizon before anyone else. Dalí thought the light on this coastline had unique qualities, more akin to Delft in the Netherlands than to the Mediterranean. In his autobiographical book, *The Secret Life of Dalí,* he writes about how the olive trees are bright and animated in the

morning, changing into motionless grey in the evenings. For him, the garden, the sea and the olive groves by day were full of gaiety, but in the evening they were bathed in nostalgia, even melancholy.

SHIFTING SPACES

The sea is visible from every room of the house at Portlligat, and Dalí gave each a name, beginning with the Hall of the Bear, reflecting a life-like stuffed bear – a gift from the writer Edward James – that stood there. Others included the Room of the Birds, where he kept canaries in cages, and the Oval Room, designed to resemble a sea urchin, with a perfect mathematical shape.

He built his studio on the corner of the building, with large windows allowing light in from both the north and the east. Here, he worked on his large canvases, which he attached to a moveable frame, so that the paintings could

ABOVE Dalí made the house at Portlligat one room at a time, while Gala decorated the furniture with garlands of aromatic *Helichrysum stoechas* that she collected from the garden and then dried.

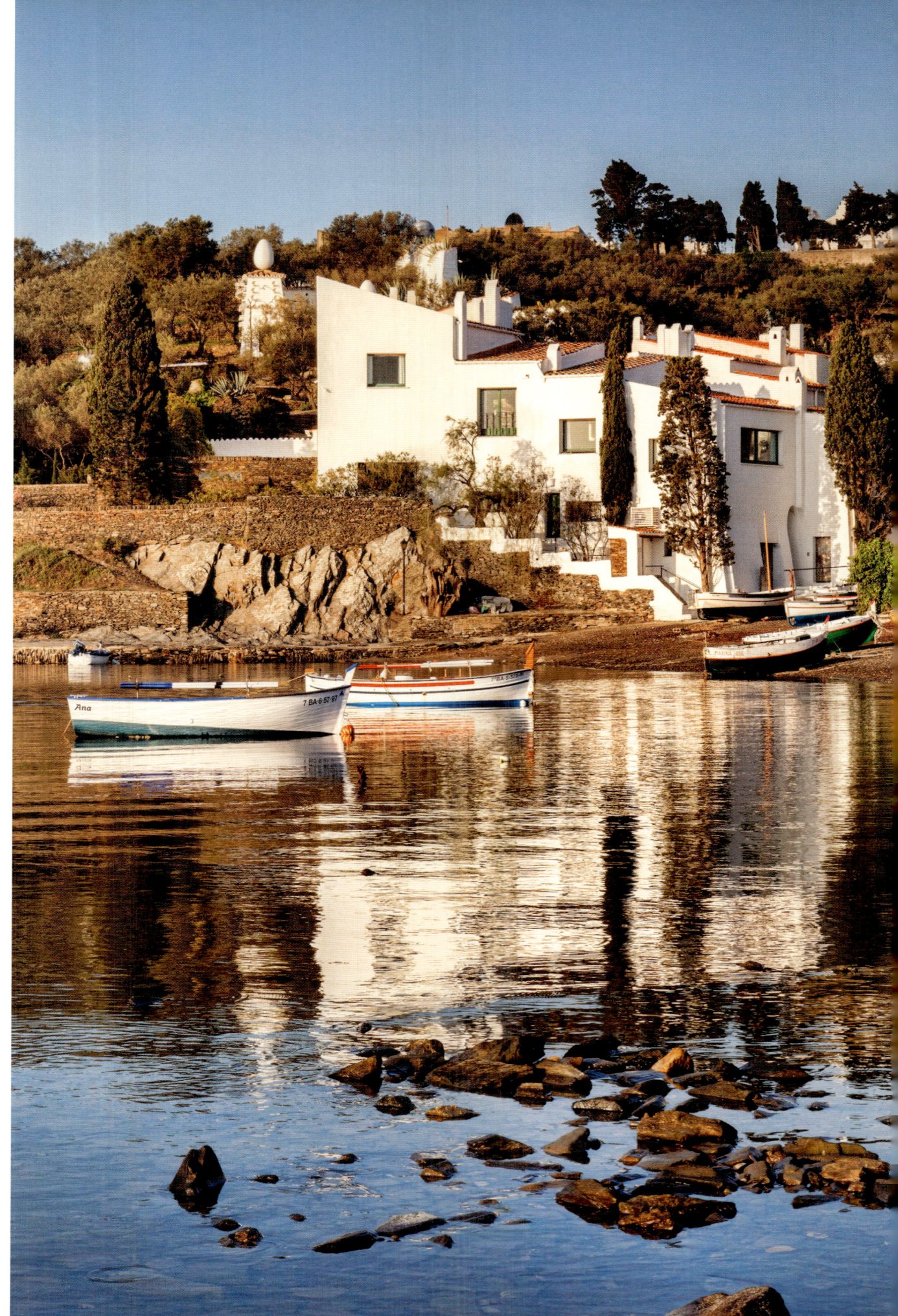

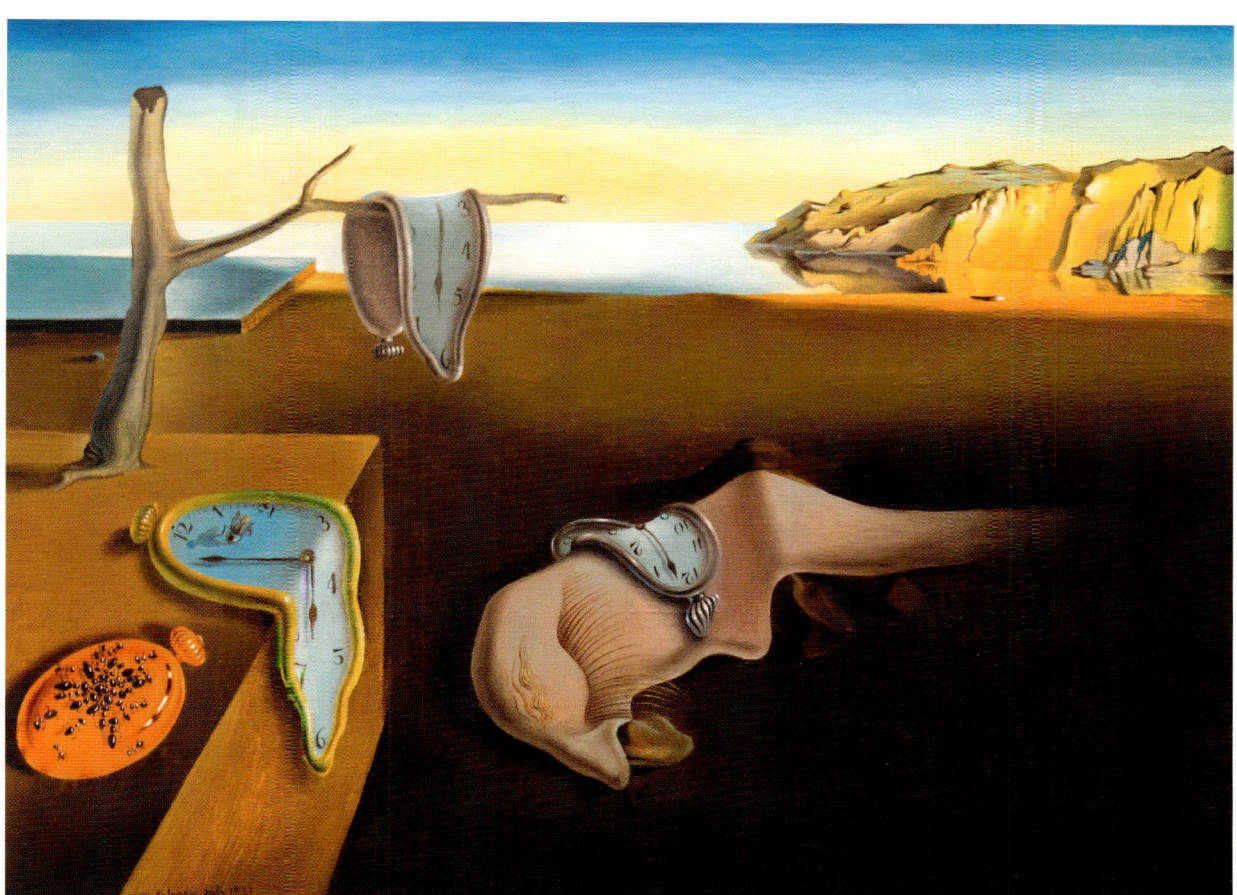

be moved up or down below floor level, allowing him to sit and work on any part of them, without the need for ladders.

Portlligat inevitably attracted more and more visitors as Dalí's international connections grew. Having made the difficult journey over the mountains, visitors were rarely turned away, but they were never admitted to the house itself. Some were famous – such as Walt Disney and the Duke and Duchess of Windsor (the former King Edward VIII and Wallis Simpson) – but as time went on, the visitors included more serious researchers and students interested in Dalí's quasi-scientific ideas

THE ARTIST AT WORK

Gala and Dalí spent the winters travelling to New York and Paris, returning to Portlligat in April or May each year, where Dalí the artist and particularly Dalí the painter – rather than Dalí the public figure – would emerge. The couple's home at Portlligat offered them a retreat, a place where they could be alone. Its protected position also suited the artist, giving him the privacy he needed when creating his art. In the evenings, when the fishermen had left, it was – and still can be – completely deserted.

The garden and surroundings of Portlligat were important to Dalí's work in three ways. Firstly, he used the landscape as actual settings in his paintings; secondly, he staged artworks and 'happenings' within the outdoor spaces; and

"I am inseparable from this sky, this sea, these rocks: linked forever with Portlligat."
SALVADOR DALÍ (1976)

ABOVE Dalí used the views from Portlligat in *The Persistence of Memory*, painted in 1931.
LEFT Every year, the light and reflections of Portlligat drew Dalí back from New York and Paris in spring to work in his studio. There, he became the private, rather than the public, Salvador Dalí.

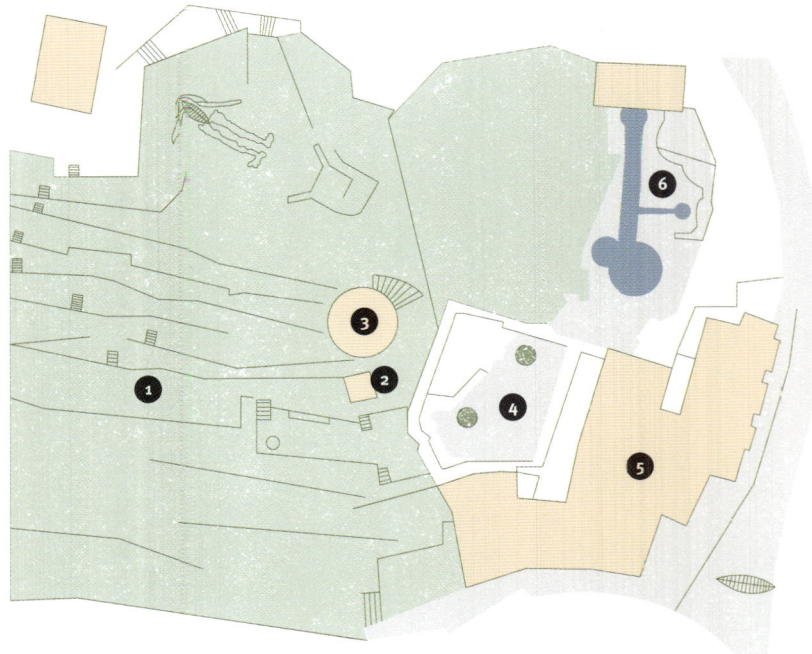

THE GARDEN AT PORTLLIGAT

KEY

1 Terraces and olive grove
2 Dovecot
3 La Torre de les Olles
  (Cooking Pot Tower)
4 Summer Courtyard
5 The house
6 Swimming pool and Shrine

RIGHT The swimming pool
with its jets of water was
inspired by Dalí's visits to
the Alhambra in Granada
and was the most sociable
space in the garden. Visitors
were welcomed in the early
evenings, when Gala and
Dalí would look on from the
covered Shrine, which features
a white fountain and a statue
of the Roman goddess Diana.

thirdly, and most crucially, the land informed his dreams and provided him with an iconography that sparked ideas from which new projects would arise.

When at home in Portlligat, Gala looked after the day-to-day running of the household, and they also employed a cook and a handyman (although not a gardener), while Dalí used local builders and craftspeople to help him with technical or physically challenging aspects of his work.

THE SPACE OUTSIDE

From the 1950s, the garden spaces at Portlligat began to assume a greater importance in the couple's lives. Dalí did not acquire all the land at the same time, but he eventually accumulated around one hectare/two-and-a-half acres of land, enclosed by traditional *pedra-seca* (drystone) walls.

The olive grove the couple bought with the *barraques* was dilapidated when they arrived in the 1930s and, although Dalí had no intention of becoming an olive farmer, he was fascinated by the soil, walls, trees and even the insects, and wanted to preserve this particular landscape for the future. In addition to the olive grove, Dalí and Gala created a new outdoor space. Known as the

Winter Terrace, the artist protected it from the wind with a whitewashed wall, into which he cut a rectangular window to capture the view. The Catalonians have many names for the winds of the region but the *tramuntana* – the cold, fierce wind that comes from the Pyrenees in winter – is the worst. It blows for days on end, smashing flower pots, ripping tiles off roofs, and affecting people's mental health – it is said that the *tramuntana* was one of the reasons Dalí's father moved away to Barcelona.

The couple also made the Summer Courtyard or '*Pati*' (patio). This is perhaps the most beautiful area in the whole property: intimate, enclosed by natural rock, the walls whitewashed with Dalí's own recipe of lime mixed with ground agaves to give it a more blueish tinge. The courtyard features giant concrete teacups and a labyrinthine walled passageway.

The final project to be completed was the swimming pool and the Shrine, the most deliberately theatrical space in the garden. Dalí had visited the water gardens in Granada and these, together with influences from the Pop Art movement of the 1960s and early 1970s, informed his design. By now, Dalí's house had become a cultural centre

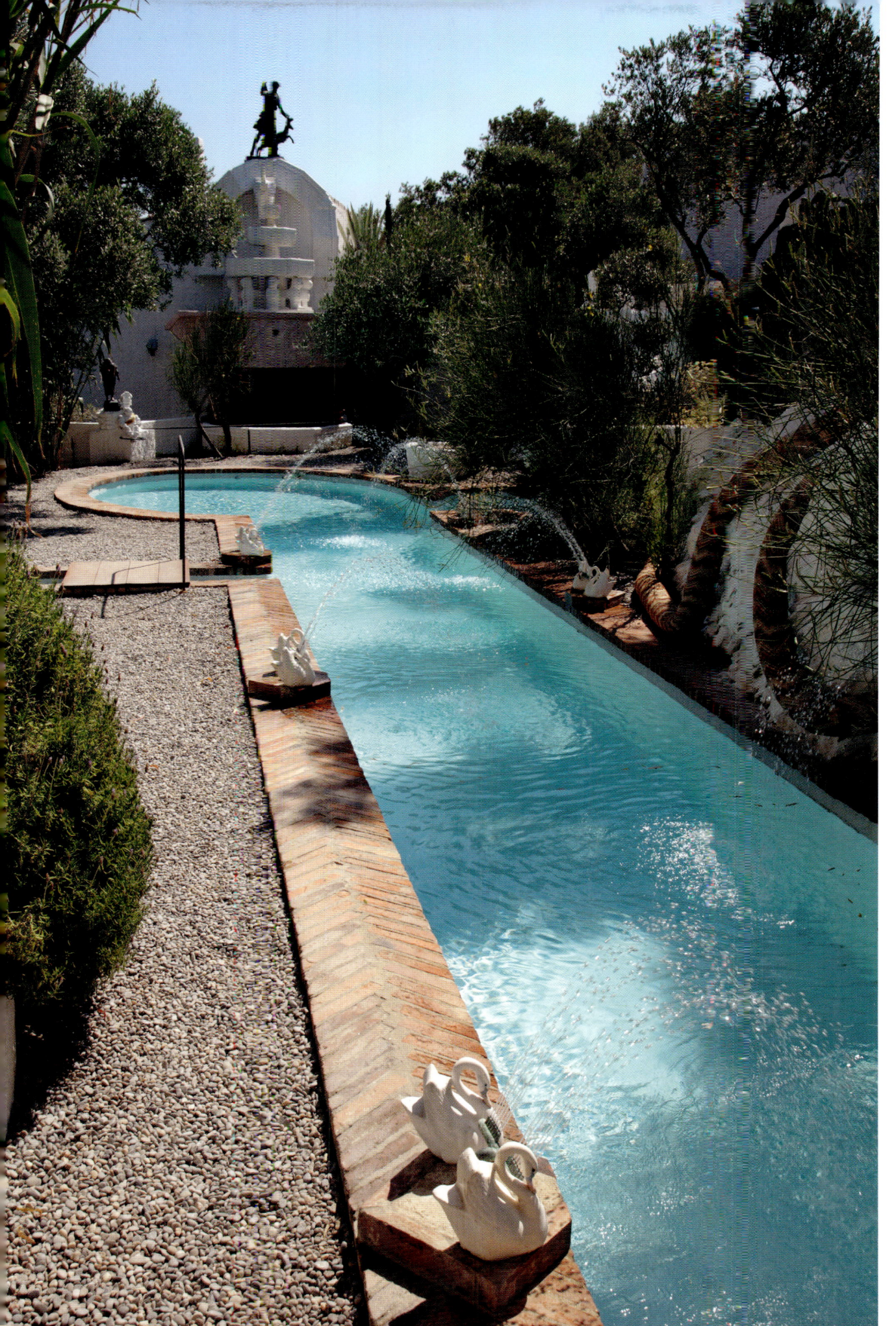

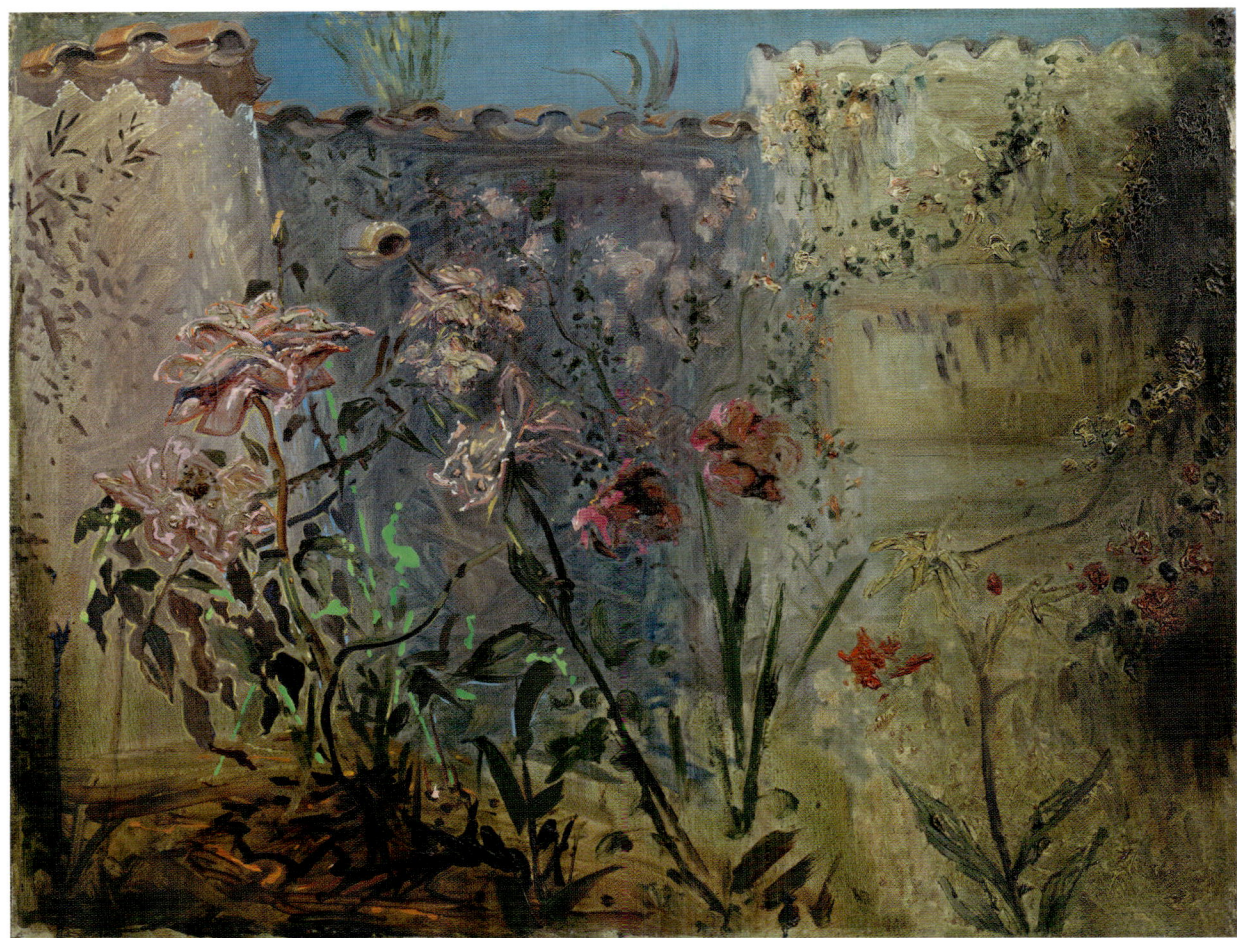

and this space was meant for their many visitors, whom the Dalís received between the hours of five and eight in the evening. The couple would then sit in the Shrine, a covered area slightly to one side, from which they could view the way people used the space.

Dalí instructed his builder, Emile Puignau, to make the rectangle of water for the swimming pool 1.5 metre-/5 foot-wide, with slightly wider semi-circles at each end, so that it looked harmonious. Although the shape, traced out in herringbone brick, is clearly phallic, the builder believed that Dalí's intention was simply for the bathers to see, and be seen from, the seating areas. The addition of water jets (inspired by the Generalife garden at the Alhambra) and lighting were all part of the theatricality. A grand waterfall

could also be switched on, and cascaded over the rocks into the pool – a spectacle reserved only for very special visitors.

Dalí also encouraged young artists to come and make artwork in the outdoor spaces, adding their art and sculpture to his own collections. He believed that gathering objects was more important than selecting or curating them and allowed a jumble of jugs, statues and figures to accumulate in corners of the garden.

PLANTS, BIRDS AND INSECTS

Dalí and Gala filled the terraces and patios with plants that were important to them. In the olive grove, they loved the Cadaqués native species that already grew there and encouraged broom, gorse, lavender and *Helichrysum*, transplanting them where needed. In the courtyards, Dalí chose white pelargoniums, jasmine and his favourite, *Polianthes tuberosa*, a scented flower grown for cutting, also known as *nardos*. The bulbs of this plant were the precious ingredient in the ointment used by Mary Magdalene to anoint the feet of Jesus Christ; everything

ABOVE *Portlligat Garden* (1968) demonstrates a more conventional side to Dalí's work and his appreciation of the flowers at his home.
ABOVE, RIGHT The courtyards at Portlligat are whitewashed to Dalí's own recipe, while the containers are filled with white and pink pelargoniums, one of the artist's favourite flowers.

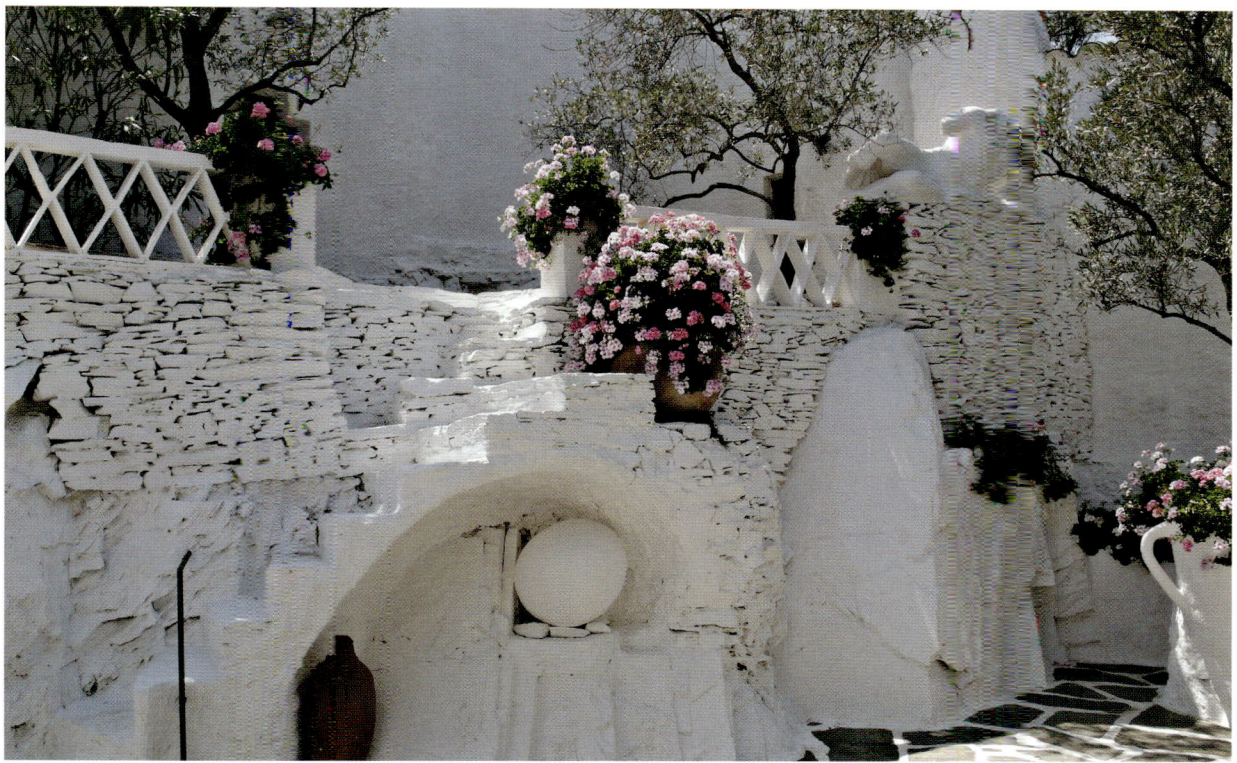

Dalí planted was chosen for his own specific reasons or because he wanted to please Gala.

Dalí's designs in the garden also focused on sound, and particularly the sound of the wind. On *Torre de les Olles* (the Cooking Pot Tower), he adapted the Catalan tradition of reusing broken or chipped terracotta cooking vessels under the eaves to create nesting sites for martins and swallows. He installed them, not for the migratory birds, but for the sound of the wind whipping in from the sea that whistled through their holes.

In fact, birds were important to Dalí, too, and in 1954 he designed a dovecote in the garden, using old wooden pitchforks as perches for his pigeons. Less palatable was his penchant for the sound of crickets, which he would catch and imprison in little cages that he suspended in the Labyrinth, Summer Courtyard and Bird Room.

It is a relatively easy task to preserve an artist's house at a particular moment in time – in this case 1982, the year Gala died and Dalí left Portlligat for good. It is less easy to capture a garden at a particular moment in time. When Dalí lived there, the garden was both an artwork in itself, and a place to create art. He also orchestrated large-scale projects outside, such as the *Crist de les Escombraries*, an interactive artwork that involved young artists and students using items they had found on the beach, such as tyres, ironwork and pieces from wooden boats.

The garden now is probably tidier and less cluttered than when Dalí and Gala lived there and the walls of the olive grove have been repaired, which he was never inclined to do. But in the courtyards, the white pelargoniums he loved still flourish – if sometimes tinged with pink. Dalí's influence is all-pervasive at Portlligat, the remote village where he seems to have been admired and loved, if not always understood.

THE CASTLE AT PÚBOL

Gala was the key to the so-called Dalí triangle, an area defined by drawing a line between Figueres, Portlligat and Púbol. While Portlligat was always the couple's home, in 1969 Dalí discovered an eleventh- to fifteenth-century castle, which was partly in ruins, next to the church in the medieval village of Púbol, and bought it for Gala. The castle was a continuation of their touching and strange relationship: Dalí offered it to her and she accepted, on the condition that he would never visit her there unless by handwritten invitation – the epitome of medieval chivalry. Dalí renovated the castle for her sole use and she would spend long periods there without him.

Gala Dalí Castle represents a milestone in the artist's approach. Portlligat was mainly a private space, created in a piecemeal fashion over decades, but always a work-in-progress. The gardens of the castle at Púbol, on the other hand, were Dalí's designs for one special client – his wife Gala – which he planned and executed within a year.

The castle grounds had an existing layout of paths and beds created in the nineteenth century by the lords of Púbol. While respecting the geometry of this underlying structure, Dalí actually planned an Italian garden. He was clearly influenced by the *Sacro Bosco* (Sacred Grove) of Bomarzo in Italy, which he had visited in 1948, where there is a surprise around each corner and the trees create mystery and intrigue. His intention was to create something similar – for example, the path leading to a statue of Venus at Púbol is flanked by trees, planted at decreasing intervals to create a false perspective and make it appear longer than it actually is. However, to please Gala, he initially planted the castle's grounds like a romantic Mediterranean garden, with flowers, oleanders, figs and small fruit trees. She wanted a garden that would remind her of summers spent on the Crimea as a child, so he also included roses and tobacco plants for scent. But he always kept an eye to the future, planting laurels, cypresses and plane trees, which he knew would grow tall and soon shade out the flowers to create something more intriguing and suited to his idea of a castle. Púbol would be his 'Sacred Grove'.

The castle was a continuation of Dalí's creative life and an extension of Portlligat, but it was, he said, a more solemn gesture of his love for his wife. On her death, Gala was buried in the crypt under the castle. Dalí then moved into the castle to be with her, putting fresh flowers on her tomb every day, a tradition that still continues today. He also worked on his last painting there, *Untitled. Swallows Tail and Cellos* (*The Catastophes Series*; circa 1983).

Gala Dalí Castle in Púbol has now become Dalí's museum – something he and Gala may or may not have intended. His trees have grown, as he knew they would, yet within the deep gloom of the evergreens, there is a tunnel of white jasmine and roses, the scent of which would have pleased the woman who allowed Dalí to become Dalí.

RIGHT, ABOVE In 1969, Dalí bought a medieval castle in Púbol as a gesture of his love for Gala and designed a garden for her there.
RIGHT, BELOW The pool in the grounds of Gala Dalí Castle was part of Dalí's homage to Bomarzo in Italy and the idea of the Sacred Grove.

DALÍ'S TIMELINE

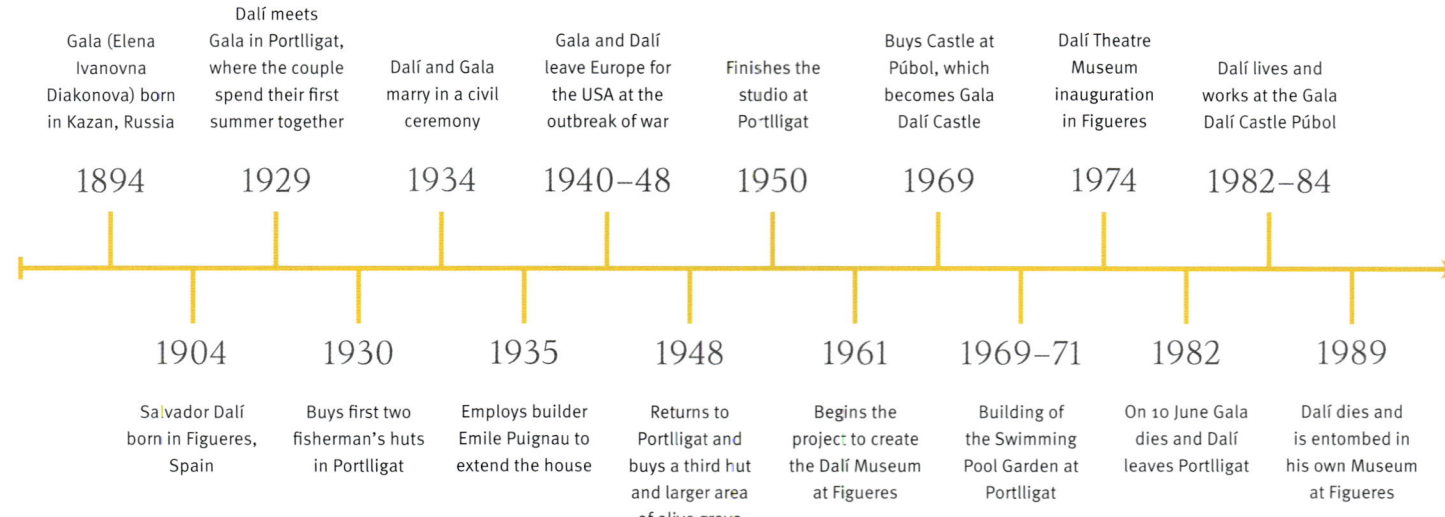

1894	1929	1934	1940–48	1950	1969	1974	1982–84
Gala (Elena Ivanovna Diakonova) born in Kazan, Russia	Dalí meets Gala in Portlligat, where the couple spend their first summer together	Dalí and Gala marry in a civil ceremony	Gala and Dalí leave Europe for the USA at the outbreak of war	Finishes the studio at Portlligat	Buys Castle at Púbol, which becomes Gala Dalí Castle	Dalí Theatre Museum inauguration in Figueres	Dalí lives and works at the Gala Dalí Castle Púbol

1904	1930	1935	1948	1961	1969–71	1982	1989
Salvador Dalí born in Figueres, Spain	Buys first two fisherman's huts in Portlligat	Employs builder Emile Puignau to extend the house	Returns to Portlligat and buys a third hut and larger area of olive grove	Begins the project to create the Dalí Museum at Figueres	Building of the Swimming Pool Garden at Portlligat	On 10 June Gala dies and Dalí leaves Portlligat	Dalí dies and is entombed in his own Museum at Figueres

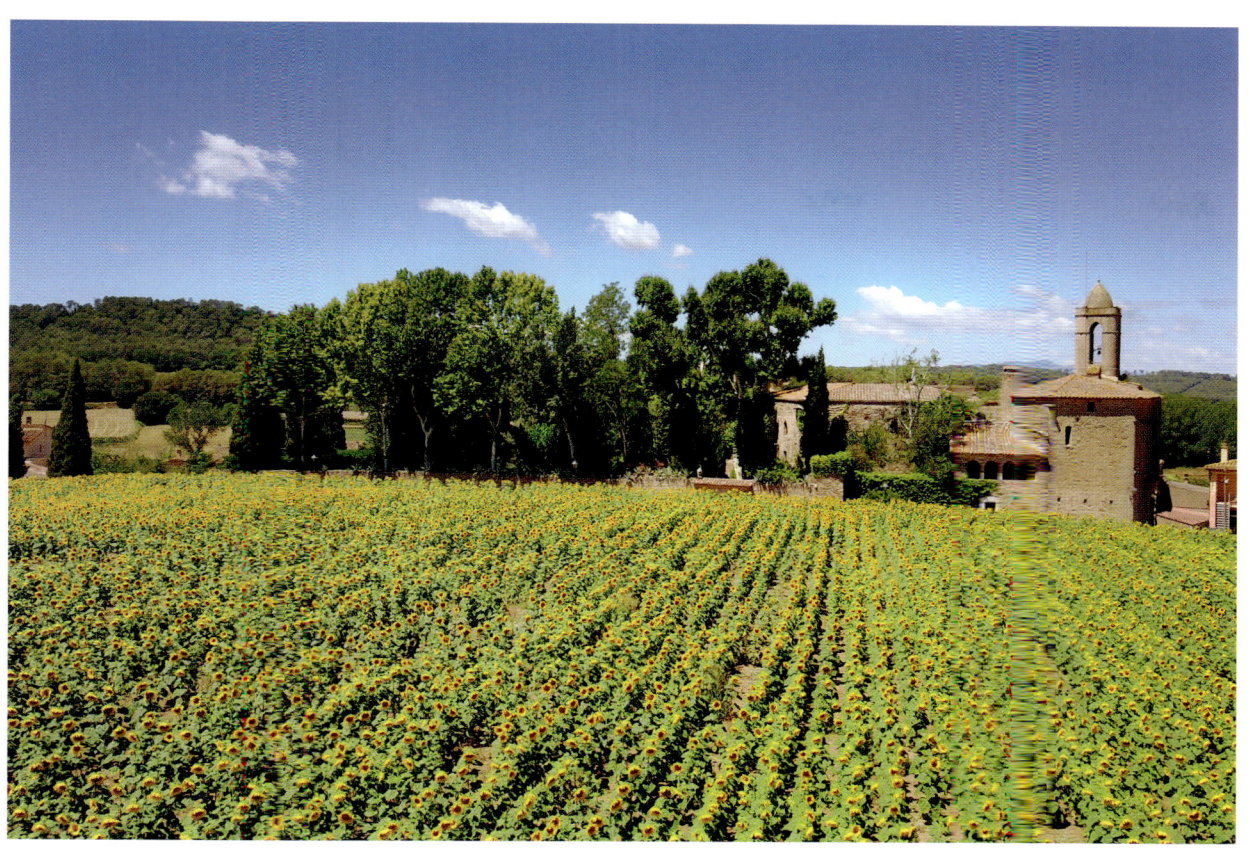

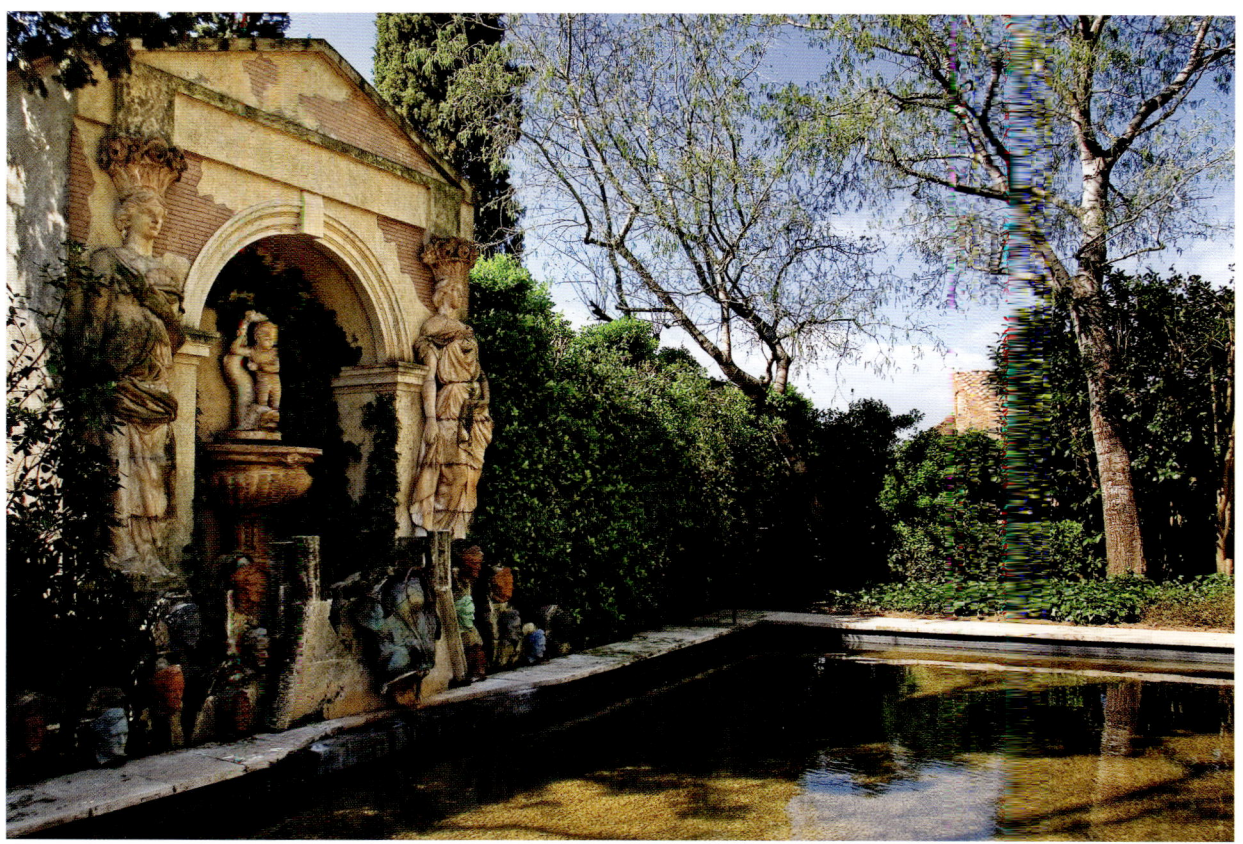

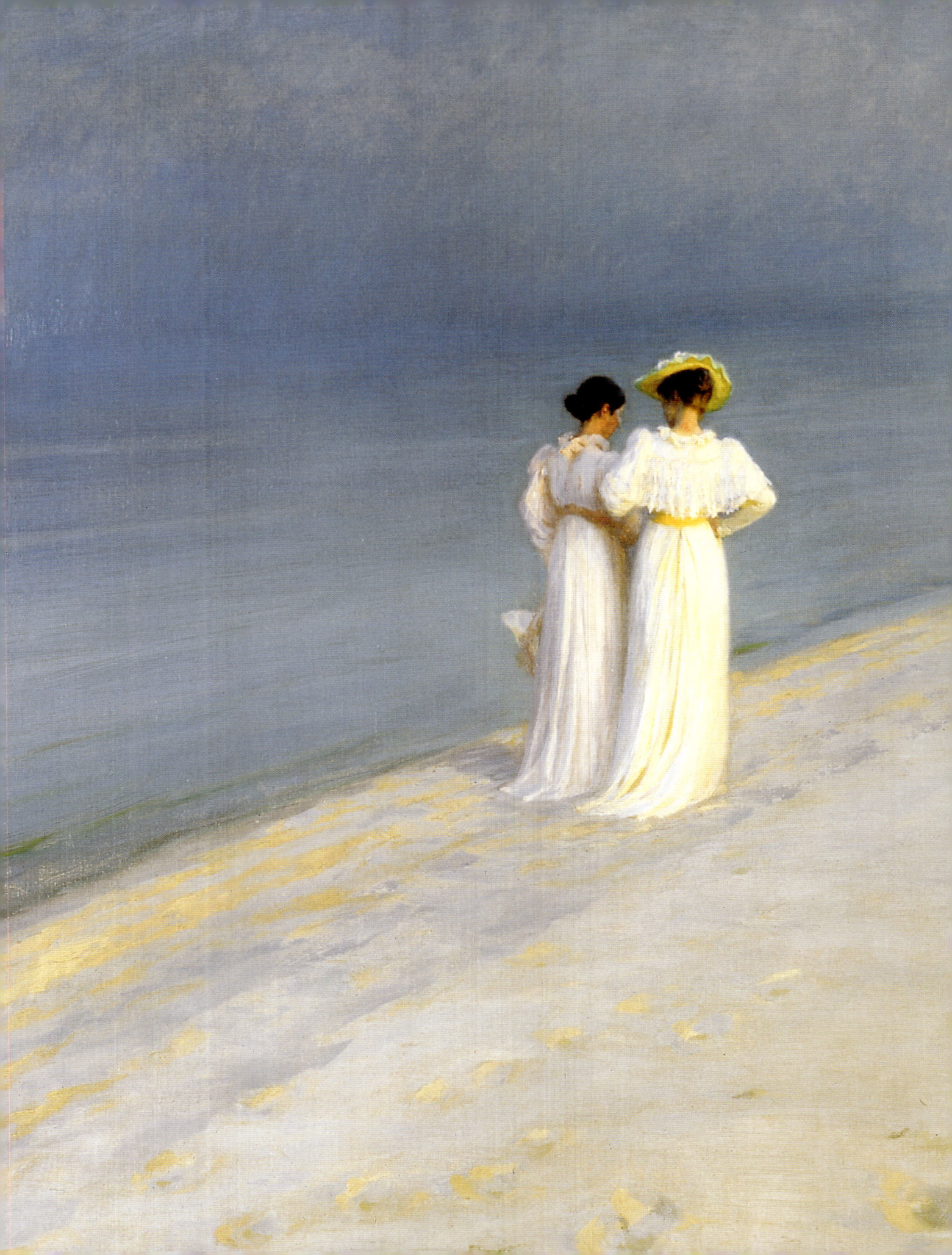

THE ARTISTS' COMMUNITY

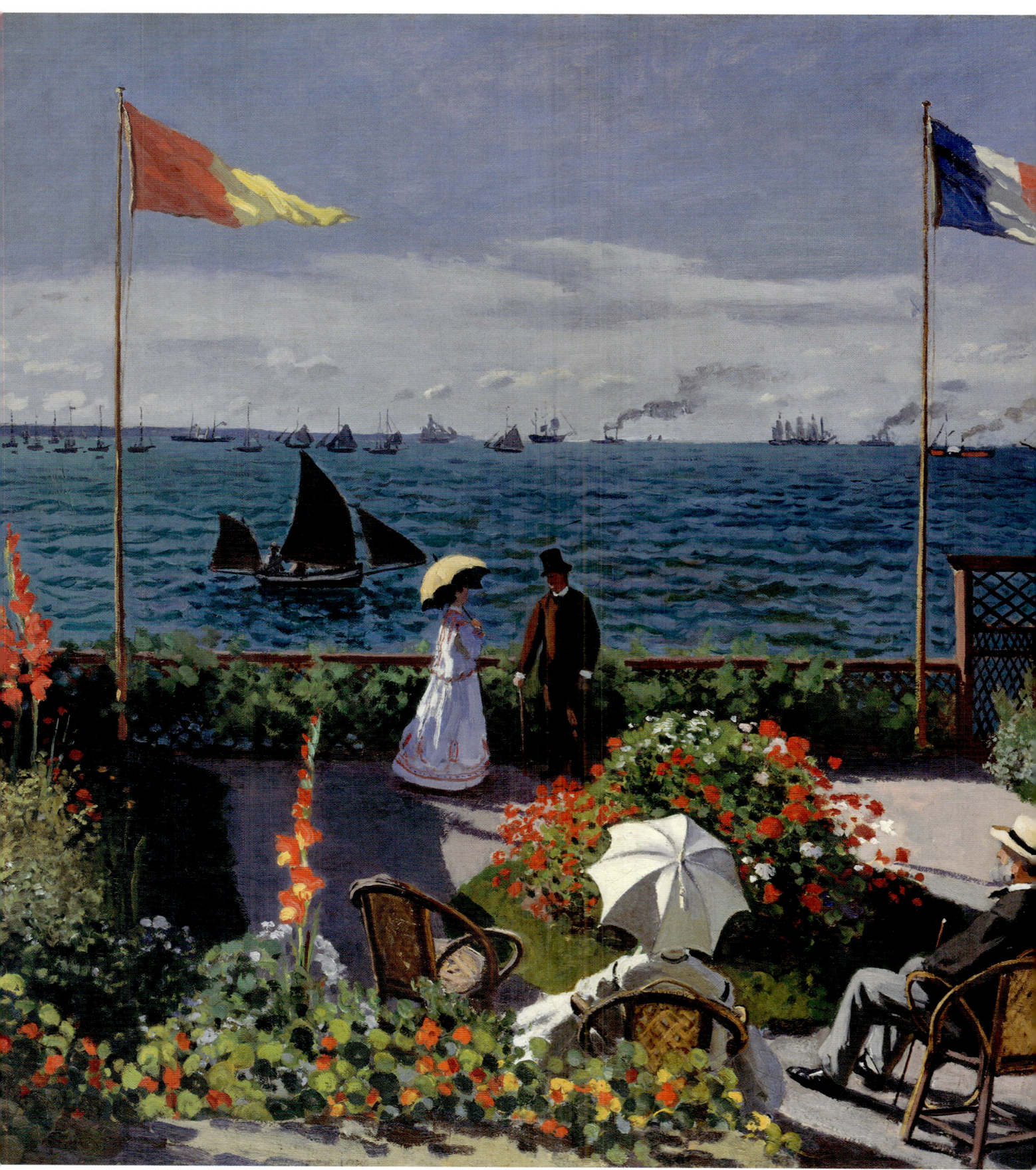

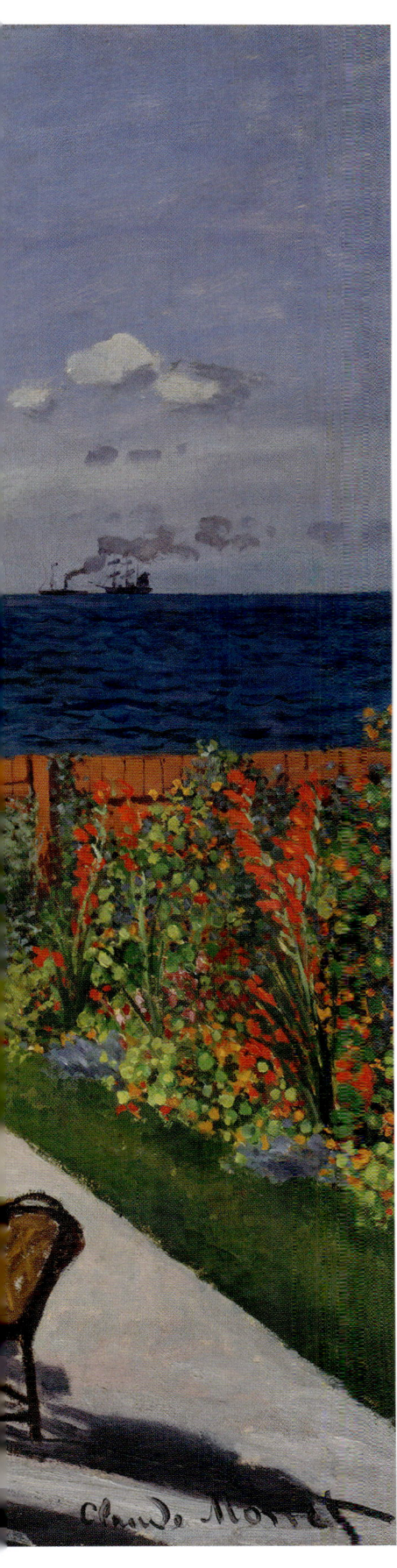

Monet and friends

Claude Monet, Berthe Morisot, Gustave Caillebotte, Pierre Bonnard and the Seine artists

Argenteuil, Vétheuil and Giverny, France

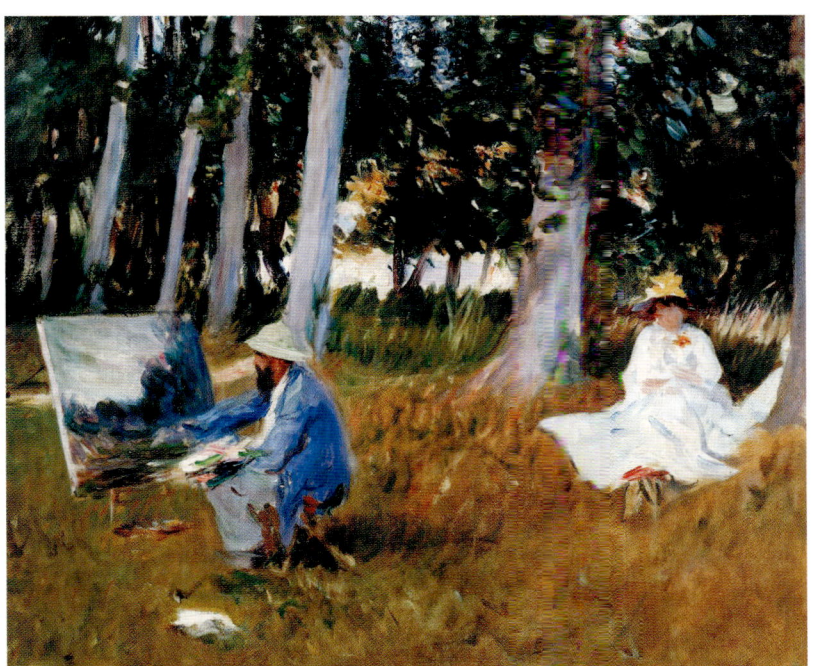

THE ART MOVEMENT that swept through France and, indeed, the world during the late nineteenth and early twentieth centuries became known as 'Impressionism'. It broke all the rules of studio-based painting and its undisputed master was Claude Monet. When we talk about art and gardening in one breath, it is largely due to Monet, who put gardens at the centre of his work. While parks, potagers, rose and suburban gardens became favourite subjects for many Impressionist painters, it was Claude Monet's fascination with garden-making that has left us the legacy of his own garden at Giverny.

LEFT The house owned by Claude Monet's aunt on the north French coast was featured in one of the artist's earliest depictions of a garden: *Jardin à Sainte-Adresse* (1867).

ABOVE John Singer Sargent came to Giverny in 1885 and captured Monet working – with his future wife, Alice Hoschedé, nearby – in his painting *Claude Monet Painting by the Edge of a Wood*.

Claude Monet
(1840–1926)

Argenteuil 1871–1878
Vétheuil 1878–1882
Giverny 1883–1926

The most famous artist of the Impressionist movement, Monet is arguably the most famous artist of all time. It was his painting *Impression, Sunrise*, exhibited in 1874, that gave birth to the label 'Impressionist' – initially a term of derision. Each period in his life, and the home in which he lived, marked a new phase in his painting style, beginning with the house at Argenteuil, then Vétheuil, and finally Giverny. He lived at Giverny with Alice Hoschedé – with Monet's two sons and Alice's six children from her marriage to Ernest Hoschedé – and the couple married after Ernest's death in 1892. At Giverny, Monet produced hundreds of landscapes, as well as his famous series of haystacks and water lilies. Towards the end of his life, he only painted the garden, producing more than one hundred images of the water garden.

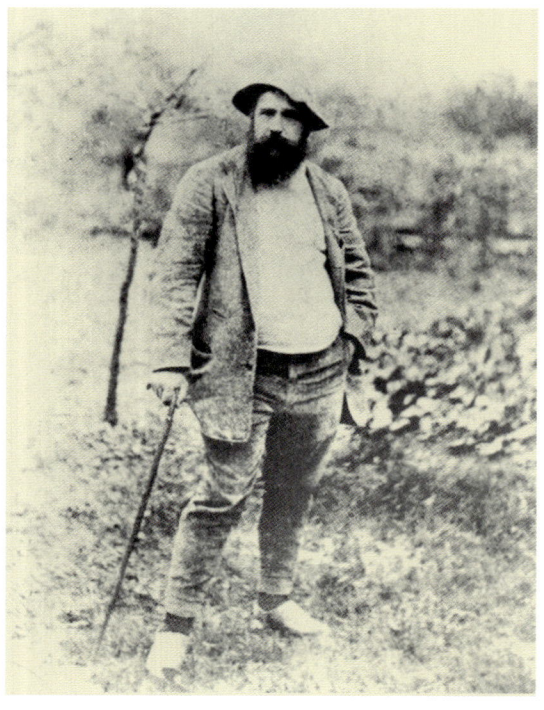

Monet, aged 49, at Giverny, photographed by Theodore Robinson.

PAINTING *EN PLEIN AIR*

The origins of the Impressionist artists' love of gardens goes back much further than Giverny. Monet and his contemporaries began painting gardens – their own and those of close friends and neighbours – long before he moved to his final home in Normandy.

Berthe Morisot was already painting the parks of Paris and would go on to use the garden at her own house at Bougival, on the outskirts of Paris, as a subject for *The Garden at Bougival* (1884). Renoir also began to use a semi-wild space behind his studio in Montmartre as an outdoor experimental studio, while in 1880 Édouard Manet painted the gardens of his summer home at Bellevue in *The Garden at Bellevue*. During the same period, Pissarro was painting many scenes of the gardens of Pontoise on the river Oise, the village where he lived for seventeen years; Pissarro's house at Quay de Pontoise was also famously captured by Gauguin in 1881.

What drew the artists together was a shared belief in the freedom that painting outside, *en plein air,* offered and a determination to put sensation and feeling into a scene, rather than just reproduce it accurately on a canvas. The Impressionists met regularly and often painted the same scene – and each other – in their gardens. Among them was Gustave Caillebotte whose parents had a house and garden at Yerres, just south-east of Paris. In 1881, Caillebotte bought his own house at Petit Gennevilliers on the Seine, where he created a garden of his own.

MONET'S EARLY GARDENS

Having a good selection of fresh flowers available to paint became essential for Monet. At first, he collected flowers from his aunt's garden near Le Havre, and its coastal view became the subject of one of his early works, *The Garden at Sainte-Adresse* (1867), in which the foreground of vivid red nasturtiums, gladioli and pelargoniums steal the show from the seascape behind.

By 1873 Monet was living with his first wife Camille Doncieux in Argenteuil on the Seine, where he rented Maison Aubry and made a garden there that became the subject of two paintings: *The Artist's House at Argenteuil*, which features pots of exotic, red-flowered orchid cacti (*Epiphyllum*), and *The Artist's Garden at Argenteuil*, with

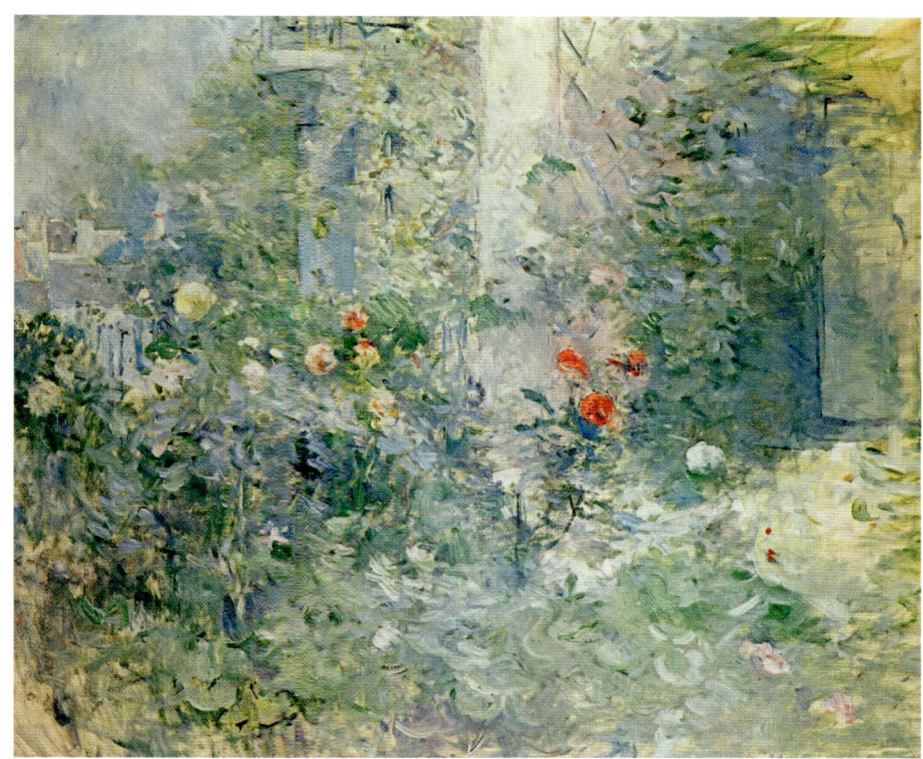

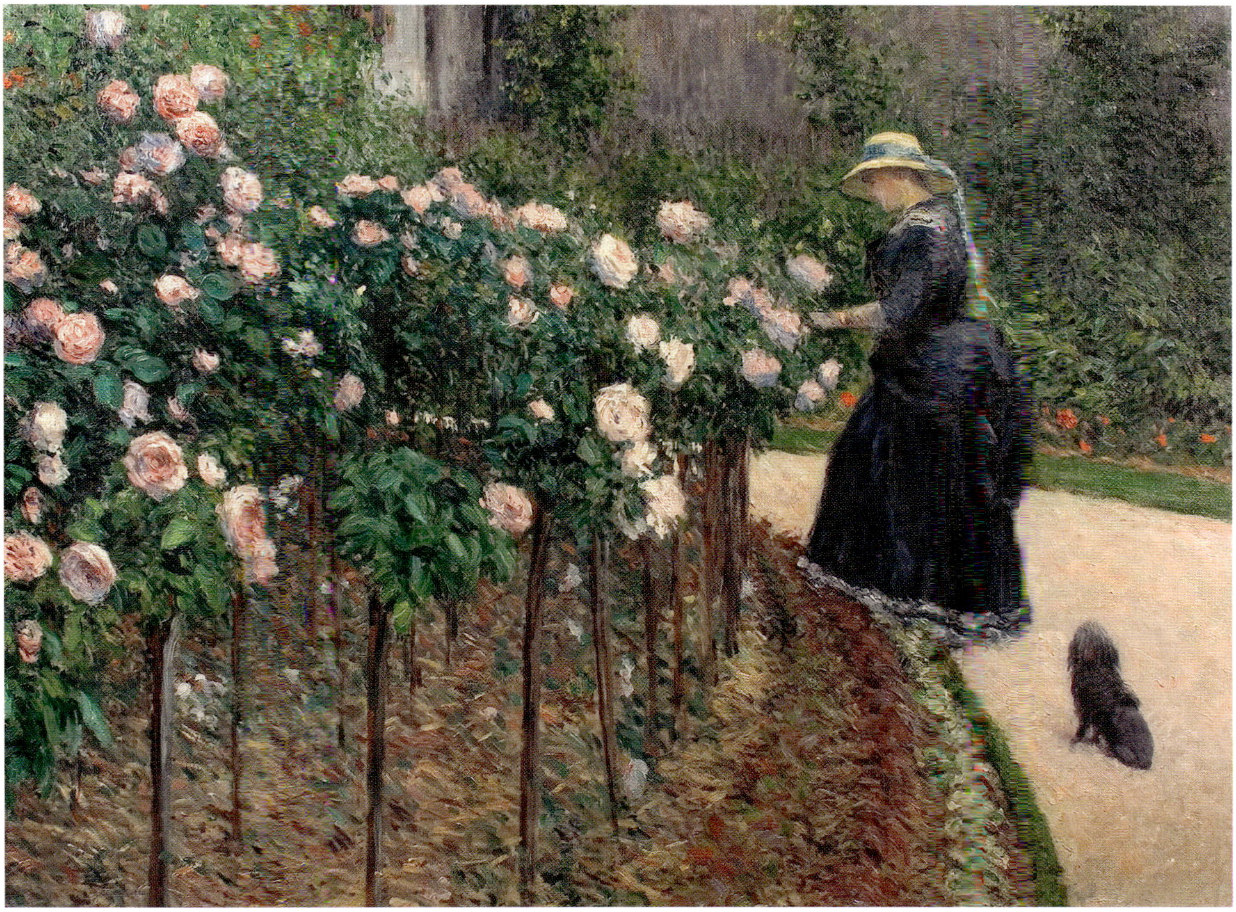

LEFT *The Garden at Bougival* (1886) by Berthe Morisot, who exhibited alongside Monet, Pissarro and Degas in the first Impressionist exhibition of 1874.

BELOW Gustave Caillebotte's *Roses in the Garden at Petit Gennevilliers* (circa 1886). Caillebotte was one of Monet's closest gardening friends.

RIGHT *Claude Monet Painting in his Garden in Argenteuil* by Renoir (1873). This was the first of Monet's three gardens.
BELOW *The Monet Family in their Garden at Argenteuil* (1874) by Édouard Manet shows Monet, Camille and son Jean. Manet visited them while spending the summer just across the Seine at Gennevilliers.
OPPOSITE After Camille Monet died in 1879, the artist threw himself into his work, making this study of their sons in the garden at Vétheuil in 1881.

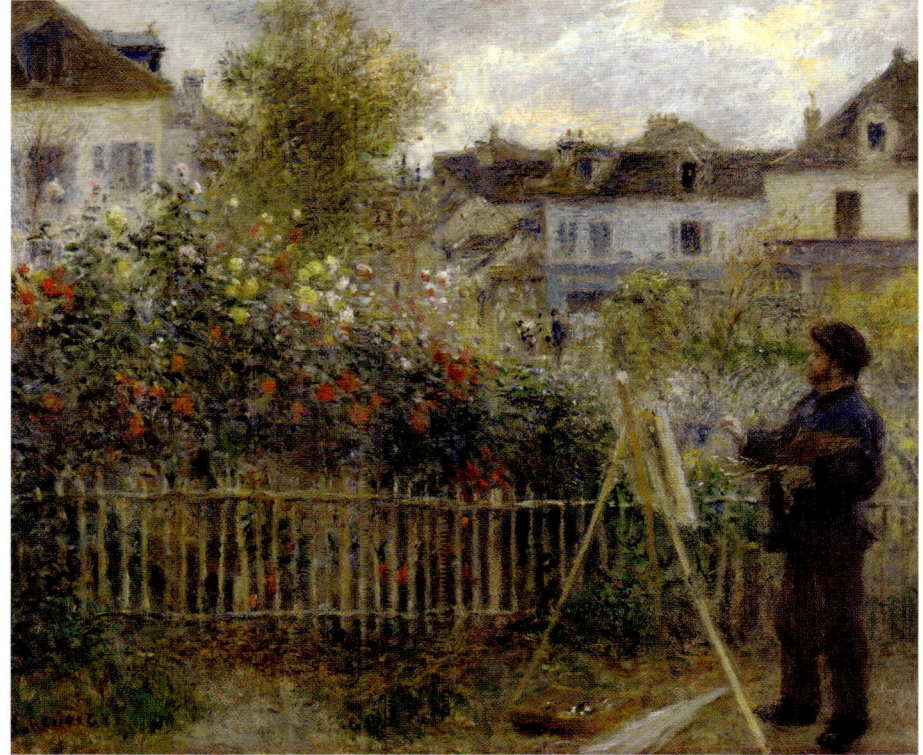

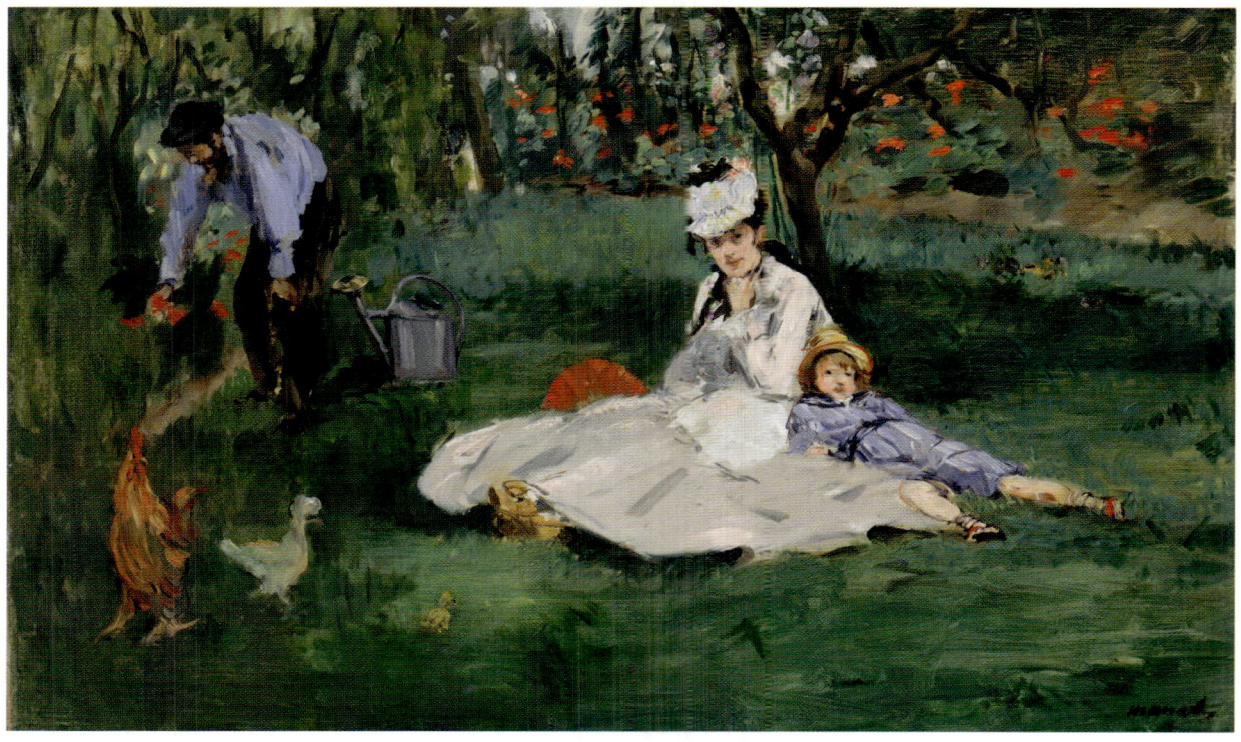

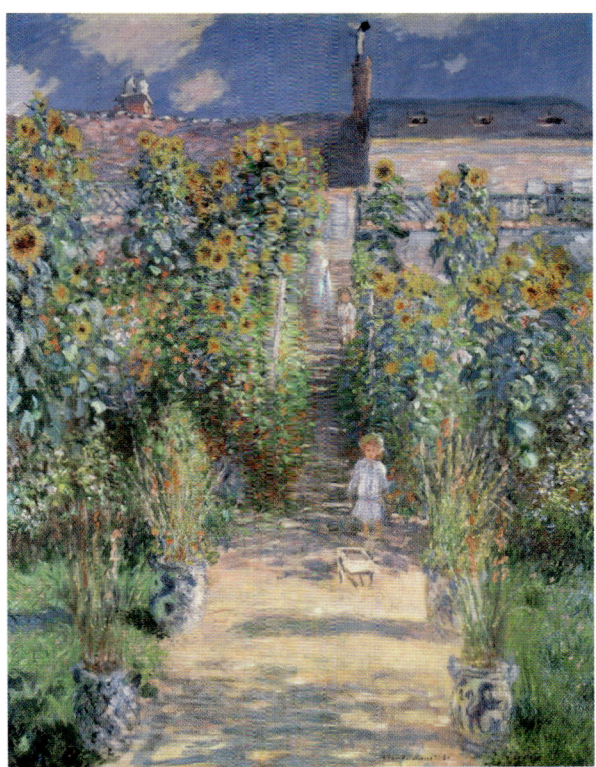

its exuberant display of dahlias. His friends, Renoir and Manet, also vied to paint Monet's flower-filled garden and his family at Argenteuil.

Monet was by no means successful at this time and in 1878, aged thirty-seven, he moved to the rural village of Vétheuil, where he and his friend Ernest Hoschedé shared the rent of 600 francs a year on a small house. Monet's wife, Camille, was already ill when the families moved and the house was barely large enough for all of them – Alice and Ernest Hoschedé had six children and the Monets had two. Nevertheless, Monet was taken with the location close to the Seine and, as there was no room in the house, he painted outdoors and stored his paints and easels on a small *bateau-atelier* (workshop boat). He worked quickly because he was desperate and depressed by his wife's illness; Camille passed away a few months after they moved in, aged just thirty-two.

After Camille's death Monet threw himself into his work, and completed some 200 paintings during his three-year stay at Vétheuil. He also saw possibilities for the garden in front of the house, with its terraces that dropped down towards the river. A journalist from *La Vie Moderne*, interviewing Monet a year after Camille's death in 1880, describes a wooden gate at the entrance to the garden, with steps leading down through apple and pear trees, the terraces abundant with vegetables to feed the children, and flowers, particularly sunflowers. When asked where his studio was, Monet just waved his hand towards the sky and his boat moored on the river just below the garden.

Monet painted at least five studies of the garden at Vétheuil, marking a new phase in his work. He began a series of the same scenes, including the garden steps flanked by sunflowers, with each painting representing a new artistic development. Figures became less important and in his last painting of the garden the small images of his sons have almost begun to fade away. After this, figures would no longer feature in Monet's paintings. His personal life changed too, as he and Alice Hoschedé, who had taken on the day-to-day care of Monet's children, began a relationship. When Ernest Hoschedé returned to Paris, a new Monet-Hoschedé family was formed and the artist began to look for a home for himself, Alice, his sons Jean and Michel, and Alice's six children.

THE GARDEN AT GIVERNY

In 1883, Monet found the home he was looking for in the village of Giverny. He initially rented the long pink house called Le Pressoir, but soon after moving he borrowed the money from his art dealer to buy it outright. He immediately set about planting flowers he could paint in the front, south-facing, sloping garden, known as Le Clos Normand. Formerly a kitchen garden, he took out the old fruit trees and replaced them with flowering cherries and apples for blossom in spring, and removed the box edging, which both he and Alice thought created too much structure. His planting was seasonal, providing colour throughout the year, while his horticultural knowledge began to deepen. He amassed a large library of gardening books, particularly on his favourite flowers – irises and dahlias.

Monet's idea was to plant flowers in blocks of colours, edging the beds with more flowers, rather than the traditional structural shrubs. He favoured large plants, such as poppies, gladioli, asters and tall daisies, each offering

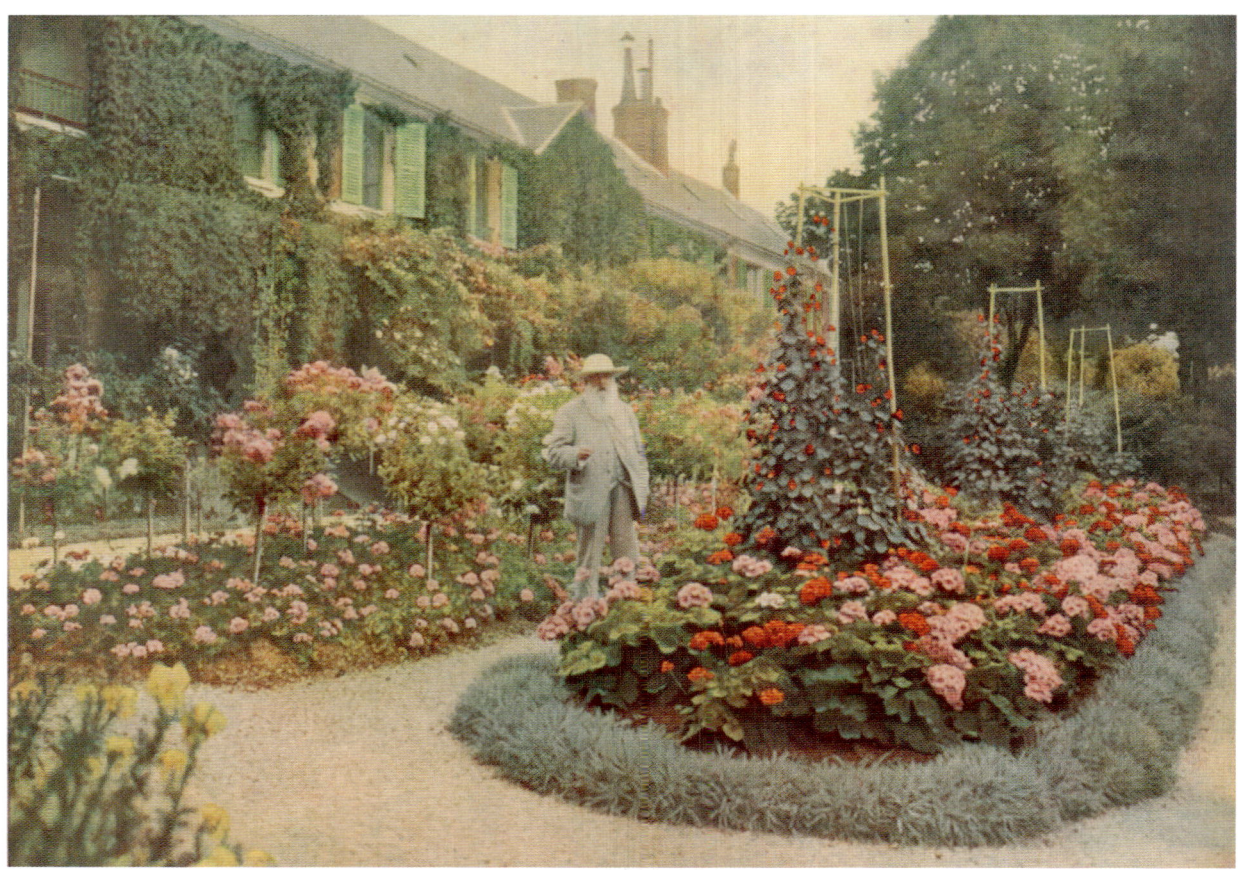

> *"I find it very hard to leave Giverny, especially now that I'm arranging the house and garden as I want them."*
>
> CLAUDE MONET (1891)

ABOVE Monet, pictured in 1905 in the flower garden or Le Clos Normand at Giverny.

RIGHT, CLOCKWISE FROM TOP LEFT View from the house over Le Clos Normand; roses and peonies were among Monet's favourite flowers; the west of the garden in spring; the regular grid of paths cut between swathes of mauve tulips, pansies and forget-me-nots; Monet fell in love with the pink painted house with green shutters; the arches in the Allée Centrale were designed to support roses, while nasturtiums almost cover the path.

a season of glory. To prevent the garden from looking too formal, the borders featured climbing structures to support *Clematis montana* and roses, which were allowed to scramble freely.

Interestingly, Monet did not attempt to paint the garden immediately after creating it. The earliest paintings of around 1887 are of the peony beds, some four years after he arrived at Giverny, but he mainly worked on landscapes in the neighbourhood during this period. It would be a further six years before he concentrated in earnest on the garden as a *motif*.

LE CLOS NORMAND

The garden closest to the house – Le Clos Normand – allowed Monet to develop his mastery of colour. On either side of the Allée Centrale that leads from the front door to the road, beds were filled with the plants that dominated his private and working lives. Here, he included the irises and dahlias he had first come to love during his time at Argenteuil, but Le Clos Normand offered greater potential and by using a wider variety of plants he was able to create a truly exuberant and spectacular flower garden.

The plan was, and still is, to extend the season of flowering for as much of the year as possible. The show begins in spring with daffodil bulbs and primroses of every colour, followed by bold tulips in a rainbow of shades. The tulips push through the emerging sword-shaped leaves of the irises, which include the varieties 'Déjazet' and 'Ma Mie' that Monet ordered from Cayeux's renowned

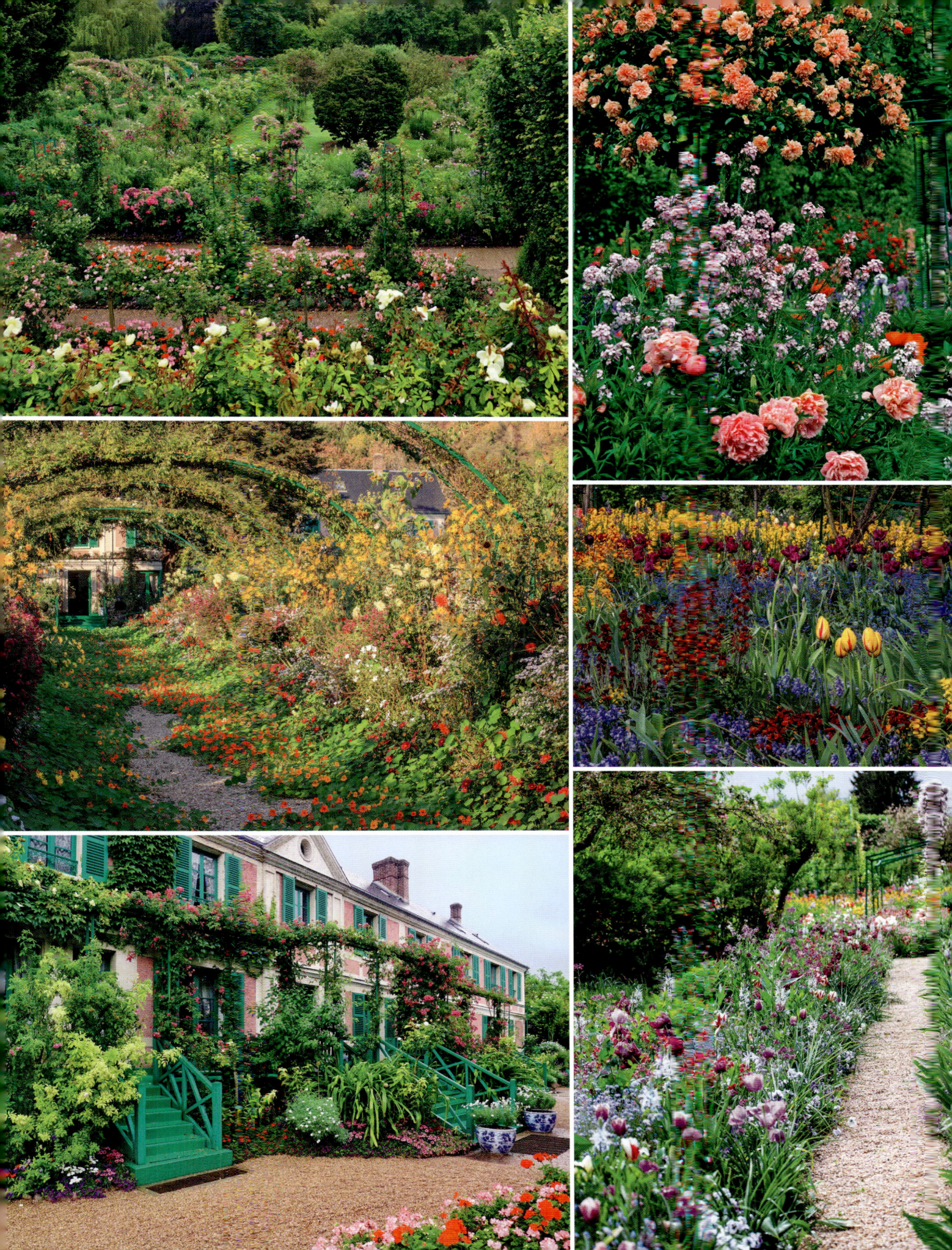

THE GARDEN AT GIVERNY

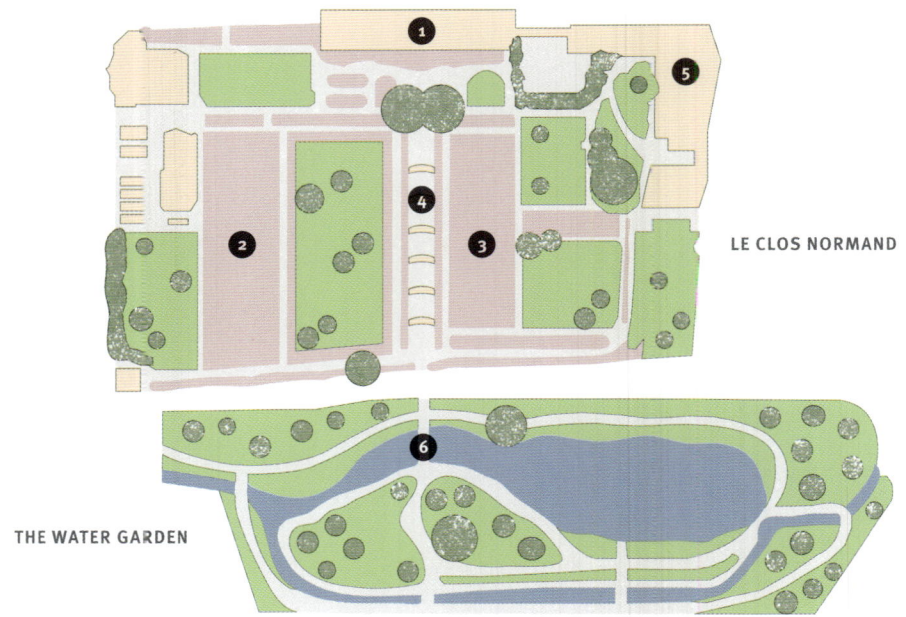

LE CLOS NORMAND

THE WATER GARDEN

KEY

1　House
2　West Garden
3　East Garden featuring
　　Paintbox Beds
4　Allée Centrale
5　Water Lily Studio
6　Japanese-style bridge

RIGHT *Water Lily Pond* (1899) was one of many paintings Monet made of this part of the garden. At the time, the bridge was not covered with wisteria, which Monet added later.

iris nursery. As always, the artist was thinking about colour, and having observed that the blue bearded irises retained their hues better in partial shade, he planted them beneath the trees in the orchard. Blue irises also tend to be the most vigorous, crowding out other colours, so they were used on their own or as edging for floppier perennials.

In summer, the perennials and annuals were given free rein, and particularly those Monet favoured, such as peonies and poppies. He preferred the simple red annual field poppy (*Papaver rhoeas*) to larger-flowered forms, but for pale and dusky pinks he turned to the flamboyant opium poppy (*Papaver somniferum*), which grows in abundance in the garden beside the Allée Centrale. Monet used the red *Paeonia lactiflora* to pick up the colour of 'Paul's Scarlet', a climbing rose bred in 1916 by Arthur Paul in England, while white and yellow single roses, such as 'Mermaid', injected brighter highlights. Monet also built up a collection of wild and species roses, bought from a nursery in Edinburgh.

The Paintbox Beds are so-called because they are set out in blocks of a single type of bloom – they also produced cut flowers for the house. Each bed was generally planted with just one colour and cultivar, although Monet did occasionally combine the same plant in two different hues.

THE WATER GARDEN

In 1893, now able to employ a full-time gardener, Monet applied to the local authorities for permission to divert the River Epte to make a water garden in the lower part of the garden. There was some opposition to his plan, but he was granted permission and channelled the water to create a pond, which he would enlarge several times during the following few years. Monet had seen a display of water lilies by the Latour-Marliac Nursery of Le Temple-sur-Lot at the 1889 Paris Exhibition, and soon he was ordering his first plants from them to fill the pond. It was the beginning of a horticultural and artistic obsession that would continue for the rest of his life.

The water garden has a totally different atmosphere to Le Clos Normand. The overriding impression is of an oriental garden, enhanced by the Japanese-style bridge that Monet installed in 1895, which was inspired by his collection of Japanese woodblock prints that hung in the house. The bridge is simple in design, painted green rather than the traditional vermilion, and Monet designed it to be viewed partly obscured by vegetation, particularly by the large weeping willows (*Salix babylonica*) along the water's edge. Monet later added a trellis to cover the bridge

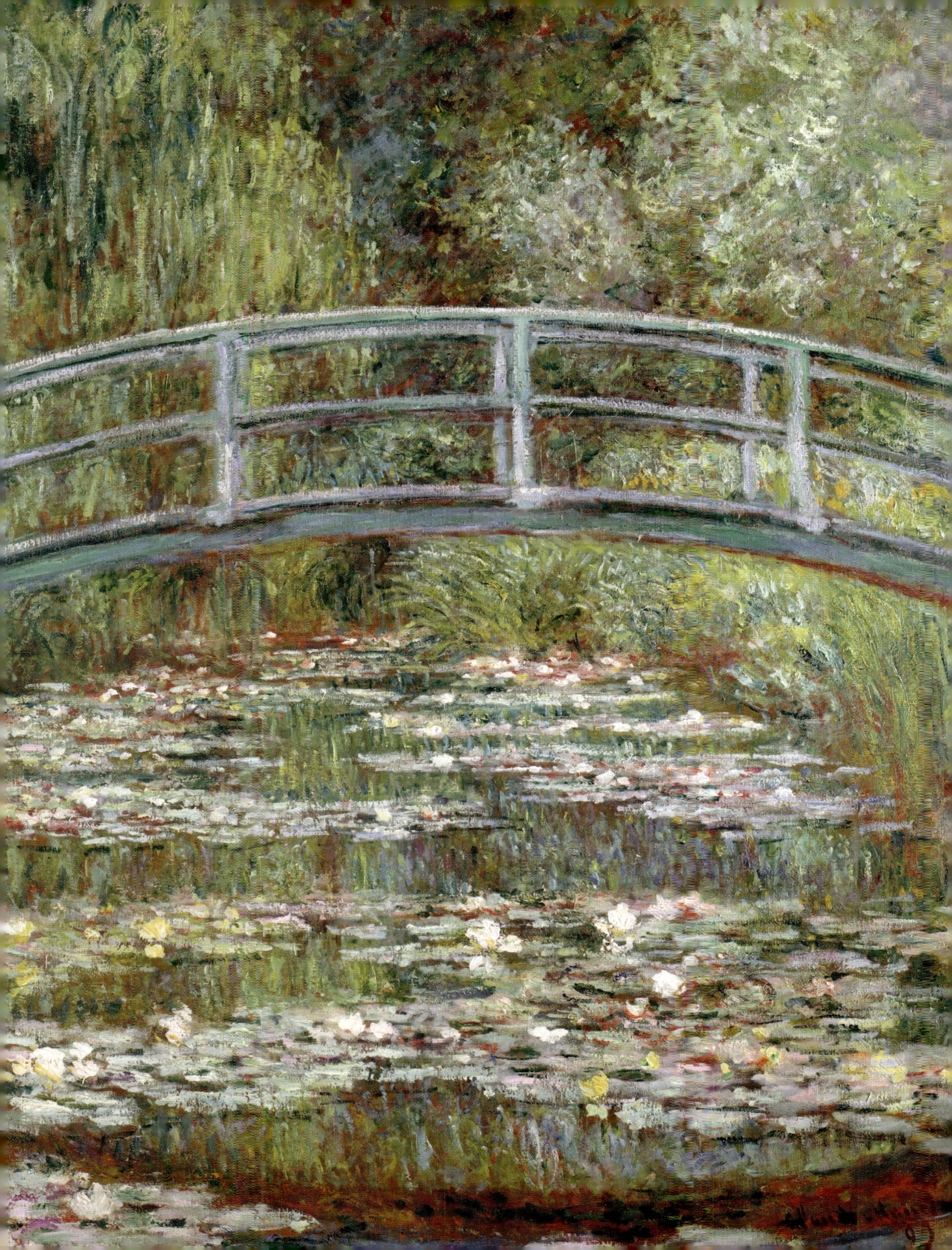

and trained white and mauve wisterias to grow over it. On the banks, bamboos, acers and tree peonies (*Paeonia* x *suffruticosa*) continued the oriental theme, together with azaleas, ferns and hydrangeas towards the margins.

THE WATER LILIES

The still water of the pool allowed Monet to indulge his passion for water lilies (which dislike fast-flowing streams). He began collecting as many different cultivars as he could find, some of which continue to thrive today. The Latour-Marliac nursery sent many hardy forms, including 'William Falconer', 'Atropurpurea' and 'James Brydon'. Monet also ordered tender species, such as the yellow *Nymphaea mexicana*, which he would have known as *Nymphaea flava*, and it is believed that he also grew the blue *Nymphaea capensis* var. *zanzibariensis* under glass.

Just as in Monet's time, maintenance of the water garden today is undertaken daily, the gardeners using a small boat to clean away the debris and pond weeds by hand. For Monet, the essential quality of the water garden was its reflective properties, so care was taken not to allow the lilies and other water plants to extend too far over the surfaces of the ponds. The planting of the banks with shrub roses, *Spiraea* and large clumps of delphiniums, creating swathes of colour reflected in the water, was as important to the overall effect as the water lilies.

In 1902, Monet had a new, larger studio built in the garden and began work on a series of water lily paintings. Unlike the garden views, his technique for these was becoming progressively more subtle, playing with light and colour from memory rather than directly from life. The resulting forty-eight canvases, which were shown in Paris in 1908 as *Grandes Décorations*, would have a lasting and profound impact on the worlds of art, music and literature. On seeing the paintings, the writer Marcel Proust was inspired to write a famous depiction of a water garden in the first volume of *À la Recherche du Temps Perdu*.

For the rest of Monet's life, the garden at Giverny, especially the water garden, would be the transformative drive for his art. The canvases got bigger and his work lost its connection to any particular viewpoint – the paintings that made Monet one of the most famous artists of all time had transcended the garden that had been their birthplace.

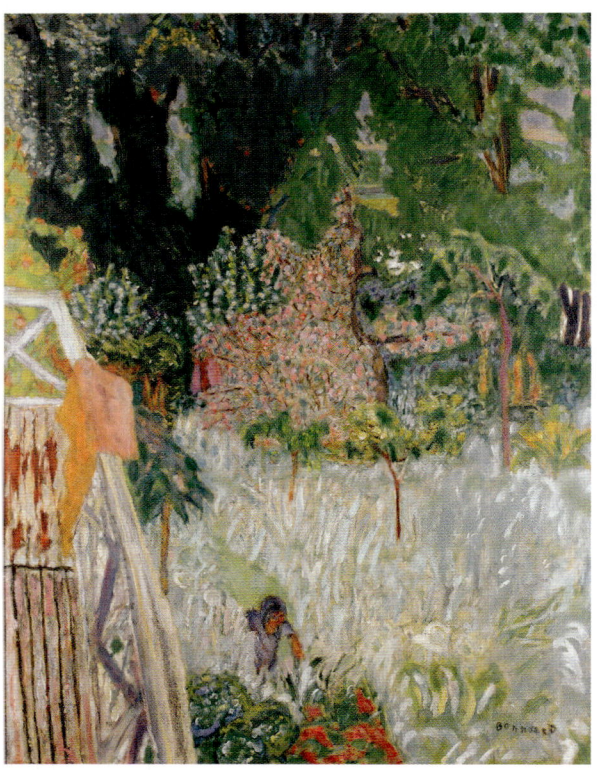

MONET'S INNER CIRCLE

Essentially a private man, Monet disliked being disturbed while working, unless it was to welcome one of his inner circle. His friends included Renoir (see page 50), with whom he had shared a studio in Paris, and Berthe Morisot, who had married Manet's brother. His favourite visitors were those who could converse knowledgeably about gardening, such as the art critic and writer Octave Mirbeau – he bred his own chrysanthemums and exchanged some of his cultivars for Monet's dahlias. Mirbeau also introduced Monet to orchids, which became an expensive passion; fortunately, his paintings were now selling well in France and in the USA, allowing him to fund it.

Another great friend was Gustave Caillebotte who, like Monet, was known as a keen and knowledgeable gardener. Unlike Monet, however, Caillebotte had never struggled for money. Born into a wealthy Parisian family, with a country estate in Yerres to the south-east of the city, in 1888 he took up permanent residence and made a garden at Petit Gennevilliers on the Seine. After taking advice

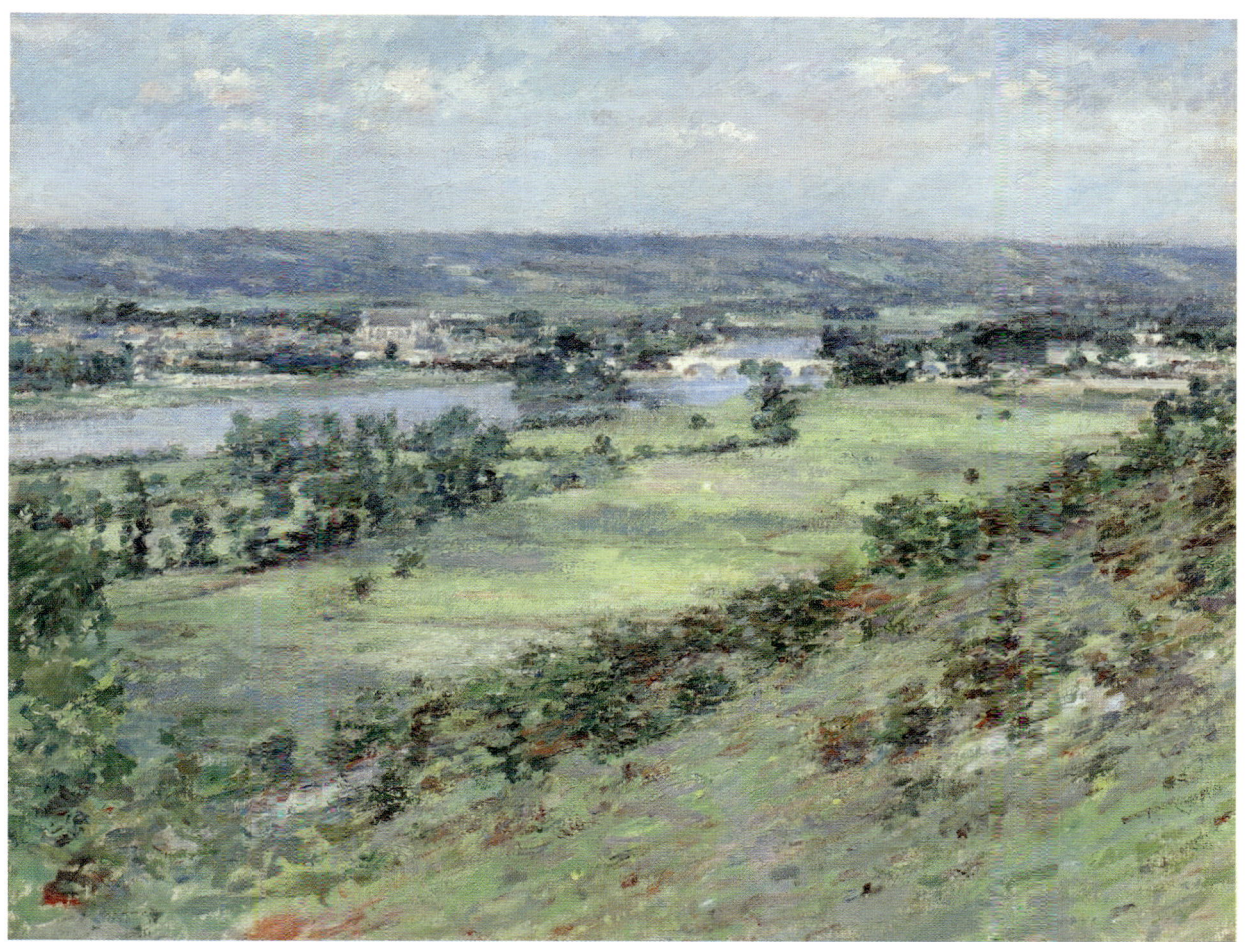

from Monet, he built a greenhouse and developed the garden for his own pleasure and also for painting. Caillebotte sadly died prematurely, collapsing in his garden aged just forty-five. If he had lived, Monet believed he would have been the most famous artist of them all.

Another artist friend, Pierre Bonnard, had moved to nearby Vernonnet, and Monet welcomed him to his house, along with other Post-Impressionist painters, Édouard Vuillard, Cézanne (see page 38) and Matisse. Bonnard's house was known as La Roulette (the caravan) and it had a more natural and rough-around-the-edges plot, which he made the subject of several paintings. Monet enjoyed showing this new guard of painters around his 'estate', dressed in the tweeds of a country gentleman.

OPPOSITE *The Balcony at Vernonnet* (1920) by Pierre Bonnard, who lived a few miles away from Monet, shows Bonnard's luxuriant garden.
ABOVE *Valley of the Seine, from the Hills of Giverny* (1892) by Theodore Robinson, who was part of the colony of American artists at Giverny.

THE AMERICAN COLONY AT GIVERNY

When Monet's art dealer, Paul Durand-Ruel, took his and other Impressionists' work to New York in 1886, he unleashed a fever for the style of painting that had still not been accepted in Europe. A few intrepid American artists – among them John Leslie Breck, John Singer Sargent, Willard Metcalf, Theodore Robinson, Mary Cassatt, and William Merritt Chase – were drawn to the rural idyll that they believed existed on the banks of the Seine. Many stayed for decades, including Frederick MacMonnies and his wife, Mary Fairchild MacMonnies, who were considered the leaders of the colony at Giverny.

Competition to produce the best paintings of the river, gardens and the haystacks was fierce, and the local Hôtel Baudy built a large studio in its garden where the artists could work on rainy days. Monet, however, remained aloof and was not in the habit of teaching or giving out advice freely, although scholars now believe that Breck may have been one of his few informal pupils, joining him to paint the same scenes around the Seine.

GIVERNY AFTER MONET

Monet's step-daughter Blanche Hoschedé-Monet was the only member of his family to take up art as a profession. She followed him in the garden and to the countryside, painting by his side. She fell in love with John Leslie Breck, one of the leading lights in the colony of American artists that formed in Giverny in the late nineteenth and early twentieth centuries. Blanche's relationship did not meet with Monet's approval and in the end the relationship was short-lived; she went on to marry Monet's biological son Jean in 1897.

Blanche's own painting, although well-respected, had to take a back seat while she ran the household, following the death of her mother Alice in 1911 – and her own husband Jean in 1914. She lived on at Giverny, caring for the gardens and Monet's legacy until 1947. The two-hectare/five-acre site (one hectare/two-and-a-half acres each of Clos Normand and the water garden), then went into a gentle decline until the 1970s, when Gérald Van der Kemp and Gilbert Vahé began restoring it, with the idea of opening it to the public, culminating in a grand re-opening in 1980.

Each year more and more visitors flow into the artist's small garden with its complex layout. Open from late March until the beginning of November, the gardens are filled with a succession of flowering plants, just as in Monet's time, from tree blossom and tulips in April, through to roses and nasturtiums in summer, followed by a crescendo of dahlias, asters, and rudbeckias at the end of the season. The idea has been to replicate Monet's intentions, while every year assessing and re-energizing the planting to make sure that it is always vibrant, no matter what month the visitor comes.

To achieve this requires a permanent staff of eleven gardeners and a huge turnover of plants. Monet himself would not have needed to garden with such intensity, and the plot would have had a wilder look under his care. Yet his spirit lingers on at Giverny. His planting style, with the irises, peonies, tulips and poppies set in blocks rather than dotted about, has been preserved and gained many followers, but Giverny is not frozen in time. The gardeners are continually updating the planting, while ensuring that the essence of the artist is retained: no double flowers, no grasses, no radical changes, just a gentle improvement each season, trying out a few different 'brushstrokes'.

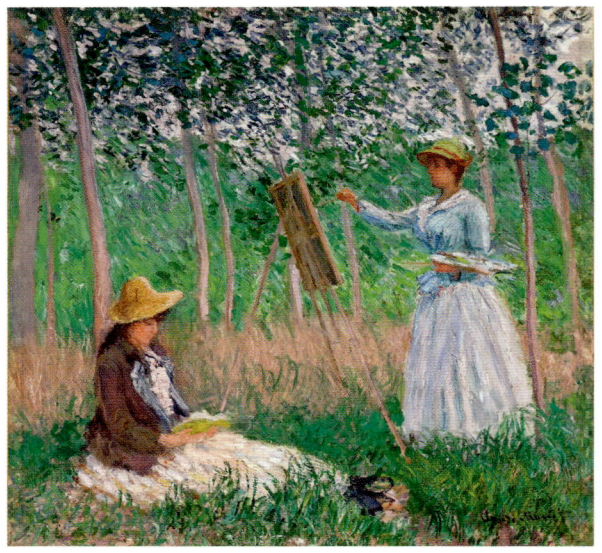

LEFT Monet's painting *In the Woods at Giverny* (1887) captures his step-children, with Blanche Hoschedé pictured at her easel – she became an artist in her own right and often painted alongside her step-father.

RIGHT The water lilies in the water garden at Giverny were the subject of Monet's last great series of paintings.

MONET'S TIMELINE

1840	1845	1862	1870	1870–71	1871	1872	1874
Oscar-Claude Monet born in Paris	Monet and his family move to the Normandy region of France	Studies under Charles Gleyre in Paris; becomes friends with Renoir, Cézanne, Degas, and Frédéric Bazille	Marries Camille Doncieux in Paris	In England, Monet sees paintings by Constable and Turner and meets Camille Pissarro	Moves to Argenteuil, France, where he lives until 1878	Paints *Impression, Sunrise* – the work that gives Impressionism its name	The first Impressionists exhibition held in Paris

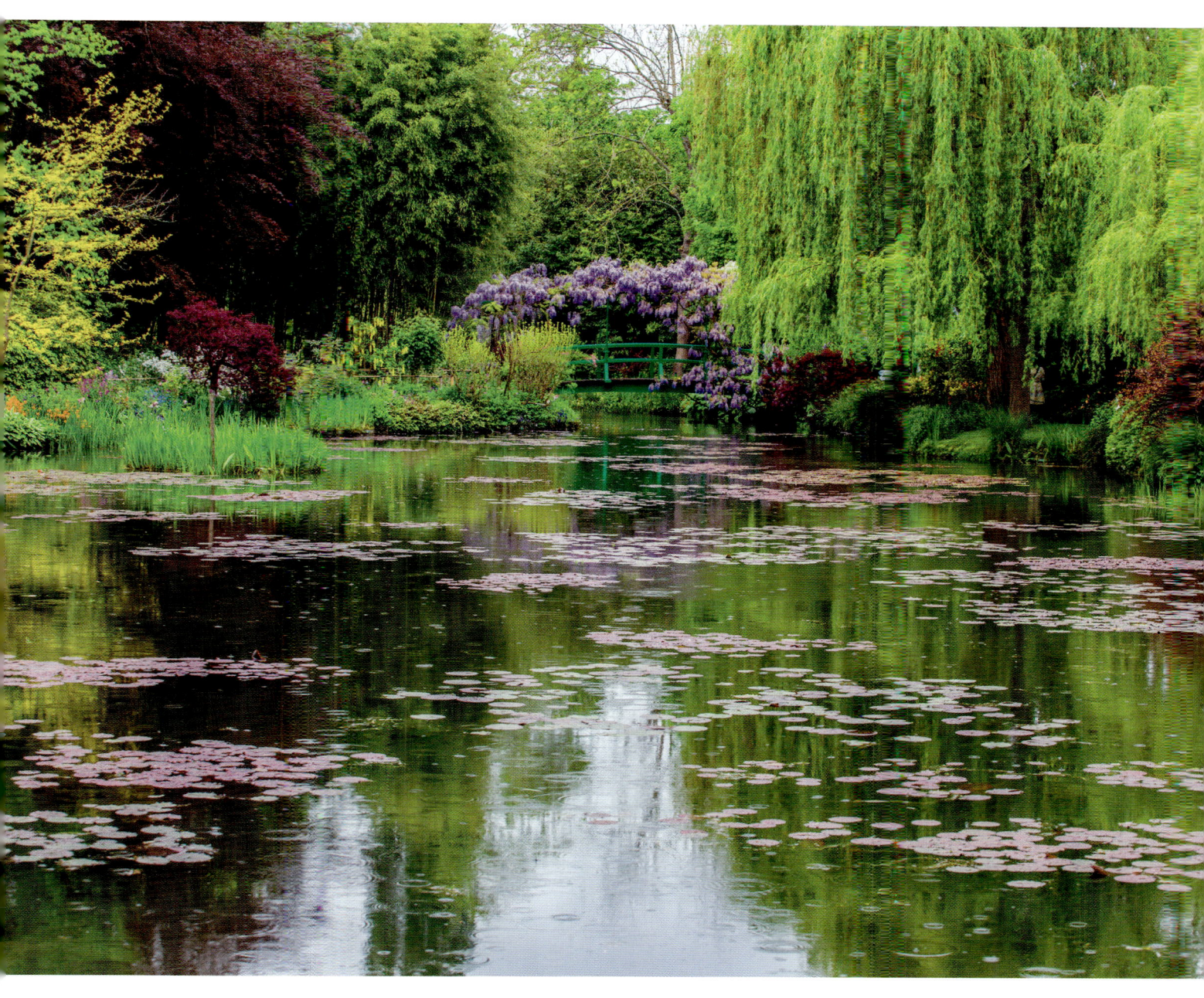

Moves to Vétheuil
with the Hoschedé
family; Camille
Monet dies in 1879

Moves to house
at Giverny

Monet marries
Alice Hoschedé

Begins to
develop the
water garden

Begins his
paintings of water
lilies, which
absorb him for
the rest of his life

Alice dies;
Jean Monet, the
artist's son, dies
three years later

Begins painting
the large *Water
Lilies*, including the
panorama paintings
and triptychs

Monet dies
of lung cancer,
aged 86

1878   1883   1892   1893   1897   1911   1916   1926

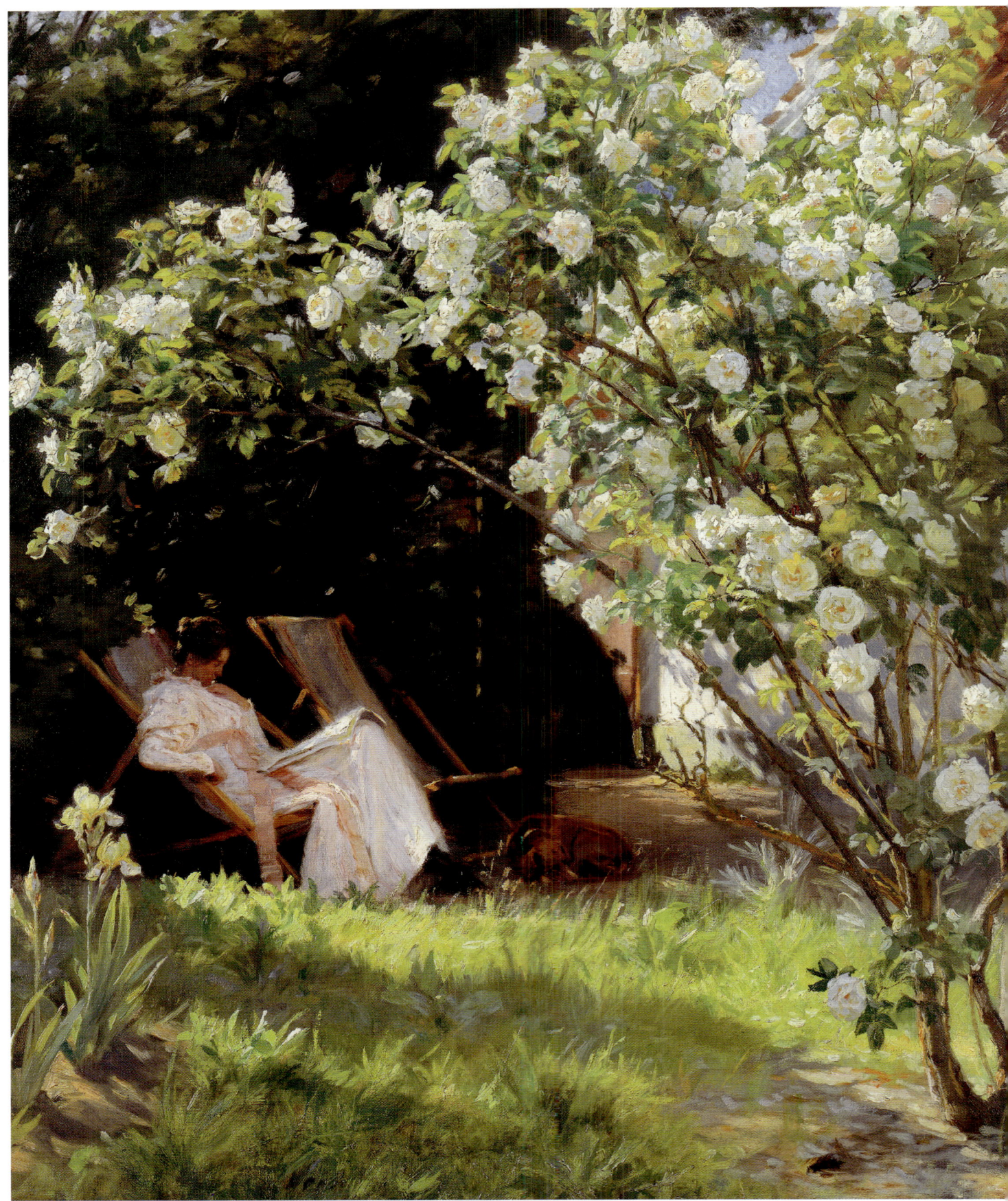

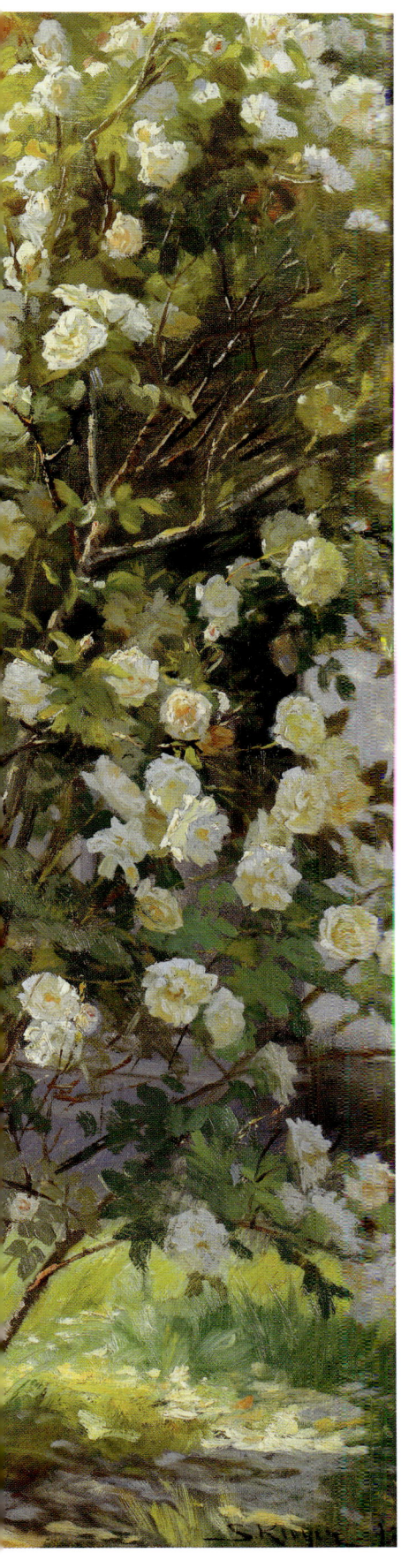

The Skagen painters

Anna and Michael Ancher, Laurits Tuxen, Marie and P.S. Krøyer, Viggo Johansen

North Jutland, Denmark

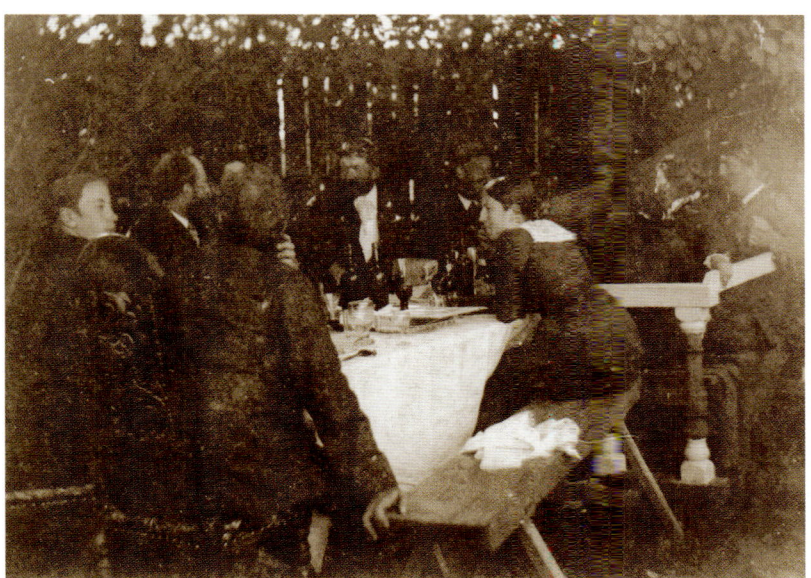

THE WIDE SKIES, sand dunes and empty seashores of northern Denmark have long been a source of inspiration for painters. In the last decades of the nineteenth century, this wild landscape attracted a group of young artists who wanted to break free from the conventions of the Royal Danish Academy of Fine Arts in Copenhagen, which they felt was stifling their artistic expression. News had reached them of a ground-breaking movement taking hold in France, dubbed 'Impressionism', named after Monet's painting of 1874, *Impression, Sunrise*. The place they chose for their 'rebellion' was a fishing village called Skagen on the northernmost tip of Jutland, where they would gather each summer in the small houses and flower-filled gardens around the Brøndums Hotel. These artists rejected the conventional teaching

ABOVE The Skagen painters: Anna Ancher (centre right), P.S. Krøyer opposite her, and others at dinner in the garden of the Anchers' house.

LEFT For three summers between 1891 and 1894, artists Marie and P.S. Krøyer rented Madame Bendsen's cottage in Skagen, where Krøyer painted one of his most celebrated images of Marie, titled *Roses* (1892), with her dog by her feet. The rose in the foreground is 'Alba Maxima'.

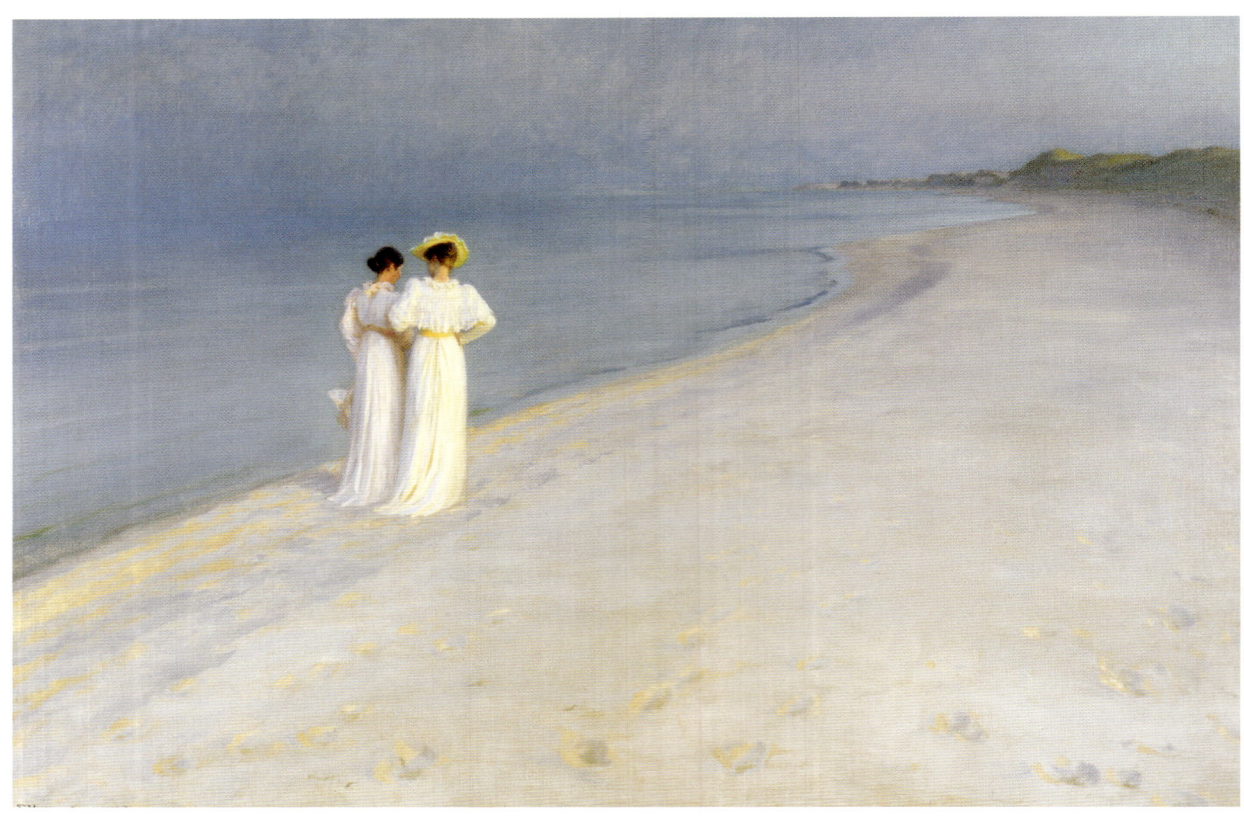

ABOVE *Summer Evening on Skagen Sønderstrand* (1893) by P.S. Krøyer portrays artists Marie Triepcke Krøyer, his wife, and Anna Ancher.
RIGHT *In the Garden* (circa 1893) by P.S. Krøyer was probably painted in Madame Bendsen's garden.
OPPOSITE *Anna Ancher Returning from the Field* (1902) by her husband Michael Ancher.

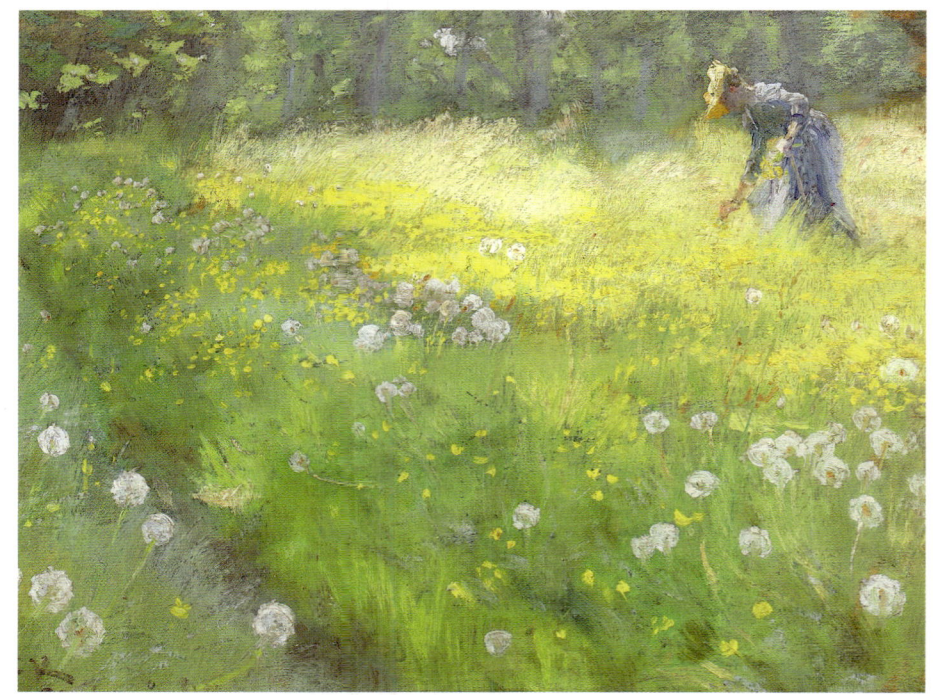

of the Academy, which was still following the realistic style of Martinus Rørbye, the foremost Danish painter of the mid-nineteenth century. In fact, it was Rørbye who had first discovered Skagen in the 1830s. At that time, the journey to this remote coastline from Copenhagen involved sea crossings and many miles of pony-and-trap rides across sandy heathlands, but when a road was built from Frederikshavn in the 1850s – and the railway reached Skagen in 1890 – the attractions of the traditional seaside village opened up to a new creative community.

FOUNDING MEMBERS

It is easy to see why the young artists loved this sandy spit of land, with its dunes, open spaces and clear light, which still draws people from all over Europe in search of a simpler life. Most of the early visitors stayed in rented houses or beach shacks, or took basic rooms to enjoy an inexpensive sojourn with the writers, poets, musicians and other artists who gathered there.

At Skagen, artists could experiment with different techniques and ways of working, particularly outdoors. Although they never became Impressionists, in terms of their brushwork, they were equally radical in their desire to change the *status quo* – choosing everyday subjects, depicting real landscapes and seascapes, and using their own homes and gardens as sources of inspiration.

The first artists to set up home at Skagen were Anna and Michael Ancher. Anna was the daughter of the Brøndums who ran the Brøndums Hotel, the only lodging house in the village. She had trained in Copenhagen (at a private school, since women were barred from the Academy) and exhibited her first painting, aged just twenty-one, at Charlottenborg, where her future husband also triumphed with his first image of Skagen – *Will He Round The Point?* (1880) – which depicted the harsh lives of the fishermen who worked there. The pair married in Skagen's church in 1880 and, as the only permanent residents (the other artists were summer visitors only), they became the unofficial leaders of the art colony.

The Anchers were soon joined by some of Denmark's most famous artists of the period, including Peder Severin Krøyer (better known as P.S. Krøyer), Laurits Tuxen and Viggo Johansen. We owe much of what we know of

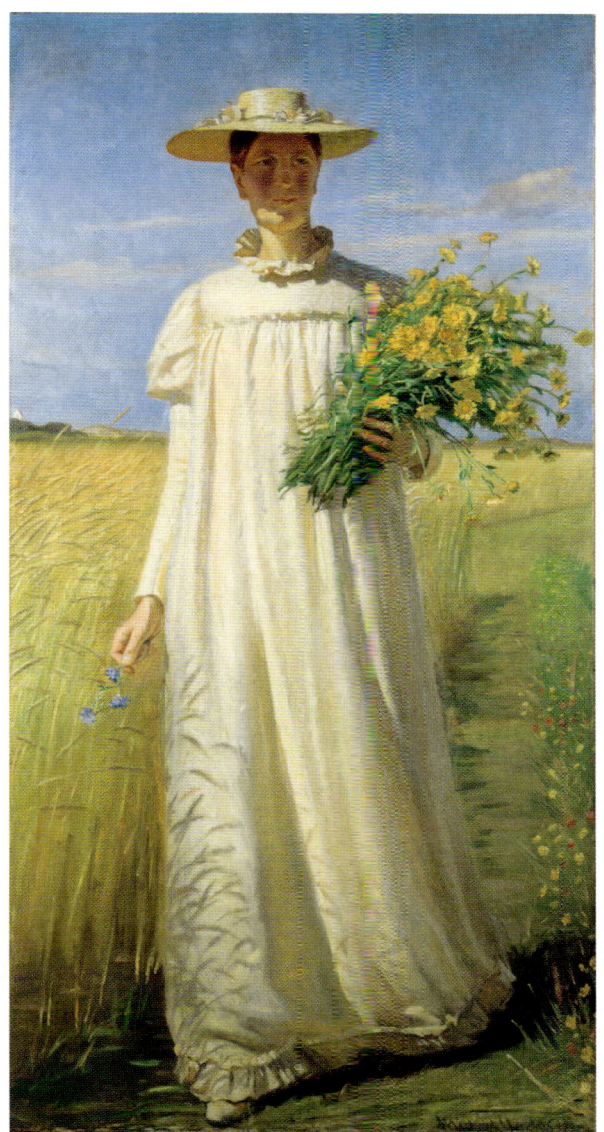

the Skagen painters to P.S. Krøyer, who was a keen photographer and often photographed his subjects before working up small oil sketches and then moving on to the final painting. He captured most of the artists at Skagen, hanging his paintings in the hotel's dining room.

P.S. Krøyer was already an established artist when he first came to Skagen in June 1882 and this helped to put the village on the map in terms of international art. He would also go on to create two of his best-known garden paintings there: *Roses (1892)* and *In the Garden* (circa 1893).

The Artists in Residence

Anna Ancher (née Brøndum) (1859–1935), Michael
Ancher (1874–1927) and Helga Ancher (1883–1964)
P.S. Krøyer (1882–1909)
Marie Krøyer (1887–1906)
Viggo Johansen (1875–1920s)
Laurits Tuxen (1870–1927)

Between the 1880s and 1920s, the Danish fishing village
of Skagen became a meeting place for Scandinavian
artists. Some came for a few weeks each summer and
rented rooms or stayed at the only inn, Brøndums
Hotel. Others resided at Skagen for months and a few,
including the leaders of the colony, Anna and Michael
Ancher, made it their permanent home. They lived close
to one another in various old houses in the village,
and met up regularly to exchange ideas. Several artists
formed couples, but it was always a shifting community.

Artists came to Skagen because of its remote, wild
nature and their interest in depicting the working
population. There, they had the freedom to develop new
ways of living and creating art. While they were inspired
by many different schools, including Impressionism
and Realism, each painter followed their own path. The
creative community in Skagen remained influential up to
the 1920s, and their work is still much sought-after today.

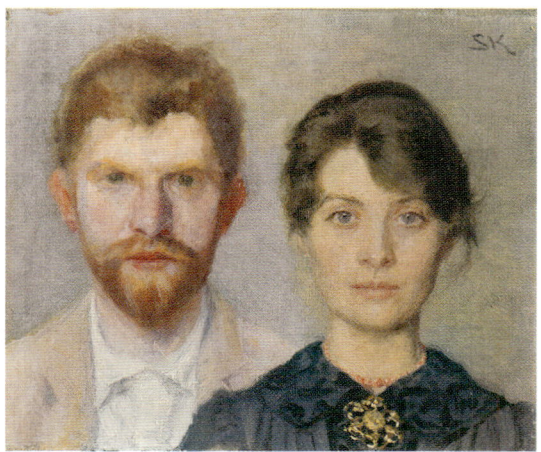

P.S. Krøyer and Marie Krøyer painted each other in this 1890
portrait, probably while on their honeymoon.

ENCLOSED SPACES

One of the central philosophies of the Skagen painters
was that they wanted to keep the distinction between the
domestic, enclosed space of a house and its garden, and
the exterior, working town. Each garden in their paintings
was enclosed by its picket fence or hedge, and belonged
to a definite genre, which the artists were adamant should
not be confused with the 'realism' of paintings illustrating
the Skagen fishermen at work.

At the centre of the community was Brøndums Hotel
and the Garden House in its grounds – this long, low
wooden building was one of the oldest in Skagen. Michael
and Anna Ancher moved into the Garden House after
their marriage and their daughter, Helga, was born there.
The couple set up a joint studio in the northern end of the
building, while Krøyer made his studio in a small grain-
drying storage barn close by, also in the hotel's grounds.

In 1883, Krøyer instigated the 'Evening Academy'. The
idea behind the Academy was for the artists and their

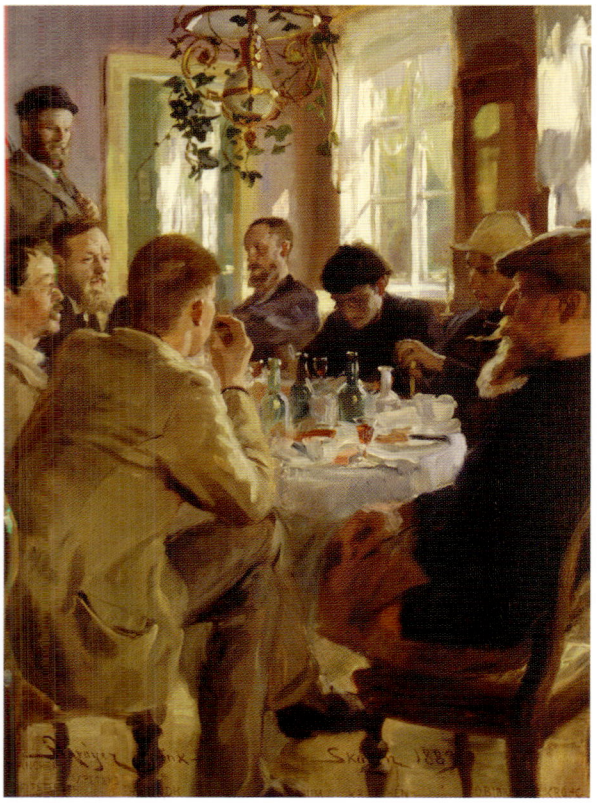

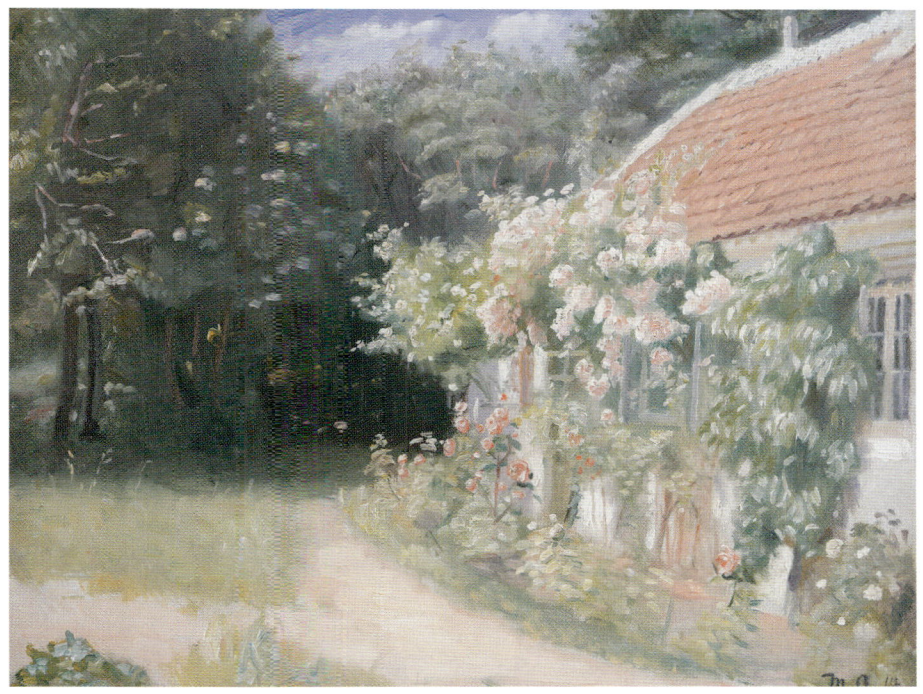

LEFT *The Old Garden House* (1914) by Michael Ancher depicts the cottage in the grounds of Brøndums Hotel, where he and his wife Anna lived and entertained friends. BELOW The Brøndum and Ancher families outside their hotel. Artists Anna and husband Michael Ancher (back row, second right and far right) were founders of the Skagen colony. OPPOSITE *Artists' Luncheon at Brøndums Hotel* (1893) by P.S. Krøyer captures one of the informal gatherings at Skagen, with Michael Ancher standing beside artists from Sweden, Denmark and Norway.

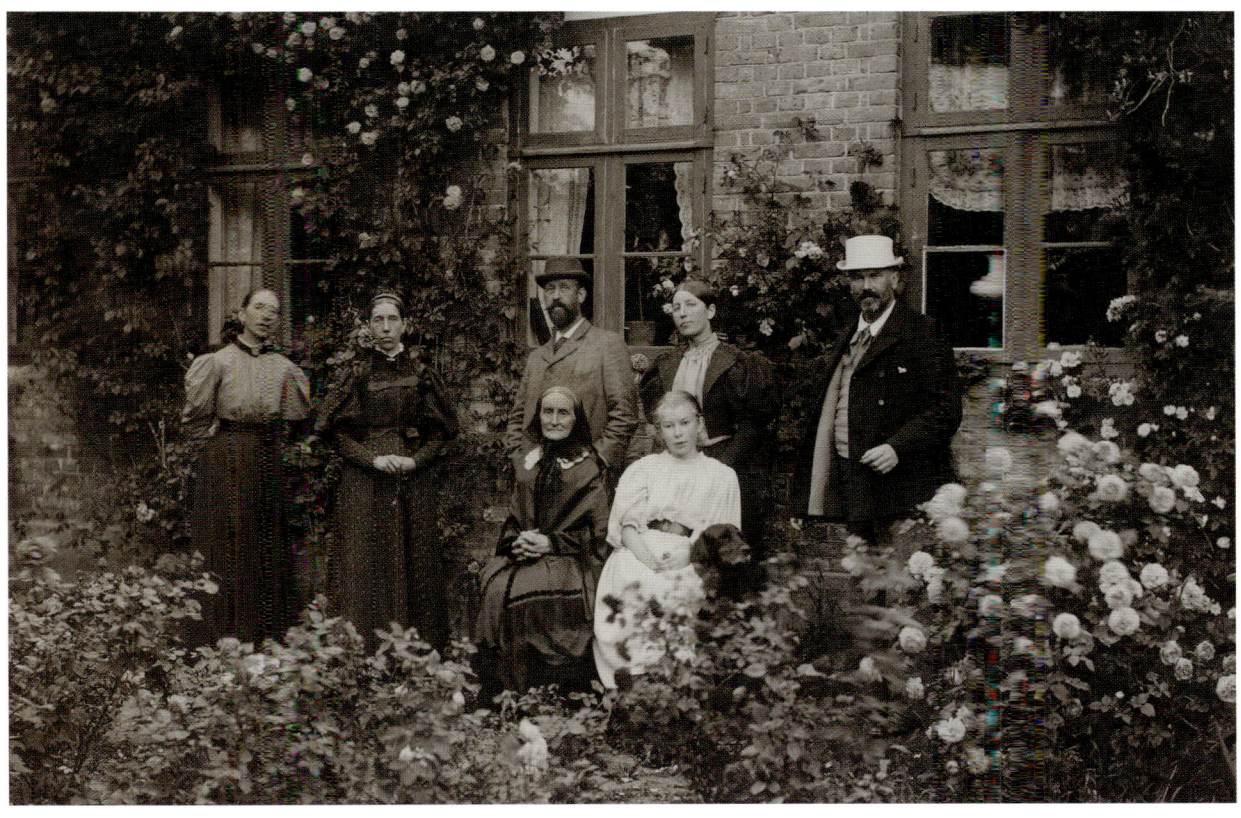

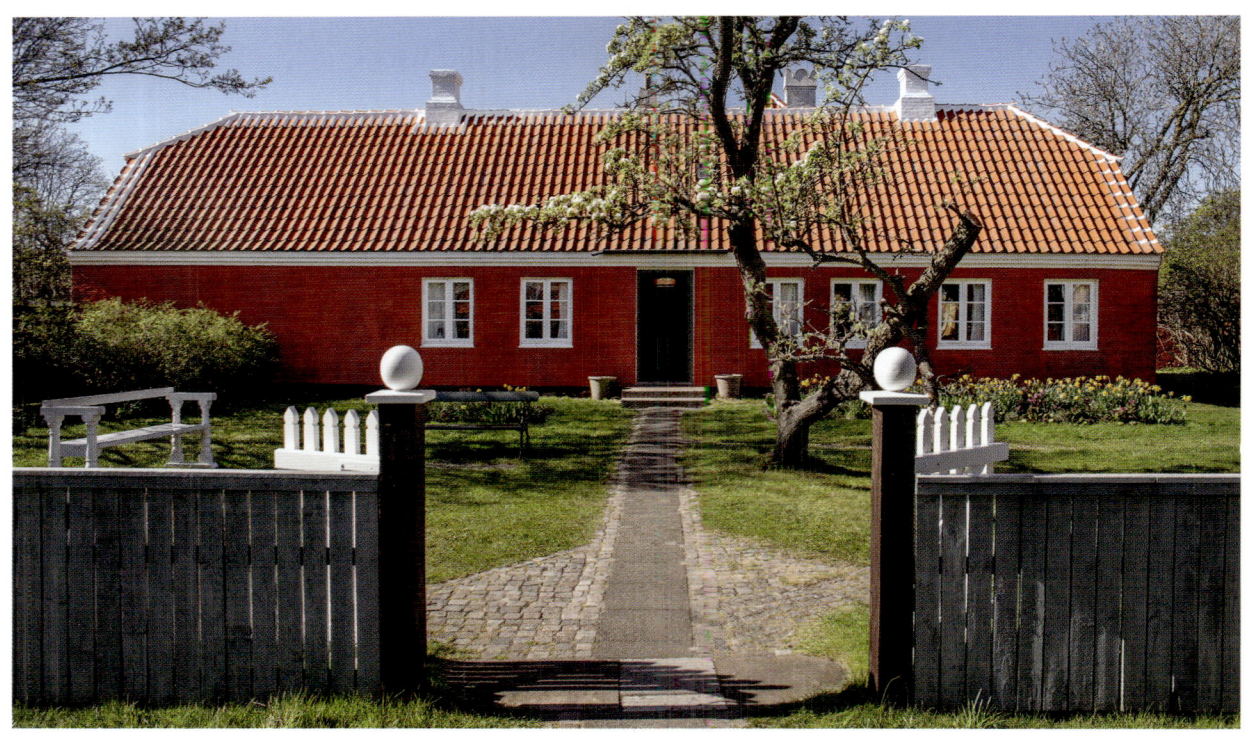

ABOVE Skagen's permanent residents, Anna and Michael Ancher, moved to No. 2 Markvej, close to her parents, who ran the Brøndums Hotel.
RIGHT *Entrance to the Anchers' Garden* (1903) by Anna Ancher; the pear tree in this painting is still standing (see above).
OPPOSITE *Hip, Hip, Hurrah!* by P.S. Krøyer (1888) was based on the artists' celebrations when his friends the Anchers moved into their house on Markvej, with its large garden.

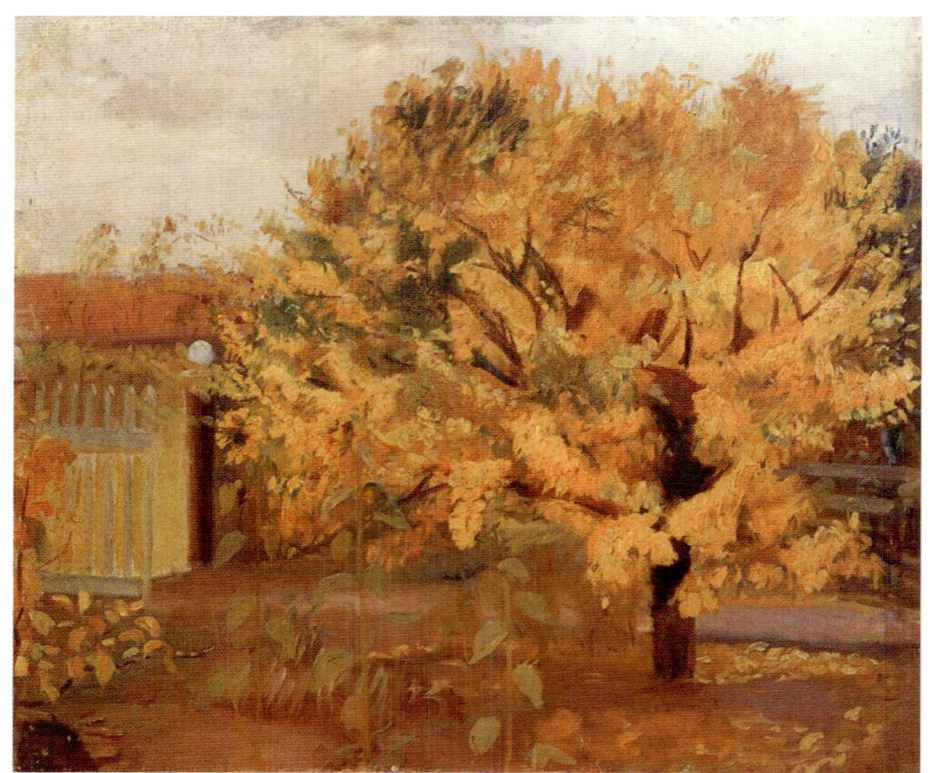

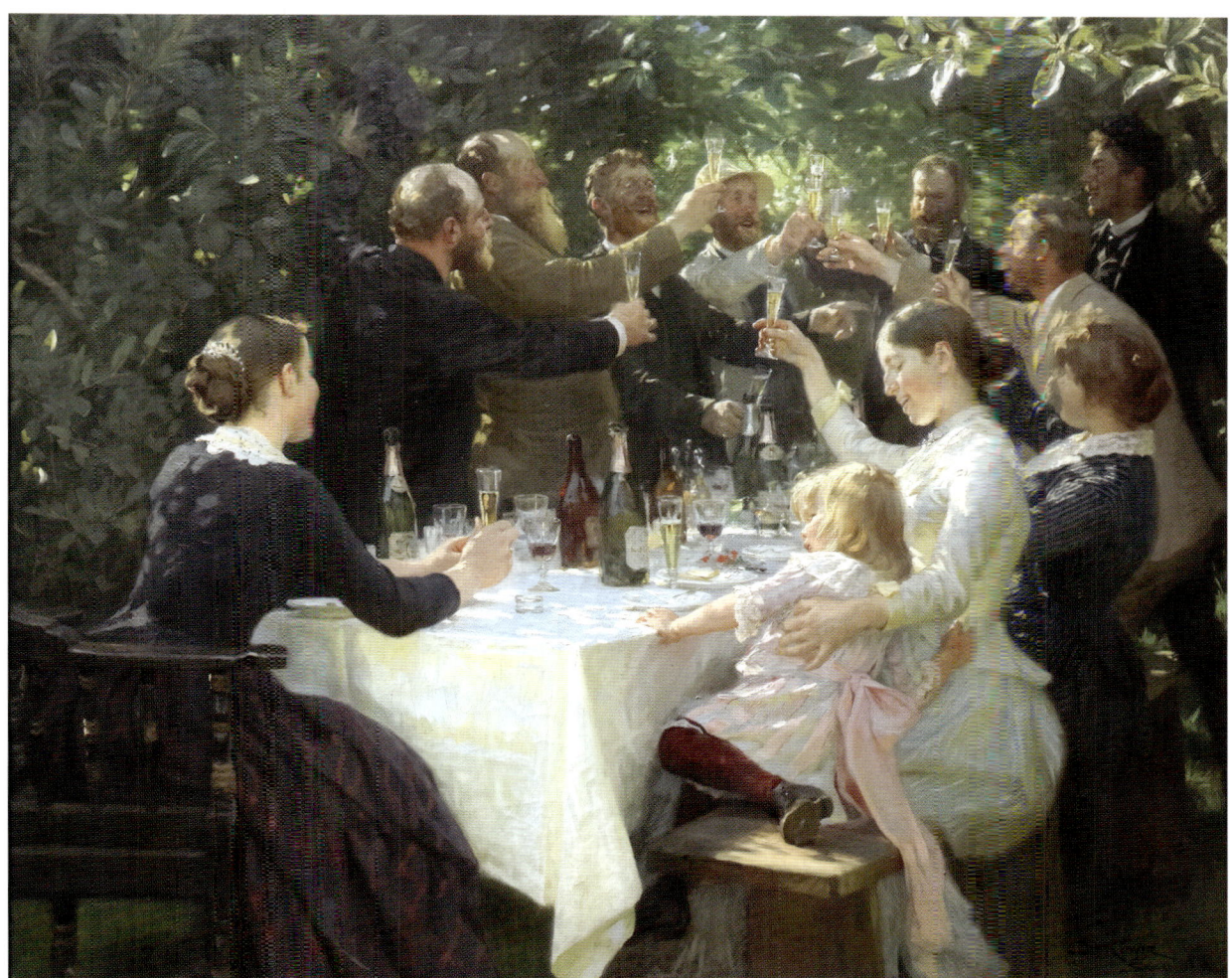

friends to take a break from their work and meet up on fine summer evenings at the Garden House to talk about their art and exchange ideas.

Gardening was very much part of this non-urban lifestyle and on 1 May 1884, Michael and Anna Ancher bought their own house at No. 2 Markvej, not far from Anna's parents at Brøndums. To celebrate, an outdoor lunch was held for all their friends and the moment was captured by P.S. Krøyer in *Hip Hip Hurrah!*, one of his most popular paintings. It was a cause for celebration, not only because the new house had a large garden with room to grow vegetables and ample space for dining tables to eat outside and entertain, but also because it had one of the few hot-water systems in the town, fired by a wood

stove that heated water for a shower above the bath. The painting would take Krøyer four years to finish, beginning probably with a photograph of the occasion, followed by repeated visits to paint in the Ancher's garden. He finally completed it in 1888 in his studio in Brøndum's garden.

Finding life at Brøndums too restrictive, Krøyer and his new wife, artist Marie Triepcke, rented part of Madame Bendsen's large farmhouse and garden, which they shared with Martha and Viggo Johansen and their family. This old property delighted the artists and was the subject of several images by Viggo of Martha working within and outside the cottage, and one by Krøyer – *Hens under the trees at Madame Bendsen's Garden* (1893) – which shows its dilapidated state, without any attempt at prettification.

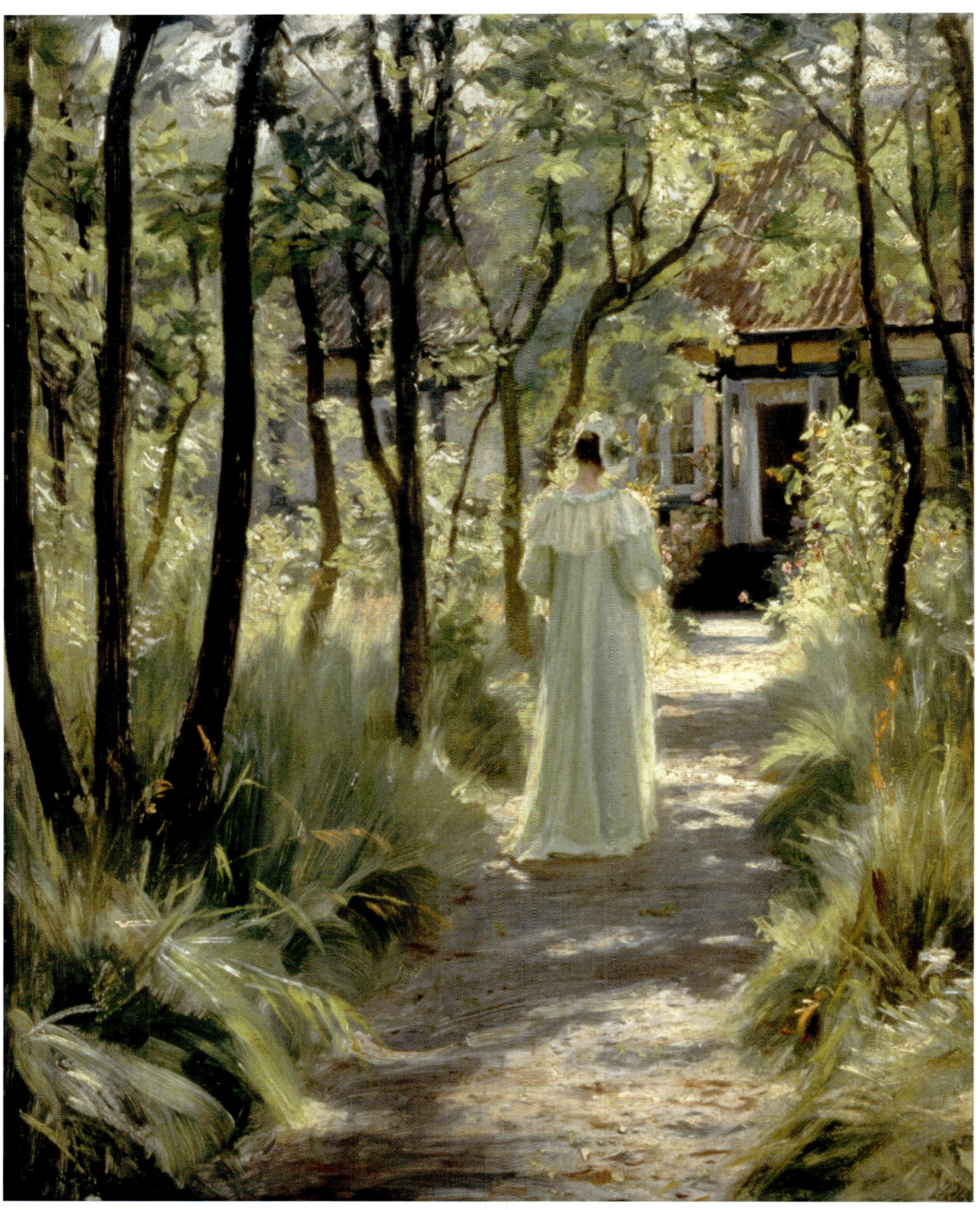

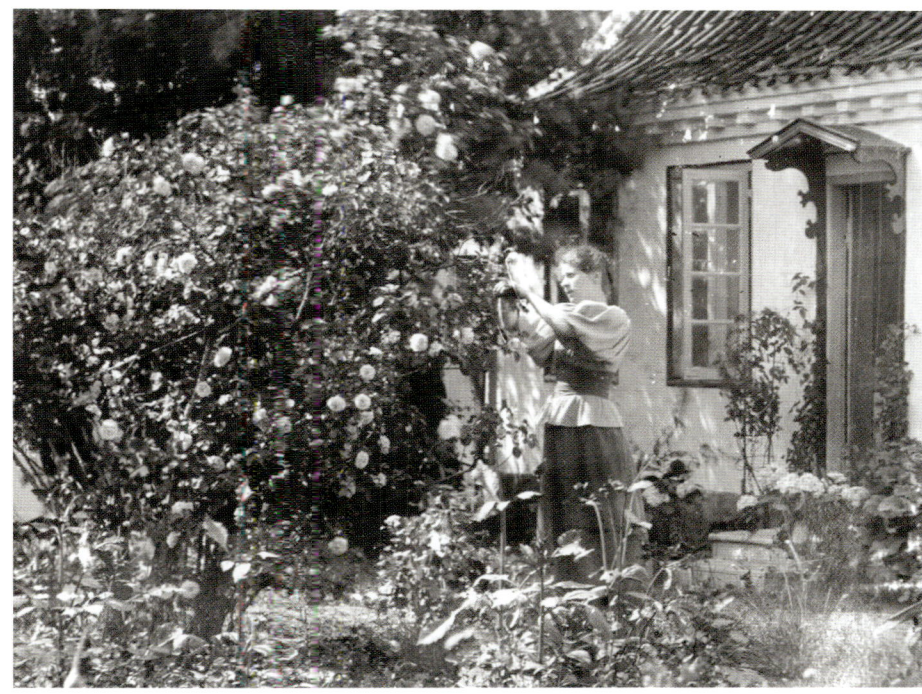

THE WIDER CIRCLE

News of the Skagen painters began to filter back to Copenhagen and soon everyone wanted to spend their summers in Jutland, particularly after the opening of the railway. P.S. Krøyer found the intrusion of holidaymakers difficult and began to distance himself by renting a house on the outskirts of town, in the Skagen Plantation, which had been allocated to the 'Inspector of Dunes' who did not need it. In 1894, Krøyer appointed the architect Plesner to remodel the interior space, while Marie masterminded the decoration, choosing furniture and making the soft furnishings – the couple were both influenced by the Arts & Crafts movement in Britain. Set within the timber plantation, the garden was deliberately left wild. Krøyer increasingly suffered periods of manic depression (probably bipolar disorder) and the couple divorced in 1906; Marie moved to Sweden, while Krøyer stayed on in the plantation house with their daughter Vibeke.

Among the artists' circle was Holger Drachmann, an eccentric writer, artist and critic, and the subject of one of Krøyer's last paintings, *Drachmann on the Beach*. In 1902, Drachmann bought a small dwelling in the village, where

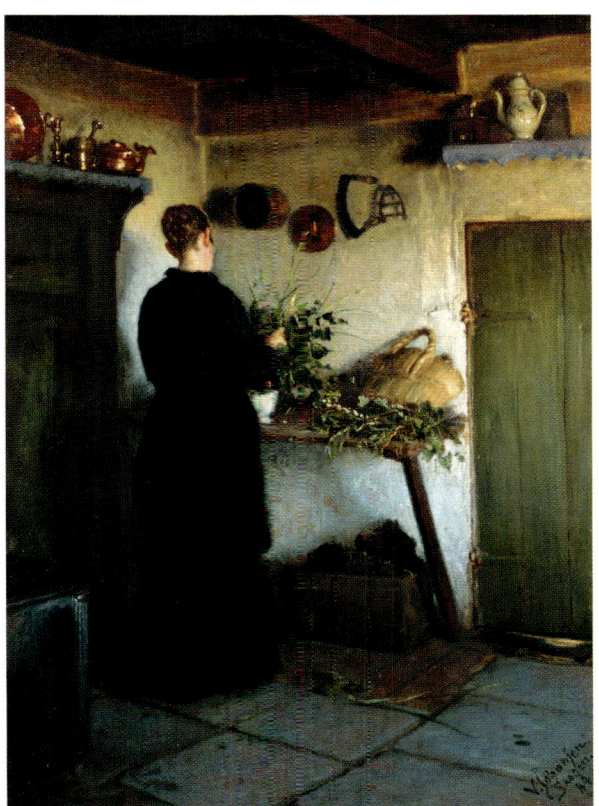

he entertained his myriad of wives and girlfriends and promoted the work of the Skagen painters. His influential newspaper columns, as well as his eccentric appearance (wearing a flowing cloak and an assortment of hats) helped bring the artists' work to a wider audience.

Laurits Tuxen was another influential member of the group. He bought Madame Bendsen's cottage in 1901 and lived there until his death in 1927. As in most of the gardens in Skagen, the soil at the cottage was acidic and sandy, like that of the surrounding heathland. Tuxen took advice from one of Skagen's most illustrious visitors, Queen Alexandra, Danish wife of the British King Edward VII, who advised him to plant rhododendrons. This he duly did, buying them from the Hartmann nursery in Ghent, and he went on to paint them repeatedly, in *Rhododendrons* (1917), *Sunshine in the Garden* (1922), and many other works.

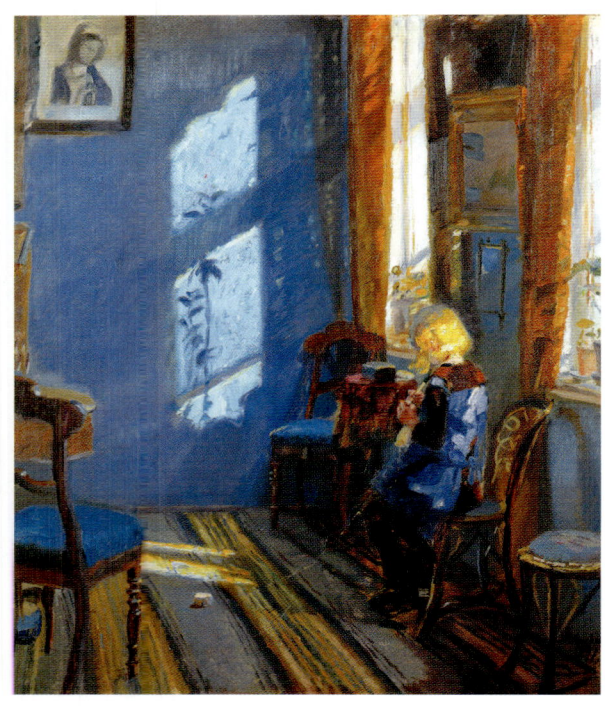

The artists started to run exhibitions for art students at the Technical School in Skagen during the summer, and in 1908 Tuxen, P.S. Krøyer, Anna's brother Degn Brøndum and others founded the Skagen Museum to house the work of the 'summer colony'. At that time artists, including Anna Ancher, began focusing on sunlight and colour, painting interiors, such as *Interior with Clematis* (1913), where she is clearly interested in the way light falls.

Anna often used her daughter Helga as a model, such as in *Sunlight in the Blue Room*, and inspired by her parents, Helga then went on to become an artist in her own right, representing a new generation at Skagen. She painted the house on Markvej, *Entrance to the Ancher House, Summer* (1922), and captured the natural chaos of Krøyer's garden in *Hogweed in the Garden behind Krøyer's House* (1927). The golden age of artists was nearing an end, but they had ensured that through the museum their work – and their houses and studios – would be preserved for the future.

THE SKAGEN PAINTERS' TIMELINE

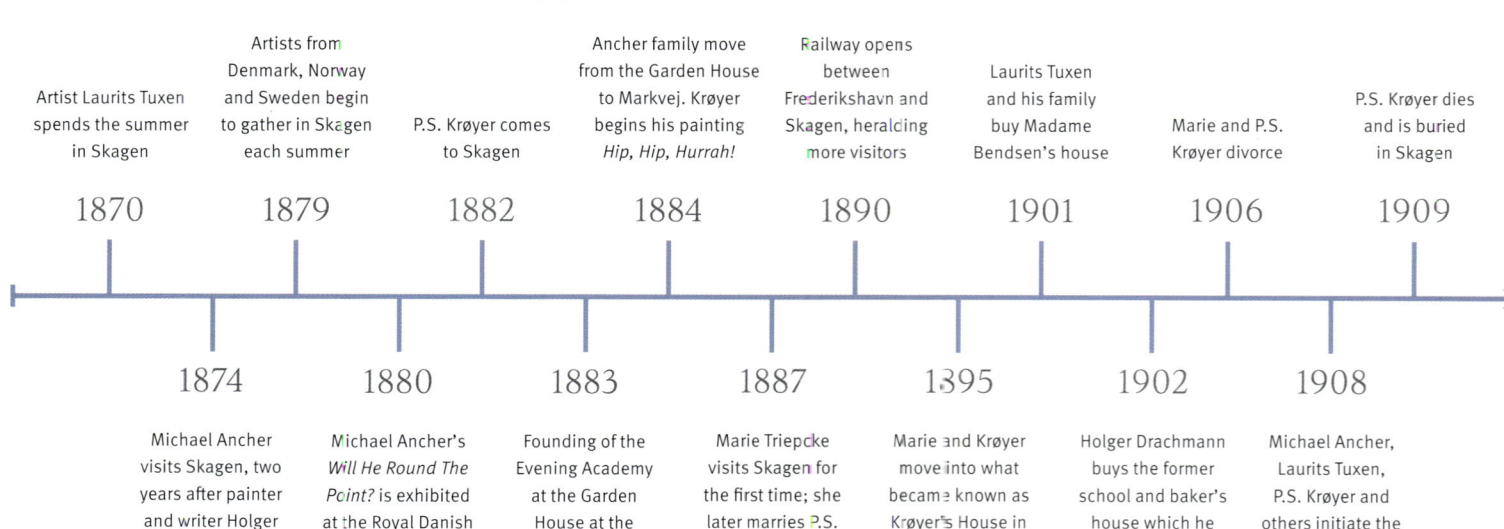

Artist Laurits Tuxen spends the summer in Skagen — 1870

Michael Ancher visits Skagen, two years after painter and writer Holger Drachmann — 1874

Artists from Denmark, Norway and Sweden begin to gather in Skagen each summer — 1879

Michael Ancher's *Will He Round The Point?* is exhibited at the Royal Danish Academy of Fine Arts — 1880

P.S. Krøyer comes to Skagen — 1882

Founding of the Evening Academy at the Garden House at the Brøndums Hotel — 1883

Ancher family move from the Garden House to Markvej. Krøyer begins his painting *Hip, Hip, Hurrah!* — 1884

Marie Triepcke visits Skagen for the first time; she later marries P.S. Krøyer in 1889 — 1887

Railway opens between Frederikshavn and Skagen, heralding more visitors — 1890

Marie and Krøyer move into what became known as Krøyer's House in Skagen Plantation — 1895

Laurits Tuxen and his family buy Madame Bendsen's house — 1901

Holger Drachmann buys the former school and baker's house which he renames *Villa Pax* — 1902

Marie and P.S. Krøyer divorce — 1906

Michael Ancher, Laurits Tuxen, P.S. Krøyer and others initiate the Skagen Museum — 1908

P.S. Krøyer dies and is buried in Skagen — 1909

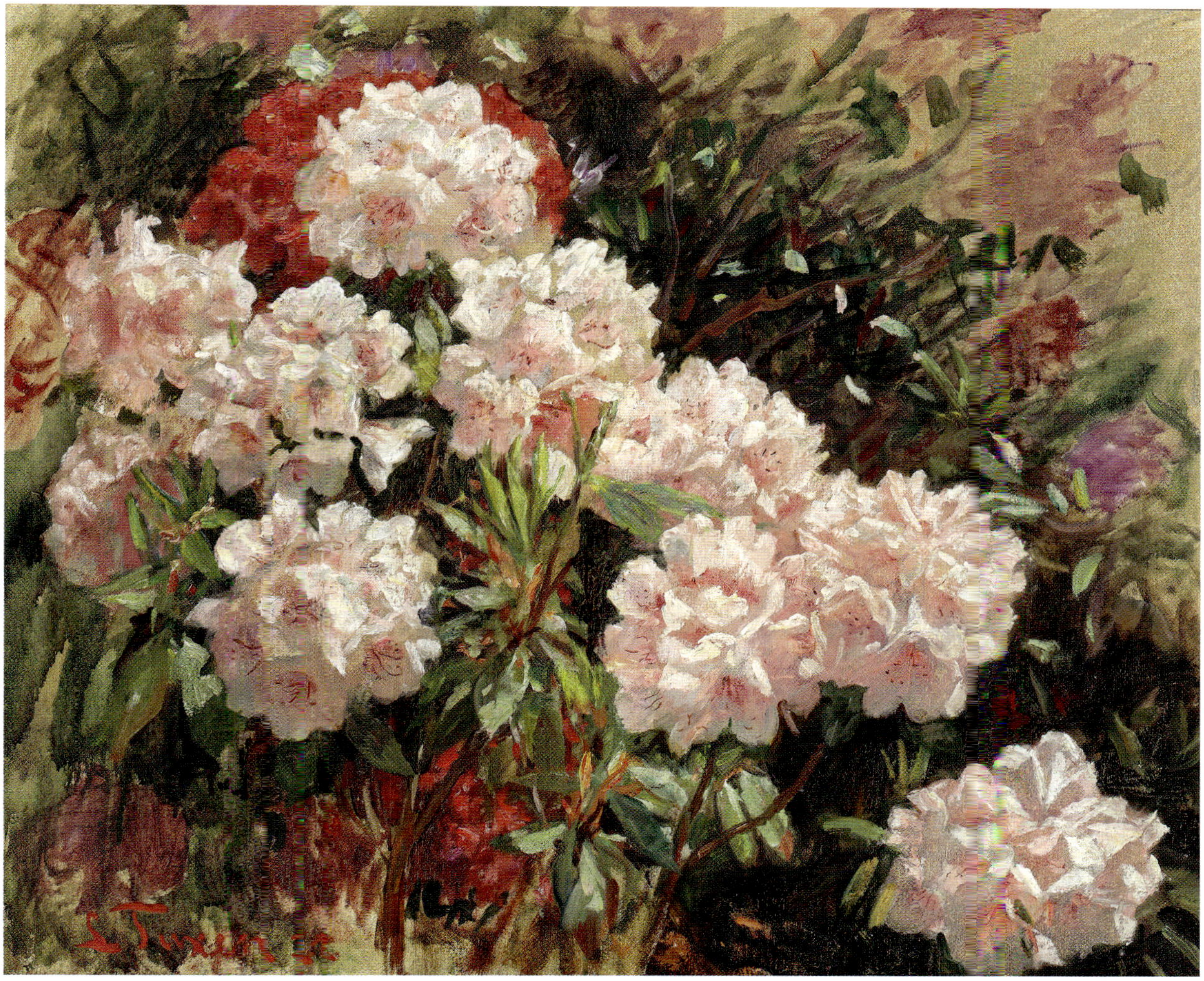

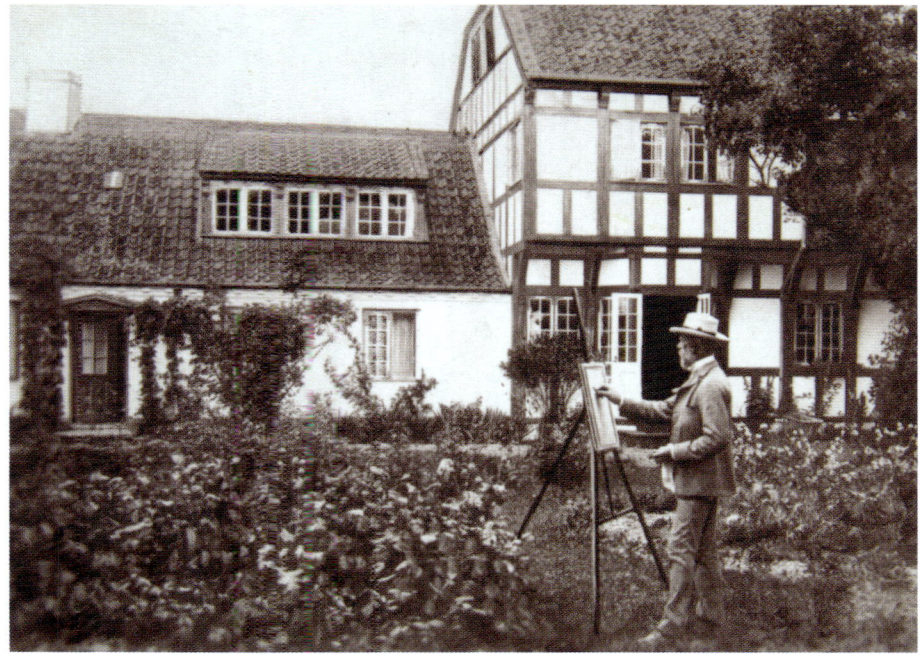

ABOVE Laurits Tuxen's
painting of *Flowering
Rhododendrons* (1911),
plants he grew on the advice
of Queen Alexandra because
they are suited to Skagen's
acid soil.

LEFT Artist Laurits Tuxen
bought Madame Bendsen's
old farmhouse in 1901 and
converted it into Villa
Dagminne, where he painted
the garden and its flowers.

OPPOSITE *Sunlight in the Blue
Room* (1891) by Anna Ancher
depicts her daughter Helga
sitting in one of the drawing
rooms of her grandparents'
hotel, Brøndums.

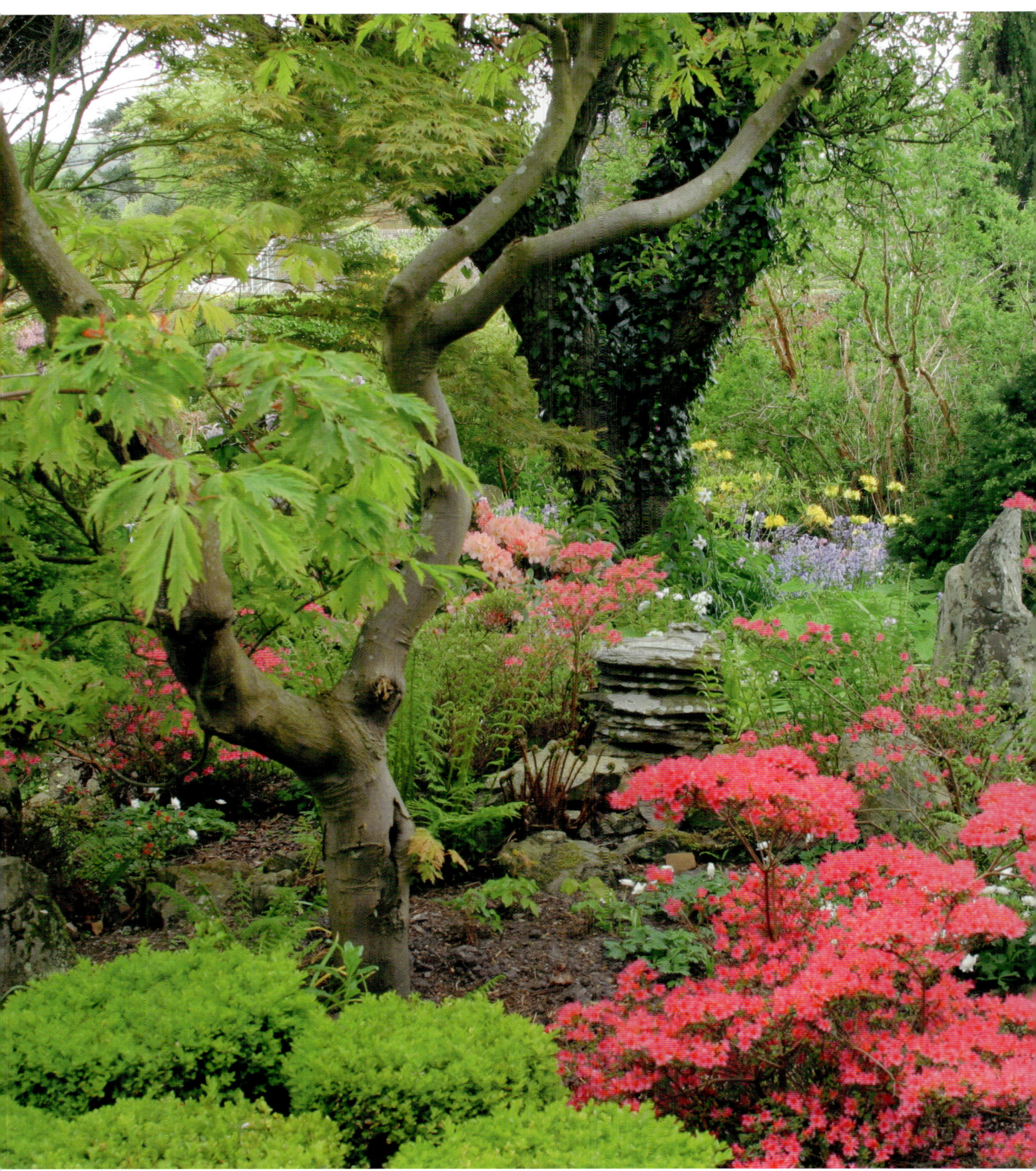

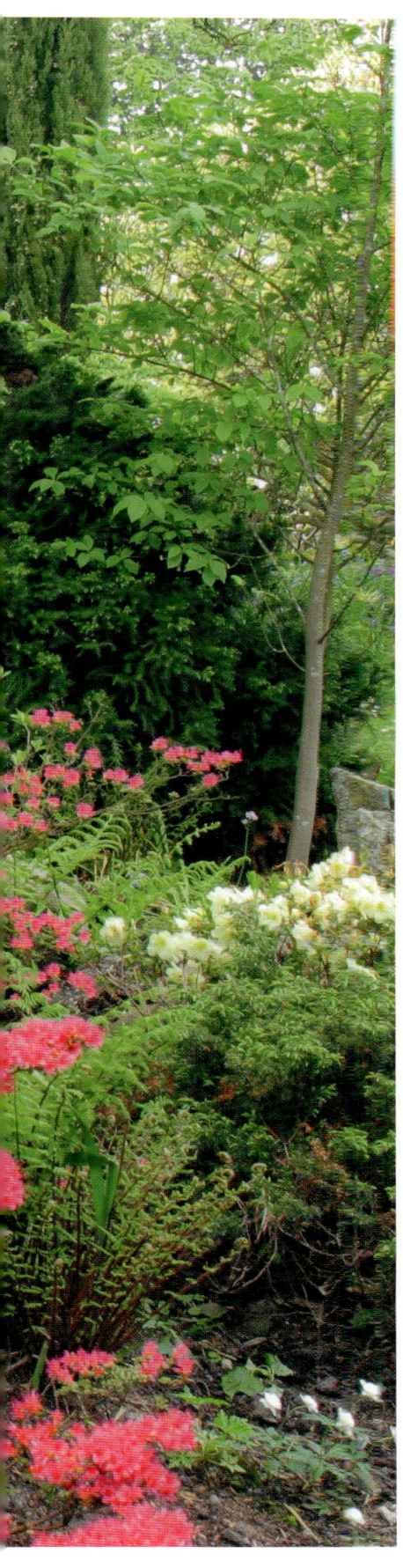

The Kirkcudbright artists

E.A. Hornel, George Henry, James Guthrie, Jessie M. King and the Glasgow School

Broughton House, Kirkcudbright, Scotland

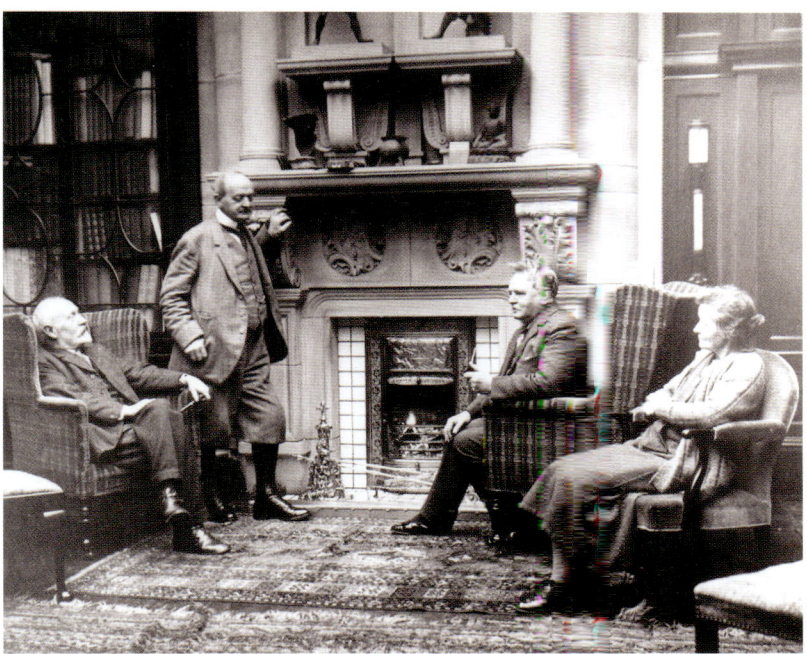

WHEN MEMBERS of the Glasgow Institute of Fine Arts gathered on a raw January day in 1885 to decide which paintings to hang in their next exhibition, they soon realized that the work of one particular group of young artists was something exceptional. Representing a new direction in Scottish and, indeed, European art, these young men would eventually become known as the 'Glasgow Boys'. James Guthrie, Edward Arthur Walton, James Paterson, William York Macgregor and others were influenced by new French ideas of painting outdoors, and had previously been rejected

ABOVE This photograph, circa 1930, shows artist E.A. Hornel (standing), his sister Tizzie, John Keppie (far left), architect of Hornel's gallery, and their family friend, Philip Halstead. LEFT Hornel travelled widely to Japan, Ceylon (Sri Lanka) and Australia, bringing home ideas for the planting of his own garden on the coast of south-west Scotland.

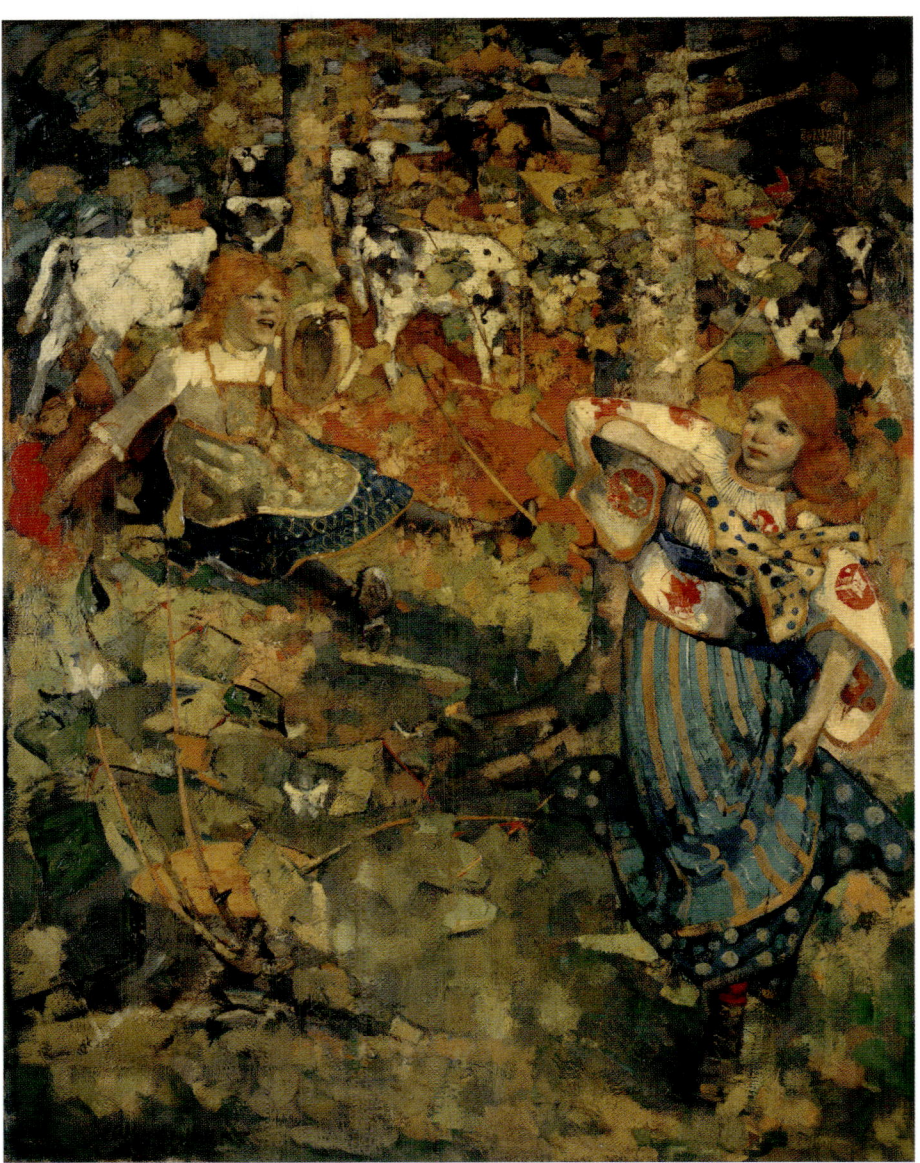

RIGHT *Summer* by E.A. Hornel, painted in 1891, demonstrates the artist's growing interest in pattern and paint texture.

by the establishment. What distinguished them from their predecessors, who had painted grand canvases of the Scottish highlands, was their choice of subjects – often modest villages or towns, where they captured the working people and landscape in a less sentimental way. While the Glasgow Boys rarely painted or, in future years, even lived in Glasgow, their nickname stuck.

From 1888, two of the younger painters, Edward Atkinson Hornel and George Henry, were forging new ways of working. Hornel and Henry probably met at one of the summer painting camps at Cockburnspath in Berwickshire, and soon they, along with James Guthrie, began meeting at Hornel's home in the small fishing port of Kirkcudbright in the south-west of Scotland. This

period also marked a change of style for the artists, as Symbolism became more important than naturalism, and they began experimenting with colour, texture and pattern. By 1890, when the last 'Glasgow Boys' exhibition was held in London's Grosvenor Gallery, a new phase in the Scottish artists' lives and work had begun.

SETTLING IN KIRKCUDBRIGHT

Edward Atkinson Hornel's family had emigrated from Scotland to Australia, but returned to Kirkcudbright when Edward was two years old. His father was a shoemaker and he was one of twelve siblings, four of whom died when children. Despite their humble beginnings, Edward's older sister, Elizabeth – or 'Tizzie' as she was known – went to

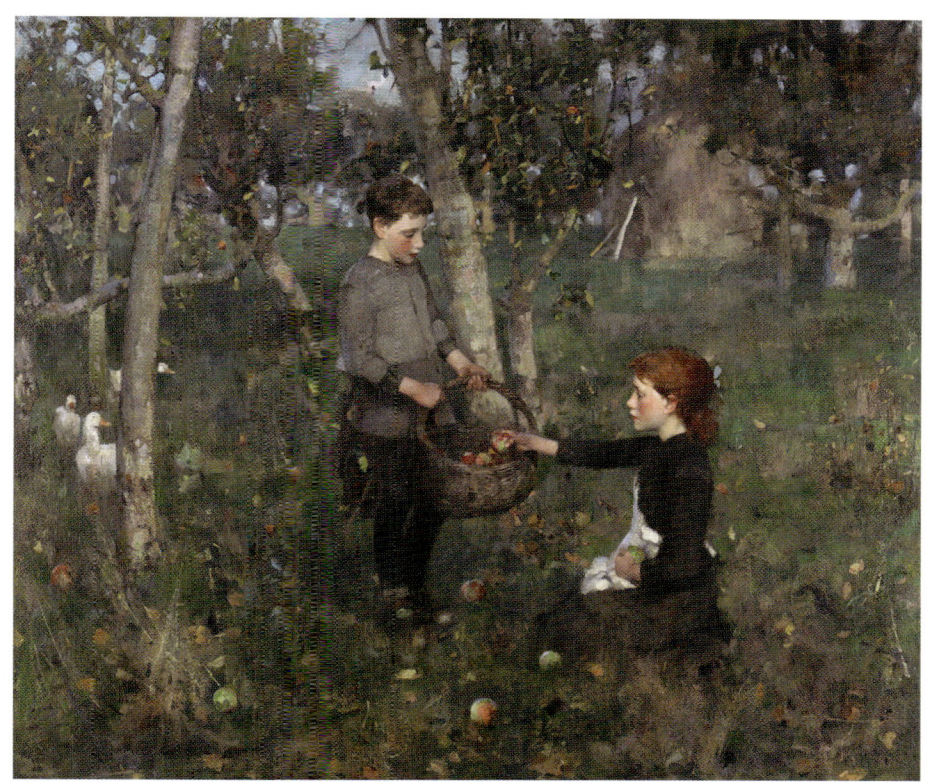

LEFT *In the Orchard* by James Guthrie (1886), who spent the summer of 1886 with E.A. Hornel and George Henry in Kirkcudbright and, like them, sought rural scenes to paint.

BELOW Painted just outside Kirkcudbright, *A Galloway Landscape* (1889) is Henry's evocative image of the region.

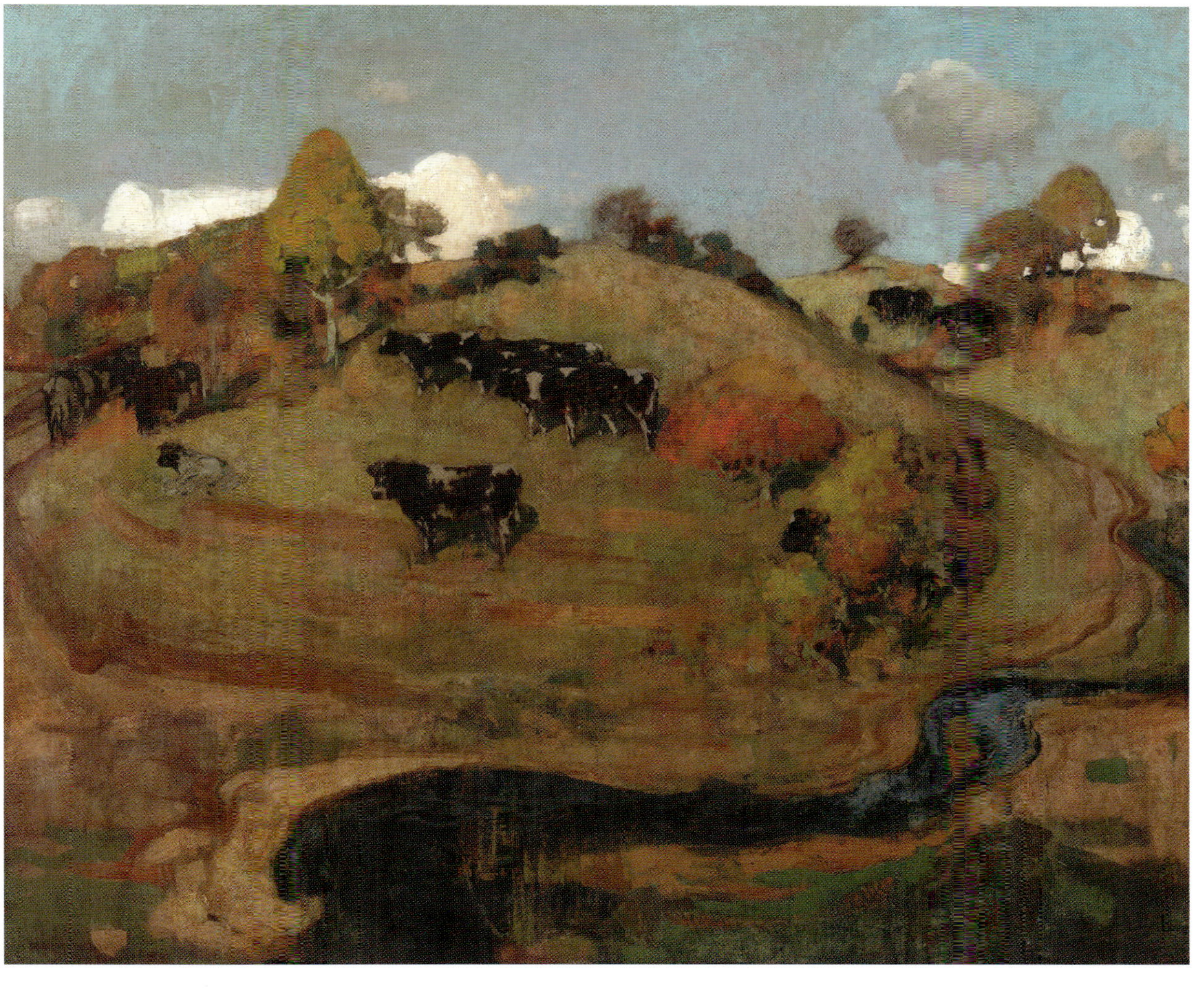

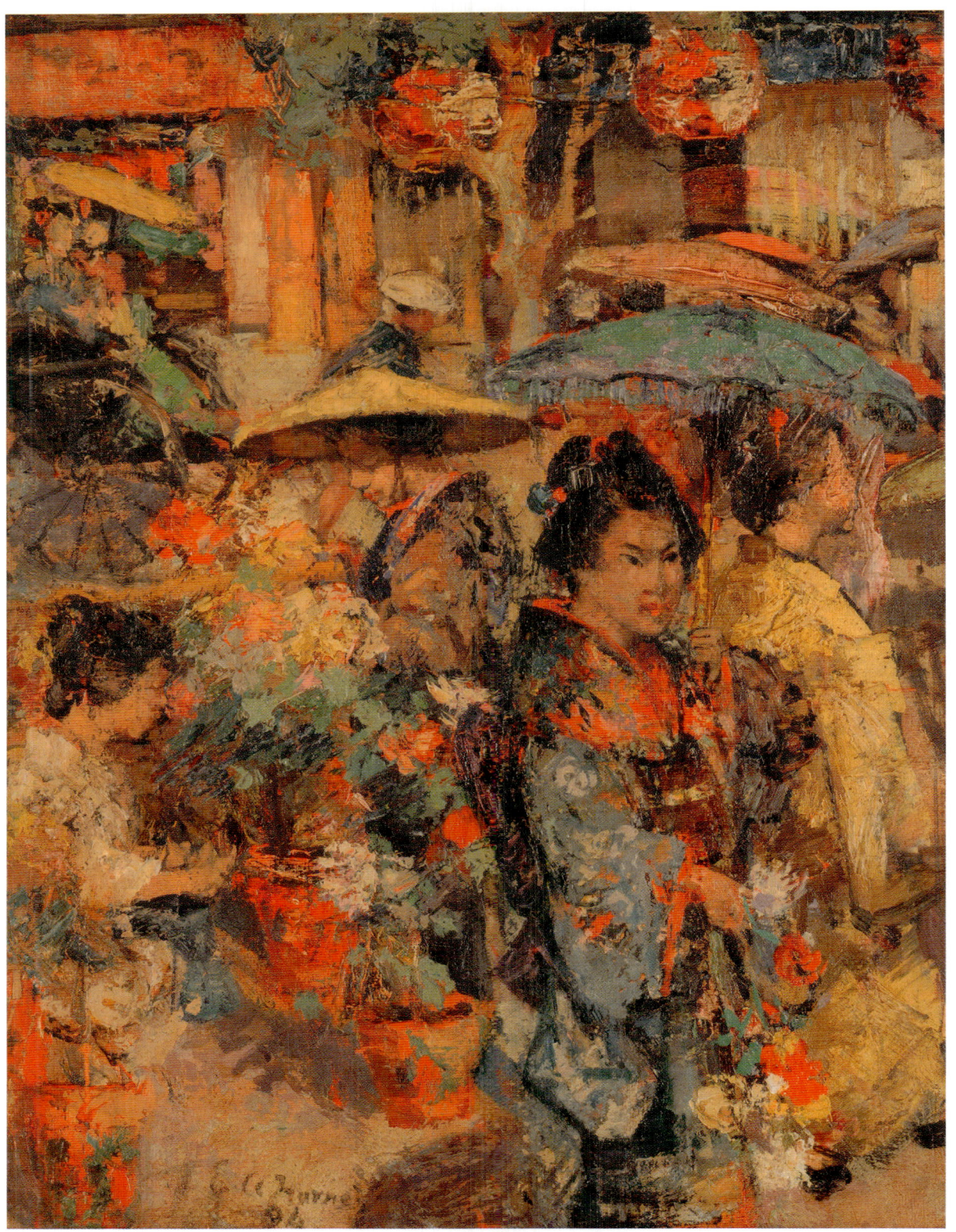

teach in Edinburgh and when Edward was sixteen he joined her there to attend the School of Art.

Aged nineteen, Edward returned to Kirkcudbright permanently, setting up a studio at 21 High Street and signing himself E.A. Hornel. He founded the first Fine Arts Association in the town, together with his long-time friends William McGeorge and John Faed and, when his father died, he took on the financial support of his sisters and began buying up property in Kirkcudbright to bring in rental income.

A JAPANESE INTERLUDE

Both Hornel and Henry shared an interest in Symbolism and had worked together on a large painting of *The Druids* (1890) which, with its use of gold paint and surface pattern, caused a sensation when it was exhibited in Munich. Their painting was said to have influenced the later work of the Austrian Symbolist painter Gustav Klimt.

In 1893, Hornel and Henry set off on a study tour of Japan, funded by the Glasgow art dealer Alexander Reid and the collector William Burrell. There they hoped to find a way of life that was fast disappearing in Scotland by this time – traditional, rural, and unsullied by industrialization.

During their eighteen-month trip, they immersed themselves in Japanese culture, staying with families and experiencing the local music, rituals and life in and around the city of Nagasaki including the cherry blossom celebration in spring, known as *Hanami*. Hornel also developed an interest and skill in photography while there, which would go on to influence his paintings. Sadly, most of George Henry's canvases were ruined on the voyage home, but, on their return Hornel exhibited his paintings of Japan at Reid's Glasgow gallery. Despite the lost work, both Henry and Hornel's reputations were made, and Japan continued to inform their art back in Kirkcudbright.

All the Kirkcudbright artists used models, particularly local agricultural workers and their children. The most famous was Willie Thompson a Kirkcudbright shoemaker, who posed for *Old Willie* by James Guthrie (1886) and

LEFT *Flower Market Nagasaki* (1894) by E.A. Hornel who, together with his colleague George Henry made an eighteen-month tour of Japan, sparking a life-long fascination with Eastern art and culture.

E.A. Hornel (1864–1933)

E.A. Hornel bought Broughton House in his Scottish home town of Kirkcudbright at the peak of his fame as one of the Glasgow School of artists, better known as the Glasgow Boys. He never married and took up residence with his elder sister Elizabeth, known as Tizzie. Buying Broughton House also marked a change in artistic direction for Hornel: leaving behind the naturalism of earlier work, he employed Symbolism and a more decorative style. After two trips to Japan, he began to imbue his paintings and his garden with ideas gleaned from the Far East. His later work was influenced by photography – he took many photographs, using local Kirkcudbright girls as models to invent a distinctive style of painting set in the gardens, woodlands, and coastal landscapes around his home. As Hornel's fame spread, many artists came to visit him, including his friend and artist George Henry, painter Charles Oppenheimer, and illustrator Jessie M. King, leading to Kirkcudbright becoming known as 'The Artist's Town'.

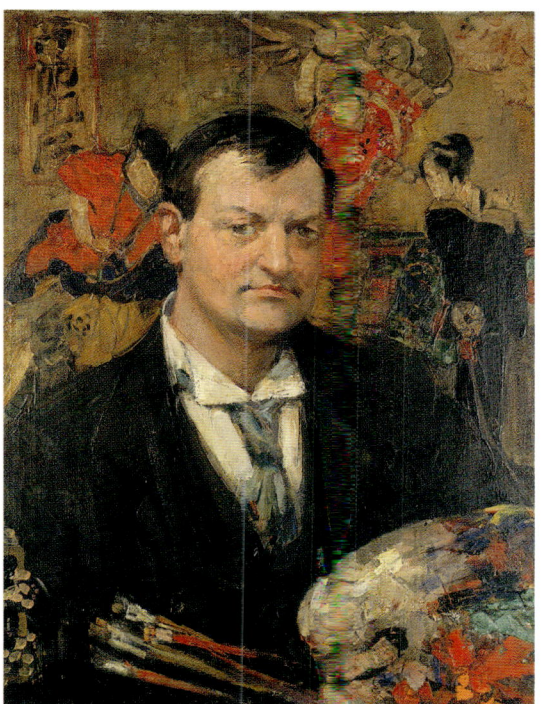

Edward Atkinson Hornel (1896) by Bessie MacNicol.

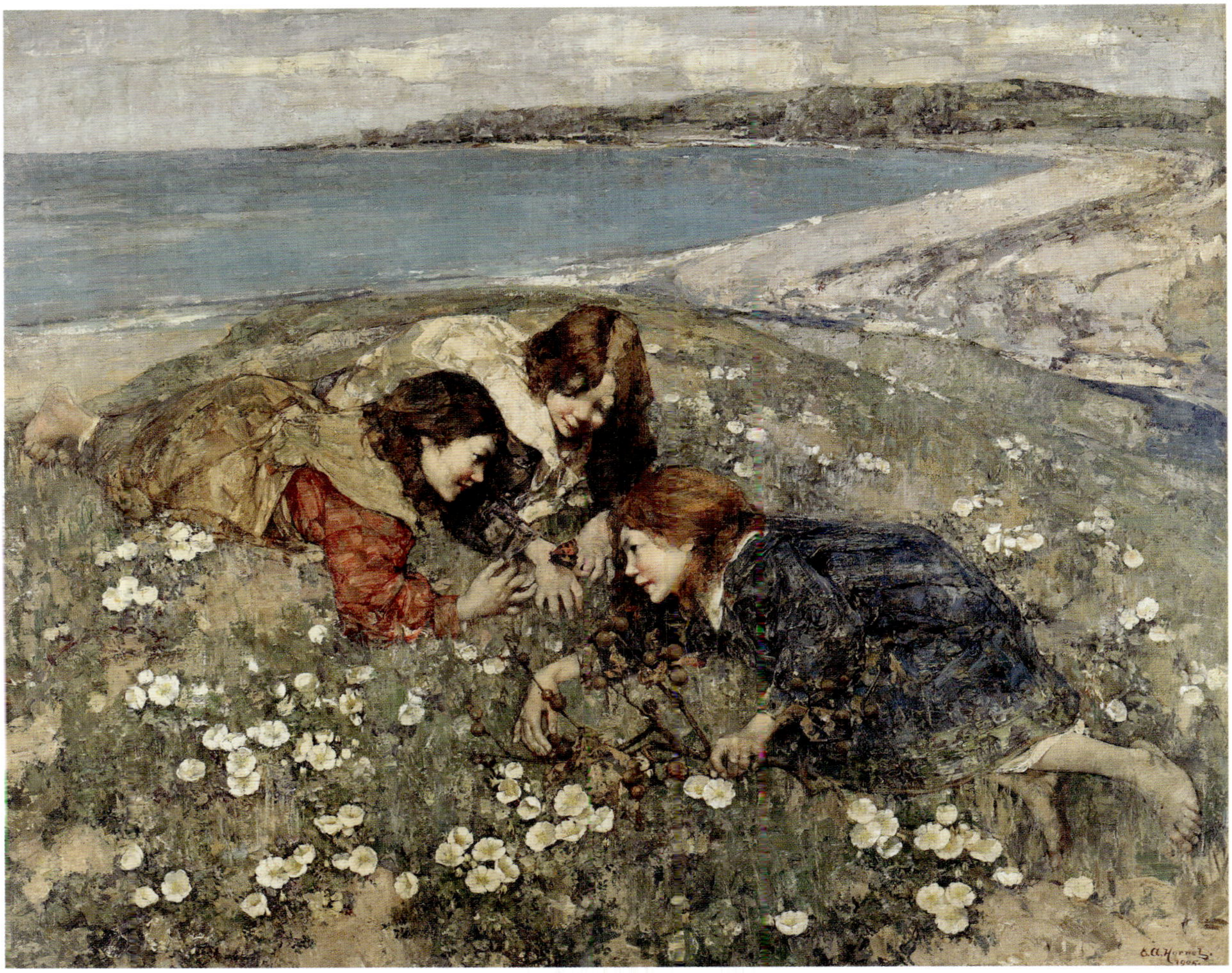

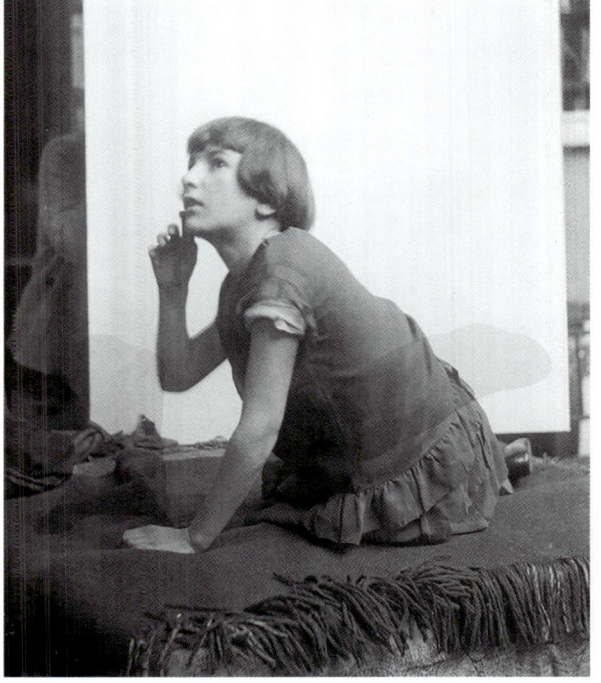

Henry's *The Hedge Cutter* (1886), which now hangs in the Hunterian Art Gallery in Glasgow.

Hornel also began photographing local girls (with sessions supervised by his sister, Tizzie), using these images of his models as references for his increasingly mystical and decorative paintings, which now looked more staged but proved very popular. He was also influenced by the photographic practice known as *Yokohama Shashin*. Named after the port in Japan, the technique involved artists delicately hand-colouring the black and white images, and Hornel built up a large collection of glass photographic slides produced in this style.

ABOVE *The Captive Butterfly* (1905) is one of several paintings Hornel made of local girls set among the wild roses at nearby Brighouse Bay.
LEFT Hornel made many photographic studies of his models, which he would later transpose on to canvases.
OPPOSITE In 1910, Hornel doubled the width of the long garden behind Broughton House by buying the adjoining property.

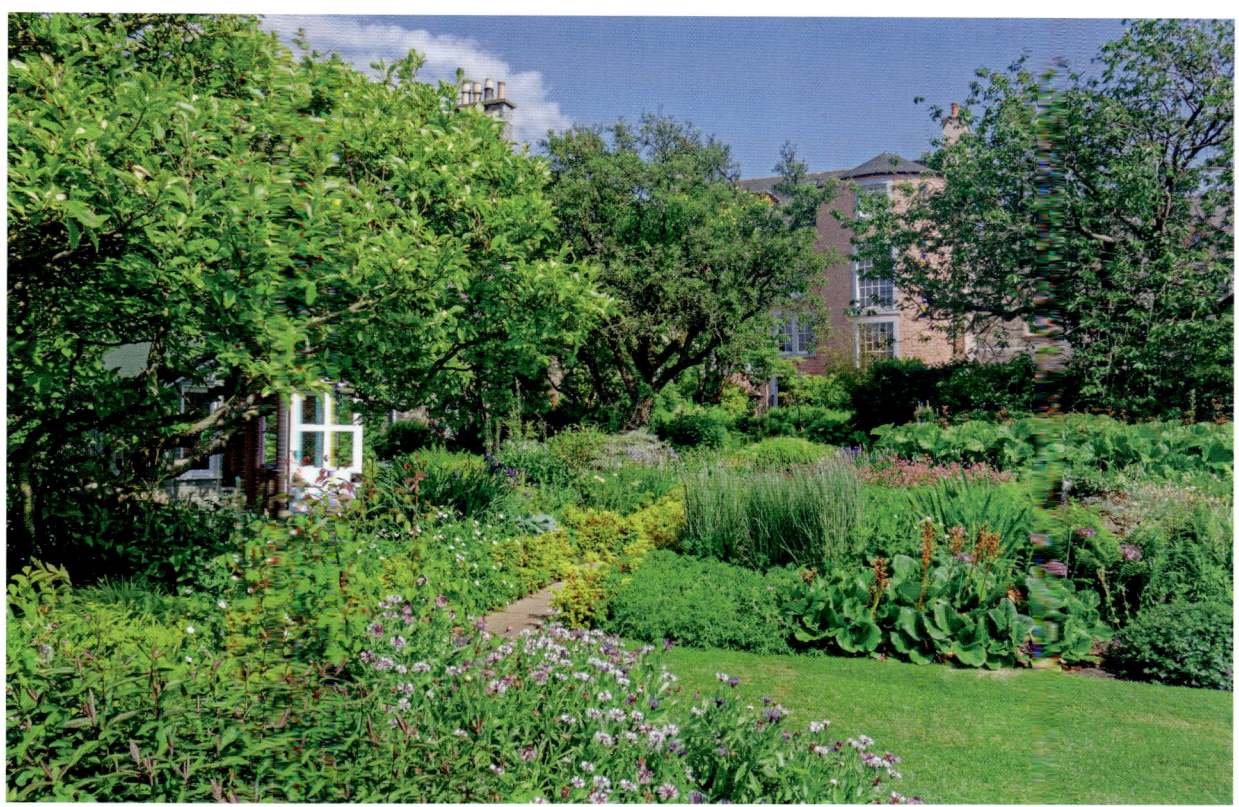

THE LANG RIG GARDEN

In 1901, Hornel was given the chance to buy a handsome property on the High Street in Kirkcudbright for £650. Broughton House had lots of potential, and Hornel felt it would make a comfortable, genteel family home for himself and Tizzie. He also liked its garden, which sloped down in a narrow strip to the river. The property included a coach house, stables and a further outbuilding, which Hornel immediately started to convert into a studio, with large roof lights and doors that opened directly on to the garden. He employed John Keppie from the famous Glasgow firm of Honeyman, Keppie & Mackintosh (who were also responsible for the Glasgow School of Art) to do the work.

The garden was, in essence, a long piece of land, known as a 'lang rig', which stretched down to the River Dee. An ordnance survey map of 1893 – the year Hornel went to Japan, but before he bought the house – shows his property with a formal early-nineteenth-century garden, which the artist preserved. Hornel employed a gardener and continued growing vegetables for the household, while also developing other aspects of the garden, including flower borders and shrubs with a Japanese influence. Through his contacts in Japan he had built up a collection of nursery catalogues, which he probably kept for their beautiful illustrations of peonies, irises, bamboos and lilies. We know from his receipts that he ordered ten bulbs of the golden-rayed lily of Japan (*Lilium auratum*) from the Glasgow firm, Leighton, for the price of £1 and it is likely that he scoured Britain for other Japanese plants that were available to buy mail order. Tizzie shared his interest in the planting of the garden, and in 1907 she travelled with him to Egypt, Ceylon, Singapore and Australia.

In 1908, Hornel was able to buy the adjoining house at No. 14. He had no intention of living in the house, but wanted it purely for the land, which would double the width of his existing garden. The following year, he rebuilt the old stables and coach house into a new full height gallery, designed by Keppie, with a flat glazed ceiling,

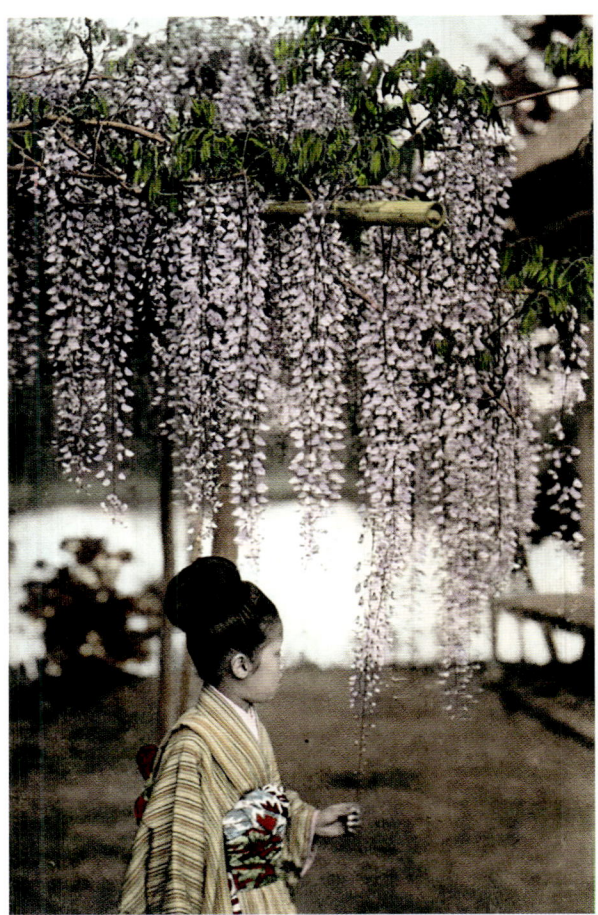

*"From letters my garden has been doing marvels.
The Peonies were magnificent & my Wisteria,
which I have longed for many weary years
to see in bloom, took advantage of my absence
and made a royal show."*

E.A. HORNEL (1907)

greenhouse – decorative and good to look at, but expensive to heat and without adequate ventilation.

Tizzie was very much a driving force in the garden, spending all day outdoors planting and propagating, and she must be given much of the credit for its creation. Overall, the garden became a combination of nineteenth-century formal and early twentieth-century ideas. Probably best summed up as an Edwardian garden of rooms, with Arts & Crafts elements, such as sundials and other traditional ornamentation, it had echoes of the Far East, rather than being a reproduction of an authentic Japanese garden.

THE GREENGATE GIRLS

At least thirty artists made their names in Kirkcudbright. Charles Oppenheimer moved into Hornel's house at No. 14 and painted the garden there, and Bessie MacNicol – one of the 'Glasgow Girls' – painted Hornel's portrait at his first studio in the High Street.

In 1908, the designer and illustrator Jessie M. King visited Kirkcudbright and, on Hornel's advice, bought a property in Greengate Close, a few doors down from him. Trained at the Glasgow School of Art, King emerged as a formidable artist and designer in the Art Nouveau style. Her new home at Greengate Close comprised the main house, four smaller cottages, a garden and a field leading down to the river. She held art classes in the main house and allowed summer groups of mainly female artists to lodge in the cottages. These included the painters Dorothy

mahogany panelling and a grand baroque fireplace, and it was this second phase of building work that probably also kick-started the design for his new Japanese-style garden.

It was not a traditional Japanese garden, with raked gravel and clipped topiary, but had a more fluid network of winding paths, raised beds and rockeries, moving water, ponds and stone artefacts. On the exterior wall of the newly reconstructed gallery, Hornel planted a Japanese climber, *Hydrangea anomala* subsp. *petiolaris*, perfect for the shady position, and elsewhere added Japanese maples (*Acer*), flowering cherries, bamboos, tree and herbaceous peonies, as well as the *Lilium auratum* bulbs and several wisterias. It was while he and Tizzie were away in 1907 that the wisteria bloomed for the first time, much to Hornel's annoyance, since he had waited years to see it flower. Hornel also commissioned a rather impractical

ABOVE, LEFT *Blossom* (circa 1890), a hand-painted print by Japanese photographer Kōzaburō Tamamura, is from Hornel's large collection of photographs and other Japanese artefacts.
RIGHT Hornel's garden combines British and Eastern ideas, with *Wisteria sinensis* cascading over traditional box hedges.

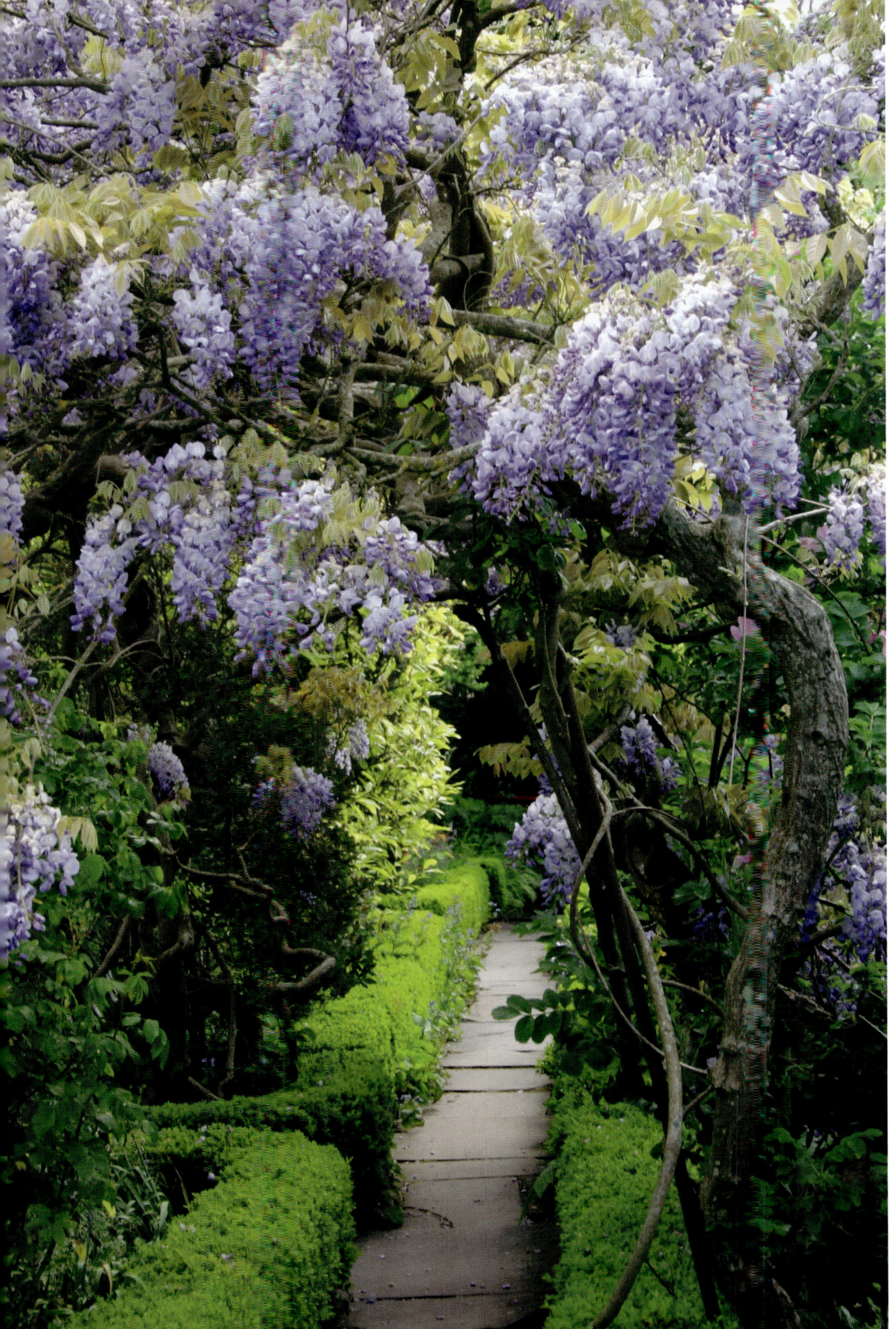

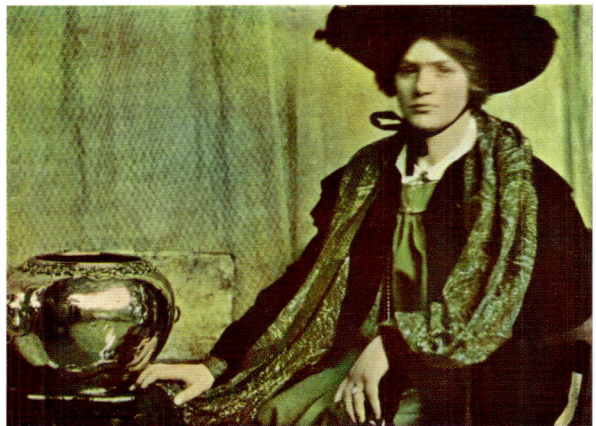

Never-Weary (1915), an innovative cut-out book designed to teach children about architecture. Attracting attention as an independent woman, she cycled everywhere and was dubbed by the locals as 'the witch on a bicycle'.

In 1931, the novelist Dorothy L. Sayers chose to send her detective Lord Peter Wimsey to Kirkcudbright to solve the murder of an artist. In *Five Red Herrings*, the town was awash with artists – while Sayers was King's friend, she had reputedly taken a dislike to several of the male artists, including Hornel, and sought her revenge in print.

The success of Kirkcudbright was its mix of amateurs and professionals – painters, writers, sculptors, designers, ceramicists and illustrators – and it never became an exclusive enclave. By the mid-twentieth century, long after Hornel's death, artists such as Dorothy Nesbitt, William Miles Johnston and Lena Alexander were still seeking out the town for their inspiration. Now, with the opening of a public art gallery in Kirkcudbright in 2018, a new phase of its artistic journey has begun, yet it is still the legacy of E.A. Hornel and his fellow Glasgow Boys that casts the most powerful spell over this small corner of Scotland.

Johnstone and Helen Stirling Johnston, the jewellery maker Mary Thew, embroiderer Helen Paxton Brown and silversmith Agnes Harvey. The cottages were basic, but the freedom from the city and its male-dominated art world would have been a great boon to their careers. The Scottish colourist Sam Peploe (S.J. Peploe), a friend of Jessie and her husband Ernest Taylor, also spent summers at Greengate Close from 1915 until 1935.

After moving to Kirkcudbright, King became more sought after as a designer for Liberty of London, and in Italy and Germany, and while continuing to teach part-time, she increasingly focused on these commissions, particularly for book covers. Yet she never moved from the Scottish port and celebrated it in *The Little White Town of*

ABOVE, LEFT A 1908 studio photograph of illustrator Jessie M. King by James Craig Annan. King created a summer school for women artists in her house at Greengate Close, near the home of E.A. Hornel.
RIGHT *A Summer's Day, Kirkcudbright* (1916) by S.J. Peploe, depicts the town that the artist visited regularly until his death in 1935.

THE KIRKCUDBRIGHT ARTISTS' TIMELINE

1864	1880	1886	1901	1908	1909–10	1933	1997
Edward Atkinson Hornel born in Australia	Hornel studies at the School of Art in Edinburgh	Hornel founds the Fine Art Association in Kirkcudbright	Hornel buys Broughton House; starts to build his studio	Illustrator Jessie M. King buys Greengate, a few doors down from Broughton House	Hornel commissions Keppie to create a gallery at Broughton for his paintings	Hornel dies; his sister Elizabeth lives on at Broughton House	The National Trust for Scotland takes over Broughton House

1866	1885	1893	1907	1908	1920–21	1950
Hornel family returns to Kirkcudbright	First Glasgow Boys exhibition at Glasgow Institute of Fine Arts	Hornel and George Henry visit Japan, and stay for eighteen months	Hornel visits Ceylon and Australia with sister Elizabeth	Hornel buys the house next door to double the size of the garden	Hornel travels to Burma (Myanmar), Japan, Canada and USA	Elizabeth Hornel dies and The Hornel Trust starts running Broughton House

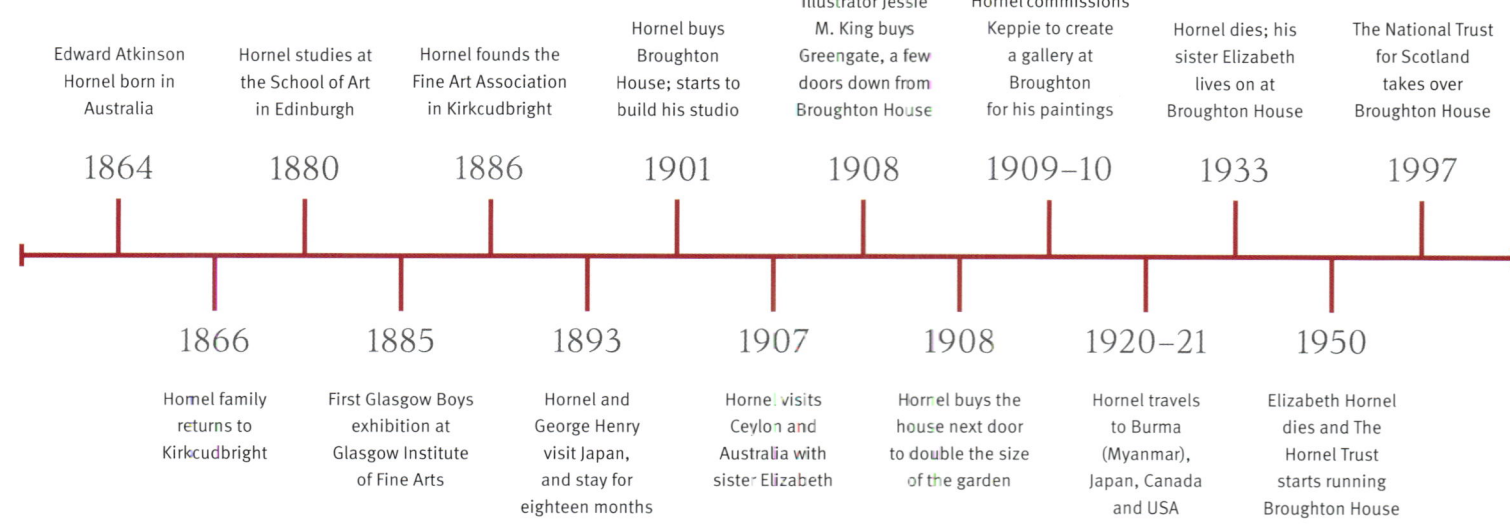

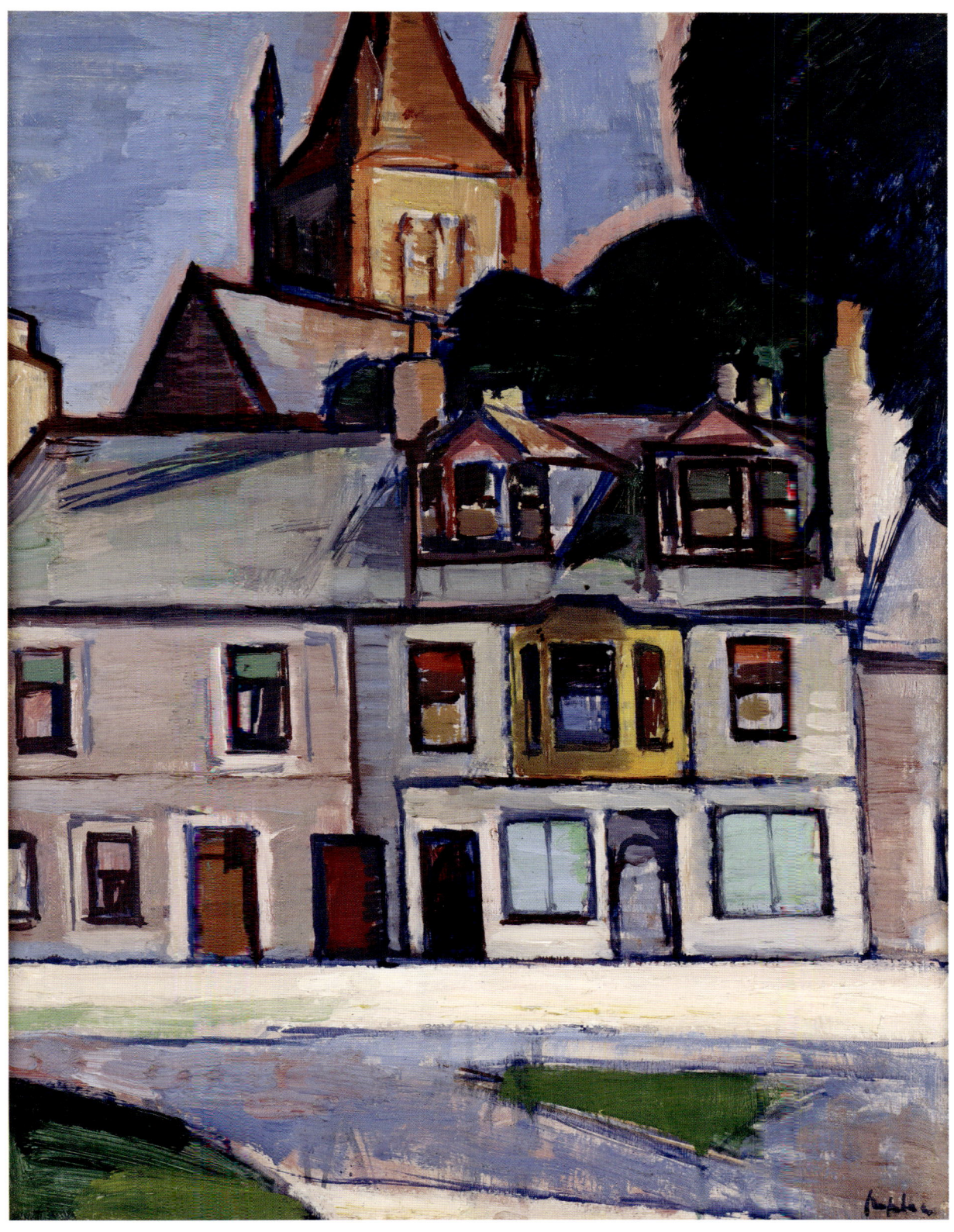

William Morris and his circle

William Morris, May Morris and Dante Gabriel Rossetti

Kelmscott Manor, Oxfordshire, England

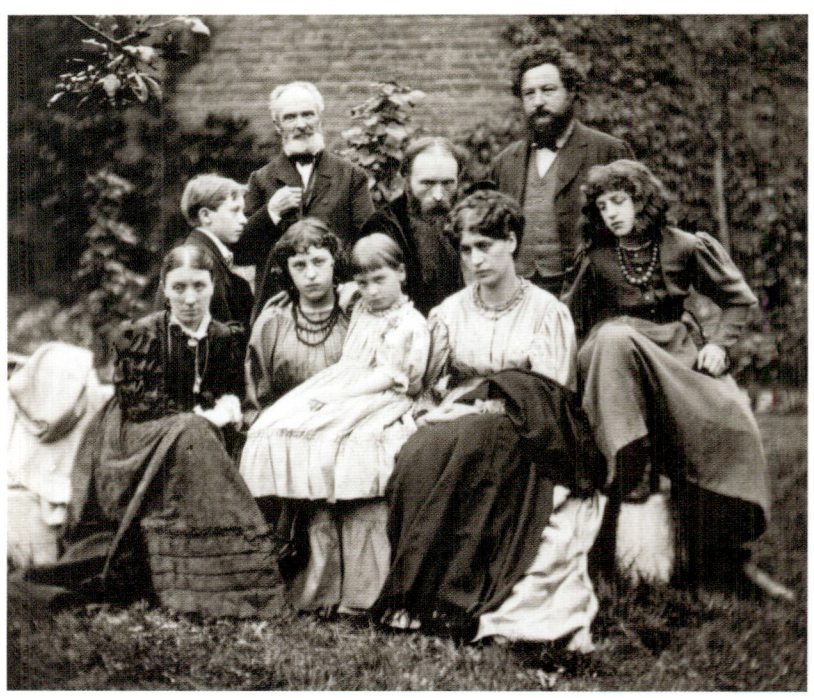

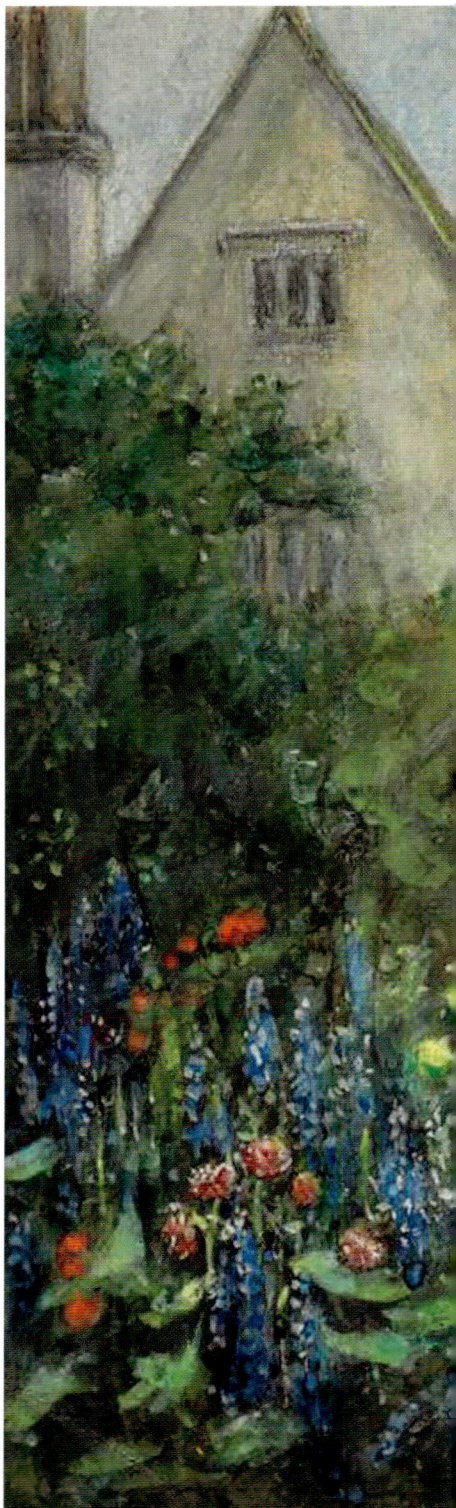

IF HOUSES HAVE MEMORIES, then Kelmscott Manor in Oxfordshire holds more than most. The early seventeenth century house and its garden played a pivotal role in the lives of three creative artists: the Arts & Crafts designer William Morris; his daughter, the painter and embroiderer May Morris; and the artist dubbed 'the last of the Pre-Raphaelites', Dante Gabriel Rossetti. There are other players in the story, too, including the artist's model and muse, Jane Burden Morris – wife of William and Rossetti's lover – as well as the artist Edward Burne-Jones and architect Philip Webb.

At the epicentre of the group was the old riverside house and garden in the village of Kelmscott, which would begin as a rural retreat for burnt-out London artists, and develop into the long-term home of May Morris and her companion of later years, Mary Lobb.

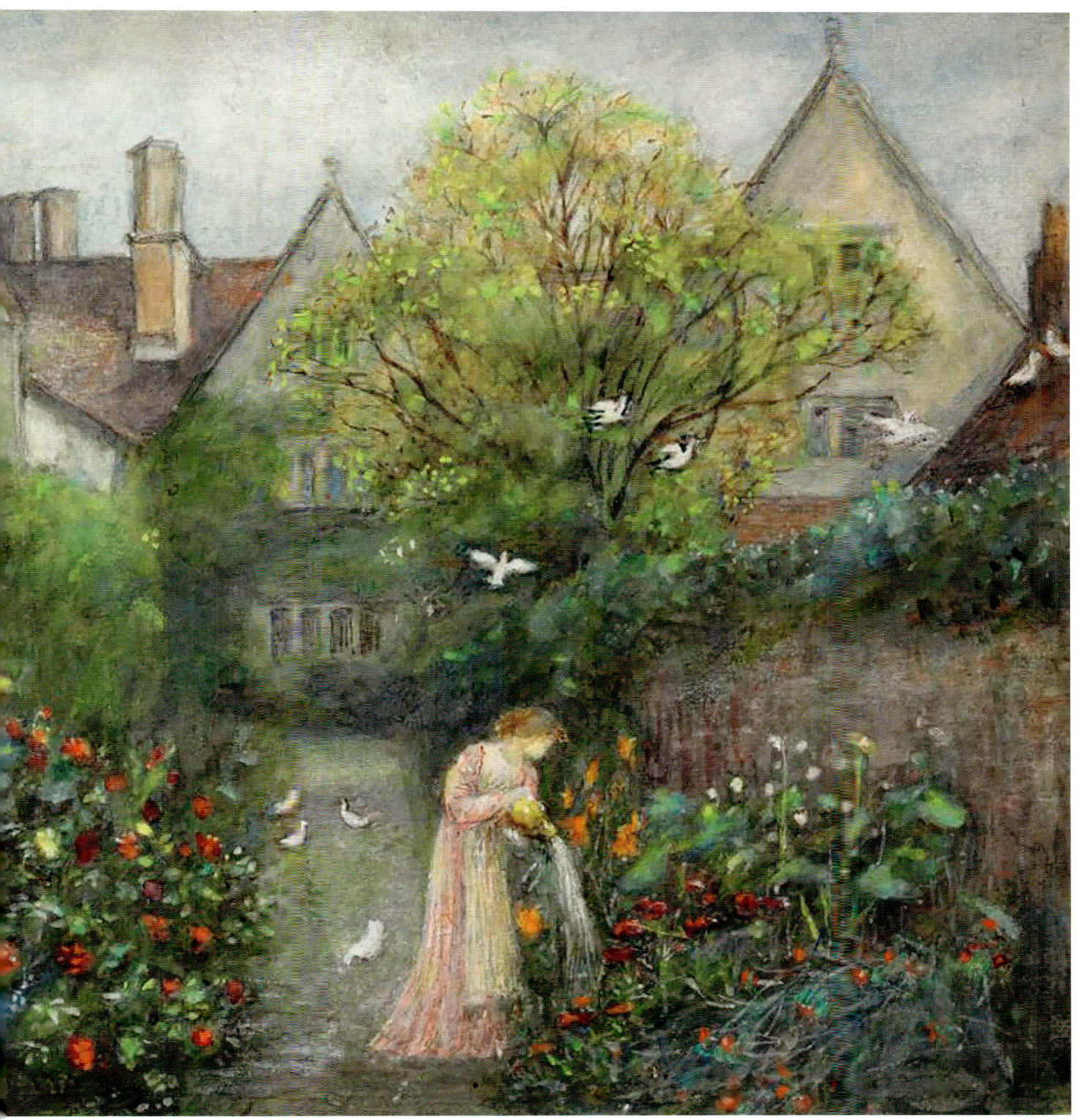

OPPOSITE This photograph was taken at the Burne-Jones's Fulham house in 1874. Back row (from left): Philip Burne-Jones, Richard Jones (Edward's father), Edward Burne-Jones, William Morris. Front row (from left): Georgiana Burne-Jones, Jenny Morris, Margaret Burne-Jones, Jane Morris, and May Morris.

ABOVE *A Lady in the Garden at Kelmscott Manor* (circa 1905) was painted by British Pre-Raphaelite artist Marie Spartali Stillman, a contemporary of May Morris. Considered one of the greatest female artists of that movement, Marie visited Kelmscott in the early years of the twentieth century and made several paintings of the gardens.

The Artists in Residence

William Morris (1871–1896)
Dante Gabriel Rossetti (1871–1874)
May Morris (1871–1938)

The part played by Kelmscott Manor in the lives of these three artists spans almost seventy years, from 1871 to 1938. William Morris used Kelmscott as his retreat, and many of his textiles and wallpapers were inspired by its plants and natural setting. His contribution to design and championing of Arts & Crafts principles made him the most famous artist/craftsman of the period. Morris's teacher and friend, Rossetti, was a founder of the Pre-Raphaelite Brotherhood and he laid the foundations for the next wave of British artists, who continued his interest in medievalism. Rossetti also fell in love with Morris's wife Jane, who features in many of his paintings. William and Jane's daughter, May, was nine when she first came to Kelmscott, where she spent time with Rossetti before training as an embroiderer and joining Morris & Co. She later became a lecturer in historic textiles, while continuing her design work and watercolour painting.

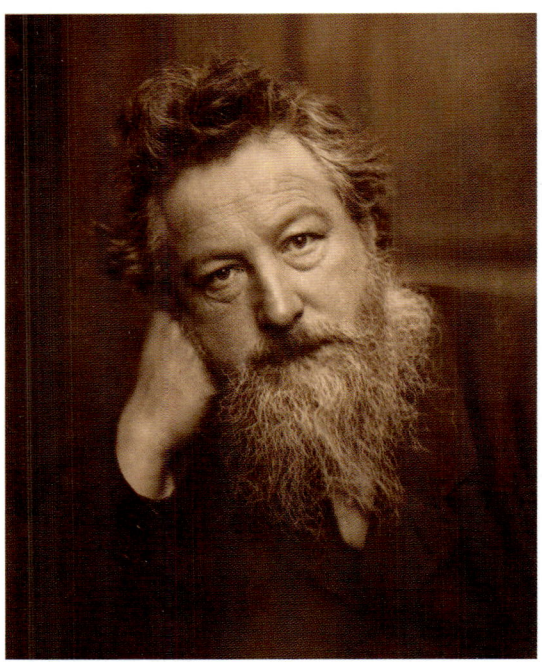

William Morris, photographed by Frederick Hollyer (1884).

EARLY INSPIRATION: WILLIAM MORRIS

When William Morris rented Kelmscott Manor in 1871, aged thirty-seven, he had already established himself as a successful artist, poet (*Earthly Paradise* had been published in 1866 to much acclaim), translator of Icelandic sagas, entrepreneur, and leader of the design revival known as the Arts & Crafts Movement.

Brought up at Woodford Hall in Epping Forest, Morris had an idyllic childhood, with the run of the grounds and the woods. It was clear that he was never going to follow his father into the City and while at Marlborough College, which he attended from the age of fifteen, he found his escape in the Savernake Forest, not far from the school, and by making pilgrimages to the ancient sites of Stonehenge and Silbury, laying the foundations for his passion for history and the natural world.

Morris went on to Oxford University and while there, in 1853, he met the artist Edward Burne-Jones, who would become a lifelong friend. His mother had wanted him to join the clergy, but after reading John Ruskin and the new ideas of Charles Darwin, he rejected the path that had been laid out for him. Having inherited the comfortable sum of £900 a year on his twenty-first birthday, he also had the financial independence to make his own way in the world.

Morris began work as an apprentice to architect George Street in Oxford, where he met the young architect Philip Webb. When the practice moved to London in 1857, Morris and Webb moved with it. Meanwhile, Dante Gabriel Rossetti had taken Burne-Jones under his wing and was teaching him to paint, and soon Morris, who was keen to practise his artistic skills, had also joined Rossetti's classes. In 1861, this group and others founded their own outlet for handmade, medieval-inspired furnishings and decorative products under the banner Morris, Marshall, Faulkner & Co. This later became the legendary Morris & Co. – known simply as 'The Firm'.

A PEACEFUL BEGINNING

One evening, on a visit to the theatre, this group of young men noticed the striking Jane Burden in the audience, and although it was Morris who married her in April 1859, it was Rossetti, six year's Morris's senior, who first earmarked Jane as his model and later became her lover.

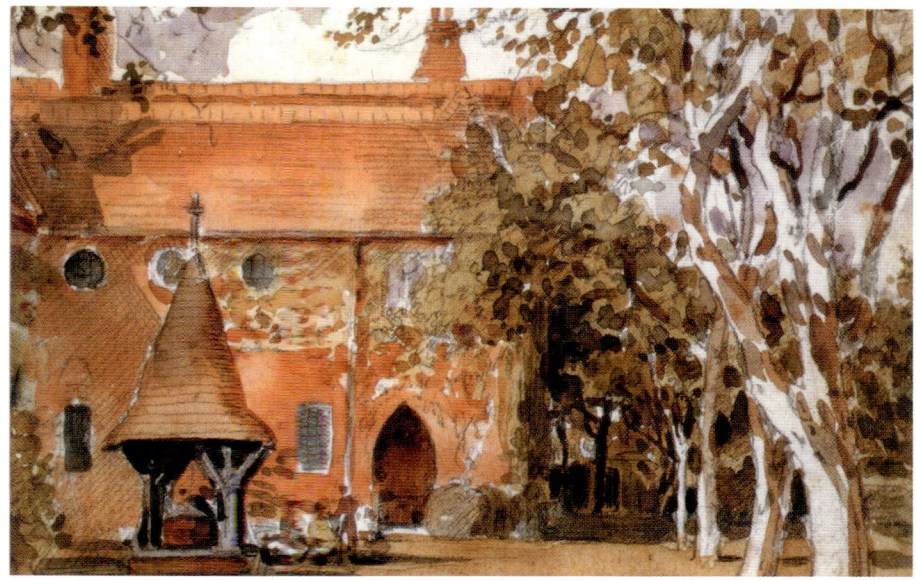

Following their marriage, Jane and William commissioned Philip Webb to design a home for them in Bexley, Kent. Known as The Red House, it was an architectural triumph and allowed the couple to develop their interests in arts and crafts. Their daughters, Jenny and May, were born at The Red House, but, as the business grew, the family moved back to London, eventually settling in Hammersmith beside the River Thames. Living in town satisfied Morris's business interests but he still believed that a different way of living was possible in the countryside. Together with Rossetti, he leased Kelmscott Manor, close to the Thames in Oxfordshire, and would go on to describe it accurately in *News from Nowhere*, his utopian novel of 1890:

'The raised way led us into a little field bounded by a backwater of the river on one side; … almost without my will my hand raised the latch of a door in the wall, and we stood presently on a stone path which led up to the old house.'

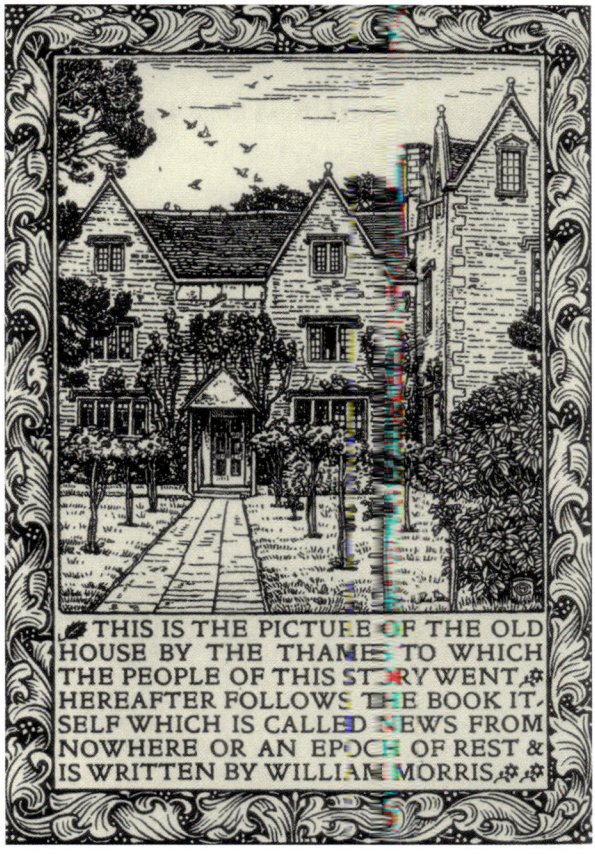

On two occasions, the Morrises arrived at Kelmscott by boat, which William much preferred to speeding trains. Jane Morris described the trips to the house as 'going on a picnic' – everything had to be brought with them from London, as the Manor was deliberately kept sparsely

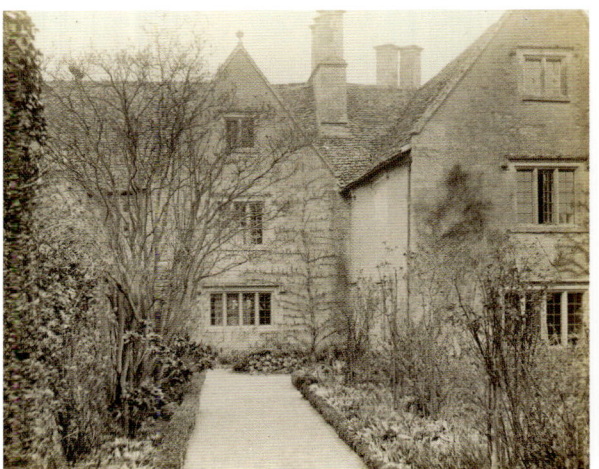
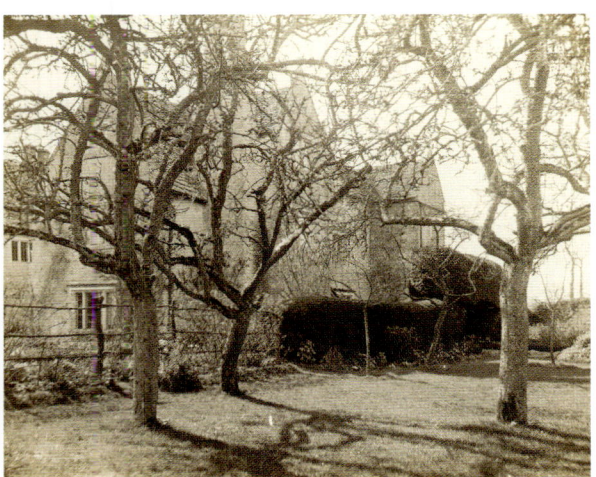

ABOVE, LEFT AND RIGHT The east façade of Kelmscott Manor and the orchard, both photographed by Frederick H. Evans in 1896.

furnished. William loved everything about the house, from the construction of its roofs, with the large tiles at the top getting progressively smaller down the pitch, to its wood-panelled interior. He loved the wildness of the garden too, and its possibilities for inspiring designs based on plants and natural features.

The original tenancy included only the house and the walled garden – the outbuildings and 'the great meadow' were still used by the farm. However, the property did come with a gardener, who lived in the garden cottage. Morris, a committed socialist, was upset that the gardener would continually doff his cap to him and pleaded with him to stop.

THE CO-TENANT: DANTE GABRIEL ROSSETTI

One of the reasons the Morrises rented Kelmscott Manor was because, by that time, Jane and Rossetti were having an intense relationship and the house allowed them to be together, away from London. In May 1871, Morris left for a study tour of Iceland and Jane and their children, Jenny and May, moved to Kelmscott with Rossetti. The artist set up his studio and bedroom in the best room on the first floor, with windows looking out over the Radcot Cut and the Thames beyond. These were turbulent times, not least because Rossetti had moved in all of his eclectic belongings, including paintings and furniture, and his many drawings of Jane. Morris, who famously disliked anything in a home that was not either useful or beautiful, found the house chaotic when he visited.

Jane's affair with Rossetti eventually ran its course and in September 1871 Morris rejoined his family and they then decamped to London, leaving Rossetti, disconsolate and alone at Kelmscott. The summer days when he had picked flowers with the Morris children had turned into the bitterly cold winter of 1872. Despite suicide attempts and unsettling behaviour towards the villagers, Rossetti would produce some of his greatest paintings while at Kelmscott, including *Proserpine*, for which Jane posed. He left the house for good in 1874.

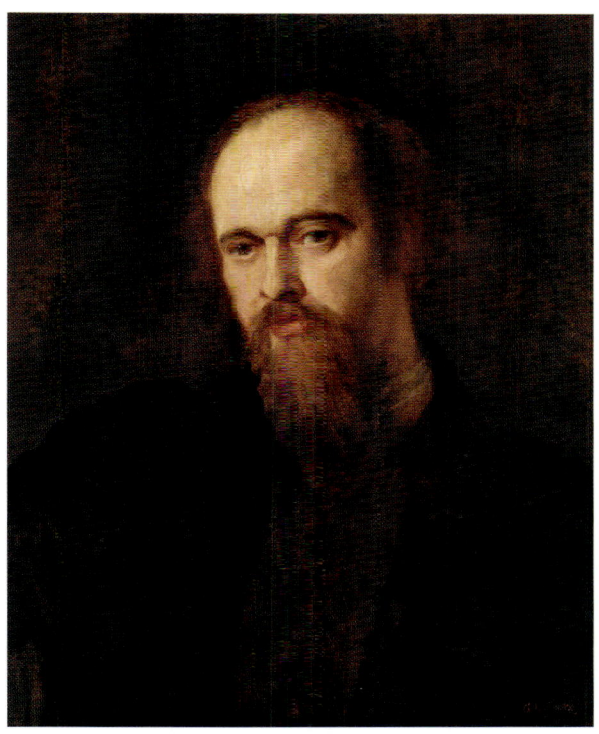

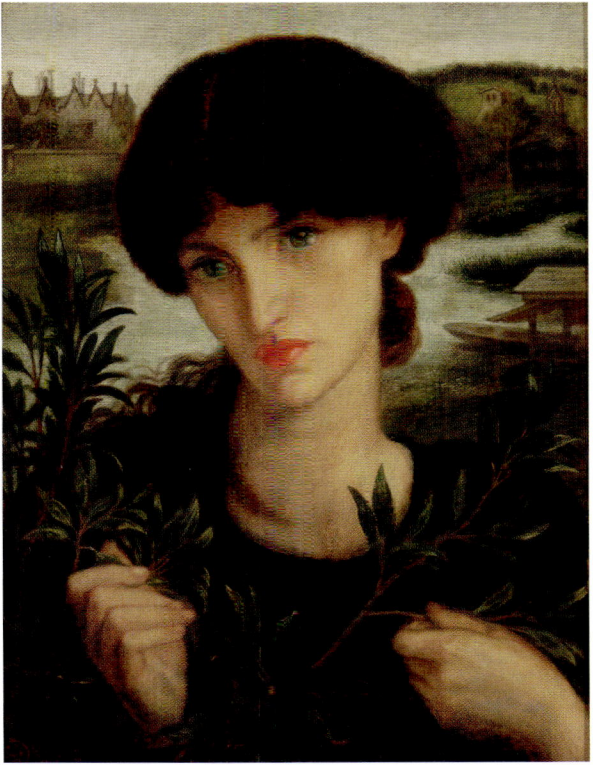

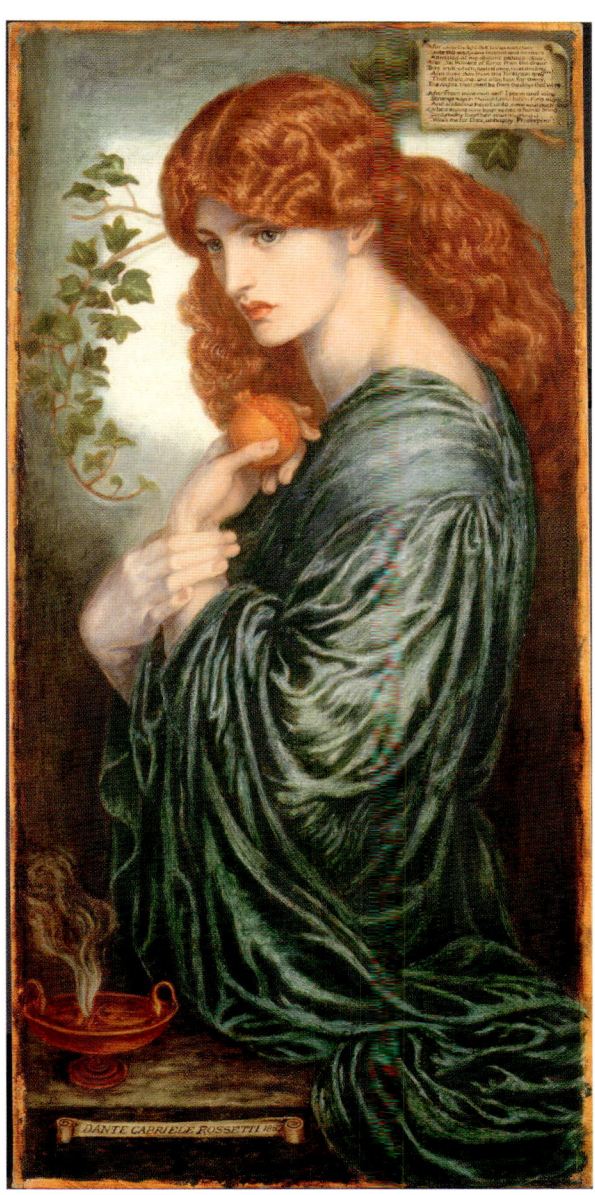

ABOVE, LEFT Dante Gabriel Rossetti became the lover of William Morris's wife Jane Burden and moved into Kelmscott Manor with her and the children. This portrait of the artist is by G.F. Watts (1871).

ABOVE, RIGHT With Jane as his muse and model, Rossetti returned to this depiction of the classical goddess Proserpine many times, making no less than eight versions. He was working on this one just before his death in 1882.

LEFT Rossetti often used Jane as his model, and this painting, titled *Water Willow* (1871), was her personal favourite. It shows her on the opposite side of the river, with Kelmscott Manor in the distance.

Designs from Nature

The Arts & Crafts Movement developed from the 1880s as a reaction against the poor quality of factory-made products that flooded the market during and after the Industrial Revolution. Practitioners in the fields of architecture, art and printing were inspired to rethink how artefacts could be made with more integrity. For Morris, this meant understanding how household items, such as curtains, bed-covers, carpets, furniture and wallpaper, were made and involving himself in the production processes. A hands-on designer, he taught himself to weave, knot carpets and embroider, and in 1878 he spent more than 500 hours weaving the *Acanthus & Vine* tapestry, which now hangs at Kelmscott.

The garden at Kelmscott was a constant source of inspiration for the designs produced by Morris & Co. Morris's daughter May remembers being allowed to experiment with natural dyes on the textiles – these were tested at Kelmscott and then taken back to London to be produced in larger quantities. William Morris studied dying with Wardle silk producers in Leek in Staffordshire and was always looking for good dyes with a natural base: indigo for blue (with woad sometimes added to 'set' the dye), madder for red, and weld for yellow.

Morris & Co.'s designs inspired by Kelmscott include The Strawberry Thief, showing thrushes attacking the strawberry patch, and Honeysuckle (see opposite) by his daughter May, often wrongly attributed to William, which was probably based on the plant growing over the porch. May also remembered her father studying the leaves of the willows by the river at Kelmscott for the Willow pattern wallpaper, produced in 1874, which led on to a more naturalized depiction in Willow Bough in 1887. Kennet was another design inspired by flowers and the flowing water of the River Thames that ran close to the house.

BACKGROUND One of Morris & Co.'s most famous designs: Violet & Columbine Furnishing Fabric (1883).

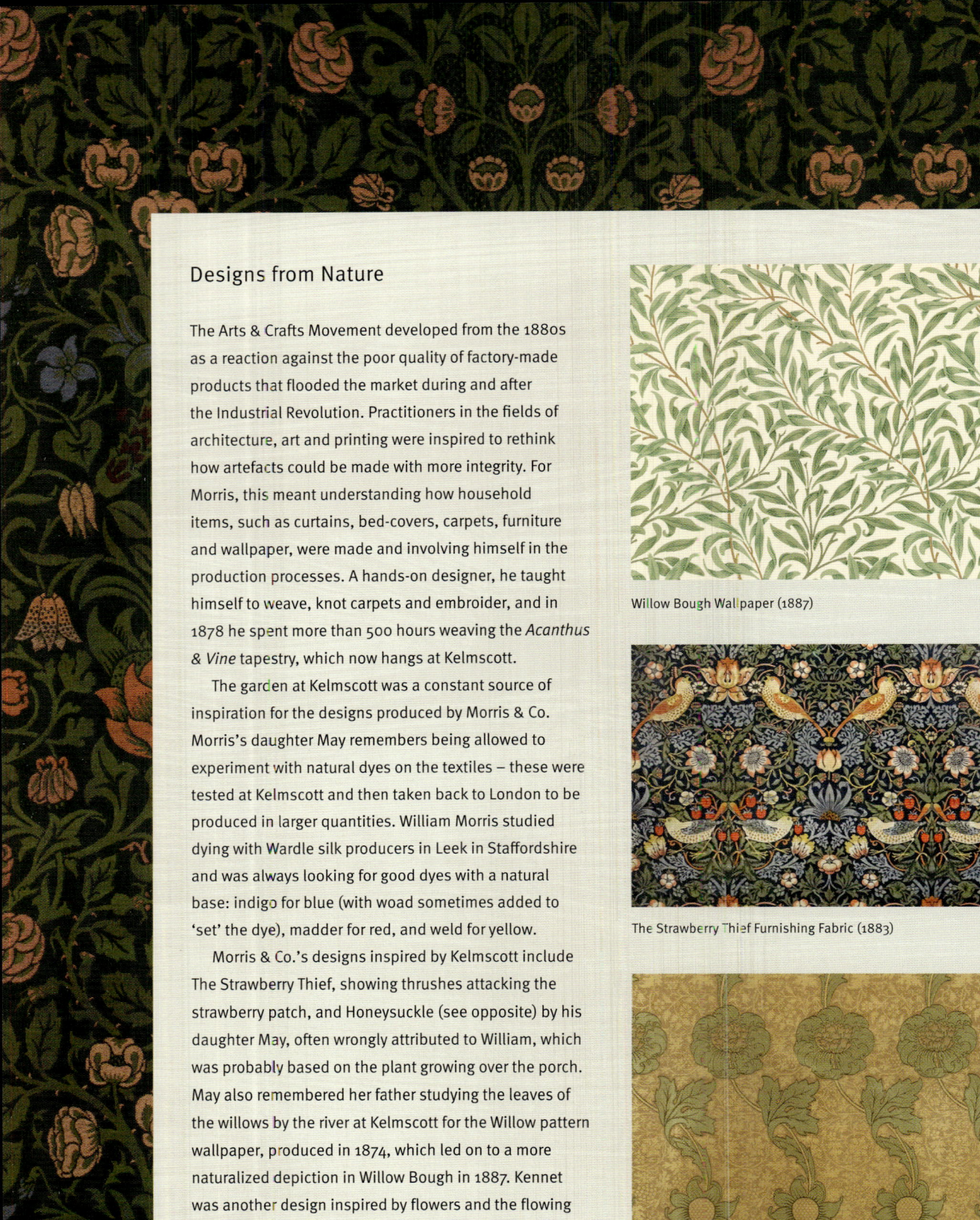

Willow Bough Wallpaper (1887)

The Strawberry Thief Furnishing Fabric (1883)

Kennet Furnishing Fabric (1883)

AN ARTIST AT HOME: MAY MORRIS

Kelmscott always remained a country retreat for William Morris, but for his daughter May it became a permanent home. May would become the longest resident of Kelmscott and the main caretaker of the garden, while also pursuing her own design career.

May had grown up surrounded by beautiful objects, creative people, interesting architecture and working crafts. She was born at The Red House in Bexley but her formative years were spent in central London next to the glass-painting workshop of Morris & Co. Her mother, aunts, friends and older sister Jenny were all involved in the stitching and embroidery of everything from wall hangings to book covers. At Kelmscott, where she lived from the age of nine, she was a favourite of Rossetti's, whom she watched paint and it would have been surprising if a little of this creativity had not rubbed off on her.

By 1878 she was enrolled at the National Art Training School (which later became the Royal College of Art) and chose embroidery, particularly medieval embroidery, as her specialism. At the age of twenty-three, she was running the embroidery department at Morris & Co. She was also a skilled watercolour artist and designed wallpapers for The Firm, including the Honeysuckle *motif*. Most of her designs were less stylized than Morris's, using meadow and hedgerow flora rather than garden flowers or exotic fruits, and her early sketchbooks show a propensity for botanical accuracy.

She followed her father's socialist ideals and became a vocal exponent of the Arts & Crafts Movement, which lasted until the outbreak of the First World War. Yet while her father was alive, her creative life was always defined by The Firm, and it was not until after his death in 1896, which gave her financial independence, that she was able to follow her own course, becoming a leading teacher and advocate of historic textiles. At the age of thirty-four, she increased her range of skills, with jewellery-making, spinning and weaving, and in 1907 she founded the Women's Guild of Arts (women were excluded from joining the Art Workers Guild at that time). In the winter of 1909–10, she embarked on a lecture tour of the USA.

Back home at Kelmscott Manor, May lived a basic life – the house had no piped water or electricity. She also

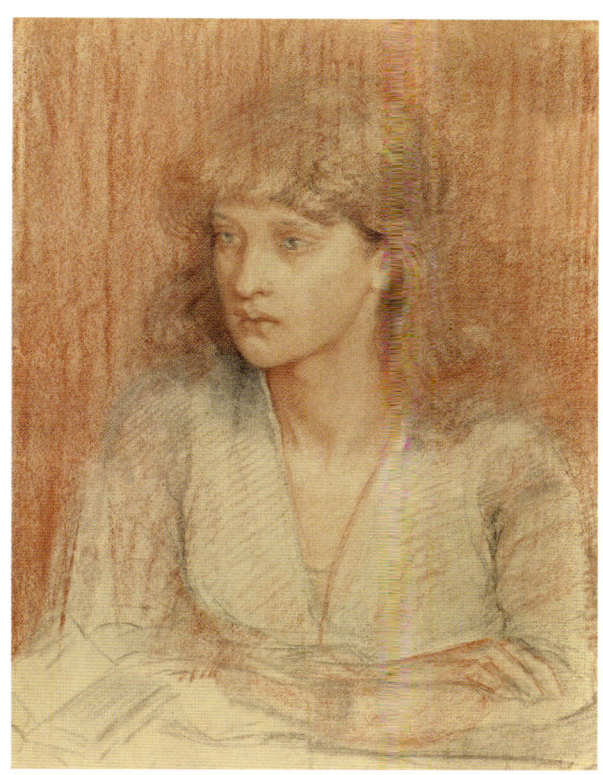

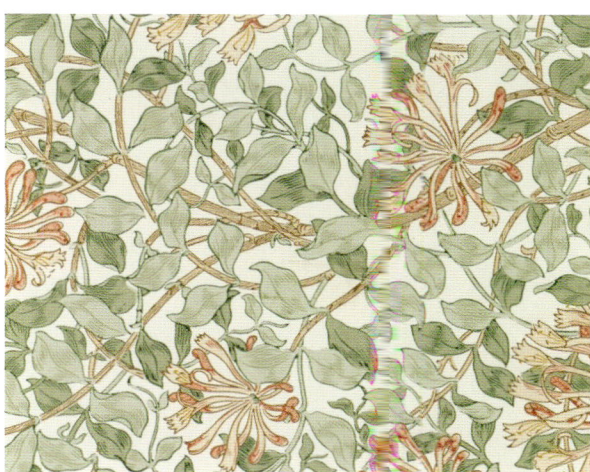

TOP May Morris was nine when Rossetti made this chalk portrait of her between 1871 and 1872, while they were living at Kelmscott Manor.
ABOVE The Honeysuckle Wallpaper was designed by May Morris for Morris & Co., circa 1883.

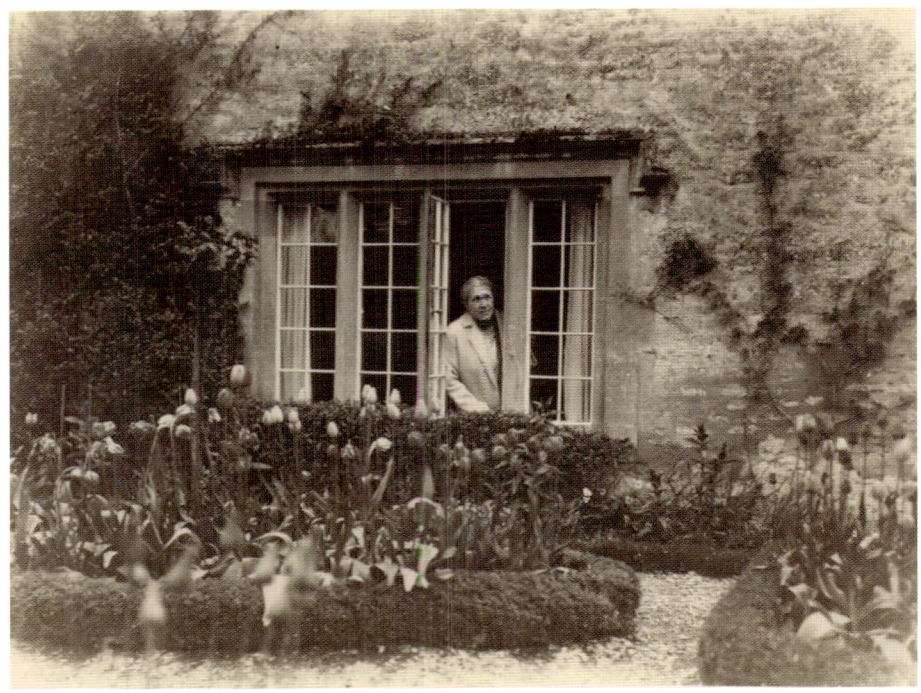

oversaw the building of new cottages in the village in honour of her mother, who had died a year after buying Kelmscott in 1913, having rented it up until then.

In 1917, May took in a Land Girl called Mary Lobb, who had been working on a nearby farm. Mary helped with the housekeeping, cooking and running of the estate, and the pair became lifelong companions, going on several epic journeys to Iceland, travelling on horseback and camping in the wilds together, and making their home at Kelmscott, where May lived until her death in 1938.

THE GARDEN YEARS

A visitor, describing May Morris and Mary Lobb's life at their Oxfordshire home between the wars, claimed that May always began the day with a walk around the garden to collect flowers for the house, and then moved on to the kitchen garden to choose the vegetables. Of the hundreds of embroideries she designed there, almost all have some kind of flower or natural *motif.*

The walled garden included an orchard, a vegetable garden, and flower borders, as well as the old mulberry tree. The standard roses that flanked the path up to the east porch are pictured on the frontispiece of *News from Nowhere*, but may well have been replanted by May in the 1920s and 1930s. On the north side of the house, old photographs show rustic fencing used to support more roses, clematis and honeysuckle. Also visible in early photographs of the garden is a lumpy topiary hedge. On returning from Iceland, William Morris had begun to shape a yew hedge into an Icelandic mythical beast – *Fáfnir* from the old Norse *Völsunga* saga. It was less dragon-shaped and more 'blobby', but later gardeners clipped it into a creature with a long tail and a serpent's head – not what Morris had intended, but more recognizable as a dragon.

The meadow beyond the garden boundary ran down to a 'cut', which was probably made in the eighteenth or nineteenth century to bring water up to the village. Paths through the meadow led to pollarded willows – an important inspiration and *motif* in William and May Morris's work. The proximity of the water was, of course, also very influential for Rossetti, who painted his famous *Water Willow* (1871) at Kelmscott, featuring Jane in the foreground, with the river and the house behind her.

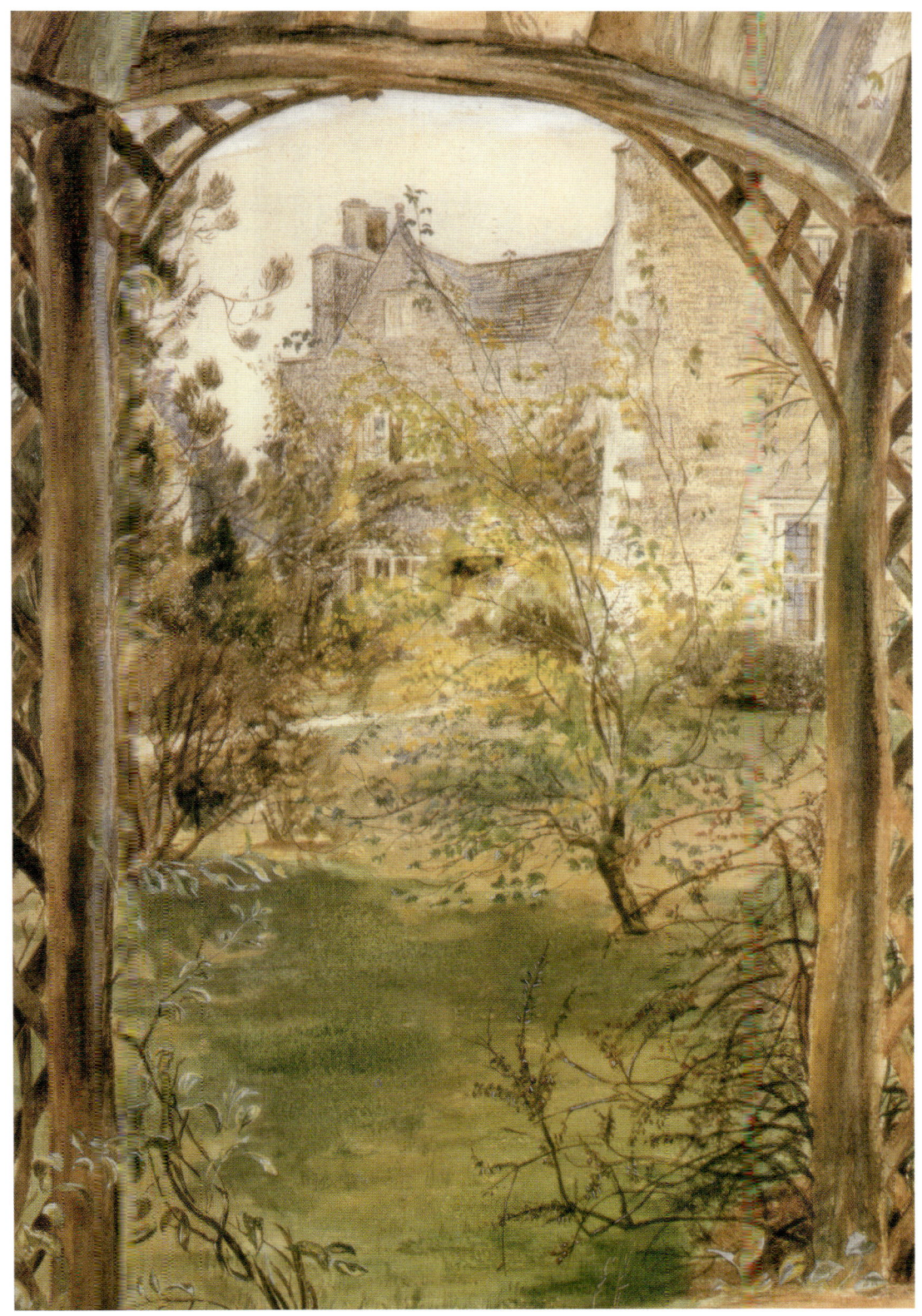

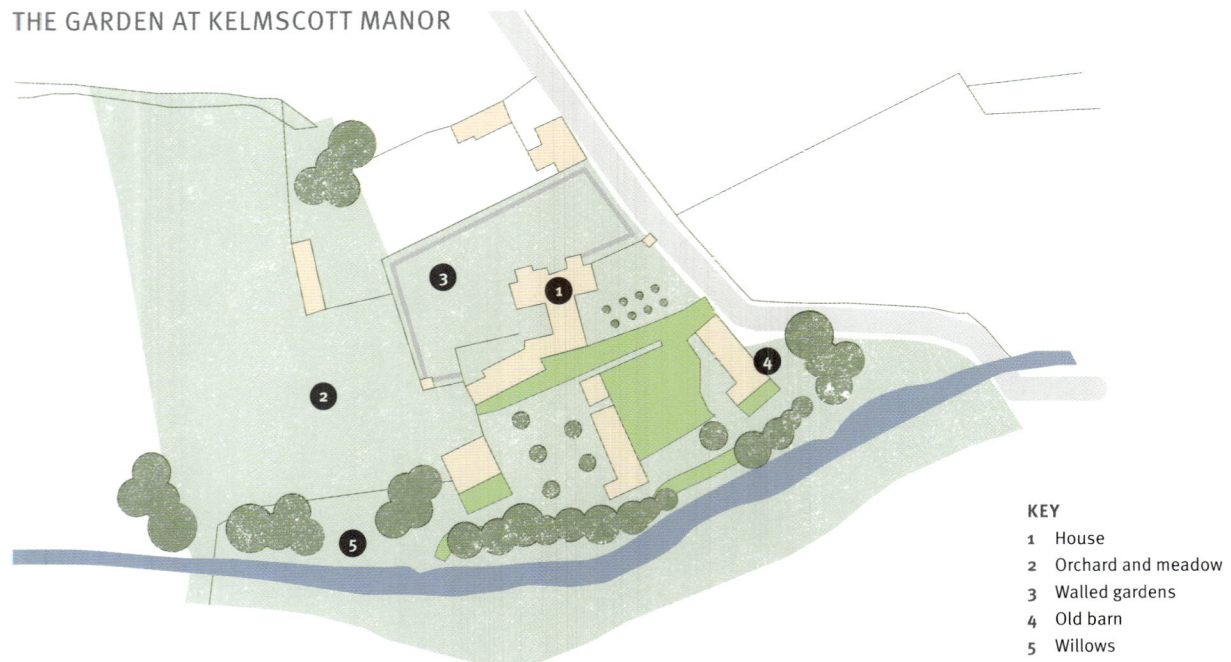

KEY
1 House
2 Orchard and meadow
3 Walled gardens
4 Old barn
5 Willows

CONSERVATION AND REVIVAL

The story of Kelmscott's revival echoes the ups and downs of historic building conservation in the twentieth century. May wanted Kelmscott to be preserved as a place of rest for artists and scholars, in honour of her father's memory. The University of Oxford found tenants, including, for a short time, the poet and campaigner John Betjeman, who made a documentary about the house in 1952. But by the 1960s, when Kelmscott passed to the Society of Antiquaries (of which William Morris had been a Fellow), the Manor was in need of extensive repair.

As the house stood, with its leaking roofs, wood rot and unsympathetic additions, May's idea was not workable. It needed full-time tenants to look after the fabric of the property and a plan was drawn up to use the south side as living quarters, and the north side as a public area. The programme of repairs involved a second organization: The Society for the Protection of Ancient Buildings (SPAB), of which William Morris was a founder and whose plea was for 'Protection in the place of restoration'. After the essential work had been completed, the house was opened to the public in 1967.

With the house repairs taking precedence, the gardens were simply laid to grass until, in 1993, the Society received funding and the firm of Brenda Colvin and Hal Moggridge were brought in to redesign them. The orchard was reinstated in its original position, and a croquet lawn was laid where the vegetables had been. A vine-covered pergola was also added, to reflect Morris's Acanthus & Vine pattern, along with many plants that reference the work of both William and May. The old standard roses that were at the

RIGHT, CLOCKWISE FROM TOP LEFT The mulberry tree was *in situ* when William Morris arrived at Kelmscott Manor in 1871; the cottage gardens to the north of the house; the shrub rose Falstaff; pollarded willows close to the river; a rustic fence that separates the orchard from the flower garden, used to support old roses; view through the Green Room window to the old mulberry.

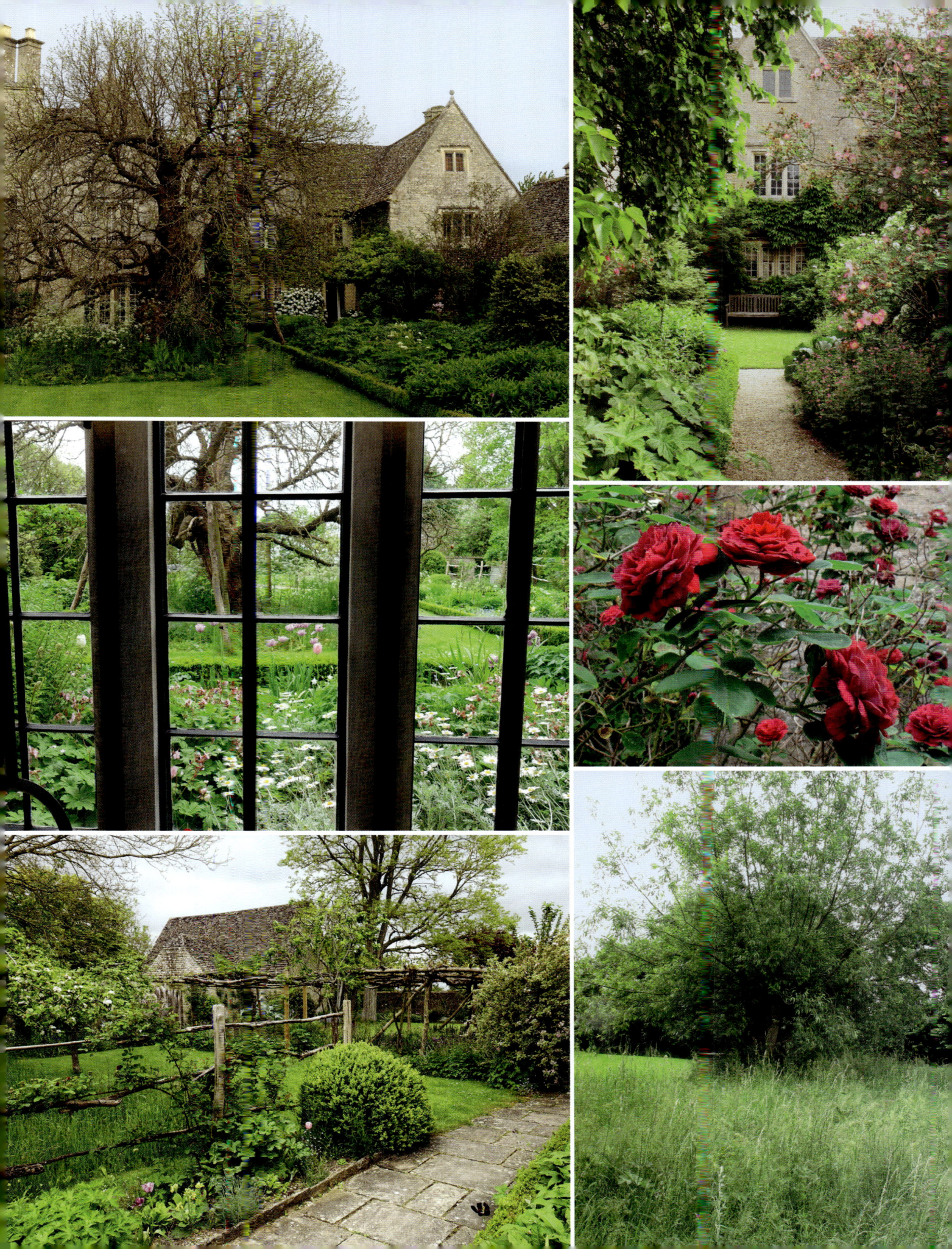

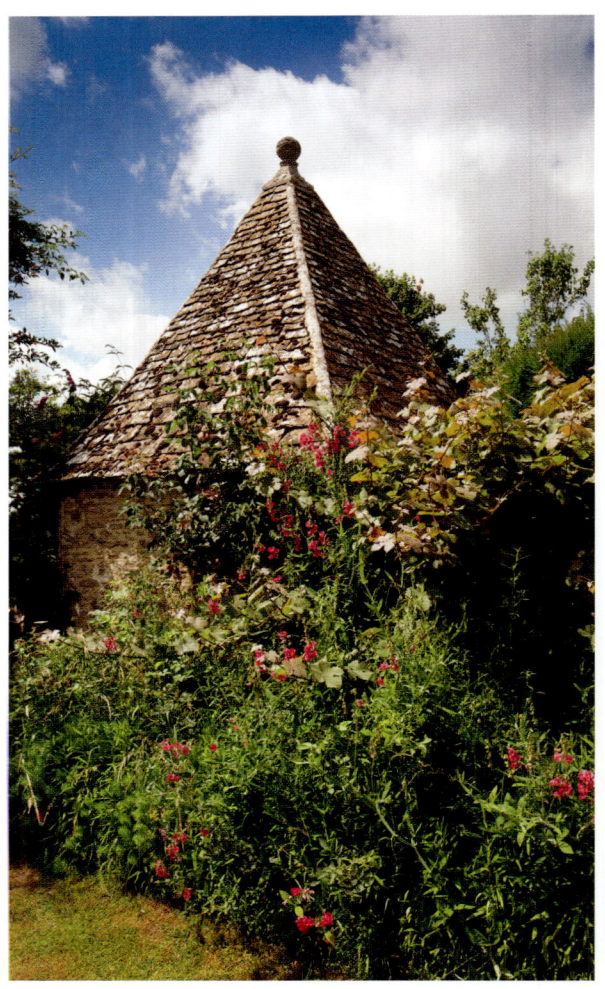

front of the house were replaced with a colour-themed scheme that progresses from pale pink roses at the gate end to dark pink in the middle and back to pale pink. On the west side of the house, dominated by an ancient mulberry, the borders are edged in box and filled with peonies, old roses, phlox, acanthus and English irises – all of which were important in the Morrises' work. For William, it was not just the visual appearance of the garden but its scent that he savoured – its herbs, lavender and lemon balm, which reminded him of the kitchen garden at Woodford Hall where he had grown up – and these plants, along with William's strawberry patch, have been reintroduced around the old earth closet.

The Morris & Co. patterns are subject to the vagaries of fashion, coming in and going out like the tide over time. While Kelmscott Manor is no shrine to The Firm, it has a deeper and more long-lasting legacy. Reflecting Morris's traditions, it has evolved into a place that embraces anyone in search of Arts & Crafts ideals: a respect for the natural world and a belief in the importance of human skill above those of the machine.

LEFT The old stone and tiled earth closet in the kitchen garden is now overgrown with climbing sweet peas.
RIGHT William Morris would have approached the house by the east porch, up the path flanked with standard roses.

THE MORRISES' TIMELINE

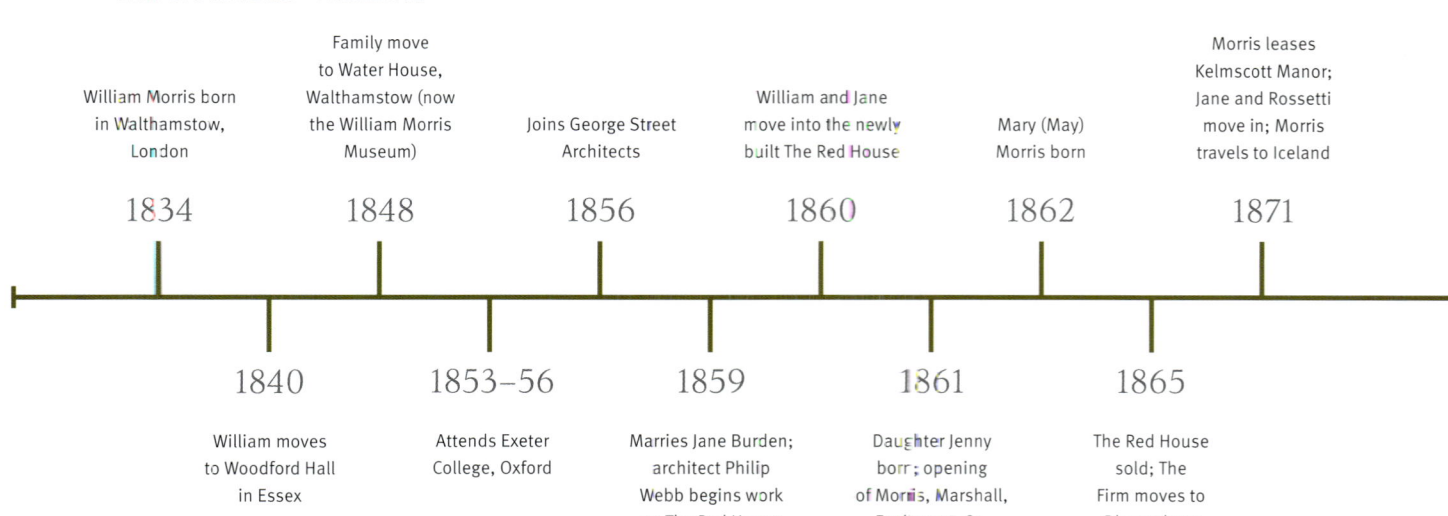

William Morris born in Walthamstow, London
1834

Family move to Water House, Walthamstow (now the William Morris Museum)
1848

Joins George Street Architects
1856

William and Jane move into the newly built The Red House
1860

Mary (May) Morris born
1862

Morris leases Kelmscott Manor; Jane and Rossetti move in; Morris travels to Iceland
1871

1840
William moves to Woodford Hall in Essex

1853–56
Attends Exeter College, Oxford

1859
Marries Jane Burden; architect Philip Webb begins work on The Red House

1861
Daughter Jenny born; opening of Morris, Marshall, Faulkner & Co. in London

1865
The Red House sold; The Firm moves to Bloomsbury

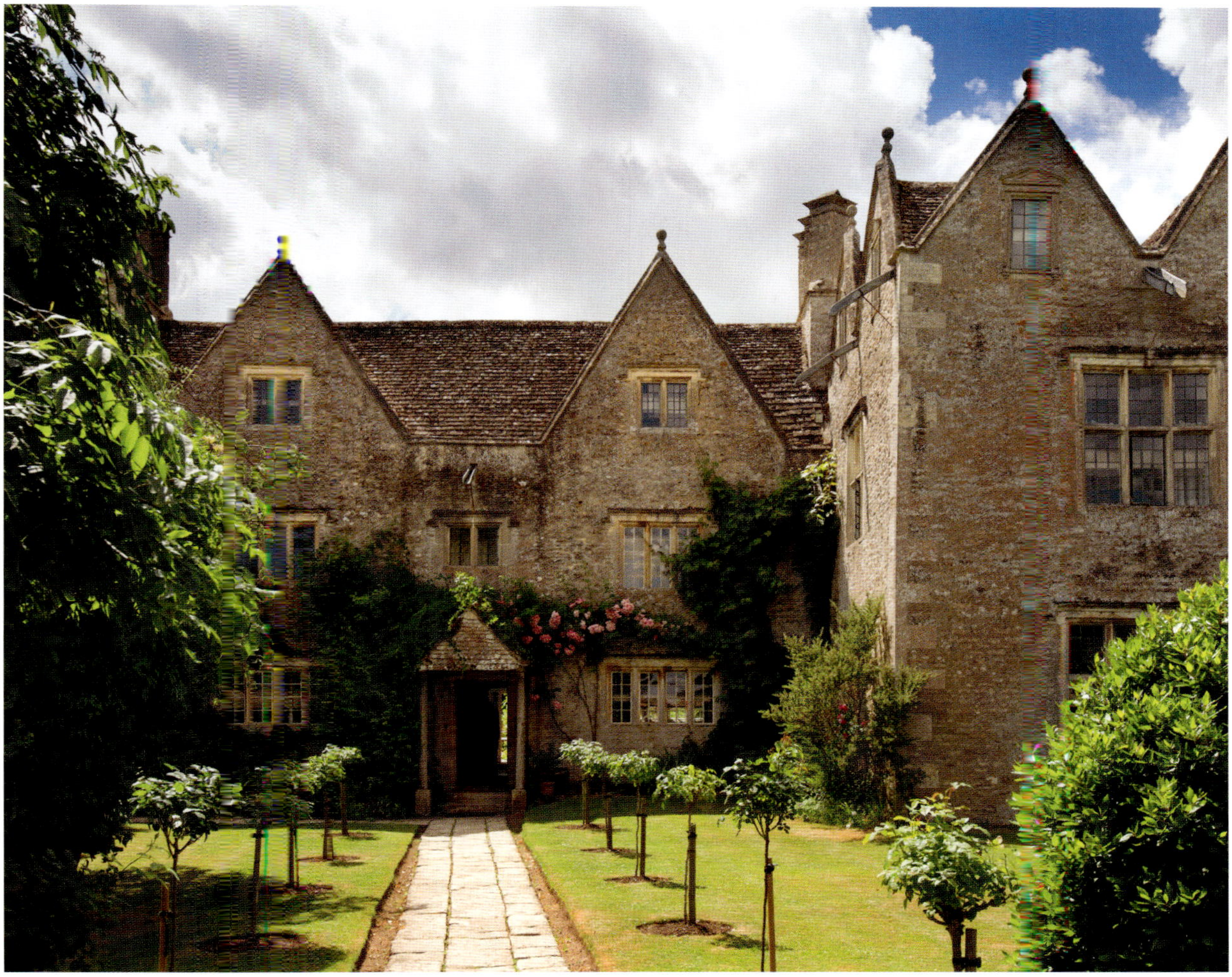

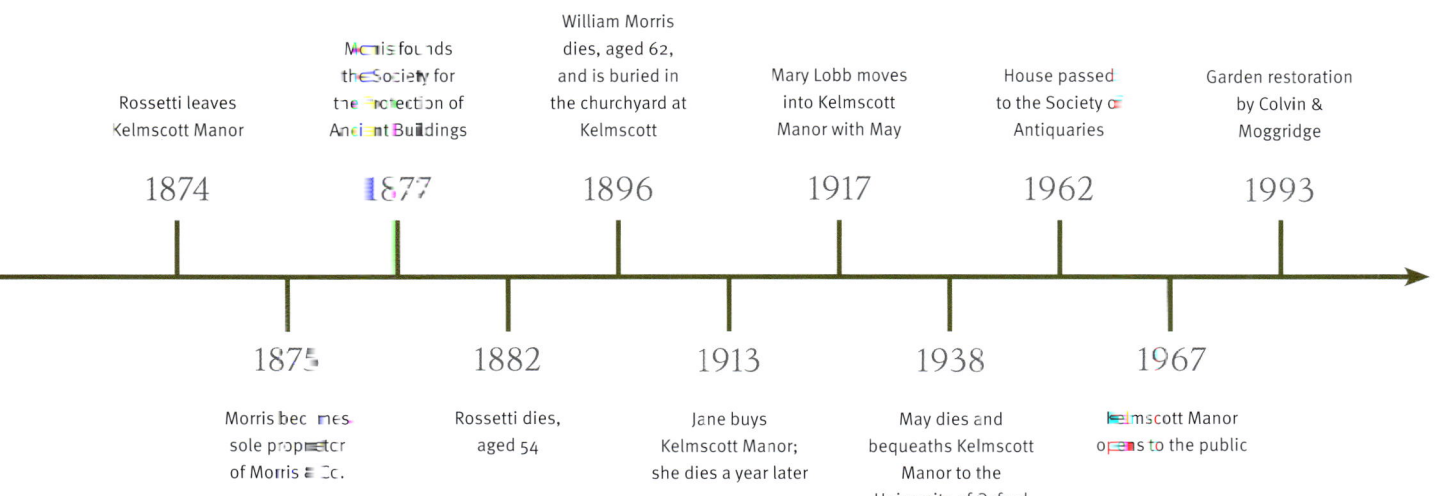

Rossetti leaves
Kelmscott Manor

Morris founds
the Society for
the Protection of
Ancient Buildings

William Morris
dies, aged 62,
and is buried in
the churchyard at
Kelmscott

Mary Lobb moves
into Kelmscott
Manor with May

House passed
to the Society of
Antiquaries

Garden restoration
by Colvin &
Moggridge

1874   **1877**   **1896**   **1917**   **1962**   **1993**

1875   **1882**   **1913**   **1938**   **1967**

Morris becomes
sole proprietor
of Morris & Co.

Rossetti dies,
aged 54

Jane buys
Kelmscott Manor;
she dies a year later

May dies and
bequeaths Kelmscott
Manor to the
University of Oxford

Kelmscott Manor
opens to the public

New England Impressionists

Frederick Childe Hassam, J. Alden Weir, Maria Oakey Dewing and the artist colonists of the USA's Eastern seaboard

Connecticut, Maine & New Hampshire, USA

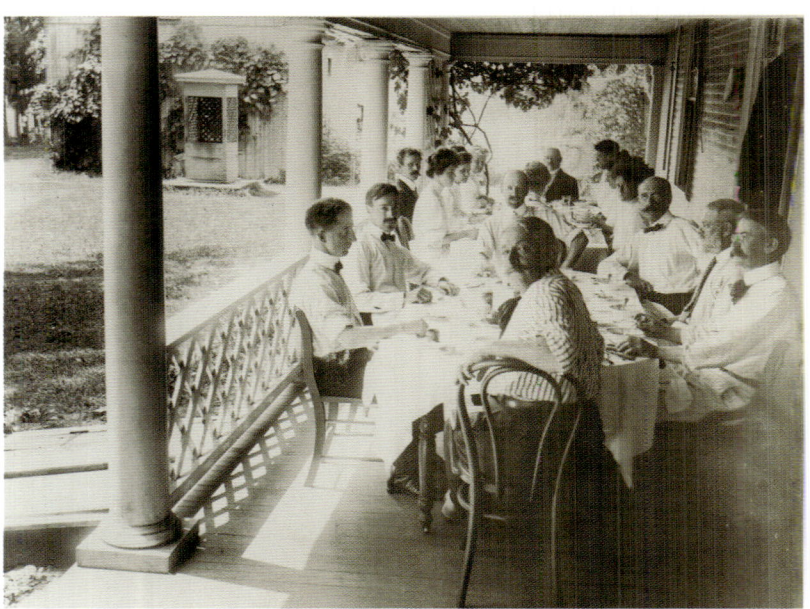

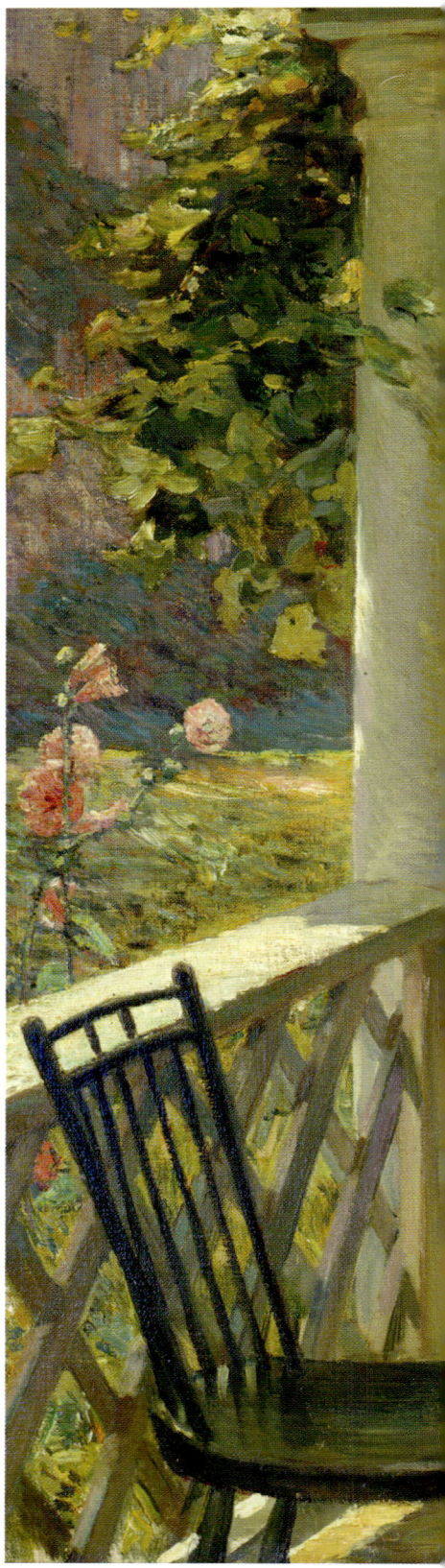

Inspired by artists working in late nineteenth-century Europe, including Monet, Renoir, Degas and Manet, American Impressionism owes its birth to the Parisian art dealer Paul Durand-Ruel. In 1883 and 1886, he brought work by French artists to the United States, and his exhibitions, along with the Americans who had gained expertise during painting trips to Europe, propelled the rise in popularity of artists such as Mary Cassatt and Theodore Robinson. These Impressionist painters were at the vanguard of a new art movement – not one that imitated its European counterpart, but one that found its own momentum, sharing with the Europeans a love of gardens and nature.

ABOVE On summer evenings, members of the Old Lyme art colony would eat outside on the porch of Florence Griswold's house. At the head of the table is major Impressionist artist Willard Metcalf while their host, Florence Griswold, can be seen on the right-hand side of the photograph (1905).

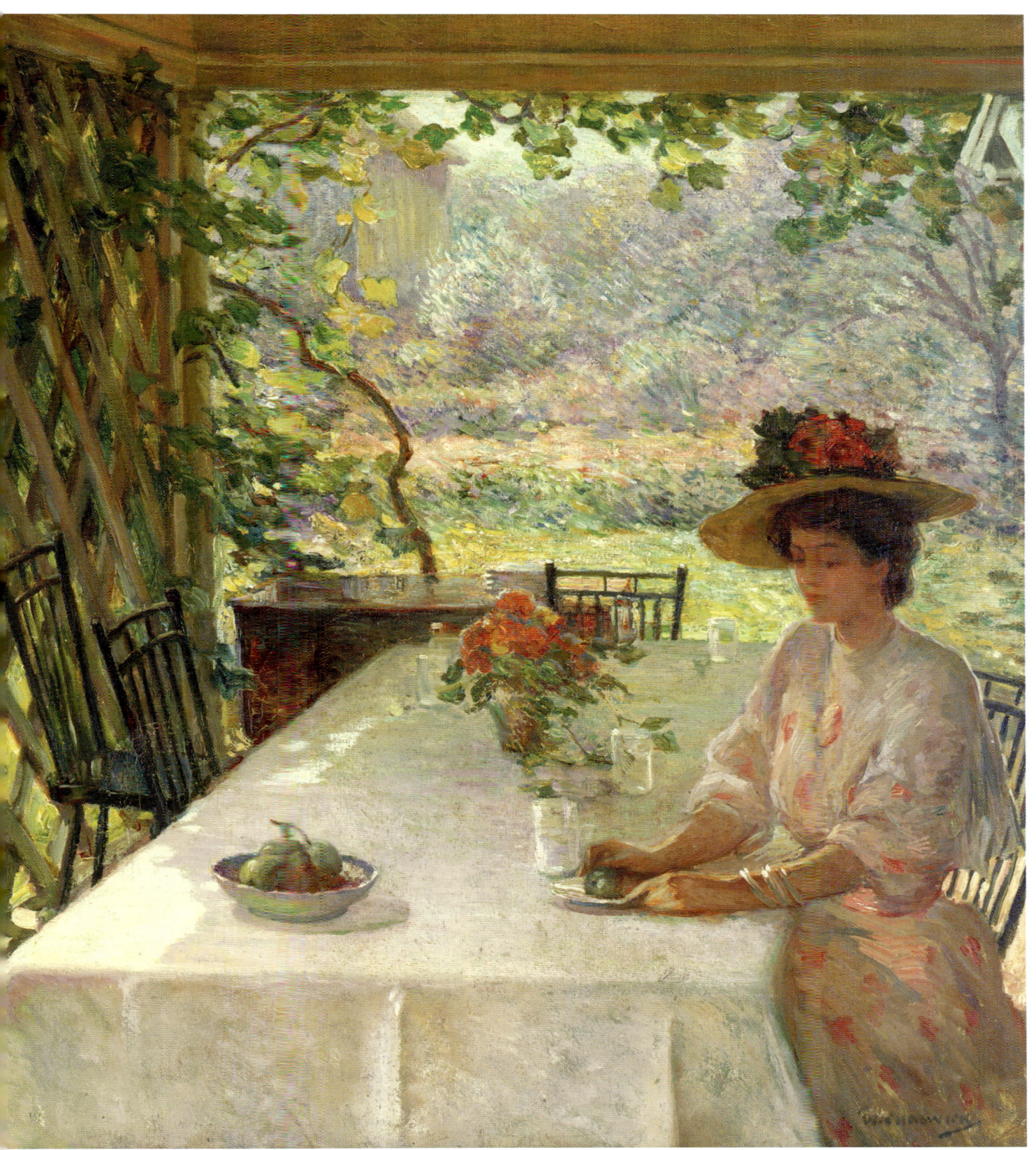

ABOVE *On the Piazza* (circa 1908, by William Chadwick, depicts the porch and garden
at Florence Griswold's house. An English-born artist, Chadwick settled in Old Lyme
and was a regular visitor to the colony in Connecticut.

The Artists in Residence
(1880–1920)

In search of garden and countryside *motifs*, American artists gathered at various colonies to learn from each other. Artists came and went – some staying a few weeks, others making permanent country homes at the colonies.

Old Lyme Colony, Florence Griswold's Boarding House Willard Metcalf, Harry Hoffman, William Chadwick, Anna Lea Merritt, Charles Vezin, Frederick Childe Hassam and Matilda Browne were the most notable artists working at this colony on the Connecticut coast.

Weir's Farm, Connecticut J. Alden Weir's farm lured many artists, including John Henry Twachtman, Childe Hassam and Morris Hunt, looking for wilder landscapes. The tradition continued with his daughter, artist Dorothy Weir Young, and her husband, sculptor Mahonri Young.

Appledore, Celia Thaxter's home Poet Celia Thaxter invited artists Childe Hassam, William Morris Hunt, and others to her house on the Isles of Shoals.

Cornish Colony, New Hampshire Maria Oakey Dewing, her husband Thomas Dewing and Willard Metcalf were drawn to the colony created by sculptor Saint-Gaudens.

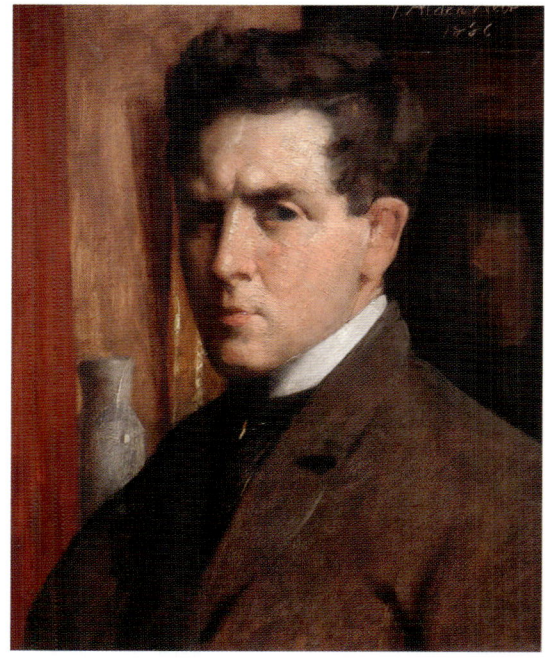

J. Alden Weir, *Self-portrait* (1886).

NEW BEGINNINGS

When Paul Durand-Ruel brought his first exhibition from Paris to Boston in September 1883, Impressionist painters were receiving mixed reviews in France. Yet in America, the works of Claude Monet, Alfred Sisley, Pierre-Auguste Renoir and Édouard Manet met with more positive critical interest. Buoyed by this limited success, Durand-Ruel brought another 300 paintings (250 of which were by French artists) to New York on the invitation of the American Art Association. He added names to this second exhibition that were not yet familiar in the United States, including Berthe Morisot, Georges Seurat and Gustave Caillebotte.

The exhibition of Impressionism continued at the National Academy in New York, with the addition of works by twenty American artists and, again, the critics liked what they saw. Many of the Americans who contributed to that exhibition had already been working with, and learning from, Impressionist painters in France when they exploded on to the new art scene in their homeland.

ART MEETS GARDENING

Mary Cassatt is thought of as the first American Impressionist painter, although she lived in Paris for most of her life, where she produced much of her work, including her famous painting, *Lydia Crocheting in the Garden at Marly* (1880). Cassatt was the first American to exhibit with the French artists and, in doing so, influenced her fellow compatriots to adopt the ideas that would guide the development of the Impressionist movement. These included employing pure colours and the free and experimental use of paint – something Cassatt practised alongside Degas, with whom she worked closely in Paris.

Durand-Ruel's exhibitions tied in neatly with the growing interest in gardens in late nineteenth-century America. There was a shift from gardens as places to grow medicinal plants and food, to those for ornament, respite and enjoyment. The gardening movement of that time was in many ways a reaction against industrialization, influenced by the Arts & Crafts Movement in Britain, particularly the designs of William Morris, the writings of the plantsman William Robinson and the painterly planting style of Gertrude Jekyll, who designed the garden of Glebe House Museum in Woodbury, Connecticut. The newly emerging American middle classes adopted this movement wholeheartedly and were now able to enjoy gardening at home as a leisure pastime.

FLORENCE GRISWOLD'S HOUSE

By the late 1880s, American artists who had spent time in France began to return to the USA with their work. In 1888, Willard Metcalf – who had spent time at Giverny, Monet's home in France (see page 130) – put on the first solo Impressionist exhibition in Boston, and many more followed. Artists began to gather in a number of locations and loose colonies were formed where painters could share their ideas and skills. One of the most successful was at a boarding house on the Connecticut coast at Old Lyme, about midway between Boston and New York.

Florence Griswold, the daughter of a ship's captain, had inherited a large New England house and a fifteen-acre estate from her family but little money. She began taking in guests to supplement her income, including the sister and mother of artist Clark Voorhees. He then spread the word to fellow artist Henry Ward Ranger, who spent the summer at Old Lyme in 1899. The following

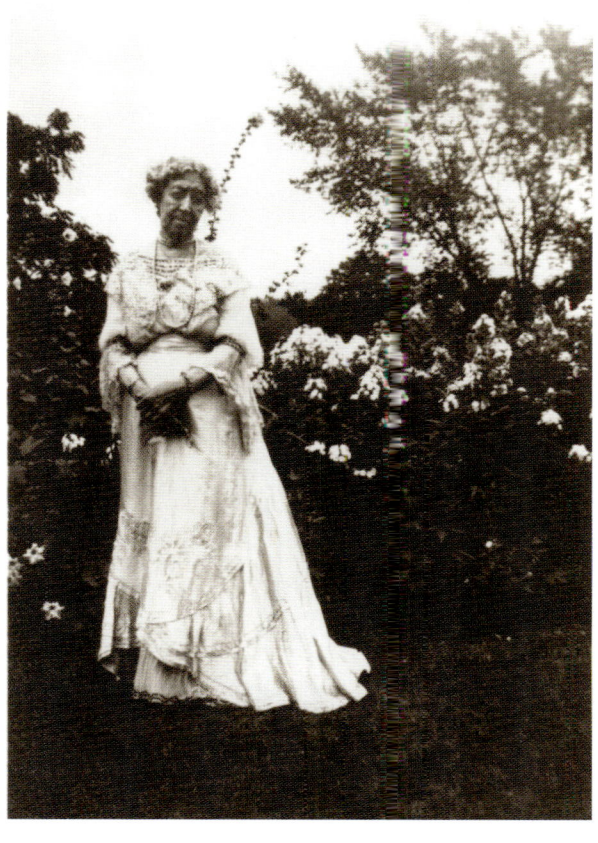

ABOVE Florence Griswold made an old-fashioned garden at her boarding house in Old Lyme, which became a summer colony for early twentieth-century Impressionist artists.

LEFT In addition to painting communally, the artists also taught pupils during classes held in the grounds.

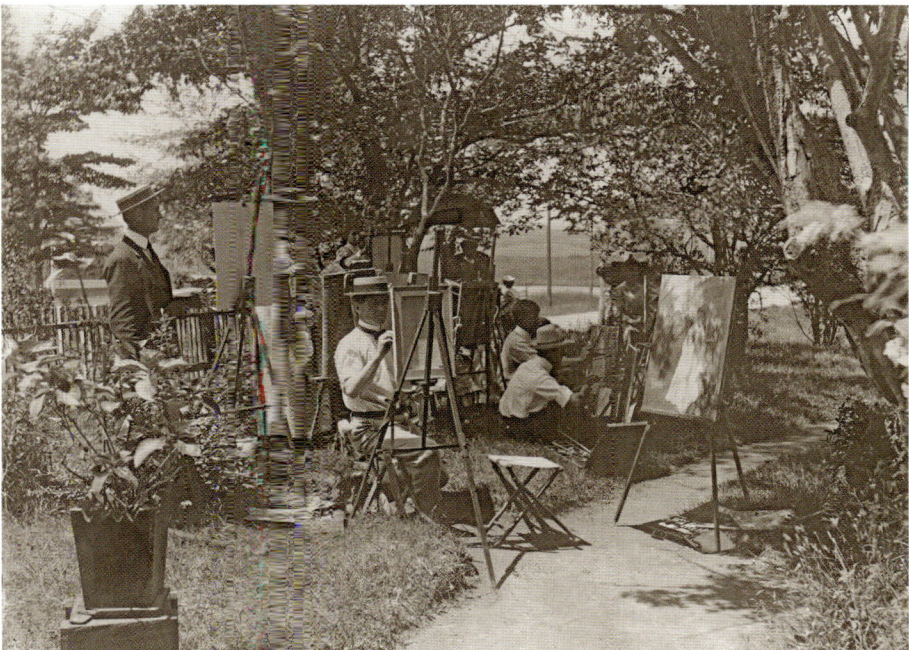

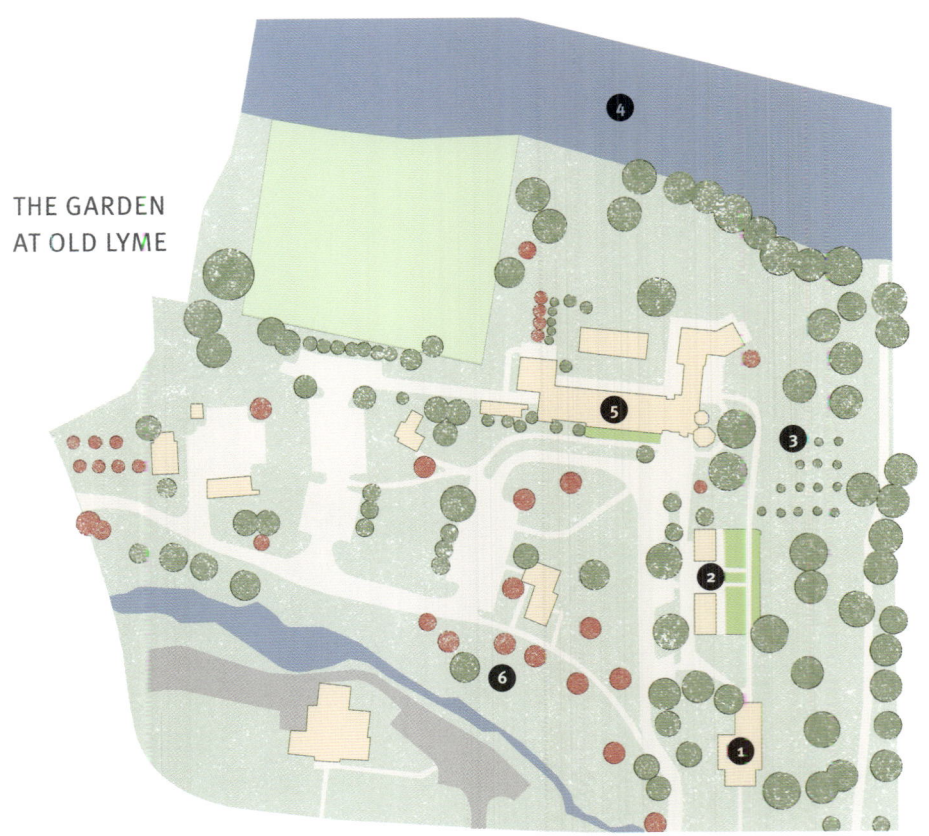

THE GARDEN AT OLD LYME

KEY

1 Florence Griswold's Boarding House (now the Florence Griswold Museum)
2 Cottage Gardens
3 Orchard
4 River Lieutenant
5 Galleries
6 Flowering dogwoods, cherries and crab apples

RIGHT *Peonies* by Matilda Browne (1907) depicts the garden of Katharine Ludington in Old Lyme. Browne visited Lyme for over a decade before buying a house there in 1917.
BELOW Florence Griswold's cottage garden includes a pergola for climbing roses.

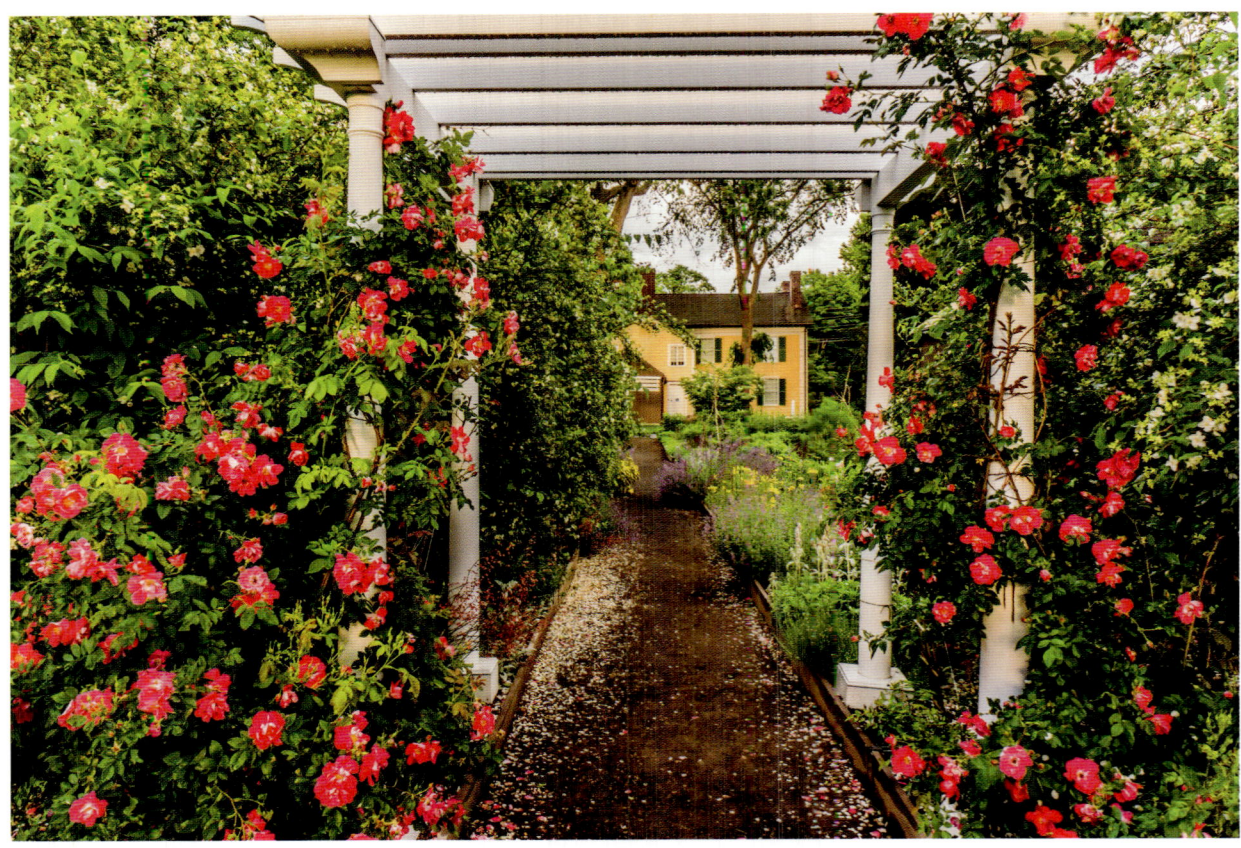

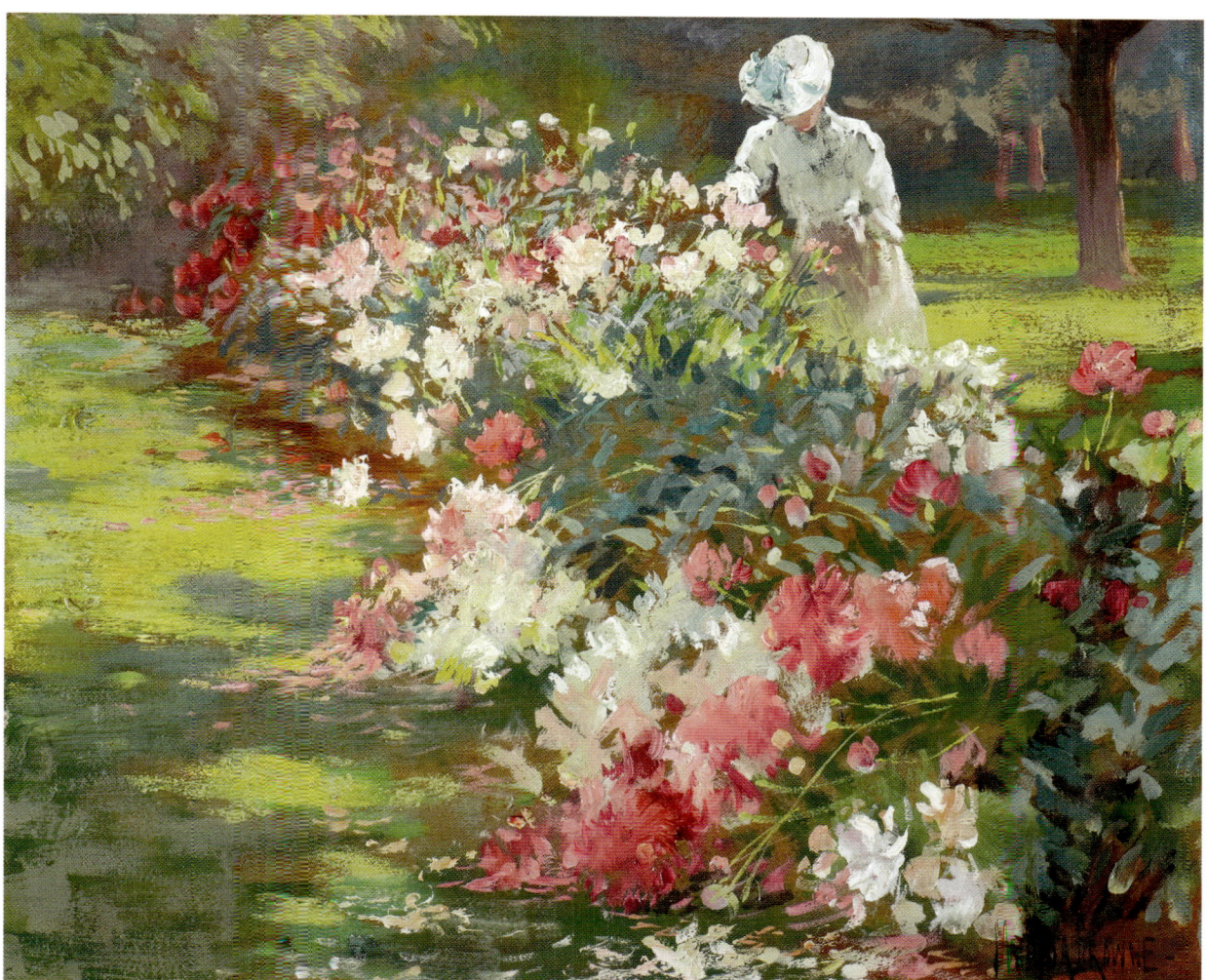

year, Ranger returned to Griswold's house with a group of artists, with the intention of establishing an American version of the Barbizon art colony in France.

The artists were looking for a calm, country setting, and found it at Florence Griswold's place. It had a small river running past the garden, a nearby woodland and fields to paint. The artists who gathered there were not students, nor in the first throes of their careers, but established professionals who valued the company of other artists. They had the run of the house and garden, taking meals on the porch when it was warm, and making temporary studios in the outbuildings and barns on the property. After breakfast, the artists would set up outdoor painting groups, employing portable easels and discussing how best to depict the garden. Flowers would be taken and arranged indoors for painting on rainy days.

Originally running the farm with hired help for the livestock, orchards, and pastureland, Griswold was also a keen gardener who cared for the plantings made by her parents. Food grown in the gardens was served to her boarding-house guests and she enhanced the flower garden using seeds from specialist catalogues and local nursery plants. The flowering plants, including lilacs, peonies, geraniums, phlox, foxgloves, hollyhocks, irises and daylilies (*Hemerocallis*), were arranged informally and grew in profusion in what we would now call a cottage or grandmothers' garden. She made an unstructured space that the artists, in their search for true nature, appreciated. As part of the colonial revival that was in vogue at that time, Griswold was always in search of heritage plant varieties and advised the artists on what to grow in their own gardens back home.

Florence Griswold's gardens were restored in the late twentieth century, after an archaeological programme helped to establish exactly where the outbuildings, paths and borders had been, bringing it back to the period of around 1910. As research is undertaken, the custodians of the Florence Griswold Museum are discovering more viewpoints depicted in the artists' paintings, so that today it is possible to find the spot where William Chadwick captured *On the Piazza* (circa 1908) and to walk along the artists' trail around the grounds.

WILD LANDSCAPES AT WEIR'S FARM

Old Lyme was not the only place early twentieth-century American artists gathered to explore their creativity. In 1882 Julian Alden Weir – who had also visited Giverny – swapped a still-life painting, plus ten dollars, for a 153-acre/70-hectare farm in Branchville, Connecticut.

A landscape of meadows, criss-crossed by stone walls and woodlands, the farm provided an alternative summer meeting place for artists in search of something less cultivated than Griswold's garden. Weir's masterstroke at Branchville was the pond, which he constructed in 1896 on a ten-acre/four-hectare plot bought with the $2,500 prize money he received for his painting, *The Truants* (also known as *The Old Rock*), at the Boston Art Club.

Among the friends who visited Weir at his farm were Childe Hassam, Albert Pinkham Ryder and John Henry Twachtman. In many ways, this group would define American Impressionism by capturing the particular light and colour of this landscape. John Twachtman was

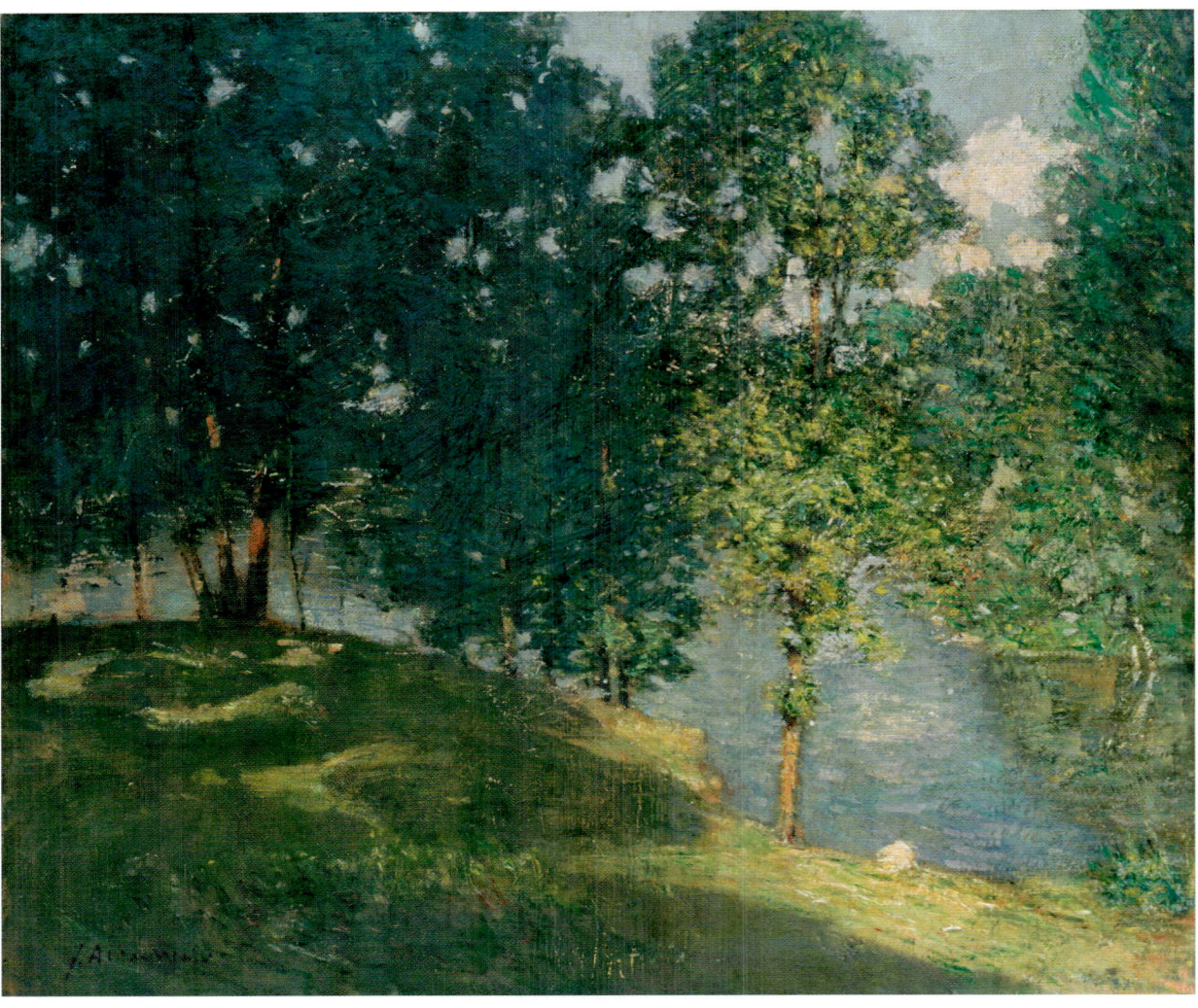

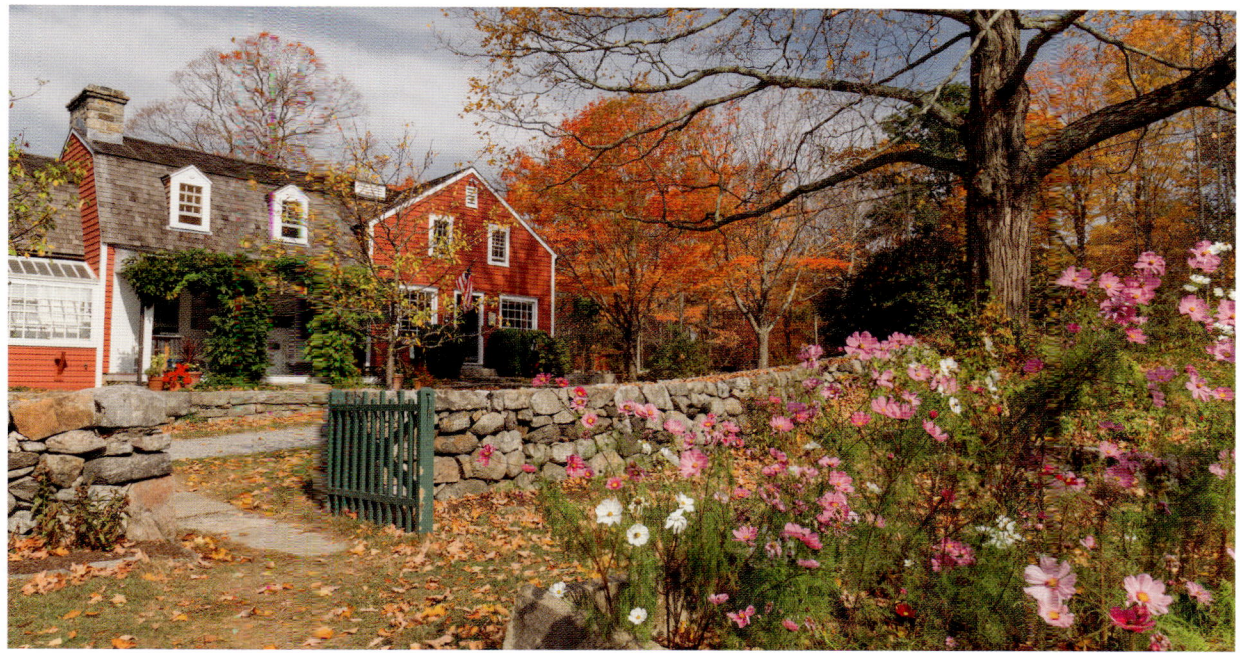

already gaining a reputation for his earthy natural tones and selection of simple themes, many of them taken from the farm. He and his family were frequent visitors and in the summer of 1888, the Twachtmans rented a house close by. Twachtman loved the isolation of Branchville and the two artists often worked alongside one another in the great outdoors. In the winter of 1888–89, Weir and Twachtman collaborated on a joint show in New York, which included the latter's painting, *Apple Trees at Branchville*. Twachtman died at the age of fifty and, after his death, Weir arranged a sale and exhibition of his friend's work, believing the late artist's talent was never fully realized.

Weir himself lived until 1915 and his daughter, Dorothy Weir Young, and her husband, sculptor Mahonri Young, carried on the artistic tradition at the farm. Weir's youngest daughter, Cora Weir Burlingham, lived in the neighbouring

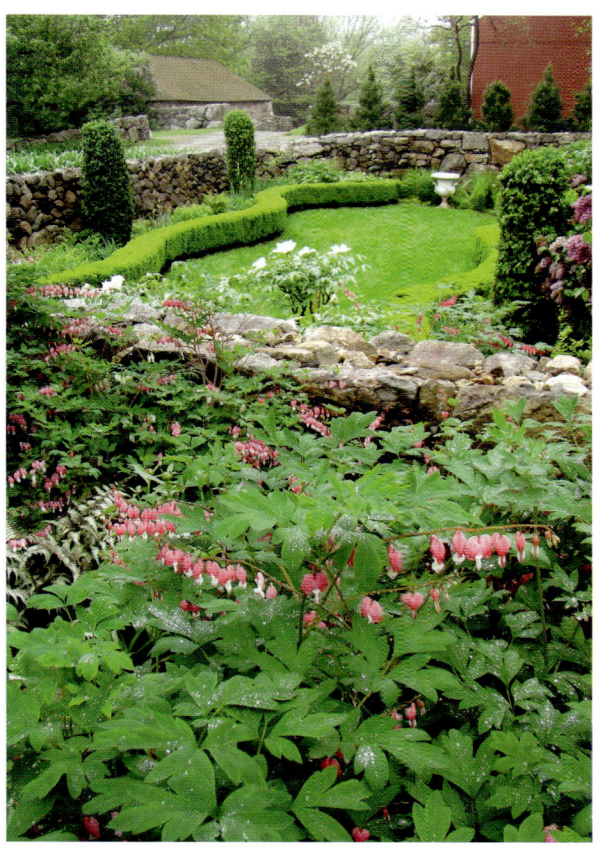

LEFT *Afternoon by the Pond (1908–09)* by J. Alden Weir, who created this huge pond at his farm in 1896; the area was one of his favourite places for painting and fishing with his friends.
ABOVE Built in the 1790s, Weir's Farm, with its red clapperboard facing, became a home for several generations of artists and their wider circle.
RIGHT The sunken garden was created in the 1930s by J. Alden Weir's youngest daughter, Cora Weir Burlingham.

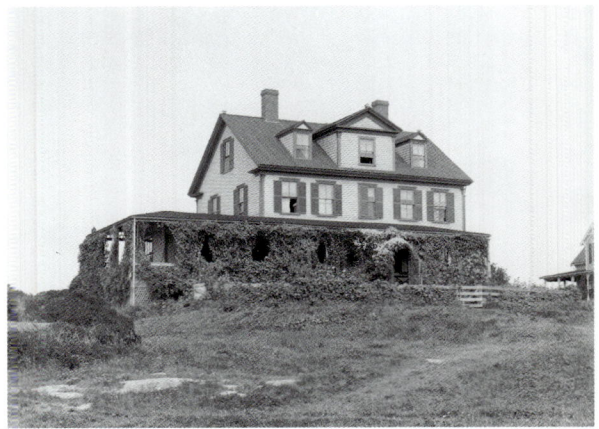

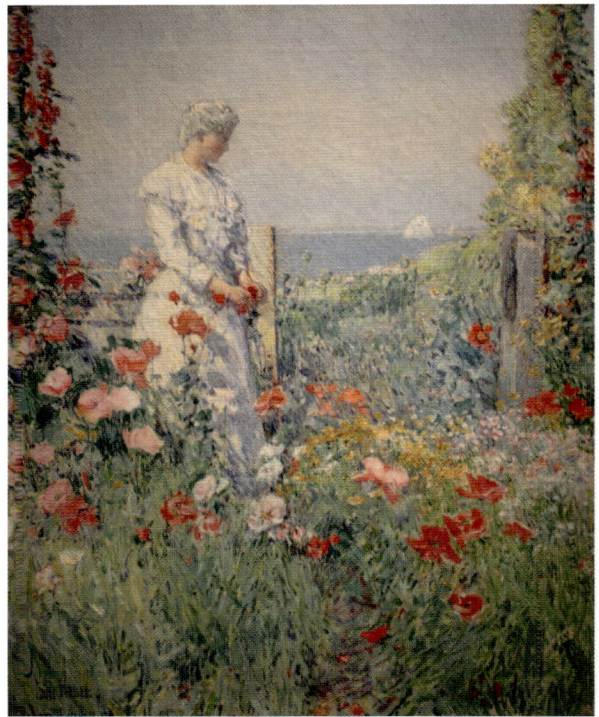

ABOVE, TOP Celia Thaxter's Cottage on Appledore Island became a key destination for Childe Hassam and other artists and writers.
ABOVE This image of Thaxter in her Appledore garden was painted by Childe Hassam for her book, *An Island Garden* (1894).
RIGHT, ABOVE *Celia Thaxter's Garden, Isles of Shoals* (1890) by Childe Hassam is one of hundreds of paintings the artist made of the garden and the wider island landscape.
RIGHT, BELOW Thaxter planted flowers to encourage pollinating insects and other wildlife into her coastal garden.

farmhouse and added the sunken garden and terraced gardens in the 1930s and 1940s. The gardens, landscape, and historic home and studios of three generations of artists, now owned by the National Park Service, includes 68 acres/28 hectares of woodland, where oaks, sugar maples and ash predominate and mountain laurel blooms in June. Today, artists continue to visit, inspired by the natural landscape and gardens that Weir loved.

HASSAM'S RETREAT AT APPLEDORE

In the early 1880s, the poet and hotelier's daughter Celia Thaxter invited the artist Frederick Childe Hassam to her home on Appledore Island in Maine, the largest of the Isles of Shoals. Hassam had spent time at all the artists' colonies in the USA and seized the opportunity with relish, going on to spend almost every summer after his first visit painting Celia and her garden.

Celia Thaxter was married to industrialist Levi Thaxter and through him met many of Boston's circle of artists and writers. Hassam's relationship with her was a close one, and his paintings of her wild garden with its poppies and daisies are among the best known of all American Impressionist paintings. In fact, such was Hassam's influence, that any group of artists he visited could call itself an 'Impressionist' colony.

The garden at Thaxter's cottage conveyed a simpler life, and Celia wrote about it lovingly in *An Island Garden* (published in 1894 by Houghton, Mifflin & Co., with illustrations by Hassam). She was also an active wildlife campaigner – the artist's image of her in the garden without a hat is a deliberate expression of her opposition to the trade in exotic bird feathers used in millinery at the time.

Celia Thaxter's garden was for pleasure – her own, and for the writers and artists who visited. The flower beds had a naturalistic look and a profusion of daylilies, cornflowers, hollyhocks and sunflowers were allowed to spill out over the garden wall. Hassam spent time at the other summer colonies, but always returned to Appledore.

After Thaxter's death in 1894, Hassam no longer painted the garden, but visited the island almost every year for a further three decades to paint its shores and seascapes, producing some 300 paintings of Appledore. In 1914, the hotel and cottage where Thaxter had lived,

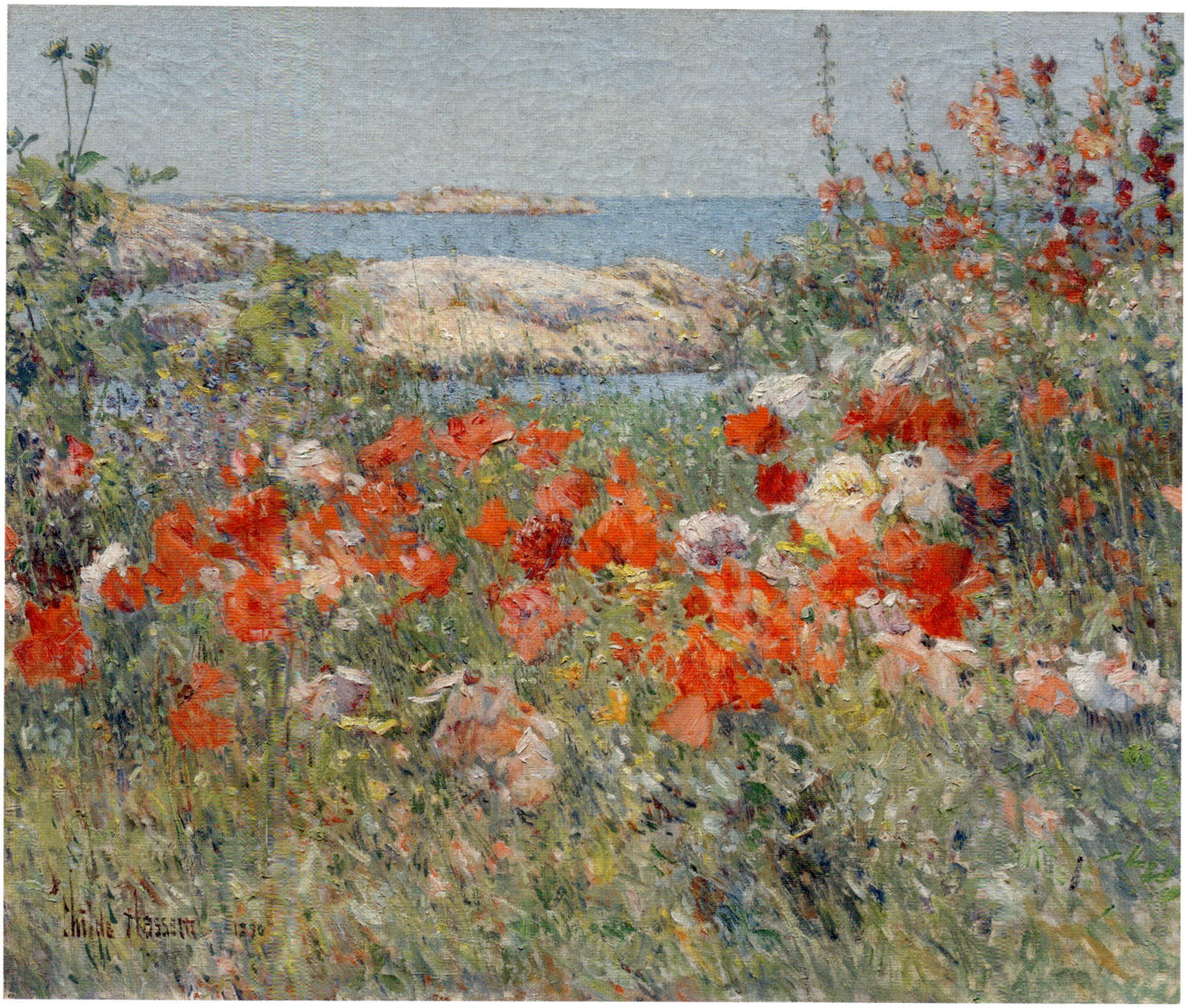

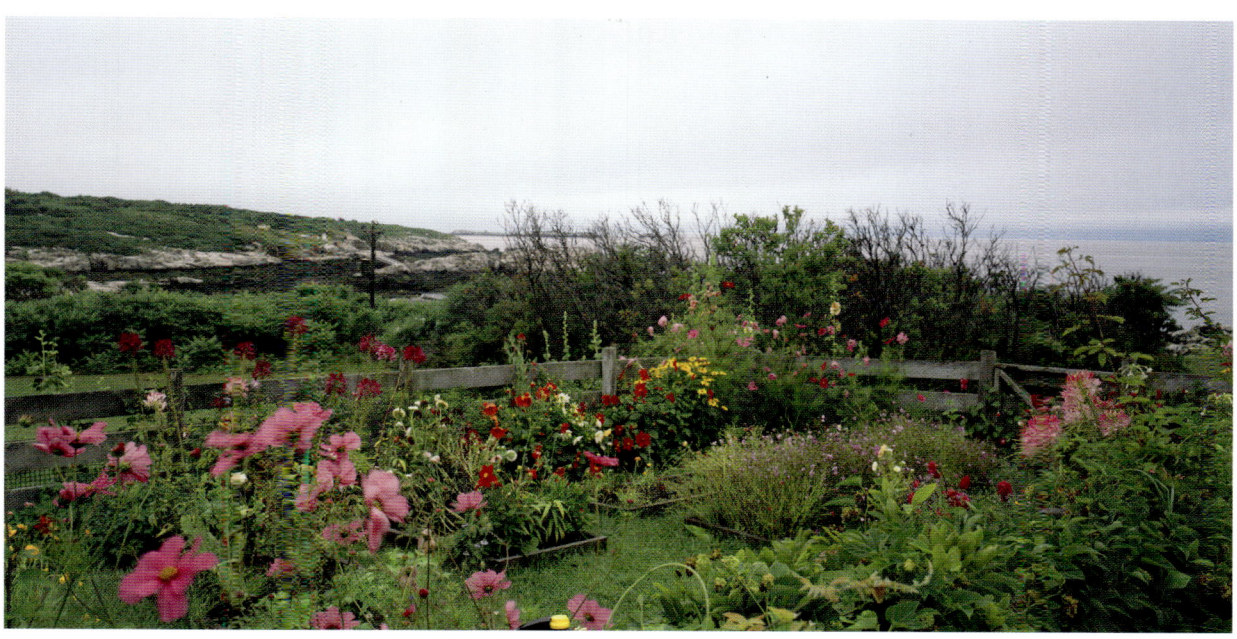

including the front porch covered with climbers, were destroyed by fire, but, in 1977, the gardens were restored by Dr John Kingsbury, founder of the Shoals Marine Laboratory, part of Cornell University and the University of New Hampshire. Incredibly, some of Thaxter's original snowdrops and daylilies (*Hemerocallis*) had survived, and the rest of the garden has now been accurately replanted according to her 1893 plan.

FLOWER PAINTING COMES OF AGE

When Celia Thaxter made her quiet but poignant wildlife protest in her garden at Appledore, American women did not have the vote and the debate over suffrage was raging. In 1898, the influential group of ten Impressionist artists, known as 'The Ten', exhibiting in New York were all men. A key painting was Philip Leslie Hale's *The Crimson Rambler* (1908). It appears to sentimentalize the female model and was read by some as an opposition to women's suffrage, while others saw it as a positive image, with a woman as its focus. (The rose itself, *Rosa* 'Crimson Rambler', bred in Japan, had come to America from England and became a runaway success.) The painting divided opinion and sparked a debate on the position of women in art.

A counter-movement began to place women as integral to the garden scene, rather than as decorative objects within it. As the new century began, more women would

"Flowers offer a removed beauty that exists only for beauty."
MARIA OAKEY DEWING (1915)

become garden-makers, garden designers and garden artists. Painters such as Maria Oakey Dewing and Anna Lea Merritt began to carve out important artistic roles for themselves. Dewing, in particular, was a colonist who made gardening and garden and flower paintings the focus of her life. Spending summers with her husband at the Cornish colony in New Hampshire (founded by the sculptor Augustus Saint-Gaudens), she planted and tended a garden there, believing that physical gardening provided the best apprenticeship for painting flowers well. Her images were in marked contrast to those of her husband, Thomas Wilmer Dewing, whose landscapes featured ethereal female figures.

Maria Oakey Dewing put women at the heart of the garden, as garden-makers. No one viewing her *Bed of Poppies* (1909) could doubt that the artist has got down on her hands and knees to study her subjects closely. Finally, an American woman was producing outdoor flower portraits to sit beside those of Van Gogh and Monet – although few over the years have given her credit for it.

NEW ENGLAND IMPRESSIONISTS' TIMELINE

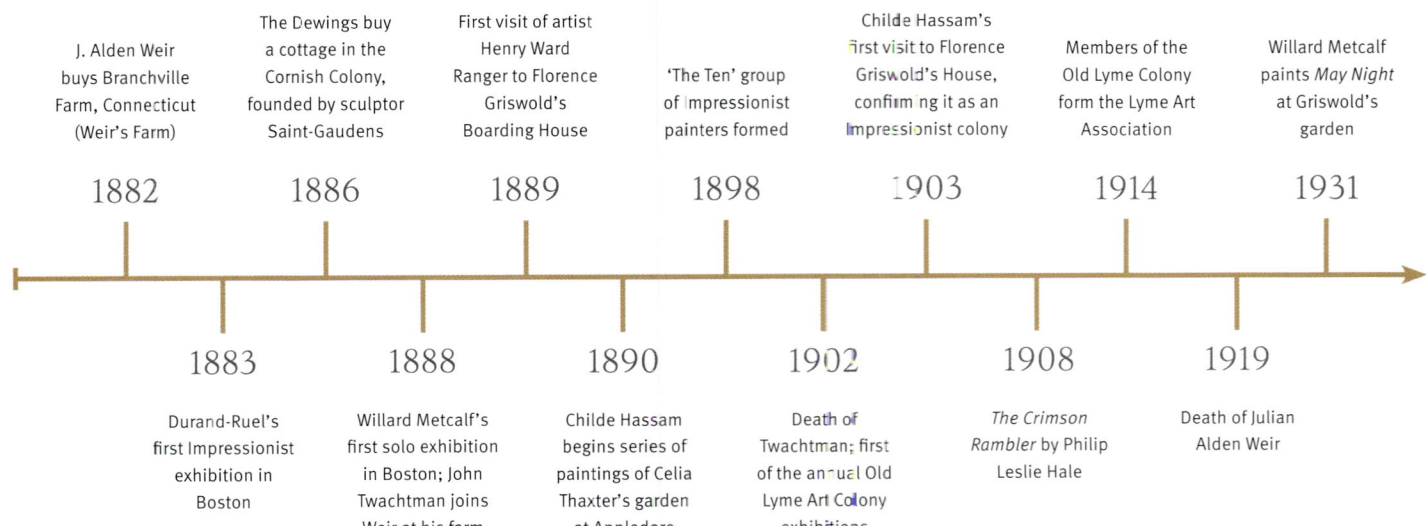

1882	1886	1889	1898	1903	1914	1931
J. Alden Weir buys Branchville Farm, Connecticut (Weir's Farm)	The Dewings buy a cottage in the Cornish Colony, founded by sculptor Saint-Gaudens	First visit of artist Henry Ward Ranger to Florence Griswold's Boarding House	'The Ten' group of Impressionist painters formed	Childe Hassam's first visit to Florence Griswold's House, confirming it as an Impressionist colony	Members of the Old Lyme Colony form the Lyme Art Association	Willard Metcalf paints *May Night* at Griswold's garden

1883	1888	1890	1902	1908	1919
Durand-Ruel's first Impressionist exhibition in Boston	Willard Metcalf's first solo exhibition in Boston; John Twachtman joins Weir at his farm	Childe Hassam begins series of paintings of Celia Thaxter's garden at Appledore	Death of Twachtman; first of the annual Old Lyme Art Colony exhibitions	*The Crimson Rambler* by Philip Leslie Hale	Death of Julian Alden Weir

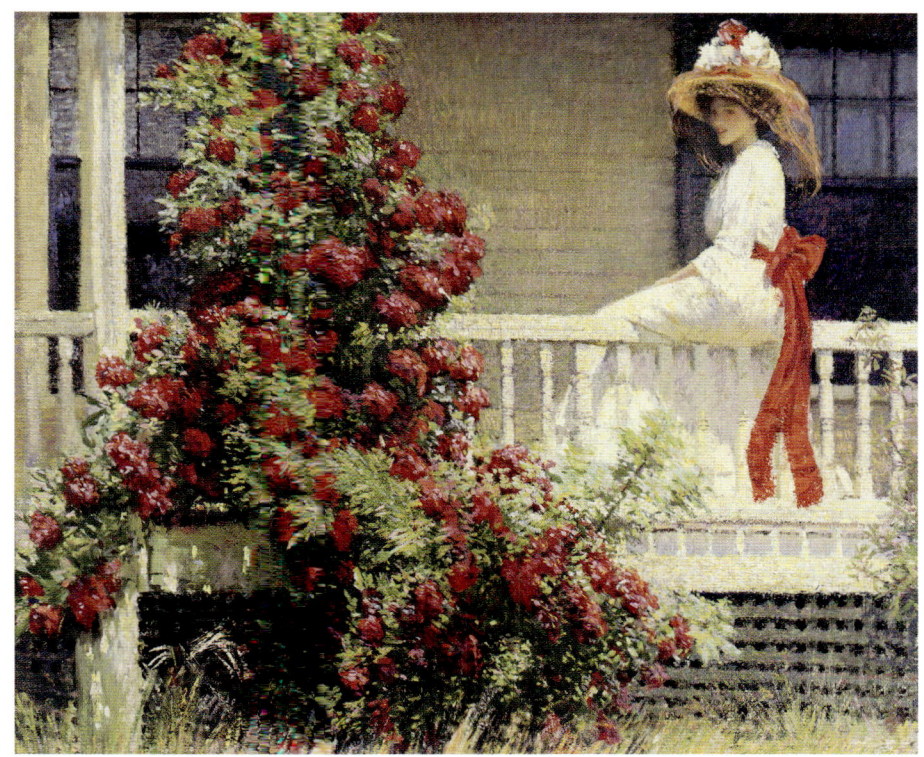

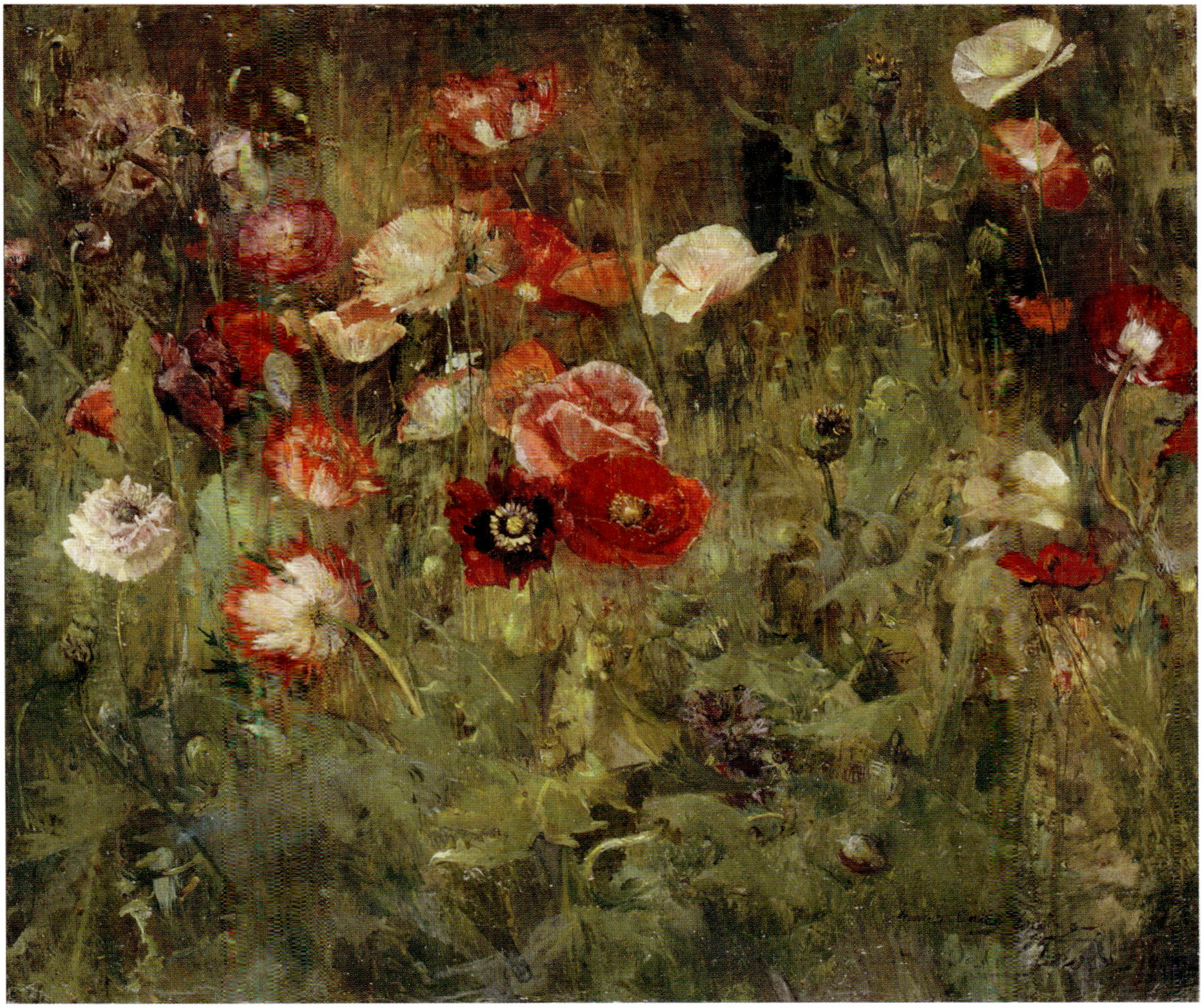

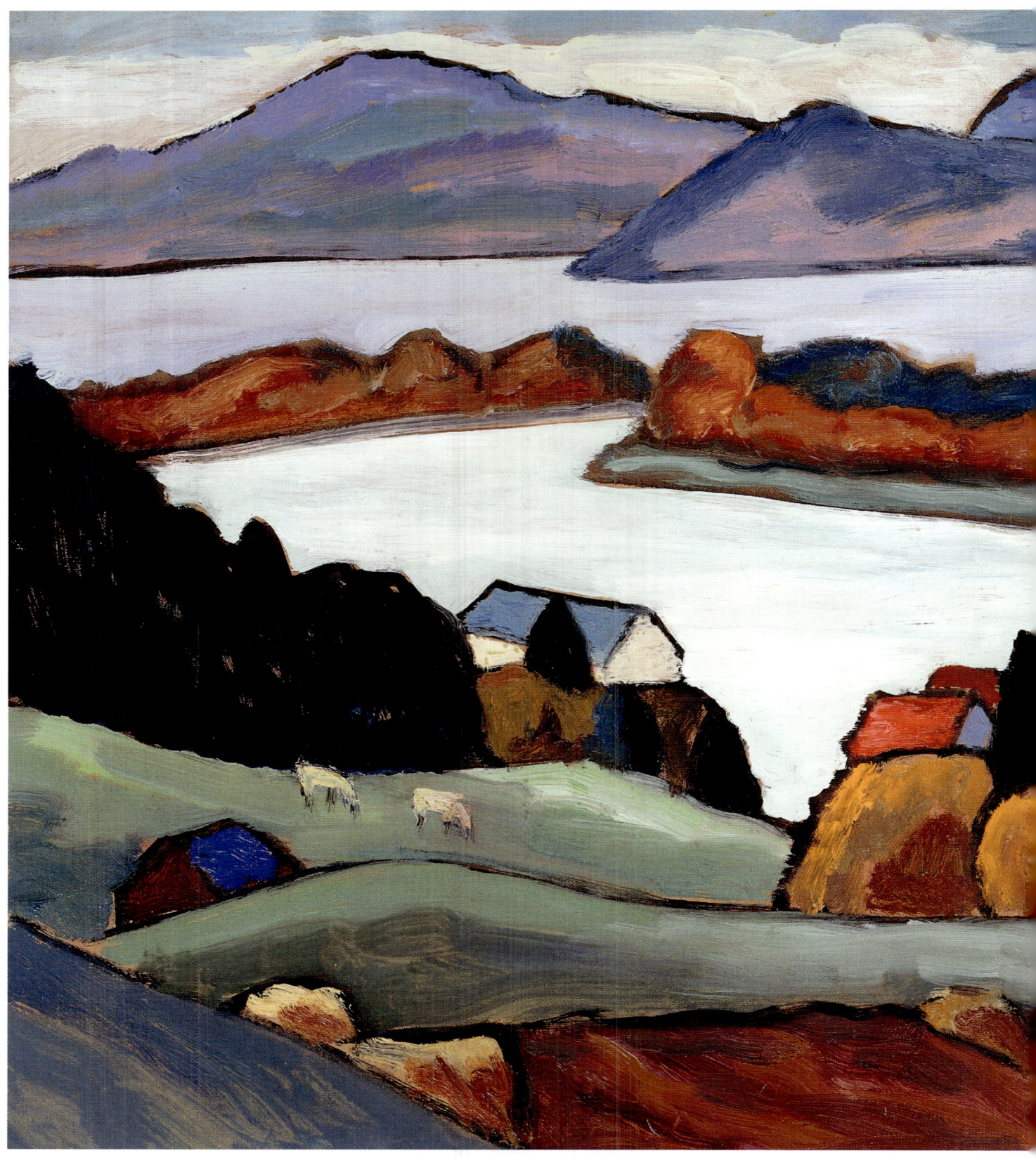

ABOVE *Staffelsee* (1935–36) by Gabriele Münter depicts the Bavarian lakes and mountains around her home in Murnau, which became a centre of German Expressionism during the twentieth century.

RIGHT Artists Wassily Kandinsky and Gabriele Münter, photographed here in 1906/07, lived together for twelve years in Munich and Murnau, until Kandinsky returned to his Russian homeland.

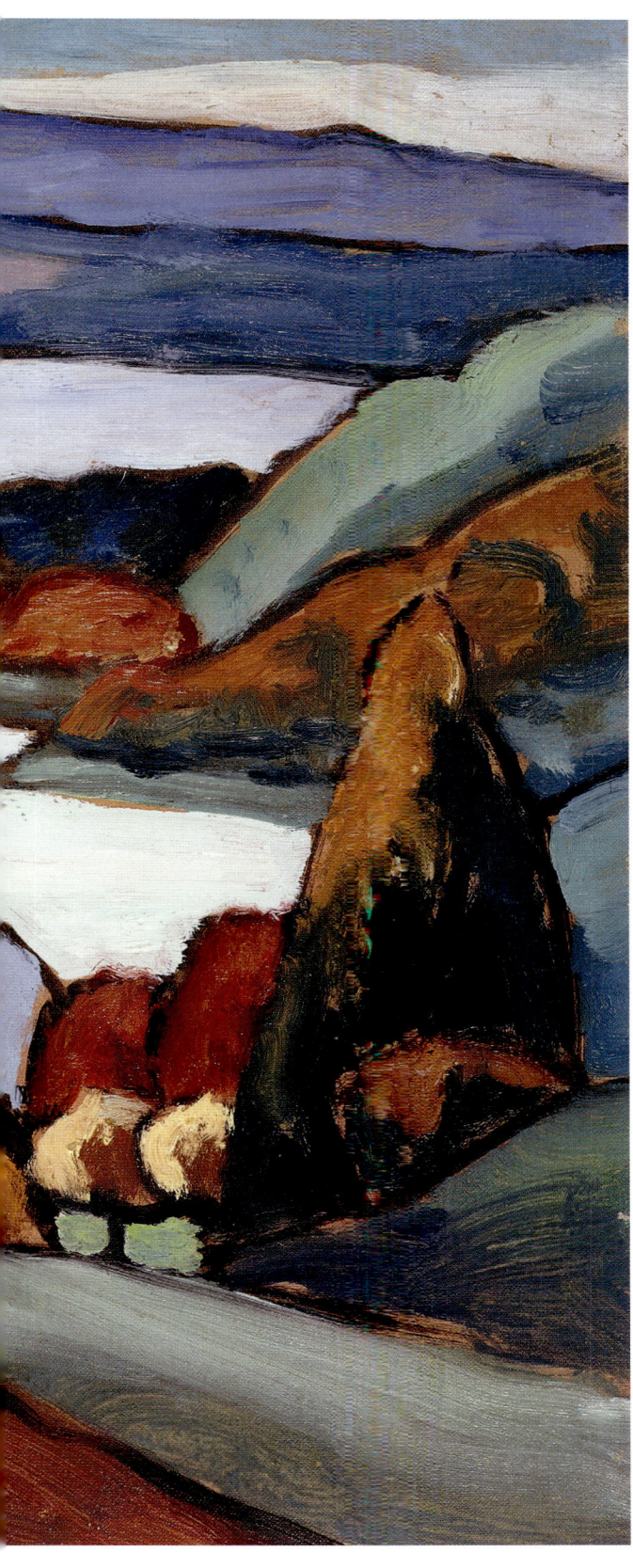

German Expressionists

Wassily Kandinsky, Gabriele Münter and The Blue Rider group

Murnau, Bavaria, Germany

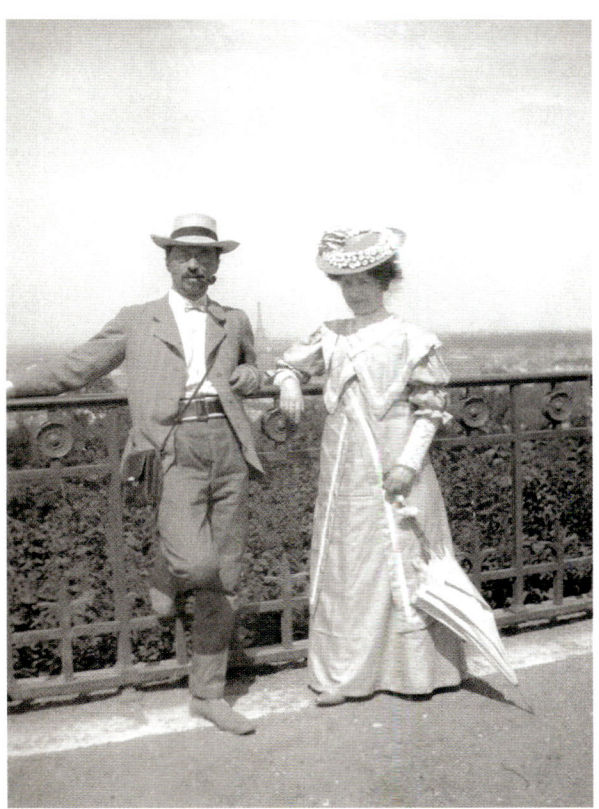

Stretching from the city to the shores of Staffelsee, Kochelsee and Walchensee, the area south of Munich in the Bavarian hills is regarded as one of the geographical centres of the German Expressionist art movement. At its heart sits a pretty house and garden in the town of Murnau, home of the late artist Gabriele Münter. Within her circle were a number of other great artists, including her partner, Russian-born

Wassily Kandinsky, their friends, Alexej von Jawlensky and Marianne von Werefkin, and their neighbour, Franz Marc.

In the early twentieth century, the house where they gathered was known by the locals as 'The Russian House', but it is now better known as the Münter House. There, Münter and Kandinsky made a garden that not only influenced their art but also opened up a way of living that inspired their friends and colleagues to form the group known as *Der Blaue Reiter* (The Blue Rider).

Münter and Kandinsky met in 1902 when Münter, aged twenty-four, was enrolled at the Phalanx in Munich, an unofficial art school (women were not admitted to the main art academies in Germany) set up by Kandinsky, where he taught painting. A love affair developed and, because Kandinsky was married, the pair fled Munich and spent four years travelling and painting together in Tunisia, the Netherlands, Italy and France. Münter was already a proficient photographer and she documented their travels with her camera and paintings. She also showed an interest in garden landscapes, capturing the Park of Saint-Cloud in Sèvres where the couple had stayed.

DISCOVERING MURNAU

Kandinsky and Münter were close to Marianne von Werefkin and Alexej von Jawlensky, who had trained with Kandinsky and had also travelled widely. In the summer of 1908, the four of them took rooms at the Gasthof Griesbräu in Murnau where they explored and painted the Bavarian landscape. For Münter, it was the start of a love affair with a place that would transcend her personal relationships and endure for the rest of her life.

After settling back in Munich, Münter and Kandinsky returned to Murnau a year after their first visit and bought a newly built house on the outskirts of town. At first, Münter was less keen than Kandinsky, but he persuaded her to buy the house as their holiday home, using money her parents had left her, and it was registered in her name on 21 August 1909.

The house was modelled on a traditional Bavarian mountain hut and it piqued the couple's interest in the folk art of the area. The house had no piped water or heating – water had to be brought in from the well – but it suited the artists and was all part of the idyllic vision they

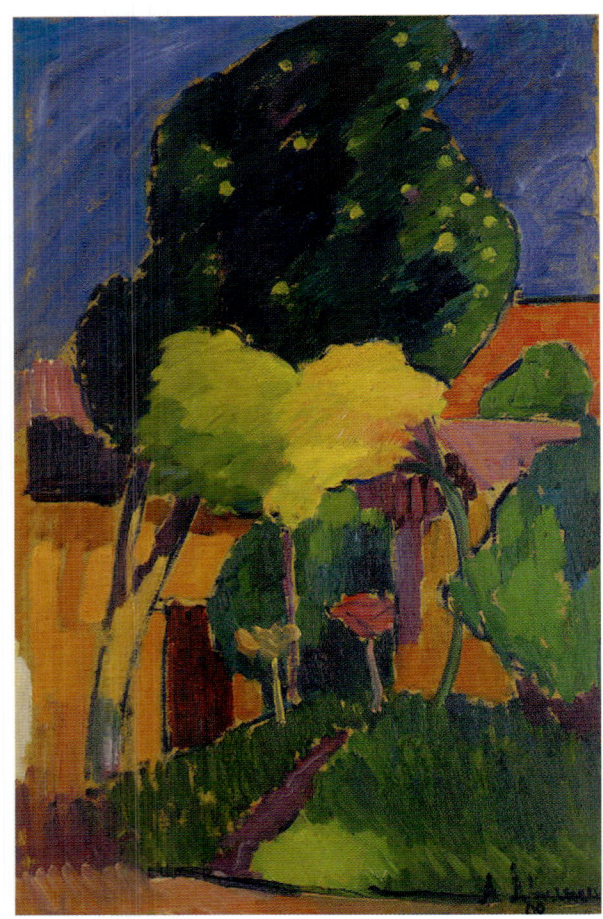

had of living in the countryside. They also liked the view, which swept down the garden and across the railway tracks towards the town, with its castle and steepled church, and then on to the hills beyond.

The interior of the house was literally a blank canvas when the couple moved in. They began by painting the kitchen deep blue, ordered floral linen curtains from Munich, and then proceeded to hand-decorate every surface of the house, including most of the furniture. Kandinsky was inspired by the tales of heroism of Saint George, the patron saint of both Murnau and Moscow, and the house was soon filled with their collections of medieval-style paintings, Russian folk art, primitive paintings from other parts of Europe, stained glass, textiles and wood carvings. In particular, they made a study of reverse-glass paintings, a tradition associated

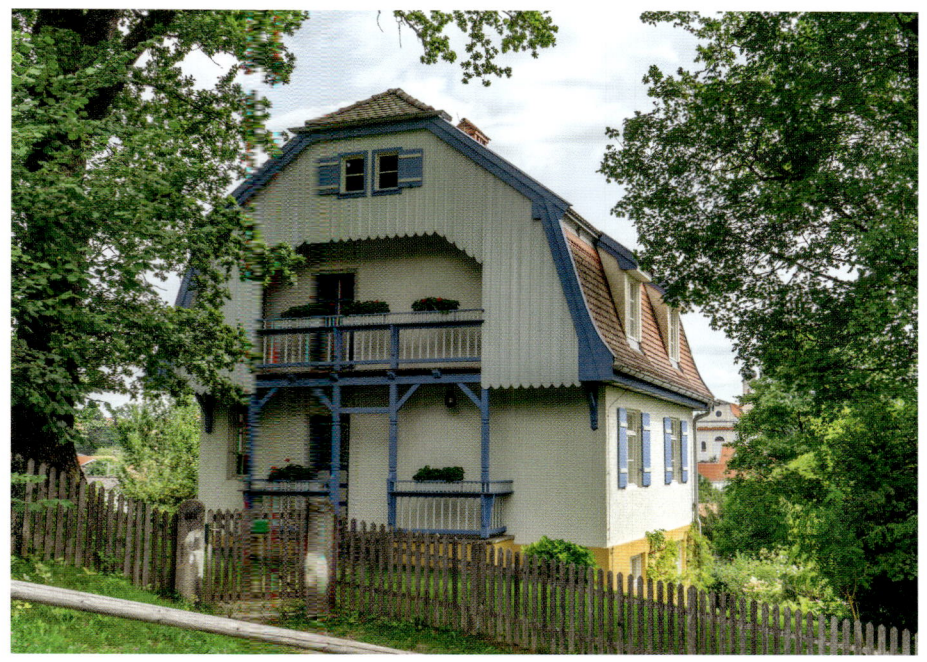

OPPOSITE *Murnau* by Alexej von Jawlensky (1908), who, together with his partner Marianne von Werefkin, were close friends of Kandinsky and Münter.
LEFT Münter and Kandinsky loved the fact that their house was modelled on a traditional Bavarian mountain hut.
BELOW, LEFT The artists gathered in the dining room in the Münter House.
BELOW RIGHT The couple decorated the surfaces of all the furniture and fittings, including the staircase, painted by Kandinsky, circa 1910.

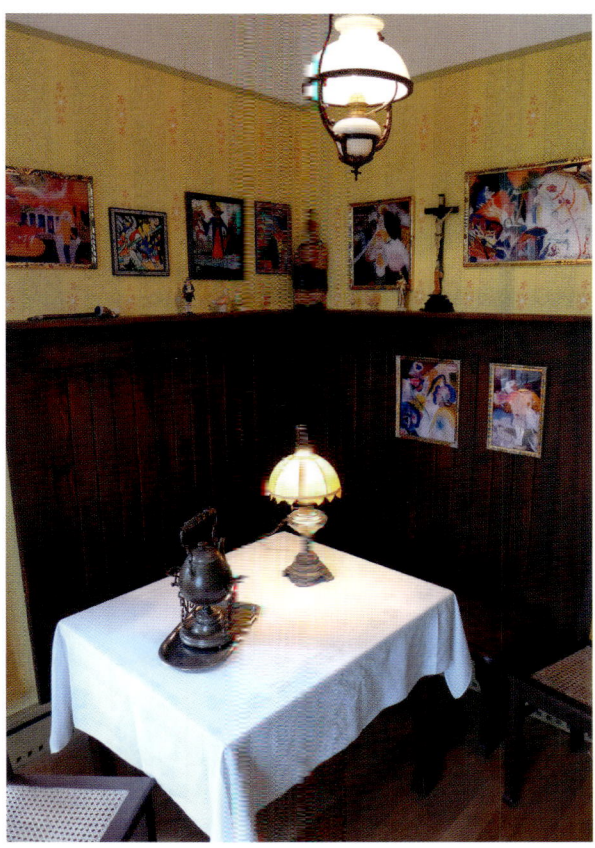

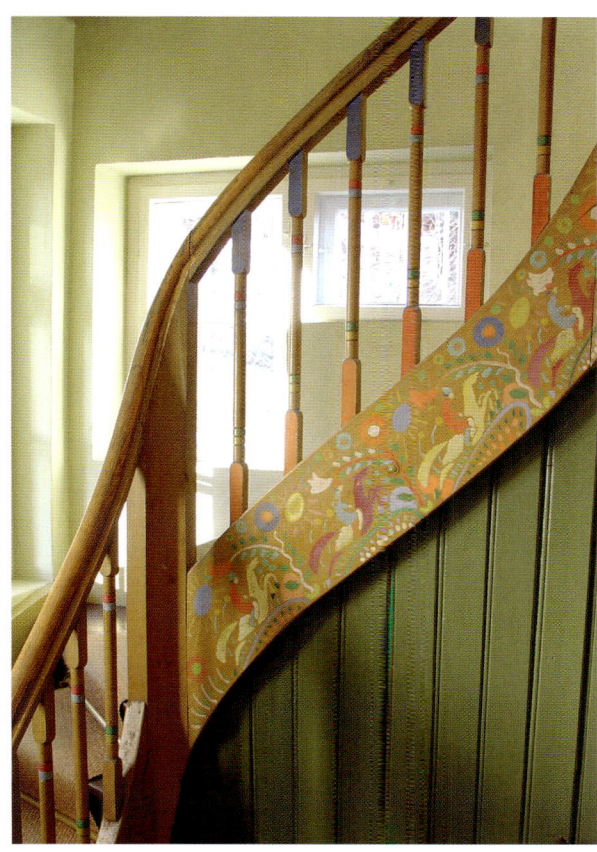

The Artists in Residence

Gabriele Münter 1909–1914, 1931–1962
Wassily Kandinsky 1909–1914
Dr Johannes Eichner 1935–1958

The artists Gabriele Münter and Wassily Kandinsky met in Munich in 1902. They became lovers and fled the city (where Kandinsky's wife lived) to travel and paint. In 1908, they visited the town of Murnau in Bavaria and Münter bought a house on the edge of town that became a meeting place for artists, writers and musicians, as well as a work of art in its own right. After Kandinsky's departure to Russia in 1914, following the outbreak of war, the house was closed up. Münter returned periodically throughout the 1920s and in 1931, she came back permanently, followed in 1935 by her new partner, the art historian, Dr Johannes Eichner.

The years 1909 to 1914 witnessed Kandinsky's move from Post-Impressionism to Abstraction and, in Münter's case, towards Expressionism. It also saw the birth of *Der Blaue Reiter*, the influential Blue Rider group, which would be key (along with *Die Brücke*, see page 98) in consolidating the German Expressionist style. For Gabriele Münter, the last thirty years of her life at Murnau would be the most productive of her career.

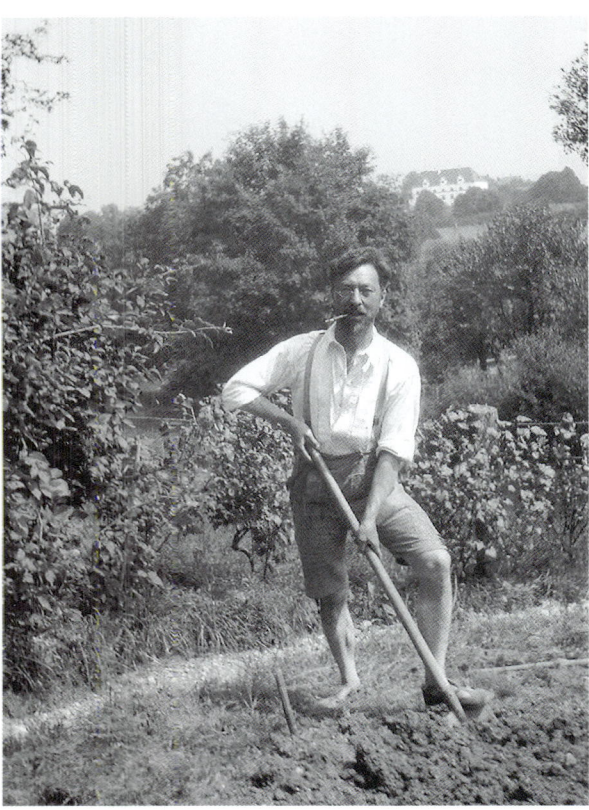

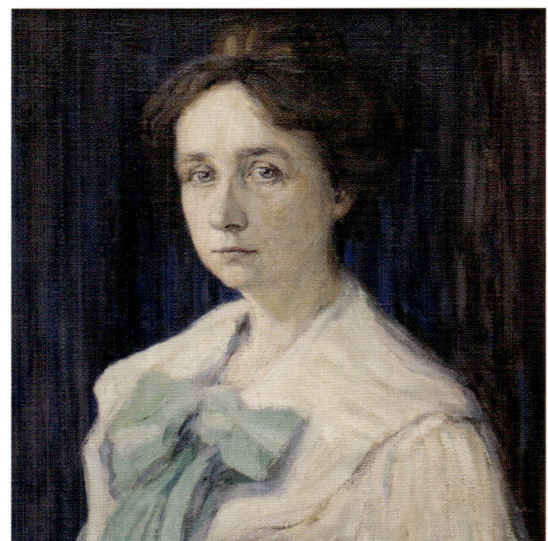

Gabriele Munter by Kandinsky (1905).

with this part of Germany, and between 1909 and 1914 Kandinsky produced thirty-three examples of paintings on glass. The couple's art collection was driven by a desire to associate themselves with 'authentic art' and the Münter House soon became a meeting place for ideas and thoughts that would later develop into *Der Blaue Reiter* (The Blue Rider).

THE GARDEN AT MURNAU

Münter and Kandinsky became enthusiastic gardeners while living at Murnau. They talked constantly and drew sketches of how the garden would look, and later kept logbooks of what they sowed and planted as it developed.

ABOVE Wassily Kandinsky digging in the garden the couple created, photographed by Gabriele Münter in 1910 or 1911.
OPPOSITE The circular garden bed in front of the house, where Münter and Kandinsky grew a mixture of vegetables and flowers for cutting, has today been reinstated in the renovated garden at Murnau.

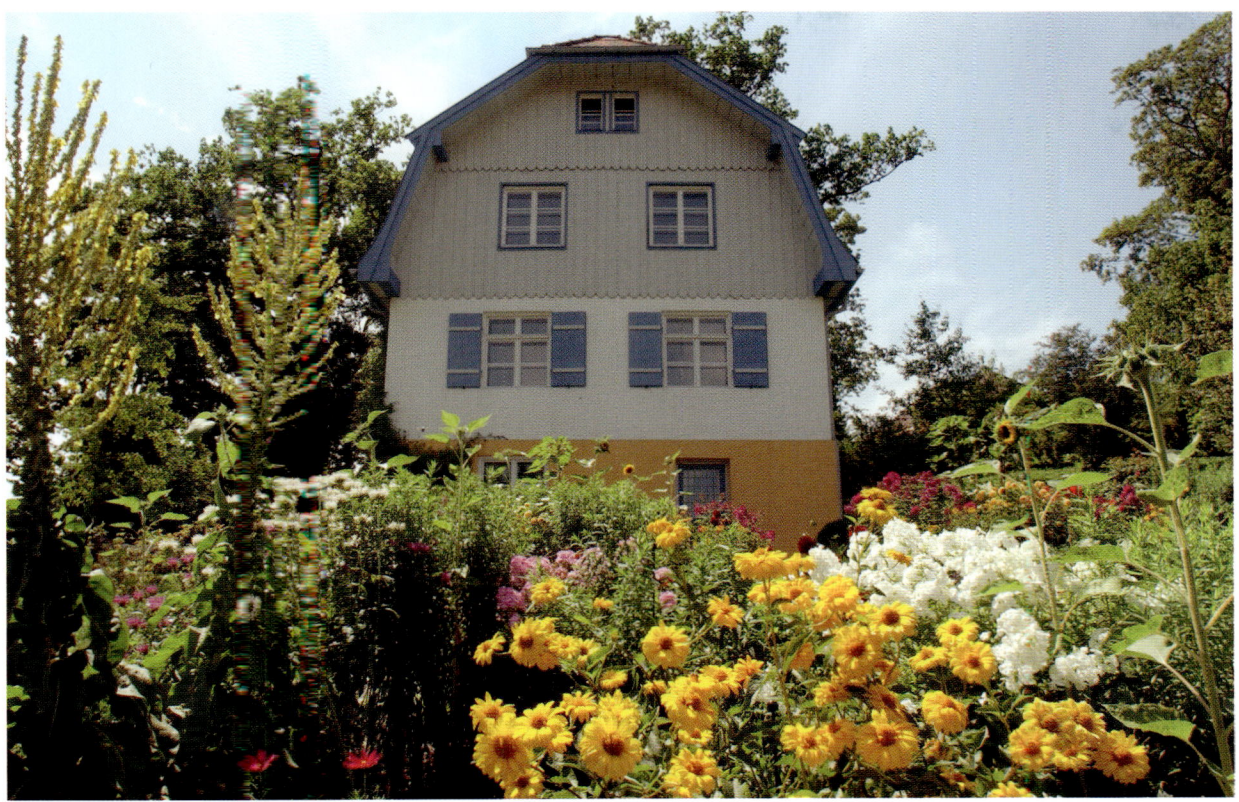

When they moved into the house in the summer of 1909, Münter's pen-and-ink drawing of 22 July shows the layout as it existed at that time, with a picket fence all the way around the property and a steep path cutting the front garden into two, from the door to a lower gate. The two large beds on either side of the path seem to have been planted with cabbages, and Münter has also drawn in the neighbour's orchard, which provided a backdrop of trees, as well as a small garden cabin.

Kandinsky initially designed a new, round bed that would take up the largest part of the garden and in 1910 they filled the centre with sunflowers, but the serious gardening did not begin until the following year. Kandinsky made several experimental sketches, one with six concentric circular beds, but he finally seems to have simplified the design, while still detailing exactly what would be grown where. Two paths intersected the central circular bed of flowers, dividing it into equal quarters, and within the four large planting areas, Kandinsky dug smaller oval beds.

This is the design that appears on the most detailed plan, drawn in 1911, that the couple finally adopted and in the photograph Münter took of the garden at that time.

Both artists loved to wear traditional Bavarian working clothes when they were toiling in the garden in Murnau. It was hard work and Kandinsky, in particular, complained that when they were there, the garden always came first, whereas in Munich there was more opportunity to pursue their art. Unused to the manual labour, in 1912, Kandinsky underwent an operation for a hernia.

The years 1911 and 1912 were the 'garden years'. Their cottage garden provided them with fresh fruit and vegetables, including raspberries and strawberries, kohl rabi, onions, peas, radish, lettuce, spinach and beans, as well as flowers, such as sunflowers, delphiniums, dahlias and roses. The detail with which Münter and Kandinsky worked out what they would grow was staggering and their logs show the exact dates that everything was sown and when their produce was harvested. The beds were

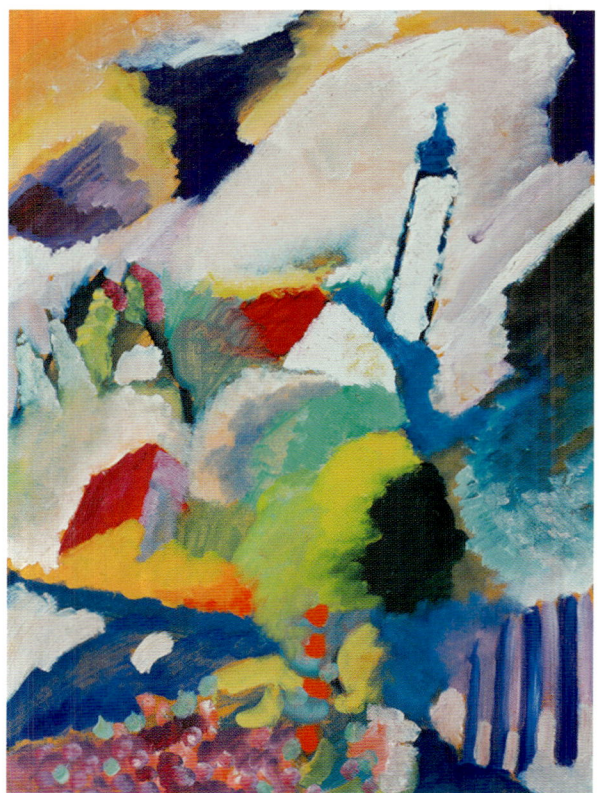

"Art today is moving in directions of which our forebears had no inkling; the Horsemen of the Apocalypse are heard galloping through the air; artistic excitement can be felt all over Europe."
FRANZ MARC (1912)

group of friends became more expressive, using explosive colour and less form, and breaking the rules by painting houses purple and trees blue, as seen in Kandinsky's *Murnau with a Church* (1910).

In 1909, Münter painted the house interior, the local landscape, and studies executed on their days in the mountains with von Jawlensky and von Werefkin. At this point, neither she nor Kandinsky used the garden very often as a *motif*, although in the summer of 1910, he painted *Garden in Murnau*, where the sunflowers and the garden bower can just be seen. This work came before Kandinsky's series, *Improvisations – Impressions – Compositions,* which would mark his move towards total Abstraction.

THE BLUE RIDER PERIOD

Visitors were welcome in Murnau and, if they stayed long enough, they were encouraged to help in the garden. As well as von Jawlensky and von Werefkin, they included Münter's artist friends, Hedwig Fröhner, Erma Bossi and Emmy Dresler. Bossi and Dresler were both members of the newly formed *Neue Künstlervereinigung München* or NKVM (New Artists' Association Munich), an organization that Kandinsky had founded with other artists, but later left. Kandinsky and Münter also became close to the artist Franz Marc and his partner Maria Franck (whom he later married), who lived at nearby Sindelsdorf.

Kandinsky and Marc had met at the beginning of 1911 and formed an immediate intellectual rapport. They would cycle or walk over to see each other whenever possible. In June of that year, Kandinsky came up with the idea of *Der Blaue Reiter* – an almanac of writings and art that would be edited jointly by the two men. The Blue Rider encapsulated all of Kandinsky's thinking of the time: blue being the colour of spirituality, combined with the Romantic idea of the free horseman, the rider who forges new paths. The meetings

numbered, with specific crops allocated to each one, and when following the progress of his vegetables, Kandinsky noted how much he had harvested, not just by weight but sometimes by counting individual peas. While Münter was travelling, he wrote to her touchingly, saying, 'I am so dreadfully sorry you're not here to enjoy the beautiful weather … and toil in our little garden, where everything is now flowering and bearing fruit.' Like the house, the garden became an expression of their love of colour and search for authenticity in the way they lived.

CHANGING DIRECTION

Before they came to Murnau in 1908, both Münter and Kandinsky were painting in what could loosely be called a late-impressionistic style, making small *en plein air* studies. Meanwhile, Alexej von Jawlensky had spent a long period in France, and brought back to the group in Murnau an interest in brightly coloured, two-dimensional painting, inspired by the work of Gauguin. Together, the

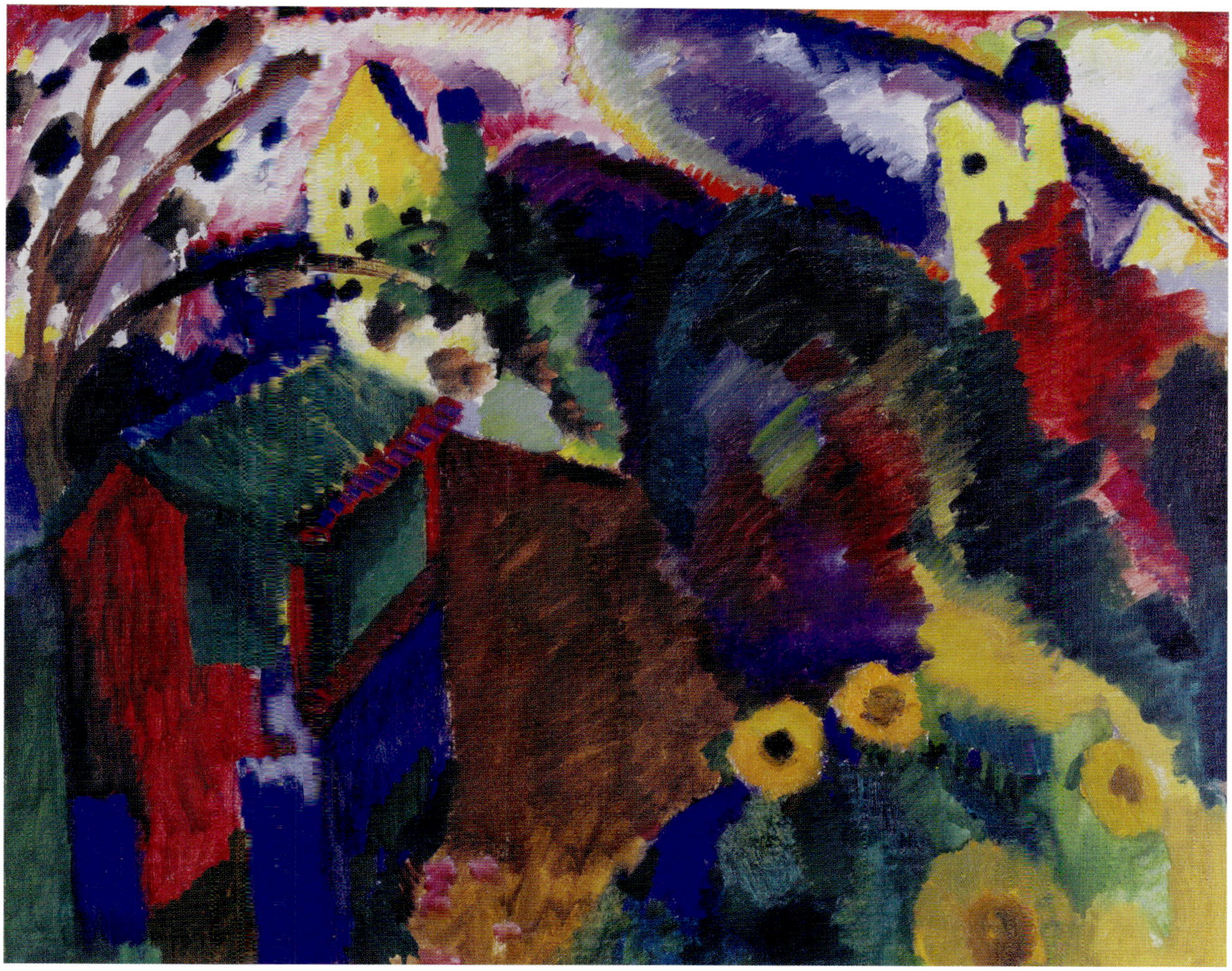

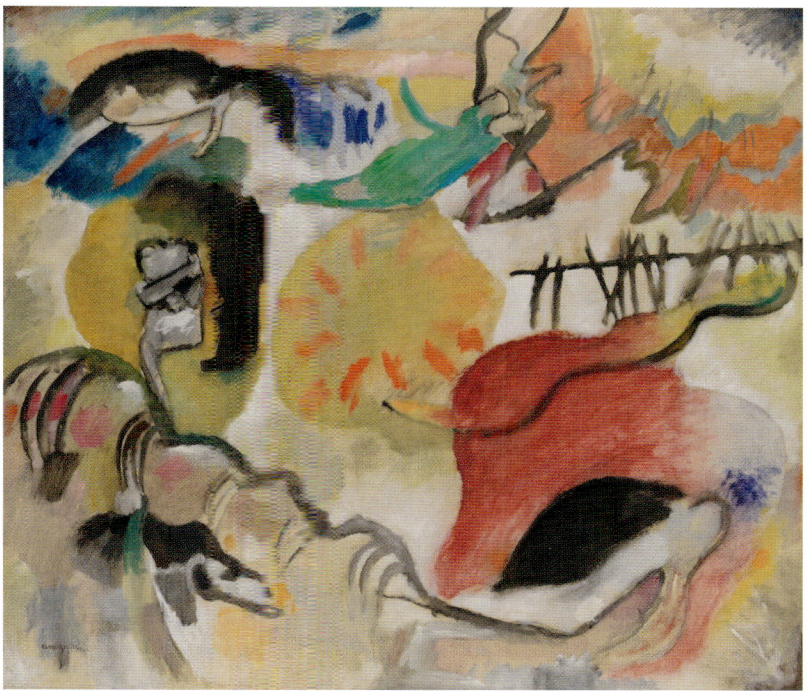

OPPOSITE *Murnau with a Church* (1910) by Kandinsky expresses his experimental use of colour and form.

ABOVE The blurred edges of *Garden in Murnau* (1910) marks Kandinsky's drift away from Realism towards Abstraction.

LEFT By 1912, Kandinsky's style had evolved into Abstraction, as seen in *Improvisation 27,* bringing him worldwide recognition.

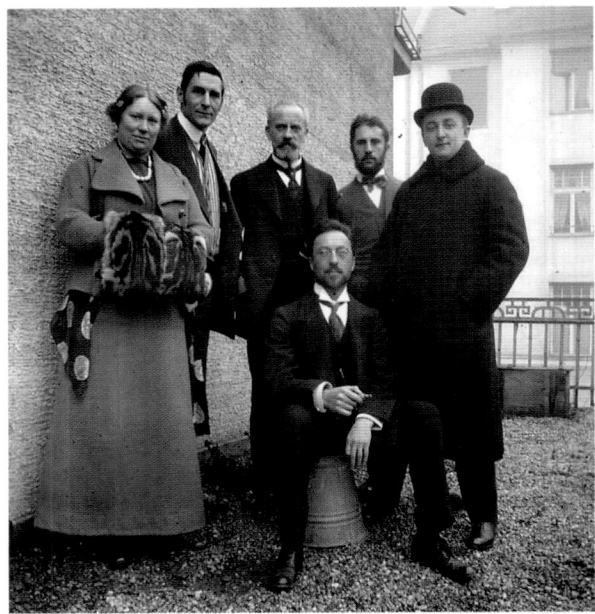

were held in October at the Münter House and were also attended by August Macke and his wife Elisabeth.

When a painting by Kandinsky was rejected by the jury of the NKVW, the newly formed group hastily organized the 'First Exhibition of the Blue Rider Editorial Board'. Held at the Thannhauser Gallery in Munich, it ran from the end of December 1911 to early 1912, and included work by Kandinsky, Münter, Macke, Marc, and the American Albert Bloch. The group held a second exhibition from February to April 1912, which included work by Paul Klee, a neighbour of Kandinsky's in Munich, and the influential *Blue Rider Almanac* was published a month later in May.

During this time Kandinsky and Münter met the composer Arnold Schoenberg and he and his wife often visited Murnau, eventually finding a holiday home there in 1914. Music had always been important to Kandinsky and he saw the potential of artistic and musical collaboration, inviting Schoenberg to submit paintings to the Almanac. Kandinsky believed passionately that the composer thought like an artist, and that the structure of musical pieces had much in common with the making of art.

Whenever friends, or increasingly art dealers, came to visit Münter and Kandinsky, they were put up in nearby lodgings and given the grand tour of Murnau and its surroundings. But this idyllic period would come to an abrupt end on 1 August 1914. With the coming of war, the couple closed the house and rushed back to Munich. Russian-born Kandinsky was now a citizen of an enemy power and he and Münter left for Switzerland two days later on 3 August 1914.

AFTER KANDINSKY

In November 1914, Kandinsky decided to return to Russia, entrusting all his belongings and paintings to Gabriele Münter. She returned to Munich in 1915 to close up their apartment and put his art works into storage in the city, where they would be safe. She then departed for neutral territory, travelling first to Sweden and then Denmark, to await his return. They met again briefly in 1915 when he visited the exhibition she had set up in Stockholm, before Kandinsky departed for good. In 1917, he broke off all contact with Münter and married a Russian, Nina Andreevskaya, never to see the house in Murnau again, or the work he had entrusted to his former partner. In 1918 and 1919, Münter held large solo exhibitions of her own work in Copenhagen, comprising one hundred paintings, as well as drawings, etchings and reverse-glass paintings.

By the 1920s, no longer feeling part of an artistic community, Münter returned to Germany, living in a series of rooms in Cologne, Berlin and Paris. In 1931, she decided to go back to Murnau and make it her permanent home. She had met art historian and philosopher Dr Johannes Eichner in Berlin a few years earlier and he then joined her in Murnau, where they became lifelong partners.

The painting Münter produced on her return to Murnau, *The Russian House* (1931), shows the garden mostly laid to lawn but still full of shrubs, with the blue painted summerhouse in its original position. Poignantly, she painted herself sitting at the window wearing red, looking out over the garden, while another, *Mein Garten* (1931), shows Eichner at work in the rectangular beds, wearing blue. Münter's output increased during this period and she no longer had to search for subjects to paint – everything she needed was right there in Murnau.

Münter and Eichner began to work on the garden again to provide themselves with fresh produce, but they never reinstated the circular beds of Kandinsky's

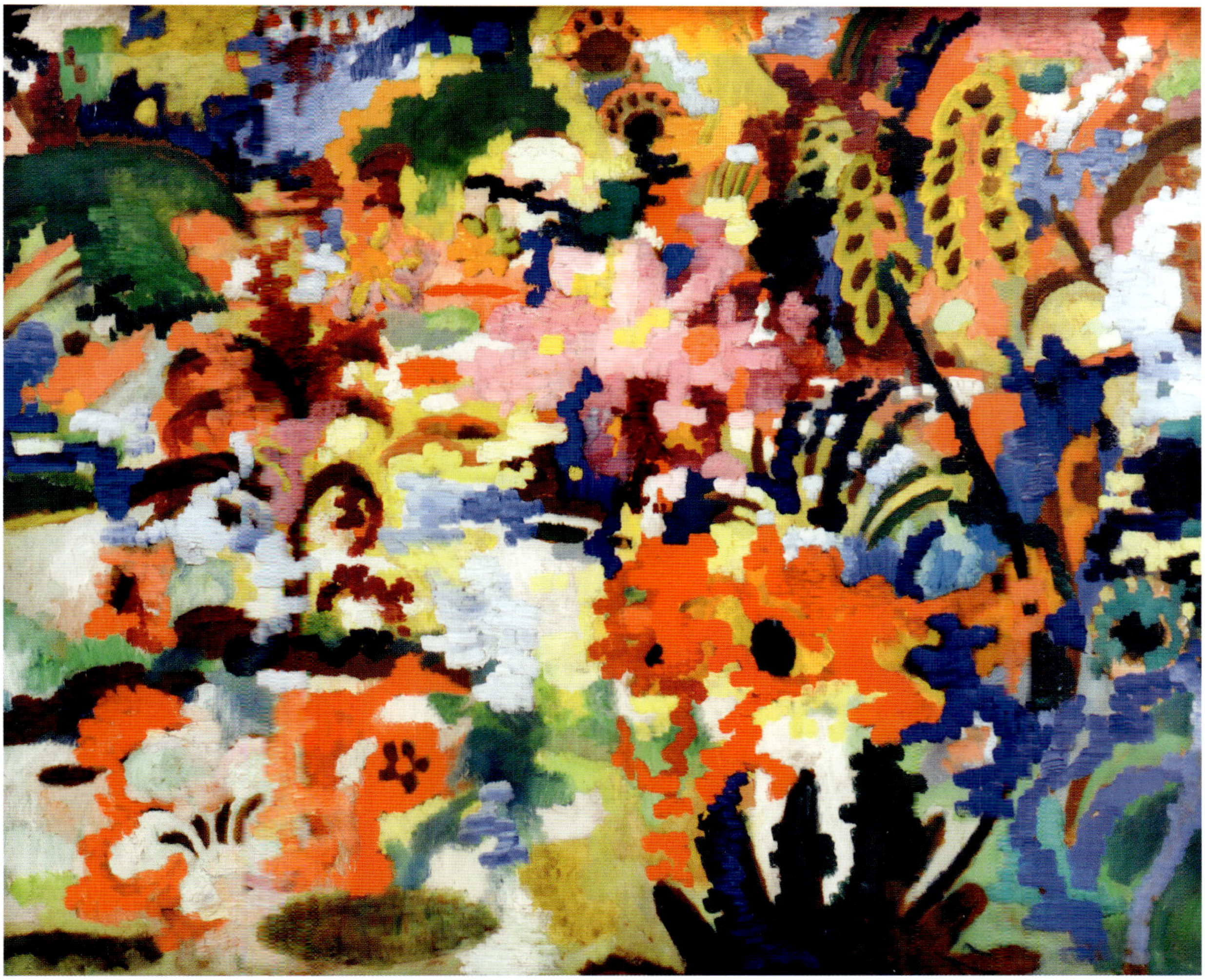

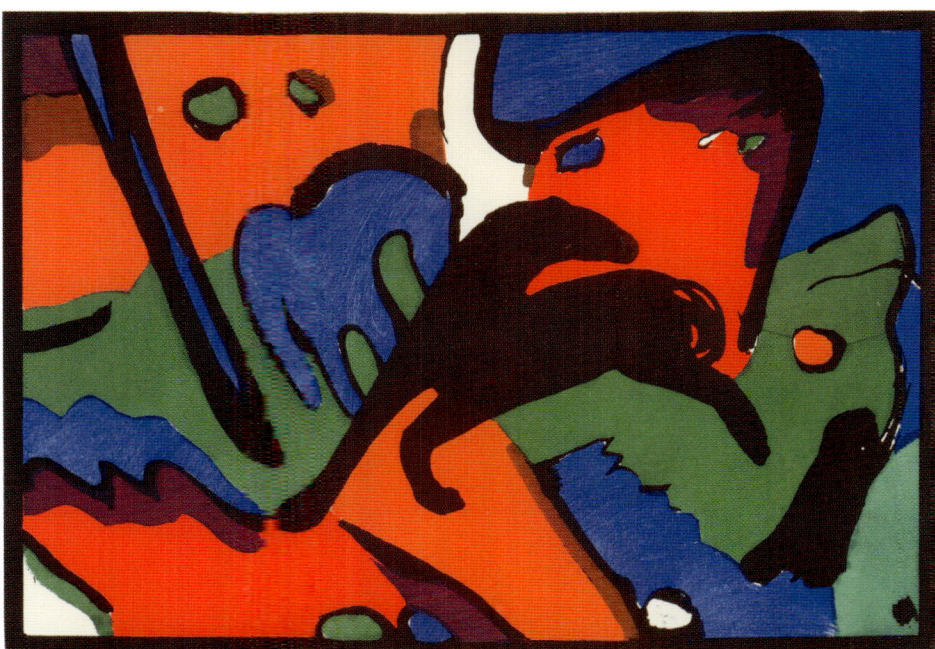

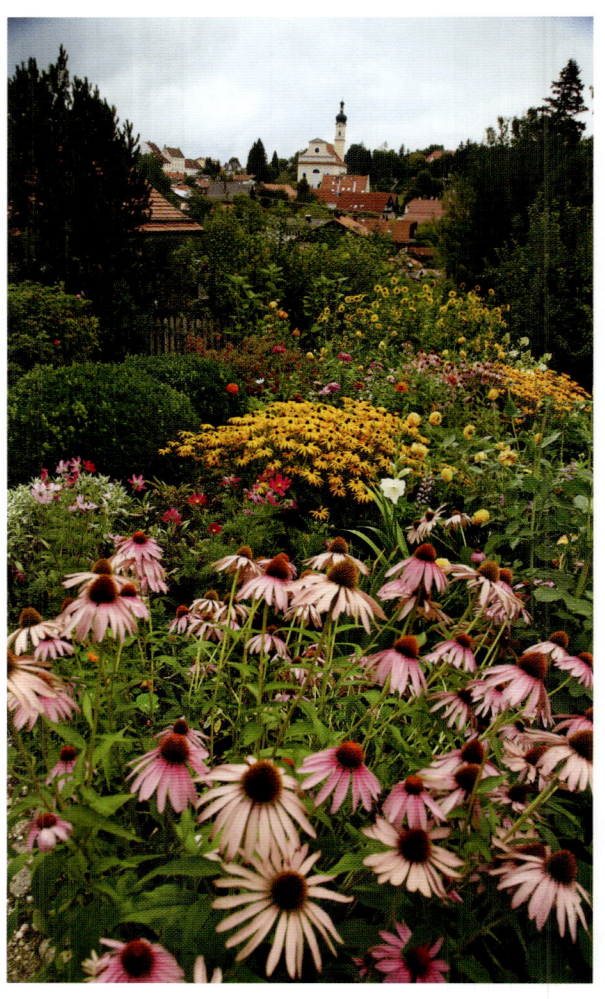

time. That would be left to a new generation. The couple always intended the house and garden to be preserved as a monument to the early period of Kandinsky's life and set up the Gabriele Münter and Johannes Eichner Foundation to look after it when they were gone. Münter also left her entire collection to the Foundation. In 1957, she made a gift of the paintings Kandinsky had left with her to the Lenbachhaus in Munich and, while Münter's art had not achieved the international recognition of Kandinsky's when she died aged eighty-five in 1962, she ensured that their artistic life together – its paintings, artefacts, house and garden – would not be forgotten.

Although Münter's work was exhibited widely in Scandinavia and Germany during her lifetime, it was not until 1992 that the first comprehensive retrospective of her art took place at the Lenbachhaus, followed in 2018 by a major exhibition of 130 paintings in Munich, Copenhagen and Cologne. Long overshadowed by Kandinsky's fame, these exhibitions reinstated Gabriele Münter to her rightful place among her Blue Rider colleagues, recognizing her skill and multi-faceted approach to her art.

LEFT The view today through the Münter House flower garden towards the church of Murnau in the town.
RIGHT Münter lived on at Murnau until her death in 1962, painting the plants and garden, including *Flowers on a Black Ground* (1953).

THE GERMAN EXPRESSIONISTS' TIMELINE

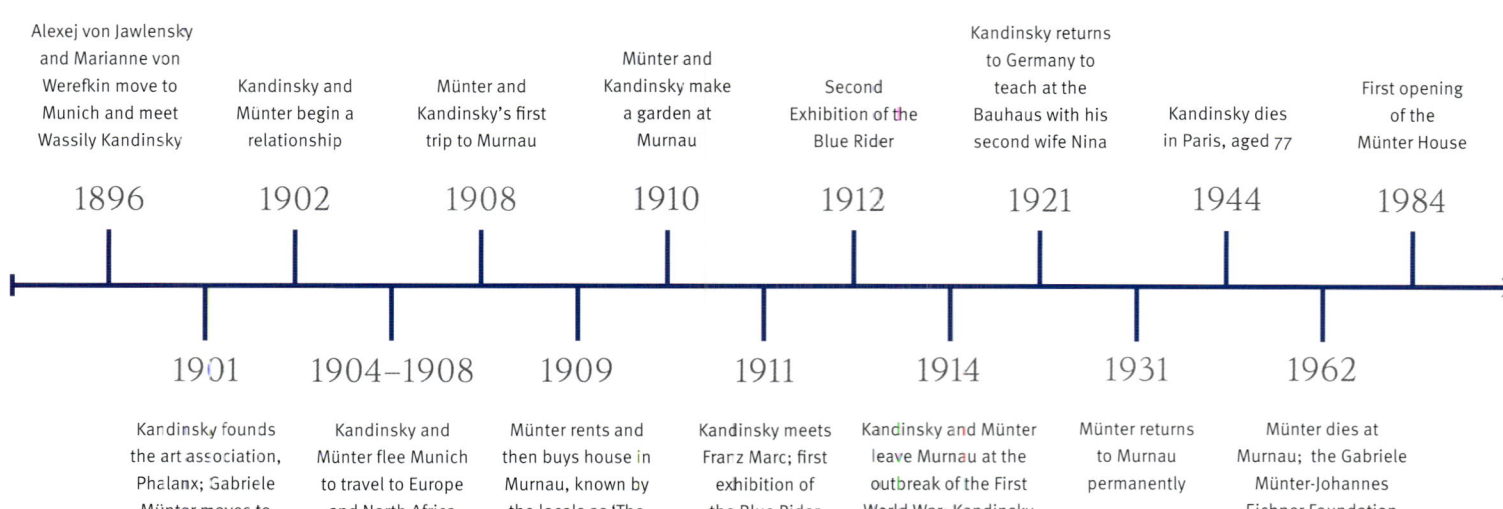

Alexej von Jawlensky and Marianne von Werefkin move to Munich and meet Wassily Kandinsky — **1896**

Kandinsky and Münter begin a relationship — **1902**

Münter and Kandinsky's first trip to Murnau — **1908**

Münter and Kandinsky make a garden at Murnau — **1910**

Second Exhibition of the Blue Rider — **1912**

Kandinsky returns to Germany to teach at the Bauhaus with his second wife Nina — **1921**

Kandinsky dies in Paris, aged 77 — **1944**

First opening of the Münter House — **1984**

1901 Kandinsky founds the art association, Phalanx; Gabriele Münter moves to Munich to study art

1904–1908 Kandinsky and Münter flee Munich to travel to Europe and North Africa

1909 Münter rents and then buys house in Murnau, known by the locals as 'The Russian House'

1911 Kandinsky meets Franz Marc; first exhibition of the Blue Rider in Munich

1914 Kandinsky and Münter leave Murnau at the outbreak of the First World War; Kandinsky returns to Russia

1931 Münter returns to Murnau permanently

1962 Münter dies at Murnau; the Gabriele Münter-Johannes Eichner Foundation established

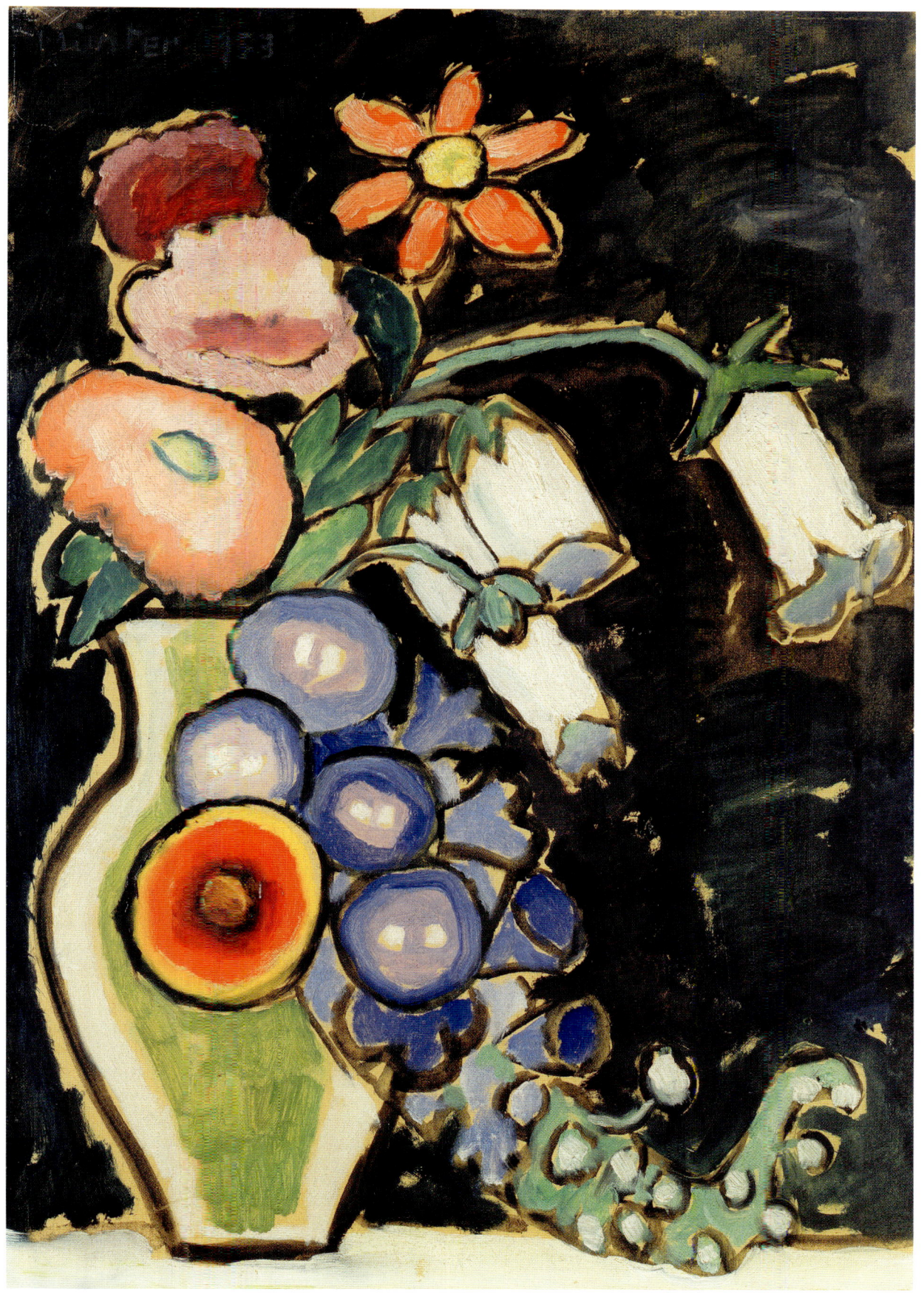

The Charleston artists

Vanessa Bell, Duncan Grant, Roger Fry and the Bloomsbury Group

Charleston, Sussex, England

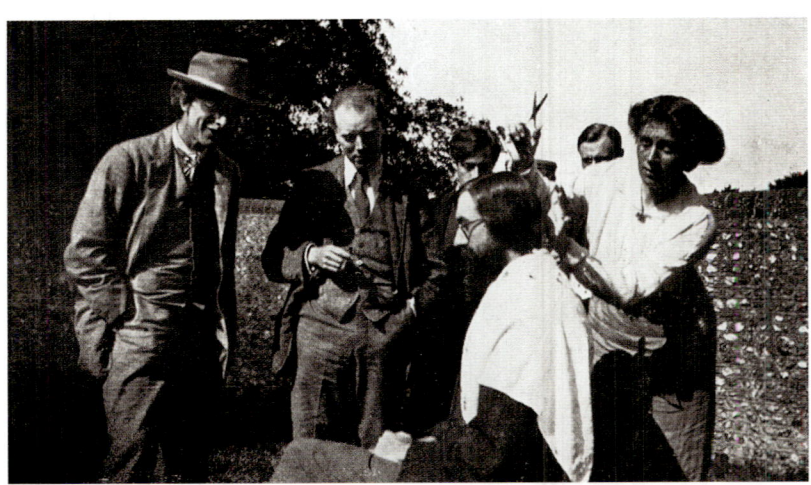

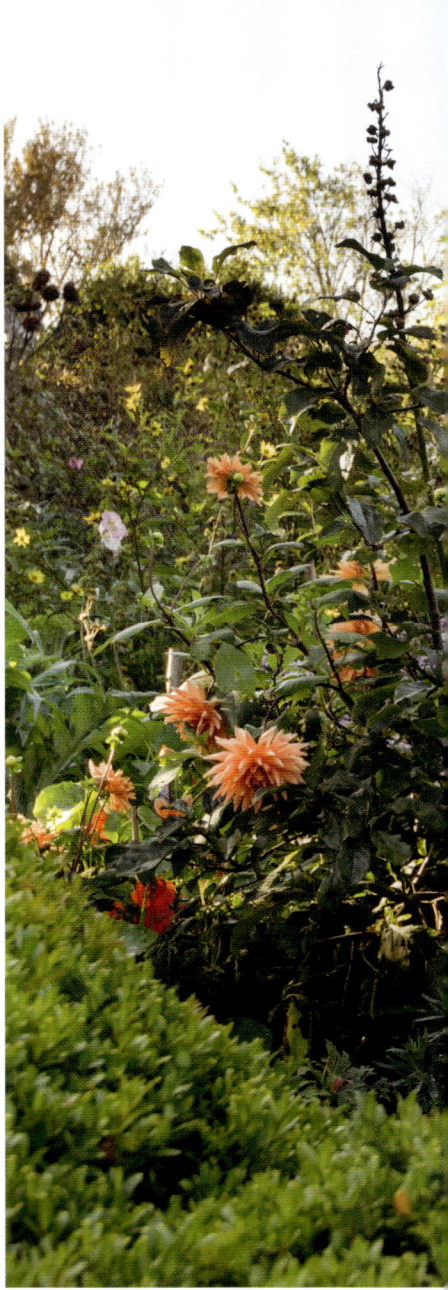

THE OUTBREAK OF THE FIRST WORLD WAR changed everything for the Bloomsbury Group of pacifist writers, artists and academics. Many left their city homes for the countryside when bombing began in London during the summer of 1915 and even more fled when conscription was introduced in January 1916, which could only be avoided by young men if they undertook work of 'national importance', such as farming.

Leonard Woolf and his wife Virginia, the novelist, were central figures in the group and already had a house called Asheham on the South Downs. Leonard discovered Charleston, an old farmhouse to rent deep in the Sussex countryside, and in May 1916 Virginia wrote to her sister, the artist Vanessa Bell, advising her to take it. Vanessa had separated from her husband, Clive Bell, and was living in Suffolk with her lover, the artist Duncan Grant. Virginia loved the idea of her sister being close and sang the praises of the house and particularly of the garden – with its pond, fruit trees and vegetable plot – which, according to the author, had run wild.

ABOVE This photograph, taken circa 1920, shows Vanessa Bell cutting Lytton Strachey's hair, watched (from left to right) by Roger Fry, Clive Bell and Duncan Grant.
RIGHT Dahlias in the walled garden at Charleston House, the country home of a diverse group of artists and writers who lived here from 1916 until the 1970s.

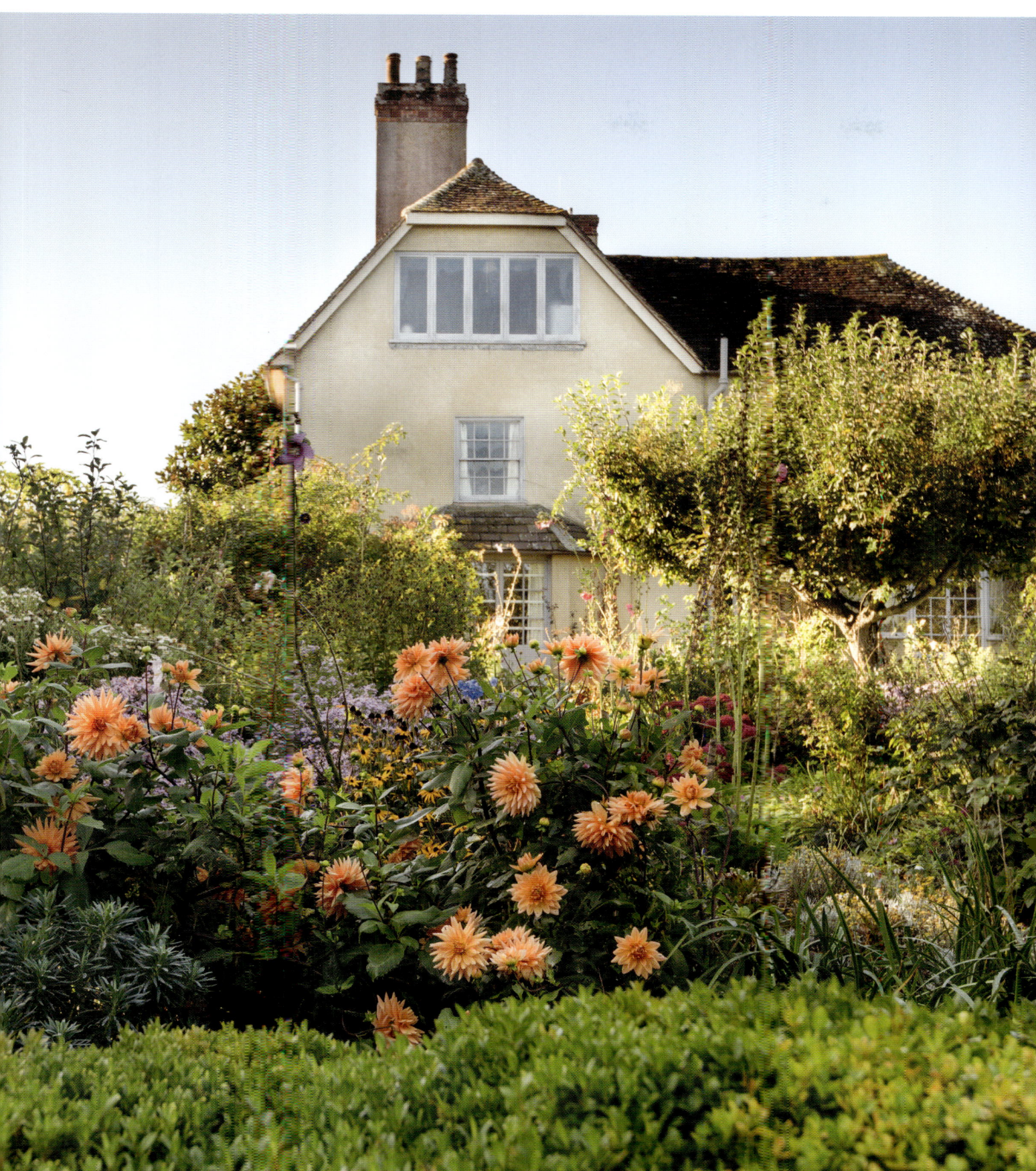

The Artists in Residence

Vanessa Bell (1916–1961)

Duncan Grant (1916–78)

Quentin Bell (1916–52)

Angelica Garnett (1918–42)

Charleston was a community of artists linked by family ties, friendship, and a shared passion for art. Although the Bloomsbury group used it as a country retreat, Charleston attracted its own set, including the art critic and designer Roger Fry, novelist David 'Bunny' Garnett (who wrote *Aspects of Love*, made into a musical by Andrew Lloyd Webber), and the economist John Maynard Keynes. Artists Vanessa Bell and Duncan Grant came to Charleston during the First World War to escape London and so that Duncan and his lover David Garnett could work on local farms to avoid conscription. The interiors of Charleston became the artists' lasting legacy, and the garden, designed by Roger Fry, was an important *motif* in their paintings, as well as being a place of invention for Vanessa's son Quentin Bell, who became a sculptor, and daughter Angelica, also a painter.

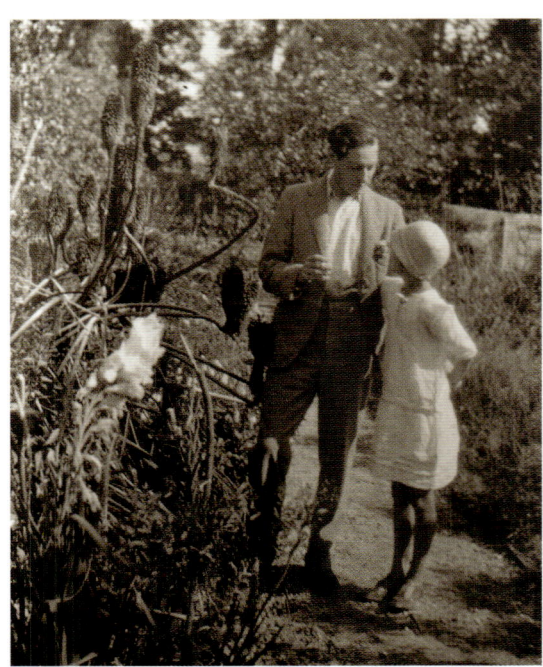

Duncan Grant and his daughter Angelica in the walled garden, 1927.

AN UNCONVENTIONAL FAMILY

In October 1916, Bell, Grant, and Bell's two children, Julian, aged eight, and six-year-old Quentin, moved into the seventeenth-century farmhouse. Grant was accompanied by his long-term boyfriend, the writer David Garnett, known as 'Bunny'. The attraction of Charleston was that it was in farming country, so Grant and Bunny, both conscientious objectors, were able to take up full-time work with a local farmer, while Bell tried to turn the cold, damp farmhouse into a home.

Bell began to paint the interior of the house, putting her own stamp on the décor. This would slowly lead to Charleston becoming a work of art in its own right, as the artists worked on the distinctive decoration that adorns every room. The process of painting walls and furniture, choosing objects and designing the rooms would continue throughout their time at Charleston.

The front of the house had been 'Victorianized', with a sweep of lawn, ivy on the walls and clipped evergreen shrubs edging the pond. Dug originally for the farm cattle to drink from, the pond was a significant feature of the house and garden; the water and large, overhanging willow tree became a playground for the children and an important *motif* in the artists' paintings.

Adjoining the house was a walled kitchen garden that produced fruit and vegetables for the household. An orchard beyond the walls became a classroom where the boys were given lessons by a series of governesses who attempted to keep them in check, as depicted in Duncan Grant's painting, *Lessons in the Orchard* (1917). In 1918, Vanessa Bell gave birth to a daughter, Angelica, by Grant, and the unconventional family was complete.

THE PAINTERS' PLACE

When the war finally ended, Bell and the family moved back to Bloomsbury in London and Charleston became their summer home. In 1925, she renegotiated a longer lease from the owner, Lord Gage, securing the farmhouse for the Bloomsbury Group for the next fifty years. After initially working in an old army hut beyond the walled garden, the longer tenure enabled Bell and Grant to build a studio on to the south-western corner of the house. Designed by their friend and London neighbour, artist

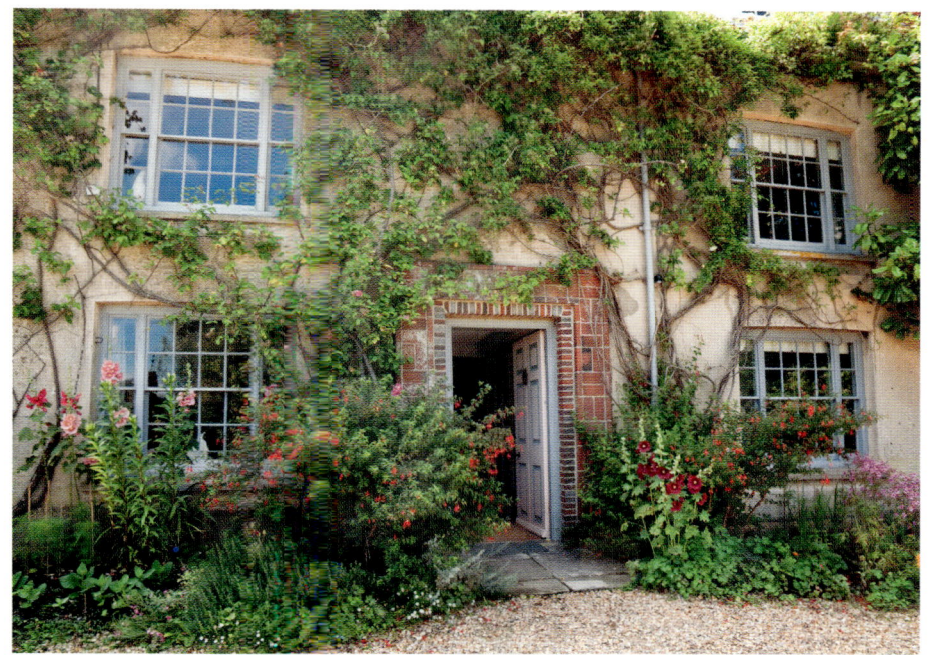

LEFT It was Virginia Woolf's husband Leonard who first saw Charleston and suggested that her sister Vanessa Bell should come to live close to them.

BELOW *The Pond at Charleston* (circa 1919). Vanessa Bell particularly loved the old cattle pond in front of the farmhouse and painted it several times.

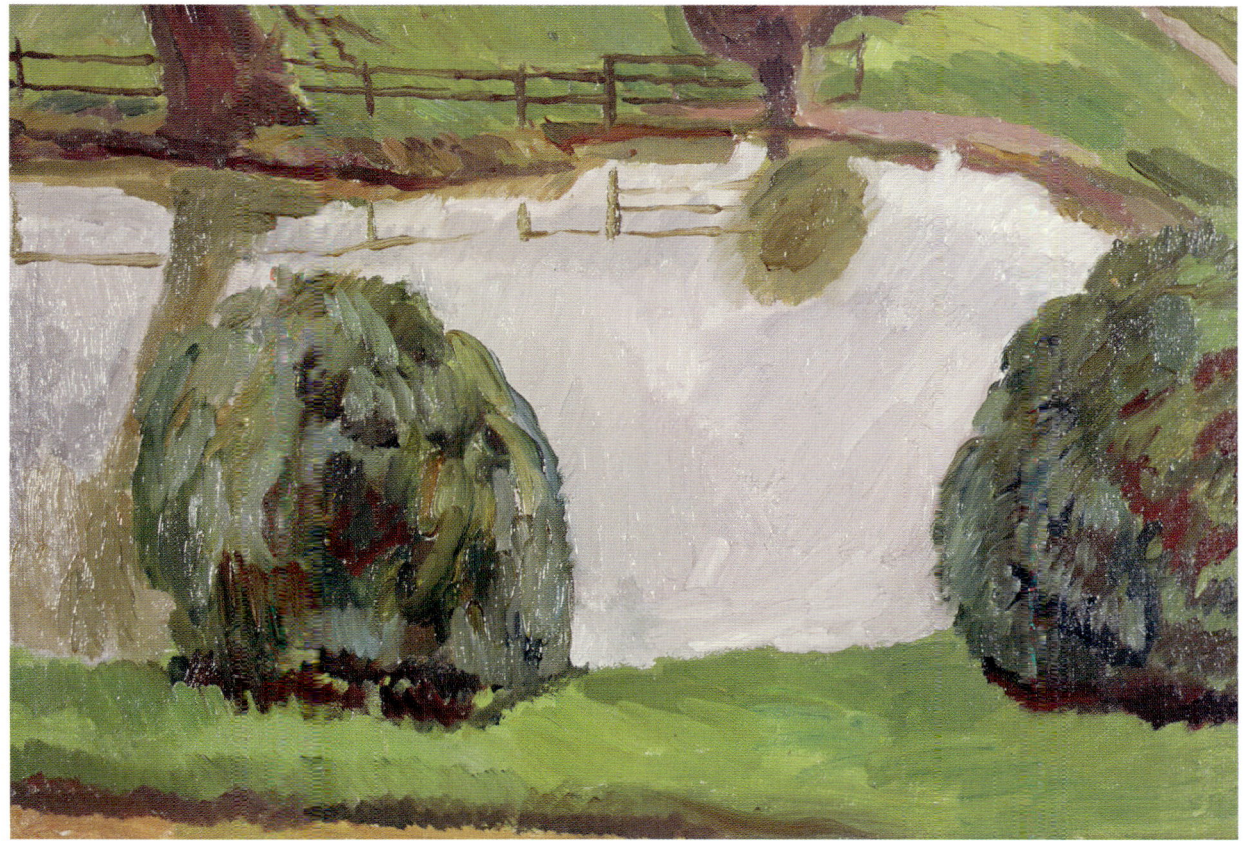

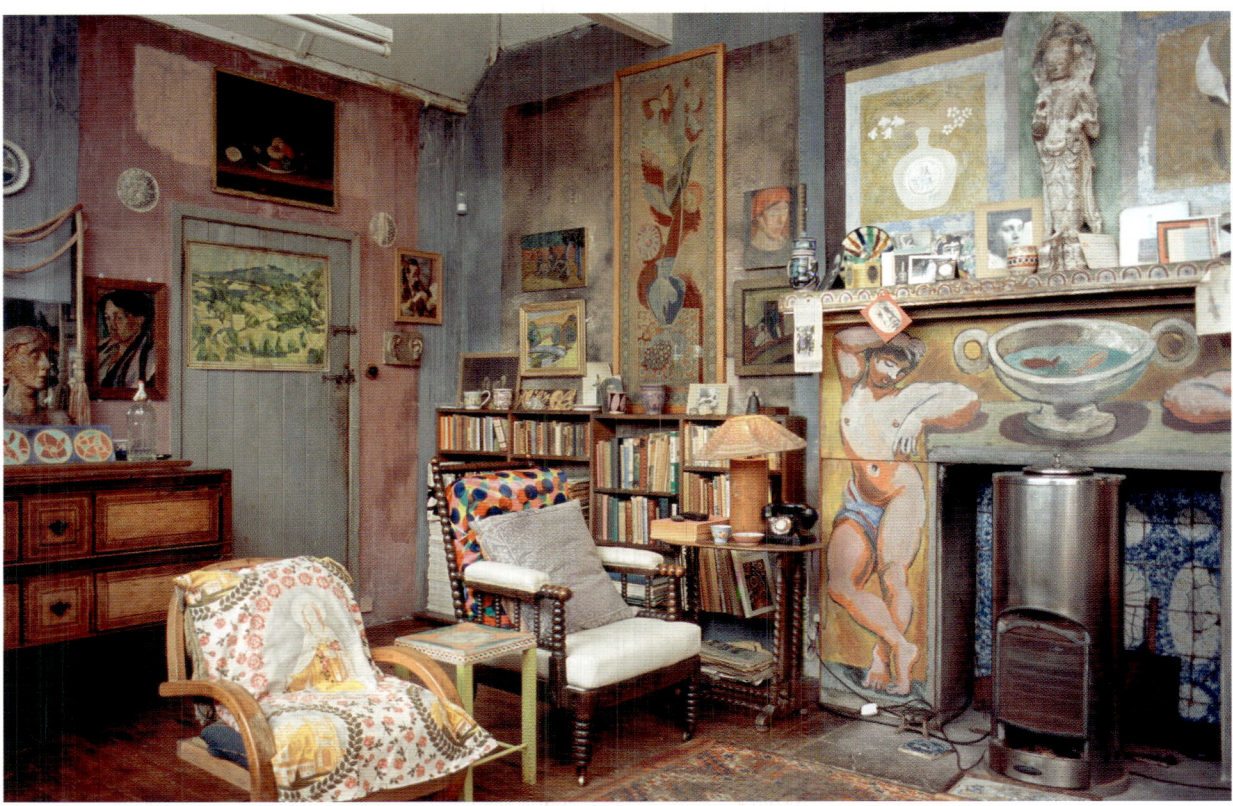

"Sitting at my open bedroom window … I look out onto the lawn which has been extended up to the terrace – Quentin's idea for making our garden a second Versailles."

VANESSA BELL (1940)

ABOVE The studio, with its efficient stove, was built in 1925 and became Duncan Grant's sitting room, as it was the warmest room in the house. He also decorated the plywood panels around the fireplace.
OPPOSITE *The Doorway* (1929) by Duncan Grant, who painted this view looking out from the studio on to the walled garden.

Roger Fry, the studio was flooded with north light and had a stove to keep them warm, offering the artists a serious and comfortable space to work.

Visitors to Charleston in these inter-war years included Virginia and Leonard Woolf, who often walked or cycled the nine miles from Monk's House in Rodmell, where the couple had moved to in 1919. The economist, John Maynard Keynes, and his wife, Lydia Lopokova, a Russian ballerina; artist Dora Carrington; and writers E.M. Forster, Lytton Strachey, Katherine Mansfield and T.S. Eliot were also welcome. However, visitors were expected to amuse themselves during the day, while the artists worked. Both Grant and Bell were busy with commercial commissions for murals, fabric designs, and ceramics for the Clarice Cliff factory, while also developing their own painting styles.

DESIGN COLLABORATIONS

One artist in particular was a very important figure in the making of Charleston and its garden. In 1910, Roger Fry had masterminded the exhibition 'Manet and the Post-Impressionists' in London, which scandalized the viewing public and had a profound influence on Vanessa Bell and Duncan Grant, who saw themselves as the British wing of the Post-Impressionist movement. In 1911, Fry and Vanessa Bell had a love affair and he was devastated when she

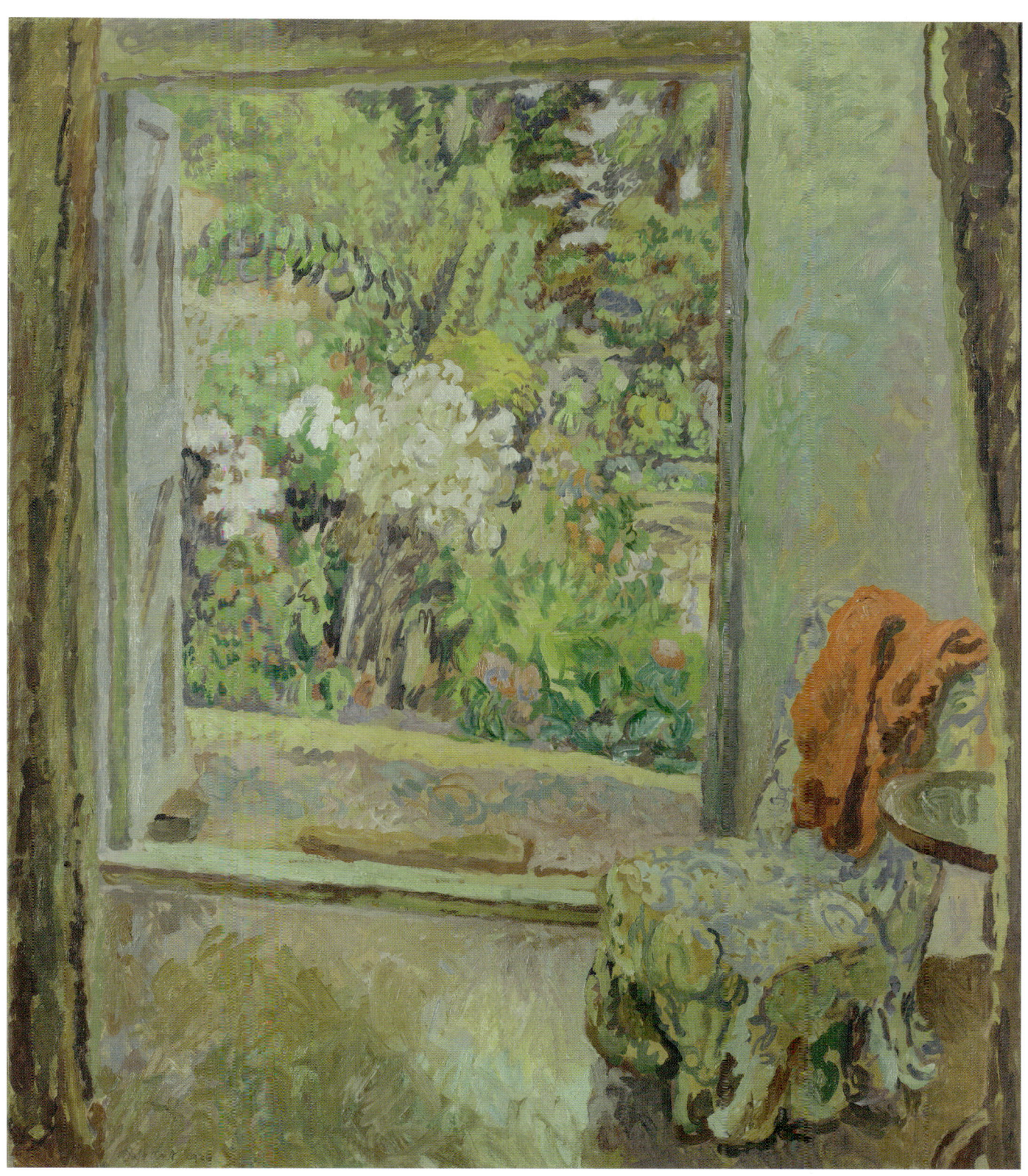

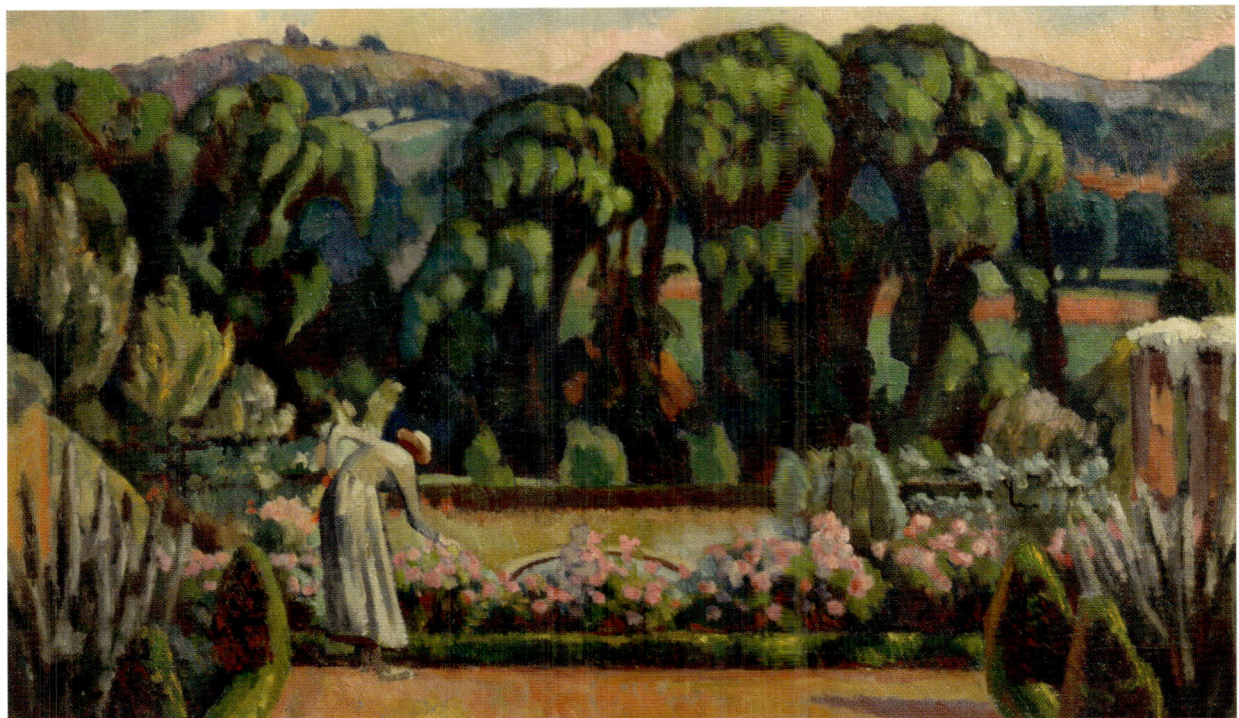

broke it off to live with Grant, but despite this, they all remained close. Fry realized that many up-and-coming artists struggled to make enough money to live, and so he set up the Omega Workshops in London in 1913 to design and make commercial products that would support them – many of Grant and Bell's early commissions came via these workshops.

In 1917 Grant and Bell asked Fry to help them design the walled garden. Fry had already designed his own house at Durbins in Guildford, where he laid out a terraced garden, aided by the famous designer and plantswoman, Gertrude Jekyll. Fry's painting, *The Artist's Garden at Durbins, Guildford*, shows a formal design that was a clear forerunner to the sloping, south-facing garden at Charleston. Both Durbins and Charleston had a generous area of lawn, a geometric pool (rectangular at Charleston; circular at Durbins), box hedges for structure, straight paths and wide, flower-filled borders.

Originally, the vegetable growing area was outside the walled garden and included edible plants, such as artichokes, which became a repeated *motif* in Bell and Grant's work. Both artists also made many still-life studies of flowers from the gardens.

Letters between Bell and Grant, and correspondence with other people, show that they were both involved in choosing the seeds they wanted to grow from Carters' Seed Catalogue. Their favourites included annuals, such as cosmos, salpiglossis, and zinnias, as well as perennials, including phlox, poppies, aquilegias and red-hot pokers. The couple were helped by a series of gardeners, including 'Young' Mr Stevens and, later, Walter Higgens, the husband of Vanessa Bell's loyal housekeeper Grace Higgens, who had been with her since 1918.

Roger Fry's plant choices for the garden were not always practical and some did not suit the site and soil conditions. The lawn was edged with cotton lavender (*Santolina chamaecyparissus*), a Mediterranean plant that suffered in the shade of the fruit trees and in the heavy clay soil. Nevertheless, the contrast of silver or grey-leaved plants, such as *Senecio* and clove pinks (*Dianthus*), was deliberate and worked well as a foil to the brightly coloured flowers – just as in the house, where grey paintwork and plain, off-

THE GARDEN AT CHARLESTON

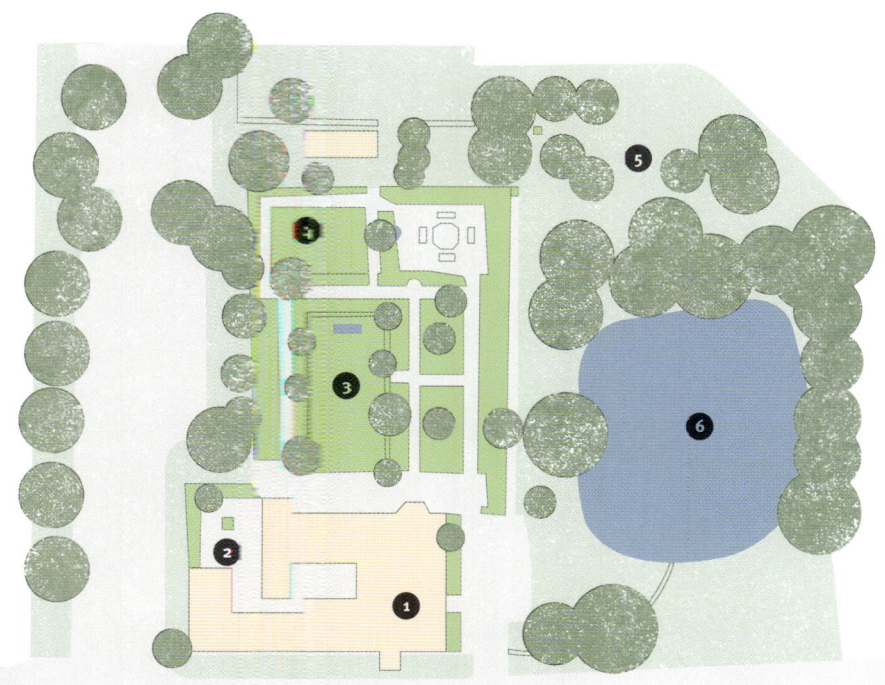

KEY

1 Charleston farmhouse
2 Grant's Folly
3 Walled garden
4 Kitchen garden
5 Orchard
6 Pond

LEFT *The Artist's Garden at Durbins, Guildford* (circa 1915), by Roger Fry, shows his own garden, which he laid out before helping to design Charleston.
BELOW The kitchen garden is now at the bottom of the sloping walled garden. Bell and Grant loved to paint the more architectural plants, such as artichokes.

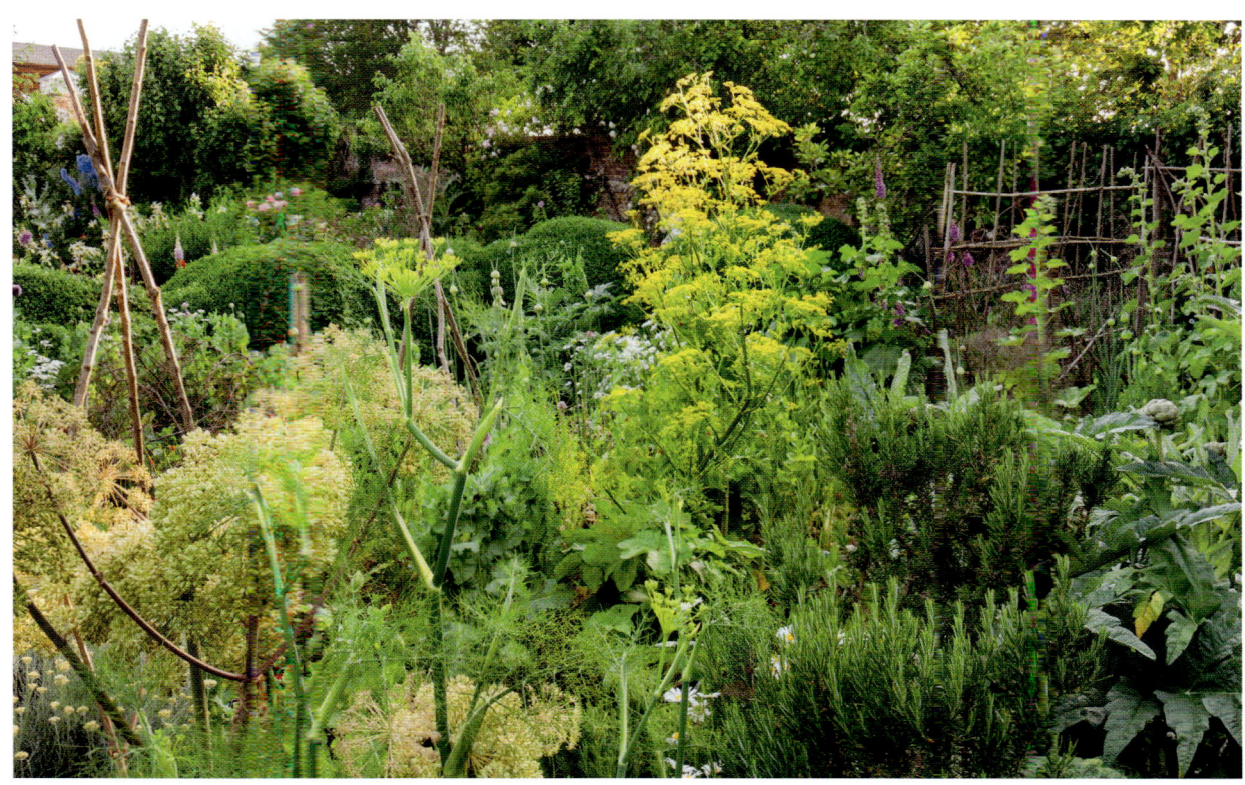

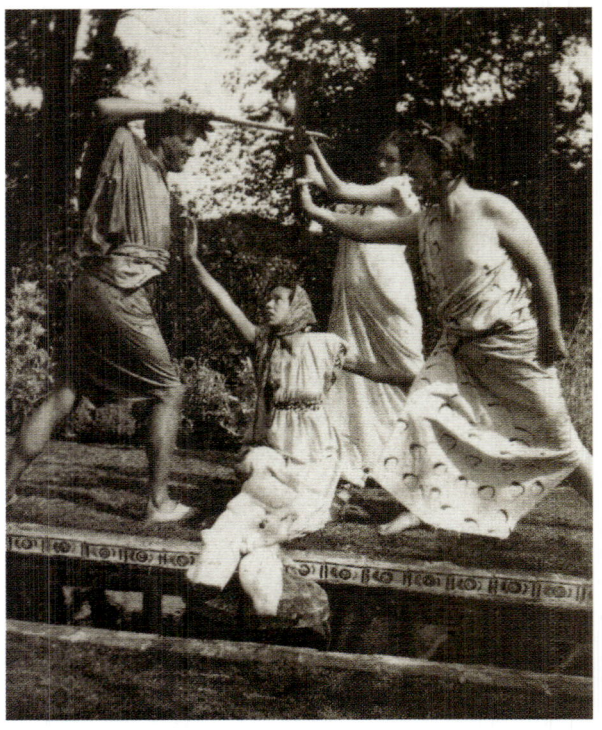

white walls in the passageways created areas of visual rest between the intensely patterned rooms.

Each person that came to Charleston added something new to the garden. Duncan Grant placed plaster busts from an art college on top of the walls. He also made the courtyard known as Grant's Folly, an enclosed space created when the studio was built. David 'Bunny' Garnett introduced bee hives to the orchard, and Vanessa's son, Quentin Bell, who became a three-dimensional artist, added sculptures, including the memorable *Levitating Lady* by the pond and the apparently unfinished brick sculpture, *The Spink*, in the orchard. Vanessa Bell also describes how young visitors would laze about the garden, enjoying its abundance, particularly the apples, pears and peaches from the trees she and Grant had planted.

LEFT This photograph taken by the pool in 1935 shows (from left) Julian Bell, Janie Bussy (niece of Lytton Strachey), Angelica and Quentin Bell.

BELOW The rectangular pool in the walled garden was a favourite place for summer gatherings of family and friends.

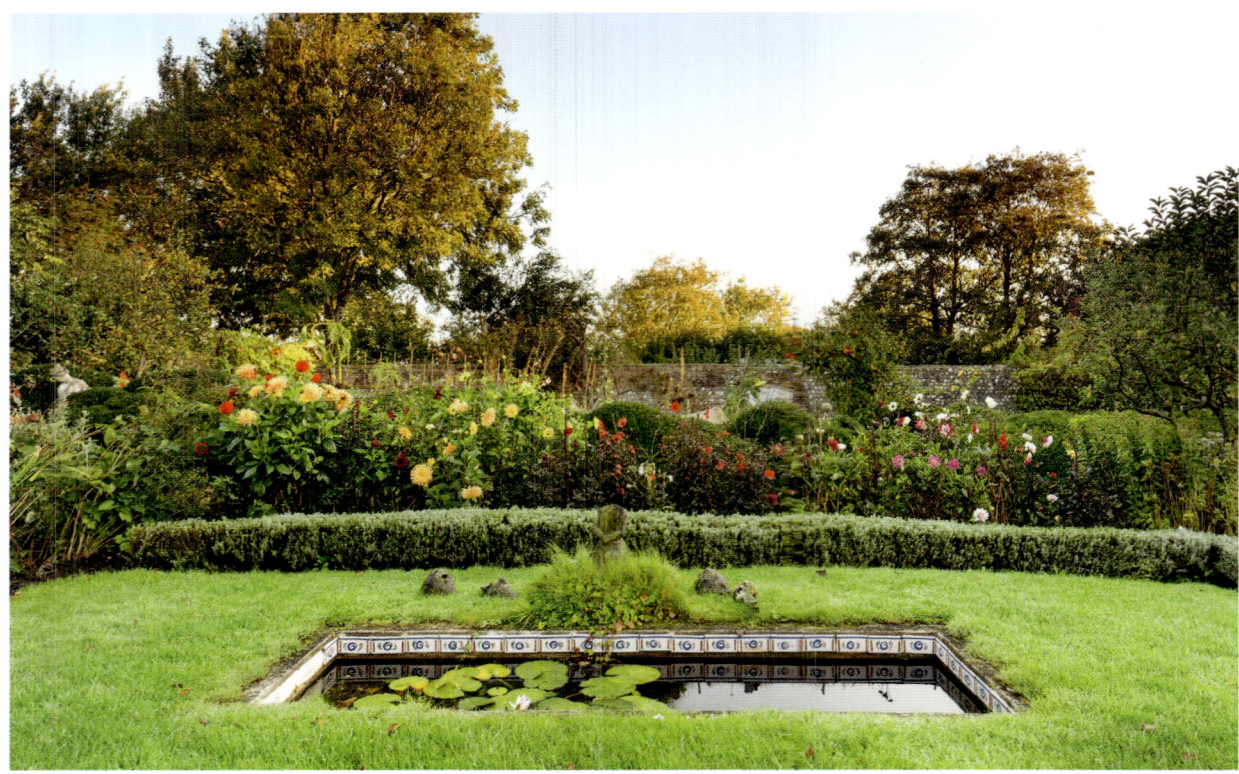

The Walled Garden

Although the picture we have of Charleston is of a wild garden with little discipline, this was not true of the walled garden in the early twentieth century. The clue is in the paintings, which reveal that, far from being uncared-for, it was planted with carefully-chosen and well-tended flowers. Vanessa Bell and Duncan Grant produced hundreds of flower paintings at Charleston, and these were almost certainly blooms they had gathered from the garden. In spring, there were tulips, narcissi, and auriculas, followed by hollyhocks and geums in early summer. From mid- to late summer, the garden was filled with cosmos, poppies, red-hot pokers (*Kniphofia*), penstemons, sweet peas, and both single- and double-flowered dahlias. Other important plants grown for painting included honesty (*Lunaria*) and everlasting flowers *Xerochrysum bracteatum*), both of which could be dried and used as subjects during the winter.

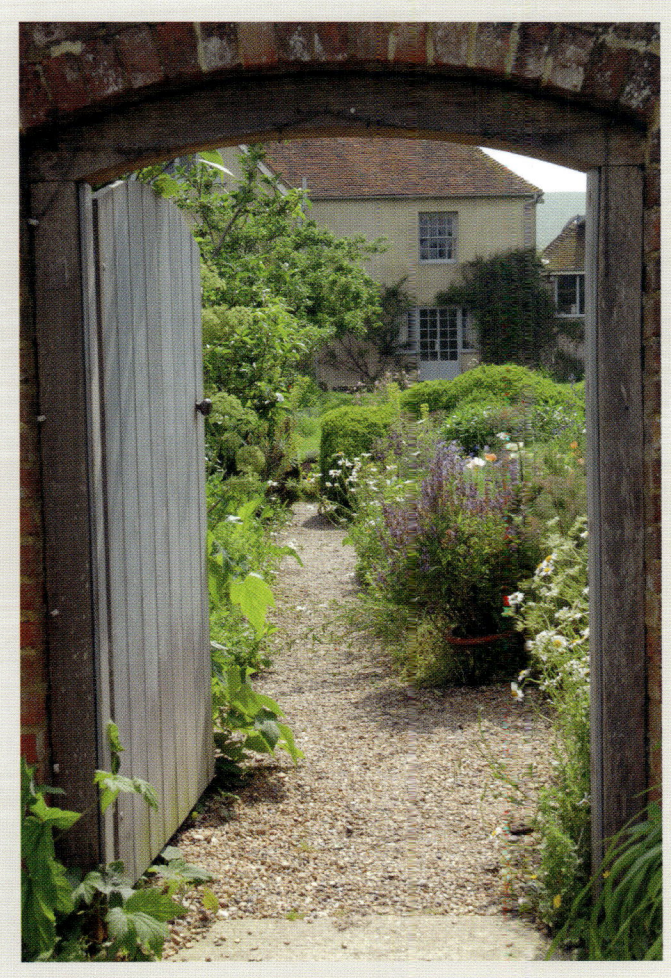

The walled garden at Charleston

INSIDE AND OUT

Other artists were encouraged to be involved in decorative schemes at Charleston, both indoors and out. Mosaics – using made from broken crockery – were a big favourite, and the earliest of these is the mosaic pavement of 1917, created by Bell, Grant and Barbara Bagenal as a base for an arbour in the south-western corner of the walled garden. Much later, in 1946–7, Quentin Bell laid out a larger work in the opposite corner known as the Piazza.

In many ways, the interiors of Charleston were Bell and Grant's biggest design project. Each room or area called for all hands on deck, with several artists working together on the design and execution. The house is widely considered to be the most complete interior design by a group of artists anywhere in the world.

The painting that perhaps shows the garden in its best light is Duncan Grant's *Garden Path in Spring* (1944), which shows the walled garden in spring, with the fruit trees in blossom and irises and pinks leading out from the French windows. The windows were in Bell's bedroom, where she describes sitting at her desk with the scent wafting in from the garden on warm summer evenings. In 1939,

Vanessa Bell's husband, the art critic Clive Bell, moved into Charleston (he had spent periods of time there, but this was a more permanent arrangement). He was given a suite of three rooms upstairs, while Vanessa took the downstairs room and installed the full-length glass doors.

Clive Bell's return to Charleston may have been prompted by the death in 1937 of his and Vanessa's eldest son, Julian, who had gone off to the Spanish Civil War and was killed within six weeks. Vanessa Bell would have needed support at this time, and during the period after her sister Virginia Woolf's suicide four years later.

Vanessa Bell lived on at Charleston with Grant and Clive until her death in 1961, aged eighty-one. She died in the room overlooking the garden – the room that Grant also moved into when he could no longer climb the stairs.

CHARLESTON REBORN

The death of Duncan Grant in 1978 marked the inevitable end of the Bloomsbury era at Charleston, where a shifting group of people had occupied the house for more than sixty years. After much negotiation, Lord Gage sold the property to the Charleston Trust, which took on an eight-year restoration. They were aided by Angelica Bell, an established artist herself, who helped to mix the paint colours; Quentin Bell, who produced replica tiles in his pottery; and his wife, the art scholar Anne Olivier Bell,

who had clear memories of the furnishings in the house. When the Trust took over the garden, it was choked with weeds, beds had been grassed over, the pond was overrun with rushes and many of the sculptures needed attention. Landscape architect, Sir Peter Shepheard, masterminded the restoration, when the flint walls were rebuilt and the pond was cleared out, while former head gardener, Mark Divall, was instrumental in restoring the planting.

For many people, it was enough to preserve the 'spirit' of the Charleston residents – its wildness and setting for a Bohemian lifestyle. But mindful of the artists who had lived there, and particularly Duncan Grant and Vanessa Bell who wanted the garden to look beautiful and be bountiful, attention turned to the paintings, which have provided references for its heyday between the 1930s and 1950s. The box hedges may have morphed into clouds, but, on either side of them, the plants have been accurately researched to reflect those that Bell and Grant painted – plants with silver foliage, a heady scent and a sprinkling of old-fashioned English cottage-garden charm.

RIGHT, ABOVE Antique heads and busts from the local art colleges were collected and placed on top of the garden walls by Duncan Grant.
RIGHT, BELOW Box hedges separate the compartments within the walled garden. A broken stone torso was converted by Duncan Grant into a container for a mophead hydrangea plant.

THE CHARLESTON ARTISTS' TIMELINE

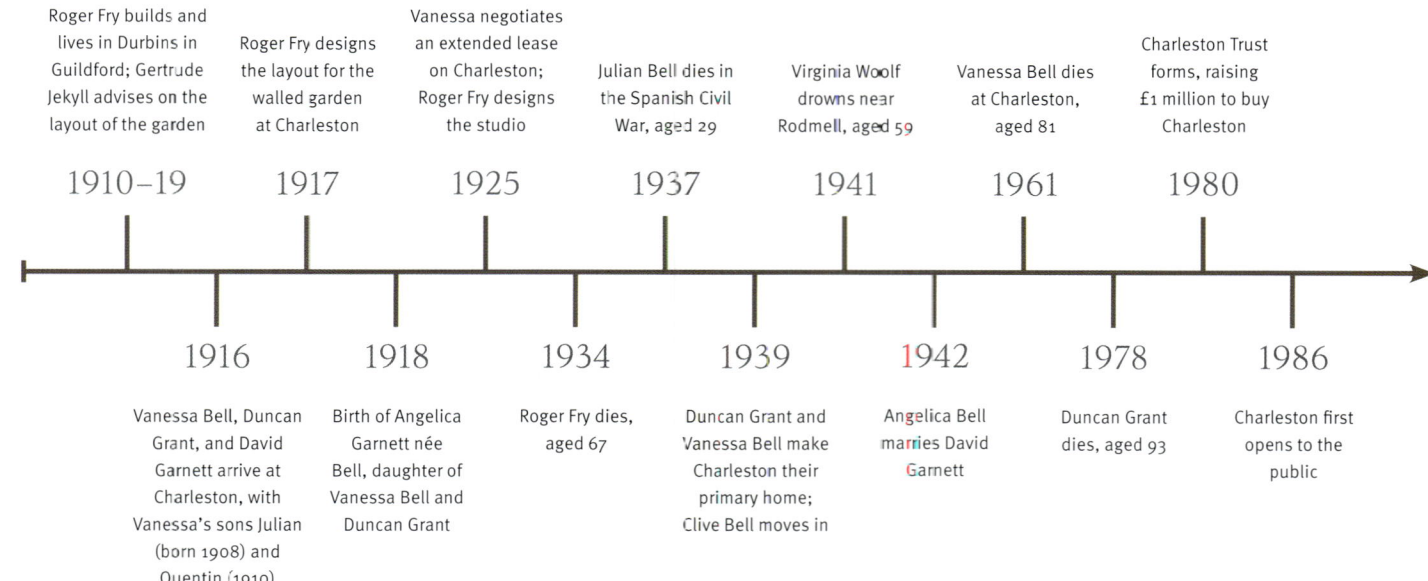

Roger Fry builds and lives in Durbins in Guildford; Gertrude Jekyll advises on the layout of the garden

Roger Fry designs the layout for the walled garden at Charleston

Vanessa negotiates an extended lease on Charleston; Roger Fry designs the studio

Julian Bell dies in the Spanish Civil War, aged 29

Virginia Woolf drowns near Rodmell, aged 59

Vanessa Bell dies at Charleston, aged 81

Charleston Trust forms, raising £1 million to buy Charleston

1910–19   1917   1925   1937   1941   1961   1980

1916   1918   1934   1939   1942   1978   1986

Vanessa Bell, Duncan Grant, and David Garnett arrive at Charleston, with Vanessa's sons Julian (born 1908) and Quentin (1910)

Birth of Angelica Garnett née Bell, daughter of Vanessa Bell and Duncan Grant

Roger Fry dies, aged 67

Duncan Grant and Vanessa Bell make Charleston their primary home; Clive Bell moves in

Angelica Bell marries David Garnett

Duncan Grant dies, aged 93

Charleston first opens to the public

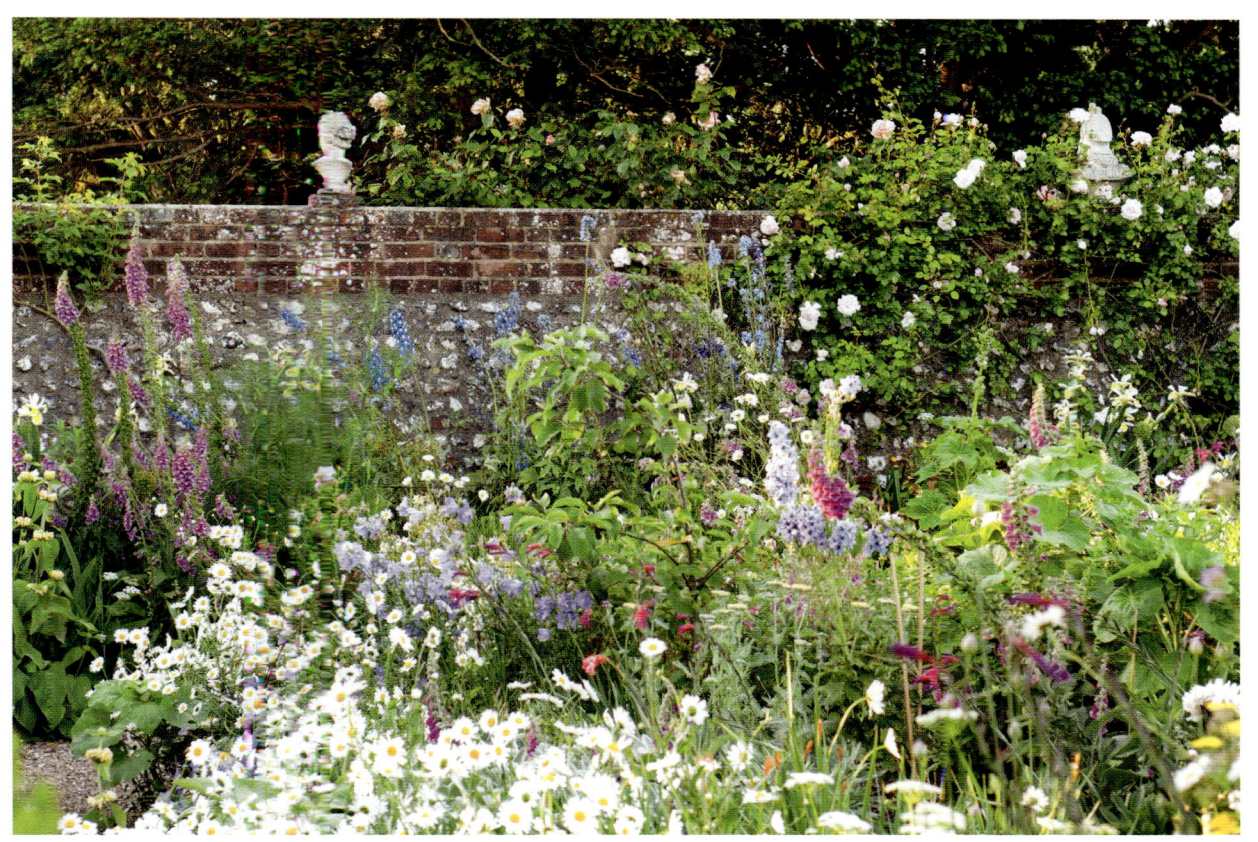

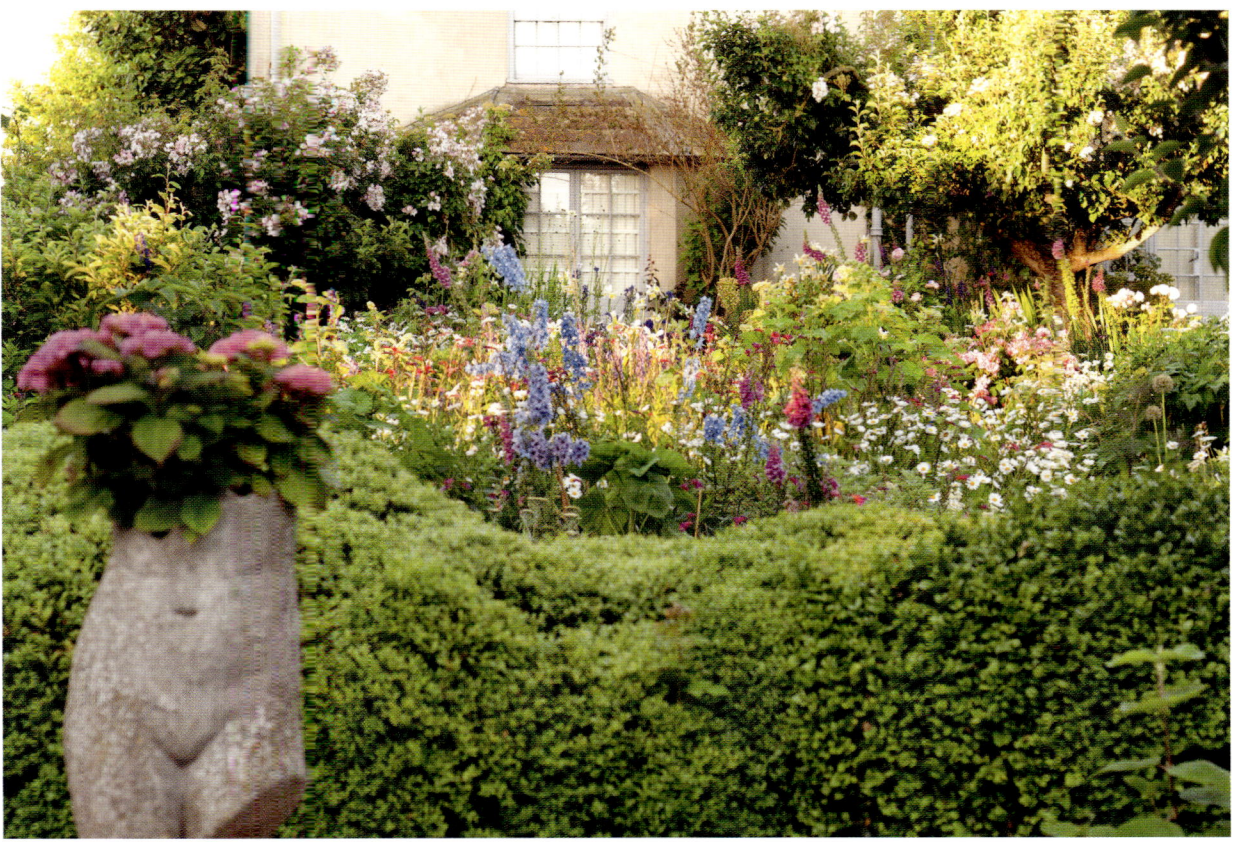

Selected reading

Bailey, Martin, *Starry Night: Van Gogh at the Asylum*, White Lion Publishing, 2018

Barbezat, Suzanne, *Frida Kahlo at Home*, Frances Lincoln, 2016

Becker, Astrid et al, *Emil Nolde Colour is Life*, National Galleries of Scotland, 2018

Bell, Quentin & Nicholson, Virginia, *Charleston: A Bloomsbury House and Garden*, Frances Lincoln, 1997 (2004 edition)

Dalí, Salvador, *Diary of a Genius 1952–1963*, Éditions de la Table Ronde, 1964 Transl: Richard Howard (Deicide Press edition 2017)

Danchev, Alex, *Cézanne: A Life*, Profile Books, 2012 (2013 edition)

Ebbesen, Lisette Vind, Jensen, Mette Bøgh, & Johansen, Annette, *The Skagen Painters*, Skagens Museums, 2009

Farinaux-Le Sidaner, Yann, *Henri Le Sidaner Paysage Intimes*, Éditions Monelle Hayot, 2013

Farinaux-Le Sidaner, Yann, *Le Sidaner L'Oeuvre Peint et Gravé*, Éditions André Sauret, 1989

Goetz, Adrien, *Monet at Giverny*, Fondation Claude Monet-Giverny, 2015

Jansen, Isabelle (ed.), *Gabriele Münter 1877–1962 Painting to the Point*, Prestel, 2018 (English Edition Lenbachhaus, Munich)

Lambirth, Andrew, *Cedric Morris: Artist Plantsman*, Garden Museum, 2018

Mason, Anna et al, *May Morris Arts & Crafts Designer*, Thames & Hudson / V&A/William Morris Gallery, London, 2017

Mondéjar, Publio López, *Sorolla in his Eden*, Fundación Museo Sorolla, Madrid, 2018

Morris, William, *News from Nowhere, 1890* (Oxford World Classics 2009 edition)

Parry-Wingfield, Catherine, *J.M.W Turner, R.A. The Artist and his House at Twickenham*, Turner's House Trust, 2012

Patin, Sylvie, *Monet's Private Picture Gallery at Giverny*, Gourcuff Gradenigo / Fondation Claude Monet-Giverny, 2016

Renoir, Jean, *Renoir, My Father*, New York Review Books, 1962 (2001 Edition)

Reuther, Manfred (ed.), *Emil Nolde: Mein Garten Voller Blumen*, Nolde Stiftung, Seebüll, 2014. English Translation: *My Garden Full of Flowers* by Michael Wolfson

Royal Academy of Arts London, *Painting the Modern Garden: Monet to Matisse*, 2015

Stoppani, Leonard et al, *William Morris and Kelmscott*, The Design Council, 1981

Visiting details

The properties and gardens featured are open to the public, unless stated. Check websites for current visiting information as these can change. As well as the artists' houses, studios and gardens, nearby and relevant museums and galleries are included.

Leonardo da Vinci (pages 16–27)
Le Château du Clos Lucé, 2 rue du Clos Lucé, 37400 Amboise, Val de Loire, France
www.vinci-closluce.com/en
Leonardo Vineyard, Corso Magenta 65, 20123 Milan, Italy
www.vignadileonardo.com/en

Peter Paul Rubens (pages 28–37)
Rubenshuis, Wapper 9–11, 2000 Antwerp, Belgium
www.rubenshuis.be/en

Paul Cézanne (pages 38–49)
Bastide du Jas de Bouffan, 17 route de Galice, 13100 Aix-en-Provence, France
Atelier de Cézanne, 9 Avenue Paul Cézanne, 13090 Aix-en-Provence, France
www.cezanne-en-provence.com

Pierre-Auguste Renoir (pages 50–63)
Du Côté des Renoir, 9 Place de la Mairie, 10360 Essoyes, France
www.renoir-essoyes.fr
Jardin du Domaine Des Collettes, Musée Renoir, Chemin des Collettes, 06800 Cagnes sur Mer, France
www.cagnes-tourisme.com

Max Liebermann (pages 64–75)
Liebermann-Villa on Lake Wannsee, Colomierstraße 3, 14109 Berlin, Germany
www.liebermann-villa.de/en/

Joaquín Sorolla (pages 76–85)
Sorolla Museum, C/ General Martínez Campos 37, 28010 Madrid, Spain
www.culturaydeporte.gob.es/msorolla

Henri Le Sidaner (pages 86–95)
Les Jardins Henri Le Sidaner, 7 rue Henri Le Sidaner, 60380 Gerberoy, France
www.lesjardinshenrilesidaner.com

Emil Nolde (pages 96–105)
Stiftung Seebüll Ada und Emil Nolde , Seebüll 31, 25927
Neukirchen, Germany
www.nolde-stiftung.de/en/

Frida Kahlo (pages 106–115)
Frida Kahlo Museum, Londres 247 Colonia Del Carmen,
Delegación Coyoacán, CP. 04100, Mexico City, Mexico
www.museofridakahlo.org.mx/en/the-blue-house/
The Anahuacalli Museum, 150 Colonia San Pablo Tepetlapa,
Delegación Coyoacán, CP. 04620, Mexico City, Mexico
www.museoanahuacalli.org.mx

Salvador Dalí (pages 116–127)
Salvador Dalí House, Portlligat E-17488 Cadaqués, Spain
Gala-Dalí Castle, Gala Dalí Square E-17120 Púbol-la Pera, Spain
Dalí Theatre-Museum, 5 Gala-Salvador Dalí Square, E-17600
Figueres, Catalonia, Spain
www.salvador-dali.org

Monet and friends (pages 130–143)
Claude Monet Foundation, 84 rue Claude Monet, 27620
Giverny, France
www.fondation-monet.com.en/
Hotel Baudy, 81 rue Claude Monet, 27620 Giverny, France
www.restaurantbaudy.com
Monet's House at Vétheuil (Private Home – Bed & Breakfast)
16 Avenue Claude Monet, 95510 Vétheuil, France
Caillebotte House, 8 rue de Concy, 91330 Yerres, France
www.proprietecaillebotte.com

The Skagen painters (pages 144–155)
Skagen Museums, Brøndumsvej 4 DK-9990 Skagen, Denmark
www.skagenskunstmuseer.dk/en/
Brøndums Hotel, Anchersvej 3, DK-9990 Skagen
broendums-hotel.dk

The Kirkcudbright artists (pages 156–167)
Broughton House & Garden, 12 High Street, Kirkcudbright,
Dumfries & Galloway, DG54JX, Scotland, UK
www.nts.org.uk/visit/places/broughton-house

William Morris and his circle (pages 168–181)
Kelmscott Manor, Kelmscott, Lechlade, Oxfordshire,
GL7 3HJ, England, UK
www.sal.org.uk/kelmscott-manor/
William Morris Gallery, Lloyd Park, Forest Road, Walthamstow,
London, E17 4PP, England, UK
www.wmgallery.org.uk

New England Impressionists (pages 182–193)
Florence Griswold Museum, 96 Lyme Street, Old Lyme,
CT 06371, USA
www.florencegriswoldmuseum.org/
Weir Farm Park, 735 Nod Hill Road, Wilton, CT 06897, USA
www.nps.gov/wefa/index.htm
Cornish Colony, Cornish, NH 03745, USA
www.cornishnh.net
Boat Tours to Celia Thaxter's Garden, Appledore and the other
Shoals Islands are run by the Shoals Marine Laboratory
(UNH/Cornell University)
www.shoalsmarinelaboratory.org/event/celia-thaxters-garden-tours

German Expressionists (pages 194–205)
Münter House, Kottmüllerallee 6, 82418 Murnau, Germany
www.muenter-stiftung.de/en/the-munter-house/
The Gabriele Münter and Johannes Eichner Foundation,
Städtische Galerie im Lenbachhaus, Luisenstraße 33,
80333 Munich, Germany
www.lenbachhaus.de
Franz Marc Museum, Franz Marc Park 8-10, 82431 Kochel am See,
Germany
www.franz-marc-museum.de

The Charleston artists (pages 206–217)
Charleston, Firle, Lewes, East Sussex, BN8 6LL, England, UK
www.charleston.org.uk

Index

Quarto

First published in 2019 by White Lion Publishing, an imprint of The Quarto Group.
One Triptych Place, London, SE1 9SH, United Kingdom
T (0)20 7700 9000
www.Quarto.com

This edition published 2026 by Frances Lincoln.

EEA Representation, WTS Tax d.o.o., Žanova ulica 3, 4000 Kranj, Slovenia
www.wts-tax.si

Text Copyright © 2019 Jackie Bennett
Garden plan illustrations © 2019 Sarah Pyke
Design Copyright © 2019, 2026 Quarto Publishing plc

Jackie Bennett has asserted her moral right to be identified as the Author of this Work in accordance with the Copyright Designs and Patents Act 1988.

All rights reserved. No part of this book may be reproduced or utilised in any form or by any means, electronic or mechanical, including photocopying, recording or by any information storage and retrieval system, without permission in writing from Frances Lincoln.

Every effort has been made to trace the copyright holders of material quoted in this book. If application is made in writing to the publisher, any omissions will be included in future editions.

A catalogue record for this book is available from the British Library.

ISBN 978-1-80570-122-4
Ebook ISBN 978-1-78131-875-1

10 9 8 7 6 5 4 3 2 1

Publisher: Jessica Axe
Editorial Director, Gardening: Helen Griffin
Designer and Picture Research: Anne Wilson
Project Editor: Laura Bulbeck
Editor: Zia Allaway
Proofreader: Annelise Evans
Indexer: Christine Shuttleworth

Printed in Guangdong, China TT012026

Acknowledgments

The author would like to thank all the custodians, museum curators and gardeners who advised and helped with this project. Special thanks go to:

Château du Clos Lucé – Parc Leonardo da Vinci
François Saint Bris, Irina Metzl, David Nabon and Carol Geoffroy

Rubenshuis, Antwerp
Dr. Ben van Beneden

Aix-en-Provence
Joëlle Benazech and Dominique Cornillet, Nick and Judi Carter

Cagnes-sur-mer
Christelle de Caires (Office de Tourisme de Cagnes-sur-Mer)
Jean-Marc Nicolaï and M. Pinkowitz (Musée du Renoir)

Du Côté des Renoir, Essoyes
Coralie Delauné, Phillipe Talbot, Françoise Tellier and Nicolas George Landscapes

Liebermann-Villa am Wannsee
Dr Martin Faass and Sandra Köhler

Museo Sorolla
Consuelo Luca de Tena

Association Henri Le Sidaner en son Jardin de Gerberoy
Dominique Le Sidaner and Tom Dabek

Stiftung Seebüll Ada und Emil Nolde
Dr. Astrid Becker

Museos Frida Kahlo y Diego Rivera Anahuacalli
Ximena Jordán

Fundació Gala-Salvador Dalí
Jordi Artigas i Cadena

Fondation Claude Monet, Giverny
Ombelline Lemaitre, Jan Huntley and Jean-Marie Avisard
Claire Gardie (Maison Claude Monet à Vétheuil)

Skagens Kunstmuseer
Niels H. Bünemann

National Trust for Scotland, Broughton House
Carol Ryall and Mike Jack

Kelmscott Manor (Society of Antiquaries)
Gavin Williams and Celia James

Florence Griswold Museum
Tammi Flynn and Amy Kurtz Lansing

Shoals Marine Laboratory
Samantha Claussen

Weir Farm National Historic Site
Kristin Lessard

Gabriele Münter-und Johannes Eichner-Stiftung
Dr Isabelle Jansen and Dr Marta Koscielniak

Charleston
Dr Darren Clarke, Fiona Dennis, Fiona Grindley and Chloe Westwood